Mediator Skills an Techniques: Trianc of Influence

The College of Law, Braboeuf Manor, St. Catherines, Portsmouth Road, Guildford, GU3 1HA
Telephone: 01483 216788   E-mail: library.gld@lawcol.co.uk

Birmingham · Chester · Guildford · London · Manchester · York

Za moji roditelji

Mediator Skills and Techniques: Triangle of Influence

Laurence Boulle AM
BA (Natal), LLB (Stellenbosch), LLM (London), PhD (Natal)
Professor of Law and Accredited Mediator

Miryana Nesic
BA (QLD), BEcon (QLD), LLB Hons (QLD), BCL (Oxon)
Accredited Mediator

Bloomsbury Professional

Bloomsbury Professional Ltd, Maxwelton House, 41–43 Boltro Road, Haywards Heath, West Sussex, RH16 1BJ

© Bloomsbury Professional 2010

A CIP Catalogue record for this book is available from the British Library.

ISBN 978 1 84766 144 9

Typeset by Phoenix Photosetting, Chatham, Kent

Printed in Great Britain by Atheneaum Press Ltd, Gateshead, Tyne & Wear

Preface

This book explains the work of a mediator. The Triangle of Influence highlights the fact that effective mediation is a combination of fair process, understanding people, the issues and the conflict, and exploring solutions. Personal needs, commercial objectives and the legal and regulatory landscape can influence each aspect.

The book provides a guide on the skills, techniques and standards of practice of mediators. It also provides an insight into the role and function of clients and their advisers, as well as other support people, in mediation.

Knowledge, skills and standards are all necessary for anyone wishing to undertake the practice of any occupation, profession or other form of skilled help. 'Knowledge' refers to the systematic theoretical understanding of a particular subject-area, and 'standards' refers to the standards and normative principles associated with its implementation in practice. 'Skills' refer to the practical activities, strategies, interventions and techniques which practitioners use as they provide their particular form of service or assistance.

In the context of a specific activity, the knowledge, skills and standards are closely related to one another and an understanding of one assists in dealing with another. However, it is sometimes useful to deal with them separately. This is the case with this book on mediation skills which does not deal with the knowledge and standards of mediation in a systematic fashion, despite their significance for actual practice. These aspects are covered in many other texts on mediation, including the authors' earlier work, *Mediation: Principles Process Practice*, Tottel Publishing, 2001 (which is referred in this book as '*MPPP*').

In attempting to be practical and pragmatic, this book deliberately avoids dealing with the major theoretical and critical issues in mediation, for example, its affinity with different models of justice. Nor does it deal with the big policy questions which the practice of mediation raises, for example the desirability of mandatory mediation or the fairness and equity of mediation outcomes. The book also does not deal in detail with the questions of when mediation is appropriate or inappropriate, although this issue is touched on when considering the timing of mediation and persuasion to mediate. It does not cover all the theory, law and policy relating to issues like confidentiality and privilege. Further understanding of the important theories, principles and social implications of mediation must be sought in the scholarly literature on this topic.

It goes without saying that a skills book on mediation does not constitute a foolproof guide to, or manual on, the subject. This is because mediators, unlike surgeons, chefs or plumbers, do not have the capacity to change things of their own accord, but only to create the circumstances in which the parties might do so themselves. In fact the only thing which mediators can do, apart from establishing the physical environment, is to change their own behaviour and language in expectation of the parties doing the same. Thus, no dot-point lists, tables, or dos and don'ts, are in themselves adequate for successful mediation practice as the mediator frequently has to respond and react to the activities of the mediating parties. This requires knowledge, skill, judgment, experience, intuition, serendipity and trial-and-error, and more than just a checklist of interventions. However, the dynamic nature of mediation cannot always be portrayed in a written text and it has been necessary to use some lists and tables to indicate possible options and strategies for mediators.

As regards its target audience, the book is aimed primarily at those who already are, or who would like to become, practising mediators. It may also be of use to those involved in mediation as disputants, or supporters or advisers of disputants. However, theirs is really a different perspective on the process of mediation, and the skills and techniques required by them to make the best use of mediation, for example in preparing for mediation, are specialised subjects in themselves. Appendix 6 provides materials to guide lawyers representing clients in mediation.

Our respective backgrounds, involving experience of a diverse range of cases, has inspired us to produce a guide which is aimed at providing insights across disciplines. With this hope also comes a great challenge, to achieve a balance between generic guidance on the one hand and the required level of detail for certain types of cases on the other. We hope that the balance is about right for a book of this nature, focusing as it does on the skills and techniques, rather than on the law, theory and policy applicable to mediation. In specialist and highly regulated practice areas, like family mediation, mediators may need access to further resources. Although the book's focus is on England and Wales, it makes reference to other jurisdictions to make comparisons.

As regards the question of style, the book is sometimes written in the second person, so as to address you, as the prospective mediator, though this is not done consistently. It is also sometimes written in the first person to emphasise that the views we have expressed are not the result of idle intellectualisation but are also based on our actual experiences as mediators.

For many years mediation workshops have emphasised the importance of 'process, process, process'. This approach has recognised the importance of a structured and ordered approach to the resolution of disputes. For this reason the mediation procedure is given significant treatment in this book. However, process alone is not always adequate for successful mediation. Sometimes the process needs to be adapted, and it always needs a range of skills, techniques and interventions. Accordingly, while the material in this book is organised in light of the ordered sequence of the mediation process, many of the strategies, skills and techniques cut across various aspects of the process.

The various case studies, illustrations and anecdotes are derived from the authors' personal experiences in specific mediations and in the accumulation of experiences from different mediations. They are also based on debriefings, anecdotes and reflections and comments from other experienced mediators. They have all been rendered anonymous in order to protect the confidentiality of the mediation process and the parties.

While the focus here is mediation as a distinct analytical model, mediation skills can be applied in numerous situations which we would not formally recognise as mediation. Parents, managers, teachers, police offers, receptionists, politicians and many other skilled helpers can all at times be seen as informal mediators of disputes. The skills and techniques referred to here are applicable in many different settings.

Thanks are due to many people for assistance in writing this book. The ideas, comments and resources of colleagues at the the Centre for Effective Dispute Resolution, ADR Group and PIMs in England, CORE Solutions Group in Scotland and the Bond Dispute Resolution Centre in Australia, as well as a hugely talented cadre of independent mediators around the world who are also our friends, have provided us with numerous valuable insights and examples. Many thanks to ADR Group, College of Mediators, Henry Brown and Barbara Wilson for their input on family mediation and to Felicity Steadman for her comments on workplace grievances. Our mediation clients and their professional advisers have provided the basis for experience, reflection and strategies. Over many years, our mediation students from all walks of life and so many professional disciplines have provided us with an amazingly rich insight into matters mediational through both their informed observations and inspired insights. Miryana is grateful to Melanie, Liz, Jennifer, John, Mary, Pat, Joy and James for their support, encouragement and wisdom. A special tribute is made to David Shapiro, a dear friend and mentor, who died suddenly in September 2009. His extraordinary tenacity in promoting mediation across the world has inspired us. Long may his memory live on.

At Bloomsbury Professional we are grateful for the patience of Andy Hill while we tried to reach the last page of this book and for the assistance of the expert team of Jane Bradford, Andrew Devine, Wendy Burford and Caroline Holme.

As is usual in a book such as this, all care has been taken in relation to legal forms and precedents but no responsibility can be accepted and legal advice should be taken on these matters.

This book acknowledges the devotion and support of our respective families. They have endured our long absences over many years so that we might share our skills and thoughts in diverse regions, cases and circumstances.

Miryana Nesic
Laurence Boulle
October 2009

About the Authors

Laurence J Boulle AM, BA, LL.B, LL.M, PhD

Laurence Boulle practised law before assuming positions in universities in Africa, Europe, North America and Australia. He is currently Director of the Mandela Institute and the Issy Wolfson Professor of Law at the University of the Witwatersrand in Johannesburg. Prior to that he was Professor of Law at Bond University, Australia, where he established the Dispute Resolution Centre, which for 20 years has provided education and training courses for mediators from around the globe. His proposals for a national system of mediator accreditation in Australia were unanimously accepted at the 2006 National Mediation Conference in Hobart. He was awarded the Order of Merit in Australia for his contribution to mediation education and development.

Miryana Nesic, BA, BEcon, LL.B (Hons), BCL

Miryana Nesic is a commercial litigation lawyer by background, a mediator and ADR consultant, who has worked on ADR cases and development across Europe, the US, Africa, the Middle East and Australasia since the early 1990s. She was the English Law Society's first Civil/Commercial Mediator Assessor, and has coached and assessed mediators, lawyers, judges and corporate representatives internationally on the skills and strategies required in mediation. She has advised governments on ADR policy and has developed ADR standards in a number of countries. She is a member of the IMI Standards Commission, Visiting Professor of ADR at NLS, a CEDR and AMA accredited mediator, and is on CORE's International Panel of Mediators.

Contents

Contents

Contents

Contents

Chapter 1

This Book's Approach to Mediation Skills and Techniques

Where there's a will there's a way

A. Basic Terminology

Defining mediation

1.1   Mediation is a rapidly developing field, recognised for its flexibility and application to many situations. In response to these positive developments, this book covers the subject of mediation in a broad and general sense to include all forms of decision-making in which the parties are assisted by someone external to the conflict, the mediator, who cannot make binding decisions for them, but assists their decision-making in various ways. It can be contrasted with those forms of dispute resolution in which the external person is the formal decision-maker for the parties, such as arbitration, adjudication, expert determination and court proceedings.

1.2   Categories of dispute resolution process include:

- *Facilitative* processes: in which a third party assists in the management of the process of dispute resolution, for example, mediation and conciliation.

- *Advisory* processes: in which a third party provides advice as to the facts, evidence and law and sometimes possible outcomes for the dispute, for example, case appraisal, early neutral evaluation and expert appraisal.

- *Determinative* processes: in which a third party makes a determination to resolve the dispute, which is potentially enforceable, for example, arbitration, expert determination and judicial decisions.

As a matter of definition, mediation is within the category of facilitative processes, but in practice it can have advisory aspects.

Basic terms in dispute resolution

1.3   Facilitative processes are known in different settings as mediation, conciliation, facilitation or assisted decision-making, and the interveners are known as mediators, conciliators, facilitators, intermediaries, go-betweens, peace-makers, brokers, and the like. We consider that the core mediation skills and techniques dealt with here are potentially applicable to all of them.

B. On learning and developing mediation skills

1.4   A book on 'mediation skills' makes a simple, but not uncontroversial, assumption that mediation skills and techniques can be learned, developed, assessed and improved. This is the assumption behind much mediation training, which usually comprises a three- or four-day workshop, with or without some form of competency assessment. It is also the assumption behind mediation skills courses being taught at universities, colleges, schools and other institutions.

In reality, many mediation figures in history have undertaken no formal training and received no accreditation as mediators, but have nevertheless been remarkable people with particular dispute resolution talents, such as Gandhi, Nelson Mandela, Benjamin Franklin and Churchill. In some cultures, mediators owe their positions to their age, experience, leadership qualities and other 'natural' talents, as opposed to their attendance at mediation workshops. There are therefore many precedents for mediators who have not learned their craft in a formal and systemised way, nor availed themselves of refined skills books on the subject.

This work, however, is not based on the view that mediation is a mystical art and that mediators are born and not made. Some of the attributes of mediators do derive from personality traits, interpersonal skills and other innate characteristics. But these are neither sufficient in themselves for successful mediation, nor is their absence necessarily fatal to the development of mediation skills. This is because mediation comprises in part a distinct procedure and a set of skills and techniques which can be understood 'scientifically', analysed, learned and practised. It is of course true that some people do appear to be naturally good at helping others resolve disputes. But just as those who are naturally good at caring for ill people require training and education to practise in health services, so too do those who are naturally good at dispute resolution.

No gain without pain

Mastery of any skill comes with study, practice and hard work. Michelangelo, the Italian artist, once stated: 'If people knew how hard I had to work to gain my mastery, it wouldn't seem wonderful at all.' Recent advances in brain science support what seems to have been known long ago, that superior performance, even what we might call genius, has as much or more to do with how much effort we put into developing a particular skill as it does with the natural aptitudes with which we are born.[1]

1.5   There is also a misconception that simply gaining experience in conducting mediations is sufficient by itself to become a quality mediator. While performing a task repetitively can lead to some increased aptitude initially, a much higher level of ability is attainable if the practitioner increases his or her knowledge of the underlying subject matter and critically evaluates his or her performance. For instance, most of us drive our car every day, but do we get much better at it simply because we have had more practice doing it? Without new knowledge about techniques or feedback about our ability, our skills remain about the same.

---

1   Philip Ross, 'The Expert Mind', *Scientific America,* August 2006, 64.

Modern brain science tells us that superior practitioners of a skill, like mediation, 'develop the capacity to break down [their] experience into multiple components and work on each of those separately'.[2] We call this reflective learning, which blends experience with critical evaluation of the quality of that experience.[3] This leads to improved performance.

This text breaks down the general skill of mediation into its component sub-skills, such as active listening, summarising, reframing, reality testing. Some of these sub-skills will come easily to you, and some will be more challenging. You must identify those sub-skills which you need to improve the most. It is through reflective practice that you will become better at the general skill of mediation.

If you wish truly to distinguish yourself as a mediator, reflective practice will be a lifelong pursuit. The concert pianist FB Busoni wrote that, 'I never neglect the opportunity to improve no matter how perfect a previous interpretation may have seemed to me. In fact, I often go directly home from a concert and practise for hours upon the very pieces that I have been playing because during the concert certain new ideas came to me.' Mastery of mediation too takes hard work and practice.

There are immense differences in *how* people learn new skills and techniques. Some learn best *cognitively*, that is, by absorbing information intellectually before applying it in concrete situations. Others learn best through *observation*, that is, through seeing others perform the particular skills and modelling their behaviour on what they have seen. And others learn best through *doing*, that is, by practising the skills clinically or in simulation and reflecting critically on their performance. A written text such as this accommodates only the first form of learning and needs to be supplemented by observation, practice and other experiential learning methods. In this respect the book provides a tool for the reflective practitioner of mediation who can evaluate their experiences in the light of its suggestions. Unfortunately, in mediation, as in many other pursuits, experience alone does not always equate with expertise.

C.   Contents and organisation

1.6   As indicated in the Preface, knowledge, skills and standards are all required for the formal practice of mediation, and this book deals extensively with only the skills element. Even here some choices have been made as regards subject matter. The book highlights three particular areas, which reflect the authors' practical experiences across case types and subject matter:

- The mediator's role in using their understanding of conflict in diagnosing, explaining and normalising the predictable features in the life-cycle of conflict.[4]

- The importance of creating the best possible climate for parties in dispute, and the need to put them at ease, make them less defensive, assist them to trust the

---

2   Richard Restak, *The New Brain* 19 (2003).
3   Nadja M. Spegel, Bernadette Rogers and Ross P. Buckley, *Negotiation: Theory and Techniques* 2–4 (1998).
4   See Chapter 4.

process and encourage them to take risks in problem-solving which they might not otherwise take.[5]

■ The mediator's role as a facilitator of negotiation and as negotiation coach. In our view this function has frequently been undervalued in manuals, training workshops and the literature, particularly in regard to the mediator's role in bargaining.[6]

Conversely, the book does not deal as comprehensively with some aspects of mediation, such as using interpreters, adapting mediation for cultural factors, the role of children in mediation, drafting agreements, and mediator debriefing. This is a result of space constraints and not of the unimportance of these factors.

As regards the organisation of the material, the book is based on the reality that mediation is not always a linear process moving from A to Z. Problem-solving, negotiation and decision-making are often recursive processes which defy neat attempts to progress them through sequential stages. If the methodology of the natural sciences is sometimes serendipitous, accidentally stumbling on important discoveries while looking for something else, then so too must be the methodology of human sciences such as mediation. Although Chapter 5 refers to the 12 stages of mediation, most of the rest of the book acknowledges in its organisation the serendipitous nature of mediation and the idea that it is not a didactic process.

D.   About mediation skills and techniques

1.7   In practice there are many different models of mediation, areas of mediation practice and styles of mediator behaviour. Mediation can also be used for many purposes: to settle disputes, define problems or disputes, manage conflict, prevent conflict, negotiate contracts, and formulate policy and standards. There are *universal* mediation skills and techniques relevant to the practice of mediation in most contexts, and *situational* skills and techniques relevant to specific situations, for example, family, workplace, personal injury, commercial, or international diplomatic disputes. This book focuses predominantly on the universal, or core, skills and techniques of mediation, with occasional references to specific practice areas as appropriate or necessary.

It is important to acknowledge that many features of mediation are common to other problem-solving processes involving managers, interviewers, arbitrators, judges, parents and many other categories of skilled helpers. Viewed individually, none of the mediation skills and techniques is unique, but their combination, organisation and inter-relation create a unique process called mediation. They also provide some challenges in their application. There is great subtlety in assisting others to communicate and negotiate well, as opposed to being a good communicator or negotiator oneself. Likewise there is sometimes only a subtle difference between assisting others to make decisions and making decisions for them.

1.8   In terms of its readership, the book assumes no, or little, experience in mediation practice or prior mediation training and education, although its

---

5   See Chapter 3.
6   See Chapter 7.

suggestions go beyond a 'beginners' manual. Experienced mediators will know that sound basics provide for sophisticated practice.

In terms of how these skills might relate to a reader's existing skills, it is worth observing that mediation is seldom a primary qualification or occupation and most beginner mediators will have skills and techniques derived from other qualifications and experience. Some of the skills developed through qualifications and experience in disciplines of origin can be readily and appropriately transposed to the mediation process, for example, active listening, appropriate questioning and plain drafting. For all prospective mediators other skills will have to be developed in addition to existing skills, depending in each case on the prior training and experience of the individuals concerned.

For some prospective mediators their prior training and experience may necessitate some 'deskilling', in the sense of consciously unlearning existing skills and approaches and replacing them with those more appropriate for mediation. For example, some experienced lawyers have an ability to reduce a complex array of circumstances to a narrow set of facts relevant to legal advocacy. This tendency needs to be subordinated in mediation and replaced with a broad notion of relevance. Likewise, some counsellors may have developed a high level of skill in refraining from imposing any pressure on their clients, which might be an inappropriate technique in some mediations. In each case the traditional approach needs to be removed from the prospective mediator's 'tool box' of skills and techniques.

1.9   It is never easy to say where mediation skills begin and end as they are closely related to many other social and professional skills, as illustrated in the following table:

Category of social or professional skill	Example
Innate common sense	Starting at the beginning Communicating clearly
Generic in many social situations	Easing awkward situations with humour Using appropriate words and language
Common among professional skilled helpers	Organising data systematically Drafting agreements in plain English
Specific, though not unique, to mediators	Managing unrealistic expectations Diagnosing and defining problems Negotiation coaching Reality testing Facilitating bargaining

E. Cultural limitations

1.10   In one sense good mediation is problem-solving with an awareness of cultural differences. Here 'cultural' is used in a broad sense to refer to differences based on class, gender, ethnicity, national origin, professional background, geography, and the like. The core process of mediation might have something of value for people with widely varying cultural attributes. However, the practical application of mediation skills and techniques is not culturally neutral. In particular, factors of ethnicity, class and gender make difficult any broad generalisations about skills and techniques since many of them are culturally derived and circumscribed.

Cultural differences may be a factor in the following issues relevant to the mediation process:[7]

- General values and beliefs, for example, attitudes to compromise.
- Language and verbal communication.
- Body language and non-verbal communication.
- Attitudes towards physical space and personal boundaries.
- Approaches to time.
- Attitudes to problems and disputes.
- Approaches to problem-solving and negotiation.
- Approaches to brainstorming.
- Decision-making styles.
- Attitudes towards privacy and involvement of third parties.
- Making offers and concessions.
- Relationship values.
- Roles of lawyers and other professional advisers.[8]

Cohen identifies specific cross-cultural roles of mediators – as interpreters who bridge communication differences; as buffers who protect the parties' face; and as co-ordinators who synchronise dissonant negotiating styles and approaches.[9] The extract in the table below provides an example in the case of Chinese culture.

Culture and mediation
Bee Chen Goh, author of *Negotiating with the Chinese*, 1996, writes as follows on the significance of culture in mediation:
'It needs to be noted that culture plays a significant role in determining and shaping one's perception of conflicts and their resolution. In the case of the Chinese, for instance, they are predominantly collectivists by nature. Collectivism favours group goals. Therefore, the Chinese are generally used to the ideals of harmony and compromise. Further, they subscribe to the anthropocosmic conception. What this means is that a conflict or a dispute is not just perceived by the Chinese as human, but it bears a cosmic dimension

---

7   Refer, for example, to C. A. Savage, 'Culture and Mediation: A Red Herring', in 5 *Am. U.J. Gender & Law* 269 (1996); S. Myers and B. Filner, *Mediation Across Cultures*, 1994.
8   Refer to Chapter 6 for a further discussion about cultural factors affecting communication.
9   R. Cohen, 'Cultural Aspects of International Mediation', in J. Bercovitch (ed), *Resolving International Conflicts – The Theory and Practice of Mediation*, 1996.

too. In the Chinese cosmological view, a conflict is seen as disrupting social harmony and disturbing the natural harmony. As such, a dispute is to be avoided lest it incurs the 'wrath of Heaven'. In ancient China, it was believed that a lack of peace on earth and human conflicts resulted in natural disasters, the most common being severe floods.

Thus, in terms of disputes, the Chinese prefer the dissolution of disputes to a resolution of disputes. In the former case, when a problem is perceived, the people involved work around the problem and try to dissipate it. The Chinese tend to act in preventative ways so that the problem does not get out of proportion and escalate into a messy conflict. It is usually messy because a conflict, in the collectivistic Chinese sense, is communal and not personal. There is a popular Chinese saying: 'Let big problems become small, and let small problems disappear'. Their general intention lies in the preservation of social harmony. In this sense, collectivists are less interested in the pursuit of individual rights. Rather, their concern is the social good.

Quite naturally, litigation essentially runs counter to the observance of harmony and the Chinese discomfort at direct confrontation. Due to this, in the event of inevitable conflicts, the prime method for solving them is conciliation or mediation. Mediation also serves the objective of the Confucian Chinese in the adherence to *li*, ie correct behaviour and ritualistic propriety. Litigation is at odds with the Confucian spirit of self-criticism. A person who practises self-criticism is considered to be morally disposed, one who does not insist on rights but who prefers to settle a dispute through the means which enables both parties to save personal embarrassment and not to lose face. A lawsuit will certainly cause one to lose face.

Confucianism has further inculcated a hierarchical social structure which establishes stability and orderliness through its members observing the rules made appropriate to rank and status. If each one observes his or her place, there will be peace in society. Mediation is regarded as congruent with this process, as the disputants can be reminded of their own specific roles.'

It can thus be seen that mediation as the primary method of conflict resolution is culturally ideal for the Chinese as it enables them to pursue their group goals of harmony and compromise, encourages face-saving behaviour, and supports the hierarchical nature of the Chinese society.[10]

1.11 In this book the skills and techniques are based on the predominant culture of English society. Although this culture is shared in part by many other inhabitants of the globe, no assumptions can be made as to the universal applicability of any particular skill or technique.[11]

---

10 In respect of Asian cultures, Pederson and Jandt have analysed over 100 case studies of mediations in various Asian cultures and have tested two models, one based on high/low context culture and the other on separating cultural expectations/stereotypes from actual behaviour. Refer to F. E. Jandt and P. B. Pederson (eds), 'Culturally Contextual Models for Creative Conflict Management' and 'The Cultural Context of Mediation and Constructive Conflict Management', in F. E. Jandt and P. B. Pederson (eds), *Constructive Conflict Management – Asia Pacific Cases*, 1996, pp 3 and 249.

11 For an explanation of how cultural differences affect negotiation, see Jeanne M. Brett, *Negotiating Globally* (2001).

F. Some assumptions

Assumptions about mediation

1.12 Although this book does not enter the definitional debate on mediation, it is important to disclose some of our assumptions about mediation.

The first assumption is that mediation is a system of exploring options and *practical decision-making*. This is represented by the apex of the Triangle of Influence. Mediation sometimes resolves disputes, it sometimes contains them, it sometimes defines them more clearly, but it always provides the opportunity for taking decisions, even if only the decision to submit the dispute to a court, the boss, an international tribunal, or some other authoritative decision-maker. We tell parties at the commencement of a mediation that 'you are here to make decisions on the issues affecting you …', not that 'you are here to resolve your disputes …'.[12] Later in the course of the mediation we suggest that the parties should consider making choices from the (sometimes limited) range of options which have emerged. Part of the mediator's function is to limit the options to those that are realistic and feasible, and to ask the parties to make practical decisions in the light of them, having had the opportunity in mediation to identify and reflect on the realities and feasibilities.[13]

Accordingly, the first assumption is that mediation is often about practical and pragmatic decision-making, for example over work conditions, money, children or over-hanging trees, which people require in order to get on with their lives. Parties should not come to mediation principally for counselling, therapy and personal transformation, though these may be secondary benefits flowing from their exposure to competent mediation practice. The skills and techniques associated with these other ideals are not dealt with in this book.[14]

1.13 A second assumption is that mediation should be primarily a *process-based* system, that is, one which regards certain core procedures as indispensable, regardless of the particular circumstances of the mediation. This is represented by the base of the Triangle of Influence. The emphasis on process operates at two levels. First, it implies that, as a matter of fact, the mediator takes the parties through a recognised process which assists the parties to make decisions but does not make decisions for them. Secondly, it has a normative element, namely that it is better for the parties to make their own decisions through a systematic decision-making process than it is to have decisions made for them. In this approach a mediator will not necessarily have done a good job merely because the parties reached a settlement. Conversely, the failure to reach a settlement will not necessarily mean that the mediator has not conducted the process satisfactorily and that the parties will not have derived some benefits or satisfaction from it. This might sound somewhat unworldly, but then mediation is as entitled to its well-reasoned premises as any other pursuit.

---

12 Other mediators think that 'taking decisions' is too vague and indeterminate, and prefer the 'dispute resolution' focus. Such is the ambiguity in this field.

13 We share the vision of mediation as a potential source of self-awareness, empowerment, forgiveness and reconciliation. However, such expectations can be too high for many disputants, many disputes, and many mediation services. High aspirations can also be a burden for the volunteer mediating a neighbourhood dispute in a draughty room, or for hard-pressed conciliators working under a statutory scheme.

14 On transformative mediation, see Bush and Folger, *The Promise of Mediation* (1994 and 2005).

1.14   A third assumption is that an *understanding of conflict – of the people and their situation –* is important for the mediator. This is represented by the middle of the Triangle of Influence. Knowledge of conflict – its sources, the ways in which it escalates and de-escalates, strategies for dealing with it, and ways in which it can be managed and resolved – not only assists mediators in terms of their choice of interventions, but also enables them to inform and educate parties about normal patterns of conflict and ways of responding to it. An understanding of the people – personalities, personal needs, commercial objectives and the relevant legal landscape – assists mediators to help the parties to communicate better, consider alternatives, generate options and make practical decisions. Needs and interests are further represented by the sides of the Triangle of Influence.

Assumptions about conflict

1.15   The mediation process is based on certain assumptions about conflict and its treatment. These assumptions are not unique or exclusive to mediation but they are consistent with its theoretical assumptions.

Conflict is not necessarily a negative phenomenon

1.16   In mediation, conflict is seen as a fact of life which, if it is handled constructively, can have positive benefits for the parties. It can provide opportunities for introspection, review and renewal, for the restoration of personal and business relationships, and for establishing new arrangements for the future.[15]

The expression of conflict is not necessarily unproductive

1.17   Skilled mediators tend to 'allow' the parties' conflict to manifest itself by not inhibiting the parties from expressing it. Here the assumption is that mediation should allow for the expression of emotions associated with conflict, in particular, anger, betrayal and lack of acknowledgment, subject to the parties adhering to the mediation guidelines[16] and not causing damage to others. In other words, the expression of negative emotions is not seen as problematic for dispute resolution.[17]

Case illustration

There had been a three-year conflict in an educational institution, involving the academic head of a department and two lecturers with differing levels of seniority. The central administration of the institution had responded to the conflict by ignoring it in the hope that it would go away. The three staff members had tried initially to deal with it, and had then not spoken to one other for two years. At the mediation there was a volatile outburst of frustration, anger and disillusionment from all three parties, much of it directed at the representative of central administration. The mediator allowed this to continue for some hours, without letting it get out of control, and then returned the discussions to plans

---

15   L. Boulle and M. Nesic, *Mediation: Principles Process Practice* ('*MPPP*') 42–3 (2001).
16   See 5.5–5.7.
17   See 3.30–3.37.

for the future. Having vented their feelings, the three parties agreed on practical arrangements for the future and the central administrator undertook to provide supervisory management services for a one-year trial period. The mediation allowed unexpressed conflict to be expressed and helped the parties to put it behind them.

It is helpful to educate parties about conflict

1.18   It is empowering for parties in dispute to have conflict normalised by being educated about its nature and resolution. Thus they can be informed about the normal causes of conflict and be asked to consider the causes of their particular dispute. Their difficulty in making decisions can be normalised as a common reality for parties in conflict, as can the 'loss of face' problem towards the end of a mediation where each side feels that they have conceded too much and are reluctant to make the final concession.[18] How and when this education takes place is a matter of judgment for the mediator, for example, some could occur before the mediation with the parties separately, some in the joint sessions with the parties together, and some in separate sessions, according to the circumstances and the type of case.

Conflicts change and are seldom static

1.19   Conflict does not stay the same over time. Often it escalates beyond its original scope because of the kinds of factors referred to in Chapter 3. When a conflict escalates it comes to involve more issues, greater intensity, and often more individuals or groups. Conversely, conflict can also de-escalate over time because it is constructively handled on all sides, there is useful intervention by outsiders, or because some participants get worn out and move on to more interesting endeavours.

Conflict can be diagnosed and defined

1.20   Finally, mediation is based on the assumptions that conflict can be diagnosed and that conflict should be comprehensively defined before it is resolved. These matters are dealt with in more detail in Chapter 4.

G.   Indicators of effective mediation

1.21   Mediation is often assessed in terms of a single criterion only, namely whether or not the parties reached a settlement, regardless of the way in which it was reached or the quality of the resolution. While this measure of effectiveness is obviously important, there is a wider range of indicators of competent mediation. By way of example, mediation could be assessed in terms of the following:

■ *Process*: the extent to which the parties are satisfied with the mediator's conduct of the mediation and their experience of the process and its fairness.

---

18   See, for example, 7.69.

- *Efficiency*: the extent to which the process is cost- and time-effective and maximised the value of the outcome.

- *Empowerment*: the extent to which the mediation educates the parties about constructive problem-solving and equips them to deal with disputes in the future.

- *Effectiveness*: the extent to which the mediation achieves a settlement outcome.

- *Durability*: the extent to which the mediation outcome endures over time.

- *Relationship*: the extent to which the mediation process increases understanding and improves the relationship between the parties.

While these, and other, indicators cannot be analysed comprehensively in this book, they constitute some of the standards by which mediator competence can be assessed. Assessing mediators in terms of the single quantitative indicator of whether they achieved a settlement can be a gross injustice to the skills of a mediator.

H. Classifying what mediators do

Note on terms

1.22   Those who are directly involved in mediation are referred to in this book as 'participants' or 'parties', although 'parties' does have a legalistic connotation. Sometimes they are referred to as mediation 'clients'. The term 'disputants' is not used because of its negative connotation. Where it is necessary to distinguish between the mediation participants, common usage is followed in referring to 'party A' and 'party B'.

Term	Meaning
Function of mediator	The broad categories of things that mediators do, for example, creating a conducive environment for dispute resolution or improving communication between the parties or facilitating the negotiations.
Techniques and skills of mediator	'Technique' and 'skill' are used interchangeably to refer to concrete acts and interventions by the mediator, such as arranging the seating, acknowledging hurt feelings, summarising, reframing and warning about certain negotiation tactics. It is through these skills and techniques that mediators come to perform their various functions.
Interventions by mediator	A term used for a combination or sequence of techniques and skills used by a mediator, for example, the mediator's response to high emotions, brainstorming options and risk analysis.

The mediator's 'toolbox'

1.23   There are many skills and techniques – sometimes referred to as a 'toolbox' of skills – employed by mediators and an almost limitless number of interventions. Mediation is an intricate set of manoeuvres involving at least three persons, and often more, and mediators initiate, react, adapt and retreat. This requires knowledge, judgment, intuition, trial and error, and occasional chance.

Mediator interventions can be categorised as either general or contingent. Interventions are *general* if they are made in all mediations, for example, explaining the process to the parties and providing structure and control. They are *contingent* when made only in specific situations, for example, shuttling messages between the participants or inviting professional advisers to discuss particular issues in general civil and commercial cases.

Similarly, mediator interventions can also be categorised as either *primary*, that is, made by the mediator as a matter of course, or *reactive*, that is, specific responses to situations or dilemmas arising in the course of the mediation.

Some mediator skills will have been developed as a result of past personal or professional experiences, while others will be more challenging. For some mediators, however, their prior training or experience may require 'deskilling' by unlearning existing skills or approaches. For example, lawyer mediators may have to learn to avoid making assumptions about the legal merits. Such assumptions need to be subordinated in mediation as all factors – personal, commercial and legal – are relevant to the parties and the potential outcome in mediation. This factor is represented by the sides of the Triangle of Influence.

Four mediator functions

1.24 As far as their functions are concerned, it is assumed in this work that all mediator interventions can be brought within the four categories of functions discussed below.

Creating favourable conditions for the parties

1.25 Mediators can contribute to the resolution of a problem or dispute by creating favourable conditions for its treatment. As (usually) independent outsiders with expertise in the nature of conflict and its management, they can do things which the parties, and their advisers, are unable to do on their own. There are at least three ways in which mediators can contribute towards a favourable climate for decision-making and dispute resolution:

- *Procedural framework*: controlling the proceedings, establishing basic ground rules, monitoring behaviour, allowing equal air time for all participants, allowing for necessary adjournments, setting parameters for the role of professional advisers, and otherwise providing a framework of control, impartiality and security. This aspect is dealt with mainly in Chapter 5.

- *Physical environment*: mediators can provide an appropriate physical environment for dispute resolution in terms of neutral venues, accessible buildings, adequate meeting rooms and amenities, and other physical facilities which provide convenience, security and symbolically appropriate seating for decision-making and problem solving. This aspect is dealt with mainly in Chapters 2 and 3.

- *Emotional environment*: mediators can contribute to an appropriate emotional environment for parties in dispute by providing a person and process in which they can trust, by ensuring an absence of threats, aggression and intimidating behaviour, by providing an aura of neutrality and impartiality, by reducing defensiveness, and by otherwise providing a hospitable emotional climate for decision-making and problem-solving. This aspect is dealt with mainly in Chapter 3.

Assisting the parties to communicate

1.26   Parties in conflict tend not to communicate accurately, comprehensively or constructively. Mediators can contribute to the communication process by modelling good speaking and listening skills, ensuring clarity and accuracy in communication, being attentive to the non-verbal communication of the parties, engaging in appropriate questioning, making use of visual communications, reframing and summarising what the parties say, and otherwise attending to communication factors which contribute to good decision-making and problem-solving. This function is dealt with mainly in Chapter 6.

Facilitating the parties' negotiations

1.27   As experts in negotiation, mediators can contribute to the parties' negotiating endeavours so as to make them more constructive, interest-driven, efficient and otherwise productive. Mediators accomplish this by ensuring that parties prepare for their negotiating roles, by focusing on the parties' needs and interests, by preventing premature offers and rejection of offers, by educating parties about good negotiation practice, by coaching the parties in separate sessions on how to negotiate, by assisting the parties with brainstorming and packaging an agreement, and by otherwise facilitating a negotiation process which is positive and productive. This aspect is dealt with mainly in Chapter 7.

Encouraging settlement

1.28   This is a controversial aspect of the mediator's role. For some disputants the mere presence of a mediator may be experienced as pressure to moderate their behaviour and come to a settlement which they would not have reached without this presence. Passive pressure to settle is a potential reality of all mediation situations. Active ways in which mediators can encourage settlement include questioning the parties about their realistic options away from the mediation, acting as the 'agent of reality', providing information and encouragement, imposing deadlines and being assertive in separate meetings. Although there is much debate about the appropriateness and ethics of the ways in which these functions are performed, they represent the reality of mediation practice.[19] This aspect is dealt with mainly in Chapter 8.

Five kinds of mediation

1.29   The particular skills and techniques used by mediators will depend in part on the type of case and in part on which model of mediation they are providing to

---

19   See Lela P. Love, 'The Top 10 Reasons that Mediators Should not Evaluate: Reflections on the Facilitative-Evaluative Debate', in 24 *Flu.St.U.L.Rev.* 937 (1997); and Marjorie Corman Aaron, 'Evaluation in Mediation', in Dwight Golann, *Mediating Legal Disputes: Effective Strategies for Lawyers and Mediators*, 267 (1996).

the parties. There are many different kinds of mediation and here it is convenient to refer to five models, each of which is associated with a different kind of mediator role.[20]

- *Settlement mediation*: The mediator encourages the parties to reach a point of compromise between their positional claims through various forms of persuasion, 'reality testing' and pressure, without any significant emphasis on the process of decision-making.

- *Facilitative mediation*: The mediator conducts the process of mediation along strict lines in order to define the problem comprehensively, focus on the parties' needs and interests and attempt to develop creative solutions which the parties can apply to the problem.

- *Therapeutic mediation*: The mediator assists the parties to deal therapeutically with the underlying causes of their problem, with a view to improving their relationship as a basis for resolving the dispute.

- *Transformative mediation*: The mediator focuses on improving communication between the parties, rather than on achieving settlement. The aim is to empower the parties; to assist the parties to recognise each other; and to improve the relationship, so that the parties can shift from destructive to constructive interactions, and find their own settlement if one is possible. The mediator allows the parties to determine the direction of the discussions.[21] The mediator listens actively, observes, provides reflection, or supportive responses, summarises and avoids directive impulses.[22]

- *Evaluative mediation*: The mediator guides and advises the parties on the basis of his or her expertise with a view to the parties reaching a settlement which accords with their legal rights and obligations, industry norms, or other objective standards.

The various terms of art used in the above descriptions are explained and illustrated in different parts of the book. It is important to note that few mediators can be neatly associated with a single form of mediation. Moreover, mediations in certain types of cases may begin in one mode, frequently facilitative, and be transformed later to another, for example, settlement or evaluative. This is a common pattern in commercial cases. As the model of mediation changes so too will the roles and techniques of the mediator.

Riskin illustrated this by developing a grid, which initially mapped facilitative and evaluative mediator styles, with broad and narrow approaches to mediation. He modified the grid in 2003 (calling it the 'New Old Grid') and replaced the facilitative-evaluative elements with directive-elicitive. His latest version of the grid (called the 'New New Grid') shifts the focus away from mediator style to how mediators and lawyers, along with their clients, influence the mediation process. Riskin considers

---

20   L. Boulle and M. Nesic, *MPPP*, 28–29.
21   R. A. Baruch Bush and J. P. Folger, *The Promise of Mediation – Responding to Conflict through Empowerment and Recognition*, 1994 and R. A. Baruch Bush and J. P. Folger, *The Promise of Mediation – The Transformative Approach to Conflict*, 2005. Refer also to www.transformativemediation.org.
22   R. A. Baruch Bush and S. Ganong Pope, 'Transformative Mediation: Principles and Practice in Divorce Mediation', in J. Folberg et al (eds), *Divorce and Family Mediation*, Guilford Press, 2004, 53.

that the point at which the mediator will be on the directive-elicitive continuum depends on the interaction with the lawyers and their clients.[23]

I. Overview of a mediation

1.30   We tend to use only those recipe books that contain good-quality colour photographs of the object of our culinary clumsiness. This is particularly helpful where the recipe goes under a foreign name and we have had no prior exposure to the particular dish.

A book on mediation is not to mediators what a recipe book is to cooks. This is because the human players in mediation do not have the objective and standardised qualities of cooking ingredients. And even if this work were like a mediation recipe book, it would be difficult to provide a picture of the final product.

Nevertheless for those eager to enter the world of mediation it is sometimes frustrating that they cannot contemplate the overall product, particularly where the process and skills are divided into so many chapters with many subheadings and numbered sections. Because of confidentiality arrangements it is not easy to observe a mediation; nor is this form of dispute resolution well represented in the media, drama or entertainment.

With this in mind, a short overview of an actual mediation is set out below. It is designed to give an overall feel of a mediation from start to finish, without of course being able to provide all the detail or human drama. It is analogous to the prologue of the Greek chorus in ancient plays, which was used to foreshadow the drama and themes in the production to come. Here the story of a mediation is presented in plain English instead of ancient Greek, and with an avoidance of the technical terms, acronyms and other jargon of mediation which is found in other parts of the book:

An example

A small business (SB) in England was in conflict with the publishers of a printed directory which was produced annually for a specific industry. The dispute originated from an ambiguous communication which led to the small business (SB) not receiving the advertising it had expected in the directory. It alleged that the omission of the directory publisher (DP) had caused loss of business and loss of income. DP rectified the problem in the next annual directory and waived all fees and charges which would otherwise have been owed by SB for another two years of the directory. SB sought damages directly from DP for their alleged losses. There was a lengthy delay in dealing with their claim because of changes of personnel in DP.

Over time SB became aware of other successful complainants who had had similar problems and decided to institute legal proceedings for breach of contract,

---

23   L. Riskin, Understanding Mediators' Orientations, Strategies and Techniques: A Grid for the Perplexed, 1 *Harv. Neg. L.R.* 7 (1996); L. Riskin, Decision-making in Mediation: the New Old Grid and the New New Grid System, *Notre Dame L.R.* (2003); L. Riskin, Who Decides What? Re-thinking the Grid of Mediator Orientations, *Disp. Resol. Mag.* 22 (2003).

claiming damages of £150,000 for additional advertising expenses, loss of business, and loss of goodwill. DP was offended by the size of the damages claim and refused to negotiate. SB made a formal offer of settlement for £75,000 and DP counter-offered with £6,000. The court encouraged the parties to mediate. The parties, on the advice of their lawyers, agreed and selected a mediator.

The mediator sent the parties written information about mediation, the mediator's profile, and an Agreement to Mediate. The mediator had telephone discussions with the parties' lawyers (one of whom sent copies of the court papers and relevant reports), explaining the nature of mediation, the role of the mediator and the responsibilities of the clients. In these discussions SB's lawyer indicated SB's intention to 'go along and see what happens' at the mediation and DP indicated an intention to reach a commercial settlement because of the bad publicity they were facing. The mediator made arrangements with the lawyers about venue, timing, the identity of participants, exchange of documents, and other housekeeping matters.

The mediation began at 10am at a neutral venue in the town of SB's business. SB was represented by the MD and a lawyer, and DP was represented by a middle manager from head office, an in-house lawyer from another city, and a regional manager. Both sides indicated that they had authority to settle. The parties were formally seated at a boardroom table with the mediator at the head.

The mediation meeting began with the mediator explaining the nature of the mediation process, the mediator's role, the order of proceedings for the mediation, and the roles of the clients and their lawyers. The lawyer for DP raised a concern about the fact that the mediator knew the owner of SB, both having grown up in the area, but agreed to proceed when it was pointed out that this fact had been conveyed to the lawyers and clients when the mediator was appointed.

The parties then made short opening statements to the mediator, with some amplification of each by their lawyers. The DP representatives acknowledged their mistake right at the outset and expressed regret for its consequences for SB. The MD of SB accepted the apology. The mediator listed a number of points for discussion and all participants then talked about these one by one. SB made use of an accountant's report in support of the monetary damages being claimed. DP criticised various aspects of the report. DP suggested possible ways of meeting SB's interests by providing new advertising products on favourable terms in the future; SB indicated some potential interest in these options but also asked for £75,000 by way of a monetary settlement.

The joint meeting then adjourned and the mediator spoke with each side separately in private meetings on a confidential basis. The representatives of DB expressed criticism over SB's 'patronising attitude' and 'gold-mining approach' and SB expressed concern over the 'terrible delays' and 'DB's lack of seriousness' in dealing with the claim. DB also indicated that they were eager to settle as it was the in-house lawyer's last day with the company. They also indicated that they could not remain at the mediation beyond 4pm because of other commitments.

A series of joint and separate meetings followed between the parties and the mediator during which the parties and their lawyers made the following offers and counter-offers:

£75,000 (again) from SB; £15,000 ('inclusive of costs') from DB; £60,000 from SB; £25,000 from DB; £45,000 from SB; £32,000 ('absolute bottom line') from DB; and £40,000 ('and not a penny less') from SB.

There was then an impasse over the gap of £8,000 and SB refused to consider the offer of new products until the impasse on the money was resolved. At 3pm DB's representatives indicated that that had to leave in an hour. The mediator met with the parties separately to explore ways of crossing the gap. At 3.50pm the parties came together and SB offered to come down to £35,000, provided payment was within seven days. On these figures the head office manager from DB shook hands with SB. DB's in-house lawyer produced a prepared contract, filled in the agreed figures and period of payment, and all parties signed the settlement, which included a confidentiality undertaking. The parties agreed verbally that a sales representative from DB would make an appointment with SB to discuss new products. There were handshakes all round and the DB representatives left the meeting at 4.01pm for their next appointments.

In follow-up phone calls to the parties a few weeks later, the mediator established that there had been full compliance with the agreement and that they all regarded the matter as fully settled.

In the chapters that follow the mechanics, procedure, skills and strategies of mediation will be discussed.

J. Summary

1.31 This chapter raises the following points of particular significance:

1. Mediation skills and techniques are not only innate and inherent, they can be learned, practised and improved.

2. Everyday interpersonal skills, and the techniques developed in many professional contexts, provide a basis for developing mediation skills, although some of these skills and techniques will have to be adapted, and they will also have to be supplemented.

3. All mediation skills and techniques are limited to particular cultural conditions and none can be applied universally in all cultural settings.

K. Tasks for beginner mediators

1.32 Listen to some podcasts by Mike McIlwrath on CPR Institute's website (www.cpradr.org) or interview a person who you know has experience of dispute resolution. Identify from the interview the particular skills and techniques which the person has found most helpful for their dispute resolution work. Which of these skills are innate and which have been developed through education and experience?

1.33 Select one or two of the skills identified above. Ask a person from a different cultural background how that skill would be regarded in their culture, and why? What are the implications of this answer for mediators?

1.34   Write out a list of some of the skills and techniques for which lawyers (or another occupational group) are renowned. Which of these do you think would be suitable for mediation and which do you think would need to be adapted or supplemented?

L. Recommended reading

Avruch K., 'Culture and Negotiation Pedagogy', in (2000) 16 *Negotiation Journal* 339.

Boulle L. and Nesic M., *Mediation: Principles Process Practice*, Tottel Publishing, 2001, Chs 1 and 2.

Bush and Folger, *The Promise of Mediation: Responding to Conflict Through Empowerment and Recognition*, Jossey-Bass, San Francisco, 1994, Chs 4, 7, 8 and 10.

Bush and Folger, *The Promise of Mediation: The Transformative Approach to Conflict*, John Wiley and Son/Jossey-Bass, San Francisco, 2005, Chs 1–4.

Charlton and Dewdney, *The Mediator's Handbook: Skills and Strategies for Practitioners*, 2nd ed, Lawbook Co, Sydney, 2004, Chs 10 and 14.

Cloke K., *Resolving Personal and Organizational Conflict: Stories of Transformation and Forgiveness*, Jossey-Bass, San Francisco, 2000.

Folberg and Taylor, *Mediation: A Comprehensive Guide to Resolving Conflicts Without Litigation*, Jossey-Bass, San Francisco, 1984, Chs 2 and 9.

Friedman G. and Himmelstein J., *Challenging Conflict: Mediation Through Understanding*. American Bar Association, 2008.

Goh B. C., *Negotiating with the Chinese*, Dartmouth Publishing Company, Aldershot UK/Brookfield USA, 1996.

Mackie K et al, *The ADR Practice Guide: Commercial Dispute Resolution*, Tottel Publishing, 2007, Chs 1 and 3.

Mareschal P.M., 'What Makes Mediation Work? Mediators' Perspectives on Resolving Disputes', in (2005) 44(3) *Industrial Relations* 509.

Moore C., *The Mediation Process: Practical Strategies for Resolving Conflict*, 3rd ed, John Wiley and Son/Jossey-Bass, San Francisco, 2003, Chs 1–2.

Palmer M. and Roberts S., *Dispute Processes: ADR and the Primary Forms of Decision-Making*. Cambridge University Press, 2005.

Spegel, Rogers and Buckley, *Negotiation: Theory and Techniques*, Butterworths, Sydney, 1998, Ch 1.

Yuan, Lim Lan, 'Impact of Cultural Differences on Dispute Resolution', (1996) 7 ADRJ 197.

Winslade J. and Another, *Narrative Mediation: A New Approach to Conflict Resolution*, Jossey-Bass, San Francisco, 2000.

Wolski B, 'Teaching and Learning Dispute Resolution by Self-Instruction', (1996) 7 *ADRJ* 218.

Chapter 2

Establishing the Foundations for Effective Mediation: Intake, Suitability Screening, Early Contact and Preparation

Failing to plan is planning to fail

A.   Introduction

2.1   This chapter deals with the roles and responsibilities of mediators in establishing the foundations for effective mediation. Mediators begin laying the foundations from the earliest stages of their involvement, and continue to strengthen and reinforce them until the final conclusion of the mediation.

The earliest phase involving intake, suitability screening or assessment of suitability for mediation and preparation gives the participants their first impression of the mediator and of mediation. The conduct of this phase sets the tone for the balance of the mediation. Accordingly, the importance of this early phase cannot be overstated.

From mediators' earliest involvements they need to be promoting the acceptability and legitimacy of themselves as mediators, developing the parties' trust in them and the mediation process, making the parties less defensive and more open to problem-solving and decision-making and managing everyone's expectations about the process, their respective roles and the goals. These objectives remain throughout the mediation and are referred to again in Chapter 5. In some cases this may also include securing a party's agreement to be involved in a mediation.

This chapter deals with the earliest stages of mediation, before the mediation meeting itself – entry into the dispute, gathering information, educating the parties about the mediation process, administrative arrangements for the mediation and other preparations for mediation.

As with the remainder of this book, this chapter seeks to distil the core skills involved in this early phase of mediation, and reference is made where the practice differs, as in specialist areas like family mediation.

B. Entering the dispute

2.2   The term 'entering the dispute' refers to the early involvement of mediators in the parties' dispute. Mediators can enter disputes in various ways. In some situations they are selected by the parties direct or by their legal or other advisers; in others they are appointed in accordance with a clause in a contract or a mediation scheme; they can be appointed by a court, tribunal or agency; or may be referred by a mediation organisation or other mediator. There are many variations on these basic forms of entry.[1]

Regardless of how a mediator enters a dispute, he or she must accomplish certain tasks during the entry stage:[2]

- building personal, institutional and procedural credibility;

- establishing a rapport with the parties;

- identifying the extent of the parties' knowledge of the mediation process;

- educating the parties about the role of the mediator, the stages of mediation and relevant aspects of the negotiation process, and the costs of the process;

- coaching parties on how to prepare effectively for mediation;

- gaining a commitment to begin mediating.[3]

2.3   In order to achieve these objectives, mediators should be attentive to the following:

- Acting at all times in a non-partisan way and not becoming an advocate of either party, even in relation to the question of whether there is to be a mediation.

- Listening to, empathising with and establishing rapport with each party through good communication and interpersonal skills.

- Promoting the credentials of mediation as a decision-making process, for example, by referring to its benefits over other methods of dispute resolution, its success rates and its levels of user satisfaction.

- Confirming their credentials as conflict managers and mediators, for example, by referring to their experience.

- Explaining the appropriate roles of the mediator and the parties.

- Preparing the parties for a constructive negotiation experience, reminding them that the process allows them to participate actively and gives them ultimate responsibility for the outcome.

---

1   As this book is not intended as a comprehensive guide for those referring clients to mediation, brief mention is made here to finding a mediator. Appendix 6 contains IMI's decision tree guide on finding a mediator. Appendix 11 contains a list of, and contact details for, mediation organisations that can be approached for assistance in finding a mediator. In relation to family mediation, refer also to the on-line search facility on the College of Mediators' website (www.collegeofmediators.co.uk). The Law Society maintains a Panel of Family Mediators and a Panel of Civil/Commercial Mediators. Refer also to www.disputesloop.com for profiles of mediators across the UK.

2   For an overview refer to C. Moore, *The Mediation Process* 3rd ed, 2003, Ch 3; and to Element 1 of the English Law Society's Competencies for Civil/Commercial Mediators which is Annex A to the Law Society's Accreditation for Civil/Commercial Mediation (included in Appendix 8).

3   These various tasks are examined in more detail throughout this chapter.

■ Building momentum by guiding the parties to consider their own aims, needs and objectives, as well as those of the other parties and any relevant outsiders.

2.4   In general civil and commercial mediations, mediators are usually selected by the parties, and some resources are dedicated for a structured entry into the dispute by the mediator, who can attend to the above activities and functions. Here mediators typically make use of standard form letters (either their own or the standard documents produced by mediation organisations) to respond to queries about their services, together with information about the mediator (usually by way of a cv) and question and answer type information about various aspects of the mediation process (see Appendix 2 for some samples). Where time, information and resources are restricted, the mediator has limited scope for attending to the above activities and functions. However, even in a brief contact in the foyer or corridor on the mediation day itself, the mediator should give effect to as many of these entry matters as possible.

In some cases, as with family and community mediations, or where the parties are referred to the process (for example, as a precondition to litigation funding), the regulatory framework prescribes the entry process, and is described further in this chapter. In relation to mediations conducted by Legal Services Commission 'LSC' (legal aid) contracted providers and in any other case adopting the LSC's standards (typically, family, workplace and community mediations), reference will be made in this chapter (and, where relevant, throughout the book) to the LSC Mediation Quality Mark Standard ('MQMS'), 2nd edition, 2009. The 2009 Standards constitute the first review of the MQMS since 2001.

Some metaphors for explaining mediation to first-time users

2.5   Because many participants have never experienced mediation before, and because this method of dispute resolution is not always easy to comprehend, mediators can make use of metaphors to explain the process during the entry stage (and later during the mediator's opening statement).[4]

Below are metaphors for explaining mediation and the mediator's role. Their suitability will depend in particular on the type of case and the personal attributes of the parties:

■ 'The mediator's role is to direct the traffic, like a traffic warden, but the parties will be doing all the driving.'

■ 'Mediation is like a jigsaw puzzle in which the mediator supervises the parties putting all the pieces in place.'

■ 'Think of the mediator as a director and the parties as the actors in a play in which the script has not yet been written.'

■ 'The mediator's role is like that of a sports umpire, controlling the game and making important decisions, but leaving the actual playing to the parties.'

■ 'The mediator is a host of the parties' event and provides comfort and safety.'

■ 'The mediator's role is to guide the parties down the path of decision-making, but which turns they actually take and how far they go depends on the parties.'

---

4   See 5.4–5.10.

- 'The mediator is a coach – the coaching helps parties to frame issues, develop options, convey offers and agree terms.'

C. Persuading a party to mediate

2.6 The MQMS process for intake and screening is outlined further below.

In general civil and commercial cases, a mediator or mediation service-provider is sometimes asked by a party to approach another to obtain the latter's agreement to mediate. Some mediators decline to undertake this task, on the grounds that they may be perceived as the agents of the initiating party and thereby lose their independence and impartiality before the mediation has begun. An alternative is for the mediator to recommend that the party should ask the other to initiate contact with the mediator direct so that the contact is free from the intermediary role of the first party. Some mediation organisations have specialised staff for the purpose of encouraging parties to mediate (sometimes called 'case advisers' or 'case managers', as in the case of organisations like CEDR, ADR Group and CORE Solutions Group), and such staff are not involved subsequently as mediators.

In many cases, though, mediators undertake the function of inviting and getting all parties to the mediation table as part of their overall service. Some commonsense guidelines for the mediator's approach to a party are as follows:

- The approach should be diplomatic and tactful.

- Disclose the nature and extent of your dealings with all other parties to minimise any suspicion in regard to your role and to promote an atmosphere of neutrality.

- Do not overstate the virtues of mediation in informing and educating a party about it.

- Be careful about disclosing your knowledge of the substantive issues in dispute in case this breaches your confidentiality undertaking to the other parties. This may require operating at a level of generality and avoiding specifics.

- Do not in any way appear to be taking the side of the initiating party or suggest that you have established a working alliance with them.

- Anticipate some resistance, ignorance or suspicion.

- In attitude and style, promote the legitimacy of mediation and the trustworthiness of the mediator.

2.7 A party will usually need to be educated about the mediation process so that they can make an informed commitment to it. The MQMS and College of Mediators' guidance on the information to be given to parties during the entry phase is outlined further below. The mediator or mediation organisation may use different forms of education: telephone conversations, printed or electronic information, videos, and face-to-face contacts.[5] For general civil and commercial cases, some sample information, letters and mediator profiles are included in Appendix 2.

---

5   See 12.20.

Inevitably, general guidelines on persuasion cannot anticipate all the complexities of this activity. For example:

- where a mediator is approaching a party in a general civil or commercial case, he or she will have to disclose some information about the dispute and will be interrogated about the initiating party's motivations and goals. The same will apply when the mediator reverts to the initiating party after the approach to the other. These matters need to be flagged up to both the initiating and approached party so that, in light of confidentiality requirements (which will discussed in later sections of this book), consent is obtained to discuss relevant matters.

- a mediator may need to resist the inclination to accept the initiating party's 'story' and regard them as all-righteous and all other parties as difficult, arrogant or suspicious.[6] This problem may require the mediator to limit the amount of information received from the initiating party in the first place.

- persistent questioning by an approached party might require the mediator to advise that the 'normal policy' is to provide the same preliminary information to all parties during the entry stage of mediation.

What if a party says no?

2.8   If a party declines mediation, their choice should clearly be respected. However, an initial refusal should not always be taken at face value; it may be motivated by a desire not to show weakness, or the need to take time out for advice, or to obtain further information, or just because the party concerned is not keen to pay the mediator's fees. As in other aspects of mediation, some probing and persistence may be necessary.

The classic problem-solving reaction to a negative response is to diagnose the reason for it. If you feel that the choice is based on ignorance, unfounded suspicion or prejudice, you may wish to consider the procedural options that might address those matters. In particular, a mediator should aim for small behavioural steps in the face of intransigence; for example, asking whether the party would agree to having a package of mediation material sent to them, or whether the party would agree to being contacted again in a week's time to discuss the matter, or whether the party can attend a 'short information meeting'.[7] Outlining the disadvantages, general risks and costs of the matter proceeding to court is another technique.[8]

2.9   There are some other procedural strategies that are worth considering depending on the circumstances in general civil and commercial cases. Where a party is reluctant to mediate, the mediator might suggest to the initiating party that they make, or remake, the approach direct. Where a party's legal adviser is reluctant to mediate, a mediator might ask for consent to speak directly to the client. If this is refused, a mediator might suggest to the initiating party that they approach the party direct, with their lawyer's knowledge.

---

6   Charlton and Dewdney, *The Mediator's Handbook*, 2004.
7   K. Slaikeu, *When Push Comes to Shove*, 1996, 61.
8   Requirement F5.3 MQMS provides that LSC contracted providers should inform clients in writing of the potential cost implications of matters proceeding to court to enable parties to asses the cost–benefit of the mediation process. These estimates must be based on the best available information. The MQMS is included in Appendix 8.

2.10   Reference to civil procedure rules might also be useful in this context. In England, various civil procedure rules encourage the take-up of mediation in general civil and commercial cases:[9]

- The Practice Direction (Pre-action Conduct) promotes settlement pre-issue by encouraging parties to consider using a form of Alternative Dispute Resolution ('ADR').[10] Although ADR is not compulsory, the PD requires parties to consider whether some form of ADR procedure might enable them to settle the matter pre-issue and the court may require evidence that the parties have considered ADR.[11]

- Pre-action protocols require parties to consider whether some form of ADR would be suitable, and if so, to endeavour to agree which form to adopt.[12] The Practice Direction (Pre-action Conduct) sets out the principles that should govern the conduct of the parties where there is no applicable pre-action protocol, in particular the exchange of information to allow informed decisions to be made about settlement and appropriate attempts to resolve the matter without starting proceedings, and in particular to consider the use of an appropriate form of ADR.

- CPR 1.4 extends case management to judicial encouragement of the parties to use an ADR procedure and facilitating its use.

- CPR 26.4 allows courts to stay cases (including on their own intiative) to enable an attempt at ADR to occur.

- Practice Direction to CPR 29 provides that courts can give directions relating to ADR on their own initiative without holding a case management conference.[13]

- In accordance with CPR 44.3 the court can take into account the parties' conduct (including adherence to protocols) on the issue of costs.[14]

- CPR 44.5 allows the court to have regard on the issue of costs to the parties' efforts before and during the proceedings to try to resolve the dispute.

In family matters, there are also various windows of opportunity for mediation in accordance with civil procedure, including after the information meeting; in response to directions of the court; and after a dispute resolution or case management hearing. The Private Law Programme provides encouragement to consider mediation at the first appointment.[15]

---

9   References to CPR are to the Civil Procedure Rules 1998 (as amended).

10   ADR is defined as methods of resolving disputes otherwise than through the normal trial process (and includes negotiation, mediation, early neutral evaluation and arbitration).

11   When considering sanctions, the court will look at the overall effect of the non-compliance. Sanctions include a stay; an order that the party at fault pays the costs of the other party; an order that the party at fault pays those costs on an indemnity basis; an order that interest be disallowed or reduced; and an order that a penalty rate of interest should apply.

12   There are pre-action protocols for construction/engineering, defamation, personal injury, clinical negligence, professional negligence, judicial review, disease/illness, housing disrepair, possession based on rent arrears and possession based on mortgage arrears cases.

13   Refer to Appendix 1 for a form of Direction.

14   Refer to *Halsey v Milton Keynes NHS Trust* [2004] EWCA Civ 291 for the considerations which the court will take into account in determining if a refusal to mediate was reasonable. For cases where courts have imposed cost sanctions for unreasonable failure to engage in ADR, see *Dyson and Field v Leeds City Council* [1999] WL 1142459, *Cowl v Plymouth City Council* [2002] 1 WLR 803, *Dunnett v Railtrack* [2002] 2 All ER 850, *Neal v Jones Motors* [2002] EWCA Civ 1731, *Leicester Circuits v Coates Brothers Plc* [2003] EWCA Civ 290, *Virani v Manuel Revert y Cia SA* (18 July 2003, Unreported, CA), *Longstaff International v Evans and Others* [2005] EWHC (Ch) 4, *McMillan Williams v Range* [2004] EWCA Civ 294, *Painting Oxford University* (*The Times*, 15 February 2005), and *Burchell v Bullard* [2005] EWCA Civ 358.

15   The recognition that courts should be a matter of last resort in family cases has prompted the launch in 2009 of a family mediation page on the Directgov website: see www.direct.gov.uk.

2.11   Although English courts consider that there are limitations on the jurisdiction to order parties to mediate (to allow parties access to courts in accordance with human rights legislation),[16] courts frequently encourage mediation. Various techniques are used at case-management stage to encourage serious consideration, and use, of mediation.[17] Courts have approved, for example, use of the Commercial Court type 'ADR Order' and the form of Order made by Master Ungley in clinical negligence cases. These 'orders' require parties to consider ADR before trial, and to file reasons for objections to engage in ADR with the court, which can be considered in relation to costs orders.[18] In the family law context, courts have encouraged mediation and conciliation for many years.[19] The EU Mediation Directive seeks to tackle the matter of persuasion by courts by recommending that courts in Member States should encourage parties to mediate or to attend mediation information sessions.[20]

The UK Government has also sought to encourage the take-up of mediation by showing its commitment to ADR via 'a pledge'.[21] Under the terms of the ADR pledge, government departments and agencies have committed to consider ADR and to use it in all suitable cases where the other party accepts it.[22]

Finally, a reference to lawyers' duties might also be helpful in the context of persuading a legally represented party to mediate: Rule 2 of the Solicitors Code of Conduct 2007 requires solicitors to discuss with clients whether mediation or other form of ADR would be more appropriate than litigation, arbitration or othe formal process. Failure to comply may later expose the client to cost sanctions (for

---

16   *Halsey v Milton Keynes NHS Trust* [2004] EWCA Civ 291, relying on Article 6 of the European Convention on European Rights. There has been considerable debate about the application of Article 6 in the mediation context as, it is argued, mediation does not prevent recourse to a trial, but postpones the parties' participation, whilst the attempt at mediation is made. The debate extends to the value of mandatory mediation schemes. Research from Ottawa, for example, where mediation is mandatory, indicates that the time and cost of litigation has reduced and, notwithstanding the mandatory nature of mediation, participants report considerable satisfaction with the process.

17   The Technology and Construction Court judges frequently warn parties that, if mediation is unsuccessful, a truncated list of issues for trial and a revised trial length estimate is required, thereby imposing some pressure on parties to take mediation seriously. Refer to Douglas, 'Mediation in complex commercial litigation', in (2008) 10(6) *ADR Bulletin*, 117.

18   Refer to Appendix 1 for sample Orders.

19   Refer to White Paper 1995, paragraphs 5.21–5.22.

20   Directive 2008/52/EC Article 5:
    (1) A court before which an action is brought may, when appropriate and having regard to all the circumstances of the case, invite the parties to use mediation in order to settle the dispute. The court may also invite the parties to attend an information session on the use of mediation if such sessions are held and are easily available.
    (2) This Directive is without prejudice to national legislation making the use of mediation compulsory or subject to incentives or sanctions, whether before or after judicial proceedings have started, provided that such legislation does not prevent the parties from exercising their right of access to the judicial system.
    The EU Recommendation on Family Mediation provides in Article V:
      b. States should set up mechanisms which would:
        i. enable legal proceedings to be interrupted for mediation to take place;
        ii. ensure that in such a case the judicial or other competent authority retains the power to make urgent decisions in order to protect the parties or their children, or their property;
        iii. inform the judicial or other competent authority whether or not the parties are continuing with mediation and whether the parties have reached an agreement.
    Both the Directive and Recommendation are in Appendix 13.

21   Refer to Ministry of Justice, *The Annual Pledge Report – Monitoring the Effectiveness of the Government's Commitment to using ADR 2006–7*, 2007.

22   Refer to www.dca.gov.uk.

unreasonable refusal to mediate) and the lawyer to wasted costs orders, even the possibility of negligence actions.[23]

Public funding of litigation

2.12   Public funding of litigation can also provide a source of persuasion to mediate, as well as indicating the timing for mediation,[24] and providing a structure for intake/screening of cases (as to which, see further below).

The Legal Services Commission (LSC) public funding covers a party's legal costs for preparing for and attending mediation.[25] Except in certain cases,[26] the LSC can require mediation before other litigation steps are taken. If the amount recovered as costs by the publicly funded party is less than costs payable to that party's solicitor, the shortfall is normally deducted from damages payable to the party, and is called 'the statutory charge'. Mediation is exempt from the statutory charge, as is legal advice provided in connection with it, provided that a settlement is reached through mediation.

The LSC provides mediation through LSC contracted providers (called franchises) under fixed fees.[27] These franchises operate in accordance with the MQMS. Provided at least one party is financially eligible, the LSC will pay for both parties' assessment/intake/screening meetings in family law matters, although each party is individually assessed/screened. Public funding is available where a mediator is satisfied that mediation is suitable to the dispute, the parties and all the circumstances. Suitability screening is discussed further below.

The National Audit Office (NAO) reported in 2007 on the use of mediation in publicly funded family cases, and confirmed that only 20% of people funded by legal aid for family breakdown opted for mediation. Among those who opted out, 33% reported that their legal adviser had not told them about the mediation option. The NAO recommended that contracts between the LSC and solicitors should reflect a presumption that mediation should normally be attempted before other remedies are tried; and that the LSC should consider paying for both parties to use mediation where a party is eligible for litigation funding.[28]

---

23 The Law Society *Family Law Protocol*, 2nd edition, 2006 (at 1.1.15) requires solicitors to keep the suitability of mediation/ADR under review throughout a family law case and to encourage clients to go to mediation/ADR when appropriate.

24 In publicly funded cases, there is a requirement to consider mediation before a General Family Help or Legal Representation Legal Certificate can be obtained.

25 In England and Wales, reasonable mediation costs (including preparation for mediation, the mediator's fee, mediation administrative charges and the legal costs associated with the mediation, including work involved in translating the outcome of mediation into a court order by consent, and any associated conveyancing involved), can be covered by LSC funding. In Scotland and Northern Ireland, the costs of civil mediation are not covered by legal aid funding, although in Scotland legal advice and assistance may be available for legal work in preparing for mediation.

26 For example, if the dispute is not suitable (as in the case of domestic abuse); where a party cannot attend mediation due to disability or other restruction; where travel time is too great; if no appointments are available; and if the other party refuses to attend..

27 In 2008/09, £13.8 million pounds was spent on publicly funded family mediation; 13,552 publicly funded family mediations commenced; and 68% of the mediations reached an agreed proposal.

28 Refer to the LSC website: www.legalservices,gov.uk

D.   Intake and screening

2.13   The term *intake* is used by some organisations and providers of mediation services. It refers to the formalised steps taken before the mediation meeting during the mediator's early entry into the dispute. *Screening* refers to one aspect of intake, involving in its broad sense an assessment of the suitability of the dispute for mediation, and in a narrower sense an assessment of those factors which make the matter unsuitable for mediation. Intake also allows for assessment of the most appropriate dispute resolution option. Each of these aspects is considered below.

Intake

Intake is a process which is designed in general terms:

- To gather information about the dispute – for example, the status of any litigation; the history of negotiations between the parties; the nature of the dispute; whether the parties are mediating voluntarily or have been compelled to do so in some way; the main points of agreement and disagreement between them; the availability of documentation; the extent of disclosure so far; and the state of relations between the parties. At a minimum, it is helpful to know the nature of the dispute. For example, if it is a landlord-tenant dispute, whether the tenant's failure to pay is due to lack of funds or a complaint about the condition of the tenanted accommodation; and in the case of a commercial contract dispute, whether the validity of the contract is being challenged or if it is a dispute over the meaning of a contract term.

- To identify the participants – the parties, any legal advisers and any other advisers or supporters – and who has the authority to settle the matter. The greater the number of participants, the longer and more complex will be the process. There is also the practical consideration, to ensure that the venue can accommodate all the participants. There is a predilection in commercial cases to 'over legalise', for example, by involving barristers, solicitors and experts.

- To educate the parties about the mediation process.[29]

- To assess the parties' negotiation styles and sources of power.

- To obtain the consent of one or more parties to participate in mediation.

- To provide a basis for diagnosing the dispute and developing theories of appropriate intervention.

- To suggest referrals to other forms of assistance in place of, or before, mediation.[30]

- To monitor for conflict of interest issues on the mediator's part.

- To decide on the most appropriate timing of mediation, the representatives who will attend the mediation and the identity of the mediator.

---

29   This is explored in further detail in this chapter. Refer also to Stage 1 of the Law Society's Competencies for Civil/Commercial Mediators which is Annex A to the Law Society's Accreditation for Civil/Commercial Mediation (included in Appendix 8).

30   Refer also to the section on Referral in the context of family mediation further below.

- To organise matters such as venue, security, refreshments, office facilities and the like.[31]

- To prepare parties for their participation in mediation.

- To identify lawyers' perceptions about their clients in general civil and commercial cases, which can provide mediators with helpful barometers (for example, regarding the client's intransigence, or preparedness to end the dispute).[32]

- To oversee the exchange documents. If the matter is in litigation, you will need to identify whether disclosure has been completed and whether any futher disclosure is required before the mediation takes place. If disclosure has not taken place, or if the matter is not in litigation, agreement has to be reached on the scope of documents that will be furnished for the mediation. Some matters will require the exchange of at least certain kinds of information before the parties are able to make informed decisions. For example, in a personal injury case, it is rare for a defendant to settle the dispute for anything more than 'nuisance value' without medical reports. In a divorce case, a settlement cannot occur until the couple's assets and financial information are considered.[33] In other cases, document requirements will be minimal. The extent to which a mediator will review the documents will depend on the kind of case or on his or her style and approach. In family cases, for example, the mediator does not independently verify the financial information provided by the parties.[34] In general civil and commercial cases, more evaluative mediators will prefer to review the key documents (in particular, statements of case, contracts, accounts and correspondence).[35] In every case, mediators should be guided in their review by what information is required to gain an understanding of the parties' concerns and needs.[36]

- To oversee the preparation and exchange of case summaries in general civil and commercial cases, which are intended to be succinct documents that summarise the background, the issues and desired outcomes from each party's perspective.[37] Although case summaries can provide useful information, inform the mediator, reduce the time required for resolution and give the parties an opportunity to vent, the summaries might also oversimplify the issues, entrench parties further, encourage legalisation of the problem and incur extra time and cost ahead of mediation. The drawbacks can be minimised by the mediator guiding the parties or their lawyers on the format and style of the case summary.[38]

- Tasking the parties to prepare costs estimates, obtain legal advice, and undertake risk assessments.[39]

---

31 Considered separately further below.
32 Family mediations are normally conducted without the presence of lawyers. Lawyers may be invited to participate in such manner as the mediator may consider useful and as the parties may agree: refer to section 5.12 Law Society Code of Practice for Family Mediation (included in Appendix 8).
33 Information about financial assets, income and future needs tend to be provided in family mediations in Form E (included in Appendix 1).
34 Refer to sections 5.7 and 5.8 Law Society Code of Practice for Family Mediation and section 6.7 College of Mediators Code of Practice (both are included in Appendix 8).
35 Although, as with family mediation, there is no obligation on a mediator in a general civil or commercial case to make independent enquiries or to undertake the verification of information supplied by the parties: see, for example, section 5.13 Law Society Code of Practice for Civil/Commercial Mediation (included in Appendix 8).
36 See also 8.6–8.7 on the mediator's role in providing information.
37 As a guide, between 8–10 pages in the case of a commercial dispute.
38 Refer to the discussion later in this chapter (2.38) and also to Chapter 4.
39 See also 6.58.

■ Being positive and identifying the potential benefits and flexibility of the process.

■ Encouraging the parties to be open to changes to their strategy or view on matters in light of any new information that is presented during the mediation and to be open to different ways of looking at the problems and potential solutions.

Screening

2.14   The intake process can be used in all cases to *screen* for unsuitability for mediation and for unsuitability of the proposed mediator for the case in question. Both aspects are outlined in this section.

Screening is essential in all family cases to ensure that parties participate in mediation willingly and uninfluenced by fears of violence or other harm.[40] As foreshadowed above in relation to litigation funding (refer to 2.12), those applying for legal aid have to meet with a recognised mediator for screening or assessment in order to consider suitability for mediation.[41]

In general terms, mediation may be unsuitable in the following broad categories of circumstances:

■ Where there is a gross imbalance of power between the mediating parties (for example, where there has been domestic violence or abuse[42] or where one party does not have the financial or personal resources needed to participate effectively in mediation, as when a party is bankrupt), which is likely to be beyond the power of a mediator to address.[43]

■ Where the cultural, community or religious dynamics make mediation inappropriate. In some family structures, gross inequality occurs due to culture or religion. In other cases, family or community networks impose undue pressure to save a marriage. In other cases, relationship counselling or marital therapy may be more appropriate at certain stages.

■ Where a party is wholly unsuited to mediation, because they are bent on revenge, or because of their inappropriate mental or psychological state, or where there has been a history of bad-faith negotiations. In family cases, it can also arise where a party is not prepared to accept the end of the relationship.

■ Where external parties have interests which might be adversely affected, or cannot adequately be addressed, in mediation, for example, where there are abused children in a matrimonial dispute; where the rights of beneficiaries or creditors cannot be adequately represented at mediation; or where consumers

---

40   Section 27 Family Law Act 1996; section 11 Law Society Code of Practice for Family Mediation; and section 4.8.1 College of Mediators Code of Practice. Refer to Appendix 8 for codes of conduct. Refer also to College of Mediators Domestic Abuse Screening Policy which is included in Appendix 2.

41   F1.1 MQMS requires LSC franchised practices to have a screening system in place. That system has to consider the clients, the dispute and the circumstances. Evidence of operation of the system will be required on audit.

42   Where there has been domestic abuse and this has resulted in a police investigation or the issuing of civil proceedings for the protection of the abused party in the last 12 months, or where a party is currently applying for a domestic violence injunction, the matter is automatically exempted from mediation in the case of family matters which are publicly funded.

43   The issue of power imbalances in mediation is addressed in more detail in Chapter 10.

in a competition law dispute require a public determination or an official response to a problem.

- Where the mediation is likely to be used for purely opportunistic reasons, as to gain some advantage in the litigation to follow.
- Where emergency procedures (like an injunction) are required or have not yet been concluded.
- Where there are policy or societal reasons why matters should not be mediated, for example, where there are allegations of terrorism, child abuse, a risk of child abduction, fraudulent or criminal behaviour, or it is the kind of dispute which should be dealt with through the public court system or requires adjudication.
- Where bail conditions are in place restricting a party having contact with another.

Screening may also reveal that the mediator proposed has an actual or potential conflict of interest,[44] or is inadequately competent for the matter in question.[45] A conflict of interest may arise in the following cases:

- Where the case involves the mediator, the mediator's firm/organisation or a member of its staff or management, or someone related to the mediator.
- Where the mediator has acquired confidential or other relevant information about the case in a private or other capacity.
- Where the mediator has a personal interest in the outcome of the mediation.
- Where the mediator or a member of the mediator's firm/organisation has acted for one of the parties.

In some cases, the conflict can be addressed by making full disclosure to the parties and if the parties consent to the mediator proceeding. In other cases, the mediator will need to withdraw from the mediation, and the matter will need to be referred to another mediator or mediation organisation.[46]

Screening may involve telephone inquiries, completion of questionnaires,[47] and personal interviews. Resource restrictions in general civil or commercial matters may

---

44 Article 2.2 of the European Code of Conduct for Mediators requires mediators to disclose conflicts, as do most other mediator codes of conduct. Refer in relation to general civil/commercial cases, for example, to section 3.4 Law Society Code of Practice for Civil/Commercial Mediation, section 4.3 of the CEDR Code, section 3 of the CORE Solutions Group Code and section 2.3 of the IMI Code. In relation to family cases, refer for example to section 4 Law Society Code of Practice for Family Mediation and section 4.4 College of Mediators Code of Practice. In relation to LSC franchised mediation practice, refer to E1.2 MQMS. Appendix 8 contains these various codes of conduct and standards. Most mediation agreements require confirmation that the mediator has disclosed any conflicts and will keep the issue under review throughout the mediation: see, for example, clauses 8–9 Law Society sample Mediation Agreement in Appendix 3.
45 Article 1.1 of the European Code of Conduct for Mediators requires mediators to be competent and knowledgeable, as do most other mediator codes of conduct. Refer in relation to general civil/commercial mediation, for example, to section 2.1 of the CEDR Code, sections 2.1 and 2.2 of the CORE Solutions Group Code and section 2.1 IMI Code. In relation to family mediation, refer, for example, to section 2 Law Society Code of Practice for Family Mediation. Appendix 8 contains a selection of codes of conduct and standards.
46 Refer to the guidance in the provisions listed in footnote 36. Refer also to referral in 2.17.
47 CMP has designed an on-line screening tool, called 'Ready to Resolve Mediation Questionnaire', which checks readiness to resolve a workplace matter using mediation (refer to www.cmpresolutions.co.uk). It has been designed in light of the new workplace dispute resolution framework (since April 2009), which encourages prevention and early resolution, and the ACAS Code of Conduct. Refer to Appendix 2 for a copy of the CMP screening questionnaire.

necessitate that intake be undertaken only by telephone. Where there are concerns about violence or abuse, an enhanced assessment process is conducted in person.

Screening has varying degrees of sophistication. In a general civil or commercial case, it is usually done by reference to an investigation about whether other attempts at ADR have been made, if the parties are willing to negotiate and whether a case is 'ripe' (in terms of timing) for mediation (which usually depends on the degree of information exchange required). In family cases, on the other hand, screening is a sophisticated process, especially in relation to the question of domestic abuse.[48] A direct inquiry as to whether there has been violence in a relationship may, for emotional or psychological reasons, elicit a negative response despite the fact that there has been a history of violence. More subtle questions and interviewing techniques are required to deal with this reticence.

LSC franchises and the member organisations of the Family Mediation Council have developed their own guidelines to aid the screening process.[49] The Law Society of England and Wales has adapted various guidelines following advice and consultation to formulate the following list of questions:[50]

1. Have you been arguing a lot recently?

2. Do you generally have a lot of arguments?

3. When you argue, what usually happens?

4. Have you or your partner been convicted of any criminal offence, in particular those including violence and/or drugs or alcohol?

5. What happens when your partner loses their temper and/or you lose your temper?

6. When you and/or your partner drink alcohol does this ever result in arguments?

7. Do you and/or your partner ever become violent after consuming alcohol or any other substance?

8. How safe or afraid do you and/or your partner feel in your current relationship?

9. Has your partner ever threatened you with a weapon and have you ever threatened him or her with a weapon?

10. Has your partner threatened to harm himself or herself and/or the children and have you ever threatened to harm yourself and/or the children?

11. Has your partner ever stalked you and have you ever stalked your partner?

---

48 Domestic abuse is 'any incident of threatening behaviour, violence or abuse (psychological, physical, sexual, financial or emotional) between adults who are or have been intimate partners or family members, regardless of gender or sexuality': Law Society, *Family Law Protocol*, 2nd edition, 2006, 94. UK College of Family Mediators, *Domestic Abuse Screening Policy*, 2000b defines domestic abuse as 'behaviour that seeks to secure power and control for the abuser and the impact of which is to undermine the safety, security, self-esteem and autonomy of the abused person. Domestic violence contains elements of the use of any or all of physical, sexual, psychological, emotional, verbal or economic intimidation, oppression or coercion.' The Policy is in Appendix 2.

49 Refer also to the College of Mediators Domestic Abuse Screening Policy in Appendix 2.

50 Law Society, *Family Law Protocol*, 2nd edition, 2006, para 6.3.1, p 98.

The Law Society has developed a further list of question for enhanced assessment/screening (where there are suspicions of domestic abuse):[51]

1. Are you afraid of your partner?

2. Why are you afraid of him or her?

3. Has there been any violence between you?

4. Have either of you been hurt by the other? If so, is the violence escalating in frequency and/or severity?

5. Were these injuries caused by someone you know?

6. Have your children ever witnessed any violence between you?

7. Are you/is your partner currently pregnant?

8. Do you have any disabilities (mental or physical)?

9. What support networks do you have in terms of friends, family or others?

There are two options as regards who undertakes the intake and screening. They can be undertaken by the mediator personally, which is common in LSC franchised, family and community mediation; or they can be undertaken by intake officers (called, for example, 'case advisers' or 'case managers'), which is common with institutional mediation service-providers in general civil and commercial cases. Intake is a specialised function, particularly where the circumstances require screening (as in family mediation), hence the need for training.[52]

The LSC pays for intake and screening where a party is publicly funded, and many family mediation franchises provide intake and screening free of charge. In other cases, intake and screening is not a cost-free activity; and requires money, resources, time and other potentially costly items. These must be paid for either by the parties, as part of the mediator's fee, or by the agency or other service provider.

2.15 Screening can lead to a determination that the case is suitable for mediation;[53] that a case is not suitable for mediation;[54] that a case should be designated to another process (called 'streaming');[55] or that the case should be referred to another mediator or mediation organisation (called 'referral').

Streaming

2.16 *Streaming* refers to the reference of disputes to appropriate dispute resolution options, such as mediation, arbitration, case appraisal or litigation.[56] The practice

---

51 Law Society, *Family Law Protocol*, 2nd edition, 2006, para 6.3.3, p 99.
52 Refer to D.5 MQMS.
53 F2.1 MQMS requires LSC franchises to provide certain information in writing as soon as possible after a decision has been made that a case is suitable for mediation, including the date/venue of mediation; name of the mediator; relevant key dates; any action to be taken by parties or mediator; and the availability of independent legal advice.
54 F1.1 MQMS requires written notification to be given to potential clients of LSC franchised services although the reasons for unsuitability do not need to be given.
55 F2.3 MQMS requires family mediation services to give parties information about complementary services, like welfare benefits suppliers, marital counselling, financial advisers, child counselling and LSC-contracted family lawyers.
56 Refer to Element 1 of the Law Society Competencies for Civil/Commercial Mediation which is Annex A to the Law Society's Accreditation for Civil/Commercial Mediation (included in Appendix 8).

has led to notions of the 'multi-door courthouse' in some jurisdictions. Streaming is not an exact science, and dispute resolution advisers in various organisations and industry bodies are required to perform this function in light of the information they have to hand. For present purposes it is sufficient to note that the streaming aspect of intake might result in a case being found unsuitable for mediation or more suitable for another dispute resolution option.[57]

Streaming

Mediation might not be the most appropriate dispute resolution option in certain circumstances; and, in others, it might be important not to use it. Pressure is sometimes exerted for a host of reasons on governments, courts, tribunals, corporations, other organisations and individuals to encourage or to use mediation, regardless of how suitable it might be for the particular case.

Unsuitability for mediation might arise where the parties' emotional or intellectual state is not conducive to mediation; where past experience suggests they will not respond to mediation, or that it will make the situation worse, and where the parties might use mediation for some ulterior purposes; where other forms of ADR have been attempted without success; where the costs or delay occasioned by the attempt at mediation might be disproportionate; and where a party considers that the merits of its case are strong.[58]

The determination that a case is unsuitable for mediation has the advantages of preventing wasteful or destructive mediation sessions, or of allowing some time to pass until conditions are more suitable for mediation, and of motivating clients to rely on, or make use of, more suitable options.

Referral

2.17

- Screening can also lead to referral to another professional, mediator or mediation organisation. LSC-franchised practices are expected to make arrangements for the party to see someone from another organisation and to meet minimum information requirements to both the party and the other organisation.[59]

---

57 And, in family cases, if the matter is appropriate for other options, like counselling, therapy and so on: refer to section 6.8 College of Mediators Code of Practice. Section 6.9 of the Code requires mediators to inform parties about the court or other formal proceedings which are available and the procedures applicable to these. However, mediators must not give legal advice or predict the outcome if the matter were referred to another process.

58 Refer to *Halsey v Milton Keynes General NHS Trust* and *Steel v Joy* [2004] EWCA Civ 576 for indictors when a refusal to mediate might not be considered unreasonable in general civil and commercial cases (the court considered this issue on the question whether cost sanctions should be imposed for refusal to mediate).

59 Refer to requirement B1.1 MQMS for staff knowledge about referral; requirement B1.2 MQMS regarding the procedures that need to be in place for conducting referral; and requirement B1.3 MQMS relating to maintenance and review of referral records and data. These requirements are aimed at LSC franchises providing the public with a seamless service, so that the public is directed to an alternative service provider where appropriate and available. The MQMS is included in Appendix 8.

E. Preparatory work in team negotiations

2.18   The term 'team negotiations' here refers to a situation in which each 'party' in mediation comprises a group of two or more individuals. In this sense a voluntary association, a community group, a trade union and even multiple claimants in general civil and commercial cases could be regarded as a team.

It is necessary for the mediator or intake staff to undertake specific preparatory work for mediation involving one or more teams. This will include attention to:

- The identification of stakeholders – who will participate in the mediation?

- Early contact with key parties.

- The nomination of advisers, spokespersons and participants for each group.

- The division of labour within each group.

- Forms of communication with members of constituent groups, which might involve modifications to the normal confidentiality arrangements.

- The desirability of appointing a process control group who can advise their constituent members of progress in the mediation.[60]

- Methods of decision-making within each group (see the case illustration below).

- A customised agreement to mediate may be required.

- Review or ratification of any mediated settlement should be discussed.

- Disclosure issues – manner, timing and comprehensiveness.

Case illustration

In a mediation involving various business associations, the mediator undertook considerable preparatory work over a number of sessions involving extensive education on the nature of conflict and interest-based negotiation.

In the preparatory stages, the mediator required the participating groups to commit to a decision-making process before any proposals were on the table. The groups committed to majority vote (which would marginalise minority dissenters and allow the groups collectively to come to a decision).

The subsequent mediation commenced well, although it soon became apparent that there was a destabilising individual in one of the team groups. It was clear that this person would not commit to any agreement and her dominant role within the particular group precluded the group from being able to do the same.

Had it not been for the preparatory work, it would have been difficult to impose a decision-making procedure on the groups once mediation had commenced and concrete proposals were on the table, especially once individuals had taken positions in respect of them.

Multi-party mediations are considered in more detail in Chapter 10.

---

60   See 10.62.

F. Authority to settle

2.19   It is always desirable that those present at the mediation table have authority to settle. Most standard mediation agreements and procedures make reference to this requirement.[61] The issue arises where the participating parties are there in a representative capacity, for example, a professional adviser on behalf of a client, a director on behalf of a company, or a public official on behalf of a government department. All veteran mediators have experienced situations where the representative party has indicated towards the conclusion of mediation that they lack authority to settle. They then request an adjournment to contact and seek ratification of the proposed agreement from their client, the company board or Minister of the government department, as the case may be. This can have fatal consequences for the mediation.

The golden rule here is for the mediator to anticipate that the 'no authority' problem may arise, and to attempt to secure the presence at the mediation table of a person or persons with the necessary authority.

2.20   This is not always straightforward, however, as there are several situations in which the no authority problem might arise:

- where the question of authority has been genuinely overlooked by the representative concerned, although this is not a common occurrence.

- where, for practical or policy reasons, it is not possible to obtain any authority at all. For example, some governmental decisions require formal approval.

- where the representative at the mediation has authority but it is limited and the proposed settlement agreement is in excess of that limit.

- where a representative at the mediation claims to have no authority as a tactic to buy time or to impose negotiation pressure on another party.

The first situation is the easiest for the mediator to deal with, by asking all participants at the earliest stage, whether they will have authority to settle at the mediation, and if not what would be necessary to obtain it.

In the second situation nothing can be done to secure authority, but the mediator can ensure that all parties are advised in advance that, say, formal approval will be required for any decision so that it does not come as a destabilising surprise in the mediation. It may also be possible to obtain an indication that the person attending the mediation is able to recommend a settlement reached at mediation to the relevant Board or Committee.

The third situation is a fact of life for many defendants who will have authority to settle up to their 'bottom line'. Here the mediator may have to engage in some reality testing to determine if the level is realistic and, in some cases, engage in doubt creation by asking whether the representative can obtain some additional

---

61   For example, in section 4 CEDR Model Mediation Procedure and in clause 2 CEDR Model Mediation Agreement; in clause 1.2 ADR Group Mediation Procedure and Rules; and in clauses 11 and 12 Law Society's sample Mediation Agreement (these various documents are included in Appendix 3).

discretion to take account of new information or disclosures from the other side or other unexpected developments.

The fourth situation is the most problematic, even where the mediator has strong grounds for believing that it is a tactic. No amount of diligence will inevitably pre-empt the tactical ploy. It is less easy to use where the mediator has remembered to raise the authority issue openly and timeously with all parties, though a party can still insist that they had only limited authority which is then exceeded at mediation. Having a warranty of authority clause in the agreement to mediate also makes it more difficult for authority isuses to be used tactically.[62]

2.21   Some experienced mediators probe in advance the limits of each representative's authority to settle. They may ask whether it extends only up to the extent of offers previously made by that side, in which case it would be expedient to suggest that further authority be obtained. They may ask whether it extends to the full amount of the other party's claim, in which case it is likely to be sufficient (unless costs will also factor into any settlement reached at mediation). They may ask to see confidentially in advance a written statement of authority to ensure that any limited authority claim is genuine and not a devious tactic. None of these strategies will guarantee that the parties are open with the mediator and that all dangers are excluded. They are, however, good risk minimisation strategies.

Accordingly, the question of authority should be canvassed as early as possible during the mediator's entry into the dispute and may need to be revisited at later stages as well. The mediator may have to act as 'reality agent' in pointing out the short-term and long-term disadvantages for the party who plays the 'no authority' card.

Similar issues arise in relation to the *ratification* problem, which is dealt with separately.[63]

G.   Preliminary meetings

2.22   In some situations there is a preliminary meeting before the mediation meeting as an occasion for building the mediation foundations.

The preliminary meeting is usually convened and chaired by the mediator and can be attended by all relevant parties. In family cases, the parties only tend to attend. In many general civil and commercial cases, only lawyers tend to attend and the parties have no direct involvement. In cases involving government or community groups, a range of stakeholders may attend. There are advantages in having the parties present at a preliminary meeting. It gives the parties an opportunity to meet the mediator and become familiar with his or her style, and it allows the mediator to assess the parties' suitability for mediation and to predict their likely attitudes and behaviour at the subsequent meetings.

2.23   The preliminary meeting can be used for many of the intake and screening functions referred to above.[64] In some cases, it can be used to persuade parties to

---

62   Refer to the sample agreements to mediate in Appendix 3.
63   See 5.75.
64   Refer, for example, to section 4 CEDR Model Mediation Procedure and to clauses 15–17 Law Society
     sample Mediation Agreement (in Appendix 3).

mediate.[65] In any case, it can provide the mediator with a good opportunity to develop the trust and confidence of the parties.

The broad functions of the preliminary meeting are:

- To provide information to the parties (and/or their lawyers) and to educate them about the nature of mediation, the respective roles in mediation, and the process which the individual mediator will follow.[66] For many participants, mediation will be a new process and they will need information about the mediation process, including its benefits and the roles and responsibilities of all participants.[67]

- To educate participants about the mediator's particular approach. Mediators have different styles and, in the case of general civil and commercial mediation, will operate somewhere along a continuum between purely facilitative and more evaluative.[68] Giving the participants an idea about what to expect promotes understanding, and overall satisfaction, in the process. It manages the parties' expectations from an early stage. It also provides an opportunity for the participants to communicate what their preferred style might be. This may happen where participants have had previous experience with mediation, as in the case of lawyers, insurers or corporate executives.[69]

---

65 Haynes and Charlesworth have reported their experience of conducting preliminary conferences in family cases with a view to persuading parties to mediate. In their experience, over 90% of parties attending those preliminary meetings chose to continue to mediation: Haynes and Charlesworth, *The Fundamentals of Family Mediation*, 1996, p 38.

66 Section 6.1 College of Mediators Code of Practice stipulates the information requirements in family cases (refer to Appendix 8). The MQMS for LSC franchises is specific (see requirement F1.2) about the information required to be given to participants ahead of mediation, including: an overview of the process; note-taking; confidentiality and waiver; the independence/impartiality of mediators; the voluntary nature of participation; other complementary services; and information about complaints procedures (refer to Appendix 8). F1.3 MQMS also requires participants to be made aware of their right to seek independent legal advice at the start of, and throughout, the mediation process. Most family mediation codes also require this: refer, for example, to section 6.10 College of Mediators Code of Practice and section 5.4 Law Society Code of Practice for Family Mediation. Element 1 of the Law Society Competencies for Civil/Commercial Mediators also addresses information requirements. The document is included as Annex A to the Law Society's Accreditation for Civil/Commercial Mediation (included in Appendix 8).

67 Refer to Stage 1 (Engaging the parties in the mediation forum) in the Law Society Civil/Commercial Mediation Competencies for a list of matters which a mediator should address with the parties at this stage. The document is Annex A to the Law Society's Accreditation for Civil/Commercial Mediation (in Appendix 8).

68 Ibid.

69 It is also likely to happen in commercial cases where the parties, or their lawyers, would like the option of the mediator expressing a view or making a non-binding written recommendation on the resolution of the dispute or difference. Refer, for example, to section 4.9 CORE Solutions Group Code of Conduct (in Appendix 8), which clarifies that the mediator is not obliged to comply with such a request or any other request to vary his or her role as independent facilitator of the process of mediation; and that the mediator may offer a non-binding recommendation if the mediator considers that he or she is competent to do so and that to do so would assist in the resolution of the dispute or difference. The Law Society's sample Mediation Agreement (refer to Appendix 3) includes provisions regarding non-binding determinations, and the Law Society's Code of Practice for Civil/Commercial Mediation addresses this matter (in the commentary under Section 5, see Appendix 8). Article 7.4 UNCITRAL Conciliation Rules (which tend to be adopted in international commercial cases) allow a facilitator to make proposals for settlement, without requiring reasons for those proposals (see Appendix 3).

- To provide information about the mediator's background and experience.[70] This helps establish credibility and authority with the participants.[71]

- To agree the mediator's fees and charges. Most mediator codes of conduct require mediators to supply the parties with complete information on the mode of remuneration, and that their appointment should not be finalised until the remuneration has been agreed by all parties.[72] In addition to the amount of fees, a mediator should address how and when, and by whom, the fees are to be paid.[73] Typically, in general civil and commercial cases, the costs of the mediation (the mediator's fees and expenses) are borne equally between the parties and each party bears their own legal costs and expenses (and unless otherwise agreed are usually costs in the case).[74] In some cases, mediation organisations require deposits and other upfront fees.[75]

- To obtain agreement on the necessary exchange of documents and other fact-finding requirements, and on the status of legal proceedings, if relevant.

- To identify the broad parameters of the mediation – to determine what issues will be discussed at mediation, and what matters are no longer in issue.

- To clarify what previous offers have been made, or where previous negotiations have got to.

- To determine who will attend the mediation meeting.[76]

- To verify that the parties at the mediation meeting will have authority to settle (refer to 2.19 above).

---

70 Refer, for example, to Article 1.2 European Code of Conduct for Mediators and section 1.3 IMI Code (both are included in Appendix 8) and to Article 3.2 ICC ADR Rules (included in Appendix 3). Refer to Appendix 2 for a sample mediator cv and generic profile.

71 Most mediator codes of conduct require mediators to promote themselves and their practices in a professional, truthful and dignified way. Refer, for example, to Article 1.4 European Code of Conduct for Mediators, section 3.1 CEDR Code, section 7 CORE Solutions Group Code, clause 3.5 IMI Code and section 6.2 College of Mediators Code (included in Appendix 8).

72 Refer, for example, to Article 1.3 European Code of Conduct. Section 3.1 CEDR Code, section 7 CORE Solutions Group Code, section 3.5 IMI Code and section 6.2 College of Mediators Code (all codes are included in Appendix 8). F5.1 MQMS requires LSC franchises to inform parties in writing at the start of the process what charges apply and, in accordance with requirement F5.2 MQMS, to update them every six months about the costs.

73 Refer to Appendix 3 for sample agreements to mediate and fee schedules. A court will not imply terms as to how fees should be split between the parties – refer to *Cable & Wireless v IBM* [2005] EWHC 873 (Comm) and *Aiton Australia Pty Ltd v Transfield Pty Ltd* (1999) NSWSC 55020. In *National Westminster Bank v Feeney & Feeney* [2006] EWHC 90066 (Costs), the Tomlin Order referred to costs assessment on the standard basis and the defendants argued that the costs of the mediation were included as part of the standard costs. The agreement to mediate provided, however, that each party should bear their own legal costs. The court found that the Tomlin Order did not override the agreement to mediate. Compare *Newcastle City Council v Paul Wieland* [2009] NSWCA 113, where an Australian court (the New South Wales Court of Appeal) considered whether the phrase 'costs of the proceedings' includes the costs associated with mediation. The court considered that, where mediation takes place as part of the court procedure, mediation is a 'step in the proceedings', and accordingly the costs associated with mediation were found to be 'costs of the proceedings'.

74 See, for example, clause 11 CEDR Model Mediation Agreement, clause 12 ADR Group Mediation Procedure and Rules, clause 2 Law Society sample Mediation Agreement, Articles 4.5 and 4.6 ICC ADR Rules and Articles 17.1–17.2 UNICTRAL Conciliation Rules (included in Appendix 3). The ICC and UNICTRAL Rules tend to be adopted in international commercial cases.

75 See, for example, Articles 4.1–4.4 ICC ADR Rules, Appendix to ICC ADR Rules called 'Schedule of ADR Costs' and Articles 18.1–18.4 UNICTRAL Conciliation Rules (included in Appendix 3).

76 Although lawyers do not generally attend family mediation sessions, most family mediation codes of conduct remind mediators about the need to inform parties to obtain independent legal advice throughout the mediation process: refer, for example, to section 6.10 College of Mediators Code of Practice (in Appendix 8).

- To make organisational arrangements relating to timing,[77] venue, facilities, seating, any special needs, and the like (refer to 2.26–2.36 below).

- To settle the agreement to mediate (refer to 2.37 below).[78]

- To guide the parties on prepartion of case summaries and opening statements (refer to 2.38 below).

- To identify any settlement formalities and review or ratification issues.[79]

- To deal with other questions and queries about mediation from the parties or their advisers.

- To start establishing a working relationship, trust and rapport with the parties, their advisers and supporters.

- To encourage good-faith participation in mediation.

- To provide the parties with guidelines on preparation for the negotiations, including cost estimates and risk assessment.[80]

- To encourage ongoing discussions.

These matters are considered further below or in later chapters. If these matters are not handled at a preliminary meeting, they are handled in pre-mediation contact, usually over the telephone, between the mediator and the parties' advisers, or the parties direct in the absence of advisers.

2.24 Apart from the overt and formal aspects relating to when, where and with whom, a number of subtle developments can take place at a preliminary meeting. Where large organisations, such as local authorities or insurers, are involved, this may be the first occasion that the mediating parties have met one another. It usually provides an opportunity for each party to meet the other's legal or other professional advisers for the first time. There is a general acclimatisation between the parties and some tentative negotiations on matters of process. In some cases, settlement has been known to occur at the preliminary meeting, or shortly thereafter.

H. Separate prior meetings with the parties

2.25 Some mediators have prior face-to-face contact with each party individually. In some cases, this happens on the mediation day, before the formal start of the mediation meeting (in which case, most of the practical matters required for preparation, outlined in the next section, are addressed beforehand).

Mediators maintain that some form of prior contact (before the formal start of a mediation session) is the most important factor in a successful mediation. Prior contact can be used to deal with many of the preliminary matters referred to in this chapter and, in addition, allows the mediator to develop a productive working relationship with each party.

---

77 Section 6.2 College of Mediators Code of Conduct requires mediators to agree with parties the anticipated length of mediation.
78 Refer also to Appendix 3 for sample mediation agreements.
79 Refer also to 5.74–5.79 and 10.74–10.77.
80 Refer to Appendix 6 for various preparation tools and guidance notes. See also Chapters 8 and 10.

In general terms, prior contact between the mediator and each party allows for:

- open communication;
- rapport building;
- frank discussions;
- party acclimatisation;
- comfort with process and roles;
- mediator diagnosis;
- negotiation planning and coaching;
- trouble shooting;
- discussion of time limits to help focus the parties' minds;
- checking on the availability of advisers and other supporters;
- time management;
- allowing questions to be asked and answered;
- motivating behavioural change;
- managing expectations;
- challenging assumptions and perceptions.

As usual, much will depend on the circumstances, including the nature of the dispute and the clients. In some cases, prior contact between the mediator and each party would create distrust and suspicion. Time, money and other resource pressures may also reduce the scope for prior contact in some cases. If prior contact takes place without lawyers, where the parties are legally represented, considerable education about what has transpired without them may be required. In family cases, although in general terms separate sessions can take place,[81] there are particular issues regarding the disclosure of discussions a party has in a separate meeting with the mediator.[82]

The following example illustrates how the prior contact system could work in a general civil or commercial case:

---

81 Refer to Chapters 5 and 9 for a more detailed discussion about separate and joint sessions.
82 For example, section 6.4 of the College of Mediators Code of Practice and sections 7.2–7.5 of the Law Society Code of Practice for Family Mediation (both codes are included in Appendix 8) address this issue. Although it may be agreed between the parties and mediator that the mediator will either report back to the parties the substance of separate meetings or maintain separate confidences, those confidences do not include any material facts which would be open if discussed in a joint meeting. All information relating to financial issues, for example, are provided on an open basis. Accordingly mediators must not guarantee that any communication from one party will be kept secret from the other (except a party's address and phone number and without prejudice offers). Where relevant information emerges in separate session which a party is not willing to have disclosed to the other, the mediator must consider whether it is appropriate to continue with mediation.

The 'prior contact' system in general civil or commercial cases

The parties (or their lawyers if they are legally represented) are contacted prior to the mediation by the mediator personally. Telephone interviews are usually used to educate the parties/their lawyers, assess their suitability for mediation, to check on information requirements, prepare the parties/their lawyers for mediation, deal with queries, and make organisational arrangements. Timings for appointments are agreed. Assume that appointments for the mediation day are made as follows: Party A with the mediator individually, 9am; Party B with the mediator individually, 10am; both parties together with the mediator, 11am. As the appointment times suggest, each party is seen separately by the mediator for approximately one hour, during which time particular emphasis is put on ascertaining their real needs and interests, in preparing them to negotiate, and in developing trust in the mediator and the process. Thereafter the mediation is conducted with both parties present, using joint and separate meetings as appropriate.

I.   Practical preparation for the mediation meeting

2.26   To complete the foundations, the following matters need to be organised prior to the actual mediation meeting.[83]

Venue and accommodation

2.27   The venue should be:

- Visible,[84] accessible to the participants, have parking facilities, provide refreshments and meals, and have lighting if mediations will be held in the evening.

- Neutral as between the parties, to prevent the 'home ground' syndrome which can provide tactical advantages for the 'home team'. Alternatively have it 'on site', for example, the place of employment in a workplace dispute or at the offices of one of the lawyers in a commercial dispute.

- Convenient, comfortable and safe for the parties.[85] If appropriate, the venue can be rotated – for example, if multiple meetings are to be held, in order to achieve balance and for the convenience of the parties.

- Suitably equipped with child facilities if appropriate.[86]

---

83   These matters are Element 4 in the Law Society's Competencies for Civil/Commercial Mediators which is an Annex A to the Law Society's Accreditation for Civil/Commercial Mediation (included in Appendix 8).
84   Especially if it is a mixed service being run out of the same premises: refer to requirement C4.3 MQMS.
85   LSC franchises must also have a written procedure/statement detailing how party and mediator safety is maintained: requirement F1.4 MQMS.
86   Requirement C4.4 MQMS.

2.28   The accommodation must also have:

- at least three meeting rooms – one for each party (assuming there are only two) and one for the mediator/any joint meetings;[87]

- soundproof rooms, or meeting places, where outsiders cannot hear what is taking place inside;[88]

- waiting rooms (separate waiting rooms are required where there has been inter-party violence).[89]

It is prudent for the mediator to provide participants with directions to the venue.

Timing

2.29   There are different views on the most appropriate timing for mediation. There has to be enough time to procure relevant information so that the case is 'ripe' for mediation, but as mediation is not fact-obsessed there does not have to be an exhaustive pursuit of information. The emotional state of the parties is also relevant to timing. Where one or more is in shock, denial, severe depression or uncontrollable anger it may not advisable to proceed with mediation at that time.[90]

Duration

2.30   The length of the mediation is another matter that is often decided during the initial phase. We believe, except where a court or other body has set the duration of the mediation by order, that the mediator should work with the parties to determine a reasonable duration of the mediation. You should use your experience with disputes to help guide the parties in setting the proper duration of the mediation as you will typically be in a better position as result of your training and experience to know how much time it will take to conduct a productive mediation.

As a general rule, the more complex the dispute and the more participants that are involved, the longer the dispute will take to resolve. Most general civil and commercial disputes can be mediated in one day. There are, however, disputes that can be handled in a half day and those that will require several days. Family mediations typically occur over two to six sessions of 1.5 hours duration.[91] Sometimes clients will advocate a block of time inappropriate for the dispute, usually shorter than necessary. For example, an employer might attempt to schedule a half-day mediation for an employment discrimination dispute, the complexity of which

---

87 Requirement C4.2 MQMS stipulates a minimum of two suitable rooms to ensure that parties can be seen separately or be separated if necessary. Refer also, for example, to section 7 CEDR Model Mediation Procedure (in Appendix 3).
88 Requirements C4.5 and F6 MQMS.
89 Requirement C4.1 MQMS. Refer also to O. J. Coogler, *Structured Mediation in Divorce Settlement*, Lexington Books, 1978; J. M. Haynes, *Divorce Mediation: A Practical Guide for Therapists and Counselors*, Springer, NY, 1981; and Folberg & Taylor, *Mediation: A Comprehensive Guide to Resolving Conflict without Mediation*, 1984.
90 See 3.5–3.7.
91 The 'hybrid' family mediation method, aimed at 'all issues' using a mediator qualified in both family and general civil/commercial mediation, is intended to run over a whole day. For more information about the operation of the 'hybrid' method, refer to ADR Group's website (www.adrgroup.co.uk).

clearly will require at least a full day of mediation. In such circumstances, the mediator should explain the need to extend the mediation time, explaining the reasons for such a request. Problem-solving and decision-making takes time.[92] Our experience is that most clients will follow advice regarding duration if it is supported with thoughtful explanation.

We believe in setting a specific duration for a mediation session (say, 2pm to 3.30pm for a family mediation session or, say, 9am to 11am for a workplace grievance or, say, 9am to 6pm, for a general civil or commercial case). This has two benefits. First, parties can plan their schedule accordingly, as well as having advisers and other support people available in person or by telephone or e-mail if necessary. The second benefit is that setting an ending time has strategic advantages. When faced with a deadline in negotiation, people have a tendency to become more flexible as that deadline approaches.[93] This potential benefit is greatly diminished when finish times are open ended.

Setting the duration in advance does not mean, however, that mediation cannot or should not be extended. If parties are making progress or the resolution of the matter appears promising with continued discussion, mediation can be continued past the planned ending time, or additional sessions/days can be scheduled in the future. These extensions should be discussed with parties and consented to by them. Moreover, there is usually a provision in the agreement to mediate regarding additional fees for extensions of the mediations so parties have the option of continuing to try to work through the conflict. If there are any additional fees for extensions, parties should be reminded of them before an extension is agreed to. There are also practical issues when working into the evening at most venues, as in the case of after-hours lighting, security, refreshments and office facilities.

Arrivals, waiting facilities and departures

2.31   Mediators must plan and supervise the arrivals, waiting and departure of all parties. Ideally, parties should arrive at the mediation venue at separate times, should be received by the mediator or a receptionist, and should be allocated to separate waiting rooms. In many cases, these arrangements are not possible, or break down. Where one party arrives before the other, the mediator should not be seen in conversation with this party when the other arrives. Attention is required regarding parties' departures where there has been high emotion in the mediation, or where there is a past history of violence between the parties. The normal practice is to allow the 'victim' or threatened party to leave the building first and complete his or her departure before the other party is allowed to leave.

Seating

2.32   There are many seating variations. The basic approach is to provide what is culturally appropriate, for example, formal tables for commercial disputes, and easy chairs for community disputes.

---

92   Leigh L. Thompson, *The Mind and Heart of the Negotiator* (3rd ed, 2005), 67.
93   Roger Dawson, *Secrets of Power Negotiating* (2nd ed, 2001), 173.

Most mediators sit at the head of the table, equidistant from the parties. The parties should have their own physical space, separate and equal. Some mediators try to avoid the parties facing one another across the table in a 'confrontational' mode, preferring round or oval settings, or seating at the corners of tables, in a less adversarial mode. Some US mediation services have custom-designed 'kitchen' layouts to symbolise the notion of 'sorting this out around the kitchen table'. However, often the facts of life provide little choice, and mediators have to make do with whatever tables are available. As regards chairs, mediators can negate the negotiation tactic of giving the opposition the lower chairs while taking the power seats for themselves, by ensuring as far as possible that the chairs for all parties are similar in size and comfort, or discomfort.

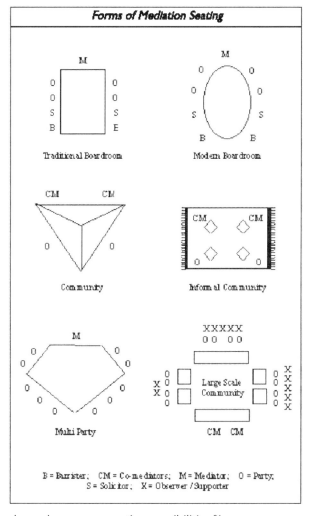

The diagram above shows some seating possibilities.[94]

2.33   Seating can change during the mediation. Initially, the parties' chairs may face each other as a basis for communicating directly across the table in later stages

---

94   Taken from L. Boulle and M. Nesic, *MPPP*, 2001, 191.

of the mediation. During separate meetings,[95] the mediator might move to sit next to a party as a way of encouraging the party to be open with the mediator and start problem-solving. In all situations mediators make practical choices based on their informed judgement.

Amenities

2.34   Communication facilities (such as telephones, fax machine and e-mail access), refreshments, tissues and other creature comforts are necessary. While the refreshment issue may seem trite, it is not just about physical comfort for the participants. Having a jug of water and empty glasses on the table provides the opportunity for some ritual serving between the parties. Even where the mediator does the pouring, it symbolises the equality of the participants and initiates a common activity for all. Where tea and coffee are available away from the mediation table, or room, there is a common activity of moving towards it and the movement provides an opportunity for informal discussion away from the table. In these ways refreshment can bring some symbolic ritual to the situation, an experience in common, which may create a bond carrying over into the negotiations.

Visuals

2.35   There is a saying in mediation that 'the visual is vital' and mediators write up important things, with varying degrees of technological sophistication. Many mediation clients benefit from seeing agendas, mathematical calculations, mud maps and sketches, points of agreement, and so on, in written or drawn form. For this purpose, mediators need to organise one or more of the following visual aids:

- flipchart – so that everything written up can be retained;

- whiteboard – enables writing to be erased;

- electronic whiteboard – allows for copies to be made and kept;

- overhead projector – for educating and informing the parties;

- VCR and monitor – to deal with 'evidence';

- PCs and computer projection – for 'high tech' versions of the above;

- writing and drawing tools.

Security

2.36   All participants in a mediation, including the mediator, require basic arrangements for their personal security.[96] Ideally, there should be a supervised waiting room, or separate rooms for each party where the circumstances require. Where circumstances require it, a vulnerable party should be allowed to leave the mediation first, so that the dominant party cannot lay in wait for him or her. These factors are likely to be most relevant in family mediation, or in cases involving a long or fraught emotional history between the parties.

---

95   See 5.56–5.66.
96   F1.4 MQMS imposes a requirement on LSC franchises to have a procedure/statement detailing how mediator and party safety is to be maintained.

J.   Settling the agreement to mediate

2.37   Most mediator standards and codes of conduct require mediators to agree terms and conditions with the parties before the mediation begins.[97] An agreement to mediate is a contractual document which defines and regulates the roles and responsibilities of the mediator and the parties.[98] It is used in many private mediations, particularly where lawyers are involved.[99] Where there is an agreement to mediate it is signed by the parties and the mediator before the mediation begins.

An agreement to mediate should be in plain English and should be as short and simple as possible so that it does not 'over-legalise' an extra-legal form of dispute resolution. Its content should be explained to those parties who might have difficulty understanding it. Sometimes this is done before the mediation, sometimes at the preliminary meeting, and sometimes as the first item in the mediation meeting. Most mediators and mediation services have standard form agreements.[100] In complex mediations the mediator and parties might negotiate an agreement which suits the specific needs of the situation, and the same applies in simple cases, like workplace grievances, requiring much less formality.[101]

There are many variations in the different agreements to mediate currently being used in practice, in particular as regards their levels of detail and legalistic orientation. The sample agreements in Appendix 3 can be adapted for various purposes in general civil and commercial cases. The basic elements include:

- appointment of mediator;
- organisational/procedural matters;
- authority to settle at mediation;
- confidentiality and privilege;
- disclosure of information;
- nature of any agreements reached;
- termination of the mediation;
- status of any litigation on foot;
- legal costs and the mediator fees and expenses;
- mediator immunity and exclusion of liability.[102]

---

97 Refer, for example, to Article 3.1 EU Code of Conduct, section 4.1 Law Society Code of Practice for Civil/Commercial Mediation, section 5 CEDR Code, section 6 CEDR Model Mediation Procedure, clauses 2.1 and 4 ADR Group Mediation Procedure and Rules, section 4.3 CORE Solutions Group Code, section 3.1 IMI Code and section 4.1 Law Society Code of Practice for Family Mediation. Refer also to Element 2 in the Competencies for Civil/Commercial Mediators which is Annex A to the Law Society's Accreditation for Civil/Commercial Mediation. The standards, codes and competencies are included in Appendix 8 and the Model Mediation Procedures are in Appendix 3.
98 See Appendix 3 for sample and standard agreements to mediate.
99 A sample letter from CORE Solutions Group is included in Appendix 2. It is used in place of the more formal standard mediation agreement included in Appendix 3 in less formal cases or where the circumstances require less formality.
100 Refer to the samples in Appendix 3.
101 See the less formal approach via the letter from CORE Solutions Group included in Appendix 2. CORE uses the letter in many workplace grievance matters.
102 Section 6.2 of the College of Mediators Code requires the following matters to be covered by any agreement to mediate: the basis on which the fees are to be charged; and anticipated length of the mediation.

K. Guidance on case summaries and other preparation

2.38   The mediator will usually provide the parties with guidance on the content of any case summary or position paper expected to be received from them ahead of the mediation, together with any other accompanying bundle of documents (normally containing key contractual documents, statements of case, any relevant orders and expert reports, along with main case law and regulations).[103] This is common in general civil and commercial mediation.[104] Where it is agreed to exchange summaries or position papers, a copy is given to the mediator and to each party, unless any documents are provided to the mediator on a confidential basis (in which case, that should be stated clearly on the papers sent to the mediator). A barrister's opinion, draft proof of evidence, an undisclosed expert's report and a confidential briefing for the mediator are common in general civil and commercial cases.[105]

Although the content of the summary will differ according to the nature of the case, the general content includes:

- name and description of parties;
- key decision-makers at the mediation;
- background – chronology;
- key technical terms or jargon;
- key issues – legal and factual;
- prior negotiations;
- status of any proceedings;
- current position –the ambit of the dispute – what is no longer in dispute;
- aims and objectives;
- costs position;
- strengths and weaknesses;
- suggested approaches;
- any review or ratification issues.

Case summaries are discussed in more detail in 4.10–4.11.

The mediator may also assist the lawyers in civil/commercial cases with guidelines on how to effectively represent clients at mediation; on how to prepare and make an opening statement; on confidentiality and privilege issues; on risk analysis

---

103 Refer to 4.10–4.11 for more information on case summaries/party statements.

104 Refer, for example, to Element 3 in the Law Society's Competencies for Civil/Commercial Mediators which is an Annex A to the Law Society's Accreditation for Civil/Commercial Mediation (included in Appendix 8). See also, for example, clauses 6.1–6.4 ADR Group Mediation Procedure and Rules (in Appendix 3).

105 In family mediation there is transparency of financial information. Addresses, phone numbers and without prejudice offers remain confidential. Refer, for example, to sections 7.2–7.4 of the Law Society Code of Practice for Family Mediation and sections 6.4–6.7 College of Mediators Code of Practice (both are included in Appendix 8). Refer also to footnote 82 above.

and on preparation of costs information. Appendix 6 contains guidance on these various topics, which will be discussed in further detail in later chapters, especially in Chapters 5, 7, 8 and 10.

L. Summary

2.39 This chapter raises the following points of particular significance:

1. When the mediator first enters the parties' dispute there are important trust-building and information-providing tasks to perform.

2. In some contexts it is imperative that the dispute and disputants be screened to assess suitability for mediation.

3. There are many practical arrangements which mediators should attend to before they convene the actual mediation meeting.

M. Tasks for beginner mediators

2.40 Develop some metaphors which might be suitable for explaining mediation to a person involved in:

- a building dispute;

- a property dispute;

- an insurance dispute;

- a maritime dispute; and

- an information technology dispute.

2.41 You are consulted by a court which is starting a pilot mediation programme. They need a checklist of factors to consider in screening cases for mediation suitability. Design an appropriate document for their use.

2.42 You are establishing a mediation centre with two mediation rooms which will need to accommodate the mediation of a wide variety of disputes. Your budget is limited. List what you will need to operate effectively.

N. Recommended reading

Boulle L. and Nesic M., *Mediation: Principles Process Practice*, Tottel Publishing, 2001, Chs 4, 5 and 6.

Charlton and Dewdney, *The Mediator's Handbook: Skills and Strategies for Practitioners*, 2nd ed, Lawbook Co, Sydney, 2004, Ch 11.

Folger J. P., Poole M. S. and Stutman R. K., *Working Through Conflict: Strategies for Relationships, Groups and Organizations*, 6th ed, Allyn & Bacon, 2008.

Hasson R. and Slaikeu K., *Controlling the Costs of Conflict: How to Design a System for your Organization*, Jossey-Bass, San Francisco, 1998.

Law Society of England and Wales, *Family Law Protocol*, 2nd ed, 2006.

LSC, *Mediation Quality Mark Standard*, 2nd ed, 2009.

Mackie K. et al, *The ADR Practice Guide: Commercial Dispute Resolution*, Tottel Publishing, 2007, Ch 12 (at 12.5–12.8).

Moore C., *The Mediation Process: Practical Strategies for Resolving Conflict,* 3rd ed, John Wiley and Son/Jossey-Bass, San Francisco, 2003, Ch 3.

Patrick, J., 'Equal Opportunities and Anti-Discriminatory Practice', in Liebmann, M. (ed), *Community and Neighbourhood Mediation.* Cavendish Publishing, London, 1998.

Payget R., 'The Purpose of an Intake Process in Mediation' (1994) 5 *ADJR* 190.

Prior A. and Thompson R., 'Are Pre-Mediation Sessions Helpful' (1990) 10 *ADJR* 285.

Roberts M., *Mediation in Family Disputes: Principles of Practice*, Ashgate, 2008.

Slaikeu K., *When Push Comes to Shove: A Practical Guide to Mediating Disputes,* Jossey-Bass, San Francisco, 1996, Chs 4 and 5.

Various mediator codes of conduct (in Appendix 8), standard mediation rules/ procedures (in Appendix 3), sample mediation agreements (in Appendix 3) and sample forms for mediation practice (in Appendix 2).

Chapter 3

Maintaining a Favourable Climate

A good beginning makes a good ending

A. The role of the mediator in 'climate control'

3.1 Mediators have a role in creating and maintaining a favourable 'climate' for the mediating parties as they communicate, negotiate and make decisions.

As with the development of the foundations referred to in the previous chapter, this is not something that occurs at only one stage of the mediation process; it has to be considered and attended to through the entire process. However, it tends to be a more important responsibility for mediators before and during the early stages of mediation when the parties are likely to be most apprehensive, confused and defensive. The mediator has the equipment and tools for 'climate control' and can modify the temperature, humidity and atmospheric pressure as the circumstances require.

This chapter focuses on some of the reasons for the discomfort of mediation clients and on some of the ways in which mediators can deal with this factor.

Mediation skills and counselling concepts

3.2 While counselling is distinguishable from mediation, counselling concepts are clearly of significance for mediators, as they are for other skilled helpers. A difficulty for a book on mediation skills is that there are many different theories of psychology and counselling on matters such as motivation, behaviour and grief. It is not possible to canvass all relevant theories; nor is it wise to link mediation skills to a particular theory in one area. Therefore the book, especially this chapter, works eclectically with counselling and psychological concepts and recommends reference to more specialised texts on these topics.[1]

---

1   As a starting point, there is a good chapter on the relevance of counselling concepts for mediators in Folberg and Taylor, *Mediation: A Comprehensive Guide to Resolving Conflicts without Litigation*, 1984, Ch 4.

B. Reasons for a poor climate

3.3   Conflict can be debilitating. To some people it appears confusing, even chaotic. It stirs the emotions and saps the energy and it almost always feels difficult to manage and resolve. Mediators can expect that parties coming into the process will be in negative emotional and psychological states. They will feel that their cause is just and that the other side has acted unfairly, or worse. They may also have invested a great deal of energy in the 'struggle' and be unwilling to negotiate towards a compromise on 'matters of principle'.

There may be several reasons for the negative state of mediation clients, which will be illustrated in the following fact scenario.

> **Ben and Southern Farms**
>
> Ben was employed by Southern Farms as a fruit picker. He had been seated on a tractor approximately 1.2m above the ground when the hydraulics failed and the seating collapsed and he fell to the ground. The fall caused him severe lower back pain. Since the accident he has not worked and has been restricted in his movements, affecting all his usual activities. He has had no treatment other than analgesics and some physiotherapy which he attended irregularly.
>
> The medical reports suggest that Ben suffered a 'significant amount' and a 'moderate degree' of pain and suffering, but not as substantial as he claimed. The reports suggest that he will ultimately be capable of resuming suitable light work.
>
> Ben alleges that since the accident he has had difficulty socialising and sleeping, relations with his wife have been disrupted and he has had to abandon plans for starting a family. He complains of constant throbbing in his back and occasional spasms and bruising. He has lost self-confidence and self-respect since the accident.
>
> Proceedings were instituted for negligence. The solicitors arranged a mediation, attended by Ben, Southern Farms and their insurer.

Reasons pertaining to pre-mediation developments

3.4   Using the example, between the time of the accident and the mediation, there could be a number of developments which contributed to a further deterioration in Ben's original negative state. Seen from his perspective, these might include:

- Insulting offers from the insurer, which have 'poisoned the well'.

- The attitude and treatment of the defendant's doctors who were abrupt, rough, disbelieving and uncaring.

- The approach of the insurer in giving him the 'run around' with gross delays in authorising payment for medical treatment or in making a 'decent' offer.

- Increasing concern that his injuries might get worse.

- Well-meaning advice from friends or relatives not to talk to the insurer, not to trust any lawyer and not to settle the case.

- His growing belief that the defendant employer treats the whole workforce badly and must be taught a lesson.

- A slow realisation that the whole system is 'loaded against him', or his rights have been unreasonably disregarded, or that the defendant will not be reasonable until the door of the court.

- The very high expectations that counsel's advice have raised in his mind, particularly in relation to the monetary amounts mentioned.

Comparable considerations could have put the insurer's representative in a negative frame of mind if, for example, Ben were from 'a certain ethnic group', or if his lawyer had a notorious reputation among insurers and there had been a 'grossly inflated' monetary claim for a 'minimal injury'. The effect of these factors is to escalate the conflict beyond its original scope, rendering mediation more problematic than it otherwise might have been.

Reasons pertaining to the individual parties

The grieving process

3.5   Most parties in conflict have experienced an actual loss or a perception of loss and are consequently undergoing a process of grieving.[2] Depending on the circumstances, the sense of loss could be over a matrimonial partnership, a promising business venture, the full use of limbs or other bodily parts, or security of employment. According to different writers on attachment theory, the grieving process could involve a number of elements, though not in any strict sequence or linear progression. Using the example above, Ben could have experienced the following emotions in his grieving process:

- *Shock*: the state of numbness in which there is no ability to analyse, understand or feel what has happened and what is going on.

- *Denial*: the inability to accept or come to terms with the loss, and the belief that his health, job and family prospects, as the case may be, will be restored to what they were before.

- *Bargaining*: an attempt, usually futile, to recover whatever has been lost by 'negotiating' with the employer, insurer, or even God, accompanied by firm commitments to reform in the future.

- *Anger*: characterised by extreme hostility towards the 'cause' of the loss, such as Ben's employer, his boss, or fate, or even the victim himself.

- *Despair and disorganisation*: a loss of hope for the future and inability by the depressed person to plan, act and make logical decisions in his best interests.

- *Acceptance and reorganisation*: in which Ben comes to terms with the loss and decides that he 'wants to get on with my life'.

---

2   See the classic account in Kubler Ross, *On Death and Dying*, 1969.

3.6   As the grieving elements do not occur in a strict linear progression, persons may move between them with some irregularity, and at times slip 'backwards', for example, from partial acceptance to denial. It is also not unusual for persons who have been in a close relationship, for example, marriage or business partners, to be in different stages of the grieving process from each other. For example, one party might be at the stage of acceptance, while the other party is still in denial. The latter party may be seen as unfeeling and the former as unable to manage, further exacerbating the dispute.

Some writers, such as Emery, talk of a cyclical theory of grief, revolving around love, anger and sadness, in which there is a constant cycling back and forth between these conflicting emotions.[3] While the intensity of these emotions lessens over time, they can involve a lengthy and confusing process with the possibility of the person becoming stuck on one of the emotions of grief. Furthermore, where there are two parties, one the 'leaver' from a personal or business relationship and the other the 'left', the guilt of the former and rejection of the latter, and the continued contact between them, can perpetuate the cyclical process. As the leaver's emotions are usually less intense than those of the left party, the same misunderstanding and exacerbation can occur as described above.

3.7   In relation to mediation, parties in all stages of grieving will be in a complicated emotional state. In some cases, for example, where there is prolonged shock or denial, it might be inappropriate to negotiate and mediation should be deferred until these stages have passed. In others, for example, where one party is in the anger phase and the other at acceptance, the mediator will have to be aware of their different emotional realities without resorting to amateur counselling. The pace of the mediation may differ for each party in such cases – the mediator may have to spend more time in separate session with the angry party.

Power imbalances

3.8   Some parties come to mediation with a perception that they are in a grossly inferior position as far as their bargaining power is concerned. This is likely to be the case for someone in Ben's position. Even if the imbalance operates only at the level of perception, it is still a reality for the party concerned. In many situations both parties might feel at a disadvantage in terms of their bargaining power, causing anxiety and defensiveness all around. Specific ways of dealing with power imbalances are referred to in Chapter 10.[4]

Fear of losing altogether

3.9   Some parties come to mediation with a perception that they might lose altogether in the course of the mediation process. Even if this is, objectively speaking, an unlikely eventuality it is not less real in the subjective world of the fearful party. Again, someone in Ben's position may have this fear. Specific ways of dealing with this fear are also referred to below.[5]

---

3   R. Emery, *Renegotiating Family Relationships*, 1994, 26–9.
4   See 10.3–10.10.
5   See 3.39–3.40.

Reasons pertaining to the mediation process

3.10   The mediation process itself can be a source of anxiety and concern. At least one of the parties in mediation has usually not experienced the system before and 'first-timers', such as Ben, are likely to have more anxieties than the 'repeat users' of mediation, as in the case of an insurer or the parties' lawyers. The negative factors relating to the mediation process could include:

- Resentment at having been forced through financial or other circumstances, or the will of a stronger party, to attend mediation.

- Ambivalence about being at mediation, even where they have chosen this option themselves.

- Unfamiliarity with and ignorance about the mediation process and the mediator.

- Uncertainty over the actual role and likely behaviour of the mediator.

- Anxiety about their negotiating abilities.

- Concern about having to compromise on 'matters of principle'.

- Concern about the impact of outcomes achieved at mediation.

Cumulatively these factors could have a deeply negative and distrustful effect on disputing parties as they come into mediation and as they begin participating in the process. The rest of this chapter deals with ways in which the mediator can change the climate to a more positive one.

C.   The trust factor

3.11   Experience suggests that a number of factors can contribute to a stormy climate for many mediations. This is compounded by the fact that parties in dispute frequently distrust each other. Here the word trust refers to one person's *willingness to believe, to be open to, and to take risks with*, another person. Another way to talk about trust is in terms of 'risk assessment'. The question then becomes, 'How can the mediation process favourably modify a party's assessment of the risks involved in coming to the negotiations, disclosing interests and needs, and exploring settlement options with the other side?'

Levels of trust may improve, deteriorate or stay the same during the course of the mediation, and a mediation is by no means a failure if the level of trust has not improved. It is too high an expectation of mediators that they turn embattled business partners or sceptical government representatives into trusting comrades. However, high levels of distrust can make it difficult or impossible to come to a joint decision. In these circumstances, mediators can generate some degree of trust in themselves and the mediation process, as a basis for getting the parties to move towards reaching an agreement with each other.

The central assumption here is that if the parties trust the mediator and the mediation process then they are more likely to remain at the negotiating table and to make attempts at settlement than if this trust were absent. Needless to say there are no guarantees.

Generating trust in the mediator

3.12   The objective is that the parties develop trust in the mediator so that they may be able to take risks with him or her which they would not take with each other. Mediators can use the following techniques to impress on the parties that they are individuals who can be trusted:

- by affirming their credentials as mediators and dispute resolvers;
- by showing respect, courtesy and concern for the parties;
- by establishing a personal rapport with the parties;
- by being attentive, through open body language, eye contact
- and appropriate matching, or mismatching, of behaviours;
- through good active listening skills and acknowledgment of the parties' concerns;
- by allowing the parties to vent and to explore their needs and objectives;
- by being impartial and even-handed in the conduct of the process;
- by addressing the parties' concerns about the process and the respective roles at mediation;
- by reassuring the parties that the environment is safe for discussion, exploration and decision-making;
- by showing an understanding of each party's positions;
- by reframing and neutralising language;
- by coaching the parties on appropriate behaviours.

Generating trust in the mediation process

3.13   Here the objective is that the parties develop trust in the mediation process so that they are more likely to remain committed to it and to persist in their attempts to reach a settlement. Mediators can use the following techniques to help the parties generate trust in the process in which they are participating:

- by explaining, normalising and validating the mediation process;
- by reassuring the parties, where possible, on their anxieties about the process;
- by providing for equality of speaking time for the parties;
- by applying the mediation guidelines appropriately;[6]
- by using the separate meetings to keep the process moving.[7]

Helping parties to develop their negotiating abilities

3.14   As negotiation experts, mediators can identify relatively minor issues on which the parties can develop trust before moving on to more substantial matters.

---

6   See 5.5.
7   See 5.56–5.66.

By initiating successful discussion and decision-making on a 'process' issue, such as the venue for the mediation or the appropriate role for advisers or outsiders, the mediator can stimulate faith in the parties' ability to negotiate successfully together. The same can be achieved by the mediator targeting and gaining negotiated agreement on 'easy' matters first, for example, on where the children will spend Christmas Day in a parenting dispute, or on how interest will be calculated in a commercial dispute.

D. Managing expectations

3.15 In our experience, managing expectations is one of the most important functions of mediators. This function is relevant in relation to the pre-mediation activities of the mediator, to developments within the mediation, and even to what occurs after the mediation.

Reference has already been made to the problems caused by parties who come to mediation in a negative frame of mind and the role of the mediator in dealing with this issue. Conversely, some parties come to mediation with wildly optimistic expectations about the process, the role of the mediator, and likely mediation outcomes. These are some of the unrealistic expectations encountered in practice:

- That the mediation will vindicate the relevant party's version of the facts; it will establish the 'truth', or 'get to the bottom of' disputed facts, or that it will establish 'who is right or wrong'.

- That the mediator will find and hold the relevant party's case to be essentially just.

- That the parties are negotiating over a 'fixed pie' which will not be diminished in mediation, litigation or any other dispute resolution process.

- That the mediation outcome will be in accordance with the party's most optimistic settlement prospects.

- That the matter can be sorted quickly, in accordance with a particular party's demands or expectations.

- That if the mediation is not successful the party will be vindicated by a judge in court and receive what they could not obtain in mediation.

These and other similar expectations are often quite unrealistic. One of the ways in which the mediator maintains a favourable climate during the mediation is by attempting throughout to manage expectations by bringing the parties to reality. This is done through the strategies and interventions referred to in this chapter, and throughout this book.

Another aspect of managing expectations is to provide parties with information that challenges 'selective perception'. People in conflict tend to see what they want to see and to distort information to support their expectations. They gather information that confirms their hypotheses and ignore information that does not support them. A mediator can change parties' perceptions through strategic use of information, appropriate questioning, reframing, paraphrasing and reality testing.[8]

---

8   L. Hall (ed), *Negotiation Strategies for Mutual Gain*, Sage, California, 1993.

E.   Strategies for improving the climate

3.16   What follows are suggestions for ways in which mediators might improve the climate in which the mediation takes place. The appropriateness of each strategy will depend on the status and circumstances of each mediation.

Providing ritual for mediation

3.17   Ritual in mediation can take many forms:[9]

> Mediation in western societies has no established tradition of rituals. In communal societies … systems of conflict management … have numerous rituals involving the exchange of gifts, eating, drinking and smoking, signs of respect, singing and movement. Ritual lends a sanctity and mystique to the proceedings, suggesting that the business at hand has a social importance greater than the interests of the individuals. It also lends a sense of purpose and even-handedness to the proceedings. In the absence of equivalent rituals in western mediation, mediators need to consider spending time on preliminary courtesies among all present, on exchanging pleasantries …, on initiating a formal round of introductions, on attending to how the parties should address one another, and on making some acknowledgment and affirmation of all parties present.
>
> Mediators may also provide food, drink and other refreshments, which can be 'ritually' served in a way which shows respect for all and the equality of all parties present. Consumption becomes a common activity, participated in equally by all participants, which temporarily distracts attention from the negative features of the dispute during the settling-in phase.

Imaginative mediators might develop additional rituals appropriate to the mediation process.

Promoting a positive tone

3.18   The mediator sets a positive tone from the outset with a quiet, confident approach and a mood of optimism. This is reinforced by emphasising and upholding the fairness of the process, highlighting its flexibility, benefits and problem-solving nature, and pointing out its ultimate goal ('to reach settlement …', 'to make decisions satisfactory to you both …'). Themes of mutuality and cooperativeness are emphasised from the beginning ('You are here to make decisions to suit both your needs and interests …'). Confidence and optimism are maintained throughout the process by emphasising progress, particularly through the intervention of summarising.[10] Positive language is used wherever possible.[11]

A positive tone can be set by acknowledging co-operation between the parties, or if any positive actions have already been taken, or if there has been a good

---

9   L. Boulle, *Mediation Principles Process Practice,* 2005, 180–1.
10   See 6.53–6.55.
11   See 6.17–6.18.

relationship in the past. Providing the parties with feedback and suggestions helps them to participate and provides comfort with the process. Asking a party 'what would it feel like if this matter were resolved today' is another technique for encouraging optimism and a future focus.

Providing structure, control and security

3.19 Mediation is not the forum to continue destructive fighting and the mediator must neutralise the situation to some extent. He or she provides a non-threatening atmosphere, controls the parties' accusations and defences to accusations, emphasises the confidentiality of the discussions and otherwise creates a secure environment for dispute resolution. The causes of destructive behaviour, and possible mediator interventions, are discussed in Chapter 6.

3.20 Mediators may encounter threats directed at the structure and control they provide. One of the ways in which mediators provide a favourable climate for decision-making is by taking charge of the mediation procedure and by keeping it moving according to the design plan in respect of which they have the expertise. This function is referred to more fully in Chapter 5. These stages are designed to ensure that the process is even-handed, that each side has sufficient 'air time', and that neither side is able to take control of the mediation or disadvantage the other through tactical manoeuvres. Therefore, at least initially, mediators should be assertive in their process control function.

3.21 The mediation guidelines are a way of asserting control and providing security for the parties.[12] They provide a simple set of standards for behaviour during the mediation and give the mediator some 'objective' criteria against which to measure party behaviour. However, where a party breaches the guidelines, the mediator has a range of possible responses, depending on the severity of the breach and other circumstances of the mediation. Thus the mediator might, in ascending degrees of assertiveness:

- Ignore the breach if it is not significant, or if it occurs very early in the mediation, and continue without any reference to it.
- Distract or disarm the party or parties with a deflective question.[13]
- Neutrally restate the guidelines and ask both parties to recommit to them.
- Rebuke or reprimand the offending party or parties.
- Break into separate meetings in order to discuss the breach.
- Terminate the mediation – a rare last resort in cases of consistent breaches.

3.22 In each case, the mediator will have to make a tactical judgment as to the appropriate intervention. The judgment is made with the overall objective of providing a good climate for decision-making through the appropriate amount and form of control. Sometimes the judgment will be correct, in others it will not, and there is no exact formula which can be applied to all situations.

---

12   See Chapter 5.
13   See 6.46.

Acknowledging concerns

3.23   Here the mediator does what might not have been done by any other professional or helper with whom the party has been involved, namely to acknowledge the nature and intensity of their concerns. This is achieved through appropriate questioning and active listening, which is dealt with further in Chapter 6.[14] Active listening is hard work. It requires being non-judgmental, picking up signals from body language, and being aware of feelings and emotions, not just the facts.

Normalising

3.24   Normalising is the other side of the acknowledging coin. While mediation clients might be convinced that their problems are unique and unprecedented in their gravity, it is appropriate at certain times to normalise their situation. Thus they might be informed that it is normal for people in business to make mistakes and normal to attribute malice to the other party. Likewise the difficulties which the parties are encountering in their negotiations can be normalised, for example, that it is usual for negotiating parties to feel that they have conceded too much and have difficulty making the final concession.

One objective of normalising is to open the parties to the notion that as other persons have been in their situation, they might consider how they have resolved the same kinds of problem. This is intended to shift them from the perception that their situation is hopeless and without remedy to one in which there are precedents and possibilities which they could be thinking about.

Getting out of the past into the future

3.25   It is normal to feel intense emotion, in particular anger, about the past, but less easy to do so about the future. A discussion about the past can be cathartic for parties. A party may feel it is necessary to explain what steps have been taken to deal with a problem. Some discussion about the past can help parties to explain the context and allow movement so that parties can then turn to a discussion about the future. While a mediation might have to devote some time to dealing with prior events, it is not obsessed with the past and with historical facts, as are other forms of dispute resolution, such as litigation or adjudication.

The mediator is gently able to redirect the parties' attention from a negative and destructive past to a future which can be different and more attractive. Focusing the party on the future also creates an atmosphere of problem-solving. It encourages parties to identify their priorities.

Mutualising the unhappiness

3.26   Charlton and Dewdney use this phrase, which highlights an important educative function of mediators.[15] Parties often assume that the unhappiness in

---

14 See 6.34.
15 Charlton and Dewdney, *The Mediator's Handbook*, 2004.

the mediation room is theirs alone, and that the other side is in a state of bliss or mild euphoria. Where this is not the case, and it seldom is, the mediator can point out that the other side is in reality unhappy about the fact that they have had to move considerably from their positions or have had to make a concession on key issues. This has the potential effect of reassuring each side on the acceptability of a proposed settlement – while it may not be what they wanted, it is not what the others wanted either. Needless to say the disclosure of the mutual unhappiness might require the consent of the parties – one or both may not wish to reveal the extent of their dissatisfaction with the way the mediation is unfolding and with an imminent settlement.

Reducing the pressure to settle

3.27   There is often a misconception by parties at mediation, especially in commercial cases, that the process is a horse-trading exercise, with pressure being imposed by the mediator and lawyers to settle. It is a considerably more subtle and powerful process. The mediator can challenge parties on their views and positions, on possible solutions and on how workable or realistic various options are.

Where there is a great sense of pressure to achieve resolution in mediation, however, it can provoke resentment, resistance and a major obstacle to settlement. One way of reducing the feeling of pressure on the parties is by reassuring them that they are not obliged to settle in the mediation. This is to emphasise the self-determination principle, namely that it is up to the parties to make decisions on all matters, including on whether mediation is the right place for them to be. In some contexts there might be drastic consequences of not reaching settlement, for example, denial of further legal aid or limited access to the court process. Nevertheless, it is a defining feature of mediation that there will only be a settlement if both parties agree, and the 'no deal unless you both accede' theme can be a reassurance for parties. It could be taken further, with a light touch, for example, 'It's OK not to agree – someone has to make up the 15% of cases that do not settle in mediation.'

This approach also alleviates pressure to rush into making demands, proposals or concessions. In turn, it avoids a rights-based focus, and can provide an opportunity to re-focus attention on parties' concerns and needs and to explore how those might be met.

Relieving tension through humour

3.28   Humour can be an appropriate way of relieving tension in many situations, from the classroom to the dentist's room. Humour provides physical relief through laughter, relaxes people emotionally, and takes them out of the characters they have been playing. Laughter is also a shared and common response from people who might not have much else in common. It can also provide insight and a change of perspective.

In mediation, the timing and focus of humour is critical. Mediators should leave their party routines at the door, and use great sensitivity in the joke-telling department. If humour is used too early it may set a flippant tone and suggest that the mediator is not taking the matter seriously enough. It should preferably be aimed at mediators' own frailties ('Please speak up, I'm deaf in one ear and can't hear out of the other') or at the situation ('No one gets to relieve their bladder until we've settled') and should not be aimed at the parties.

Acknowledging autonomy, status and roles

3.29 Fisher and Shapiro provide a model for creating a positive emotional environment, which recognises that:

- Parties need freedom and space to make decisions.
- Parties need acknowledgement of their status and expertise to effectively engage in negotiations.
- Parties need to feel that they have fulfilled a role in negotiations.[16]

F. Dealing with intense emotions

3.30 Emotion can be triggered more quickly than it takes the rational mind to assess a situation and decide how to react. While 'positive' emotions, such as joy and contentment, are not a major problem ,'negative' emotions, such as fear and anger, are a difficult challenge for most mediators.

Intense and strongly expressed emotions can seriously affect the climate of a mediation. Strong emotions are often expressed in mediation, despite the naive view that because mediation is a 'collaborative' and 'non-adversarial' process all destructive and negative elements are miraculously avoided. This view confuses structure, on one hand, with style and behaviour, on the other. Mediation is collaborative in structure, but this will not always prevent parties from being positional, adversarial and bloody-minded in style and behaviour.

3.31 Some mediators attempt to prohibit the expression of negative emotion as it is seen to be dysfunctional in the mediation, although one suspects that it might also be because they feel uncomfortable with high emotion themselves or do not feel professionally equipped to deal with it.[17] Suppressing emotion is not normally effective:

- Any attempt to suppress emotion may not work.
- Suppressing emotions can impair a person's cognitive skills.
- Avoiding or suppressing emotion can lead to poor physical and mental health.
- Avoiding emotion can lead to poor outcomes, ongoing conflict and difficulties with compliance with agreements reached.[18]

---

16 Roger Fisher and Daniel Shapiro, *Beyond Reason – Using Emotion as you Negotiate*, Viking, New York, 2005. Refer also to Robert S. Adler et al, 'Emotions in Negotiation – how to Manage Fear and Anger', in 14 *Negotiation Journal* 16 (1998).
17 See also H. S. Golann and D. Golann, 'Why is it Hard for Lawyers to Deal with Emotional Issues?' in (2003) 9 *Disp. Resol. Mag.* 26
18 C Freshmen et al, 'The Lawyer-Negotiator as Mood Scientist: What we Know and don't Know about how Mood Relates to Successful Negotiation' in (2002) *J Disp Resol* 1.

As the expression of emotion is an important form of communication, a blanket prohibition policy will restrict certain forms of communication and undermine many of the potential benefits of mediation. Legitimately expressed anger can have the advantage of indicating to others a depth of feeling, and even sincerity. However, anger can also change the parties' focus from the problem to the emotion, cloud their objectivity, lead to angry retaliation and entrenchment.

3.32   There are various ways of dealing with strongly expressed emotions during the course of a mediation. There are differing views in the literature and among mediation practitioners about the most appropriate interventions. In keeping with the style of this book, no attempt is made to indicate whether a particular approach is suitable or not. Instead some suggestions are made as to the potential advantages and disadvantages of each. As usual, these responses shade into one another and there may be elements of more than one in a single mediator intervention.

Some ways in which mediators might respond to intense feelings are set out below. Reference will be made to the following workplace fact scenario in assessing each approach.

Fact scenario

Ian, a supervisor, has demoted and changed the sales areas of Patricia, a salesperson, for not meeting her specified performance criteria. Patricia has lodged a complaint over the demotion and changed sales areas. In terms of company policy the matter has been referred, in the first instance, to the HR director, who undertakes an internal mediation. Patricia has just had an intense outburst of anger and frustration over victimisation, discrimination and lack of training, allegedly arising from Ian's actions and inactions.

Discourage the expression of intense emotion

3.33   Mediator: 'Patricia, it's not going to help here if you get angry and shout. Let's talk about how you calculated your sales figures against the target figures for the last six months.'

As suggested above, this is often the practice of mediators who feel unable to deal with high emotion or regard it as irrelevant to the problem, and therefore attempt to prevent its expression as soon as it commences. This might be advantageous where resource limitations necessitate only a very short mediation and the parties need to be kept focused. It has the potential disadvantage, however, of causing further frustration and discontent for the emotive party and of jeopardising the longer term success of the mediation.

Ignore the emotion and proceed with the mediation

3.34   Mediator: 'Patricia and Ian, I thought you were trying to provide some answers to the second question on the flipchart, namely how can the sales areas be divided in a way which is fair to Patricia and other salespersons. Let's see how this can be done ...'

Here the mediator does not intervene to suppress the expression of emotion, but ignores it and moves on. He uses the visuals on the whiteboard to focus the parties' attention on the problem, and distracts them from the interpersonal hostility. This has much the same advantages and disadvantages as the policy of discouraging the expression of emotions in the first place. A refinement on this strategy involves distinguishing between positive and negative emotions: mediators acknowledge and validate the former, for example, the optimism and hope present in the early stages of a joint initiative between the mediating parties, and ignore and disregard the latter, for example, intense anger over a party feeling betrayed.

Acknowledge the emotion, and then continue

3.35   Mediator: 'Patricia, it sounds as though your treatment has made you extremely frustrated and angry and that your last four months at work have been exceptionally difficult....'.

Here the mediator explicitly acknowledges the presence of the emotions, and their intensity, whether they are expressed directly by the party, or are merely evident from behaviour, tone of voice or body language. This approach is designed to give the emotive party the experience of being heard and understood by at least one professional. There is an expectation that this validation will encourage Patricia to move forward from the emotional state to practical decision-making. This intervention (if it happens in a joint meeting) also results in the other party having to listen to the emotion being identified and named by the mediator. Some mediators are nervous that such acknowledgment might provide a licence for more extensive emotional outbursts and further complicate the dispute. However, acknowledgment does not equate with approval, and in our experience, continued emotiveness is a rare occurrence where strongly felt emotions are expressed and acknowledged. The mediator might wish to add an educational dimension to this approach by indicating that mediation in itself might not resolve the intense hurt or anger and that other forms of assistance would be appropriate for these goals.

Encourage venting of the emotion

3.36   Mediator: 'Patricia, tell Ian exactly what you felt about the demotion and what effect it had on you emotionally and physically ...'.

Here the mediator explicitly invites an expression of emotion: in turn, the mediator might (if this is in a joint session) invite Ian to explain how he felt about making the demotion decision or how he feels now about Patricia's condition. The advantage of this approach is that it allows the parties to get things off their chests, to release pent-up feelings and, after an emotional catharsis, to move on to the problem at hand. Judgment and control is required if this is done in a joint session to ensure that neither party is injured by the other's emotional venting, and there also needs to be a limit on the duration of this exercise. This approach has the same potential benefits and disadvantages as the previous one. It might be particularly valuable where a party is inhibited or uncomfortable about expressing emotion without some encouragement from the mediator. It can also be a particularly valuable way to start a private session following a highly emotional opening.

Identify and deal with the underlying problem therapeutically

3.37 Mediator: 'Patricia, it sounds as though you have been traumatised by this ordeal, and that you have lost confidence and self-esteem. You may also be clinically depressed. Those issues need to be dealt with first ...'.

This response is something that can only be undertaken by those professionally qualified to do so. It has the advantage of dealing with underlying emotional or relationship difficulties which might prevent the parties from coming to a decision, or which might jeopardise the long-term durability of any decision reached. It has the disadvantage of delaying the making of decisions on matters requiring immediate attention, and of blurring the boundaries between mediation and counselling. Many mediators would adjourn the mediation and refer Patricia to another professional if they decided that the problem needed therapeutic handling.

In selecting a strategy the mediator needs to recognise the emotion distinct from the symptoms (for example, a party may be attempting to suppress fear or anger), diagnose it tentatively, and test out an intervention:

- If the diagnosis is that a party is deliberately using anger to force a compromise, the appropriate response may be to ignore it.

- If the mediator diagnoses a potential build-up in emotion, he or she may attempt to defuse it.

- If the emotion is genuine but not too serious the mediator might use behavioural techniques such as calling for an adjournment, bringing in refreshments, conducting a round of separate meetings, getting the parties to write points on the whiteboard and making other changes in the process to allow for a cooling-off.

Ultimately, mediators are providing a secure environment in which the dispute can be played out in a constructive manner. As with other skilled helpers, mediators also need to be attuned to their own responses to emotional outbursts and develop mechanisms to manage those without affecting the mediation.

G. Dealing with criticism

3.38 Because of the way in which mediating parties view the dispute and each other, they often expressly or impliedly engage in criticism. Many people deal poorly with criticism as it is often experienced as an attack on the innate value of the person.[19] This provokes an angry, defensive or diversionary response.

Ideally, mediators should attempt to keep the parties out of a cycle of criticism, defence, justification and counter-criticism, though this may not always be possible or even wise. Indeed, they should try to understand better what the criticism is about and acknowledge the underlying emotional feelings.

Where there is strong criticism, mediators need to judge which of the following strategies, or combination of strategies, might be appropriate. The responses are

---

19   Sheehy, *Pathfinders*, 1982.

based on a manufacturer criticising a supplier for being 'slack, inept and unreliable' over times for the delivery of supplies:

■ Reframe the criticism in terms of actions, events or views and not in terms of the innate value of the criticised party:[20] 'Are you saying that the late deliveries affected your production schedule?'

■ Ask the criticised party to make a response in relation to the action, behaviour or idea, and deflect attention from the self: 'Are you able to explain what made it difficult to deliver the goods on time?'

■ Ask the criticising party to move from the general to the specific and to avoid imputing motives to the other. 'In relation to timing of deliveries, can you give some examples of when the goods arrived after the date on which you expected them?'

■ Ask the criticised party to indicate how they feel about the criticism, and get the criticising party to respond to the other's feeling statement: 'How does the manufacturer's criticism make you feel?'

■ Ask the parties to suggest ways of dealing with the criticism in the present and for the future: 'Are there ways in which you can ensure reliable deliveries in the future?'

H.   Overcoming clients' fundamental fears

3.39   It is clear from the previous sections in this chapter that mediators can have an important role in reducing the defensiveness of the negotiating parties. Many parties in mediation anticipate the worst possible outcome (for example, that they will never see their children or that they will receive no compensation for their injuries or that their business might not survive) which causes them to defend their positional claims at all costs. Of course, there may be some realism to this anxiety, but a party could also be negatively obsessed with an outcome which has not been decided and is not inevitable. In either event, this fear-induced defensiveness is not conducive to constructive problem-solving.

3.40   Haynes and Charlesworth refer to the need for mediators to attempt to reduce the defensiveness of the parties.[21] They suggest that the mediator can reduce fear early in the process by asking the parties, 'What is the worst possible outcome of working with me?'

When a party outlines any fear, it is usually an unrealistic concern, that is, one based not on fact but on emotion. The mediator then asks each party if they can agree that the worst fear of the other party will not materialise in the mediation. For example, in a family dispute, if both parents state that the worst possible outcome would be 'losing the children', the mediator asks each parent to affirm that the other will not lose their role in parenting the children in the negotiations. As this is understood and accepted by each parent, the need to defend against the possibility is diminished, and each parent can spend their energy thinking about new solutions rather than defending against old fears.

---

20   On reframing, see 6.38–6.44 and the examples in Appendix 5.
21   Haynes and Charlesworth, *The Fundamentals of Family Mediation*, 1995, 163.

The same strategy can be adopted in respect of any mediation where the 'fundamental fear' syndrome is evident or suspected.

I. Preserving face and avoiding loss of face

3.41   Here the term 'face' is used in a loose way to refer to the need which people have to retain a sense of dignity and self-worth in the eyes of others and in their own eyes. Conversely, a loss of face involves a perceived loss of dignity and self-worth. The 'face' issue can be a major factor in the continuation, escalation or even origins of conflict, whether between two siblings over their academic achievements or between two countries over their performances in a soccer match.

A mediating party might feel they have lost face where they have made significant concessions from their original position; and their refusal to make further concessions, however commercially logical, might be motivated by the need to maintain vestiges of face. Another common occurrence is for a party to be motivated by the fear of how they will appear to outside 'ratifiers' if they make further concessions.[22] In each case this subjective factor becomes the dominant interest of the party, as opposed to the objective factors over which they are negotiating.

While the 'face' phenomenon is probably common to all strands of humanity, it does have different significance in different cultures. In some cultures any notion of compromise or concession on principle involves a loss of face, whereas in others the problem is less acute.

3.42   The ideal is that in mediation everyone should preserve face, and conversely, that no-one should lose face. Mediators can contribute to these goals by conducting the mediation along best-practice lines in terms of the principles referred in this book. In addition, there are some specific techniques which can be adopted:

- Using 'objective criteria' as a basis for getting a party's agreement rather than having them feel that they are conceding to the other side's proposal.[23]

- Using the technique of blaming a third party, such as the bank or the government or an external factor, such as the economy, in order to remove blame and a sense of responsibility from the disputing parties.

- Using the 'scapegoat strategy'. This is where the mediator engineers things so that the parties can blame him or her for a proposal or outcome, thereby justifying their own conduct. Alternatively, the mediator might personally endorse a mediated outcome, even in writing, in order to assist one of the parties to deal with outside ratifiers or constituents. This is, however, a risky strategy and might lead to the mediator being held liable for the outcome.[24]

---

22 See 5.75.
23 'Open to reason, closed to pressure' to use the language of Fisher and Ury in *Getting to Yes*, Hutchinson, 1992. See also 7.43–7.45.
24 On liability issues, refer to the Australian case of *Tapoohi v Lewenberg and Others* [2003] VSC 379 (10 October 2003) and the New Zealand case of *McCosh v Williams* [2003] NZCA 192 (12 August 2003). Refer also to Chapter 12.

- Using the technique of 'mediator vulnerability'. If one party does not understand a term, ask for your sake that it be explained. If the parties continually interrupt each other, explain that you are having difficulty in hearing or concentrating on what is said. Again, there are obvious limitations on this technique, lest you appear feeble.

- Providing reasons for a change in negotiating position, for example, 'in the light of the new information which you have heard for the first time today ...', or 'in light of the concessions you have heard them make ...'. These can be useful interventions for professional advisers who need face-saving reasons for departing from the advice they have previously given to their clients.

- Using interim agreements. This is a classical negotiation strategy and is used to get deals accepted on a short-term basis ('say for the next two months ...') without making any face-losing concessions on matters of principle which can still be negotiated on in the future. In some cases 'the temporary becomes the permanent' and the interim agreement is ratified without problem because it can be done without loss of face.

3.43   The following scenario illustrates some of the above principles.

Case illustration: improving the climate

A young child had died during surgery to correct a heart defect and the parents brought an action against the public hospital. After a lengthy coronial inquiry, legal proceedings had been instituted by the parents. The mediation was conducted in difficult circumstances because of the grief of the parents, the continuing semi-denial of the mother over the death of her son, the seeming intransigence of the hospital and the government's concern about adverse publicity which was escalating in the media.

The following steps were taken to improve the climate for the parents:

1. A relaxed, informal venue was chosen for the mediation (namely, the clubhouse on a golf-course).

2. Care was taken in restricting the number of professionals at the mediation; all parties agreed to exclude barristers, technical experts and accountants who might otherwise have been present.

3. The parents were educated extensively by their lawyers and the mediator about the nature of the mediation process and about their own roles in it.

4. Through prior agreement of the professionals, the parents were given extensive time to talk about the circumstances of the accident, the effect of the loss on their lives and their outrage at official responses to their plight, without any restrictions in relation to length or relevance.

5. There was considerable acknowledgment by the hospital's solicitor, who had undertaken mediation training, of the parents' loss, anger and frustration.

6. During the 'technical' discussions on liability and quantum of damages the parents were allowed to leave the room and wander around the grounds, returning in their own time.

> 7. When agreement was reached on all matters, it was further decided to allow the parents 24 hours in which to consider the agreement before committing to it.

While these actions were mainly for the benefit of one party only, they had the support of the others, and illustrate the practical application of some of this chapter's principles.

J. Summary

3.44   This chapter raises the following points of particular significance:

- Mediators need to be aware of a range of negative emotions or feelings which mediating parties may have.

- In order to generate an improvement in the climate of the mediation and manage the clients' expectations, mediators need to develop their clients' trust both in themselves and in the mediation process.

- While the mediator is not acting as a counsellor or psychologist, he or she needs to draw from a broad range of techniques inherent in the mediation process to improve the problem-solving climate for the parties.

K. Tasks for beginner mediators

3.45   Identify a dispute of some magnitude in which you have been involved as an employee, a consumer, a tenant or a student. Write out a list of the things which the employer, retailer, landlord or educational institution did or did not do between the emergence of the dispute and its 'resolution' and describe the effect these factors had on your emotional state.

3.46   Assume you are the mediator between Ben and Southern Farms. What steps would you take to create a favourable climate for Ben? What effect might these steps have on the representative of Southern Farms?

3.47   Discuss with a friend or colleague how each of you responds to intense sadness and anger. Develop some strategies you might use for dealing with these emotions if you were working as a professional mediator.

L. Recommended reading

Adler, Rosen and Silverstein, 'Emotions in Negotiation: How to Manage Fear and Anger' (1998) 14 *Negotiation Journal* 161.

Axelrod R., *The Evolution of Cooperation,* Basic Books, New York, 2006.

Barry, Fulmer and Coates, 'Bargaining with Feeling: Emotionality in and around Negotiation', in L. Thomas (ed), *Negotiation Theory and Research,* Psychology Press, New York, 2006 (pp 99–127).

Boulle L. and Nesic M., *Mediation: Principles Process Practice*, Tottel Publishing, 2001, Ch 5.

Bowling D. and Hoffman D., *Bringing Peace Into the Room: How the Personal Qualities of the Mediator Impact the Process of Conflict Resolution*, Jossey-Bass, San Francisco, 2003.

Charlton R. and Dewdney M., *The Mediator's Handbook*, 2nd ed, Lawbook Co, Sydney, 2004, Ch 2.

Cloke K., *Resolving Personal and Organizational Conflict: Stories of Transformation and Forgiveness*, Jossey-Bass, San Francisco, 2000.

Covey S., *7 Habits of Highly Effective People*, Simon and Schuster, New York, 1989.

Doherty N. and Guyler, M., *The Essential Guide to Workplace Mediation and Conflict Resolution: Rebuilding Working Relationships*, Kogan Page, 2008.

Ellis A., 'Rational Emotional Behaviour Therapy' in Corsini and Wedding (eds), *Current Psychotherapies*, 6th ed, F. E. Peacock, Itasca, 2000.

Emery R., *Renegotiating Family Relationships – Divorce, Child Custody and Mediation*, The Guildford Press, New York, 1994, Chs 1 and 2.

Fisher R. and Brown S., *Getting Together – Building a Relationship that Gets to Yes*, Business Books, London, 1989, Chs 1–3.

Fisher R. and Shapiro, D., *Beyond Reason: Using Emotions as You Negotiate*, Viking Penguin, 2005.

Folberg J. and Taylor A., *Mediation: A Comprehensive Guide to Resolving Conflicts without Litigation*, Jossey-Bass, San Francisco, 1984, Ch 2.

Folger J. P., Poole, M. S. and Stutman, R. K., *Working Through Conflict: Strategies for Relationships, Groups and Organizations*, 6th ed, Allyn & Bacon, 2008.

Friedman G. and Himmelstein J., *Challenging Conflict: Mediation Through Understanding*, American Bar Association, 2008.

Frijda N. H., *The Emotions*, Cambridge University Press, 1986.

Goleman D., *Working with Emotional Intelligence*, Bantam, New York, 1998.

Kubler, Ross E., *On Death and Dying*, Macmillan, New York, 1969, Ch 2.

Levy D., *The Role of Apology in Mediation*, New York University Law Review, 1997, 72(5), p 1165.

Mackie K. et al, *The ADR Practice Guide: Commercial Dispute Resolution*, Tottel Publishing, London, 2007, Ch 13 (at 13.3, 13.4, 13.5.2, 13.6.2, 13.7.2).

Roberts M., *Mediation in Family Disputes: Principles of Practice*, Ashgate, 2008.

Serventy N., 'Understanding Shame in Mediation and Dispute Resolution' (1998) 9 *ADRJ* 150.

Sheehy G., *Pathfinders*, Bantam Books, New York, 1982.

Stulberg J., *Taking Charge/Managing Conflict*, Lexington Books, Massachusetts, 1987, Ch 3.

Ury W., *The Power of a Positive No: How to Say No and Still Get to Yes*. Bantam, 2007.

van Dijk and others, 'A Social Functional Approach to Emotions in Bargaining: when Communicating Anger Pays and when it Backfires', in (2008) 94 *Journal of Personality and Social Psychology* 600.

Van Kleef and Cote, 'Expressing Anger in Conflicts: when it Helps and when it Hurts', in (2007) 92 *Journal of Applied Psychology* 1557.

Chapter 4

Diagnosing, Defining, Designing

A picture paints a thousand words

A. Introduction

4.1   Mediators can make contributions in the following aspects of sound conflict resolution:

- in *diagnosing* the nature of the conflict;

- in *defining* the issues in dispute (and defining out what is not in dispute);

- in *designing* an appropriate model of mediation for the particular dispute;

- in assisting the parties to *develop options* for settlement.

The first three functions are dealt with in this chapter (the last, in later chapters). Each of these functions makes assumptions about the resources, such as time, information, expertise and money, available for the mediation. The greater the resources, the greater the scope for the mediator to diagnose, define, design and develop; the fewer the resources, the less feasible this becomes. However, there is also a relativity about this: where resources are extensive there will still be limitations on how effective these functions can be, and where resources are restricted they can still be performed in a limited way.

The Triangle of Influence serves as a graphic reminder of these functions. The base represents design of the appropriate process; the middle portion focuses on the diagnosis of the conflict and definition of the issues; and the apex represents assistance with option generation.

B. Developing a 'conflict road map'

4.2   In order for mediators to make appropriate interventions in the disputes of others they need to develop a 'conflict road map', or hypothesis, on which to base each intervention. A road map is a framework for understanding the dispute and the disputants. All the activities referred to in this chapter contribute towards the development of that road map. The road map is always tentative in nature, given the fact that conflict resolution is not an exact science and new actions or behaviours by the parties might require revision of the mediator's initial understanding of the conflict.

At the most general level, all forms of problem solving, such as engineering, firefighting and mediation, deal with the following three questions:[1]

■ Where are we now?

■ Where do we want to be?

■ How do we get there?

Where mediation is being used to deal with problems, the hypothesis can be put at a more specific level:

■ What are the *causes* of the problem facing the parties?

■ What are the appropriate *interventions* which a mediator might make to assist in resolving or managing it?

■ What are the possible *outcomes* of the problem-solving process?

■ What potential *problems* could emerge in the mediation?

4.3   The mediation hypothesis is different from a legal or social science hypothesis. To illustrate these differences, let us take, by way of example, a dispute between a small internet service provider (ISP) company and a former employee, Edward. After 18 months' employment Edward has set up an independent part-time business in a related, but not identical, area of internet service. The employer alleges that this is in breach of the employment agreement which restricts former employees from setting up a competitive service within six months of their employment ending.

The following table shows how, with a little poetic licence, this problem might be approached and understood from the perspectives of law, counselling and mediation:

	Discipline		
	Law	**Counselling**	**Mediation**
Hypothesis on the causes of the dispute	Possible breach of the employment agreement giving rise to probable cause of action; alternatively illegal restraint on Edward's right to work giving rise to valid legal defence.	Personal relationship breakdown between parties because of employer's sense of betrayal by a trusted worker and employee feeling unacknowledged for contributions to the business.	Dispute apparently caused by poor communication between the parties, by differing interpretations of the employment agreement, and by competition over scarce resources in the market.

---

1   See Costanzo, *Problem-Solving*, 1995, 54.

	Discipline		
	Law	**Counselling**	**Mediation**
Hypothesis on appropriate forms of intervention	Probable need for adjudication to resolve disputes of fact, to select relevant legal rules, and to apply rules to fact situation in a decision binding on both parties.	A period of professional counselling is indicated in order to heal the sense of wrong suffered by each party and to restore their personal relationship.	Mediation meeting required involving mediator with expertise in communication with understanding of small business, with parties advised on the legal issues.
Hypothesis on outcome	Possible injunction to discontinue with new business for a certain period and potential payment of damages for the employer's losses; alternatively order invalidating parts of service agreement.	The parties might be able to resume their business association on the basis of restored sense of trust, or decide to part ways after resolving personal differences.	The parties might be able to negotiate a termination of legal proceedings, consider options for doing business together in future, and/or make monetary adjustments for past actions.

For present purposes it is the mediation hypothesis which is of importance. How this is developed and used is explained in the following sections.

C.   Gathering information

4.4   All dispute-resolution methods need some amount of data and information with which to operate. Some, like litigation, are obsessed with data and information and have structures and procedures for identifying, obtaining, exchanging and validating them. Generally, mediation has relatively few mechanisms for doing this, partly because it is not obsessed with questions of fact and partly because most mediators do not have the authority to order the production and verification of documents and other forms of evidence. In certain situations, mediators may have some authority in terms of legislation, rules of court or referral orders[2] and in some situations they derive such authority from the agreement to mediate,[3] or mediator standards or codes of practice,[4] but in many others they have to rely on the moral authority deriving from their position as a basis for being involved in this aspect of the dispute resolution process.

Some obligations to provide information

4.5   Increasingly, legislation, rules of court, standards, codes of conduct and court orders will seek to regulate aspects of mediation, including the provision of documents and other information.

---

2   Refer to Appendix 1.
3   Refer to Appendix 3.
4   Refer to Appendix 8.

The European Code of Conduct for Mediators, for example, requires a mediator to ensure that:

- The parties understand the mediation process and the role of each participant.[5]

- The parties understand and agree the terms of a mediation agreement before the mediation commences.[6] A specific agreement on the mediator's fees is required ahead of commencement.[7]

- The parties are informed if the mediator considers that any proposed settlement is unenforceable.[8]

- The parties understand the terms of any agreement reached at mediation.[9]

- The parties are informed about how the agreement reached in mediation might be formalised and made enforceable.[10]

Court mediation referral orders sometimes require the parties to exchange information with one another, or to bring specified documents to the mediation, or even allow the mediator to call for the production of documentation.[11] For example, the Commercial Court's 'ADR order', set out in Appendix 7 to the Admiralty and Commercial Court Guide, requires parties to exchange lists of mediators (with a view to providing a mechanism for selection of the mediator)[12] and provision as to costs sharing.[13] The court's 'ADR order' also typically includes provisions as to exchange of mediation case summaries and supporting bundles of documents.

In the family context, where financial or property claims are involved, the parties provide financial statements, frequently referred to as 'Form E', although some mediation services providers use their own forms.[14] Agreements relating to financial or property matters in family matters, which are embodied in court consent orders, need to be supported by full and frank disclosure.[15] Most mediator codes of conduct also remind family mediators about the requirement for full and frank disclosure[16] and the need to inform parties about the desirability of independent legal advice.[17] Although family mediators do not verify financial information, or give legal advice about such matters, they can give information about the disclosure requirements.[18]

Agreements to mediate typically require the parties to submit to each other and the mediator all information and documentation that would usually be available through the disclosure process in legal proceedings. For example, CEDR's Model Medition Procedure (which is referred in its Model Mediation Agreement) requires each party to prepare and exchange a case summary and endeavour to agree with

---

5   Article 3.1.
6   Ibid.
7   Article 1.3.
8   Article 3.2.
9   Article 3.3.
10 Ibid.
11 See a sample Order in Appendix 1.
12 Paragraph 1.
13 Paragraph 6.
14 Refer to Appendix 1 for 'Form E'.
15 Rule 76A revised by Rule 9 Matrimonial Causes (Amendment No 2) Rules 1985.
16 For example, sections 6.4 and 6.16 UK College of Family Mediators Code of Practice: see Appendix 8.
17 For example, section 11.4 Law Society Code of Practice for Family Mediation: see Appendix 8. Also refer to 8.6–8.7.
18 For example, section 6.7 UK College of Family Mediators Code of Practice: see Appendix 8. Also refer to 8.6–8.7.

all other parties what documents are needed for the mediation; and to send to the mediator a copy of the case summary and two copies of the document bundles no later than two weeks before the date set for the mediation.[19]

LSC contracted providers, and those complying with the LSC Mediation Quality Mark Standards ('MQMS'), are required to give information about the process before the mediation begins;[20] to inform parties about the right to seek independent legal advice;[21] to provide various details as soon as the decision to mediate is made;[22] to give various forms of information during the mediation;[23] and to provide information about supplementary services.[24]

4.6   Accordingly, mediators need to be attentive to any legislative, court procedural or contractual obligations pertaining to the disclosure of information by the parties or themselves.

Assuming there are no such obligations, mediators should, at the minimum, ask the parties what information or facts are essential to enable them to make decisions in the mediation, and where these are missing have the parties consider ways of obtaining them. The obvious example of such essential information would be reports from valuers where the parties need to negotiate over the division of property, a business, shares, or similar objects of disputed value. One advantage of the mediator being involved in obtaining, say, the different valuations is that consideration can be given to ways of avoiding the 'duelling experts' phenomenon which occurs where each side obtains widely differing valuations.[25] The same applies to other expert reports.

4.7   For lawyer-mediators a change of mind-set is needed on the information question. The reason why facts and documents are needed in mediation is not in order to resolve liability for past events, but so that the parties can make personal and commercial decisions relating to their present circumstances and future plans. This is a different perspective to the information issue to that normally encountered in the legal system.

Generally, mediators should be mindful of the following aspects of information and data gathering, though their exact role in relation to each will depend on the context and circumstances of the mediation:

- Procuring necessary documents, reports, tables, books of account and other forms of documentation.

- Securing exchange of relevant information between the parties to the dispute.

- Co-ordinating the verification of the data's accuracy.

- Examining ways of dealing with uncertain, contradictory or missing information.

- Encouraging agreements on facts, or obtaining clarity on fact differences between the parties.

---

19 For example, section 4 CEDR Model Mediation Procedure (10th ed): see Appendix 3.
20 Requirement F1.2 MQMS (in Appendix 8).
21 Requirement F1.3.
22 Requirement F2.1.
23 Requirement F2.2.
24 Requirement F2.3.
25 See 10.39–10.43.

- Exchanging summaries of cases, witness statements and experts' reports in order to cut down on documents and paper.

4.8   To some extent this may be a limited exercise, in that the mediator has no way of ensuring that the information gathered is accurate, comprehensive or properly understood by all parties concerned. Moreover, where mediation occurs in the context of litigation or in other adversarial situations, there may be a reluctance to provide information (where there has not yet been the required disclosure) as it will be seen as weakening that side's case. Information is a source of power and mediating parties cannot be expected to relinquish their power merely because they have entered the mediation process. However, here the mediator can use some gentle persuasion by indicating to the parties that the issue is not *whether* they will exchange information, but *when* they will exchange it, that is, either at the mediation or when ordered to do so by a court or tribunal.

How much does the mediator need to know about the facts of the dispute?

4.9   Some mediators consider that they do not need to know much about the facts of the dispute. In some cases, mediators merely ask parties:

(a) Who initiated the mediation and why?

(b) When/how did the problems occur?

(c) How did the other parties respond when they first heard about the problems?

(d) How does each party feel now?

(e) What does each party want?

This is a *minimalist* model of mediator knowledge and is also more appropriate for *facilitative* mediation where the main role of the mediator is to assist the parties to exchange information and ideas for settlement with each other. It is also more common in certain practice areas, like family and workplace matters.

Most commercial mediators, for example, would ask for much more information, in particular, the statements of case, disclosed documents, contractual documents, experts' reports, witness statements and even correspondence. This is based on the assumption that there might be complex issues of fact and law on which the mediator needs to be prepared in order to assist the parties appropriately. This is a *maximalist* model of mediator knowledge and is also appropriate for more *evaluative* mediation or where the mediator plays a more 'interventionist' role in the parties' negotiations and decision-making process.

What are the benefits and drawbacks of party case summaries?

4.10   Some mediators ask the parties for, and oversee the exchange of, 'case summaries', 'party statements' or 'issue statements'.[26] These documents are intended to be short in length and to summarise the background, issues and intended outcomes from each side's perspective. The intention is that, regardless of prior definitions of the problem and information exchanges between the parties,

---

26   See also 2.38.

these statements will provide an up-to-date summary of the problem, from each side's point of view, for the benefit of the parties and the mediator.

While the statements may encourage the parties and lawyers to 'get to the point' in a focused and disciplined way, they also tend to provide simplistic definitions of and solutions to the problem which the parties might regurgitate later.[27]

Some of the other potential benefits and drawbacks of position statements are set out in the table below:

Potential benefits	Potential drawbacks
Succinct statement of the problem	Over-simplification of the problem
Up-to-date version of issues and demands	Positional and adversarially worded style
Efficient way of informing mediator	Legalistic definition of the problem
Shortens time needed for mediation	Extra pre-mediation time and costs
Gets parties prepared for mediation	Reinforces parties in entrenched positions

One way of attempting to derive the benefits and minimise the drawbacks of issue statements is for mediators to give instructions to the parties on the desired format and style of the documents. A guide on the format of a case summary might include the following items:

Format of case summary
Name and description of parties
Key decision makers at the mediation
Nature of the dispute
Chronology
Key technical terms
What's agreed – no longer in issue
What's still outstanding and each party's views on those issues
Status of any litigation
Previous negotiations and offers
What the parties want to achieve at mediation
Costs position
Stengths/weaknesses
Suggested approaches
Whether the mediation is voluntary or has been compelled
Any deadlines/time issues/limitation and any settlement formality or ratification/review issues

---

27 As K. Slaikeu (*When Push Comes to Shove*, 1996, p 60) points out, the issue statement can lead to more emotional investment in a party's position ('I told you in my issue statement I wanted a million dollars and now you don't seem to be taking that seriously …'), making the mediator's job more difficult later. Instead, he suggests asking the parties to submit and exchange only materials that have already been generated beforehand.

What are the benefits and drawbacks of chronologies of the dispute?

4.11   Some mediators ask the parties to provide them with a chronological history of the dispute, with dates and major events listed in a format provided to them. This approach has the benefit of avoiding the positional nature of an issue statement and providing a succinct account of the factors significant for the mediation. It has the drawback, however, of highlighting the selective and sometimes biased ways in which individuals view their own history. There are classic examples of party chronologies which make it difficult to recognise that they are talking about the same marriage, business partnership or work situation, as the case may be. These divergences nevertheless assist the mediator in selecting appropriate strategies for conducting the mediation.

D.   Distinguishing between positions and interests

4.12   Before examining the mediator's role in diagnosing and defining the problem, it is necessary to define some basic terms relevant to these functions:

■ *Positions*: the demands or claims which parties in dispute make of the other side; positions are also known as *solutions* or *outcomes*, that is, the things a party wants to get out of the mediation. Other terms might be *wish lists* or *wants*.

■ *Interests*: the factors which underlie the parties' positional claims; those things which are actually motivating the parties in the negotiations. Interests can also be referred to as the *motivations* or *needs* of the parties.

Positions and interests, in these senses, are often closely connected, sometimes different sides of the same coin. However, a positional claim may disguise or conceal the party's real interests. Thus, a residential parent in a family mediation might make the positional claim that the children should have no overnight contact with the other parent, when their real interest is in having one night to themselves every weekend. Likewise a farmer in a mediation over the farm's debts might make the positional claim that he wants a loan restructured, when his real interest might be to leave the farm with a sense of dignity after the next crop is harvested. The positional claims could be motivated by revenge, fear, ignorance or professional advice, and they could disguise the parties' real interests even from themselves.

4.13   One way of turning a position into an interest is to ask the question, 'Why is the position important for you?' This is not to suggest that mediators should regularly ask the 'why' question as it might elicit a defensive or protective response, but it indicates the relationship between positions and interests.

Moore refers to three kinds of interests – substantive, procedural and psychological:[28]

■ *Substantive* interests are those which relate to concrete factors, such as money or conditions of employment, or a specific kind of performance, as the case might be.

---

28   C. Moore, *The Mediation Process*, 3rd ed, 2003.

- *Procedural* interests are those relating to the way in which the dispute has been dealt with, or not dealt with; for example, a lack of response to complaints, refusal to be flexible in dealing with exceptional circumstances, or inequality in the treatment of similar people.

- *Psychological* interests refer to emotional needs, such as desire for vindication in respect of past actions or acknowledgment for hurts and injuries suffered.

Each type of interest is depicted by a side of the Triangle of Influence.[29] The way in which these interests are identified, explored and addressed is depicted by the sections within (or phases represented by) the Triangle of Influence (at the bottom, preparation; in the middle, exploration; and, at the apex, bargaining). The process factors are considered in detail in Chapter 5.

4.14   In focusing on the interests behind positions, the parties may discover that there are matters on which they are not in conflict. Some interests may be shared by the parties, and there may be some interests of one party which are not incompatible with those of any other. Even where interests are in conflict, it may be more feasible to develop creative options when focusing on the interests than it would be where the focus is only on irreconcilable positions. For every interest there may be several possible solutions (options) which could satisfy it.

These factors can be illustrated by reference to a dispute between an employee and his employer over the employee's claim for promotion and the employer's refusal of the claim:

	Employee	**Employer**
Positions	Immediate promotion	No promotion at present
Interests	Increased remuneration and other benefits Recognition for past contributions Scope for contributing more to the firm Increased status within the organisation Comparable treatment to other employees Know whether there is a future in the firm	Keep to budget and planned payroll Retention of employee in workforce Avoid a precedent for other workers Maintenance of managerial prerogatives Best use of available human resources Stable and harmonious workplace

4.15   As can be seen from this example, there is more negotiability in relation to the various interests than there is in relation to the single positional factor of promotion. The employee's interest in increased remuneration and other benefits can be met in various ways, not just by promotion. Within the two lists there are interests which are highly subjective (increased status) and generalised (stable workplace), and therefore more open to creative settlement options than the objective and concrete positional claims of 'promotion' and 'no promotion'.

4.16   Some further refinements can be provided in relation to the term *interests*, as follows:

---

29   Refer also to 1.12–1.14.

- *Objective and subjective interests*: A *subjective* interest is something a party wants, for example, a personal injury claimant wants to buy a car and go on an extended holiday and therefore claims a quick lump-sum payment (position). Here the subjective interest is in the nature of a 'want' or a 'wish'. However, their *objective* interest might be in rehabilitation, retraining and other educational arrangements for future security which would be better secured by instalment payments, subsidies, and the like. Here the interest is in the nature of an objective 'need'.

- *Instrumental and ultimate interests*: An *instrumental* interest is one which is required in order to achieve other interests. An *ultimate* interest is one which is needed in itself and not as means of obtaining another interest. Money is usually an instrumental interest, that is, a means of obtaining security, another car, a sense of vindication, and the like. An ultimate interest is usually very subjective, such as vindication, maintaining dignity and upholding of principle.

4.17   Maslow believes that people's motivation will depend on whether their basic needs are being satisfied.[30] He classifies these needs in a another 'triangular' form, with five basic levels:

- Physiological needs – the most fundamental needs at the base of the 'triangle', including food and shelter.

- Safety needs – including security, stability, freedom from fear and need for order.

- Love and belongingness needs – the need for a place in a group and the affection of a partner, children and friends. This level in particular may be a motivating factor in many mediations as disputing parties have often experienced some kind of loss of a relationship with the other party.

- Esteem needs – this level can be divided into two layers; first, self-respect and the need for confidence, achievement, independence and freedom; second, respect or esteem from others, that is, reputation or prestige.

- Need for self-actualisation – it is at this level, the apex of the 'triangle', that individual differences are greatest, as people try to be true to their own nature and aim for self-fulfilment.

Using the Triangle of Influence, these issues are depicted by the sides of the Triangle (each side representing different interests), as well as the middle of the Triangle (representing the process of diagnosis of the conflict and the definition of motivations, needs and issues through exploration).

This rudimentary insight into mediating parties' possible motivations is part of the context, of which mediators need to take account when defining and diagnosing the dispute.

E. Diagnosing the dispute

4.18   It is imperative for mediators, on a continuing basis, to analyse and diagnose conflict situations in order to develop a theory on which they can base an intervention. Any diagnosis is always tentative. Conflict is not a static phenomenon

---

30   Maslow, *Motivation and Personality*, 2nd ed, 1987, 35.

and it can escalate and de-escalate over time, necessitating a continual diagnostic assessment by mediators.

Diagnosis can be done intuitively, as some mediator trainees would like to have it, or it can be done in a structured manner. As there is more to dealing with conflict than only gut-feeling, the structured approach is recommended. It is more appropriate for beginner mediators to learn through this, rather than through the intestinal, method. Structured diagnosis involves asking the following questions:

Who are the parties to the conflict?

4.19   Mediators need to ensure that all relevant parties are playing an appropriate role in the mediation. In some cases, it is self-evident who they are and what their roles should be; for example, the person asking for something and the person being asked to provide it. In others, the situation is more complex and requires some investigation, analysis and consultation with the parties directly involved to ascertain what other categories of parties should be included. In a mediation over a disputed planning application, for example, there might be a first category of parties, the developer, the objectors and the local council, and also a second category, comprising residents, council tax payers, environmental groups and business associations.

There may be a difference between the parties to the conflict and appropriate parties for the mediation. For example, a doctor might not technically be a party to a medical negligence dispute between a patient and medical insurer, but his or her presence at the mediation might be an important ingredient for its success. Likewise, a party to the conflict might not be the appropriate person to attend the mediation. For example, a middle manager in a business dispute might have too many self-interests to be a useful participant in the mediation, which could be attended by a higher-ranking manager instead.

4.20   A related question is who, apart from the parties to the dispute, should attend the mediation as observers, support persons or in some other capacities. Where legal counsel has given an opinion it is preferable for them to be present, particularly if the opinion has created a firm expectation in the mind of the relevant party, for example, on an amount of damages. If the barrister is not present to 'condone' a reduction in the quantum it may not be possible to settle the matter.

In Chapter 2, reference was made to the need to identify representatives and spokespersons in 'team negotiations' and for the mediator to deal with the question of authority within teams from an early stage.[31] Further attention is given to the problem of 'ratifiers' and other external parties in later chapters.[32]

Why are the parties in conflict?

4.21   Mediators need to develop an understanding as to what has caused the parties' conflict.[33] A sample analysis is set out in the table below.

---

31   See 2.18.
32   See 5.75 and 10.29.
33   See C. Moore, *The Mediation Process*, 3rd ed, 2003.

4.22   In reality most conflicts have more than one cause. Nevertheless, mediators need to develop an understanding of the probable causes of conflict because the mediation interventions and strategies will differ for each cause. For example:

- in 'data' disputes the parties need to consider ways of obtaining comprehensive and accurate data, or of obtaining a single expert interpretation of the data, to tackle misinformation, different views on relevance or different interpretations of the same information.

- in 'relationship' disputes the parties may require extensive interpersonal communication (venting, acknowledgment, clarification and encouragement) to air feelings and explore new arrangements for the relationship.

- in 'value' disputes the parties might have to consider ways in which they can 'live and let live' on their value differences or discuss procedures for having an authority adjudicate on the differences.

The various options can be canvassed in the course of a mediation.

Conflict category	Cause of conflict	Illustration
Goals/objectives	Parties have different goals and cannot achieve them without assistance from each other.	The marketing department requires more products for new customers, while production wants fewer to ensure reliability of quality.
Information/data	Figures, data or documents are incorrect, incomplete, lost or differently interpreted.	Valuers have different methods for assessing the value of goodwill in a business and produce widely different valuations.
Communication	Written, verbal or vocal communications unclear, incomplete, misunderstood, misfiled or ignored.	Subcontractor is accustomed to verbal agreements and does not understand the content of a written contract.
Resources	Competition over limited amounts of money, goods, services, time or other matters of substantive value.	There is a fixed amount of matrimonial property and the more one party receives the more the other will give up.
Structural	Unequal access to authority, information, resources, professional advice, time and other sources of power.	The bank is seen to have unlimited resources and access to power, while the borrower is battling in the current economic climate.
Relationship	Patterns of negative behaviour, untreated emotions, the grieving process, stereotypes, psychological problems.	Women bosses in an organisation are regarded by male employees as biased, rigid, unreasonable and unwilling to take risks.
Values/principles	Competing ideologies, world views, religious and cultural values, basic assumptions about life and the universe.	Employer and employee differ over whether touching on the shoulder constitutes collegial affection or harassment.

Why have past attempts at settlement failed?

4.23 Past patterns of interaction, or inaction, between the parties assists in developing an understanding of the conflict. As there was no resolution of the parties' differences in the past, present attempts at resolution should be informed by the reasons for past failures. This may reinforce the diagnosis on the causes of the dispute referred to above, and pick up on some of the factors which caused the dispute to escalate. Reasons for failure to settle in the past could include:

- *Lack of communication*: misunderstanding and confusion between the parties.

- *Rule differences*: where the parties alone or with expert advice interpret the rules, standards, policies or other relevant norms differently.

- *Unhelpful involvement of outsiders*: where neighbours, in-laws, bosses, lawyers and others provide 'assistance' which escalates the conflict and obstructs constructive problem solving.

- *Restrictions on resources*: lack of knowledge, experts' opinions, professional advice and the like which has made it difficult to come to an agreed settlement.

- *Lack of opportunity*: there has been no structured opportunity for all relevant parties with all relevant information to get together to resolve the matter.

By diagnosing both the causes of conflict and the reasons why past attempts at settlement have failed, the mediator can design appropriate interventions for achieving settlement.

Interventions are depicted by the area of (the stages/phases within) the Triangle of Influence. Chistopher Moore suggests different interventions for the various causes of conflict, as illustrated in the table below.[34] Some interventions, like collation of information, are depicted by the base of the Triangle; others, like identification of interests, by the middle portion; and others, like agreement to disagree on values, by the apex.

Cause of conflict	Possible interventions
Data conflicts	Process for collecting information Criteria for assessing information Third party to give opinion
Interest conflicts	Identify interests Develop a range of options Search for objective criteria Develop trade-offs to satisfy interests
Value conflicts	Change definition of problem away from values Agree to disagree in relation to values Search for common goals/interests
Structural conflicts	Move from positions to interests Ensure fairness of process Ensure even-handedness Find ways to deal with structural issues (eg modify external pressures, change time constraints, allow legal advice to be obtained etc).

---

34 Refer to C. Moore, *The Mediation Process*, 3rd ed, 2003.

Cause of conflict	Possible interventions
Relationship conflicts	Allow expression of emotion Clarify perceptions Improve communication Coach on behaviour modification

Some useful mediator questions to ask parties prior to the mediation meeting

4.24   In order to assist them to diagnose a dispute, mediators might ask the parties one or more of the following questions:

- What has prevented you from settling the dispute in the past? How do you see the background? What impact has it had on you?

- What are your concerns/fears about negotiating with the other parties? What do you think are the other parties' concerns?

- What's at stake here for you? For the other parties?

- What problems are likely to arise in the mediation negotiations? Where have misunderstandings arisen in the past?

- What do you need to achieve in mediation? What do you think the other parties need to achieve?

- What do you think is needed at the mediation to bring you and the other party to a satisfactory settlement of the dispute?

- How have other people settled disputes similar to this?

- How would things be for you if you did settle in the mediation?

- What would be the consequences for you of not settling the dispute in mediation? What would be the consequences for the other parties?

- What would be an outcome you could live with?

The responses to these questions will give the mediator useful information in preparing for the mediation.

What are the parties' current interests, needs and concerns?

4.25   As indicated at 4.12, the parties before mediation might have concealed their real needs, concerns and interests. This occurs for two main reasons. The first is because the disclosure of interests can make that party vulnerable, in negotiating terms, to the other side and therefore they need to bluff and posture. The second is that parties in conflict have difficulty in understanding and articulating their real needs, and it is quicker and easier to be positional. In either event, they become locked into positional claims and demands and during the mediation process they may conceal their needs from their opponents, their professional advisers and even themselves. The undisclosed interests can include not only substantive matters, as referred to above, but emotional and procedural needs as well.

Mediators can attempt to elicit the parties' needs, concerns and interests through the following interventions before and during the mediation:

- by reassuring them of confidentiality;
- by asking open and clarifying questions (about facts and feelings);[35]
- by engaging in active listening;[36]
- through the device of reframing;[37]
- through the use of separate meetings;[38]
- by probing for parties' objectives;
- by strategic exchange of information;
- by avoiding narrow focus on a single answer, option or solution;
- by summarising;
- by asking whether there is 'anything else'?
- by tasking a party to consider needs, concerns and interests when the mediator is in private session with another party.

However, it is naive to expect that even skilled mediator interventions will elicit from the parties all their interests. In reality, there will only be a tentative understanding of the parties' interests in the early stages of conflict diagnosis.

What are the parties' alternatives to a mediated settlement?

4.26   All participants in mediation have options away from the negotiating table, such as going to court, appealing to higher authority (the company board, the cabinet) or engaging in hostilities (for instance, going to the press or engaging in strike action). These alternatives are relevant in assisting the parties to assess whether they would be better off not accepting a particular offer of settlement in mediation and pursuing their cause elsewhere. This notion has been immortalised by Fisher and Ury in the form of the acronym BATNA (best alternative to a negotiated agreement).[39] Consideration might also be given to the notion of the worst alternative to a negotiated agreement (WATNA), and even the most realistic alternative (RATNA).

Mediators, mindful of their acronyms, routinely ask parties from the earliest stages of the mediation to consider these factors as a way of focusing their minds on the value of a mediated settlement, relative to what might happen away from the mediation room. If their BATNA or RATNA is worse than that which is on offer in the mediation, it would be wise to accept the latter; if their WATNA or RATNA is better than that which is on offer in the mediation, it would be wise to reject the latter.

---

35   See 6.46.
36   See 6.34–6.35.
37   See 6.38 6.43.
38   See 5.56–5.66.
39   *Getting to Yes*, 2nd ed, 1996, Ch 6.

What are possible solutions?

4.27   While there is an infinite number of potential outcomes to mediation, unlike litigation, these can be categorised into the following groups:

- Compensation/restitution, that is, the making good of past damage, injury or loss through the provision of money, goods, services, repairs, replacements or other forms of reparation.

- Plans of action for the future, for example, arrangements for joint parenting of children, new conditions of employment in a particular enterprise, or a joint business venture. Further examples are improving the quality of quantity of communication; encouraging positive problem-solving attitudes in the future; and blocking negative repetitive behaviours.

- Dealing with emotional/psychological issues, for example, through acknowledgment of others' feelings, apologies and forgiveness, and other aspects of reconciliation.

Mapping the conflict

4.28   Sometimes it is useful to draw the answers to the above questions and factors in a consolidated map, chart or grid which provides an overview of the conflict for the benefit of the mediator and the parties.[40] Assume, for example, that there has been a long-running dispute between the governing board of a school and the school head over matters relating to subjects offered in the curriculum, student discipline and uniforms, and the naming of the new bell tower. Past students, through their official association, and parents, through petitioning, have also become involved. Taking just that part of the dispute relating to curriculum and subject offerings, the conflict might be mapped as shown below.[41] 'Other facts' below refers to external environmental realities which have implications for the way in which the dispute is managed.

Party	School board	School principal	Parents	Past students
Positions	Principal must consult experts on the board about curriculum changes.	Head alone should make all decisions on curriculum matters.	School must introduce new subjects relevant to future careers.	School should stick to traditional subjects studied in their day.
Interests	Avoidance of bad publicity for school. Need to contain costs in tight budget.	Support of most teachers on subject decisions. Harmonious environment in school.	School to cater for diverse needs of students. School to keep up with new competitors.	Avoidance of bad publicity for school. Greater success in sporting competitions.

---

40   The various questions above are recorded on a 'conflict analysis sheet' in Appendix 5. This sheet can be adapted to suit the particular case or circumstances.

41   See K. Slaikeu, *When Push Comes to Shove*, 1996, 23–45.

Party	School board	School principal	Parents	Past students
Other facts	Increased fees already provided for in budget.	Only two years until retirement and pension.	Severe discontent over entrenched teachers' skills.	Deep divisions in the management committee.
BATNAS	Offer head an exit package and replace.	Appeal to religious hierarchy to which school is affiliated.	Lobby for new subjects through formal committees.	Indicate lack of confidence in board and withhold donations.
Possible solutions, options	Appoint consultant on curriculum matters.	Impose fee levy for expensive new subjects.	Private external tuition for special subjects.	Generate further contributions to school foundation.

4.29   The conflict mapping concept can be used in different ways in mediation. The map can be used exclusively by the mediator to provide a sense of structure within which he or she makes judgements over strategies and interventions. Where resources allow, it can be suggested to the parties that they engage in conflict mapping as part of their negotiation preparation. Where trust has developed there can even be some sharing of map information between the parties. And it can be used with constituents, ratifiers and other parties not at the mediation table to explain the realities in as objective and economical a way as possible.

F.   Defining the problem appropriately: identifying issues or questions

4.30   The procedural steps of mediation are designed to define disputes comprehensively before moving on to their resolution.[42] As has been pointed out in this chapter, parties in conflict often 'present' their problem in simplistic and positional terms which obscure their real needs, interests and desires. By redefining the problem in all its complexity, mediation allows the parties to deal with their needs, interests and desires, to have more issues over which to negotiate, and to exploit all potential value at the negotiating table. A problem well-defined, say mediators, is a problem half-resolved.

4.31   Mediators need to assume a significant leadership role in the defining stage of mediation as it is a sophisticated art. It is not something which would come naturally to most people. It is also counter-intuitive in that people in dispute are inclined to define the problem one-sidedly in a way which implies that the other party is at fault and must rectify the problem. This creates a naturally defensive reaction from the other person, who develops his or her own one-sided definition. Mediators must attempt to move beyond such one-sided definitions and to obtain the parties' acceptance of a mutual and generalised definition which puts the onus for resolving the problem on both parties.

---

42   See Chapter 5.

To revert to the dispute between the school board and the head, referred to above, the following different definitions of the problem by the two main parties and mediator might be found:

- *School board's definition of the problem*: The head is not faithfully applying school policy set by the board and does not communicate adequately with the board. (Implication: the head must change.)

- *School head's definition of the problem*: The board is going beyond its policy-making role and continually interferes in matters of day-to-day school administration. (Implication: the board must back off.)

- *Mediator's definition of the problem*: What is an appropriate division of functions and responsibilities between the board and the principal and how should future communication and co-operation take place between them? (Implication: they both have to work on the problem.)

The last definition implies no blame, provides a single common definition, is future-oriented, and presents the problem as an open-ended question which can be used to invite possible answers from the parties. By contrast, the other two definitions each have a one-sided approach to the problem which implies that the other side must fix it.

The mediator's initiatives in defining the problem

4.32   As has been pointed out, parties will make positional claims in mediation and impute blame to everyone other than themselves. An important mediator function is to direct the parties' perceptions away from positional claims towards underlying interests, and to get the parties to accept a definition of the problem which reflects these interests.[43] To achieve this mediators must attempt to:

- Restate or reframe positional claims to reflect underlying interests and clarify and make explicit the parties' needs: for example, a claim for the family car may be motivated by a more general need for adequate transportation.[44]

- Change from one-sided views of the dispute towards views which reflect both sides of the problem. If two parents each claim exclusive residence of the children, the mediator might suggest that they see the problem as one of reconciling each parent's need for appropriate involvement in the children's lives and having a good relationship with them.

- Move from a specific definition of the problem to one which is more generalised and tentative. Thus a claim for 60% of the property might be depicted by the mediator as a need for a fair and equitable division of property which takes into account past contributions and future requirements. By ignoring the specific figure, the mediator opens up the negotiating process to more options.

- Include both sides' interests in the definition of the problem. For example, in the school problem referred to above, the mediator might suggest that what is needed is the consideration of solutions which allow the school board to have overall supervision of policy-making in the school and allow the head to have a say on matters of administrative management.

---

43 For further discussion on this function, see 5.37–5.49.
44 On reframing, see 6.38–6.43 and the examples in Appendix 5.

■ Use neutral and non-laden language. Thus a claim that 'the fascist managers must give us a pay rise or there will be rivers of blood on the factory floor' could be redefined as 'You want management to pay you an appropriate wage for the kind of work you do.'

■ By casting positions and interests in open-ended problem solving questions, for example, 'How can the loan be repaid in a way which satisfies both parties?', or 'How can you each be assured as to the reliability of future performances?'

■ By 'de-legalising' the problem. Lawyers might define a problem as one of liability and quantum, whereas a mediator should attempt to define it in non-legal terms. In a personal injury case, the mediator might redefine liability and quantum as 'How can you deal with different versions of the accident?', 'How have the various parties been affected by the accident?' and 'What actions are required to make good any losses suffered?'

■ By 'de-monetising' the problem. In litigation, interests and issues are usually incorporated into a monetary claim, whereas in mediation it might be better not to define the dispute in monetary terms so that other non-monetary factors are encouraged to emerge. Thus an employee's claim for damages for wrongful dismissal might be redefined as 'What actions should the employer undertake in order to resolve the employee's grievances?'

The mediator skill most pertinent to the above interventions is that of *reframing*.[45]

Different levels of defining

4.33   Mediators have some discretion in relation to the *level* at which the dispute is defined, and the discretion will be exercised in the light of the circumstances of the parties and the mediator's background and training. To revert, this time, to the dispute between the ISP employer and former employee Edward, referred to above, there are three potential levels at which it could be defined (though they are not entirely mutually exclusive), using the three sides of the Triangle of Influence:

■ The *legal* level: has there been a breach of the employment agreement between the two?

■ The *commercial* level: what is an appropriate commercial arrangement to take account of past conduct and future business possibilities?

■ The *personal* level: how can the employer's sense of betrayal and the employee's lack of acknowledgment be dealt with?[46]

4.34   As indicated previously, mediators normally avoid legalistic definitions because they do not promote negotiated decision-making, although they might be appropriate in some circumstances. Which of the other approaches, or combination of approaches, will be taken depends on the needs and wishes of the parties, the circumstances of the dispute and the skills of the mediator.

---

45   See 6.38–6.43. Refer also to the reframing examples in Appendix 5.
46   See J. Wade, 'Levels of Problem Definition', in (2001) 4(1) *ADR Bulletin*, 7.

Terminology on positions, interests and issues

4.35   The following table further illustrates how the terms positions, interests and issues/questions are used in this book:

	Positions	**Interests**	**Issues**
Also known as	Solutions, wants, answers, outcomes	Needs, motivations, requirements, concerns	Agenda items, problems, questions to be answered
Definition	How a party wants to come out of a dispute, what it demands of the other party	The underlying needs a party wants satisfied, what is really motivating them	A mutually acceptable definition of the problem which needs treatment
Characteristics	Narrowly focused, defined by each side in extreme and mutually exclusive terms	Broadly focused, more subjective, more likelihood of common grounds between parties	Defined generally, non-judgementally, and mutually, which both sides can accept
Examples	'I want a million pounds ...'	Financial security for the future, vindication for past behaviour	What financial arrangements would be reasonable for the parties?
	'I want residence (custody) of the children ...'	Significant involvement in parenting the child	How should the parents share their parenting responsibilities?
	'That bloody employee must be terminated at once ...'	Stability in workplace, fewer disruptions in production	What should the future involvement of the employee be in the firm?

G. Designing an appropriate form of mediation

4.36   Because of the number of variables in the structure and procedure of mediation, there should be a design effort by the mediator both before and during its course (depicted by the base of the Triangle of Influence). Mediators may be able to impose their design on the process without the parties' consent, or even consciousness, they may recommend it to the parties, or they may consult them openly and seek their input into how the mediation is designed.[47] The stronger the mediator's understanding of the conflict, the more assertive he or she can be in designing the mediation process.

Here are some of the factors which should be considered in the design function:

- How many mediators are required, with what professional background, training and experience, and with what cultural, gender, age or class attributes?

---

47   Some mediator codes of conduct provide guidance. For example, section 5 CEDR Code of Conduct, section 4 CORE Solutions Group Code of Conduct and section 6 College of Mediators Code of Practice. Refer to Appendix 8.

- What is the appropriate role of advisers such as lawyers and accountants before, during and after the mediation?

- To what extent should constituents, supporters, partners, friends or other parties be involved in the mediation?

- What degree of 'interventionism' by the mediator does the situation require?

- What rules and procedures should be followed, and how much formality and flexibility should there be?

- What rooms, seating, amenities, visual aids and other facilities should there be?

- Should there be interpreters, and what qualifications and experience should they have?

- What status should the outcome of the mediation have?

4.37   In respect of these, and many other factors, the experienced mediator can provide leadership and guidance in designing a particular form of mediation for a particular dispute.

Case illustration

Brigitte had inherited money and decided to invest it by developing property. A professional valuer, Stephen, was retained and valued the relevant property at £2 million, in reliance on which a bank lent her £960,000. Four months later, after making only one repayment, Brigitte defaulted on the loan and the bank took possession. The bank sold the property for almost £1.1 million, which covered the loan, interest and the agent's commission, and there was nothing remaining for Brigitte. The personal guarantors had gone bankrupt shortly after the loan was made. Brigitte sued the valuer (who had no professional indemnity insurance), alleging professional negligence, and the parties agreed to mediate.

Diagnosing: The dispute was caused by: data conflict (different understandings of the instructions to the valuer, different interpretations of the valuation, and different professional advice on the law and likely court outcome) and structural factors (the high risks and relative lack of security).

Defining: While the legal definition of the dispute was whether the valuer was professionally negligent and if so what were the damages, the mediation definition was:

- How should the differences in valuation be dealt with?

- How should the losses/damages of the parties be dealt with?

- How can further losses for the parties be contained?

- What else is required to finalise the matter?

Design: The following design steps were taken: exchange of valuations, obtaining a third valuation, attendance of Brigitte's barrister at the mediation, a mediator with strong facilitative skills, short pre-mediation contact with each side before coming together, ample

---

	opportunity for Brigitte to speak her mind and Stephen to respond, with prior agreement of advisers ample opportunity for parties to speak extensively with each other and to meet with mediator without advisers present.
Developing options and reaching outcome:	A settlement satisfactory to both parties after six hours of mediation.

H.   Summary

4.38   This chapter raises the following points of particular significance:

■ Mediators need to continually diagnose, and re-diagnose, a dispute on the basis of the changing information which they have. The diagnosis relies on data provided by the parties and on an existing set of concepts which mediators can use to process it.

■ A dispute appropriately defined is a dispute half-resolved, and mediators need to take care in defining conflicts in ways which are suited to their resolution through mediation, as opposed to definitions which might be suited to litigation or other dispute resolution processes.

■ On the basis of their diagnosis and definition of the dispute, mediators can make informed judgements about strategies, interventions and other aspects of the mediation process which they are responsible for designing and putting into effect.

I.   Tasks for beginner mediators

4.39   Identify a dispute in which you have been involved personally and analyse it in terms of the sources of conflict referred to in this chapter. What other factors not referred to here might have caused the conflict to occur? What interventions worked and did not work in relation to resolving the dispute? How might a mediation have been designed to deal with the particular nature of this dispute?

4.40   Consult a newspaper for a news report on a dispute of some magnitude. What are the positional claims made by the parties to the dispute? What might be the interests and needs underlying these positions? As the dispute continues to be reported in the media, how do the parties' positions and interests change?

4.41   Refer to a classic court decision (for example, *Donoghue v Stevenson* (1932) AC 562). How was this dispute defined for purposes of the litigation? If the same dispute were to be mediated, how might it be defined for purposes of the mediation?

J. Recommended reading

Boulle L. and Nesic M., *Mediation: Principles Process Practice*, Tottel Publishing, 2001, Ch 6.

Cooley J. W., *The Mediator's Handbook*, National Institute for Trial Advocacy, 2006.

Costanzo M., *Problem-Solving*, Cavendish Publishing, London, 1995, Ch 4.

Fisher R. and Ury W., *Getting to Yes*, 2nd ed, Pantheon Books, US, 1996, Chs 2, 3, 6.

Jeong H., *Understanding Conflict and Conflict Analysis*, Sage Publications Ltd, 2008.

Justice T. and Jamieson D., *The Facilitator's Fieldbook: Step-by-Step Procedures, Checklists and Guidelines*, AMACOM, 2006.

Mackie K. et al, *The ADR Practice Guide: Commercial Dispute Resolution*, Tottel Publishing, 2007, at 13.6 and 13.7.

Maslow A., *Motivation and Personality*, 3rd ed, Addison Wesley Publishing Co, New York, 1987, Ch 4.

Moore C., *The Mediation Process*, 3rd ed, John Wiley and Son/Jossey-Bass, San Francisco, 2003, Chs 4–6.

Slaikeu K., *When Push Comes to Shove – A Practical Guide to Mediating Disputes*, Jossey Bass, San Francisco, 1996, Ch 4.

Tillet G., *Resolving Conflict – A Practical Approach*, 2nd ed, Oxford UP, Melbourne, 1999, Ch 2.

Chapter 5

Managing the Mediation Process

More haste, less speed

A. The power of process

5.1   This chapter deals with the stages of mediation and the role of the mediator in conducting the mediation process. Variations to the process, and across practice areas, are outlined in Chapter 9. The mediator assumes multiple identities in mediation, as chairperson, manager, guide, conductor, leader, controller, umpire and police officer. All these roles of influence are based on the distinction between *process* and *content*, unreliable and misleading as that distinction is: the mediator is responsible for conducting and managing the process of dispute resolution, while the parties are responsible for making decisions on its substantive content.

In Chapter 4 reference was made to the roles of mediators before the commencement of the mediation meeting. Here the focus is on their roles during the mediation meeting itself, and also in relation to post-mediation activities. Clearly, the more work that has been done prior to the meeting, the more the mediator will be able to abbreviate some of the stages without a major threat to the process.

A mediation has the following typical stages:

- meeting, greeting and seating;
- mediator's opening statement;
- parties' initial statements;
- definition of the problem;
- generating solutions, negotiation and problem solving;
- final decisions and closure;
- post-mediation activities.

B. Meeting, greeting and seating

5.2   Mediators greet the parties, engage in pleasantries and small talk, and seat them according to the mediator's sense of what is appropriate.[1] This may also

---

1   On seating, see Chapter 2.

involve some introductions: first, of the mediator where he or she is unknown to the parties; and second, of professional advisers who are present or of other parties not known to one another (for example, a claimant may not know the insurer's representative). In large mediations this can be facilitated with a mediator-prepared list of those who will be present, or even name or place cards. In commercial mediations there can be an exchange of business cards.

5.3   In this early stage, mediators should also indicate what would be considered suitable forms of address, in particular where it seems appropriate to use first names. It is also the time to establish any constraints for the meeting: time commitments, breaks for the parking meter, limits on mobile phones, and the like. The question of small talk at this stage will depend very much on questions of culture, time and personality. Where it is appropriate in terms of those three factors, small talk can personalise the relationships between the parties and the mediator and assist the parties to settle in.

Case illustration

In an industrial dispute between a trade union and five employers in a particular industry, considerable preparatory attention was given to the question of who would be present at the mediation as representatives, advisers and resource persons. As this was an important issue for all concerned, the mediator tabled a document at the mediation listing all those present, together with a description of the capacity in which they were participating. Despite the need for this diligence, most of the participants had negotiated with one another previously and the culture allowed for considerable small talk and banter from the earliest stages of the mediation.

C. Mediator's opening statement

5.4   The first formal part of the mediation comprises an opening statement by the mediator. Experience indicates that this is an important stage of the process, particularly for first-time clients of mediation, regardless of how much prior contact there has been with the mediator.

What are the functions of the mediator's opening statement?

5.5   The opening statement:

- allows the parties to settle in, puts them at ease as their role is limited to listening, and provides a mini mediation ritual;
- builds rapport between the parties and mediator;
- reassures the parties on their choice of mediation (if relevant) and commends them on their commitment;
- acknowledges the significance of the matter to all parties;

- informs them about the nature of mediation, the mediator's role, and their role;

- can be used to distinguish mediation from other forms of help or intervention, like counselling and arbitration;

- explains the order of events for the rest of the mediation meeting;

- stresses the flexibility in the process;

- explains the rationale for the party statements and provides an order for the presentations;

- establishes the mediator's control and the parties' commitment to the mediation guidelines – the 'table manners' for the meeting;

- allows the mediator to establish his/her credentials and trustworthiness;

- establishes positive goals and an optimistic tone for the proceedings;

- identifies common ground and common goals;

- encourages parties actively to participate and reminds them that they are in control of the outcome;

- deals with the confidentiality issue;

- confirms the mediator's neutrality and impartiality;

- establishes that the parties have authority to settle (if relevant);

- clarifies special conditions, for example, on the need for agreements to be reduced to writing;

- addresses any other formalities regarding settlement, for example, review or ratification that might be required;

- manages expectations, for example, by reminding the parties that they might reach impasse and that compromise will be required;

- encourages openess and information exchange;

- allows for clarification on the roles of lawyers, witnesses and other support parties present (and those who may be at the end of the telephone).

In almost all cases the statement is presented orally. In some cases, points are distributed in written form or shown on an overhead projector which the parties can follow as the mediator works through them in more detail.

What are the main principles to be followed in the mediator's opening statement?

5.6 The main principles to be applied are:

- It should be clear and understandable in positive, goal-oriented language. By projecting a positive tone for the mediation, a productive atmosphere can be created. This does not mean that the mediator should promise a favourable outcome, but to be hopeful about what mediation can deliver.

- It should be in plain English and avoid legal or technical terms. It should not be overly formal and is best delivered in a more conversational style, whilst ensuring that it is polished and professional. It should not be read verbatim from

97

notes. The delivery should be confident as that helps to establish the mediator's authority and credibility.

■ It should be concise – keeping it short will ensure that the participants listen to it. The mediator should assume, however, that important elements of it may need to be at later stages in the process.

■ It should be made in all cases, even where the parties are repeated users of mediation such as insurers, banks and government departments.

■ It should be made in all cases, even where the elements have been told to the parties beforehand, so that they all hear the same thing at the same time.

Form of a model mediator's opening statement

5.7   Every mediator's opening statement needs to be adapted to what is suitable to the parties, the dispute, the circumstances of the mediation and other relevant factors. The following is an example of a statement which has implicit assumptions about all of the above matters. It would require amendments, including abbreviation, in many circumstances.

Sample opening statement[2]

Preliminaries – welcome and introductions

Welcome to the mediation, my name is Angela Smith and I am the mediator. You both know each other, but you may not know each other's solicitors. Jane, this is Robert Baker, who is assisting Peter. Peter, this is Alan Nolan, who is Jane's solicitor. Please call me Angela. Are you also comfortable with first names?

Time constraints and settlement authority

Before we get going I would like to check with you about timing matters. We originally agreed to meet today for up to four hours, can you all recommit to that ...? Do you have any parking limits, or other time constraints ...? Do you both have authority to resolve this matter today?

Extent of prior contact with the parties

By way of background, Jane you approached me about having a mediation and I spent some time talking to you on the phone and sent you some written information about mediation, and Peter I did the same with you. You both know that I have spoken to your solicitors by telephone and have received the papers which you prepared for me. That is all the contact I have had about this matter, and I have had about the same access to both of you. Are there any queries about that?

---

2   Refer to Appendix 5 for a mediator's opening statement checklist. For another model of a mediator's opening Statement, see Charlton and Dewdney, *The Mediator's Handbook*, 2nd ed, 2004, Ch 1.

Nature of mediation and role of mediator

You've made the decision to come to mediation yourselves and generally this is a better way of dealing with problems than going into battle. So that's a commendable start. Let me tell you briefly a few things about mediation, although I appreciate that you may have heard some of this before.

Mediation is a structured opportunity for those with a problem to make decisions about it themselves. My role as the mediator is not to make those decisions for you; nor is it to tell you what decisions to make or to advise you on the law or on technical matters. My role is to assist you along the way in your own decision-making. Sometimes emotion or poor communication makes it difficult for people to deal with problems. The mediator's role is to guide them down the path of decision-making and help them to avoid the obstacles and pitfalls. Peter and Jane, you will be discussing the situation and making the decisions, and your advisers will assist you in that process.

Experience/credibility statement

As you know from the materials sent through to you, I have practised for ten years as a mediator. While every situation is unique, I have considerable experience of working through the kind of problems we will be discussing.

Neutrality and impartiality statement

I am a neutral and impartial party in the mediation and you do not have to try and persuade me about the merits of your case. If at any stage you feel a lack of impartiality, please let me know.

Checking understanding

The objective today is for you to make decisions on the issues you are facing, and my role is to assist you in that process. Are there any questions?

Mediation process

This is what will happen in the mediation process. Shortly I shall ask each of you in turn to explain to me your main concerns. This need only be a brief overview as there will be time later to go into the detail. After you have each made a statement I shall summarise it back to you and then we shall confirm the matters in respect of which there already is agreement and what matters still require decisions. I shall then write these issues on the whiteboard/flipchart and we can use it as an agenda for the meeting. You will then work through the issues on the board/chart, looking at options for dealing with them, and making as many decisions as you can.

Separate meetings[3]

A normal part of the mediation process is for the mediator to meet separately with each of the parties. As you have advisers, I would meet with Jane and Alan

---

3   Some family mediators meet with parties jointly only. In workplace mediators, the parties are usually seen separately prior to the start of the mediation, and the mediation session itself may proceed in joint session only. Variations in practice are outlined in Chapter 9.

together, and with Peter and Pat together. This gives me an opportunity to see how the mediation is going for each of you, it allows you to raise matters which have not come up when we were together, and it allows the other party to have a break and to think about settlement options. It is also an opportunity for refreshments and to make any calls if you need to. Are there any questions? Of course this is a flexible process and anyone can ask for an adjournment at any reasonable time.

Guidelines and obtaining commitment to the guidelines

In my experience mediation works best if some basic guidelines are observed. It helps if we speak one at a time, and even where emotions run high it is useful if no-one denigrates the other. As you know this is a non-smoking building, and we should probably also make it a mobile-free zone while we are together. We could call these the table manners for the mediation. Can you commit to them, Jane …? Peter …?

Confidentiality

I need to refer to one more matter before we begin. Mediation is conducted confidentially, which means that, in so far as the law allows, I will not disclose anything said here today. I will be taking some brief written notes, but these will be destroyed after the mediation and cannot be accessed by either of you. Mediation is also conducted on a 'without prejudice' basis which means that should the matter go to court, which we hope it will not do, then neither of you can lead evidence about what the other said at the mediation or produce documents which they made for the mediation.[4] Do you understand these basic principles …? Please check with your solicitors if you require more advice on these points.

Agreement binding when signed[5]

As regards the outcome, the situation today is that any agreements will not be binding until they have been reduced to writing and signed by both of you. Is that understood?

Questions and commitment

Before we begin, are there any questions which either of you have about mediation generally, or about what will happen here today?

Good, are you both then prepared to continue along the lines I have outlined?

Transition to parties' initial statements

Thank you. Peter, can you tell me what your concerns are here today …?

---

4   In relation to family mediation, there is transparency in relation to financial/property information. Refer to Chapter 10 for a further discussion in relation to confidentiality issues.
5   In some contexts like family mediation, a memorandum of understanding is produced, which the parties take to lawyers for advice and to create legally binding agreements and consent orders. Refer to 5.69–5.72 and 10.74–10.77.

Delivery of the mediator's opening statement where there are two or more mediators

5.8   There should be no sense of hierarchy between co-mediators, which entails that they should share the statement and not leave all or most of it to one mediator.[6] How they divide it up is a matter of logic, convenience and training, subject only to the necessity of operating as a team. Because a division of tasks is more important during this stage of co-mediation than in later stages, co-mediators require a clear understanding of who will say what, and what their 'cues' are, in order to operate as a team in delivering the statement.[7]

Questions arising out of the mediator's opening statement

5.9   Questions asked at the invitation of the mediator at the end of the statement should be dealt with as clearly, but briefly, as possible. Solicited or unsolicited questions during the presentation of the statement can be dealt with there and then in like manner, or the mediator can advise that they will be answered later in his or her opening. A delicate balance is required between satisfying the needs of the questioner, on one hand, and avoiding over-elaborate answers and delay, on the other.

Omissions from the mediator's opening statement

5.10   Much will depend on when the mediator discovers that an omission has been made. Generally, a missing element can be added at any stage of the mediation, provided the mediator openly acknowledges the oversight and emphasises its 'normality' in mediation. For example, 'I'm sorry that I forgot to tell you in the beginning that it is a normal feature of mediation for the mediator to see the parties separately ...'. After a certain stage in the mediation, it will be too late to deal with the omission , and this might have little impact on the final product.

D. The party statements

5.11   In most mediations the parties, and/or their representatives, will be invited to make a statement early in the proceedings. Here the mediator hands over to the parties and they have the dominant role in the process for the first time, but in a controlled and structured way.

Purpose of party statements

5.12   The purposes of party statements are:

- To allow each party to make their first contribution without interruption or confrontation and to satisfy their need to have their say and be heard.

---

6   See Charlton and Dewdney, *The Mediator's Handbook*, 2nd ed, 2004, Ch 1.
7   See further on the roles of co-mediators at 9.17–9.35.

- To provide information to the mediator about the parties' concerns, particularly where the mediator has had no prior contact with the parties, as a basis for understanding the dispute and developing an agenda.

- To provide a basis for the mediator to acknowledge what the parties have said so as to satisfy their need to be listened to and know that they have been heard.

- To provide an opportunity for each party to hear the other's presentation in the latter's own words and thereby understand what their current concerns are.

- To give everyone the 'big picture'.

- To give each party an opportunity to assess the credibility, sincerity and other qualities of the principals and decision-makers.

- To confront each party with some aspects of the other's case, in order to create doubt about their own position.

- To achieve a 'day in court' benefit for the parties.

- To allow venting and for cathartic benefits.

- To give the mediator a sense of the dynamics – who leads, who influences and who is respected.

- To allow the parties to acknowledge, if appropriate, the relevance of their relationship.

It is not within the purposes of the party statements to encourage discussion, negotiation or altercation between the parties at this stage, nor to encourage the parties to propose and accept solutions. Experience suggests these aims and objectives could be premature and counter-productive at the early stages. Timing is important in mediation and the mediator has control of the timer.

Scope of party statements

5.13   The party statements should deal with broad themes. This means that they need only be brief. These requirements should be explained to the parties, and where the statements become long-winded, repetitive or excessively detailed the mediator should refer back to these constraints. Loquacious parties might need to be reassured that matters of detail can be dealt with comprehensively at later stages of the mediation.

This topic raises the question of the extent to which mediation clients should be able to 'tell their stories'. There are many advantages in encouraging storytelling by clients. It allows them to present things in their own words, it discloses relevant details, it allows the listener to identify the speaker's interests, and it provides satisfaction for the teller.[8] It can also help to clarify or overcome misunderstandings, miscommunication or misperceptions. Roger Schank, an artificial intelligence researcher, explains that human memory is story-based, so that to disallow storytelling is to disallow effective conversation and communication.[9] Donald

---

8   See Spegel, Rogers and Buckley, *Negotiation – Theory and Techniques,* 1998, paras 3.7–3.9.
9   R. Shank, *Tell me a Story: Narrative and Intelligence,* Northwestern University Press, Evanston, 1990.

Schon of MIT and Chris Argyris of Harvard Business School depicted the impact of storytelling via a 'ladder of inference'.[10]

On the other hand, stories tend to focus on the past and the differences in perceptions about when and how the conflict started. Stories also tend to reinforce blame and other negative judgements and they may have no impact on the other negotiating party. The teller of a story tends to cast himself as the hero and the counterpart as the villain or problem-maker, sometimes referred to as the 'stereotype bias'. Most storytelling is about linear recollections about the past, whereby the party casts him- or herself as the defender and the counterpart as the aggressor. Frequently, there is no acceptance of any contribution made by the party to the problem.

Lawyers and courts tend not to allow free storytelling and rather encourage structured disclosures from clients. In mediation there should be more scope for storytelling. However, this need not all occur in the party statements. Our own preference is to keep the opening statements relatively short and to allow further storytelling when parties exchange information and views on the issues identified as part of the agenda.[11]

Focus of party statements

5.14   Mediators can invite the parties to focus on different factors in their statements, though the extent to which this guidance will affect what the parties actually say is unpredictable. Thus mediators can attempt to make the focus and content of the opening statement:

- *Fact-based*: 'Tell me the history and facts in this case as you see them ...'

- *Rights-based*: 'Tell me what your arguments and evidence are ...'

- *Positional*: 'Tell me what you are here for, what would you like to achieve in the mediation ...'

- *Legalistic*: 'Tell me what the issues are between you today ...'

- *Narrative*: 'Tell me what happened and what effect it had on you ...'

- *Interest-based*: 'Tell me what your concerns are today ...'

- *Problem solving*: 'Tell me what decisions need to be made today ...'

- *Procedure-based*: 'Tell me first how you think we should go about resolving the problems that we are dealing with ...'

5.15   Each approach has its advantages and disadvantages. Most mediators would generally regard the last four approaches as more appropriate than the first four. Each of the last four is in keeping with the philosophical assumptions of mediation. They will be counter-intuitive for many mediation clients who want to be positional, legalistic or rights-based, and will require some explanation and justification if the mediator wishes the parties to adopt one of them. For example, 'In my experience it helps if, instead of getting into a debate over who did or said what to whom, you each tell me briefly what your current concerns are that you would like dealt with in the mediation ...'.

---

10   See, Stone, Patton and Ileen, *Difficult Conversations – How to Discuss what Matters Most*, Penguin, New York, 1999.
11   See 5.51–5.52.

Who makes the party statements?

5.16   Usually the parties themselves make the statements in oral form. Where there are professional advisers present, the practice varies. Some mediators insist that the parties make the statements and invite the lawyers or other advisers to supplement them if necessary. This is consistent with the philosophical assumptions of mediation and the need for the parties to feel that they have control over their own dispute. A client may be able to articulate his concerns and his interests more persuasively. In addition, there is a tendency for parties to 'tune out' comments from opposing lawyers. In certain cases, like personal injury and employment cases, where a claimant's pain and suffering or distress is an element of the claim, a description by the claimant of his suffering can be particularly persuasive. Where an ongoing relationship is likely, in the business or personal context, a party's direct presentation can affect the other party's willingness to commit to an ongoing or working relationship. A willingness to settle a case can be more forcefully addressed via a direct party presentation.

Other mediators request the advisers to make the statements, and then invite the parties themselves to add their contributions. Where there are multiple lawyers, there is sometimes a 'hierarchical' order of presentation, with barristers speaking first, if they are present, followed by solicitors. These arrangements give a dominant role to lawyers in the mediation process and reassure them that their clients will not prejudice their cases by admitting liability or making other detrimental statements. However, mediators should be careful about establishing a strong sense of hierarchy, lawyer domination and exclusive focus on legal rights, at the expense of client interests and party participation.

5.17   Where there is more than one party on a side, the mediator will normally invite each side to nominate a spokesperson to speak and will be wary of inviting the others to add to it for fear that this stage of the mediation will become too protracted. The mediator can reassure the other participants that they will have later opportunities to speak.

Dangers of excluding clients from making the opening presentations

The mediation of a complex commercial dispute was held during the course of litigation and conducted in a vacant court room. The barrister mediator sat at the bar table, with the barristers and solicitors on an adjoining table, and the clients seated in the public gallery. The mediator invited the various lawyers to make 'submissions' to him and did not give the parties an opportunity to speak. The submissions, and some argument over them, proceeded for some hours, after which the mediator announced that there had been no progress in the mediation, and as the agreed time for the process had expired, he terminated proceedings. After a formal complaint to the organisation that appointed the mediator, another mediator was supplied at no cost and the matter settled after full participation by the clients (who were seated at the mediation table) at the second attempt.

Which party makes the first statement?

5.18   There is some significance, albeit limited, in who makes the first party statement. Research shows that the first speaker establishes a narrative framework which can predominate and be more influential on listening parties than subsequent statements. This is referred to as the 'tenacity of the first voice'.[12] Mediators might also be more inclined to believe the first speaker than the second or subsequent speakers where their versions differ from the first. Although mediators do not make binding decisions, their first impressions may unintentionally affect the way in which they conduct the process.

5.19   Another point of significance is that the second speaker is likely to be defensive and to *deny, justify* or *excuse* what has been said by the first, instead of giving his or her own statement. This detracts from the objectives of the party statements and, as indicated below, mediators often indicate clearly to later speakers that they are to give their own versions of events and not to respond to what they have heard.

Nevertheless, mediators would be wise to downplay the significance of speaking first. They should remember that while the mediator is responsible for conducting the process fairly and even-handedly, this depends on the overall conduct of the mediation and not on a single decision early in the piece. And they should inform the parties that:

■ There is no major disadvantage in speaking second, and each party will have an approximate equality of speaking time.

■ There will be other occasions for parties to go first, for example, in the separate meetings, so that 'going first' can be rotated.

Who should decide on who speaks first?

5.20   Most mediators decide themselves who should make the first party statement. This is the preferred practice. It shows that the mediator is in charge of the process, and it prevents any conflict between the parties at an early stage. In making their decisions, it is useful for mediators to have both a private rationale for their decision, and a public explanation for it.

Private rationales for who speaks first

5.21   As in all other interventions, mediators require a hypothesis to support their decision on who should speak first. The following are some potential hypotheses:

■ The 'weaker' party should speak first, to reassure them about the fairness of the process.

■ The more anxious party should speak first, to settle them down.

■ The less anxious party should speak first, so that the other can settle down.

■ The party not legally represented should speak first, so that they do not feel disadvantaged.

---

12   M. Costanzo, *Problem Solving*, 1995, 27.

■ The party claiming something from the other should speak first, because they need to set the parameters of the negotiations.

Public explanations for who speaks first

5.22 In order to legitimise their decision, and retain the parties' trust and confidence, mediators should give a brief explanation for their choice of first speaker. Clearly, mediators would not always express publicly their underlying rationale for asking one party to speak first. However, they need to provide a plausible public reason, which may involve some mediator licence, for example:

■ 'I should like John to begin because he is the claimant in the litigation proceedings …'

■ 'I should like to hear from Mary first, because she instigated the mediation …'

■ 'I should like to hear from Fred first, because Mary instigated the mediation …'

5.23 Some mediators avoid making a choice between the parties out of fear of losing the trust and confidence of the second speaker. They might ask the parties to decide themselves who should speak first: this may work well in some cases, but create its own conflict in others. Mediators should show leadership in selecting the first speaker and to use appropriate explanations to help the parties accept their decision, without making too big an issue of it. In practice the mediator's choice is seldom challenged.

Preventing a defensive response from the second speaker

5.24 Mediators should not invite the second speaker to reply to the first party's statement (for example, 'Mary how do you respond to what Fred has said?'). That approach will allow the first speaker's definition of the problem to predominate and the second speaker is likely to justify, deny or excuse in response. Rather, mediators should direct the second party to give their statement without reference to what they have just heard. They can also specifically instruct the second speaker not to respond to the first (for example, 'Mary, without responding to Fred, can you tell us in your words what your concerns are today …').

To whom are the party statements addressed?

5.25 There are two options for the direction of the party statements. As has already been indicated, the party statements can be addressed to the mediator directly and not to the other party. This avoids heated, or even hostile, interaction between the parties in the early stages of a mediation and affords the mediator the opportunity to use good attending and following skills to ensure that the early communications are accurately heard and each speaker feels listened to.[13]

---

13   See 6.34.

On the other hand, where the parties are experienced in, or comfortable with, the mediation process, are professionals, or are articulate, the mediator may encourage them to speak directly to each other at the opening stage. Encouraging direct statements can give an opportunity for parties to reconnect with those with whom they have worked or had a relationship in the past, and can encourage co-operation at an early stage of the mediation.

Mediator's role during the party statements

5.26   The mediator's main role during party presentations is to listen actively. This requires mediators to exercise good listening skills and display appropriate non-verbal language during the party statements.[14]

They may also have to ask questions, but these should mainly be open questions.[15] Some clarifying questions may be necessary where a party is unclear or ambiguous, but this is not the time for seeking detailed information, asking probing questions, or otherwise embarking on a series of leading questions which either detract from the party telling their own story or make them defensive. When a speaker stops talking, after only speaking very briefly, the mediator invites more information by asking in an open-ended way, 'Is there anything else?' or 'Would you like to go on?'

5.27   As suggested above, mediator intervention will also be required where a party statement is excessively long or descends into unnecessary detail for this stage of the process. Here the mediator should restate the purpose of the party statements as being to provide only an overview of the problem, and reassure the speaker that there will be a later opportunity to go into detail. Where there is repetition of a particular fact or theme, the mediator will need to acknowledge the point being made, and even write it down, to cure the 'broken record' symptom.

5.28   Another role for mediators during the party statements is that of note-taker. Most mediators take only brief notes, usually words or phrases to record key concerns and interests, common ground and areas of potential agreement, and prospective concessions. It is difficult to practise good listening skills and take comprehensive notes at the same time, though there can be a division of these labours between two co-mediators.

A common form of note-taking is as follows. The mediator divides a page with a vertical line and heads each column with the name of a different party. As the mediator records words or phrases under the appropriate column, he or she can connect concerns common to both parties with a line or numbered asterisk, to assist with the later development of the agenda.

5.29   For purposes of illustrating this mediator function, and others to follow, the following fact scenario will be assumed.

---

14   See 6.28–6.36.
15   See 6.45–6.46.

Case illustration

There is a professional business partnership involving two partners, Simon and Jonathan. Simon is the older partner in a firm established by his father many years ago. Jonathan is the younger partner who was taken into the business when Simon's son 'defected' to another profession. The two have been in dispute over a number of issues for the past seven months and finally agree to sort things out at mediation.

This is what the mediator's notes might look like at the end of the party statements:

Partner Simon
Retain the partnership and name
Retain existing profit-sharing arrangement
Golf is an important rain-making activity
Wants to settle dispute here privately
Jonathan has bad attitude
Jonathan's clients are late in paying bills

Partner Jonathan
Wants greater share of profits
More professional workplace needed
Needs client diversity
Does not want this to get out of hand
Simon should spend less time on golf
Simon should use support staff less for private activities
Is committed to retaining partnership

These notes allow the mediator to identify the parties' common interests in retaining the partnership and avoiding a court battle, and to recognise the fact that some other interests of Simon, for example, the payment of bills, are not incompatible with those of Jonathan.

Mediators should be consistent with note-taking in that speakers will be conscious of sudden changes, such as the mediator stopping writing, or recommencing writing. Some mediators use note-taking as a way of reducing anger or a stream of consciousness; by insisting that they need to make more detailed notes, the mediator gets the speaker to talk more slowly and less emotionally.

Request for a 'right of reply'

5.30 The first speaker, or their adviser, might ask for a right of reply after listening to the second speaker. In most circumstances, this should be denied for the same reasons that the second speaker was asked not to respond to the statement of the first. A mediation is not a debate or a court-room combat, and a reply is likely to involve justification, denial or excuse and lead to an adversarial confrontation too early in the piece. A summary of the party statements is a more appropriate development at this stage.

Mediator's summary of the party statements

5.31   Mediators typically thank each party for listening to the presentations, and for each party's openess and frankness. Some, but not all, mediators summarise the parties' statements, normally after both have made them. To summarise the first statement directly after it has been made would be to devote excessive attention to that party and to leave the other in the cold. The statement summaries serve several functions, to:

■ reassure the parties that they have been heard correctly as regards the content of what they have said;

■ provide some acknowledgment and validation of the emotional side of the parties' statements;

■ enable mediators to check the accuracy of their understanding of what has been said and provide feedback if they have got things wrong;

■ require each party to hear what the other has said for a second time;

■ allow a party to add to their statement when they realise from the summary that it is deficient.

5.32   There are three types of summaries:

■ *Actual summary*: some of the parties' actual words are used so that they hear from the mediator's mouth the same terms they have used themselves. Early words and phrases, in particular, are restated in their original form. For example, in the Simon and Jonathan dispute a summary of this kind would begin:

   'Jonathan, you began by saying that this matter was quite simple, and that Simon annoyed you over his old-fashioned ways and needed to change to a more professional style ...'

■ *Reframed summary*: the mediator reframes the parties' statements so as to shift to interests, remove the sting from any comments and focus on the future.[16] In this method, the mediator avoids the actual words of the parties and provides a sanitised summary. For example, in the Simon/Jonathan example:

   'Jonathan, you began by suggesting that this matter should resolve easily, and that you wished to discuss how the firm could adapt its practices for the future ...'

■ *Cross-summaries:* the mediator asks each side to summarise what they have heard from the other in order for them to walk in each other's shoes. In the example of Simon and Jonathan:

   'Simon, as I foreshadowed earlier, I would like you to summarise what you heard Jonathan say, and then I shall ask Jonathan to summarise your statement.'

5.33   *Actual* summaries give the parties the experience of being heard. In actual summary the mediator should use the second person and reported speech ('By way of summary, you told us that Simon was ...'). This distances the mediator from statements which are hostile to the other party. Therefore the mediator should not say 'By way of summary, Simon annoys you over his old-fashioned ways ...'. *Cross-summaries* involve several risks for limited potential gain.

---

16   See 6.38–6.44.

E.   Defining the problem

Purpose

5.34   The mediator next defines the problem, by identifying and prioritising the issues. Definition of the problem provides a structure to the mediation. It can set an agenda for the mediation, providing a sense of direction and purpose for all participants. It also reassures the parties that their concerns have been heard and noted from the outset.

Identifying areas of agreement (the common ground)

5.35   Where parties are in conflict, mutual antagonism and poor communication can cause them to think that they are in dispute on all matters. The mediator can perform an affirming role by pointing out areas in which agreement already exists. This serves to give the parties a positive perspective on the problem, to delineate matters on which no decisions need to be made, and to provide a platform for discussion, co-operation, further agreement and decision-making. These are sometimes called 'easy agreements' or 'cheap agreements' and they can generate a 'climate of consent'. They may include:

- substantive issues, for example, agreement on the amount of damages suffered;

- procedural issues, for example, that both parties will accept a particular valuer's figures; and

- objective standards for decision-making, for example, that any agreement should measure up to current industry practices.

In the partnership mediation being referred to in this chapter, the mediator might indicate the common ground between the parties in the following way:

> You may not realise it, Jonathan and Simon, but there are many things on which you are agreed. You both agree that this is a profitable partnership which needs to remain competitive in the future. You agree that you have different professional strengths which you contribute to the firm, and you agree that there are different categories of clients being serviced. And finally you are both agreed that you would like to sort things out today so that you can get on with the business. Is that correct? Now let's look at the things you still have to work on …

The mediator describes the common ground in terms of the information provided in the party statements, so that it does not appear contrived or imposed (or incorrect). The mediator's notes and summaries are instruments for achieving this goal. The mediator may present the areas of agreement visually on a board or flipchart and use them subsequently to emphasise progress and maintain a sense of momentum. The list can also be added to as new agreements are achieved.

5.36   Sometimes it may only be possible to identify agreements at a high level of generality; for example, that the interests of the children should prevail, or that any outcome should uphold the principle of ecological sustainability, or that both parties would like an outcome that is fair and minimises transaction costs. In these cases, the mediator must exercise a judgement about whether to leave out this stage on the grounds that, because of its high level of generality, it may appear trite, patronising or absurd. However, our experience is that it is an important stage in the process and should be attempted in at least some form.

Developing the list of issues/setting the agenda

5.37   Mediators can make a valuable contribution to the parties' negotiations by assisting them to list and prioritise the issues which require decisions. While setting the agenda is something which many parties would find difficult to achieve on their own, it is also a complicated exercise for most mediators, whether early trainees or grey eminences. For this reason some mediators lapse into ad hoc agenda-setting, allowing the parties to talk about issues randomly as they arise. At the other extreme is a very structured and elaborate approach, involving considerable leadership and finesse from the mediator, in consultation with the parties. Dispute-resolution theory points to the benefits of the latter approach, which is what is described here. However, it is a difficult ideal, which requires sound understanding and extensive practice to realise.

Purposes

5.38   This stage in the mediation process serves the following purposes:

- It provides structure and clarity to a problem which might have been presented and perceived in chaotic and confused terms.

- It defines the dispute in neutral terms and not according to the one-eyed perceptions of each party.

- It subdivides the dispute into smaller individual parts to make it less formidable and easier to negotiate on.

- It reassures each party that their concerns have been noted and will be dealt with during the course of the mediation.

- It serves as an agenda for the rest of the mediation and allows the mediator to check off matters that have been discussed and finalised.

- It symbolises the fact that the dispute is finite, as depicted by the list, and not over all matters under the sun.

- It provides a basis for the parties to prioritise the order in which issues will be dealt with.

- It provides an indication of the futher work, information and documents required.

Appropriate wording for the list of issues

5.39   In Chapter 4 reference was made to the importance of how the issues are worded. It was pointed out, with illustrations, that mediators should ensure some principles are followed in wording items on the list of issues. In short, mediators should:

■ Restate or reframe positional claims to reflect underlying interests and clarify and make explicit the parties' needs. For example, 'transportation is an issue' in a claim over the family car in a matrimonial case.

■ Change from one-sided views of the dispute towards views which reflect both sides of the problem. For example, 'each parent has a need for involvement in the children's lives' where both parents are claiming sole custody.

■ Move from a specific definition of the problem to one which is more generalised and tentative. For example, 'you need a fair division of the property that takes into account your past contributions' in a claim for 80% of the matrimonial property.

■ Include both sides' interests in the definition of the problem. For example, 'solutions that allow the children to live with one parent and allow the other to have a say on their education and upbringing is required'.

■ Use neutral and non-judgmental language. For example, 'you need to receive a monthly sum to cover the school fees, clothing and food'.

■ Cast positions and interests in open-ended problem solving questions which do not imply solutions. For example, 'how can the debts be repaid in a way that satisfies you both?'

■ 'De-legalise' the problem. For example, 'how can you deal with the different versions of events?'

■ 'De-monetise' the problem. For example, 'what actions are required to make good the losses?'

Different forms for the list of issues

5.40   Some mediators use single words or phrases to define the parties' issues. The main advantage of this system is that it is easy to learn and quick to perform.

Other mediators convert the issues into a series of problem-solving questions. The main advantage of this system is that questions beg answers and they provide the mediator subsequently with a useful source of leverage for soliciting the parties' responses. For example, the mediator might say 'Simon and Jonathan, we are looking for possible ways of answering the third question, "What is an appropriate client base for the firm?" What suggestions do either of you have?'

Questions are also dynamic ways of presenting the issues because they contain action words, namely verbs (newspaper sub-editors know about this when writing headlines). They give the issue some 'lift', a sense of purpose, something in which the parties can get involved. It is not easy to ignore a dynamically written question ('How Can We Improve Teachers' Working Conditions so that Schools and Students will Benefit?'), just as it is not easy to ignore an action-packed newspaper headline ('Mediator Solves Bitter Teachers' Dispute in One Dramatic Night').

The following table depicts the different approaches to issue identification in the same partnership dispute:

Single term	Phrase	Problem-solving question
Profits	Future profit shares	How should the partners share profits in the future?
Support staff	Appropriate use of support staff	What is an appropriate use of support staff?
Billing	Faster billing	How can the billing system be made more efficient?
Retirement	Timing of Simon's retirement	How should each partner's involvement with the firm be arranged over time?

How can the mediator avoid single issue lists?

5.41 In some cases the parties might attempt to restrict the list of issues to one matter only. For example, in an action for personal injuries arising out of a workplace accident, the parties might be agreed on the damages and be in dispute on the question of liability. The single issue of liability, and even the question 'is the employer/insurer liable?', are both problematic for mediation. The mediator should attempt to generate more issues to prevent the parties becoming stuck in positional bargaining on a single issue only. In the above case, the following issues might be developed:

■ What were the circumstances surrounding the accident?

■ What has been the effect of the accident on the employee?

■ What is the basis for past claims and offers?

■ In what proportion should the parties bear the losses suffered?

The object of this expansion is to open up the problem solving process and to prevent it becoming too narrowly focused too soon. While a narrow focus might be inevitable at a later stage, the mediator strives to keep the problem open-ended in the beginning to encourage broader thinking about the problem.

'One-party' issues?

5.42 In some situations one of the mediating parties wishes a matter to be included in the list of issues, but the other insists that it is not something requiring any decisions, or even discussion. There are risks both in including the issue on the board, and in excluding it. Our view is that the latter risk is the greater. To minimise the problems inherent in the former, the mediator could say, in the Simon and Jonathan dispute, something along the following lines:

Simon, the use of support staff time is something that Jonathan would like to talk about and although you feel that it is not a matter requiring any decisions, it seems necessary to refer to it in order to have all the issues between you resolved. Likewise, you may wish to talk about some matters which Jonathan does not think are necessary for today's decisions. Is that a reasonable arrangement for you both?

5.43   This choice of words is designed to have the topic dealt with in some degree, to marginalise slightly its importance, and to make the arrangement mutual and reciprocal so that it can potentially operate for both parties' benefit.

This problem can also be pre-empted, where time and resources allow, by advising both parties before the problem-defining begins that this difficulty sometimes arises and by indicating how it will be dealt with should it arise in the present case. This has the advantage of giving the mediator's 'rule' greater impartiality, as it has been given before either party stands to 'gain' or 'lose' from it.

Presenting the list of issues visually

5.44   The list of issues is often presented visually on a whiteboard or flipchart. This provides a point of common focus for the parties, a public checklist of matters to be dealt with, and a visible and a visual point of reference for the mediator.

There are a number of important techniques relating to this apparently simple function:

- Identify its purpose so that the parties do not assume that substantive agreements about the matters in dispute are being reached. Similarly, it should be explained that creating a 'wish list' is not its purpose.

- Agenda matters should not be written up before they have been agreed to verbally between the mediator and the parties.

- Particular attention should be given to not including any judgmental or inflammatory terms in public view on the board.

- Care should be taken in erasing items from the board, as they might have symbolic significance to one party.

- The mediator's handwriting needs to accommodate the visually challenged. Using appropriate colours can be helpful. Avoid numbering so that no issue is given priority over others by the mediator.

- Stand to the side of the chart, and sit down between making additions to it, to avoid being in teacher or lecturing mode.

- The board should be cleaned, or the paper disposed of, at the termination of the mediation so that it is not accessible to cleaners or whoever will be using the room subsequently.

- Practical experience has taught us to be conscious of the fact that a proportion of adults are not literate.

Prioritising the issues

5.45   Thus far the mediator has written up various issues on a board in no particular order and the question now arises as to how they should be prioritised for purposes of the discussions. There are two approaches.

The first is that the mediator invites the parties to examine and together prioritise the issues. This approach acknowledges that the parties are in control of the dispute and that their subjective priorities are more important than the objective priorities of the mediator. Thus the parties might want to talk first about urgent debts and insistent creditors, before working through assets and valuations. The parties' priorities can be shown visually on the board against the list of issues. In practice there is usually little problem in the parties reaching agreement on priorities. However, where there are difficulties, the mediator is required to intervene, and is advised to try and move through this stage quickly. He/she might suggest alternating priorities, two 'first' priorities with each dealt with for a limited time, or some random choice (flip a coin) on priorities.

5.46   The second approach involves the mediator taking the initiative in prioritising the issues. This avoids any problems of the parties not agreeing on priorities. It also allows the mediator to use his or expertise to guide the parties. For example, the mediator might explain that good negotiating practice involves dealing with 'easier' matters first, before moving to those which are most difficult, so that the parties develop some early success and confidence and avoid becoming deadlocked too soon. In this approach it would be problematic to allow the parties to self-select the most difficult issue with which to start their negotiations.

Each approach has its strengths and its shortcomings. There is also scope for reconciling the approaches in practice by balancing user choice with expert guidance. Circumstances will provide the mediator with the clues for exercising this task and it should be accomplished as efficiently, and with as little argument and pedantry, as possible. As with other aspects of agenda setting, this involves some delicate leadership by the mediator. As the expert in dispute resolution, the mediator is alert to the best practice in this exercise. However, the mediator should not appear to be imposing his or her list of issues and priorities on the parties.

In addition, the mediator may need to decide if issues are best addressed separately or together, sometimes called 'packaging issues'. Packaging can provide opportunities for trade-offs or integrative solutions.

Standard issue lists

5.47   Experienced mediators can anticipate the predictable issues in their fields of expertise, even where they have no prior knowledge of the particular dispute. Doing so is useful where the parties are hesitant about presenting the issues themselves. Normally, through appropriate questioning, the mediator is able to draw out of the parties those issues which he or she knows, if only at a level of generality, are normal for the particular category of dispute. Where there is pressure of time the mediator may even commence the mediation with the standard issues on the board, ask the parties whether they are relevant to their case, and invite them to add additional issues. The following is a standard list of issues in a dispute involving the dissolution of a professional partnership.

Standard issues: partnership dissolution

1. What are the assets and liabilities of the partnership?

2. How should the assets be divided among the partners?

3. What needs to be done in relation to the liabilities?

4. How should the clients of the partnership be dealt with?

5. What legal formalities are required for the dissolution?

6. What else is required to finalise the matter?

7. How should post-dissolution problems be dealt with?

In family cases, for example, standard issues include the possibility of reconciliation; disclosure in relation to property and finances; the welfare of the children (residence, maintenance, education and health issues); division of assets; sale of assets and division of proceeds; oustanding debts; future issues; and the associated formalities.

Using the list of issues

5.48 As has already been suggested, mediators can use the list of issues in various ways. They can direct the parties' attention to them when there is acrimony in the room, they can tick off completed issues to give a visual sense of progress, they can write up optional solutions next to each issue, and they can use the issues as a checklist to verify that the drafted agreement is comprehensive. They can add to the list if additional issues arise during the course of the mediation and can use the list in any other way that causes the mediation to progress.

Dangers with developing the list of issues

5.49 There are dangers in developing a list of issues:

- Where time is spent on the list and it is not used again, it may appear to have been a futile exercise.

- Where the mediator gets the list, or any specific wording, wrong it presents a very visible source of grievance to the affected party.

- The mediator may be tempted to stand at the whiteboard or flipchart for too long, assuming an authoritarian position.

- The mediator's writing may be illegible.

- The list could entrench a party or make the differences between the parties more stark.

F. Generating options, negotiation and problem-solving

5.50 Once a prioritised list of issues is available, the mediation moves to the stages of discussing the various issues, delving into the parties' interests, considering options for resolution, and negotiating specific outcomes. Generically we might refer to this as the 'problem-solving' stage of the mediation. Some of this is just semantics, but there are some important variations in practice. Thus problem-solving, involving option generation and creative negotiation, might be used in commercial or neighbourhood disputes but be less evident in personal injury disputes which might only involve a haggle over money. As much of this stage has to do with different aspects of negotiation and bargaining, this section should be read in conjunction with Chapter 7.

There are two broad modes of mediator involvement during this phase of the mediation. A facilitative mediator style is somewhat like 'directing the traffic', whereas an evaluative style is more like 'driving the bus'. Put differently, the first style can be called 'orchestrator' mode, and the latter the 'deal-maker' mode. The characteristics of each style are summarised in the table:

Mode	Characteristics	Advantages	Shortcomings
'Directing the traffic' (sometimes called 'orchestrator' mode)	Maintain order, provide structure, encourage discussion, summarise and reframe, keep notes of agreements reached.	Mediator stays out of the fray, parties assume responsibility for solutions, mediator can observe bigger picture.	Lack of direction, parties might be unable to progress on their own, mediation might be over-lengthy and unproductive.
'Driving the bus' (sometimes called 'deal-maker' mode)[17]	Control communications, extensive questioning, suggestion of options, encouragement and pressure to settle.	Mediator's experience is used to guide parties, parties feel more secure coming to settlements, outcome more likely to be achieved.	Confusing for parties, mediator acts as quasi-arbitrator, parties might become resistant or later blame mediator for outcome.

Exchange of information and views – storytelling

5.51   While mediation is primarily concerned with the present and future, if the parties exchange their understandings and perceptions of past events it may be useful in clearing the air, correcting misunderstandings and opening the way for dealing with current and future issues. This involves encouraging storytelling, as referred to above.[18] Each party can explain their motivations for past conduct and the significance to them of important events. Where emotions are high there may be considerable venting of feelings as parties communicate with one another about the past. It can help to identify important interests.

---

17   Encountered in commercial mediation.
18   See 5.13.

For example, mediators might say to parties in workplace disputes:

> Tell me a little about how the workplace was for each of you before the problems began to arise …

Likewise they may say in a family dispute:

> Tell me first of all about the children, can you each give me a thumbnail sketch of each child …

5.52   However, mediators are advised to limit the time spent on discussing past events so that things do not become too protracted and complex. Such exchanges will often not lead to agreement about the past. Mediation is not good at discovering the 'historical truth', nor is that its purpose. Accordingly, where there are several grievances over historical events, the mediator might advise the parties to select a few to deal with (one of each party say), before closing the book on the past.

It can be useful to manage the parties' expectations about the purpose of storytelling, by allowing them to be heard, provide the mediator with information to start defining the problem and to gather information that may be useful in developing options and solutions.

In this regard, it is useful for the mediator to provide the parties with some basic guidelines:

- Emphasise that each party should 'tell your version' of the past, or 'explain your understanding' or 'how things seemed to you', as opposed to asking them 'to tell the others what happened' or 'to state what are the facts'.

- Discourage statements that assign blame and ecourage a description of events. For example, ask a party 'to discuss your version of events and the effect this had on you', without referring to the motivations, invariably negative if not conspiratorial, of the other party. Another way of directing the parties is to ask them 'to discuss your experiences without saying why the other party acted like they did'.

- Discourage generalisations, like 'they never' or 'they always', by reframing to focus on the consequences of the behaviour. For example, 'tell us why that upset you'.

- Control interruptions and avoid a party monopolising air time. Imbalance may create the perception that the mediator is biased in favour of the person monopolising the air time.

> **Case illustration**
>
> An employment dispute was set down for trial in which the statements of case identified a major dispute of fact (and law): had there, or had there not, been an oral variation of the service agreement? The case involved a substantial damages claim and was set down for three days of trial; each party had a number of witnesses to support their case. At mediation there was about 30 minutes discussion over the question of what the employer, the manager of a finance company, and the employee, an accountant, had said to each other three years earlier. While there was some clarification of the factual issues, there was no agreement on the essential dispute of fact. This factor was acknowledged, and the parties moved on to find a commercial accommodation involving the finance company re-deploying the accountant in one of its subsidiaries. This was achieved without ever reconciling the different versions of the facts.

Uncovering interests and developing and exploring options

5.53   Positions are the parties' demands or claims, whereas interests are the concerns, needs or fears that underlie those demands. The parties' interests are not always easy to uncover as people in conflict tend to be positional and make no distinction between demands and interests. In other cases, parties obscure their interests, believing that disclosure would make them appear weak. The mediator can uncover interests by asking questions focused on each party's concerns, needs or fears. The mediator may need to explain to the parties the benefits of discussing their interests to encourage them to be open. Often, separate meetings are required to uncover interests. These meetings are discussed further below.

Having an understanding of interests assists parties to develop options for settling the dispute. The mediator can assist the parties through the device of *brainstorming*. Here all parties are invited to identify possible options for dealing with the dispute, regardless of how practical, reasonable or viable they may or may not be. The objective is to get the parties to think imaginatively about solutions and to feed off each other's ideas, without the twin fears of being judged as stupid or being committed to their suggestions. All options are noted, usually by the mediator.[19]

Other ways of encouraging the parties to come up with options are by the mediator asking hypothetical questions ('What could you think of in relation to ...?'), or analogous reasoning ('Can you think of ways in which other people have dealt with this kind of problem ...?'). A further way is encouraging creativity, as to which see the frequently cited example in the box below. Other techniques for encouraging creativity include:

- use of analogy and metaphor;
- use of concepts and ideas from other disciplines;
- role reversal;
- challenging assumptions;
- visualisation;
- reframing problems from a different perspective.

---

19   For a further discussion about brainstorming, see 7.38–7.39.

Thinking creatively

A man left 17 camels to his 3 sons. He left half to his eldest son; a third to his middle son; and a ninth to his youngest son. The brothers couldn't negotiate a solution as 17 could not be divided by 2, 3 or 9. The sons consulted a wise village elder, who asked 'what would happen if you took my camel'. The brothers had 18 camels. The eldest took 9 (a half); the middle brother took 6 (a third); and the youngest brother took 2 (a ninth). 9, 6 and 2 camels makes a total of 17 camels. The wise elder got back her camel.[20]

Evaluation and selection of options

5.54   The mediator should encourage the parties to evaluate options in terms of those interests and objective standards of fairness and reasonableness. The mediator should also invite the parties to consider the practical consequences of various options. Where no options satisfy both parties, the mediator may attempt to gain agreement at a level of principle. This type of mediator intervention is discussed further in Chapter 7.[21]

Case illustration

A mediation involved a local authority and a property owner who had been affected by a major extension to the council's sewerage works which affected the property's future residential use. The council had offered to purchase the property, but no agreement could be reached on the purchase price. After other issues had been discussed, a brainstorm was held over options for the land. No fewer than ten options were listed, including a joint commercial development between the council and owner, and the development of an environmental park named after the owner. The brainstorm ended with an evaluation of the options, resulting in mutual choice of the original option of a council purchase with the price to be decided by an agreed valuer. While the exercise ended with the option they had first thought of, the process adopted gave it greater legitimacy and prompted them to fine-tune ways of achieving it.

Positional bargaining

5.55   There will often be hard positional bargaining towards the end of a mediation. Here the parties have to use concessions, packaging, compromises and splitting the difference to reach agreement. The mediator's role in the positional bargaining process is considered in Chapter 7.[22]

---

20 William Ury, *Getting Past No: Negotiating Your Way from Confrontation to Co-operation,* Bantam Books.
21 See 7.38–7.39.
22 See 7.16–7.31.

G. Separate meetings

5.56 In some contexts, as in family disputes, arguments abound that mediation should be conducted in joint session only to encourage direct negotiation between the parties.[23]

Even in the family context, there is a recognition that changes in format can serve useful purposes,[24] although the mediator must discuss arrangements about confidentiality with the parties before holding separate meetings.[25]

In other cases, there are many ways in which mediators can change the format of the mediation from the joint session. Here the term 'separate meetings' is used to refer to the meetings between the mediator, on one hand, and each party and their advisers, on the other. Other terms used for this part of the process are 'private meetings', 'separate sessions' and 'caucuses'. There are many variations regarding these meetings and the table below suggests distinguishing terms for different kinds of meetings:

Name	Those involved	Objective
Separate meetings	Mediator and each party with their own advisers	See discussion in text
Side meetings	Mediator and each party individually without advisers	To give parties an opportunity to talk directly without adviser influence or pressure
Party meetings	Mediator and all parties without advisers	To avoid negative role of advisers, to get parties talking unadvised, to get parties focused on personal or commercial (rather than purely legal) goals

---

23 A model developed by Dr John Haynes, an American mediator, who trained many mediators in the UK throughout the 1990s.

24 The Coogler Model, taken from the US in the late 1970s, for example, gives the mediator a more modest profile, focusing on party autonomy, with advance agreement on guidelines and structure to ensure an orderly process and fairness. Although joint sessions and direct negotiation is the common practice, separate time for each party is included. For further information, refer to M. Roberts, *Mediation in Family Disputes: Principles of Practice*, Ashgate, 2008. In addition, a hybrid mediation model is developing for family mediation cases, utilising mediators who are trained as both family and civil/commercial mediators, with the aim of resolving more efficiently 'all issues'. ADR Group explain the model in this way (refer to their website: www.adrgroup.co.uk):

This approach is particularly appropriate where parties:

- would like lawyers or other professionals present to advise during the mediation itself;

- want to mediate over a half or full-day rather than several 90 minute sessions spread over several months, as is normal practice in mainstream family mediation, civil mediation or divorce mediation;

- their lawyers have been working collaboratively and resolution may be reached more cost effectively and quickly via this service.

25 The parties may agree that the mediator will either report back the substance of the separate meetings or maintain separate confidences, provided that information material to financial/property matters must be provided on an open basis. Refer to Law Society Code of Practice for Family Mediation (sections 7.3 and 7.5) and College of Mediators Code of Practice (sections 4.6.2 and 6.5) in Appendix 8.

Adviser meetings	Mediators with all advisers without parties	To explore realistic settlement options where both clients are 'problematic', to explore merits, to discuss alternatives if the matter does not settle at mediation

The terms used above are by no means standard, but are adopted here so as to distinguish among the different kinds of meetings which could be convened at this stage in the proceedings. In what follows, the emphasis is on *separate meetings*, as defined above, though many of the principles are equally applicable to other kinds of meetings.

Purpose of separate meetings

5.57   There should always be a reason for calling separate meetings, and these reasons will vary according to the stage that the mediation has reached. Strictly speaking, they should be called to serve the requirements of the parties and the negotiations, and not in terms of the mediator's comfort needs or his or her uncertainty about what to do next. Adjournments can be used to deal with the mediator's problems, ranging from confusion to thirst.

Some of the purposes for calling separate meetings are:

- to build trust and rapport with the parties;
- to ask a party for impressions of the process and progress made;
- to provide relief from destructive emotions and high tension and allow the relevant party to vent their feelings;
- to acknowledge the strength of feelings;
- to provide space and time for a weaker or disempowered party to recover;
- to establish whether there are any concerns which have not yet been raised but which might need to be addressed for the resolution of the dispute;
- to clarify the issues, and to 'drill further down' on each issue;
- to identify what is at stake for each party generally and if the matter does not settle at mediation;
- to attempt to understand the motivations of the parties and their priorities;
- where the mediator believes that there is additional information which he or she will not obtain in joint session;
- to check assumptions (made by the parties or the mediator);
- to deal with breaches of the mediation guidelines and threatened disruption of the process and to get the parties recommitted to the process;
- to attempt to break a deadlock by changing the dynamics of the negotiation process;
- to help manage the parties' expectations about the process and what can be achieved in mediation;

- to ascertain whether an apparently inflexible and intransigent party is open to further negotiation;

- to test 'deal breakers' and 'bottom lines';

- to engage in 'reality testing' with a positional or intransigent party or to encourage settlement in other ways;[26]

- to probe the legal strengths and weaknesses and cost implications of various alternatives;

- to coach the parties in constructive communication and productive negotiation strategies;

- where the parties are unable to come up with settlement options in each other's presence, to provide a risk-free environment for considering such options;

- to encourage 'brainstorming' and creativity;[27]

- to work up offers or concessions and consider the timing of their relay;

- to check out privately the acceptability of an imminent agreement;

- to allow for last-minute consultation with the parties before the mediator terminates the mediation without agreement being reached;

- to apply more pressure to the parties in a confidential setting;

- to test the parties' perceptions of each other, for example, to ask party A how they view party B's interests and position;

- to check confidentiality and identify what information can be relayed;

- to task a party in relation to further work, information, decisions or advice that might be helpful to progress the negotiations;

- to summarise progress made.

Timing of separate meetings

5.58   Here there are no hard and fast rules and practice varies. Where one of the above purposes can be pursued, it is an appropriate time to call separate meetings. Where the parties or their advisers request them, it is appropriate to respond to the request, provided that it does not appear to be allowing the requesting party to control or manipulate the process. It should be pointed out that in some mediations separate meetings are called as a matter of routine, regardless of whether there is an overt need for them.[28] In others they are called as a matter of discretion.

In some styles of mediation, mediators call separate meetings directly after the party statements to establish whether there are any concerns which have not yet been raised or to gather information which has not been disclosed. Other mediators commence the mediation with separate meetings, a practice referred to above.[29]

---

26   See 8.14–8.15.
27   For further information refer to C. Menkel-Meadow, 'AHA? Is Creativity Possible in Legal Problem Solving and Teachable in Legal Education' in 6 *Harv. Negot. L. Rev.* 97 and J. G. Brown, 'Creativity and Problem-Solving' in (2004) 87 *Marq L Rev* 697.
28   This is particularly the case in commercial mediations.
29   See 2.22 and 2.25.

Some mediations are conducted exclusively through separate meetings, but this involves a different concept, referred in this book as 'shuttle mediation'.[30]

5.59 All the variations have their strengths and shortcomings. Our own preference is to follow the 'orthodox' approach and convene separate meetings after at least some of the issues have been discussed in joint session, at least provisionally. Our concerns with calling separate meetings immediately after the party statements are that it artificially prevents the conflict from occurring, it allows the parties to relapse into positional thinking, it introduces the confidentiality of the separate meetings too early in the process, it gives the mediator immense power, and it involves a default shuttle mediation system without that option being expressly considered and chosen. However, in reality many lawyer mediators, unpersuaded by this logic, call separate meetings immediately after the party statements, especially in commercial mediations.

Separate meetings and shuttle mediation

5.60 Sometimes a mediator may conduct a series of separate meetings and begin shuttling messages back and forth between the parties. This is particularly the case in the commercial context where separate meetings are commenced when parties reach the stage of making offers and counter-offers to each other. While it might be necessary for parties to be able to confer alone, and to consult with their advisers, before making or responding to offers, it is not necessary that this be done through separate meetings. It is feasible to adjourn the mediation for such deliberations to take place, and to resume the joint session thereafter.

The concern is that the process should not move by default into shuttle mode, and should involve a conscious strategic decision of the mediator, after some consultation with the parties. It may be entirely appropriate to adopt shuttle mediation, but that should involve a deliberate and transparent decision. This is because the mediator's role in shuttle is different to that in non-shuttle mediation. He or she becomes the sole messenger for offers and counter-offers and the sole conveyer of other information on the attitudes and behaviour of the parties. There are necessary limits on the confidentiality principle in this context and the mediator acquires immense power.[31]

Separate meetings and physical space

5.61 Mediators should ensure that the room in which a separate meeting is being conducted is soundproofed from those outside. Where the accommodation allows it, the parties can each be offered their own separate rooms and the mediator will move between them.[32] This gives the mediator their own space in the room where the joint meeting was held. It also provides the best image of equality as between the parties.

---

30 See 9.6–9.16.
31 For a further discussion of shuttle mediation, see 9.6–9.16.
32 Requirement C4.2 MQMS stipulates (for LSC contracted providers and those complying with the MQMS) a minimum of two suitable rooms to ensure that parties can be seen separately or be separated if necessary. Refer to Appendix 8. Refer also, for example, to section 7 CEDR Model Mediation Procedure (in Appendix 3).

Change of dynamics in separate meetings

5.62   As compared with the joint sessions, there are two potential, yet contradictory, changes in the separate meetings. These may be extremely subtle changes, or very pronounced, depending on the style of the mediator and the requirements of the mediation:

■ In a more relaxed setting, the mediator can identify with the relevant person and empathise with their situation. This is sometimes referred to as 'alliance formation', in that the mediator builds an alliance with the person so that he or she is perceived as their ally in relation to the problem they are facing. It might also be considered the 'guardian angel' function.

■ In a confidential setting, the mediator can be a harsher critic of the relevant person and be more forceful in pointing out the downside of their position. This is sometimes referred to as 'reality testing' in that the mediator uses a wide range of tactics to disenchant the person with their positional claims. It might also be considered as the 'devil's advocate' function.

5.63   While many mediators regard at least one separate meeting with each party as a fundamental stage of the mediation process, they may have a limited bearing on the outcome in some cases, as illustrated in the following case study, although in every case they should help to build trust and rapport between the parties and mediator.

Case illustration

In a mediation involving a division of matrimonial property, one party was being particularly intransigent and requested a separate meeting. In the meeting he informed the mediator that the reason for his attitude was that he had recently been diagnosed with glaucoma, that he worked in the surveillance industry, and that he would lose his work within the next 12 months. He did not want this disclosed to the other side (and had not even told his professional adviser until then). The mediator empathised with the predicament and the desire not to disclose it. The mediator could not use the information in any other way, but the interest of the party in explaining and justifying his behaviour to the mediator was satisfied and the matter moved to quick resolution in the next joint session.

When to end separate meetings

5.64   Separate meetings may be ended:

■ When they have served the purpose for which they were called.

■ When the party involved has nothing further to say and the mediator nothing more to contribute.

■ Where new information, threats or final offers emerge – resuming the joint session might return responsibility to the parties in those circumstances.

■ When the mediator decides to terminate the mediation without agreement.

The separate meeting transitions

5.65 There are four significant transitions in relation to the separate meetings. As the transitions may invoke some anxiety and suspicion on the part of clients, the mediator should give an explanation to justify the change and to reassure the parties. Here is a model mediator explanation for each transition, based on the scenario of Simon and Jonathan referred to earlier in this chapter.

Transition 1: Breaking into separate meetings

As indicated earlier, it is normal practice for the mediator to meet with each of the parties separately, and to give the other some time out, and I should now like to do that with you. I shall probably meet with you each for about 20 minutes, and if I am going to be significantly longer than that with either of you I shall let the other person know. These are confidential meetings and I shall not disclose what either of you has said unless you ask me to do so. Jonathan, as I heard from you first when the mediation began I shall speak to Simon first now. Would you like to go into the other room, have a coffee and think about options for the billing system. I shall come to see you when I have finished with Simon.

Transition 2: Commencing a separate meeting

Simon, thanks for meeting with me separately. Can I reassure you again that what is said here will be kept confidential unless you ask me to convey some offer or message to Jonathan ... Let's start by hearing how the mediation has been going for you so far ...? Thanks, Simon, now is there anything new you would like to raise with me which hasn't come up in the joint session ...?

Transition 3: Ending a separate meeting

As I understand it, Simon, you would like to make an offer to Jonathan when we resume in joint session along the lines that if he is willing to set up a more effective billing system for his clients then you are prepared to spend only two afternoons a week on the golf course. You also said that while you were on your own you would consider ways of increasing Jonathan's share of the profits on a phased basis. Is that correct?

Transition 4: Resuming the joint session

Thank you, Simon and Jonathan, for meeting with me separately. That can sometimes be an important stage in a mediation, and it gave you time to consider settlement options and do some other homework. Now as a result of those meetings, is there anything which either of you would like to say to the other ...?

Potential dangers with separate meetings and ways of handling them

5.66 There are risks relating to separate meetings; and ways of limiting and dealing with the risks. The following table deals with the separate meeting risks only:

Potential risk	Ways of dealing
Breach of confidential disclosure in separate meeting	Make written notes of confidences, limit length of meetings
Development of suspicion and distrust ('What is going on without me ...?')	Educate parties, normalise this stage, keep to times, meet with both sides, give withdrawing party task to perform
Mediator mis-communicates an offer or information or money figure	Write down details and check with party before conveying them
Party becomes anxious over length of other side's separate meeting	Advise of likely duration, and tell waiting party if longer than expected
Party thinks mediator is on their side	Avoid sympathy, too much bonding and encouragement of their position
Creates too much power for mediator	Have your assistant (if you are mediating with an assistant) 'keep you honest' and require mediator debriefing
No progress on resumption of joint sessions	Prepare parties at end of separate meetings for subsequent negotiations
Detachment of parties from each other and lack of 'constructive confrontation'	Do not hold too early, resume joint sessions after served purpose

Due to these risks, and in particular the potential loss of trust by one or both parties, some mediators conduct few separate meetings. In our experience, this precaution is unwarranted. However, the concern underlying this practice should be understood and dealt with through the expediencies of advance notice, explanation, confidentiality and equality referred to in the above pages.

Learning lessons

5.67 In a mediation simulation conducted by law school students one of the participants learnt a dramatic lesson. On returning to the mediation room for a separate session, the participant saw the mediator's notes on the table, including a description of the other side's forthcoming offer. The student was struck by how easy it is to break the confidences of separate sessions through inadvertence. It is a useful lesson about being careful about the confidentiality of the mediator's notes.

H.   Final decision-making

5.68 It is customary, and usually desirable, for the parties to be brought together again (if there has been a separate meeting or several separate meetings) for further discharge, consideration of options and final bargaining. Here the mediator should discharge the parties from re-opening matters already resolved or from going over old history again. The mediator should ensure that all issues in dispute have been dealt with,[33] that no agreements have been overlooked, that the parties can live with the final settlement, and that unforeseen contingencies have been considered. The mediator's role in dealing with the dynamics of this stage of negotiation are discussed in more detail in Chapter 7.

I. Recording the decisions

5.69   In most mediations the agreement, if one is reached, is reduced to writing. It is a term of most mediation agreements in general civil and commercial cases that the agreement will only be binding once it has been reduced to writing.[34] This is an important precaution against any disputes over whether agreement has been reached or not.

In some situations, heads of agreement or memoranda of understanding are drafted, to be subsequently refined into formal arrangements, whether as a deed of agreement, terms of settlement or consent orders which will be ratified by a court. In the family context, it is usual to set out what has been agreed and the reasons if appropriate, accompanied by the documents required for full disclosure of assets and income if relevant, so that the terms can then be reviewed by independent legal advisers. The terms are variously called, 'parenting plan', 'outcome statement' or 'memorandum of understanding', and are 'without prejudice' until formulated into legally binding contracts or court consent orders.[35] No financial or other mediated outcome is binding on the parties until approved by the court as a consent order or made legally binding in some other way.

In other cases, where there has not been full agreement on all issues, the lawyers may agree to exchange correspondence on some limited matters or to make interim arrangements or obtain interim orders.

In other cases, the parties may prefer an oral agreement, especially where the type of agreement is too vague to have legal enforceability. For example, in a dispute between supervisor and employee, they might 'agree to respect each other's work styles' or 'agree that the administrative assistant should give Jonathan's work priority in the mornings and Simon's work priority in the afternoons'. Even in those cases, it is usual to have a simple form of agreement which is signed.

Chapter 10 reviews settlement formalities across practice areas.[36] Sample mediated settlement agreements and a Tomlin Order are in Appendix 4. For family law

---

33 Whilst retaining impartiality and neutrality, there are cases, where mediators have to ensure that agreements include certain matters and cover certain content. For example, family mediators are required to have regard by virtue of the Family Law Act 1996 to the principles in section 1 of the Act. In particular, they are required to have special concern for the welfare of children of the family; and must keep the possibility of reconciliation under review throughout the mediation.

34 See, for example, section 9 CEDR Model Mediation Procedure, section 8 ADR Group Model Mediation Procedure and Rules, clause 8 in the sample Agreement to Mediate (for a general civil case) and clause 9 CEDR Model Mediation Agreement. Refer to Appendix 3 for these various documents.

35 Council of Europe Recommendation on Family Mediation No R(98)1 refers to agreements reached at family mediation not normally being legally binding and that Member States should facilitate the approval of mediated agreements via judicial authorities. The Recommendation is included in Appendix 13. Refer also to 10.74–10.77. In addition, see sections 6.10 and 6.17 College of Mediators Code of Practice and section 5.13 Law Society Code of Practice for Family Mediation (both are in Appendix 8).

36 See 10.74–10.77.

precedents, refer to Resolution's *Precedents for Consent Orders* which are universally used and accepted and have been approved by judges.[37]

Who does the drafting?

5.70   Where lawyers or other advisers are involved they usually draft the agreement and the mediator has only a limited role of checking for completeness, accuracy and lack of ambiguity.

Where the mediator assists with drafting of the agreement the following principles should apply:

- There should be close consultation with the parties over its precise wording.

- All drafting should be done in plain English and where possible the parties' own words and terms should be used.

- Aim to put positive commitments and mutual obligations first.

- Use non-judgemental language.

- There should be a sense of balance in the agreement in that the parties' names are used alternatively and their rights and obligations are balanced against each other.

- Ensure that there are clear and verifiable methods of performance. Be specific about payment terms and timeframes.

- Each page, and any alterations, should be initialled and the final page should be signed by the parties; some mediators sign as witness to the parties' signatures.

- A list of unresolved issues can be drafted to assist the parties in future dispute-resolution efforts.

Content of the agreement

5.71   Inevitably the content of the written document will reflect the parties' agreement. However, there are many different styles in which this can be recorded, from a flourishing aspirational style which deals with matters of principle in broad generality, to a focused legalistic style which records minute detail with a view to legal enforceability. The context and circumstances of the mediation will determine which of these styles, and the many variations in between, should be used.[38]

Most agreements are likely to contain the following elements:

- names of the parties;

- date of the agreement;

- a description of the dispute or conflict which is the subject of the agreement;

- responsibilities of each party;

- if payment is part of the settlement, terms about amount, timing and form of payment are required;

---

37   Refer to Appendix 11 for Resolution contact details (formerly, the SFLA).
38   Refer also to 10.74–10.77 for variations across practice areas.

- what is to happen to any litigation that is on foot;

- signature by the parties (or any other formality required by the nature of the agreement).

5.72   In some cases, the mediator might suggest consideration of the following matters for inclusion:

- *Cooling-off period*: 'This agreement will become effective after a period of [x hours or y days] unless one party notifies the other in writing …'

- *Return to mediation*: 'In the event of the parties encountering any difficulties in the application of this agreement they will use their best endeavours to settle the problems with the assistance of the mediator.'

- *Supervision of any performance*: 'The mediator will supervise the performance of any obligations or duties required in terms of this agreement.'

- *Goodwill statement for the future*: 'The parties agree that they will treat each other with courtesy and respect in the future and avoid any actions which might cause the conflict to recur.'

J. Closing statement and termination

5.73   Mediators should take some care in terminating the mediation, even if agreement has been reached on all matters requiring decisions. A short closing statement can perform some of the following functions:

- Conclude the proceedings on a positive note.

- Commend the parties for what they have achieved.

- Encourage compliance with the agreement.

- Normalise the 'post-settlement blues' (that is, the prospect of the parties having subsequent misgivings over concessions they have made).

- Thank the lawyers or other advisers for their contributions.

- Reassure the parties as to the confidentiality of the mediation.

- Invite the parties's lawyers to contact the mediator if there are any issues regarding implementation of the agreement.

- Invite the parties to return to mediation should that be necessary.

The closing statement should be tailored to the circumstances. For example, 'Through your commitment and hard work you were able to reach agreement. I commend you for your efforts. You have worked through the problem thoroughly, with the able assistance of your lawyers. I reassure you of confidentiality and will destroy the notes that I have taken during the mediation….'.[39]

---

[39] This chapter deals with termination where there is resolution. For termination in cases where there is no agreement, refer to 10.78–10.80. Although there are various factors when mediation may be terminated in the absence of resolution, most mediation agreements and codes of conduct provide at least that the mediator can terminate a mediation where the process is unlikely to result in resolution. See, for example, section 7.2 CEDR Code of Conduct and section 5 CORE Solutions Group Code of Conduct (both are in Appendix 8).

K. Post-mediation activities

5.74 The mediator's responsibilities might not end with the termination of the mediation meeting. Some of the post-mediation functions which mediators might perform are described below.

Ratification and review

5.75 There are different forms of post-mediation review and ratification by bodies or individuals external to the mediation meeting, such as boards, local authorities or government and even courts.[40] While this is primarily the responsibility of the parties, the mediator might discuss with them ways of securing the necessary ratification.

The same consideration applies to the review of a mediated settlement agreement by lawyers, accountants or other professional advisers. For a settlement of an employment matter to be legally valid, the employee or worker must (among other things) have received independent advice from an adviser falling within one of the permitted categories of advisers.

In some cases, it might be advisable for the mediator, with the client's permission, to contact the adviser in order to provide a balanced version of what had occurred in the mediation.[41] Mediators can also write to advisers explaining the dynamics of the process so that the agreement is not reviewed with too much clinical detachment.

Case illustration

In a mediation between a local authority, represented by the an in-house lawyer, and a property developer, it was decided that the mediator should address a closed meeting of the authority in order to promote the ratification of a controversial proposed agreement. The developer agreed to waive the confidentiality of the mediation for this purpose only. At the meeting, the authority's external lawyer first explained the nature of the proposed agreement and its benefits, after which the mediator addressed the full meeting of council and answered questions. This served to bring some of the context and dynamics of the mediation to the attention of the ratifiers. The local authority subsequently ratified the agreement.

Reporting obligations

5.76 Where there are legislative or other requirements for mediators to report to persons or bodies outside the mediation, this reporting function should be disclosed

---

40 For example, finance/property aspects in an agreement reached in family mediation are open to review by the court (*Jessel v Jessel* [1979] 1 WLR 1158), although the court is reluctant to interfere where the parties have received independent legal advice.
41 Family mediators cannot discuss or correspond with a party's lawyer without the express consent of each party. Where both parties have lawyers, nothing can be said or written to one adviser that is not also said or written to the other, unless at the specific request of both parties. Refer to section 4.5.2 College of Mediators Code of Practice (in Appendix 8).

to the parties in advance and might be subject to agreed confidentiality constraints in the mediation agreement and mediator standards and codes of conduct.[42] Some relevant reporting requirements are as follows:

- *Court-referred or encouraged mediations*: the court may require advice in general terms of the outcome (for example, that the parties attended the mediation; that the parties prepared for the mediation; or that the matter was settled at the mediation). Where there has been a Commercial Court 'ADR Order', the parties report to the court what steps they have taken towards ADR and why such steps have failed. That enquiry does not extend to whether a party acted reasonably in mediation.

- *Community mediators*: mediators usually report on the mediation in the form of a debriefing document which they complete after terminating the mediation. This is submitted to the director of the programme.

- *Family mediators*: mediators may disclose information gained in their role as mediator if they feel it is necessary to protect a child, to prevent or lessen a significant harm, and to report the commission or prevent the likely commission of a crime involving a risk of significant harm.[43]

- *Workplace mediators*: in case of a breach of organisational policy which amounts to gross misconduct, the relevant authorities are usually notified.[44]

- *Legal services funding*: the service may require some reporting back, including comment on the reasonableness of the legally funded client, a factor which can be taken into account when a decision is taken on whether to extend funding.[45]

- *Other*: occasionally a report is made to an external body or person paying for the mediation, such as a government, an employer or an association. In most workplace mediation cases, although HR and line managers will know that a mediation has taken place, the content or outcome is not normally disclosed unless the agreement reached in mediation requires support of management and the parties' consent to disclosure has been obtained.[46]

- *In all cases*: where a mediator becomes aware of any criminal activity, involving risk of significant harm, the mediator can report to the relevant authority.

Debriefing

5.77   Debriefing involves a review and reflection on a mediation which has recently been conducted.[47] It can take place between co-mediators, between a mediator and supervisor, or by a mediator on his or her own.[48] In some situations

---

42   Refer to 10.81–10.82.
43   Refer, for example, to sections 4.5.3–4 and 4.7.1–2 College of Mediators Code of Practice and section 8.2 Law Society Code of Practice for Family Mediation (both are in Appendix 8).
44   Refer, for example, to section 4.4.5 College of Mediators Code of Practice (see Appendix 8).
45   See 10.70 and refer, generally, to LSC *Disclosure of Information Regulations* 2000 (regulation 4).
46   Refer to ACAS, *Mediation: Guide for Employers*, 2009.
47   Refer also to Chapter 12 for a further outline of debriefing and self reflection (especially 12.14 and 12.62).
48   In contexts like workplace mediation, a mediator might debrief with the HR manager, whilst retaining the confidentiality of information imparted in the mediation, or with a co-mediator where internal mediation is conducted in pairs.

mediation clients, and their advisers, are asked to complete evaluation forms immediately after the mediation has concluded.[49]

Debriefing serves several purposes for mediators:

■ It allows them to deal with their own emotional needs, particularly where there has been anger, sadness or other emotions in the mediation session.

■ It encourages self-awareness as a basis for improving mediator performance.

■ It assists with supervision, accountability and quality control, and with responding to complaints from consumers of mediation services.

■ It provides statistical information for survey use.

5.78   Successful debriefing is a sophisticated art and requires training and resources.[50] Some of the requirements for successful debriefing are:

■ It needs to be structured, preferably in the form of a written report.

■ It should have an appropriately specific focus, and not be over-generalised.

■ It requires diplomacy in giving, and self-confidence in receiving, criticism and feedback.

■ It works best in co-mediation where a mediator targets in advance those matters on which feedback is desired.[51]

■ It needs to respect the confidentiality of all involved.

Shepherding

5.79   Some mediators follow up on mediation agreements and supervise aspects of their implementation. This is sometimes referred to as *shepherding*. This may include monitoring a mediated agreement's progress, up to the making of consent orders by the relevant tribunal or court. In practical terms this is usually done through a series of telephone calls. This may also involve offering mediation assistance where the parties are having difficulty in the implementation of the agreement.

L. Variations in the process

5.80   There are numerous potential variations in the conventional mediation process described in this chapter. The most important of the variations, for example, multiple meetings and shuttle mediation, are dealt with in Chapter 10. Chapter 10 also describes variations across practice areas.

---

49 A sample is at Appendix 7. Refer also to 12.14 and 12.62.
50 In family mediation, supervision (or professional practice consultancy, 'PPC') is recognised in the standards of the UK College of Family Mediators (2000a and 2003) and in LSC's MQMS. Refer to MQMS Requirements D3.1 (the position of supervisor), D3.2 (supervision skills) and D4.1–4.3 (how supervision works).
51 See 9.35.

M. Summary

5.81   This chapter raises the following points of particular significance:

- There is an internal logic to the stages and sequence of the mediation process and mediators, as the experts in dispute resolution, should guide the parties through the process in order to achieve its benefits.

- Despite the logic of the process, there are many points at which mediators have important discretions to exercise and on which they can consult the parties on the design of the process.

- As many mediation clients will be unfamiliar with the process, mediators should explain the stages to them, in other words they should make it transparent for the client.

N. Tasks for beginner mediators

5.82   Find (or appoint) a volunteer and ask them to role play a party in a mediation who has no prior knowledge of the process. Make a mediator's opening statement to them (use some poetic licence to pretend that there are two persons present). Respond to their questions or concerns. After making the statement ask them to give you feedback on what you did well and what you could have done differently. Evaluate your own performance against the standards in this chapter.

5.83   With the same volunteer as before, practise the transition patterns for the separate meetings. In light of this experience, modify the explanations for your use.

5.84   Watch a video of a real or simulated mediation (see section (B) in Appendix 10 for a list) and identify differences in the structure of that process, compared with that described here. Write out possible reasons for why the structures differ.

O. Recommended reading

ACAS, *Mediation: Guide for Employers*, 2009.

Albin C., 'The Role of Fairness in Negotiation', in (1993) 9 *Negotiation Journal* 223.

Boulle L. and Nesic M., *Mediation: Principles Process Practice*, Tottel Publishing, 2001, Ch 4.

Charlton R. and Dewdney M., *A Mediator's Handbook*, 2nd ed, Lawbook Co, Sydney, 2004, Ch 2.

Cooley J. W., *The Mediator's Handbook*. National Institute for Trial Advocacy, 2006.

Mackie K. et al, *The ADR Practice Guide: Commercial Dispute Resolution*, Tottel Publishing, 2007, Ch 13.

Costanzo M., *Problem Solving*, Cavendish Publishing, London, 1995.

Moore C., *The Mediation Process: Practical Strategies for Resolving Conflict*, 3rd ed, John Wiley and Son/Jossey-Bass, San Francisco, 2003, Chs 8, 9, 10, 11 and 14.

Folberg J. and Taylor A., *Mediation: A Comprehensive Guide to Resolving Disputes without Litigation*, Jossey-Bass, San Francisco, 1984, Ch 3.

Pirie A., *Alternative Dispute Resolution: Skill, Science and the Law,* Irwin Law, Toronto, 2000.

Pruitt D. G. and Another, in Afzalur M. F. (ed.),*The Process of Mediation: Caucusing, Control and Problem Solving*, Praiger Publishers, New York, 1989.

Riskin L., Understanding Mediators' Orientations, Strategies and Techniques: a Grid for the Perplexed' *Harvard Negotiation Law Review*, 1996, Vol 1, p 38.

Roberts M., *Mediation in Family Disputes: Principles of Practice*, Ashgate, 2008.

Roberts, M. *Developing the Craft of Mediation: Reflections on Theory and Practice,* Jessica Kingsley Publishers, 2007.

Schank R. C., *Tell me a Story: Narrative and Intelligence,* Northwestern University Press, Evanston, 1990.

Sharp G., 'In Praise of Joint Sessions', in (2009) 11(4) *ADR Bulletin* 69.

Spegel N., Rogers B. and Buckley R., *Negotiation: Theory and Techniques*, Butterworths, Sydney, 1998, Ch 3.

Stone D., Patton B. and Heen S., *Difficult Conversations – How to Discuss what Matters Most*, Penguin, New York, 1999.

Various videos listed in section B in Appendix 10.

Chapter 6

Assisting the Communication Process

There's none so deaf as they who will not hear

A. Introduction

6.1   One of the most important functions of mediators is to provide a context in which good communication can take place. Parties in conflict tend to communicate poorly, and disputes can be the result of bad communication. The goal of good communication is mutual understanding, that is, a meeting of the minds of those engaged in communicating with one another.

This chapter deals with the mediator's roles in assisting the parties to communicate appropriately. The skills referred to here are clearly not peculiar to mediating. Many prospective mediators have good communication skills from past training and experience, which they need to adapt to the requirements of mediation. Many others do not have those skills and need to begin with the basics.

6.2   There are several broad responsibilities for mediators in relation to their communication roles:

- to be good communicators and model good communication practices, with words as their main, but not their only, tool;
- to intervene in the parties' communications to make them more accurate, explicit, comprehensible and appropriate;
- to 'educate' the parties in good communication techniques;
- to provide an environment which encourages effective communication.

Communication is an important ingredient in all forms of professional practice. Communication is also a major discipline in its own right and a book on mediation skills can only deal with some aspects of communication particularly relevant to that practice. Dedicated students of communication should consult the specialised literature on this subject for more theoretical and practical insights than can be provided here.

B. Communication and culture

6.3   As referred to in the preface and Chapter 1, this book does not attempt to deal in any significant way with the relevance of culture to many aspects of mediation. However, in respect of communication some reference, no matter how brief, needs to be made to the significance of cross-cultural realities.

Styles and methods of communication are affected by many factors, including class, gender, ethnicity, education and emotional state. Even the meaning of simple words or phrases can be different for people from middle class or working class backgrounds, or for members of the different genders, for example, 'to negotiate', 'matter of principle', 'compromise', 'agreement' and 'commitment'. Here reference is made only to the factor of culture and its significance for communication, but the general principles referred to have much wider applicability.

6.4   Culture is understood as the habits, behaviour, attitudes, values and unconscious knowledge of different social groups, in the present context, groups of identifiable ethnic or racial background. One could also talk about different business cultures. Culture shapes and affects approaches to many different facets of life, including the approach towards 'negotiation' and 'mediation'. Hofstede, a Dutch researcher, suggests five culturally varied dimensions of human behaviour:[1]

- Degree to which a culture accepts differences of power – for example, how is authority decided and what degree of deference is shown to others during negotiation.

- The emphasis a culture places on collectivism and individualism – for example, how is information shared when negotiating.

- Modesty versus assertiveness or masculinity versus femininity – for example, modesty or assertiveness in demands or demeanour when negotiating.

- Degree of comfort with ambiguity – for example, degree to which rules, detailed agreements and implementation oversight are required.

- Short-term versus long-term orientation – for example, expectations, interests and priorities are all affected by the time frame adopted in negotiation.

In relation to negotiation and mediation, culture specifically affects:

- process choice;
- issues to be negotiated;
- level of detail required;
- exchange of information;
- choice and level of authority;
- concession patterns;
- manner of decision-making.[2]

Different cultures also speak different languages and while it is possible to translate the spoken word from one language to another, this will not necessarily convey the intended meaning across cultures. As Goh points out, language may translate words but not meaning because, particularly across cultures, communication consists of more than words alone. Where cultural factors are the less visible, and even unconscious, part of behaviour, they may lead to serious communication

---

1   G. Hofstede, *Culture and Organizations: Software of the Mind*, 2nd ed, McGraw-Hill, New York, 2005.
2   Refer to Chapter 1 for a further discussion about culture.

breakdowns as each side judges and evaluates the other in terms of their own cultural realities.[3]

6.5   Goh develops this theme in relation to the different outlooks and perceptions of the Chinese and Western cultures.[4] Chinese society has a collectivist (homocentric) conception in which the individual inhabits a web of relationships and conformity is highly regarded. Western society has an individualistic (egocentric) conception in which the individual self is of prime importance and self-actualisation is admired. While harmony and inter-dependent relationships are a feature of collectivist societies, individualistic societies emphasise self-centredness and competition.

6.6   Given the contrasts between the cultures, communication can be expected to be highly different as between collectivist and individualistic societies. Collectivist cultures tend to have 'high-text' communication and individualistic cultures tend to have 'low-text' communication.[5]

- In *low-text* communication, most information is conveyed in explicit verbal messages, with less focus on situational context. Communicators state opinions and desires directly and strive to persuade others to accept their viewpoint. Clear, accurate speech and verbal fluency are admired.

- In *high-text* communication, important information is conveyed in contextual cues (time, relationship, situation), with less reliance on verbal messages. Communicators state opinions indirectly and abstain from saying 'no' directly. Talking around the point, ambiguity and silence are admired.

6.7   While there can be a tendency to stereotype cultural factors, and while not all individuals in a culture behave in identical fashion, the differences between high- and low-text communication styles are highly significant in mediation. This book is based on the low-text communication style which is part of the dominant British culture. In this context, mediators strive to get the parties to come to the point, say what they mean and be explicit, direct and unambiguous. This is highly appropriate for some cultural contexts, and highly inappropriate for others where indirectness, ambiguity and situation are more relevant. In the latter context, mediators must adapt the suggestions in this chapter to take account of the subtleties of high-text communication.

Case illustration

Multicultural miscommunication

In a commercial lease dispute, a shopping centre was represented by its commercial manager, an Englishman, and the lessee, a new immigrant from India, was representing himself. During the exchange of information the manager gave a lengthy account of why factors beyond the centre's control had led to reduced numbers of customers and how the centre had no responsibility for the lessee's substantial drop in turnover during the past year. Throughout this presentation the lessee listened attentively, nodded his head continuously

---

3   Goh *Negotiating with the Chinese*, 1996, 20.
4   See 1.10.
5   Adler and Rodman, *Understanding Human Communication*, 1994, 102.

and made occasional affirmative noises. As soon as he began to speak it became apparent that he did not accept any of the landlord's explanations and the manager was outraged. During the separate meeting the manager vented his anger to the mediator and asked how the other party could be so inconsistent. The mediator explained the cross-cultural misunderstanding and that, for the lessee, his attending and nodding indicated that he was listening, but not that he was giving his assent.

Bennett suggests that there are six stages of development in tolerance towards, and understanding of, cultural differences:[6]

- Denial – people are ignorant of another's culture or believe that their own culture is a template for the situation in question.

- Defence – people believe their own culture is superior and other cultures are inferior.

- Minimisation – people lump everyone together by assuming all people are much the same and any differences are trivial.

- Acceptance – people recognise that others have their own way of seeing things.

- Adaptation – people can make adjustments to their understanding of a situation.

- Integration – people can change depending on the cultural context.

In the example above, the mediator was assisting one party to accept the different cultural behaviour, to adapt their analysis of it and to integrate that understanding in order to formulate a response in the mediation.

C. When communication counts

6.8 Communication assistance by the mediator is necessary during all stages of the mediation. Where communication is unclear, negative or over-emotional, then his or her intervention is required.[7] Where communications break down entirely the mediator tries to keep them going, for example, by relying on the advisers or using informal channels. However, in some phases of mediation the mediator's communication function is of particular significance because of the peculiar needs of these stages:

- During the introductory rituals, the mediator's opening statement, party statements and defining of the agenda – here it is important for the mediator to connect with the parties through communication which they understand, to convey understanding of the parties, to assure them that they have been heard, and to use appropriate and precise terms in defining the issues.

---

6   M. J. Bennett, 'Towards Ethnorelativism' in R. M. Paige (ed) *Education of the Intercultural Experience*, Intercultural Press, Yarmouth, 1993.
7   In some cases, such as workplace grievances, improvement in the communication between parties, rather than the resolution of a particular dispute, is required, and the skills in this chapter have additional significance.

- During the separate meetings – the mediator uses communication suitable for reassuring the parties, for forming alliances with them, and for encouraging them to settle by acting as agents of reality.

- During the closing stages – communication is required which ensures comprehensiveness in the agreement, accuracy in its drafting, a positive tone to see things through to conclusion and a congratulatory note without appearing patronising.

6.9   Despite these critical junctures, good communication, as pointed out, is important at all stages of mediation. All dispute resolution processes rely on good information and where the mediator can enhance communication it can serve the purpose of obtaining and making use of the best information. However, this is not a narrow instrumental role. Good communication is enhanced as much by context as it is by a good reframe or appropriate question. The other mediator skills required in building the foundations for mediation and conducting the process effectively are all significant in achieving good communication.

D.   Basic issues in communication

6.10   The beginner's guide to communication would inform us that human communication involves (at least) two parties, a 'sender' and a 'receiver'. The sender wishes to transmit a message to the receiver and sends it by way of verbal, vocal and visual elements. The receiver takes delivery of the message, and the communication is complete. Unfortunately it is not quite as simple as beginners' guides like to suggest.

6.11   The passing of a message from one person to another is not as mechanical as the passing of a ball from one player to another. This is because both the sender and receiver are affected in the way they communicate by a range of factors: the context of the communication, the respective emotions of the parties, cultural expectations, past experiences, and assumptions and prejudices. These are all subjective and highly variable factors which can differ significantly from one person to the other, even where they are from the same cultural background. This means that the sender will 'encode' his or her message, that is, the words used, the vocal effects and the body language will be based on his or her perceptions of the world. Likewise, the receiver will 'decode' the message in terms of his or her perceptions and frame of reference. Because of the subjective nature of both the encoding and decoding, there may be a substantial difference between what the sender thought they were communicating and what the receiver thought was being communicated. Hence the need for advanced guides to communication.

6.12   Of course, in reality communication seldom consists of a single message from one person to another. Particularly in the mediation context it involves a series of ongoing messages between three or more people. This makes things both easier and more complex at the same time. It is easier because the receiver of a message usually responds to it and this response can help to clarify things. Receivers can give feedback to the sender through verbal, vocal or visual means. Thus the receiver may ask a question which gives the sender an opportunity to resend the message more clearly, more slowly or more accurately than before. Moreover, the sender may detect from the body language of the receiver that the message has not been understood, or has been misunderstood, and immediately clarify it.

6.13   Things are more complex in the mediation context because, as in any other conversation, all parties continually swap the roles of sender and receiver. During these exchanges many different facts, ideas, emotions and attitudes are being exchanged, and if the situation is tense and the communication fast and furious the encoding of each party may be clumsy and the decoding may be faulty. Thus where a receiver is intently focused on the words being used by the sender, he or she might pick up on the factual information of the message but fail to pick up on attitudes and feelings surrounding it. Likewise, where a sender uses aggressive body language this may cause the receiver to overlook important objective information being conveyed verbally.

6.14   Professional frameworks also affect communication, whether lawyers, accountants or psychologists are involved. Thus lawyers use accepted and well-understood terms to communicate in a kind of shorthand which is highly accurate and appropriate when they converse with one another. For example, lawyers in a personal injury mediation may happily swap terms such as 'without prejudice', 'liability and quantum', 'special damages', 'future economic loss' with both ease and understanding. Unfortunately, these terms add another layer of complexity to the involvement of laypersons for whom legalese is unintelligible at best and alienating at worst.

Mediators also have their in-house jargon such as 'BATNA', 'caucus' and 'conditional linked bargaining' which should be used with caution in front of parties.

6.15   Egan points out that clients of the helping professionals tend to talk about three things:[8]

- Experiences – what happened to them, for example, an employee says she has just been reprimanded and put on notice by her supervisor.

- Behaviour – what they do or refrain from doing, for example, that the employee arrives at work late, makes long personal phone calls and often misses deadlines.

- Affect – feelings and emotions that arise from or are associated with experiences and behaviour, for example, the employee's frustration about job advancement or anger over her treatment.

Most people are willing to talk about their *experiences*, and are less willing to talk about their *behaviour* and *feelings*. Experiences are easier to discuss because they usually involve something which has happened *to* the speaker and they entail no acceptance of responsibility. However, in mediation, communication is required on experiences, behaviour and affect in so far as this will promote resolution of the dispute.

6.16   In facilitating the parties' communication, the mediator should be attentive to the common tendency for people to talk about others' motives and to talk about the facts as though there is only one version of 'what happened'. The mediator might instruct the parties at an early stage of the mediation that they cannot claim to talk about 'what happened' but only about 'your memory of events'. This builds

---

8   G. Egan, *The Skilled Helper*, 8th ed, 2006.

in a qualification to whatever they might say. Likewise, the mediator might instruct them not to talk about what they perceive the other party's motives to be, but only about 'your own motives and internal feelings' relating to past events.

E. Communication style and terminology

6.17 Mediators need to develop an appropriate communication style and use of terminology. The style is an art, the terminology a science.

As regards style, much will depend on culture and context. In most British contexts mediators need to speak fluently, in a quiet and confident manner, and to give complete and specific messages. They should use plain and intelligible words and avoid legal jargon and technical terms where these would not be understood by the parties they are helping.

As regards terminology, some words and phrases are redolent of conflict, contest and struggle, and are best avoided by mediators. Others could be seen as threatening or challenging to particular parties. There is much emphasis in mediation manuals on the need for 'reframing' the inappropriate language of the parties to words and phrases which are positive instead of negative, constructive instead of destructive, and problem-solving rather than problem-reinforcing. However, instead of only being reactive through reframing, mediators should proactively use appropriate language as a model for that of the parties.[9] This can be illustrated in the following table.

Framing	
Mediators might say	**Instead of saying**
Matter/situation	Dispute/conflict
Discussions	Negotiations
Current hopes	Claims/demands
Other party or use person's name	Opponent/defendant
Agree to	Concede
Give us your understanding of [ ]	Tell us the facts
Your ways of dealing with [ ]	Make compromises/concessions
Make decisions	Reach agreement
So this is important for you	It's a matter of principle
Ways of addressing/making good	Damages/award
Important matter for you	Fundamental to claim
I'm having trouble understanding you	I don't believe you

6.18 These and other positive terms are second nature to veteran mediators and are used from the earliest stages of mediation. This use of positive terms is designed to get parties to think about the dispute constructively. It attempts to restructure their perceptions. Where the positive term is adopted by the parties it

---

9   See 6.38–6.43.

can open them up to a more constructive form of problem solving. Mediators also use a number of constructive 'weasel' words such as 'reasonable', 'satisfactory', 'appropriate' and 'productive'. These again lend a positive tone to the discussions. Where a negative term is used by the parties, the mediator reframes to the positive replacement term.[10] The power of framing is highlighted by a psychological experiment. One group played 'The Wall Street Game', whereas the other played 'The Community Game'. The rules of the game were identical. Those who played the former co-operated only one-third of the time, whereas those who played the latter co-operated two-thirds of the time. The framing of the game caused participants to construct a different story of what was going on.[11]

F. Non-verbal communication in mediation

6.19   Verbal communication is only one form of communication. Non-verbal communication is another. Non-verbal communication consists of those aspects of communication which can be seen by the other party, the visuals, and other forms of non-verbal communication which can be heard, namely vocals.

Visuals

6.20   The term 'visuals' refers to all aspects of communication which are observed, as opposed to heard, by the receiver and which convey messages to him or her.

Body language is the most prominent form of visual communication. It involves all aspects of bodily appearance and movement which convey attitudes, feelings, emotions and other important dimensions of communication. In practical terms it could include a person's clothing, posture, body and limb movements, hand gestures, facial expressions, eye motions, and physiological responses such as blushing and quickened breathing. The face and eyes are often portrayed as the most important conveyers of body language, but micro-signals in these areas are not always easy to read and interpret.

While parties can fake body language to some degree, this is not always easy, for example, in relation to eye signals, tone of voice, blushing or shortness of breath. Children in particular find it difficult to conceal body language and the crossed legs or averted eyes can betray the apparent innocence of their spoken words. Unlike verbal communication, body language never stops, and when a person is verbally silent it remains the only way in which they are communicating.

6.21   Some generalised features of body language in Western societies are:

■ Open limb positions – receptivity towards what is being said.

■ Crossed or folded limbs – defensiveness towards what is being said.

---

10 Reframing is dealt with in 6.38–6.43.
11 L. Ross and A. Ward, 'Naïve Realism in Everyday Life: Implications for Social Conflict and Misunderstanding' in E. S. Reed and others (eds), *Values and Knowledge*, Erlbaum, NJ, 1996. See also D. Schon and M. Rein, *Frame Reflection: Toward the Resolution of Intractable Policy Controversies*, Basic Books, New York, 1994.

- Forward-leaning body posture – attentiveness to speaker.

- Backward stance – indifference to speaker.

- Open hands – plain dealing and honesty.

- Closed fists, pointed fingers – aggression, threatening attitude.

- Direct eye contact – sincerity, openness, honest dealing.

- Averted gaze, avoidance of eye contact – deceit, guilt, embarrassment.

Paul Ekman's work shows that physical sensations and facial expressions can reveal distinct emotions. For example, when a party feels contempt, he or she is likely to smile with one side of the face only; and when a party is angry, his or her eyelids may draw down, but the eyes will remain open and glare.[12]

Body language can either confirm or contradict what is being said verbally, or it might simply confuse. As mentioned below, when it comes to interpreting body language it is dangerous to put too much weight on a single factor. As Egan suggests, the trick is to spot the messages without making too much or too little of them.[13] Folberg and Taylor refer to studies finding that people in the helping professions often misinterpret the non-verbal messages implicit in a series of photographs, while untrained people pick them correctly.[14] Lawyers have highly trained listening skills, but are not trained in observing behaviour and are among the offenders.

6.22   Pease makes the following observations about body language:[15]

- More than 65% of a message is conveyed non-verbally.

- Non-verbal communication has a significance in communication five times that of verbal communication.

- In general, non-verbal communication conveys interpersonal attitudes, while verbal communication is used to impart information.

- Some non-verbal signals are learned and some are inborn.

- A single gesture may have many meanings and should be interpreted in the context of associated verbal and non-verbal communication, the person's culture, and the environment in which it takes place.

6.23   'Visuals' also refers to messages received from the broader environment, such as the size of an office, the shape of a table, the size and height of chairs, seating arrangements, spatial configurations, lighting, and the like. These factors can convey power, strength, status, influence, domination or equality, and other such messages more emphatically and unequivocally than words. The director Stanley Kubrik is reported to have spent five days arranging the lighting for a single scene in his last film *Eyes Wide Shut*; mediators seldom have such time, or flair. Nevertheless, without any language, body movement or other overt communication, a whole

---

12   P. Ekman, *Emotions Revealed*, 2003, Times Books, New York, 2003.
13   G. Egan, *The Skilled Helper*, 8th ed, 2006.
14   Folberg and Taylor, *Mediation*, 1988, 117.
15   Allan Pease, *Body Language: How to Read Others' Thoughts by their Gestures*, Camel Publishing Co, Avalon Beach, 1991. Refer also to Allan Pease, *The Definitive Book on Body Language*, Bantam Books, New York, 2006.

mood and atmosphere can be conveyed by the environment and surroundings. The mediator is usually responsible for the mediation environment.[16]

Vocals

6.24   Vocal communication refers to the many oral messages which can be sent without using words and language. It is sometimes referred to as paralanguage. It refers to volume, pitch, pace, tone, inflection, emphasis, intonation, rhythm, resonance, inflection and silence.[17] One may add laughter, sighs, gestures and shouting. All of these disclose emotion, attitude and other states of mind which are not conveyed through verbal communication.

6.25   As the vocals are all auditory signals, except the silence part, they are difficult to demonstrate through written words in a textbook. However, the following illustration shows the different meanings which the same five words can have, depending on where the emphasis is placed by the speaker:

- *Their* mediation book is good (but not all the other mediation books).
- Their *mediation* book is good (but not their books on other topics).
- Their mediation *book* is good (but not their mediation video).
- Their mediation book *is* good (I had my doubts, but now I've read it).
- Their mediation book is *good* (it is recommended).

As with body language, some forms of vocal communication are difficult to disguise. Where the vocal messages contradict the spoken words, listeners tend to be influenced more by the former. This can be demonstrated in relation to sarcasm, where emphasis and tone can give spoken words a meaning diametrically opposed to their literal meaning.

The mediator's role in relation to visuals and vocals

6.26   One of the mediator's functions is to observe and interpret vocal messages and body language, though much micro-language in the face and eyes is not easy to read. From their observations, mediators need to make inferences, for example, that blushing or crossing of the limbs indicates anxiety or defensiveness, and plan their next intervention accordingly. This is part of the mediator's mapping or hypothesis development function, referred to in Chapter 4. It is also part of the mediator's wider role of managing a favourable climate, referred to in Chapter 3.

However, observing behaviour and inferring meaning are separate activities and it is possible accurately to observe but assign a mistaken meaning to that behaviour. Mediators therefore need to make tentative interpretations of behaviour and check to see if they are correct. They should not read too much into a single cue. A sudden bodily movement by a young attendee at mediation, may be caused as much by discomfort, habit or a medical condition as by anger or boredom. When an elderly party frowns at a document, she might be upset at what the paper says

---

16   See generally Chapter 2.
17   Spegel, Rogers and Buckley, *Negotiation: Theory and Techniques*, 1998, 151.

or be unable to see clearly without her glasses. Where behavioural signals occur in clusters, for example, dilation of the pupils, heavier breathing and distressed hand movements, they are easier for mediators to diagnose tentatively than where they are single occurrences.

6.27   Non-verbal signals are most significant where they are incongruent with the verbal message, for example, where the words signify assent but the crossed legs or nervous eyes suggest resistance, or where the words suggest honesty but the voice's higher pitch suggests an untruth. Mediators can use the separate meetings to raise and deal with incongruent factors such as these. They can check whether their understanding of a party's signals is correct, and whether the other side might be aware of the message being sent.

The mediator's own non-verbal communication

6.28   Mediators need to be attentive to their own body language and vocals, which could reveal bias, impatience or boredom. Some actions will be generally appropriate in mediation, for example, open body positions, direct eye contact and congruent facial expressions. Others will usually be inappropriate, for example, frowning when a party is making their opening statement or folding the arms when a party is proclaiming the truth of their version of events. Yet others require the mediator to make judgments and adaptations for particular circumstances; for example, choice of clothing, handshakes, touch and facial expressions. Silence can be an effective tool to add emphasis, get attention, allow space for consideration and create pressure for a response.

Some long-held habits, which could disconcert or mislead the parties, may be unknown to mediators and the use of videotapes of actual or simulated mediations provides a useful insight into reality. That said, some long-held habits are notoriously difficult for even earnest mediators to change.

Just as contradictions between a party's language and non-verbals is of significance for mediators, so should mediators strive to achieve consistency in their verbal, vocal and visual communication. However, some 'censorship' of body language might be required, for example, where the mediator feels annoyance or disbelief, he or she might have to control facial expressions so as not to display this inner reality. 'Censorship' can develop into manipulation where mediators deliberately provide non-verbal signals which they think might be appropriate; for example, a shake of the head to indicate disagreement with a party's proposal.

6.29   Mediators need to be attentive to their own physiological reactions, for example, tensing of the muscles or clenching of the fists. By being aware of these the mediator can control his or her bodily reactions and prevent communicating anxiety, disapproval or anger, as the case may be. Experienced mediators can also use body language as a form of constructive intervention, for example, to guide the conversation between the parties with simple hand directions to ensure that they are speaking to each other and not to the mediator.

Appearance is an important issue for mediators, though not entirely within their control. Appearance creates initial impressions which are difficult to change. Clothing can be changed but height and grooming cannot. Some male commercial mediators remove their suit jacket at the earliest opportunity to convey the message, without saying it, that this is an informal process. However, few would remove the tie as this might convey lack of commercial experience. Likewise, the initial handshake can convey domination (crushed phalanxes), weakness (wet fish) or strength (firm grip).

6.30 How mediators arrange the physical space is also significant. Reference was made in Chapter 4 to a number of variations in relation to how people are seated in mediation. Physical arrangements should always respect personal space. In a professional relationship there is usually more physical space between persons than in a personal relationship. Where the mediator knows a lawyer personally it might be appropriate to maintain a professional distance when the clients are present.

G. Effective listening

6.31 In the kingdom of Camelot, mediation would not be necessary, as parties would listen to each other effectively. They would hear the messages which are 'on the lines', usually factual content, and they would hear the messages which are 'between the lines', usually emotions and feelings. Mediators would not be required to remind the parties to listen to each other to achieve proper understanding. However, outside Camelot, mediators are required for these purposes.

Most of a mediator's time should be spent listening to the parties and effective listening skills are of major importance to mediators. They must listen effectively before they can get the parties to listen to each other. Effective listening involves more than hearing spoken words. It involves properly understanding the meaning of messages, by both grasping facts and information analytically and picking up on their emotional content and the broad patterns and themes which they convey.

Causes of ineffective listening

6.32 Listening may prove to be ineffective in relation to the following factors:

- The speaker – inaudibility, annoying mannerisms, physical appearance, tone of voice, speed of delivery, presentation, contentious content, interruptions by others.

- The listener – inattention, discomfort, fatigue, stress/anxiety, thinking ahead, focus on responding to the speaker, ignorance of subject matter, psychological deafness, emotional involvement, lack of comprehension, inability to absorb, judgemental attitude, and 'inner noise' from your own thoughts.

- Environmental factors – external noise, bad lighting, poor accoustics, uncomfortable seating, outside interruptions and other distractions.

Listening effectively

6.33 There is a lot of hard work involved in listening effectively. It is not just a passive exercise, hence the use of the phrase 'active listening'. The listener must be physically attentive, concentrate on and encourage the speaker, display an attitude of interest and concern, be non-judgmental, not be preoccupied with responding to or questioning the speaker, and not be distracted by non-relevant matters. The effective listener is concentrating not only on words and sentences, but on patterns of thought, the organisation of ideas and the themes implicit in the speaker's communication. This requires considerable effort. Active listening is important for mediators in relation to a number of other functions, such as summarising, defining the issues and making the best use of any valuable communications by the parties for settlement.

Elements of active listening

6.34   There are three elements to active listening:

- *Attending skills*: being with a party, physically and psychologically, making them feel important and trustful by use of physical attention, display of interest, appropriate body movements, encouraging noises ('I see ...', 'Uhuh ...', 'Yes ...'), and encouraging the speaker to say more. Gerard Egan refers to the macroskills of listening in terms of the acronym SOLER:[18]
  - *Squarely* face the client to show involvement
  - Adopt an *Open* posture, literally and metaphorically
  - *Lean* towards the client at times
  - Maintain *Eye* contact most of the time
  - *Relax*, be natural in these behaviours.

- *Following skills*: indicating that the listener is following the speaker by providing cues, not interrupting, asking clarifying questions, taking notes, summarising and refraining from giving advice.

- *Reflecting skills*: giving feedback to the speaker on the listener's understanding of their meaning, with reference to feeling and content; identifying and acknowledging content and feeling, summarising content and feeling, and asking empathic questions.[19]

6.35   The speaker's frame of reference is always important in relation to listening. The listener needs to try and understand and comprehend this frame of reference and to look for themes and patterns in the speaker's speech. The mediator also needs to be aware of his or her own frame of reference. In some situations the mediator needs to modify the speaker's frame of reference through reframing.[20]

Reading body language and vocal communication is an important element in active listening. As referred to above, the trick is to spot the messages in non-verbal behaviours, without making too much or too little of them. They can confirm the verbal message, contradict it, or confuse it. Much will depend on context.

---

18 G. Egan, *The Skilled Helper*, 8th ed, 2006.
19 Refer also to R. Salem, *The Benefits of Empathic Listening*, Conflict Research Consortium, University of Colorado, 2003.
20 G. Egan, *The Skilled Helper*, 8th ed, 2006.

Detracting from effective listening

6.36 Some of the natural impulses which detract from good listening by the mediator include:[21]

- Focusing on facts and information and ignoring the feeling and emotions: 'So you want £93,475.12 as compensation?'

- Asking too many questions, in particular closed, leading or cross-examining questions: 'But didn't you tell me earlier that you had not obtained a valuation at the time?'

- Being judgmental and moralising: 'You did okay ...'; 'Everyone has to take the ups with the downs.'

- Analysing the reasons for parties' behaviour: 'You were obviously in denial when you refused help.'

- Lapsing into cliches: 'I hear what you're saying ...'; 'I know how you must have felt ...'.

- Becoming hooked into the other's emotions, values or judgments: 'So you felt you were entitled to some self-help against the fraudster?'

- Engaging in self-exposure: 'The same thing happened to me ...'.

- Finishing the parties' sentences.

Difficult communication situations

6.37 Some difficult communication situations may arise:

- In telephone mediations the mediator is entirely dependent on verbal and vocal communication and is unaware of the speaker's body language. It is also more difficult to maintain equality of air time in the absence of visual cues available in face-to-face mediation. Here active listening may require the mediator to step up their encouraging vocal and verbal signals to indicate that the speaker is being heard. Frequent summarising and paraphrasing are important to ensure that each party has been properly and fully understood and asking for clarification avoids misunderstandings. Having an agenda and engaging less vocal parties are also necessary.

- In shuttle mediations the mediator is aware of all three forms of communication but has to decide what aspects of non-verbal communication to convey to the other side, who relies entirely on the mediator.

- In using interpreters – where the mediator does not speak the language of one or both parties he or she is reliant solely on the interpreter's version of a speaker's language and, because of cultural differences in this context, will have to be cautious about interpreting vocals and visuals.

- In internet mediations, the mediator is exclusively dependent on electronic communication for understanding a distant party.

---

21 Bolton, *People Skills*, 1987, 15–16.

H. Reframing

6.38   Reframing is closely related to active listening and is an important skill for mediators.[22] It is the other side of the 'framing' coin. Whereas framing is carried out proactively, reframing is a reactive mediator intervention. All parties communicate within a certain frame of reference, based on how they see the world in terms of their culture, experiences and sense of justice. The goal of reframing is to change this frame of reference in order to get the parties to think differently about things, or at least to get them to see things in a different light. It is based on the fact that the language we use affects how we perceive the world, that by changing language we can change perceptions, and that changed perceptions can lead to changed behaviour.

Slaikeu defines reframing as a *translation exercise* through which the mediator changes the communication by moving it from one language to another, with the hope that in the second language the comment may be more palatable to the parties or more conducive to collaborative problem solving.[23] This then is another role for the mediator, that of 'translator'.

6.39   Reframing takes place through the mediator using different words, concepts and terms, using different emphases and intonations, and otherwise qualifying what the parties have themselves said to provide a different frame of reference. As Charlton and Dewdney point out, reframing is used not only to change the words being used but also the context of a party's statement, for example, from positions to interests or from the past to the future[24] and from threats or problems to opportunities. The shift in emphasis is aimed at helping parties to consider another frame of reference, for example, from a 'claim for £100,000' to a recognition of the relevant interest, say, 'your desire to retire next year and be fairly compensated'. When successful, it leads to a change in perspective or perception on the parties' behalf and this altered attitude or view of the dispute can lead to changes in behaviour. While the original frame of reference may have had a negative effect on the resolution of the dispute, the new frame of reference is conducive to constructive conflict management.

To illustrate the importance of framing and reframing, the Kahneman effect, or 'the endowment effect', is the phenomenon that more is required to compensate someone who thinks that they are losing something in negotiations.[25] A possible way around the effect is to demonstrate how, and what, the person will gain in the process. This should be done from the outset, and throughout, the negotiations. In this way, through appropriate framing and reframing, a party's reference point can be altered, by ensuring that settlement is seen as a gain of something (for example, the ending of litigation, stress or uncertainty), rather than a loss (for example, giving up a right to pursue a claim).

6.40   It must be emphasised that reframing is not just a terminological exercise. It is about orienting the whole tone of the discussions. Where a party points out

---

22   A joke in mediation circles: 'How many mediators does it take to hang a picture?' Answer: 'None. Mediators don't hang pictures, they reframe them.'
23   K. Slaikeu *When Push Comes to Shove*, 1996, 232.
24   Charlton and Dewdney, *The Mediator's Handbook*, 2nd ed, 2004.
25   D. Kahneman and A. Tverksy, Prospect Theory: An Analysis of Decision under Risk, in *Econometrica* (1979), Volume 47, p 263.

what is wrong, the mediator asks them to indicate what would be right for them. Where a party continually emphasises what they do not want, the mediator gets them to talk about what they do want. Where a party goes on about what the other party wants, the mediator asks them to state what they themselves want.[26]

6.41   There is similarity between reframing and the design of jokes, as explained in the box below.

A joke-teller encourages a certain point of view, but when the punch line is delivered the listener is able to see the preceding story in a different light. On the face of it, the punch line is incongruous, but when the listener catches the joke by seeing the previous narrative in a different light, then the incongruous becomes congruous. The humour is caused by the surprise, relief or delight which occurs when the punch line is delivered and the listener has to change his or her erroneous expectation. In other words, a scene is first described from one viewpoint, and then rearranged, sometimes by a single word. Likewise, mediators, through reframing, have the capacity to restructure the parties' perceptions of a dispute situation. In joke-telling the switch-over is temporary and gives rise to humour, whereas in mediation it can be permanent and give rise to insight. While the joke-teller reframes to achieve laughter, the mediator reframes to contribute to problem-solving.[27]

Reframing case illustration

In a lengthy family mediation both parents began positionally by demanding 'residence' of their two children and denying that the other was a suitable 'residence parent'. The mediator reframed this language to that of 'discussing the most appropriate parenting arrangements for Mark and Matthew'. Initially the parents resisted this definition of the problem and continued to assert their claim for residence. The mediator persisted, and eventually one party, then the other, began using the new language. This shifted the focus from the parents to the children. It led to a constructive discussion of the children's needs and to eventual agreement on a parenting regime. In light of this arrangement the legal concepts of residence and contact were dealt with in the final agreement.

Functions and examples of reframing

6.42   Reframing can serve a number of different functions. Clearly, no single reframe can perform each one of the functions at the same time. Nor is reframing a constant form of mediator intervention; it is used selectively where it can perform one of the stated purposes.

Here the various functions of reframing are illustrated in the context of a hypothetical dispute between a house owner and the builder who was contracted to repair the chimney. The repairs were faulty, causing rain to leak into the reception room and on to expensive furnishings.

---

26   See K. Bryant and D. L. Curtis, *Reframing*, 2004.
27   L. Boulle and M. Nesic, *MPPP*, 2001, 206.

Function of reframe	Statement by party	Reframe by mediator
It can detoxify language, by removing accusations, judgments and other verbal stings.	'The builder is an idiot whose appalling workmanship has ruined my carpets.'	'So this repair job has been a bad experience for both of you?'
It can focus on the positive, by removing references to negatives and other destructive elements in the language.	'The damage to the roof has caused me enormous losses ...'	'So getting the roof fixed properly is important to you?'
It can focus on interests, by removing references to positions and solutions and reframing to underlying needs and requirements.	'He must fix that roof tomorrow and give me £20,000 for the ruined carpets.'	'So you need to stop the leaking as soon as possible and sort out your furnishings.'
It can focus on the future, by removing references to the past and reframing to future needs and interests.	'He was always late, never returned my calls and left a mess all over the place.'	'So you would like the future work to be done on a professional basis?'
It can mutualise problems, by avoiding one-sided definitions and reframing to dual-sided formulations.	'His stupid negligence has made me look a fool among friends and neighbours.'	'So we also need to see how both your damaged reputations can be repaired.'
It can soften and qualify demands, threats and negotiate 'bottom lines'.	'If he does not pay me £20,000 within 3 days I'll take him to court.'	'So you're looking for a settlement within a short time.'
It can turn an absolute demand or a position into one possible option.	'I demand the repair of the roof, £20 000, and a full apology.'	'So your preferred option right now is an acknowledgement, money and repairs.'

Some further standard terms encountered in mediation, and ways in which mediators can reframe them, are contained in Appendix 5.

Potential problems with reframing

6.43   There are a number of potential problems with mediator reframing. The problems could arise because a suspicious or distrustful party finds it an alien experience, or it could be because the mediator does not carry out the reframing appropriately. In either event, the party's subjective assessment will be the same, namely that the reframing intervention has not contributed positively to the mediation. Thus:

■ Reframing is a difficult art and if performed badly may be seen as mere parroting of the parties. ('Why does he/she keep repeating everything I say ...?')

■ Reframing could be seen as manipulating. ('That's not what I said, he/she keeps twisting my words ...')

■ Reframing could be perceived as the mediator favouring one party and losing the non-partisan role. ('He/she seems to be agreeing with the other party all the time ...')

6.44   Nevertheless, appropriate reframing is a powerful mediator intervention and it can be readily improved through practice. One of the golden rules for avoiding the potential problems is to retain neutrality in the reframing role and to use the intervention in relation to both parties' language. However, it takes some trial and error to achieve the correct balance, as illustrated in the following example.

Case illustration – finding the balance in reframing

The mediator's first reframe might be unsuccessful, in the sense that it is 'rejected' by the party to whom it is directed. She could then try again. However, there are dangers in being too persistent. Assume in the following exchange that the mediator wants to soften, or at least qualify, Bill's positional claim in order to get some flexibility into his thinking:

Bill: I want a million pounds.

Mediator: So you want to be reasonably compensated to settle this?

Bill: No, I told you I want a million pounds.

Clearly the reframe has not worked as Bill has restated his positional claim, and he is also not happy with the mediator. The mediator could persist with a softer reframe in the hope that Bill will accept it:

Bill: No, I told you I want a million pounds.

Mediator: So at this point in time a million pounds would be reasonable compensation for you?

Bill: Yes ... I guess that is the case.

The mediator now has two flexible concepts to work with, 'this point in time' and 'reasonable compensation'. At a later stage she could make use of these concepts:

Mediator: Bill, now that you have heard from the other side, what do you think a reasonable compensation would be?

However, Bill might also reject the second reframe, with greater insistence than before, for example:

Mediator: So at this point in time a million pounds would be reasonable compensation for you?

Bill: No, I've already told you twice, I will only ever settle for a million pounds, not a penny less.

Here Bill has entrenched himself in his positional claim and the mediator may decide not to make matters worse, acknowledge Bill, and move on. Alternatively, with some risk of losing Bill's trust, he/she might try with the softest of reframes:

Mediator: So Bill your preferred option is one million pounds, let's now look at Mary's options and see where you can both get to ...

This has not contradicted Bill's positional claim, but is calling it something else, namely a preferred option, and is opening the way for a consideration of other options.

Where to draw the line when reframing? It is impossible to define this in the abstract. There is inevitably some trial and error in this area. Our own preference is to be as persistent with reframing as the circumstances suggest is feasible.

I. Appropriate questioning

6.45   There are different views as to the nature and extent of the questioning mediators should engage in. In some models of mediation the mediator conducts the process almost entirely through the use of questioning. In others, mediators ask very few questions of the parties, but encourage them to explain certain facts or feelings directly to each other. The degree of questioning (and not the third degree) may also depend on the stage and phase of the mediation. Mediators may be reluctant to ask certain kinds of questions in joint session or early in the mediation, but feel it is appropriate to ask them in separate session or towards the end of the mediation. The mediator also needs to keep a check on questioning by professional advisers who may seek to interrogate or cross-examine the other party.

Types of questions

6.46   The following table provides some of the different categories of questions, an illustration of each, the objectives for which the category can be used, and the circumstances in which the particular category might be appropriate. They are based on a hypothetical mediation involving Kate, an employee, and Graham, the employer, over Kate's claim arising out of an injury sustained on the factory floor.

Type of question	Illustration of question	Objectives of question	Circumstances of potential suitability
Open	Kate, would you like to describe in your own words how the accident at work has affected your life?	General disclosure and exchange of information in open-ended way; to get things started; non-threatening.	Commencement of joint and separate sessions; whenever the mediator seeks a non-defensive response.
Focused	Kate, can you tell me how the accident affected your work performance in the last 12 months?	Disclosure of more detailed facts or information about a specific aspect of an event, incident, etc.	When there is time pressure or parties are rambling and the mediator needs to achieve direction.
Closed	Could you tell me, Graham, whether your method of working contributed to the accident in any way?	Controlled disclosure of information through affirmative or negative response ('yes' or 'no').	Not in opening stages; only later in mediation or during separate meetings. When decisions are required on matters.
Clarifying	Is it correct, Graham, that you were under the impression that the machine had been serviced shortly before the accident?	Verify or correct the listener's understanding of a communication; either general or specific information.	Where parties are not being sufficiently clear or specific on important matters, in particular during separate meetings.

Type of question	Illustration of question	Objectives of question	Circumstances of potential suitability
Reflective/ empathic	So at the present time, Kate, you feel that you have little power?	Select and validate an important emotion or fact and highlight it.	Appropriate at all times when active listening and reframing called for.
Probing	Kate, if you are retrained how will you deal with the new technology which was a problem in the past?	Obtain further specificity or justification from speaker, or to test option being considered.	More appropriate in separate meetings to avoid defensive response; or towards end of mediation to 'road test' options.
Leading	Graham, you were responsible for health and safety in the company when the accident happened, isn't that so?	To elicit information which the questioner already knows, to lead the speaker to a pre-determined outcome.	Only when uncontroversial information needs to be elicited, but not otherwise.
Cross-examining	Graham, you are saying that there were adequate safety precautions, but did you not refer earlier to other accidents on this same machine?	To test a party's accuracy, reliability and general credibility; to expose contradictions and inconsistencies.	Generally not appropriate in mediation, either for the mediator or for the lawyers.
Hypothetical	Kate, if we could agree on the matter of compensation, what would you like to have done on the question of safety training?	To get parties to consider options hypothetically without feeling committed to them.	When there are impasses or break downs in the negotiation process.
Disarming/ distracting	How many employees were there in the company at the time?	To deflect attention from a destructive interchange between parties.	Whenever there is a need to deflect from high emotions or destructive exchanges.
Rhetorical	Graham and Kate, who of you really wants to go through a tortuous trial?	To make a point dramatically or to produce an effect.	When the parties need to be confronted with an obvious reality.
Suggestive	Graham, would it be possible for company resources to be used to assist in making alterations to Kate's house?	To suggest possible or obvious options for settlement, to float options with out parties feeling committed to them	As a last resort, where the parties are making no headway on their own

Choosing the appropriate question

6.47   At a broad level, no type of question is unsuitable, it all depends on context and circumstances. However, Folberg and Taylor suggest that questions for gaining information are the most overused tool in the novice mediator's toolbox.[28] 'If questions are used to the exclusion of other techniques, the conversation will cease to be an exchange and will become an unsatisfactory form of verbal ping-pong or interrogation.' We agree with this view. Thus, in the early stages of mediation open questions are needed so that the parties can tell their story without any suggestive leading questions. Only rarely will closed questions of the either/or variety, associated with selling techniques, be appropriate. Thus the question 'Do you want to settle at mediation or go to litigation?' has a powerful rhetorical effect but could be experienced as manipulative, and might even receive an unexpected answer.

Hypothetical questions

6.48 The 'what-if' or 'if-what' question is in the mediator's top-ten list of interventions. As illustrated above, it is used to get the parties to consider options hypothetically without feeling committed to them. The two forms of the hypothetical question are as follows:

> Mediator: Graham, *what if* Kate were to agree to accept the clerical position – would you then be able to make a commitment in relation to her retraining needs?
>
> A more elegant version looks like this:
>
> Mediator: Kate, *if* Graham would agree to pay for your retraining programme, *what* would you be willing to accept in relation to the clerical position?

In each case the question allows the relevant party to make a settlement suggestion on one issue in the knowledge that it will not be binding unless the pre-condition on another issue is satisfied. If the condition is not satisfied, the party's concession can be withdrawn. This is related to the negotiation strategy of conditional linked bargaining.

Empathic versus probing questioning

6.49 Covey names empathic communication, through actions, comments and questions, as one of the seven habits of effective people.[29] Empathy refers to the ability to put oneself in the shoes of another, to understand things from their perspective. Empathy does not signify agreement; nor does it amount to sympathy with, or compassion for, another. It involves convincing a person that the listener has entered their world of perceptions, if only temporarily. Empathic questions show a sender that the receiver has understood what they said. They involve reflecting a feeling, or an act and a feeling, from the sender's statement.

---

28 Folberg and Taylor, *Mediation*, 1988, p 109.
29 Covey, *The Seven Habits of Highly Effective People*, 1990, 253.

> ### Examples of empathic questions
>
> **1.** Kate, you felt unappreciated for a long period of time because you were not acknowledged in the reports ...?
>
> **2.** Is it correct, Kate, that you became more determined from then on ...?
>
> **3.** It sounds, Graham, as if you were concerned about safety conditions after the accident ...?

While empathic questions seek to check out the feeling or attitude behind a statement, probing or clarifying questions seek confirmation of facts and information. Probing questions seek more focus, more concreteness, more specificity or more accuracy. While they may be entirely appropriate in some circumstances, mediation is not the appropriate venue for an inquisition, whether by the parties, their advisers or the mediator. It is likely to make the parties defensive and adversarial.

In addition, as Charlton and Dewdney point out, mediators do not need to know the full facts in order to fulfil their facilitation role.[30] If there is a genuine need for additional facts, the mediator might discuss with the parties ways of engaging in a fact-finding exercise. Therefore, empathic questions are generally more important for mediators to understand and use than probing questions.

J. Reiterating

6.50   Mediators need to prevent anything of value 'falling off' the negotiation table. In the heat of the moment it is possible for an apology, a concession or a significant offer not to be heard by the non-speaking party because of their anger, psychological deafness or emotional state. Here it is wise for mediators to ask the speaker to repeat the statement, when the timing is appropriate for this intervention:

> *Mediator:*   Graham, I think you were making an offer about redeployment to Kate a few moments ago when we got side-tracked by the question of management attitudes to staff and I'd like you to repeat that offer now ...
>
> Alternatively, mediators might themselves reiterate the statement of value when circumstances allow, for example:
>
> *Mediator:*   A few minutes ago I heard Graham say that he would redeploy Kate in the sales department as part of a package of agreements involving other matters. Is that correct, Graham?
>
> Reiteration can be used to step up a weak signal from one party that is not being heard by the other, for example:

---

30   Charlton and Dewdney, *The Mediator's Handbook*, 2nd ed, 2004.

> *Mediator:* Kate, Graham has indicated on a number of occasions that you have been a valuable and trustworthy employee, and the conflict has arisen over broader pressures affecting the company. Is that your understanding too?

Generally reiteration is one of the tools in the mediator's toolbox which can be used in all situations in which the parties are talking past each other and not picking up on important messages.

K. Paraphrasing

6.51   Paraphrasing involves the mediator closely controlling the dialogue between the parties and picking up on important issues, in particular, the emotional content of a message, and ensuring that there is a response to them. Because it involves the mediator intervening in the dialogue and reframing some of the language, it requires some delicacy and discretion in choice of language.

6.52   The following hypothetical dialogue is from a mediation involving a farmer and a bank representative, in which the representative of the bank, Mr Peters, is negotiating with the farmer, Mr Bianco, as a step prior to foreclosing on the family farm. It illustrates the paraphrasing method:

> *Mediator:*   Mr Peters, Mr Bianco is saying that although the bank was legally justified in its actions, the way it went about things caused him considerable stress and embarrassment in the community. Can you respond to him on that?
>
> *Mr Peters:*   Yes, we do regret any embarrassment caused to you, Mr Bianco, you were always a good customer and we acknowledge that the collapse of your farming business was not altogether your fault. But at the end of the day a bank is a business not a charity and we need to get our money back.
>
> *Mediator:*   Mr Bianco, Mr Peters has expressed his regret at the upset this has caused you and has emphasised that you were a good customer. Can you tell him how you feel now that you have heard that?
>
> *Mr Bianco:*   Well, it's the first time I've ever heard that kind of language from a bank, but I'd still like to keep the farm .

Paraphrasing should be done in an even-handed way so that both parties' communications are paraphrased. It can be used to set up a pattern of direct communication between the parties. It can break what Charlton and Dewdney call the 'Oh but', 'Yes but' pattern of communication: 'Oh but I didn't understand that's what you wanted.' 'Yes but I had told you only two days before ...'[31] However, if this is the only way of keeping the parties communicating constructively it will become strained and artificial.

---

31   Charlton and Dewdney, *The Mediator's Handbook*, 2nd ed, 2004.

L. **Summarising**

6.53   Reference has already been made to the mediator's function of summarising the parties' statements.[32] In that context, the summary is intended to provide an accurate account of what each party has said in order to demonstrate that they have been heard and to allow the mediator to verify his or her understanding of what has been said. Summarising can also be used in later stages of the mediation, and it will take on a different complexion in different contexts. Generally, summarising involves the mediator briefly restating or recapping important features of the preceding discussion and identifying the dominant feelings of the parties.

Summarising can be a powerful intervention which can achieve one or more of the following objectives:

■ Provide a neutral and organised version of a course of discussion.

■ Pick up on key issues which might otherwise have been overlooked.

■ Simplify convoluted exchanges.

■ Remind the parties that progress is being made.

■ Provide acknowledgment to the parties that they have been understood.

■ Establish a platform for the next round of discussion.

■ Assist the mediator to establish trust by using key words spoken by the parties.

6.54   Good summarising requires a range of micro skills, such as retaining important information, recalling it and condensing it. It is always a selective process, that is, the mediator picks up on the progress to date and presents this in a positive summarised statement. It is also selective in that the mediator picks up only on what is useful for mediation, as opposed to what would be useful for law or counselling. The reason why the mediator is selective in the summaries is that it provides a positive and encouraging basis for the parties to move forward with their negotiations. However, the summary also needs to be balanced in the sense that it deals fairly with what each party has said. The following is an example of a summary from the Bianco and Peters mediation:

> Mediator: Mr Bianco, you've told us that your financial difficulties were caused by wider economic factors, and that you felt the bank could have dealt with you more directly and sympathetically. You also acknowledged that you may not be able to trade out of your difficulties but that you would like to restructure finances for the short term so that you can consider your options for the future. And Mr Peters, you said that things could have been handled differently with Mr Bianco, particularly as he was a longstanding customer of yours. You also said that banks have some discretion in these circumstances and that you would be prepared to look at some short-term financial arrangements, provided that these were appropriately monitored and reviewed. Is that correct ...? Mr Peters and Mr Bianco, let's move forward and look at some options for the finances in the short term.

---

32   See 5.31–5.33.

6.55 There are two situations in which summarising is particularly appropriate. It is useful after an adjournment or when a joint session resumes after separate sessions; here it has the function of refocusing the parties on the state of the negotiations. It should also be used when the parties reach an impasse in their negotiations; here it has the function of emphasising the positive progress to date and providing building blocks for the future.

Despite the fact that good summarising can be one of the most effective interventions for mediators, it is probably one of the most under-utilised. It should be added to the toolbox.

M. Note-taking

6.56 Reference has been made in Chapter 5 to the mediator's role of note-taking during the party statements.[33] During the rest of the mediation most mediators take only brief notes despite the fact that it is rare for proceedings to be recorded and a transcript to be produced. The following notes would ordinarily be required at the different stages of the process:

■ *Preliminaries*: names of parties and advisers, time of commencement, special conditions for mediation, nature of queries by parties during this stage.

■ *Mediator's opening statement*: important matters dealt with, such as confidentiality, separate meetings – can be checked off on a list.

■ *Party statements*: main concerns, important facts, some record of feelings.

■ *List of issues*: the mediator should keep a separate list in case that on the whiteboard is erased or changed.

■ *Negotiation stages*: settlement options, concessions, acknowledgments, apologies, figures and amounts, sequence and timing of offers and counter-offers.

■ *Separate meetings*: time of start and conclusion, exact offers if they are to be communicated by mediator, record of matters to be kept confidential.

N. Exchange of information

6.57 Mediators play a pivotal role in conveying information, proposals and offers, whilst maintaining the integrity of the neutral role, and preserving confidentiality. The exchange of information by the mediator involves clarifying what each party wants to be conveyed, assisting them to couch the exchange in appropriate language, and to ensure the accurate, strategic and effective relay of that information.

Accordingly, information exchange involves the following mediator skills:

■ careful listening;

■ checking the information being given and referring it back to the party giving it to ensure accuracy;

---

33   See 5.28–5.29.

- checking confidentiality;
- checking authority to exchange;
- clarifying the ambit of the authority to exchange;
- coaching parties on the exchange – its purpose and possible effects or implications, the language to be used, and the timing of the exchange;
- framing and reframing of the language;
- timing of exchange;
- preparation of the mediator for the exchange – the mediator is not a mere messenger, and aims to skilfully and strategically impart information;
- consideration of tone to be used in the exchange;
- effective presentation skills.

Information collation, disclosure and information exchange have an additional dimension in certain contexts, like family mediation. For example, mediators are required to inform parties of the need for full and frank disclosure, in particular in relation to financial matters and property, and to assist them to identify the relevant information and request any relevant documentation.[34] Mediators have no obligation to make independent enquiries or to undertake verification. They may assist parties as to the ways in which parties may make such enquiries.[35]

O. Tasking

6.58 Throughout a mediation, the mediator may task each party in order to assist the progress of the negotiations, For example, the mediator may task the parties to consider:

- the strong and weak points in a party's legal case;
- the uncertainties at trial;
- the cost implications of going to trial;
- other implications of the matter not settling at mediation;
- the pros and cons of settling and of going to trial;
- the range of options;
- the alternatives available;
- objective criteria;
- obtaining or reviewing figures;
- obtaining advice or technical or other reports and documentation;
- clarifying authority;

---

34   See, for example, sections 6.14 and 6.16 College of Mediators Code of Practice (in Appendix 8).
35   See, for example, section 5.7 Law Society Code of Practice for Family Mediation (in Appendix 8). Refer also to 8.6–8.7.

- formulating offers or concessions and the wording of any acknowledgements;

- making a visual presentation to assist a joint meeting.

Where the mediator tasks a party, it is important to ensure that the results of the task are picked up in a subsequent meeting with that party and not forgotten.

P. Drafting

6.59 As referred to in Chapter 5,[36] most mediated agreements are recorded in writing. Practice varies as to whether mediated agreements are drafted by mediators or by the parties and their advisers. In both situations, mediators require drafting skills, whether as drafters, advisers or supervisors to those doing the drafting.

The principles which mediators need to take account of in relation to their drafting function, and some specific drafting and content issues are outlined in Chapters 5 and 10.[37]

Q. Summary

6.60 This chapter raises the following points of particular significance:

- Mediators have important communication functions, in particular, in modelling appropriate mediation language, modifying inappropriate words and terms, being attentive to the many forms of communication taking place and making their own communication clear, unambiguous and consistent.

- The mediator's communication functions have the goal of opening up the channels of communication between the parties, allowing them to communicate directly with each other and avoiding ambiguity and confusion in their dialogue.

- All communication skills, in particular non-verbal communication, are dependent on the cultural assumptions and understandings of the parties involved in mediation.

R. Tasks for beginner mediators

6.61 Develop a list of terms and words associated with conflict in your professional practice, work, educational institution or home. Write out at least two positive replacement terms for the negative words or phrases, and ask someone to assess their suitability. Try using the replacement terms in your particular situation.

6.62 Assume that an insurer's lawyer attempts to ask clarifying and probing questions of the claimant. You as the mediator are concerned that this might lead to a hostile interrogation. What procedures could you use to allow the lawyer to ask legitimate questions without the claimant being cross-examined?

---

36   See 5.69.
37   See 5.71, 10.74–10.77 and Appendix 4.

6.63   Form pairs and have one person begin talking about a subject of interest to them. The other person should match the speaker's body language (for example, fold their arms when the speaker folds their arms; smile when the speaker smiles, without parroting). After a few minutes, swap roles. At the end of this exercise both speaker and imitator should discuss what effect non-verbal communication can have on a conversation.

S.   Recommended reading

Adachi Y., 'The Effects of Semantic Difference on Cross-cultural Business Negotiation: a Japanese and American Case Study', in (1998) 9 *Journal of Language for International Business* 43.

Adair W., 'Integrative Sequences and Outcome in Same and Mixed-culture Negotiations', in (2003) 14 *International Journal of Conflict Management* 273.

Adler Ronald B., and Rodman George, *Understanding Human Communication*, 5th ed, Harcourt Brace College, Fort Worth, 1994.

Avruch K., *Culture and Conflict Resolution*, Institute of Peace, Washington DC, 1998.

Bolton R., *People Skills: How to Assert Yourself, Listen to others, and Resolve Conflict*, Simon and Schuster Australia, Sydney, 1987.

Boulle L. and Nesic M., *Mediation: Principles Process Practice*, Tottel Publishing, 2001, 201–217.

Charlton R., *Dispute Resolution Guidelines*, LBC Information Services, Sydney, 2000, Ch 5.

Charlton R. and Dewdney M., *The Mediator's Handbook: Skills and Strategies for Practitioners*, 2nd ed, Lawbook Co, Sydney, 2004, Ch 10.

Cohen R., *Negotiating Across Cultures*, Institute of Peace, Washington DC, 1991.

Covey S. R., *The Seven Habits of Highly Effective People: Restoring the Character Ethic*, The Business Library, Melbourne, 1989.

Crano W. D. and Prislin R., 'Attitudes and Persuasion', in (2006) 57 *Annual Review of Psychology* 345.

Egan G., *The Skilled Helper: A Problem Management Approach to Helping*, 8th ed, Brooks/Cole Publishing Co, 2006, Chs 4–6.

Folberg J. and Taylor A., *Mediation: A Comprehensive Guide to Resolving Conflicts without Litigation*, Jossey-Bass, San Francisco, 1984, Ch 5.

Goh Bee Chen, *Negotiating with the Chinese*, Dartmouth Publishing Co, Brookfield, 1996.

Hofstede G., *Culture and Organisations: Software of the Mind*, 2nd ed, McGraw-Hill, New York, 2005.

Moore C., *The Mediation Process: Practical Strategies for Resolving Conflict*, 3rd ed, John Wiley and Son/Jossey-Bass, San Francisco, 2003, Ch 7.

Pease A., *Body Language: How to Read others' Thoughts by their Gestures*, Camel Publishing Co, Avalon Beach, 2001.

Pease A., *The Definitive Book on Body Language*, Bantam Books, New York, 2006.

Roberts M., *Developing the Craft of Mediation: Reflections on Theory and Practice*, Jessica Kingsley Publishers, 2007.

Rothschild, J. H. Dispute Transformation, the Influence of a Communication Paradigm of Disputing, and the San Francisco Community Boards Program, in Engle Merry, S. and Milner, N. (eds), *The Possibility of Popular Justice: A Case Study of Community Mediation in the United States*, University of Michigan Press, Ann Arbor, 1995.

Schon and Rein, *Frame Reflection: Toward the Resolution of Intractable Policy Controversies*, Basic Books, New York, 1994.

Slaikeu K. A., *When Push Comes to Shove: A Practical Guide to Mediating Disputes*, Jossey-Bass, San Francisco, 1996.

Spegel, Rogers and Buckley, *Negotiation: Theory and Techniques*, Butterworths, Sydney, 1998, Ch 8.

Stone D., Patton B. and Heen S., *Difficult Conversations: How to Discuss What Matters Most*, Penguin Books, New York, 1999.

Wertheim E., Love A., Peck C. and Littlefield L., *Skills for Resolving Conflict*, Eruditions Publishing, Victoria, 1998.

Chapter 7

Facilitating the Negotiations

Two heads are better than one

A. Introduction

7.1   Mediation is often defined as a form of assisted negotiation; the mediation process is portrayed as an extension and elaboration of the unassisted negotiation process. This suggests that the mediator is not a negotiator in the direct sense, but is able to use his or her negotiation expertise to improve the negotiations that the parties are undertaking. If there are any 'golden rules' for contemporary mediators one would be that they need to become aware of both the 'art' and the 'science' of negotiation in order to perform their role adequately.

7.2   This chapter deals with the mediator's role as facilitator of the parties' negotiations. As with the previous chapter, the present one provides only a brief overview of general negotiation strategies and styles and deals mainly with the particular role of the mediator in the negotiation process. More insights into negotiation itself can be gained from the specialist literature on this subject, from training courses, and from reflecting on real negotiation experiences. Mediators are privileged observers of negotiation practice conducted by the parties and their advisers.

How mediators use their negotiation expertise to assist the parties is not a straightforward matter. It is a subtle and demanding mediator skill requiring a balance between strong intervention and 'benign neglect'.[1]

B. On negotiation generally

The stages of negotiation

7.3   The stages of negotiation are only described in brief overview here, with the important disclaimer that negotiation is often not a strict sequential process and, in any particular negotiation, one or more of the stages may be missed or come at an unpredictable time. Furthermore, the existence of the stages, and their sequence, will depend partly on which 'style' of negotiation the parties adopt.

---

1   Haynes and Haynes, *Mediating Divorce*, 1989, 46.

7.4   Notwithstanding these qualifications, it is still possible to list the potential stages of negotiation:

- *Initial process decisions*: these are the 'who', 'where', 'when' and 'what' matters, namely the identification of the negotiation parties, the venue, the timing and the topics to be negotiated. Behaviour during this stage can affect later stages; successful agreements on process issues (where the mediation will be held and when) can provide a sound platform for later negotiations on content issues (the money, the barking dog, the children, the apology).

- *Opening rituals*: negotiation can have its own rituals, which depend very much on culture and context. In some situations there may be extensive inter-personal rituals involving the exchange of pleasantries, refreshments, and symbolic acts of acknowledgment, and in others there may be only brief greetings and handshakes and perfunctory small-talk, after which the parties proceed directly to business.

- *Exchange of information and views*: this refers to the mutual exchange of stories, information, data and perspectives by all the parties. Sometimes this occurs in concentrated form in the beginning of the negotiations; in others it is interspersed throughout the process.

- *Development of the issues*: this refers to the process of defining what is and what is not to be negotiated over, especially where this has not been resolved beforehand and the circumstances either do not make it self-evident or render it a matter of contention.

- *Opening and signalling*: this refers to the voicing of demands and claims, often involving financial sums, and the surrounding signalling designed to reinforce the claim or indicate that it is only an initial position. There may be some tactical manoeuvring between the parties over who makes the opening bid; and regarding the level of the opening offer.

- *Development and exploration of options*: this involves the parties considering possible ways of dealing with the problem facing them; again, this can be a dynamic creative process or a limited and narrow one.

- *Evaluation and selection of options*: here the parties assess the value of the various options from their own points of view or in terms of agreed standards, and select those of potential relevance to them. Alternatives to reaching agreement are also considered. The risks associated with different approaches and outcomes are assessed.

- *Bargaining from options*: here each party attempts to persuade the other side to accept their preferred options and attempts to package a deal involving linkages and trade-offs favourable to them. Strategies for breaking impasses are used.

- *Crossing the last gap*: this refers to dealing with the last amount of value still to be negotiated over, where the parties frequently haggle over who will make the final concession.

- *Recording and documentation*: here the parties reduce the agreement to some form of written document and decide on other relevant matters.

- *Termination and closure*: here the parties conclude the negotiations and go their (usually) separate ways.

As already indicated, there is no A–Z of negotiation, and even if there was, some negotiations would only include steps K, Q and W. Nevertheless the mediator needs to be aware of the various possible stages of negotiation in order to be able to assist the parties as they work through the process.

Styles of negotiation

7.5   There are different styles of negotiation with relevant terms to refer to the different styles. Different terminology is used to refer to these different styles. As this is not a text on negotiation itself, particular reference is made to two broad styles of negotiation, namely positional bargaining and interest-based bargaining, as a basis for discussing the role of the mediator within each style.

The two styles are not, however, mutually exclusive and a single negotiation may display elements of both. The styles are described, illustrated and assessed in the table below:

Positional and interest-based negotiation			
Style of negotiation	*Some features*	*Some advantages*	*Some disadvantages*
Positional also known as • Solution • Competitive • Distributive	Extreme opening offers	May require little preparation	May not be efficient in exploiting all potential value
	A process of incremental concession-making by the parties	Relatively easy to perform	
		Culturally understood in many contexts	May escalate the conflict with inexperienced negotiators
	Compromise somewhere between opening positions	Does not require many resources	May overlook key interests which would permit settlement
		Initially impresses client when used by professional adviser	
	Accompanied by competitive tactics (bluffs, lies, threats and tricks) designed to 'create doubt' in mind of other party		Parties may not be able to cross the 'last gap'
		Allows each side to track concessions of other side	
		Can be successful for more powerful party	Could damage parties' relationship and leave long-term bitterness
	If not adequate concessions by parties, there is no settlement		

Interest-based			
Also known as • Collaborative • Integrative • Constructive	Focused on parties' personal and commercial needs and interests	Deals with real needs and interests of the parties	Requires extensive, uncommon skills
		No competitive tactics to create problems	Needs time and resources
	Avoids extreme positional claims		May create image of weakness
	Involves search for additional 'chips' over which to negotiate	Likely to retain or improve parties' relationship	May require disclosure of sensitive information
		Possibility of creative settlements	
	Attempts to achieve creative, mutually-beneficial outcomes		Could lead to exploitation if other party is positional
		Aims to maximise value at the negotiation table	May still leave a 'last gap' which is difficult to cross

The additional 'chips' or value adding referred to in the table above may include, for example:

- identifying shared goals or interests to encourage the parties to move on to identify options to meet those goals or interests;

- searching for differences in priorities or timeframes, which can be used to facilitate a trade-off;

- allocation of risk depending on each party's level of risk tolerance.[2]

More detail on the elements and dynamics of the two styles of bargaining follows in the discussion of the mediator's role in negotiations.

C.   The mediator's role in negotiations

7.6   Mediators can assist the parties with their negotiations before the mediation, during the joint sessions, during the separate sessions and shuttle stages, during the closing stages, and even after the mediation has been terminated. They can educate, advise, demonstrate, coach and rehearse. How they go about these tasks involves the use of discretion, some important judgements and a sense of timing. For instance, there are clearly restrictions on what can be done in joint sessions, while there is greater latitude for the mediator in separate sessions. There will also be some trial and error as the mediator revises or refines the hypothesis on which an intervention was made in the light of its impact and effectiveness.

In most negotiations there will be some scope for the mediator to assist the parties in:

- Planning and preparing to negotiate – usually via the pre-mediation contact. Guidance should be specific; plans should be simple and tailored to the particular

---

2   Refer to R. Mnookin and others, *Beyond Winning: Negotiating to Create Value in Deals and Disputes*, Belknap Press, Cambridge Mass., 2000.

mediation; and flexibility will be required given that preparation will occur in the context of incomplete information.

■ Avoiding a narrow approach to negotiation, whilst preserving the parties' confidences and remaining impartial.

■ Developing cohesive strategies within negotiation teams.

■ Moving through the rituals and other opening stages.

■ Avoiding the difficulties of negotiation tactics, such as different sized chairs, planned interruptions, or the 'no authority' strategy.

■ Emphasising common ground between the parties to provide a positive tone to the negotiations and a platform for further agreement.

■ Getting the parties to deal with the 'easy' issues first, for example, sorting out basic facts or documentation.

■ Coaching parties on negotiation skills and techniques, for example, the pros and cons of making the first offer; the level of offers and concessions; helping the parties to consider numbers in different ways; helping parties to assess the alternatives to settlement; and managing their expectations about the process and likely outcomes.

■ Anticipating post-settlement blues (subsequent regrets about the agreement) and advising on ways of dealing with this syndrome.

■ Considering strategies for dealing with outside parties who need to ratify agreements or who could jeopardise their success.

7.7   Thus, regardless of the style of negotiation, it is often useful to negotiate about procedural matters first before moving on to matters of substance. This makes practical sense in that matters of venue, timing, identity of participants and other process issues need to be sorted out before the negotiations proper begin. But more than this, decision-making on these issues gives the parties opportunities to find out about each other's styles, to have some early negotiation successes, and to develop confidence in their ability to negotiate successfully with each other.

The mediator can encourage this emphasis on 'procedure first'. Likewise, in most styles of negotiation it makes sense to deal with the 'easier' substantive issues first, and to postpone the more difficult issues for later. Again the mediator can guide or educate the parties about this reality of the negotiation process.

The mediator's more specific roles can be best described in the context of a discussion of the two styles of negotiation referred to in the previous section.

D.   Role in positional bargaining

7.8   The table above refers to some of the features of positional or distributive bargaining. This style of negotiation is commonly encountered in mediations which involve deciding 'who gets what' in relation to money, shares, chattels and other benefits whose number or quantity are restricted in one way or another. In this kind of negotiation there are limited compatible or mutual interests, and the more one side obtains the less the other will receive. It is the 'more for you must mean less for me' scenario. These situations are referred to as 'zero-sum' disputes – if you add the gain of one party to the loss of the other party, it will equal zero. Positional bargaining is often encountered in buying and selling in the market bazaar, and in dispute situations in which is there is no future relationship between the parties.

7.9 The typical pattern of positional bargaining is depicted in the following diagrams.

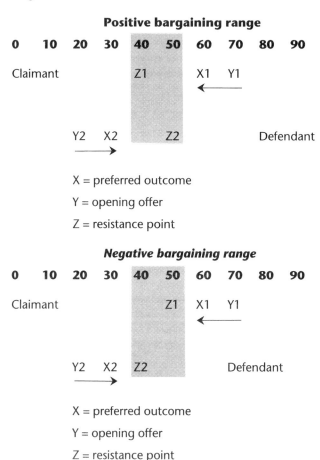

Positive bargaining range

| 0 | 10 | 20 | 30 | 40 | 50 | 60 | 70 | 80 | 90 |

Claimant   Z1   X1   Y1
                                     ←

        Y2   X2   Z2   Defendant
        ——→

X = preferred outcome

Y = opening offer

Z = resistance point

Negative bargaining range

| 0 | 10 | 20 | 30 | 40 | 50 | 60 | 70 | 80 | 90 |

Claimant   Z1 X1   Y1
                                ←

        Y2   X2 Z2   Defendant
        ——→

X = preferred outcome

Y = opening offer

Z = resistance point

The distance between the two resistance points Z1 and Z2 constitutes the *bargaining range*. There can be a *positive bargaining range* (as in the first diagram above), in which case there is likely to be an outcome through positional bargaining. Alternatively, there can be a *negative bargaining range* (as in the second diagram above), in which case there is unlikely to be a settlement through positional bargaining, unless one or both parties change their resistance point.

Lewicki, Barry and Saunders make various propositions referring to the effect of the resistence point on distributive bargaining. For example:

- The higher a party's estimate of the cost to another party of delay or impasse, the stronger will be their resistence point.

- The higher a party's estimate of their own cost of delay or impasse, the weaker their resistence point will be.

- The less value a party places on an issue, the lower will be their resistence point.[3]

Characteristics of positional bargaining

7.10 There are several predictable characteristics of positional bargaining.

Extreme opening offers

Both parties make extreme opening offers (points Y1 and Y2 in the diagrams above), in the expectation that this will impose pressure on the other side, allow them to keep something up their sleeves with which to trade and bargain, and lead to a more favourable point of compromise. Studies show that in many cases an extreme positional demand (ambit claim) at the beginning, provided it does not fall in the 'insult zone', which will result in the other party leaving the negotiating table, will result in a better outcome for that party.

Incremental concessions

There will be a series of 'incremental concessions' from each side, sometimes referred to as a 'negotiation dance'. This involves each party making a number of concessions on their original position, and on each subsequent position, until they reach agreement (somewhere between points Z1 and Z2 on the first diagram) or until they refuse to concede any further and fail to settle (somewhere between points Z1 and Z2 on the second diagram above).

In an attempt to influence the other side to back off their opening position, and each succeeding position, the parties use a range of tactics, including stonewalls, threats, anger, intimidation, ridicule and tricks (sometimes referred to as the LBT factors – lies, bluffs and tricks). Parties will use these tactics, where they have the aptitude, power and incentive to do so, in order to 'create doubt' in the mind of the other party. Where there is an inequality of bargaining power these tactics may be highly successful for the more powerful party in achieving an outcome close to their own X point. The weaker or more vulnerable party makes concessions as a result of the pressures and tactics applied by the other side, as they change their perceptions of their negotiation prospects and their own best interests.

7.11 While there is no uniformity in concession making, the following patterns can occur:

- *Matching*: this often occurs at the beginning of concession making, where each side matches the other's concessions (for example, Party A concedes £5,000, Party B concedes £5,000), and at the end of the negotiations, where parties are prepared to match each other by 'splitting the difference'.[4]

---

3   Lewicki, Barry and Saunders, *Negotiation*, 6th ed, McGraw Hill International, New York, 2010.
4   See 7.70.

- *Mismatching*: this occurs where there is an impasse in the negotiations, and the weaker party, or party more in need of a settlement, makes a large concession to prevent the negotiations from failing and the other side, sensing 'victory', makes a smaller one (for example, Party A concedes £5,000 and Party B concedes only £1,000).

- *Decreasing increments*: this means that each successive concession is smaller than the previous one (for example, £2,000, £1,000, £500), and usually takes longer to obtain ('half the size, twice the time' is seen in practice), though occasionally the successive increments are of equal size (for example, £1,000, £1,000, £1,000).

Signalling

7.12   The pattern and sequence of concessions involves a form of *signalling* between the parties in that they convey to each party some insight into the other's intentions. Thus a series of equal concessions (for example, £10,000, £10,000 and £10,000) suggests that further concessions can be anticipated, while diminishing concessions (£10,000, £6,000 and £2,000) suggest that the relevant party is reaching its resistance point (Z1 or Z2 on the diagrams above). Of course there is no science to this kind of prediction and it is indicative only of the way the negotiations might develop.

There may be a 'last gap' which is difficult, and in some cases impossible, to bridge. This can be because each party feels that it has conceded too much already, neither party wants to make the final concession, and both are concerned about 'losing face'. The last gap is depicted by the negative bargaining range between points Z1 and Z2 in the second diagram above.[5]

The context and benefits of positional bargaining

7.13   There are several reasons why parties might engage in positional bargaining in certain contexts. The system has deep cultural roots in that it is the pattern of negotiation encountered in the marketplace, for example, in buying a house or car. It is a system of negotiation which can be conducted with little preparation and which does not assume any educational background or require any special skills. Once commenced, positional bargaining is difficult to get out of, as it is a *reactive* model of negotiating with continual 'tit-for-tat' exchanges between the parties. It also has some short-term emotional advantages where there is a need to appear strong and forceful to the opposition.

7.14   Where parties are in competition with each other over scarce resources, it is entirely logical for them to make extreme opening claims (points X1 and X2 on the diagrams above) and to be secretive and uncompromising in the negotiations. If they are not as extreme as possible at the beginning of the negotiations, the chances of their having conceded too much by the end are increased. Positional bargaining appears to make sense in terms of protecting each party's interests and information. In a competitive situation it does not make sense to disclose information unilaterally, to make concessions and to be exploited.

---

5   See 7.69.

This is illustrated in a negotiation exercise called 'The Prisoner's Dilemma' which is played at many mediation workshops; it shows that where one party is collaborative (interest-based) and the other is competitive (positional), the former will lose out. In order to avoiding losing, the collaborative party is likely to resort to competitive strategies as well; but where both parties adopt competitive strategies they both lose out. The object of the exercise is to discover ways of getting both parties to engage in collaborative bargaining which serves both their interests simultaneously and leaves them both better off than if they had bargained competitively.

7.15   As already indicated, positional negotiation is typically used where there is little likelihood of a future relationship between the parties. This includes personal injury disputes, dissolution of partnerships, building disputes and debt claims. It can also be more likely where the negotiating parties are using intermediaries such as lawyers, or where they have to appear tough in the eyes of outside persons, such as managers and trade union officials in industrial disputes, and council tax payers in planning and development disputes.

The role of mediators in positional bargaining

7.16   Mediators may be able to intervene in some aspects of positional or distributive bargaining (some of these interventions might also be appropriate for interest-based bargaining).

Making the first offer

7.17   There are different views as to the benefits and shortcomings of making the first offer in positional bargaining. Assume, in the following illustrations, that the parties are bargaining over the price of a used car, a classic positional bargaining situation.

7.18   Where a party wishes to establish one end of the bargaining range they may decide to make the first offer and attempt to influence the other side by making it as extreme as the circumstances will allow. This can have an 'anchoring' effect on the perceptions of the other side, and influence them to make a less extreme opening offer than intended. Thus the seller of the car might reflect, 'I was going to ask £2,000 for this lemon of a car, but they got in first and offered only £800 so perhaps it would be wiser for me to ask for £1,600.' It can also serve to detract attention from weak issues, with the view that these will be wrapped up as part of the ultimate deal. If an opening offer is too extreme, there is a risk that the other party will 'walk away' or will attempt to re-anchor by an equally extreme response.

7.19   Some parties will resist making the first offer as they wish to work out what their opening should be in the light of the other side's opening bid. They therefore wait for the other side to make the first offer so that they can calculate at what level they should open so as to make the point of final compromise more favourable to them than to the other party. Thus, the seller could reason, 'They only offered £800, so now I know that I should begin at £1,800 and not £1,600 so that I have more up my sleeve with which to force up the price.' Which of these differing approaches a party adopts will be determined by a number of factors, including their perception of how powerful they are in relation to the other.

7.20   Mediators may have no control over who makes the opening offer in a mediation. However, they need to be aware of the different approaches and tactics which may be operating. Normally, there is not a problem in having one of the parties make the first offer in positional bargaining. Occasionally both parties adopt the delay strategy, the defendant saying, 'Tell me first what you want', and the claimant saying, 'Well tell me first what you are prepared to offer.' Where neither is prepared to begin, some mediators suggest that both parties give their first offers confidentially to the mediator, without knowing what the other is offering, and the mediator then exchanges them between the parties at the same time. In this arrangement there are no 'first' offers, only two simultaneous offers with neither affected by the other.

The type of opening offer

7.21   Before referring to the various types of opening offers in positional bargaining, it is useful to elaborate on two concepts referred to above, namely the 'insult zone' and the 'credible zone'. In the above diagrams above, the 'insult zone' refers to points above the Z point of the claimant and below the Z point of the respondent which would be insulting to the other party. Thus a claimant may say to a respondent who makes an opening offer in the insult zone, 'You have offered me so little that it is a joke; I am leaving, let me know when you are serious.' The 'credible' zone begins where the insult zone ends, though there can clearly be no precise point of differentiation between the two.

7.22   There are two ways in which parties can open positional negotiations:

■ With *high/soft* or *low/soft* opening offers, where a party's opening offer is as far from their preferred outcome (the points X1 and X2 in the diagrams above) and as close to the insult zone as possible (the points Y1 and Y2). Here the expectation is that both parties will move off their high/low opening offers to a series of more reasonable positions during the course of the negotiation – in this sense their first offers, whether high or low, contain 'soft' numbers.

■ With *reasonable/firm* opening offers, where a party's opening offer is close to both their preferred outcome and resistance point (that is, the relevant party's X, Y and Z points are close together). Because this is regarded as a reasonable proposal by the relevant party they stick to it firmly and there is little scope for concessions in the negotiation. In this sense, the figures contained in the offer are 'firm'.

7.23   There are several potential roles for mediators in relation to the types of opening offers. They can educate the parties about the different kinds of openings and explain their implications. Thus a claimant who has made a high/soft offer needs to understand why the reasonable/firm approach of the other side leaves the impression that she is making all the concessions and feels as though she is negotiating against herself (see case illustration below). Mediators can point out to the parties the problems of opening in the insult zone, for example, that it may cause the other party to walk out, or give them the reputation of negotiators whose first offers need not be taken seriously, or it is likely to lead to an opening insulting offer from the other party. Mediators can further educate clients who are unfamiliar with the low/soft strategies of some large defendants, such as insurers and governments, to advise them not to allow this to exacerbate the conflict: 'I can see you are aggrieved by their offer, and don't worry, the ABC Insurance Company always start like that; if you hang in for a while, in my experience, they are likely to improve their offer.'

Case illustration – 'reasonable firm' approach

A dissolution of partnership mediation was conducted between the partners, Chris and Robert. Chris began the positional bargaining with a high/soft claim of 55% of the value of the assets and made three incremental concessions in moving down to 45%. Robert commenced with a claim of 58% and had not moved from this position at all. During a separate session with the mediator Chris complained about the lack of movement from Robert and about the fact that he had been 'negotiating against myself'. The mediator explained that Robert was operating under the 'reasonable/firm' system and this made the situation at least understandable to Chris. They both made some further small concessions and settled.

To avoid this problem mediators can educate parties who are adopting the reasonable/firm approach to signal this fact, for example, by saying 'After careful consideration, and in light of all the circumstances I am asking for 58% of the assets because …' Some lawyers hold themselves out as reasonable/firm negotiators who only ever make 'one offer'.

The timing of offers and acceptances

7.24   There is a negotiation saying that, 'The right offer at the wrong time is the wrong offer'. Despite being rather simplistic, the maxim is useful to bear in mind. Where a negotiating party receives a 'favourable' offer too early in positional bargaining there is a tendency to devalue what the other side has offered (called 'reactive devaluation') and to attempt to secure something additional from the negotiations. This might involve them backtracking and trying to recover even more than they initially sought. Thus in the used car example above, if the purchaser were to offer the seller the ticket price of £1,800 immediately on seeing the car, the seller might decide that he had asked for too little and should have asked for more: 'I was going to accept £1,500 but the offer of £1,800 suggests the car is more valuable than I thought.' The seller's reaction might be to explain that of course the price did not include the tyres, for which he would require an extra amount.

7.25   The same principle applies to the acceptance of offers. Where an offer is, in the perception of the offeror, accepted too eagerly by the offeree the former may likewise have second thoughts about the wisdom of their offer and attempt to complicate the dispute in other ways. Thus in the used car example, if the purchaser offered £800 and this was immediately accepted by the seller, the former might become suspicious about the quality of the vehicle: 'He seemed to jump at that offer rather quickly, perhaps I should take things a bit more cautiously here.'

We have encountered commercial negotiators who, in conscious or unconscious application of the above maxim, deliberately idle away some time before making or accepting offers. They are waiting for the timing to be 'ripe'. While this is hardly an exact science, mediators can discuss with the parties the possible implications of making offers or accepting them at particular times in the negotiations.

Ways of responding to claims and offers

7.26 Negotiations are complicated systems of actions, reactions and interactions. Where a negotiating party is unhappy with a claim or offer there is a risk that he or she will react in a retaliatory way and exacerbate the conflict. Thus in the mediation involving Chris and Robert, referred to in the preceding box, Robert's claim for 58% of the assets could invoke a strongly negative reaction from Chris. The mediator can adopt strategies to avoid problems in situations such as these and can assist a party to make the rejection of an offer in a constructive way. Thus the mediator may suggest that the response be made in a way that identifies the level of principle at which there is agreement, before rejecting the detail: 'You are entitled to more than I am, but I cannot agree to 58% at this stage.'

Alternatively, where there is only a partial rejection, the form of the response could identify first the areas of agreement and then specify what is being rejected: 'I can agree to you getting 50%, but am not happy with giving you more.' Mediators can also coach the parties in the art of informing each other *why* an offer is being rejected so that the rejection can be better understood: 'The reasons I cannot agree to 58% are that I don't accept the way you are valuing the business or your contributions to it.' The reasons provide an indication of what the claimant needs to work on (in the last example, the valuations), in order to persuade the offeree to accept.

Ways of packaging offers and presenting offers

7.27 Because of the difficulties referred to in the previous section, mediators should consider assisting the parties to package offers and counter-offers in the most constructive way in the first place, in order to avoid negative reactions from the other party in the second place:

- For the reasons already explained, any offer should be accompanied by an explanation and not consist of cold hard figures alone. The explanation serves to give some 'rationality' to the offer and creates an opening for the offeree should they wish to respond constructively to it. A person is more likely to listen to another when reasons or explanations to rationalise the offer are given before the offer.

- The offer should be packaged in such a way that the most palatable parts are heard or seen first and those least attractive to the other side are presented last. This is sometimes referred to as 'gift wrapping' the offer and is particularly feasible where the mediator is shuttling offers and counter-offers between the parties when they are in separate rooms. Thus the mediator in private session might say, 'Robert, when I take to Chris your claim for 58% of the assets, it would assist if I could first indicate what you agree with in relation to his arguments over his contributions and valuations, before disclosing to him your actual figure.'

Patterns of concession-making

7.28 Reference has been made above to some of the patterns of concession-making in positional bargaining. It was indicated that where the concessions are equal in size, more might be expected, whereas where they are decreasing in size, that party might be reaching their limit. Where a larger concession follows smaller ones, this might indicate a last desperate attempt by the conceding party (or mere confusion).

Mediators should always keep a written record of the parties' concessions. They can be the honest keepers of accurate figures. This will assist them assess the extent to which the parties might be approaching their resistance points. It can also be used to show one party how much the other has conceded – it is a common feature of negotiations that each party feels that they have conceded more than the other and objective facts and figures can be used to challenge this perception. In the above scenario the mediator might say, 'You may not realise it, Robert, but Chris has moved down from a 55% claim at the beginning of the mediation to one of 45% now'.

It is part of a mediator's function to coach the parties on the signals that might be sent with concessions made, patterns of concession making, the appropriate timing for concessions and the trade-off potential with concession making.[6]

Dealing with the tactics of positional bargaining

7.29   Mediators need to be familiar with the predictable tactics associated with positional or distributive bargaining. As suggested earlier, these include:

■ Intimidation or threats by the more powerful party: 'Robert, if you don't become more reasonable, I'll call in the lawyers and take you to court.'

■ Stonewalling and refusal to make concessions: 'Chris, my offer is eminently fair and reasonable and under no circumstances am I going to offer you another penny.'

■ Data manipulation regarding facts, figures, evidence and other relevant factors: 'Robert, the goodwill in the business has dropped by 50% because of the new competition in the industry and my accountant's assessment of the impact of the latest tax changes.'

■ Last minute add-ons, where a negotiator makes a request on an item that has not been discussed before: 'I'll sign the agreement now, Chris, but only if you pay all my costs.'

■ The 'phantom' trade, in which a negotiator pretends that an issue of little importance to them is of great value when conceded: 'Well, I really wanted the office sofa, Chris, but I suppose I'll let you have it if you give me the business vehicle.'

■ A deliberate claim of lack of authority, aimed at imposing pressure or gaining an adjournment: 'Well, that looks fine in principle, Robert, but I first need to consult my advisers, who couldn't attend today.'

■ The 'take it or leave it' ultimatum or threat of a walk out: 'If the agreement doesn't include payment of my costs, Robert, I'll try my luck in court'.

---

6   See T. O'Connor, *Planning and Executing an Effective Concession Strategy*, Bay Group International, 2003.

7.30   As with their other functions in the mediation process, mediators have a range of tools in their toolboxes for dealing with these tactics. It will be a question of judgement as to which is appropriate, and there can never be any certainty that a specific intervention will work. Mediators need to use the strengths of the mediation process and their understanding of negotiation to attempt to counteract the use of these tactics. By way of example, they might:

- Recognise the tactic and its implication and potential effect.

- Point out the downsides of a particular strategy, particularly in the separate sessions: 'Chris, in my experience those kinds of threats normally make the other side even more resistant.' 'Chris, in my experience, that's likely to be countered by an equally bullish response.'

- Anticipate some of the tactics and pre-empt them by alerting the parties generally to their possibility: 'Chris and Robert, we are getting closer to agreement and in order to prevent any late surprises, could you advise each other at this point whether you wish to raise any matters not already on the agenda.'

- Enforce the mediation guidelines and intervene strongly when they are breached: 'I have mentioned before that mediation works best when you speak one at a time and avoid personal attacks. Can you both recommit to those principles?'

- Identify the tactic ('name the game') as a way of shaming the relevant party: 'Robert, that deal over the sofa and the business vehicle sounds like a phantom trade to me. Do you think it's wise to persist with it?'

- Use separate meetings to ascertain how the targeted party is dealing with the other's tactics: 'Chris, Robert seems to be stonewalling now, how are you feeling about that and what can you do about it?'

- Ask for a party's reasoning for a tactic; or how a demand, stance, postion or offer is supported or rationalised. Probe for details.

- Encourage interest-based negotiation techniques.

- Remind parties of progress made and their aims and objectives. Assist the parties to assess the alternatives should agreement not be reached at mediation.

Creating doubt

7.31   While the mediator is not negotiating as such with the parties, he or she may become involved in the 'doubt creation' tactics associated with positional bargaining. The object of creating doubt in a negotiating party's mind is to cause them to move off their current positional claim to one which is more likely to result in settlement. There can be doubt creation over the facts, over evidence, over rules and precedents, over likely court outcomes, and even over the personality and behaviour of the other party. This is also referred to as the mediator acting as the 'agent of reality'. Some of the ways in which the mediator can exercise the doubt creation, or reality testing, function are considered in Chapter 8.[7]

---

7   See 8.14–8.16 and refer to risk analysis guide in Appendix 6. See J. Wade, 'Persuasion in negotiation and mediation', in (2007) 10(1) *ADR Bulletin* 8.

E. Role in promoting interest-based bargaining

7.32   Much mediator training and mediation literature focuses on the roles and functions of mediators in shifting the parties' negotiations away from positional and towards interest-based bargaining. Mediation shares the same assumptions as this form of negotiation, and some mediator guidelines require mediators to promote 'interest-based bargaining'.

Interest-based negotiation is encountered in mediations involving partnership conflicts, business disputes, organisational conflict, planning disputes and parenting disputes, and in many other situations in which there is an ongoing relationship between the parties. Here the mediator's roles are looked at in terms of the concepts developed by Fisher, Ury and Patten.[8]

To aid this approach, mediators typically assist parties to prepare effectively for the negotiations by suggesting that they gather information about matters, like their interests, alternatives, objective standards and the range of possible solutions/ options. Each issue is discussed futher below. A checklist to help mediators with the organisation and oversight of this information is at Appendix 5. Each party can be given a separate worksheet.

Focusing on interests instead of positions

7.33   The following scenario will be used to illustrate points made in this section.

Case illustration

A large corporation, Resources International, supplies raw materials to a medium-sized manufacturer, Home Supplies Ltd, which exports most of its products abroad. Before expiration of the supply contract, Home Supplies indicates that it will make use of an alternative supplier in the future. Resources International immediately stops delivery of raw materials and Home Supplies sues for damages arising from the breach of contract. Both sides agree to mediation, where Resources International is represented by Ms Greene and Home Supplies by Mr White.

7.34   The distinction between the terms 'positions' and 'interests' has been explained already.[9] It was shown that positional claims can easily lead to impasses and can obscure what people really want. Shell points out that skilled negotiators spend up to four times the amont of time thinking about the needs and interests of the other parties than average negotiators.[10] Mediation provides a process in which the focus can be changed to the underlying interests, that is, the motivating needs, desires, concerns and fears of the parties. When the focus shifts to interests, the problem becomes better defined and better understood by all concerned. The

---

8   *Getting to Yes*, 1996. Refer also to Spegel, Rogers and Buckley, *Negotiation: Theory and Techniques*, 1998, on 'constructive negotiation'.
9   See 4.12–4.17.
10   G Richard Shell, *Bargaining for Advantage* (2nd ed 2006), 78.

disclosure of interests also reveals what is really motivating the parties and what is preventing a resolution of the dispute. As people are motivated mainly by self-interest, this approach opens the way to dealing with the dispute creatively in terms of the parties' own priorities.

The main stratagem of interest-based bargaining is to put more 'negotiating chips' on the table[11] or to 'create value' in the negotiations before value is claimed or to 'make the pie bigger before it is cut up'. Doing so avoids the 'negotiator's dilemma' which arises on account of the competition between value creating and claiming techniques (because value claiming impedes the creation of value and value creation risks exploitation by value claiming tactics).[12]

Accordingly, where the parties make positional claims over money, the interest-based approach seeks to disclose the interests underlying that claim and make them objects of negotiation. In the above scenario between Resources International and Home Supplies, the 'chips' could include:

- preservation of a tough image by Resources International;
- Home Supplies being able to deal with its pressing creditors;
- a quick and confidential settlement for both parties;
- reducing opportunity costs for Home Supplies and transaction costs for Resources International;
- keeping open Home Supplies' prospect of future business dealings with Resources International;
- avoiding precedents with other customers for Resources International;
- maintaining face for Home Supplies with overseas customers.

These multiple interests, dealing with the present and the future, provide a more constructive basis for fashioning a negotiated settlement than the single-issue obsession with financial damages.

7.35   The role of the mediator is therefore to try and get the parties to negotiate in terms of their own and each other's interests. One way in which the mediator can get the parties to focus on their interests is to ask them why a position is important to them. He or she can also help the parties to try to persuade each other on the mutual benefits of requests, rather than try to convince the mediator of the justice of their cause. In some cases the mediator might be able to point out why certain settlement options could in fact be in both the parties' interests. Mediators might also resort to 'role reversal', by asking a party to imagine that they are in the position of the other party, as a way for them to identify that other party's interests. This can be uncomfortable for some parties and might be resisted. Explaining the benefits of role reversal might overcome intransigence.

Understanding interests

Understanding interests also requires the mediator to assist the parties to sort and prioritise their interests. By identifying areas of common ground, parties are more

---

11   See 7.5.
12   David A. Lax and James K. Sebenius, *The Manager as Negotiator*, 1987, 38.

likely to work towards proposals that meet those common interests. In the case of divergent interests, or different values placed on the same interests, trade-offs are possible. For example, one party might value the amount of payment, the other the form or timing of payment. In a dispute between a company and one of its departing executives, the company might be willing to pay £100,000 in severance provided that it is payable in shares but less than £100,000 if the severance is paid in cash. If the executive has no preference between cash and shares, both sides benefit from a severance in shares.

Generating creative settlement options

7.36　Mediators can encourage the parties to be creative in fashioning their settlement outcomes. In order to be creative there needs to be a broad consideration of possible settlement options. This involves three facets:

- developing options;

- evaluating options;

- selecting options.

This rarely happens in an orderly textbook fashion but there is an important underlying principle: good negotiation requires expansionary thinking before contractionist thinking takes place. Mediators can educate the parties about this principle and its possible applications. Thus in the distribution of property, in a matrimonial or partnership mediation, a positional approach might lead to a crude 50:50 division, whereas a creative interests approach could allocate specific chattels, assets or other forms of property to the party which places the most value on them.

Developing options

7.37　There are a number of strategies for assisting the parties to be creative in developing options. Thus mediators might use a direct strategy in asking the parties, in the above scenario, 'Ms Greene and Mr White, can you think about and suggest possible options?' They may do it analogously, by asking, 'Mr White and Ms Greene, can you think of ways in which other people have dealt with the problem in question?' Or they may proffer a contribution themselves by saying, 'I can share some creative ideas with you about what others in similar situations have considered …'[13]

There are several factors which might make it difficult for the parties on their own to develop options creatively. One is the assumption that there is only a single answer to the problem, a second is the perception that there is a 'fixed pie' to negotiate over, and a third is the tendency for a party in dispute to judge negatively options mentioned by the other party (called 'negative transference' or 'reactive devaluation').

Brainstorming

7.38　Brainstorming is one technique designed to overcome these obstacles and to assist the parties to think creatively and constructively about settlement.

13　See Haynes and Charlesworth, *The Fundamentals of Family Mediation*, 1996, 41.

The objective of brainstorming is for the parties to develop and consider a wide range of alternatives for resolving the problem at hand. In brainstorming, parties are invited to think creatively and laterally and to propose settlement options, however unrealistic they might be, without having to justify or defend their suggestions. Other parties are not allowed to comment on, evaluate or criticise the option so as to reduce defensiveness and inhibitions and to provide for risk-free ideas without any party being committed to specific proposals. The technique is designed to get the parties to feed off each other's insights and to illustrate the wide number of conceivable ways of dealing with the problem.

Brainstorming guidelines

Guidelines for the *first stage* of brainstorming

1. all ideas, without exception, are allowed;

2. parties are encouraged to feed off one another's ideas;

3. no interruption or criticism of others is permitted;

4. no evaluation or ranking of options is allowed.

Guidelines for the *second stage* of brainstorming

5. categorise the options into relevant groups;

6. develop some interest-based criteria for evaluating them;

7. discard the worst options, in terms of those criteria;

8. undertake a cost–benefit analysis of the best options.

7.39   In the context of a mediation, the mediator can suggest brainstorming as a way of moving forward when the negotiations have bogged down. When the first stage of brainstorming is complete, the options can be evaluated and selected in terms of their desirability, practicality and cost. Even where this brings the parties back to the unpalatable option first thought of, this option is shown to be the only realistic one in the circumstances and it therefore acquires more credibility.

For a case illustration of brainstorming, see 5.54. In the dispute between the supplier and manufacturer referred to, brainstorming could lead to a range of creative options. For example, it could be agreed that, while the manufacturer Home Supplies would abide by its decision to use the alternative supplier, it would purchase another product from Resources International but at a discount which would 'compensate' it for losses suffered, and that both parties would enter a joint research and development project for new export products.

Separating people issues from problem issues

7.40   During the course of negotiations personality factors and destructive emotions frequently become entangled with the objective merits of a dispute. Each party portrays the other negatively, dubious motives are attributed, and personal accusations and recriminations occur. Even where there is a negotiated settlement, ongoing relationships may be seriously damaged by the destructive exchanges.

7.41   The mediator may decide that it is necessary to deal first with the 'people' side of the problem before the substantive issues can be considered. This may involve acknowledging, validating and giving face to each side. As Fisher, Ury and Patten put it, 'Be hard on the problem and soft on the people'.[14] Mediators can provide a lead in showing respect for all parties and in acknowledging deep-seated emotions. Ideally this will lead to a situation in which the disputants stand aside from the inter-personal aspects of the dispute and see it as an objective problem outside of themselves. If this happens, they can build a working relationship and jointly face a common task.

7.42   A mediator can use the following techniques in attempting to achieve this joint working system (with reference to the supply contract scenario at 7.33):

- Using an appropriate metaphor to describe the mediation process, for example: 'Ms Greene and Mr White, we are here to put the pieces of the jigsaw puzzle in place and I shall help you do that together ...'

- Setting up the room and other aspects of the environment to symbolise the fact that the parties should collaborate against the problem and not engage in armed combat with each other, for example, using a round or oval table.

- Using the whiteboard or flipchart to focus the parties' attention on the 'problem' and away from the personal antagonism: 'Mr White and Ms Greene, we are trying to look for answers to the fourth question here on the board, what could be done about using your respective strengths in a joint venture in the future?'

- Using appropriate terminology and language to emphasise the mutuality of the problem and the need for both parties to resolve it: 'Ms Greene and Mr White, what can we do about a discounting system for other products?'

- Reframing from the personal (Mr White says, 'Ms Greene always treated me with contempt when I queried delays') to external behaviour (Mediator says, 'So you would like to be treated differently in the future?').

- Changing the process, for example, calling separate meetings and saying: 'Mr White, Ms Greene seems to be reacting badly to your persistent accusations against her, can we look at ways of overcoming that?'

Evaluating options

7.43   Much negotiation involves a battle of wills. Each side attempts to persuade the other to accept their particular set of facts, values, perspectives, or sense of fairness. Where one side can persuade the other to accept these factors there will be a settlement, but where they cannot there will be a deadlock. Even where the criteria advanced by one party are 'objective' they can be contaminated by the fact that they come from the 'opposition'.

7.44   Ideally mediators should help the parties apply criteria which are independent of, and external to, either of them for justifying a particular option or settlement proposal. The criteria can include: market value, custom and policy within an organisation, normal business practice, industry standards, legal rules, and the like. The main advantage of these objective standards is that neither party feels that they are 'giving in' to the other, they are merely acceding to external

---

14   *Getting to Yes*, 1996, 31.

norms. Other advantages are that it is more difficult for parties to resist the notion of an objective standard applicable in similar situations, and it provides some protection to weaker parties.

7.45   The mediator can attempt to introduce external criteria into the negotiations in several ways. He or she can educate the parties about their usefulness, can suggest that they consider appropriate objective standards by which to evaluate settlement options, and can explore with the parties ways of obtaining outside input on relevant criteria. Thus in the scenario being referred to in this section, the mediator could encourage the parties to consider the use of standard pricing systems and industry-wide discounting practices to put together a settlement and to refer for expert assessment by a consultant the feasibility of joint venture proposals.

Where there are two sets of 'objective' criteria provided by different specialists such as engineers or doctors, the mediatior is faced with the problem of 'duelling experts', a problem dealt with elsewhere in this book.[15]

Deciding amongst options

7.46   When deciding amongst the options available at mediation, parties will also need to consider the alternatives to achieving a deal at the mediation.[16] Without knowing those alternatives (best and worst – BATNA and WATNA), parties will be making decisions at mediation in the dark. The alternatives are different to the 'reservation point' – sometimes referred to as the 'bottom line'. The alternatives are also different to the 'aspiration level' – sometimes referred to as the 'target'. Typically, the 'reservation point' is better than a party's BATNA and the 'aspiration' level is usually much higher than the BATNA. For example:

- BATNA – 'the court will order a 50% split in the assets'.

- Reservation point – 'I will accept 55% to take account of the costs I've expended to date.'

- Aspiration level – 'I want to aim for 65% as I feel I contributed more than he did.'[17]

The analysis of BATNA is more complex where the alternative is litigation. To determine whether it is in a party's interests to pursue the litigation route, consideration is necessary of the risks, costs and benefits of that alternative. Risk analysis is considered in further detail in Chapter 8.

F.   Special techniques in negotiation

7.47   The following techniques are potentially appropriate for all kinds and styles of negotiation and their use is a matter for the mediator's wise discretion. The

---

15   See 10.39–10.43.
16   Refer to Chapters 4 and 8 for further discussion of BATNA.
17   Richard Shell's research showed that the higher the aspiration level, the higher the outcome achieved (provided that the aspiration level could be substantiated): G. Richard Shell, *Bargaining for Advantage – Negotiation Strategies for Reasonable People*, Viking, New York, 1999.

illustrations below are made in relation to a workplace mediation between Jo, the supervisor, and Mary, an employee, where it is common ground that the two will continue working with each other in the future.

Reframing to enhance 'negotiability'

7.48   Reframing has particular application in the fiery crucible of negotiation.[18] Here it has the objective of reorienting the parties' perceptions towards a more 'negotiable' view of the problem. There are many possibilities, of which the following are just examples:

- Where a negotiator makes blanket demands. Mary says, 'I need more training and assistance to be able to cope with the new demands of the job'. The mediator can focus them on the underlying needs which would be served by the training and resources: 'Tell us what the new demands of the job are over a weekly period and how training would assist you in coping with them.'

- Where a party is continuously complaining about what they do not want from the negotiations, the mediator can reframe to focus them on what they do want from the process: 'Mary, don't tell Jo what you don't want her to do when you bring problems to her, tell us what you do want her to do.'

- Where a party talks only in broad generalities. Mary says, 'The supervisor always gives the good projects to other employees'. The mediator can focus them on the specifics, 'What do you mean by always, and what for you constitute good projects?'

- Where a party is focused on the past, the mediator can refocus them on the future: 'Jo, you've told us about the difficulties in supervising Mary in the past, now tell us what a good working relationship between you would look like in the future.'

Issue proliferation

7.49   In many negotiations there appears to be only a single issue at stake – which is often the question of how much money should be paid by one party to the other. In these situations mediators require techniques to get the parties to identify and deal with other issues as well. This is referred to as issue proliferation or issue enlargement. The additional issues could be substantive, procedural or emotional. They might include non-material factors such as positive publicity, confidentiality to avoid embarrassment and future business dealings. Multiple issues are easier to bargain with than single issues. They provide more scope for trade-offs, reciprocal concessions and packaging, and are less likely to result in the dreaded 'last gap' that is often difficult to bridge.

7.50   This principle can be illustrated in relation to money claims. Assume, in the above employment scenario, that all matters have been settled, except for a monetary payment to the employee Mary in relation to past services for which she was not remunerated. Here the mediator should be alert to potential sub-issues

---

18   See 6.38–6.44.

which can be added to the main issue in question, namely the financial amount to be paid. The sub-issues could (with some poetic licence in this scenario) include:

- timing of payment (immediate, 21 days, and so on);
- method of payment (electronic, bank cheque, cash, payment in kind – extra day's holiday);
- nature of payment (lump sum, instalments);
- variations with instalments (number, quantum, timing);
- place of payment (local, overseas);
- effectiveness of payment (in relation to taxation or pension);
- security for deferred payments;
- interest to accrue on default of deferred payments;
- legal and other professional costs;
- the mediator's fees (see case illustration below).

7.51   While all these issues will be subordinate to the central issue of the amount of money to be paid, they may constitute sufficient value to one or both parties to be helpful in reaching an agreement on the money. They also allow the party making the final monetary concession to save face through being able to prevail on a lesser issue. Thus Mary might say, 'I had to accept Jo's final offer on the amount of back pay, but at least she agreed to give me a bank cheque within 48 hours.' All disputes can be converted into multiple issue disputes to some degree.

Case illustration

In a matrimonial property mediation the parties had worked through the list of assets and liabilities, valuations, apportionment of chattels, and some short-term financial arrangements. They were deadlocked on the proportions in which the value in the pool of assets would be divided between them. There was about £600,000 to share between them, and a major impasse was reached when they were £6,000 apart. There were no sub-issues on the table, until the husband asked the mediator what his fee for the mediation would be. When told by the mediator that it would be about £2,200, the husband offered to pay the full fee instead of the 50:50 fee sharing arrangement set out in the mediation agreement. The wife responded by accepting his prior offer on the division of the property. The sub-issue of the mediator's fee had created additional 'value' to allow them to cross the last gap, despite the fact it was considerably smaller than the gap itself. It might, however, have given the wife the procedural and emotional satisfaction of being able to say, 'He caused the break-up, so at least he was obliged to pay for the mediation. I can live with that.'

'Forcing the issue'

7.52   Where there are a number of negotiating items and the parties are moving through them one by one in a positional way, the mediator might decide to 'force the issue', either because little progress is being made or because there is a serious time limitation. As with any other mediator intervention this requires some delicate judgement and there is always a chance that it will not work as intended. However, where the mediator makes this choice, he or she might move things along as follows.

Case illustration

Assume that there is a dispute between leaseholders in a period block and their management company involving a number of matters, of which the following four remain to be resolved: establishment of a residents' association, amount of increase in the service charges, parking arrangements, and limits on noise in the block. The mediator writes these issues up on the flipchart in two lists, apparently in random order, but with the actual goal of having the more important issues at the head of each list. The table might look as follows:

Remaining issues

Residents' association	Service charges
Parking arrangements	Noise complaints

7.53   The mediator then indicates that each party will be asked the same questions. He or she points to the column on the left and asks the leaseholders' representative, Andrew, which is the more important of the two issues in that column for the leaseholders. If Andrew indicates the residents' association, the mediator then asks him whether, if his preferred option is accepted on this issue, the leaseholders would be prepared to accept the management's proposal on the parking issue. If there is an affirmative answer, the mediator asks the same two questions of management's representative, Bernard, in relation to the second column. If both parties accept the proposals, it allows each to be successful on their 'first' priority and have their way on another issue, in a reciprocal package which is nominally equal to them both: Andrew gets his way on the residents' association and the noise, and Bernard gets his way on the service charges and the parking. This avoids the feeling that one party is conceding to the other and prevents the problem of having one issue only left for negotiation.

7.54   Another way of 'forcing the issue' is to ask one of three different kinds of questions to each party. Each question has the same objective, namely to get the parties out of entrenched positions, to open up the negotiations, and to get the parties to think in terms of trading off one preference for another.

First way of asking the question

Mediator: I am now going to ask you each a similar question so that we can explore the scope for structuring a package here. Andrew, you have said that the leaseholders insist on having a residents' association formed. What are you prepared to offer Bernard to get him to agree to that position? ... Bernard, you have said that management's proposal on the service charges should be accepted, what are you prepared to offer the leaseholders to get Andrew to agree to that proposal? ...

Second way of asking the question

Mediator: Andrew, assume that I was a tribunal and allowed the formation of the residents' association, but that you could build in some safeguards as regards its functions and review of performance, what would you be asking for along those lines...? Bernard, assume that I was a tribunal and ...

Third way of asking the question

Mediator: Bernard, you have heard that the leaseholders want a residents' association, which is not your preferred choice, but what would you want from the leaseholders to get you to agree to his position on that ...? Andrew, you have heard that Bernard ...

7.55   In each case the mediator is using 'dissonance theory' to get the relevant party to consider and talk about options which are not immediately palatable to them.[19] It gets them to think about the issues from the other side's point of view, to 'walk in their shoes' and to consider options which they have so far resisted. By articulating things from the other side's perspective, it is less easy for that party to hold rigidly to their own preferred position. It could also result in the mediator being regarded as the 'scapegoat'.[20]

Shifting between principle and detail

7.56   Where the parties are stuck on matters of detail, the mediator can attempt to move the discussion to a more abstract level in order to achieve agreement 'in principle'. For example, in the dispute between leaseholders and management over noise complaints, the mediator might attempt to get the parties to agree in principle on the need for all children in the block to have 'reasonable time to play and express themselves'. With the 'in principle' framework in place, the parties can then work on the detail of times, kinds of activities and decibel levels.

Conversely, where the parties cannot agree on matters of principle, because it is seen as too abstract or too compromising, the mediator can attempt to move the

---

19   Haynes and Charlesworth, *The Fundamentals of Family Mediation*, 1996, 168–70.
20   See 3.42.

discussion to a more concrete level and try to reach agreement on some of the details. Thus in the above example, neither party might want to agree to the 'in principle' arrangement and the mediator can then focus on the specific detail of activities, times and noise levels. In dealing with the detail, the parties might creep up to the level of 'in principle' agreement. In our experience the mediator's ability to move the discussions between principle and detail is a significant way of keeping them moving productively.

Making more than one offer

7.57   There are two views on the benefits of making more than one offer in mediation. Some mediators find it useful to encourage the parties, in particular defendants or respondents, to make more than one offer at an appropriate time. This gives the other side, usually a claimant, a sense of power and control through the choice, albeit limited, that is being provided. Thus in a matrimonial property mediation a party might be encouraged to say:

> I offer either 60% of the asset pool based on my valuations, or 54% based on your valuations.

In a mediation involving the payment of damages, the defendant might be encouraged to say:

> I offer £20,000 lump sum within 14 days and 24 monthly instalments of £3,000, or £50,000 lump sum within 14 days and 36 monthly instalments of £1,000.

Apart from the choice element which these offers provide, there can also be value for a claimant who is not receiving what they really want from the defendant in money terms. They can at least opt for the scheme which is otherwise best suited to their needs, for example, in relation to taxation or cash flow.

On the other hand, having a choice amongst alternative offers can make some negotiations more difficult due to the following psychological phenomena:

■ Option devaluation – for some people, the attractiveness of all options might be diminished the more options there are.

■ Avoidance – some people are unable to make a choice when faced with several options.

■ Decision deferral – some people postpone decision making when faced with several options.[21]

---

21 See C. Guthrie, 'Panacea or Pandora's Box?', in *Iowa Law Review* (2003), Volume 8, p 601; A. Tversy and E. Shafir, 'Choice under conflict – the dynamics of deferred decision', in *Psychological Science* (1992), Volume 3, p358; and S. S. Lyengar and M. R. Lepper, 'When choice is demotivating: can one desire too much of a good thing?', in *Journal of Personality and Social Psychology*, 2000, 76.

- Dissatisfaction or regret – as the number of options increases, a party's satisfaction from the chosen option can be eroded; and negotiators who choose from a number of options can experience post-decision regret.[22]

Bringing in reciprocity

7.58

Case illustration
A contact parent may insist on being notified immediately by the resident parent about any illness or sickness of the children, on receiving medical reports and on having access to the treating doctors. If this condition can be made applicable to both parties, it is more likely to be accepted by the resident parent. This is because it is easier to commit to something if the other party is making the same commitment – it creates a nominal equality even though the arrangement is more significant for one side than it is for the other. The same principle can be applied to other common demands in parenting mediations, for example, that the contact parent give written notice if they intend to take the children on holiday or that the resident parent make their telephone number available to the other parent. In all these cases the request is more likely to be accepted if the obligation is made reciprocally binding on both parents.

A party's approach in negotiation – positive or negative – provokes a similar response from the others.[23] A favour given is usually a favour returned. Co-operation, once established, can endure. An aggressive stance is likely to be returned in kind. Accordingly, a constructive or unproductive cycle of reciprocity (as the case may be) can occur. The mediator's role is to coach the parties on the possible effects of their behaviour. In this way, a party might be persuaded to reconsider a tactic, approach, offer or concession.

The impact of reciprocity is particularly evident in patterns of concession-making. Mediators can help parties consider the signals that they are sending through their pattern of concessions, both in terms of timing and magnitude. A concession needs to be substantial enough to engage the other party to reciprocate. In terms of timing, gradual concessions tend to produce better results. Parties expect some 'dance', or reciprocity, in the negotiations.

Linked bargaining

7.59   Linked bargaining involves the conditional coupling of one negotiation issue with another. It is sometimes called 'conditional linked bargaining', which highlights its two closely related elements. The first is the *linking* of one negotiation issue to another so that there is a package of two issues; the second is the *conditional* way in which the linked issues are presented. It is best illustrated by way of example.

---

22   B. Schwartz, *The Paradox of Choice: Why More is Less*, Harper Collins, NY, 2004.
23   Robert Caldini, *Influence: Science and Practice*, 4th ed, 2001, 20.

Case illustration

Suppose that there is a mediation in a tenancy dispute involving the rental agent, Alex, and the assured shorthold tenant, Catherine. The agent is seeking compensation for early termination of the tenancy agreement by the tenant and for damage to the carpets beyond normal wear and tear. The tenant is claiming that the landlord was in breach of the tenancy agreement and is also claiming for damage allegedly caused to the tenant's furniture by the landlord. The following dialogue indicates how linked bargaining could be pursued in respect of two of these issues:

Mediator: Catherine, if you were to get a satisfactory outcome on Alex's claim for compensation, what would you be prepared to offer Alex in relation to the carpets?

Catherine: Well, I suppose if I could be really satisfied on the compensation issue, I would be prepared to get the carpets cleaned at my expense.

Mediator: Alex, if Catherine is prepared to pay for the carpet cleaning, what could you do about the contract issue?

Alex: If she undertakes to have the cleaning done immediately at her expense, and if I approve of the quality, I might be able to write off most of the compensation claim. Not all of it though.

7.60   This strategy is closely related to the 'what … if' and 'if … what' hypothetical questions referred to above.[24] Its objective is to free up some space in which either Catherine or Alex might feel free to make an offer on one issue in the knowledge that it is contingent on them being satisfied on another. It is designed to open up the process without either side feeling that they are at risk. If Catherine makes a constructive suggestion on the question of the carpets it will not constitute a unilateral concession to the agent and the mediator can then focus attention on the conditional factor, namely the compensation. Likewise if Alex concedes conditionally on the compensation issue, the mediator can focus on the carpets as the way of ensuring that the concession can be attained. If the conditions are not met on either side, the relevant party can withdraw their offer without being inconsistent or losing face.

7.61   This approach forces the parties to focus on a specific issue, without sliding off into other issues, as frequently happens in negotiations. For example, Catherine might ordinarily say, 'I'm not prepared to talk about the carpets while he wants damages in lieu of rent.' The mediator's intervention makes her concentrate on one issue by reassuring her on the other. It also involves a key reframe by the mediator, through the use of words such as 'reasonable', 'fair' and 'appropriate' in the conditional term. This avoids an expectation in Catherine's mind that she will get what she wants on the compensation issue; it reduces the expectation to a 'satisfactory outcome'.

If this method of bargaining is initiated by the mediator, it can become a pattern for the deal-making phase of the negotiations.

---

24   See 6.48.

Unilateral concessions

7.62   Linked bargaining is a way of avoiding 'wasted' concessions being made by one or both parties. Mediators often observe a party or their lawyer making an early concession on a seemingly unimportant issue, 'Yes, we'll agree to the terms of settlement being made confidential if that is what you would like …' Often, this is done without extracting a reciprocal concession for their own benefit or keeping it up their sleeve to trade with later.

There are two basic approaches to dealing with multiple negotiation issues. The first is the *building block* approach where each issue constitutes a block in the wall being constructed and the blocks are put in place one by one. In this model each concession a party makes means good progress as another block is cemented into place. In this approach the mediator might encourage unilateral concessions. The main problem with this approach is that the final block might have to be put in place on its own without the possibility of rearranging the other blocks and this might be difficult or impossible to achieve.

7.63   The other approach is the *juggling balls* approach. Here the various negotiation issues are kept in the air for as long as possible so that there are always multiple issues to negotiate over, and conditional offers and linked bargaining can lead to mutually satisfying trade-offs and packaging. In this approach the mediator would not encourage unilateral concessions. However, a problem with this model is that it may become too complicated, the parties might be discouraged, and all the balls could fall to the ground with nothing settled. As usual each approach has its strengths and shortcomings and circumstances will dictate which is used.

Even if the juggling balls approach is being followed, there is one good reason why an early unilateral concession might be appropriate. It could constitute a sign of good faith and dramatically improve the climate of the negotiations.

Accommodating future contingencies

7.64   A recurring problem in negotiations is that decisions have to be made in the face of uncertain future contingencies. The contingencies could relate to many kinds of external factors, involving other parties, the establishment of facts, or developments in the economy or the marketplace. There are many examples: a grandparent has to be asked to transport children at the beginning and the conclusion of contact; property has to be sold and distributed and the sale price, and even the likelihood of a sale, are unknown factors; a bank has to be asked to release a debtor from personal guarantees in a partnership dissolution.

7.65   Where this problem arises in a mediation, there are various ways in which mediators might guide the parties on dealing with the future unknowns. As with other difficulties in mediation, they should first normalise the situation: in many negotiations, and other life situations, the relevant people, and often their professional helpers as well, have to make decisions in circumstances of uncertainty. In addition mediators could guide the parties to:

■ Reach agreement on matters that can be settled, adjourn the mediation, and resume it when the formerly uncertain events have become clear – the 'wait and see' method.

- Make an assumption as to what will occur, and base the settlement on this assumption, with a covenant that if the assumption proves to be incorrect the parties will revisit their agreement on which it was based – the 'default' method.

- Develop a formula, involving percentages, proportions or ratios, which can be applied to facts or figures when they eventuate – the 'formula' approach.

- Develop a process for resolving the uncertainty, involving the parties, fact finding, external experts, and the like – the 'process' method.

- Have the parties base their agreement on an average or median price or other relevant factor, using their own figures or the estimates of their advisers or experts – the 'rough as guts' approach.

Taking account of parties' perceptions

7.66   The focus in this chapter is on how the mediator can assist the parties to negotiate constructively. This requires the mediator to observe what is happening and to make some judgements and decisions on the basis of the observed phenomena. Mediators should also be alert to the factor of how the parties are subjectively experiencing the negotiations, though this is less easy for an outsider to detect and understand. However, the mediator should be conscious of several possible factors:

- Where Party A makes a concession 'too easily', and Party B feels that it has not been given in response to their demands, Party B may devalue the significance of the concession (known as 'reactive devaluation'). This points to the need for appropriate timing in the negotiation process, a matter referred to earlier. It is repeated here because it is important for mediators to be mindful of the parties' possible perceptions accompanying the 'objective' developments.

- Concessions made by Party A on a 'take it or leave it' basis, without any apparent recognition of Party B's arguments or needs, might be rejected by Party B, even though they are objectively valuable, because they did not materialise out of a reciprocal process of give and take between the two.

- Offers or concessions made by the 'wrong person' may be rejected, for example, a worker does not accept anything emanating from the human resources manager, or a claimant refuses to consider suggestions from the other defendant's lawyer (known as 'negative transference'), whereas they would be receptive to the same offers from other individuals.

- Where Party A feels powerless and forced into making compromises ('perceptual disempowerment'), they might become resistant and recalcitrant, even though the concessions being made by Party B are objectively valuable.

- Party A, who has consistently made strong positional demands, may find it possible to change their mind only where 'legitimate' reasons for doing so are provided and identified, for example, new documents have been produced of which they were previously unaware.

- Some parties require a protracted sense of struggle before they will be satisfied with any outcome. In these situations a series of incremental concessions will be more 'satisfying' to them than a single large concession.

- A settlement will be easier to accept where it is perceived as a 'gain' and not a 'loss' (known as 'loss aversion'), which might require consideration of the bigger picture surrounding the specific dispute, including such factors as legal costs and opportunity costs.

7.67   Mediators should use the familiar formula in dealing with these dynamics. They observe what is happening, make a tentative diagnosis, plan an intervention and implement it. The intervention could involve normalising the situation so as to empower the parties, educating the parties about its significance, and using separate meetings to discuss with them ways of dealing with it. If this intervention does not work, they re-diagnose the problem, reach into the toolbox and try another intervention.

Working with numbers

7.68   A mediator who has an understanding of the psychology of numbers can help parties work flexibly with numbers. Numbers can be viewed in many different ways, for example:

- as a percentage ('would you consider increasing your offer by 10% to reflect their 10% decrease in the claim?');

- as a range ('would you be prepared to consider a settlement between £300,000 and £350,000?');

- as beginning with a particular digit ('are you looking for a settlement beginning with a 3 or 4?');

- as containing a certain number of digits ('are you looking for a 6 figure settlement?');

- as being higher or lower than a target ('are you aiming to recover at least your costs?').

Flexibility with numbers can provide momentum for the negotiations. Another useful technique is to assist the parties to move from an approach based on specific items or figures to a global approach or lump sum. This approach can change the dynamic and encourage movement.

Crossing the last gap

7.69   The last gap is a special type of deadlock that can be encountered in both positional and interest-based bargaining.[25] It occurs where the parties have made decisions on all issues except one, and have reached a deadlock on that one. It usually involves an amount of money – the last ten pounds or the last one million pounds, as the case may be. The last gap is difficult to cross because both parties feel that they have conceded too much, and they feel that they would show weakness and lose face if they made the final concession. Even where it makes commercial sense to compromise on the last gap, these non-commercial factors make it difficult to do so.

---

25   See 7.5.

There are clearly no guaranteed strategies for dealing with the last gap. Mediations do sometimes fail to reach settlement. Mediators can, however, be mindful of the following possible approaches for dealing with it:

- Splitting the difference: the classical compromise arrangement in which the parties meet each other halfway.

- Using random chance: spin a coin, draw straws, or write out a series of figures between the last two offers (for example, £2,000, £3,000, £4,000 up to £10,000) and have one selected randomly with the agreement that it will constitute the settlement figure.

- Giving the benefit or value being argued over to a third party, for example, to charity or to the children, or to purchase a lottery ticket.

- Subdividing the gap: develop sub-issues, as discussed above.

- Using the 'You cut, I choose' routine: one party divides up the chattels or other objects of value and the other party has first pick of the 'piles'.

- Making last confidential offers: each party gives the mediator their best offer in private and if the gap between these last offers is less than a predetermined amount the mediation proceeds, otherwise it is discontinued.

- Deciding on appropriate procedural options:

  - Referring the liability or quantum question to an expert and continue the mediation in light of their opinion.

  - Changing the process (for example to 'med-arb').[26]

  - Referring the issue to a 'higher authority', such as an arbitrator, tribunal, board or court.

  - Deferring treatment of the last gap to a fixed time and implementing the remainder of the agreement in the interim.

- Adjourning and getting both parties to exchange 'final offers' directly with each other, or through the mediator, within a specific period.

- Adjourning and getting one party to accept or reject the 'final offer' of the other party at a specified date and time.

- Asking the solicitors to put the same question to their clients, namely whether, if the other party moves up/down to a specified figure, they will move down/up.

- Shaming the parties by focusing on the progress made and testing whether the parties wish to walk away.

Ultimately, of course, it is best to anticipate and avoid the last gap phenomenon. Mediators should consider warning the parties early in the mediation about the potential problem and discuss ways of avoiding it, for example, by keeping more than one issue to negotiate over.

A note on splitting the difference

7.70   Splitting the difference is useful, in the right circumstances. It is the classical form of compromise and might be the appropriate strategy in some cases,

---

26   See 9.54.

even though compromise is sometimes looked on as too simplistic. Splitting the difference may well reward the 'bigger liar', in that the point of compromise will favour the party who made the more extreme opening demand. Nevertheless, in the right circumstances it might be highly appropriate. It can be introduced by the mediator as an honourable option, 'You need to give a little to get a little', or with a small homily, 'In my view a little give and take by each of you will settle this matter.'

7.71   Mediators should be alert to the problem of only one party offering to come halfway to cross the last gap; the danger is that the other party will then split the remaining difference, and so on. For example, if there is a last gap of £10,000 and one party offers to move £5,000 the other might respond with an offer of only £2,500. Therefore, in joint session the mediator might say, 'Are you both prepared to meet halfway …?' or in separate session, 'Are you prepared to concede half the disputed amount on condition that the other side also does so …?' Care should also be taken with language on this issue, as the term 'compromise' might not be appropriate in some cultural contexts where it might suggest the sacrifice of principle.

Dealing with the last-minute add-on

7.72   This additional claim, where settlement has been reached on all declared issues, shortens the temper of the other party, and the life expectancy of the mediator. Thus, in a matrimonial property dispute where agreement had been reached on all the assets, on the debts and on the resources such as the pension, one party raised the question of the family pet. It took another 90 minutes to finalise the issue of the pet's residence.

The add-on should not be judged too quickly as it might be the result of a genuine oversight by the relevant party. Usually, though, it is raised as a deliberate strategy to save face by extracting the last concession, or even to destabilise the whole settlement because the party concerned did not want to settle at all.

7.73   Thus the mediator's first responsibility is to attempt to diagnose the significance of the add-on and to base an intervention on that provisional diagnosis. If it appears to be an oversight, then some explanation and face-saving is required. If it is a tactical ploy then several interventions can be considered: asking the other party if they also have any additional items, re-opening earlier issues to discuss together with the additional one, resorting to separate meetings, confronting the party who raised it, or using some of the techniques discussed in relation to the last gap.

Where a mediator suspects in advance that the add-on problem might occur, he or she can inform the parties about the problem in a generalised way, thereby lessening the chances of its being used as a tactical ploy. The mediator could even ask the parties to agree at that point on how to deal with the problem should it arise. Another way of pre-empting the problem is by asking the parties periodically whether all relevant issues have been disclosed, in an attempt to make it less easy to sabotage the process at the end.

Recognising negotiation bias

7.74   Bias in negotiation can arise in the following cases:

- If a party has chosen the wrong 'anchor' based on faulty or incomplete information.

- If a party devalues a recommendation made by another solely on the grounds that it was made by another party (called, 'reactive devaluation').

- Where a party is overly confident about the likely outcome should the negotiations fail.[27]

- When a party's 'objective criteria' are self-serving or a party places more weight on factors consistent with its desired outcome.

- If a party has over-committed to a prior course of action (called, 'entrapment'). This is also referred to as 'escalation commitment' or 'throwing good money after bad'.

- Where a party takes a short-term, narrow, or rights-based approach.

- Where a party is affected by 'loss aversion' – a loss has more of an impact on choice than an equivalent gain.[28]

- Where the 'winner's curse' operates – a party feels discomfort at an easy or quick settlement.

Being aware of the operation of bias and challenging parties to overcome bias is a useful mediator skill. This can be done in many civil/commercial cases by, for example:

- Raising awareness among lawyers and parties of bias traits, and coaching parties on negotiation behaviour.

- Role reversal – asking each party to 'step into another's shoes', allowing the party to consider the arguments that might be presented by any other party should the matter go to court.

- Asking the lawyer to place himself in the role of a 'disagreeable adjudicator', challenging the lawyer to give reasons why the case might not be successful if it went to court.

- A 'mini hearing' that encourages each party to make short presentations to the others, giving everyone a chance to hear the stength of each party's case, and to identify any bias or re-evaluate their positions.

---

27   Many studies confirm lawyer overconfidence when advising on cases in litigation. An ABA study found that on average lawyers rated themselves in the top 80th percentile on their ability to predict the outcome of a case, negotiation skills and cooperation; and that high self-regard leads to inflated values assigned to cases. Refer to R. Birke, 'Settlement Psychology: When Decision-making Processes Fail', in (2000) 18 *Alternatives* 203.

28   For example, most people think that a 50% chance of gaining X is not sufficient to compensate for a 50% chance of losing X, so that most people would need a 50% chance of gaining 2X or 3X to offset the 50% chance of losing X. Framing offers as gains increases the chance of having the offer accepted. Refer also to the 'endowment effect', described at 6.39.

■ Reality testing, or playing 'devil's advocate', with a party in private meeting (this technique is discussed in further detail in Chapter 8).

G. Dealing with impasses

A note on terminology

7.75   Terminology is crucial, as detailed here. Different words are used for the situation in which the mediating parties 'get stuck'. Some mediators avoid the word *deadlock* as it implies a complete breakdown in negotiations and is too negative; the same applies to *stalemate* which suggests that there can be no resolution. The term *logjam* suggests that with some jostling, it might be possible to find a solution, although the metaphor might not be universally understood. The term *impasse* is rather abstract, but does not have any of the negative connotations of the others. It is the term used (mainly) here but might not be appropriate for some clients.

7.76   Impasses are situations in which one or both negotiating parties refuse to make further concessions and the negotiations are threatened with termination. Some mediation texts provide long lists of 'things to do' in the face of impasses, such as 'move on to another issue', 'take an adjournment', and 'have a drink'. There is some value in these suggestions, but they all require concrete circumstances to indicate their appropriateness. Here the list system is also used, with an attempt to provide a more systematic approach to the problem.

7.77   As with other problems in mediation, the mediator needs to diagnose the situation and develop a hypothesis about the reason for the impasse, before selecting an intervention. There can be three broad types of impasses.[29] They can arise over:

■ *substantive* issues, where parties will not shift from their positional demands because their monetary or other substantive interests are not being met.

■ *procedural* issues, where the parties' interests in a fair and appropriate procedure are not being satisfied.

■ *emotional* issues, where a party's emotional interests are not being met.

In each situation the affected party will engage in grand-standing, table-thumping, threatened walk-outs, and the other dramatic symptoms of negotiation impasses.

7.78   Based on their tentative hypothesis, mediators decide on an appropriate intervention. What follows are some possible mediator interventions in lists which recap on many of the tactics discussed in this book. At the end of each subsection an illustration is provided from the tenancy mediation involving Alex and Catherine above.

7.79   In the case of *substantive* impasses:

■ Challenge the assumption that there is only a 'fixed pie' over which to negotiate.

---

29   See Spegel, Rogers and Buckley, *Negotiation: Theory and Techniques*, 1998, 75–7.

- Refocus the parties' attention on interests (what they need) and away from their positions (what they are publicly stating to be their demands/wants).

- Investigate the possibility of a further exchange of information and data.

- Shift from the substantive issues to alternative processes for dealing with the problem.

- Go back to exploration, as appropriate, to re-open the discussion.

- Conduct brainstorming or another creative option exercise.

- Clarify communication and the understanding of the parties.

- Develop sub-issues (issue proliferation).

- Link negotiation issues in a packaged system.

- Review figures in a different way – encourage parties to be flexible in their approach with the figures.

- Consider any non-monetary considerations, concessions or offers.

- Emphasise the costs and other downsides of not settling.

- Consider the alternatives if the matter does not settle at mediation.

- Have one key witness give 'evidence' after which the parties discuss its significance.

- 'Role reversal' – ask a party to step into the shoes of another and consider their position, interests, perspectives and approach.[30]

- Hypothesise – use the 'what if?' question to test ideas.

- Park difficult issues.

- Seek permission to relay information obtained in private meeting where it could be helpful to encourage movement in other parties.

- Review, search for or make reference to objective criteria.

- Probe if legal, financial or expert advice might assist the parties.

- Consider if explanations, acknowledgements or an apology would be appropriate.[31]

Case illustration

If Alex and Catherine are in dispute over questions of fact relating to what happened during the tenancy, the mediator might suggest that they invite the resident manager of the units, a relatively independent party in the eyes of both agent and tenant, to provide some information at the mediation and to be asked questions of clarification, after which Alex and Catherine could resume their discussions.

---

30 Through role reversal a party can gain insight and empathy for another party in a way that might help to tailor arguments or approaches to make them more persuasive.

31 The value of apologies has been documented, see for example, J. K. Robbennolt, 'Apologies and Legal Settlement: An Empirical Examination' (2004) *Mich L Rev*.102.

7.80 In the case of *procedural* impasses:

- 'Normalise' the situation – remind the parties that it is a normal party of the mediation process to get stuck.
- Summarise progress in a positive way and invite the parties to continue.
- Reassess the effect of the venue, seating, comfort factors, visual aids, and the like.
- Use separate meetings to ascertain why and how the process is not satisfying the parties.
- A lawyers' only, or a principals' only, meeting can provide momentum.
- Re-convene a joint meeting to encourage airing of differences, brainstorming and narrowing. Before the meeting is convened, the mediator should outline its purpose, obtain permission to reconvene, allow the parties to prepare and then manage the meeting effectively.
- Explain and make transparent aspects of the mediation and negotiation processes.
- Use visuals/the flip chart to depict the situation more graphically.
- Ensure stronger enforcement of the mediation guidelines.
- Encourage parties to take responsibility – 'how will you resolve this impasse?' or 'what can you do to make a difference?'
- Encourage a concession that is easy to make for one party and valuable for another to receive.
- Offer to make a non-binding recommendation.
- Suggest that the parties make 'blind offers' – one or more confidential offers to the mediator on the condition if the offers are close (an agreed percentage) that the mediator will split the difference.
- Ask the parties for their final offers.
- Investigate the possibility of changing the mediator or terminating the mediation (as a last resort).
- Introduce a deadline to decision-making.

Case illustration

If Alex and Catherine have reached an impasse because Alex is dominating the process, talking over Catherine and otherwise ignoring the mediation guidelines, the mediator might identify the problem, restate the guidelines, get the parties to recommit to them, and resume the process with a more forceful application of the rules than before.

7.81 In the case of *emotional* impasses:

- Acknowledge the emotional issues and feelings.
- Remind the parties of their objectives.
- Consider changing the principal negotiators, or support persons.

- Allow some controlled venting of feelings.

- Acknowledge deeply experienced emotions of the parties.

- Deal with destructive tactics being used by one or both parties.

- Consider appropriateness of language, terminology and non-verbals.

- Consider the relevance of mutual apologies.

- Attempt to quantify value disputes.

- Identify an exception or other basis to change the rules or dynamic, and help the parties to save face.

- Suggest a break and reconvene at a later time or date.

- Remain positive and confident.

- Consider whether confidentiality undertakings might help to overcome deadlock concerns.

> ### Case illustration
>
> If Alex and Catherine have reached an impasse because Alex cannot afford to lose face in the eyes of other tenants, the mediator might discuss with him in separate session a basis for distinguishing Catherine's situation from those of other tenants so that he can have a reason for bending the rules, for example, that she has an unmodernised flat or has been in the building for considerably longer than other tenants.

In the case of all impasses the mediator always has the option of bringing 'pressure' to bear on the parties to settle – this topic is dealt with in Chapter 8.

H.   Different methods of performing these functions

7.82   There are many different methods which mediators can adopt for assisting the parties to accomplish the goals of good negotiation. Here are some examples of these methods:

- *Educating*: Mediators can explain to the parties before the mediation about negotiation's normal features and predictable problems. This can be done via email, in writing, in personal or telephone contacts, or, where there are many individuals on each side, by conducting a negotiation workshop for each group. Likewise during the course of the mediation the mediator may give a 'mini-lecture' to the parties on a specific aspect of negotiation.

- *'Advising'*: Mediators may 'advise' both parties in a generalised way, for example, that mediation works best when they are all prepared for the negotiations. They may add some specific recommendations, for example, that preparation on the valuation of disputed goods can help negotiations run more smoothly. At a more 'interventionist' level mediators may advise one of the parties in a separate meeting that if they accept the other side's offer with too much alacrity the offeror might feel that they have offered too much and attempt to recover some of it.

- *Coaching*: During the separate sessions mediators can coach the relevant party in appropriate ways of linking offers, presenting offers and responding to offers once the joint session resumes. The coaching can include short demonstrations and rehearsals for the real thing. Clearly, mediators need to be mindful of the neutrality issue when undertaking this role; they should not become the 'advocates' of either party.

- *Modelling*: Co-mediators can model appropriate negotiation styles by dealing openly with their differences and focusing on underlying interests. In more subtle ways solo mediators can model good negotiation techniques when they are 'negotiating' with one or both of the parties over a procedural issue or other problem.

- *Pre-empting*: Where mediators are concerned that specific problems may materialise they may attempt to pre-empt the problems. For example, where they are suspicious about a last-minute add-on they might say, well before this can occur: 'In my experience people sometimes think of something they want at the last moment and this can threaten all the good work that has been done. Might either of you have overlooked anything like that?'

- *Illustrating*: Mediators can provide examples from their practical experiences, without actually suggesting them as solutions, for example: 'In another workplace dispute in which I was involved the parties agreed to implement the wages and safety agreements immediately and to defer the training issue until they could each come up with fuller training proposals.'

I.   Summary

7.83   This chapter raises the following points of particular significance:

- Mediators have a role in all styles and strategies of negotiation in order to make them more productive, efficient and likely to result in wise agreements for the parties.

- The mediator's role requires an extensive understanding of the art and science of negotiation – he or she is the negotiation expert and specialist at the mediation table.

- The standard mediator responsibility is to develop a hypothesis on a negotiation issue, plan an intervention, carry out the intervention, and in the light of the effectiveness of the intervention revise or refine the hypothesis.

J.   Tasks for beginner mediators

7.84   Reflect on the last time that you bought or sold a house or car. What one specific insight from this chapter would cause you to negotiate differently if you were to take part in that same transaction again? What principle of negotiation did you learn in that encounter that is not referred to in this chapter?

7.85   Role play with a partner a negotiation between a consumer and a retailer over the former's attempt to return a vacuum cleaner on the grounds that it is defective. Each of you must use a range of relevant tactics, including lies, bluffs and threats, to 'create doubt' in the mind of the other. Use great poetic licence. Debrief each other on the effects of these tactics on each of you. How might a mediator have dealt with the doubt-creating tactics, and their effects, which you experienced?

7.86   You have been appointed to mediate a dispute between two factions in a voluntary organisation. They have the time and resources to allow you to have preliminary meetings with each faction at which you plan to educate them about and train them in negotiation skills. Write out a list of the *five* negotiation principles which you think are the most important and which you will enlighten them on in the preliminary meetings.

K. Recommended reading

Adair W.L. et.al., 'Culture and negotiation strategy', in (2004) 20 *Negotiation Journal* 87.

Adair W.L. and Brett J.M., 'The negotiation dance: time, culture and behavioural sequences in negotiation', in (2005) 16(1) *Organisation Science* 33.

Adair W.L. et.al., 'The timing and function of offers in US and Japanese negotiations' in (2007) 92 *Journal of Applied Psychology* 1056.

Amabile T.M. and others, 'Creativity under the gun', in (August 2002) *Harvard Business Review* 52.

Babcock L. and Loewenstein G., 'Explaining bargaining impasse: the role of self-serving biases', in (1997) 11(1) *Journal of Economic Perspectives* 109.

Bazerman M. H. and Neale M. A., *Negotiating Rationally*, Free Press, New York, 1994.

Caldini R., *Influence: The Psychology of Persuasion*, Harper-Collins, NY, 1998.

Carnevale P.J., 'Creativity in the outcome of conflict', in M. Deutsh (et. al.) eds, *The Handbook of Conflict: Theory and Practice*, 2nd ed, Jossey-Bass, San Francisco, 44-35.

Charlton R., *Dispute Resolution Guidebook*, LBC Information Services, Sydney, 2000.

Charlton and Dewdney, *The Mediator's Handbook: Skills and Strategies for Practitioners*, 2nd ed, Lawbook Co, Sydney, 2004.

Craver C. B., *Effective Legal Negotiation and Settlement* (5th ed), Lexis Nexis, Danvers, 2005.

Davis R., 'Negotiating Personal Injury Cases: A Survey of the Attitudes and Beliefs of Personal Injury Lawyers' in (1994) 68 *Australian Law Journal* 734–50.

Dawson, R. *Secrets of Power Negotiating: Inside Secrets from a Master Negotiator*, Career Press, 1999.

Emery R., *Renegotiating Family Relationships – Divorce, Child Custody and Mediation*, Guildford Press, New York, 1994.

Fisher R., Ury W. and Patton, *Getting to Yes*, 2nd ed, Pantheon Books, US, 1996.

Foo M.D. et.al., 'Emotional intelligence and negotiation: the tension between creating and claiming value', in (2004) 15 *International Journal of Conflict Management* 411.

Folberg, J. & Golann, D. *Lawyer Negotiation: Theory, Practice and Law*, Aspen Publishers, 2006.

Galinsky A.D. & Mussweiler T., 'First offers as anchors: the role of perspective-taking and negotiator focus', in (2001) 81(4) *Journal of Personality and Social Psychology* 657.

Kristensen H. and Garling T., 'Anchor points, reference points and counteroffers in negotiations', in (2000) 9 *Group Decision and Negotiation* 493.

Kurtzburg T.R., 'Creative thinking, cognitive aptitude and integrative joint gains: a study of negotiator creativity', in (1998) 11 *Creativity Research Journal* 283.

Langner L.A. and Winter D.G., 'The motivational basis of concessions and compromise: archival and laboratory studies', in (2001) 81 *Journal of Personality and Social Psychology* 711.

Lax D. and Sebenius J., *The Manager as Negotiator: Bargaining for Cooperation and Competitive Gain*, Free Press, NY, 1987.

Lax D. and Sebenius J., *3-D Negotiation: Powerful Tools to Change the Game in your most important Negotiations*, Harvard Business School Press, 2006.

Lewicki et.al., *Negotiation* (3rd ed), McGraw Hill, NY, 1999.

Lewicki et.al., *Essentials of Negotiation* (4th ed), McGraw Hill/Irwin, Chicago, 2004.

Lewicki et.al., *Negotiation: Readings, Exercises and Cases* (4th ed), McGraw Hill, NY, 2004.

Lewicki et.al., *Negotiation*, 6th ed, McGraw Hill International, New York, 2010.

Lovenheim P., *How to Mediate your Dispute*, Nolo Press, Berkeley, 1996.

Magee J.C. et.al., 'Power, propensity to negotiate, and moving first in competitive interactions', in (2007) 33(2) *Personality and Social Psychology Bulletin* 200.

Menkel-Meadow C., 'Lawyer Negotiations: Theories and Realities – What we Learn from Mediation' in (1993) 56 *Modern Law Review* 361–379.

Mnookin R., 'Why Negotiations Fail: An Exploration of Barriers to the Resolution of Conflict' (1993) 8 *Ohio Journal of Dispute Resolution* 313–349.

Olekalns M. and Smith P., 'Loose with the truth: predicting deception in negotiation', in (2007) 76 *Journal of Business Ethics* 225.

Raiffa H., *The Art and Science of Negotiation*, Belknap Press, 2005.

Raiffa H. et.al., *Negotiation Analysis: The Science and Art of Collaborative Decision Making*, Harvard University Press, Cambridge Mass., 2007.

Schneider A.K., 'Shattering negotiation myths: empirical evidence on effectiveness of negotiation style', in (2002) 7 *Harvard Law Review* 143.

Schwarz B., *The Paradox of Choice: Why More is Less*, HarperCollins, NY, 2004.

Spegel, Rogers and Buckley, *Negotiation: Theory and Techniques*, Butterworths, Sydney, 1998, Ch 2.

Stone D., Patton B. and Heen S., *Difficult Conversations: How to Discuss What Matters Most*, Penguin Books, NY, 1999.

Tesler P., *Collaborative Law*, ABA Section on Family Law, Chicago, 2001.

Thomson L., *The Mind and Heart of the Negotiator*, 4th ed, Prentice Hall, NJ, 2008.

Wade J., 'The Last Gap in Negotiations – Why is it Important? How can it be crossed?' (1995) 6 *ADRJ* 93.

Wade J., 'Persuasion in negotiation and mediation', in (2007) 10(1) *ADR Bulletin* 8.

Williams G. R., *Legal Negotiation and Settlement*, West Publishing, St Paul Minn, 1983.

Wolski B., 'The Role and the Limitations of Fisher and Ury's Model of Interest-based Negotiation in Mediation (1994) 5 *ADRJ* 210.

Chapter 8

Encouraging Settlement

The longest journey starts with a single step

A. Introduction

8.1   Another way in which mediators can add value to the parties' negotiations and decision-making is by 'encouraging settlement'.[1] This chapter looks more closely at this mediator role.

Most modern mediation training is based on the distinction between process and content.[2] This distinction implies that the mediator should conduct the mediation process and allow the parties, in terms of the principle of self-determination, to come to their own decisions on matters of content. There is an assumption that in conducting the process the mediator does not 'coerce', 'pressure' or otherwise 'influence' the parties to reach their decisions. This assumption, however, requires some scrutiny and analysis.

8.2   This is another area in which terminology is problematic, given the inherent flexibility of words and the different connotations which the same terms have for different people. Here is a 'starter kit' glossary for present purposes, although it is by no means a definitive list of definitions:

- *Power* – the ability to affect the perceptions, attitudes and behaviour of others.

- *Influence* – to affect mildly the perceptions, attitudes and behaviour of others.[3]

- *Pressure* – to affect more strongly the perceptions, attitudes and behaviour of others.

- *Coerce* – to impose forceful pressure on others which is difficult, or impossible, to resist.

- *Encourage* – a generic term for using power to influence, pressure or coerce.

8.3   Whether a mediator's intervention to encourage settlement or other decision-making involves influence, pressure or coercion will depend on the nature of the intervention, on the circumstances and timing of the mediation, the nature of the case, and on the subjective reaction of the parties concerned. Where, for example, a mediator directly or indirectly expresses pleasure or displeasure at the

---

1   See 1.28.
2   See 1.13.
3   On influence, see R. Cialdini, *Influence: Science and Practice,* 4th ed, 2001. Refer to D. Coggiola, 'Cialdini's Six in Mediation', in (2008) 10(7) *ADR Bulletin* 134.

state of the negotiations, different parties will experience it differently. For some it might be a major source of pressure or coercion, and for others it might be of little significance at all. There is therefore a significant element of subjectivity to the topics discussed in this chapter.

The term 'encouraging settlement' is used to refer to all interventions in which the mediator uses power to promote settlement by the parties. Ways in which mediators *could* encourage settlement or the making of other relevant decisions will be reviewed. The difficult evaluative question of the extent to which mediators *should* perform this function is discussed at the end of the chapter.

B.   Sources of mediator power and influence

8.4   While mediators have limited formal authority (for example, they cannot impose binding decisions on the parties), they have considerable potential 'power'.[4] As indicated above, power is the ability to affect the perceptions, attitudes and behaviour of others.

Some of the sources of mediators' power are as follows:

- *Associational status* – the power they derive from their membership of a mediation service or professional association which 'accredits' mediators, or from a court or agency which appoints them to mediate.

- *Expertise* – the power that derives from their knowledge and understanding of conflict, of the mediation process, of negotiation behaviour and of other aspects of dispute resolution, and, in some situations, their substantive knowledge about the matters in dispute.

- *Control of the process* – the power deriving from their role as chair and manager of the mediation process, including the ability to make decisions on procedural matters, such as who speaks first, when to move from the discussion of one issue to another, or when to adjourn.

- *Personal attributes and skills* – the power deriving from their personality, inter-personal skills, intellectual capacity, linguistic abilities, and the like.

- *Access to restricted information* – the power which derives from knowing the parties' strengths, weaknesses, resistance points,[5] their priorities, the factors which are motivating them, and other information they may disclose to the mediator on a confidential basis.

- *Ability to transmit messages* – mediators derive considerable power from their position as the source of communication between the parties where they are in separate session or if the mediation is being conducted on a shuttle basis.

- *Ability to evaluate and sanction* – if mediators have structural sources of power, for example, if they were required to evaluate mediation behaviour or make any observations or recommendations (which could lead to sanctions for one or both parties) to outside bodies.[6]

---

4   L. Boulle and M. Nesic, *MPPP*, 2001, 137.
5   See 7.9.
6   Sanctions could include costs orders and, in funded cases, decisions regarding the nature and extent of ongoing funding.

- *Moral pressure* – mediators have power where, by virtue of their neutrality and independent status, they can invoke ethical standards or moral judgements which might affect and influence the parties.

At least some of these sources of power exist in all mediations. The next question for discussion is how mediator power can be used to encourage settlement and the making of other relevant decisions.

C. Categories of encouragement to settle

8.5   There are many potential ways in which mediators could use their power to encourage settlement. Here reference is made to five categories of encouraging settlement, namely providing information, expressing an opinion, advising, being judgemental, and acting as the agent of reality. It is not always easy, however, to be precise about the distinction between the provision of 'information' and the furnishing of an 'opinion', or between expressing an 'opinion' and giving 'advice'. Thus most of the following categories have some potential overlap with one another.

By providing 'information'

8.6   The first way in which mediators can encourage settlement is by providing 'information' to the parties.

Here 'information' is understood as referring to statements asserting the objective truth about matters, as opposed to providing an evaluation or expression of opinion.

Mediators can provide information in this sense in relation to:

- The mediation process ('In mediation we first define the problem before considering options for its settlement …').[7]

- Negotiation behaviour ('Negotiations work best where there are no last-minute add-ons as this can prejudice the progress made …').[8]

---

7   In some cases, the mediator has to provide certain information to the parties. For example, LSC contracted providers (and those complying with the MQMS) are required to provide information about the mediation process before and during mediation (Requirements F1.2, F2.1 and F2.2), on the right to seek independent legal advice (Requirement F1.3) and about complementary services (Requirement F2.3). Refer to Appendix 8 for the MQMS. The EU Recommendation on Family Mediation proposes an EU-wide requirement that family mediators should give legal information and inform parties of the possibility for them to consult a lawyer or any other relevant professional person at any time (refer to Article III (x) in Appendix 13).

8   In family mediation, mediators are required to inform parties of the need for full and frank disclosure (especially in relation to finance and property matters) before issues can be negotiated and agreed. Refer, for example, to sections 6.4 and 6.16 College of Mediators Code of Practice (in Appendix 8). In all cases, mediators may assist the parties to identify what information and documents might help resolution and how such information and documentation may be obtained. Refer, for example, to section 5.13 Law Society Code of Practice for Civil/Commercial Mediation (in Appendix 8).

- Legal rules or principles ('there is a cap on recovery at the tribunal...').[9]

- The legal system ('You would have to bring this kind of claim before the tribunal rather than the court').[10]

- Aspects of human behaviour ('Executives normally benefit from professional counselling after they have been retrenched').

- Realities of the situation ('Don't forget that while you are arguing over the sizes of the slices, the "cake" is getter smaller because of legal fees and other expenses').

- About the situation ('I have permission to tell you that, if your claim is successful, they will need to petition for insolvency and they are prepared to show you their financial information').

8.7   Clearly some kinds of information will be more 'objective' than others. The statement that 'In this jurisdiction you cannot get damages for [...]' will, if correct, be more objective than the statement that 'It's normal for depression to lift once the anxiety of a court hearing is removed.' Similarly some kinds of information when furnished by the mediator will have a greater effect in encouraging settlement than others.

By expressing an 'opinion'

8.8   The second way in which mediators can encourage settlement is by expressing an 'opinion' to the parties on a particular matter.

Here an 'opinion' refers to a considered view on some matter or a personal evaluation about a state of affairs, but without any firm advice or recommendation on which course of action to pursue. Opinions can be expressed on the same matters as those on which information can be provided. It is sometimes used when parties reach impasse and other interventions have failed.[11]

The expression of an opinion would normally be a more 'interventionist' contribution by a mediator than the provision of information, and therefore more likely to encourage settlement. Some mediators distinguish between a *professional* opinion (for example, the statement, 'As an engineer my view is that there was probably insufficient ballast for the size of the ship ...') and a personal opinion (for example, the statement, 'If I were you I'd probably forget about trying to get

---

9   For example, in family mediation, the mediator has to inform the parties of the impact on their arrangements of the Child Maintenance and Other Payments Act. Section 6.6 College of Mediators Code of Practice provides that mediators are required to promote parties' understanding of information before final agreement is reached. More generally, section 4.2 of the Code confirms that mediators may help parties to identify options available to them and the feasibility of those options. Refer to Appendix 8 for the Code.

10 For example, section 6.9 College of Mediators Code of Practice provides that mediators are required to inform parties about the court or other formal proceedings available without giving legal or other advice and without predicting the outcome of court or other proceedings. Refer to Appendix 8 for the Code.

11 For example, the mediator might ask if the parties would find it helpful if the mediator indicated a figure or range in which the negotiations might settle, given how the particular mediation has evolved.

them to apologise if they agree to more than £120,000 in damages …'). Some mediators feel that their professional opinions are more appropriate in mediation than their personal opinions. However, the subtleties of this distinction may not be appreciated by mediation clients for whom any expression of opinion by an authoritative mediator might influence them into making decisions in accordance with the opinion.

By 'advising'

8.9   The third way in which mediators can encourage settlement is by advising one or both parties on a particular issue or course of action.

Here the term 'advise' refers to the mediator making a suggestion or recommendation based on their professional assessment of the situation or on their personal experience. Advice denotes more than just an expression of opinion – it denotes an attitude as well.

8.10   In a mediation, advice can relate to one or more of a number of things:

■ Substantive advice: '£120,000 does not sound like adequate compensation for your injuries when your medical problems could continue for many years to come.'

■ Procedural advice: 'You would have difficulty getting most of that evidence admitted in court, but in mediation you may be able to use it to convince the other side to settle.'

■ Legal advice: 'You might find that you have a tax problem later if you formalise the agreement in that way.'

■ Advice on conflict: 'This dispute was the result of a breakdown in your working relationship caused by poor communication and now that you have demonised each other you should look at your relationship before discussing the money.'

■ Negotiation advice: 'In this type of negotiation it would be best for you to keep something up your sleeve and not to make your best offer at this stage.'

■ Advice on court behaviour: 'Judges here are not very sympathetic to those kinds of arguments and you would be advised to drop the idea that you can pursue them there.'

■ Advice on the facts: 'Your facts about the accident are disorganised and inconsistent and will have to be presented in a comprehensive and systematic way if you are to persuade anyone on the liability question.'

8.11   Probably one of the most discernible trends in certain areas of contemporary mediation practice, particularly in mediations relating to matters which are the subject of court proceedings, is that of the mediator 'advising' the parties in some or other way. The question of whether mediators should ever, or sometimes, give advice in one of the forms above is a major one in mediation circles. As with the other categories of encouraging settlement, it is dealt with further below.[12]

---

12   See 8.27–8.31.

By being 'critical or judgmental'

8.12   The fourth way in which mediators can encourage settlement is by being 'critical or judgmental' of one or both parties on a particular issue or proposed course of action.

This category is closely connected to that of the mediator advising, but implies a more severe evaluation of the parties' statements or behaviour. There are many ways in which mediators can encourage settlement by being critical or judgmental of the parties. Apart from direct judgmental or critical statements, one of the most likely ways is by asking certain categories of questions. When asked in the relevant context and with the appropriate tone, questions which are critical, suggestive or judgemental could be a significant factor in encouraging settlement by the parties.

8.13   The following are examples of such questions:

- Rhetorical questions: 'Do you want to settle on those terms now, or do you want to spend more time and money and settle in a year's time on the court steps?'

- Closed questions: 'Do you want to take either the reduced amount in cash or do you want the larger sum of money in instalments over three years?'

- Suggestive questions: 'Would it be possible for you to agree on the amount of damages if, for the purposes of mediation, the liability question remains unanswered?'

- Cross-examining questions: 'Didn't you say previously that you did not want to pursue that point any further?'

- Probing questions: 'You've said that you are strong on the liability question, but could you tell me what case law supports the defence you are raising?'

By acting as the 'agent of reality'

8.14   Mediators can encourage settlement by acting as 'agents of reality'.

The term 'agent of reality' is used frequently in relation to the role of mediators. The phrase suggests that they can encourage parties to face the realities of their situations where they are being unrealistic, uninformed or just intransigent. The purpose of reality testing is to make the relevant party reflect on a position, behaviour or attitude, to think of future consequences which they have not considered before, and to change their behaviour. The phrase is part of the jargon of mediation and is usually used in a way which denotes a sacred legitimacy to the function. In negotiation terms it is the mediator's way of 'creating doubt': he or she is the 'devil's advocate'.[13]

8.15   In fact the 'agent of reality' terminology is a loose and rather unhelpful description for many of the interventions referred to in this section. Thus the mediator can perform the agent of reality function by:

- providing information;

- advising one or both parties;

---

13   See 7.31.

- expressing an opinion on the matters in dispute;

- asking critical or judgemental questions;

- asking a party to think about another party's perspective;

- asking what would happen if the matter went to trial;

- helping parties to test the rationale for options;

- considering how proposals might affect non-parties.

Essentially, the mediator is inviting each party to see the weaknesses as well as the strengths of their case, the downsides as well as the upsides. Parties tend to minimise facts that weaken their position. Mediators seek to address that tendency. As reality testing is relatively interventionist, its extent and timing should be considered carefully. Parties can also perceive questions about the assessment of their case as a form of criticism, so reality testing is done in private meeting.[14]

The following table provides examples of how reality testing may be done in general civil and commercial cases. Appendix 6 contains a comprehensive guide on this topic.

Examples of reality testing methods

- Asking a party if a demand is a 'deal breaker'.

- Asking a party how they would react if the figures were considered in a different way eg – as a lump sum or on a global basis rather than item per item.

- A consideration of BATNA/WATNA/RATNA (ie – the best, worst and most realistic alternatives) if the matter were not to settle at the mediation.[15]

- A review of the stress, time and cost associated with litigation.

- A review of the prospects of success if the matter were to go to trial. This can be done formally via decision-tree analysis (see further below).

- A review of the facts, law or evidence.

- If there's a contributory negligence claim, a consideration of the outcome at trial if, say, a 20%, 50% or 80% contribution were found.

- A consideration of quantum issues, leaving to one side liability issues. Alternatively, a consideration of the liability issues, leaving to one side the quantum issues.

- In relation to a claim for goodwill, profits or consequential loss, a consideration of how such a claim will be proved.

- In relation to other money claims, a consideration of how these will be substantiated (eg – receipts).

- A review of the credibility of witnesses or experts.

- Even in 'strong cases', a review of litigation risks.

---

14 On some of the further ways in which mediators can exercise their reality testing function see 7.79–7.81.

15 Chapter 7 outlines these concepts.

- Even if a party were to win at trial, a review of what would be recovered, and how quickly and easily.

- A consideration of the financial viability of any party against whom a judgment will be sought if the matter did not settle at the mediation.

- A consideration of the effect of any offers should the matter go to trial.

- A consideration of the effect of any conditional fee agreement.

- A review of the publicity and reputation risks; and risks to relationships.

- Level of inconvenience for any relevant third parties if the matter did not resolve.

- A consideration of how each party would feel to have the whole matter behind them.

- The effect of delays in reaching settlement.

- 'Role reversal' – asking a party to put themselves in the shoes of another to consider their perspective.

- De Bono's 'six hats' technique – where each party has a number of team members, asking each member to 'wear a different coloured hat' and consider the perspective denoted by the colour of that hat (ie – red for emotional issues; white for factual matters; yellow for all the positive aspects; green for future implications, black for critique and blue for process).[16]

- Asking 'hypothetical questions' – 'what if…?' to test ideas and options.

- Consideration of the costs to date and the likely costs to trial. Identifying the level of irrecoverable costs. Refer to Appendix 6 for further guidance.

- Asking 'in principle, would you….?' as a further way of testing ideas and options.

- Making reference to policies, principles, precedents or customs to test the rationale for suggestions, offers and proposals.

- Referring to legal, expert, technical or other advice.

D. Methods and styles of encouraging settlement

8.16   As with most other mediator functions there are many methods and styles of encouraging settlement.

Verbal

8.17   There are numerous ways in which mediators can encourage settlement through verbal interventions. They include questioning, reframing, summarising and wording of the list of issues. As words are the main tool of the mediator, most encouragement to settle is likely to be provided in verbal form.

---

16   Edward de Bono, *Six Thinking Hats*, Little Brown, Boston, 1999.

Non-verbal

8.18   The various vocal and non-verbal forms of communication relevant to mediation have been referred to in Chapter 6.[17] They too can all potentially be used to encourage settlement, for example, through a mediator's sarcastic or disbelieving tone of voice, or through their shrug of the shoulders or raised eye-brow, with or without verbal accompaniment.

Another non-verbal form of pressure is the use of silence. Mediators can use silence strategically to induce one or other party to make an offer or proposal which might not otherwise have been forthcoming. The circumstances will determine whether this is an appropriate method of furthering the negotiations. It could be a manipulative strategy where one party is uncomfortable or embarrassed by silence and, in order to 'fill the vacuum', volunteers information which might otherwise have remained confidential or makes an offer, concession or compromise which they might not otherwise have made.

Procedural and structural

8.19   Again, there is a wide variety of procedural interventions which mediators might use to encourage settlement, for example, hurrying the parties quickly through the list of issues, keeping them at the negotiation table for lengthy periods, imposing deadlines on them, or resorting to shuttle mediation so that they can use their mediator power more forcefully. This is to acknowledge that even the standard process tasks of mediators are not always neutral and passive functions but can be experienced by the parties as influencing, pressuring or even coercing them into making decisions.

Environmental

8.20   Design and manipulation of the environment can also be factors in encouraging the parties to settle. This includes the choice of venue, use of space, seating arrangements, and the like. However, even where time is limited, mediators are not advised to provide the parties with uncomfortable seats so that they are pressured by discomfort to agree and get out of there.

Visual

8.21   Mediators can use visual effects to make a point about a proposed settlement. For example, in a parenting dispute, they could visually represent the days and weeks on a flipchart to depict graphically the overall effect, and its fairness or unfairness, of a proposed plan. Likewise in a commercial mediation they can write up lists of offers and counter-offers to show how much each party has conceded since the negotiations commenced, or perform mathematical calculations which can be more easily assimilated by the parties.

---

17   See 6.19–6.30.

Styles of encouraging settlement

8.22   Each of the different methods of encouraging settlement can vary in style and intensity. An intervention could be very tentative, very assertive, and so on, along a continuum of high to low intensity. The point at which it is located on this continuum will depend on the nature of the intervention, the intention of the mediator and the perception of the party or parties concerned.

8.23   Here are some points on this continuum, based on a contractual dispute. They range from the strictly non-interventionist to the forcefully interventionist style. These styles overlap to some extent with the categories of encouraging settlement referred to above, but they are provided to illustrate degrees of intensity and not the different categories as such.

- Non-interventionist: 'No, I cannot advise you in any way on what you should do about the indemnity, nor on your legal rights. If you need that kind of advice, we shall have to adjourn and you can approach someone who can assist with that.'

- Minimal interventionist: 'Well, I cannot give you any advice, but in my experience of these disputes there are three basic ways of dealing with the indemnity issue. Shall I tell you what they are and you can decide if you will opt for one of them?'

- Mildly interventionist: 'Of course it's not for me to say what you should do, but as an outsider I might be inclined to drop the request for the indemnity if you can get a warranty.'

- Moderately interventionist: 'You know, it's up to you to decide, but in my experience in these situations, an indemnity is not common.'

- Reluctantly interventionist: 'I won't be recommending anything now about that issue, but sometimes if both parties ask me late in the day I will make a suggestion, but it would clearly not be binding on you.'

- Strongly interventionist: 'You have more chance of winning the lottery than having a court award that.'

- Forcefully interventionist: 'You're crazy to think about it, no court would order that.'

Again, the extent to which the different styles of encouraging settlement are appropriate or inappropriate will be covered below.[18]

E. Using power to encourage settlement: some illustrations

8.24   Following are some further illustrations of ways in which mediators could encourage settlement through influence, pressure or other uses of mediator power. They involve the application of principles referred to in this chapter. It should be emphasised that *some of these examples might be highly inappropriate in some circumstances and in some types of cases*. Mediators *need to be selective in choosing* from them.[19]

---

18   See 8.27–8.34.
19   Refer also to L. R. Lowry, 'To Evaluate or Not – That is Not the Question!', in (1997) 2 *Resolutions* (Pepperdine University) 2.

8.25   The illustrations are based on a workplace dispute over the introduction of new information technology systems into the production and management system of a small publishing company. Those involved in the mediation are Bernadette, representing the chief executive officer; Ray, the human resources manager; Leigh, representing the workers; and John, a union official.

Case illustration

Congratulations, flattery:

> Well done to you all on coming to mediation, which avoids the downsides of a fight in court.

Setting high expectations:

> Most disputes settle and very few ever go to formal adjudication. In mediation, typically 75% of cases are settled.

Shaming:

> Well Ray, Bernadette, John and Leigh, you've been arguing for seven hours now with plenty of acrimony but very little progress. Do you think that sort of behaviour is of any benefit to the business or to the workers employed in it?

Using time limits:

> Unfortunately there are only 15 minutes of mediation time left, after which there will be no further opportunity to mediate, so why don't you use the time productively.

Referring to BATNA:

> If you don't reach an agreement here today this matter will go to adjudication and an umpire you have not chosen will make decisions about the business and working conditions about which he or she will know very little. Have you considered this alternative?

Depict a limited range of options:

> You all want the business to remain profitable and competitive. From what you have said, there are two options – to introduce the new technologies or to look for other ways of cutting expenses and being more productive. Which of those options do you want to work on?

Becoming evaluative:

> It seems to me that you're all going to have to be more flexible. Bernadette and Ray, you'll have to consider conceding on the employees' demand for more training within working hours, and Leigh and John, you're going to have to consider conceding on the introduction of electronic forms of production as has happened throughout the industry.

'Gift-wrapping' offers or counter-offers (during private meetings):

> Ray and Bernadette, you're making good progress; Leigh and John are still committed to coming to an agreement, they're now prepared for the company to introduce some new technology, and they're committed in principle to seeking worker support for what is agreed today. However, at this point in time they can't quite agree on the nature and timing of the new systems you propose, and you'll also have to do some further work on the training issue.

Educating and coaching (in separate session):

> John and Leigh, in negotiations it's usual for one side to make a concession in response to the first concession of the other side. This keeps the negotiations moving, is a sign of good faith, and can establish a pattern for the rest of the negotiations. John and Leigh, would you like me to assist you in making a counter-offer to Bernadette and Ray in a way which is most favourable to you?

Trivialising differences:

> You're arguing over whether the new system will be introduced on 23 October or 30 October. How important is that difference in light of all the other factors you have largely agreed on?

Emphasising common objective standards:

> You're all committed to the continuing viability of the company. All the expertise indicates that new technology requires adequate training in order for it to be used to the optimum extent. And the suppliers have standard training packages that can be purchased by users. Let's focus on the details of those packages.

Creating doubt over professional advice:

> You both have good legal advisers, but it is logically not possible for both lawyers to be right. At least one is wrong, and it may be that both are wrong. However, it is logically impossible for both to be right.

Creating dissonance:

> John and Leigh, what would you need from Bernadette and Ray in order to get you to agree to their proposal on when the new systems should come into effect?

> John and Leigh, what could you offer Bernadette and Ray to get them to agree to your proposal on the new remuneration package?

> Bernadette and Ray, if I was an adjudicator here and I was to say that there was going to be the kind of training and support being requested by Leigh and John, but that you could define the timing and extent of that training, then what would you suggest should be those terms and conditions?

> **Threatening to quit:**
>
> You've been arguing on that point for several hours, and not only are you making no progress, but you seem to be slipping backwards. It seems that there is no real negotiability between you. Unless either of you can come up with a proposal, I may have to terminate the mediation.

As already indicated, there are dangers in the use of these forms of encouraging settlement and these are referred to in section G below.

F. Risk assessment

8.26   Risk assessment is an important tool in preparation of a party for mediation. It provides an 'illumination' of the risks should the matter not settle at the mediation. It also provides a realistic basis for assessing the BATNA, WATNA and RATNA (ie – the best, worst and most realistic alternatives). It is a form of reality testing (discussed above). Risk assessment requires experience, good judgement, and a review of the law and evidence. An accurate assessment of the chances of success if the matter were to go to trial is essential. A common way of capturing uncertainties in a case is via a decision tree. It overcomes the tendency for parties to oversimplify their risk decisions. A decision tree analysis involves the following basic steps:[20]

- Identify all the uncertainties – in relation to the facts, the law, the witnesses, the other parties' witnesses, the costs and the procedure:

  - For example, in relation to the facts, a list of all factual matters in issue, even if they are not disputed, is a first step. For risk purposes, the factual basis for each legal claim is analysed. A consideration of how the facts can be proved is the next step. The areas of uncertainty allow an assessment to be made of the chances of success.

  - Even assuming that the facts are clear and can be proved, the question then becomes whether the facts establish a legal action. For risk purposes, the effects on the case of various decisions on the law are factored in.

  - Some account must then be taken of how the witnesses will come across at trial. Will the judge be sympathetic towards a particular witness? How credible are the witnesses?

  - In relation to costs, the effect of any offers made, and the issue of proportionality of costs, will need to be considered. The ability to recover costs from an opponent is also considered.

  - Procedural risks need to be factored in as well, for example, the effect of limitation issues, pre-action protocols, and other procedural requirements.

- Probabilities are then assigned for each outcome. A discussion of percentages may also reveal differences between the way descriptive phrases about risk were

---

20 For a further discussion of decision tree analysis, refer to Aaron and Hoffer, 'Decision Analysis as a Method of Evaluating the Trial Alternative', in Dwight Golann (ed), *Mediating Legal Disputes*, Aspen, 1996, 307; and Hoffer, 'Decision Analysis as a Mediator's Tool', in (1996) *1 Harv. Neg. L.R.* 113.

intended by a lawyer and the way these have been understood by a client. For example, legal advice that a case 'is quite strong' might be interpreted by a client to mean 90% chance of success, whereas the lawyer might have meant 60%.

- If there is a Part 36 offer, the chances of beating that offer are also evaluated.

- The value of the claim is based on the various assessments made above. It is calculated by multiplying the pound value of the possible outcomes by the probability that each will occur and adding them together. It represents an average of all the possible outcomes, weighted by the probability that each outcome will occur. The expected value of the claim is not the likely judgment at trial, but an average award that would be made if the party ran 100 identical claims to trial. In other words, it is just an estimate based on many other estimates along the branches. The calculation also does not take into account less tangible costs, like management time required for a trial or the stress occasioned by preparation for a trial.

- The cost effectiveness of litigation, and other alternatives, can then be evaluated. When comparing alternatives, all alternatives need to be identified first. Although the decision tree will usually deal with one alternative, the litigation route, there might be many others, for example, sale of a business or going to the Press.

A mediator uses risk assessment to highlight the risks of litigation to the parties. A simple decision tree is in the diagram below. Usually, a decision tree analysis is not so straightforward and can contain many branches along the path of each option to accommodate the various elements that will need to proved in most cases, for example, a breach of duty, causation and loss in the case of a negligence action. If the chance of proving liability is 70%, causation 70% and loss 100%, the chance of proving all three is 70 x 70 x 100 = 49%. In addition, if there is a Part 36 offer, and if the chance of beating that offer is 50%, the chance of beating the offer is 49 x 50 = 24.5%.

To describe the structure of the tree, each decision node (when a party has a choice to make) is represented by a square (for example, the decision to settle or to litigate). The party then reaches a chance node (when the party cannot control the outcome), which is represented by a circle. The chance node is followed by the number of branches needed to represent what might happen at each stage. There are usually a number of chance nodes along a branch.

There are limits to and risks in tree analysis. In particular, the analysis depends on a comprehensive analysis and sound judgement. In addition, not everything is quantifiable. There are many less formal ways to conduct a risk assessment. Refer to Appendix 6 for a further guide.[21]

G.   Dangers in encouraging settlement

8.27   There are a number of potential dangers in any situation in which a mediator uses his or her power to influence or pressure the parties to enter an agreement which they might not otherwise have entered. Some of the dangers

---

21   The guide in Appendix 6 has been reprinted with the kind permission of John Wade.

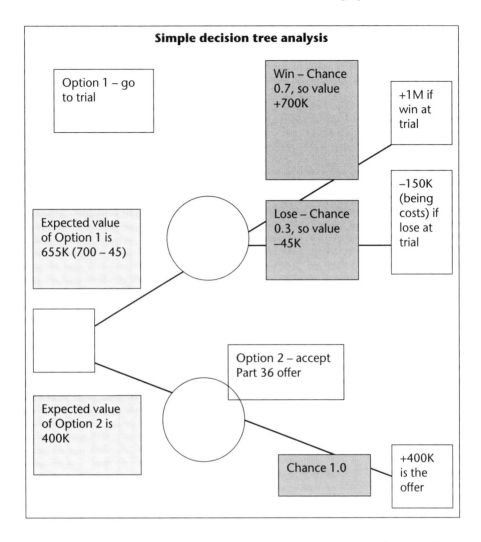

Simple decision tree analysis

Option 1 – go to trial

Win – Chance 0.7, so value +700K

+1M if win at trial

Expected value of Option 1 is 655K (700 – 45)

Lose – Chance 0.3, so value –45K

–150K (being costs) if lose at trial

Option 2 – accept Part 36 offer

Expected value of Option 2 is 400K

Chance 1.0

+400K is the offer

relate to the parties and their agreement, others relate to the mediator, and yet others relate to the reputation of mediation as a whole.

Dangers relating to the parties and their agreement

8.28 Some of the dangers might be:

- The mediator's own interests in achieving a mediated settlement, such as his or her success rate and reputation, could take precedence over the interests of the parties.

- The mediator's own perceptions, values and preferences about what is appropriate might come to the fore and affect the outcome more than the parties' views affect it.

- There is a possibility of greater pressure being applied to, or experienced by, the weaker party because they are the ones more likely to be affected by mediator power and more likely to make concessions.

- The mediator's pressure could be based on objective, normative standards (legal rules, company policies, and so on) and not on the subjective interests and needs of the parties.

- One or both parties might not abide by the mediated agreement because they feel that they were pressured and forced to compromise in the mediation.

- The legal validity of the mediated agreement might be challenged on grounds of duress or undue influence.

Case illustration: too much encouragement

In a mediation involving a bank's attempt to foreclose on the family property, all parties were legally represented. The mediator was determined to maintain the momentum when the parties were making progress and continued the mediation without significant breaks into the late hours of the night. Eventually settlement was reached and all parties signed the mediated agreement. Some time later the owner of the property brought legal proceedings in an attempt to have the mediated agreement set aside as not being valid in law. The court was asked to review the contract in the light of the undue influence and duress which was allegedly affecting the owner when the agreement was signed. The court found that the party had established these factors and refused to uphold the agreement. The action was brought against the party's own solicitor and not against the mediator, but the argument was that the circumstances of the mediation created an oppressive climate for this party.[22]

Dangers relating to the mediator

8.29   Dangers relating to the mediator are:

- The mediator might lose his or her status of independence and neutrality in the eyes of a party who felt pressured into reaching settlement.

- Disciplinary action might be brought against the mediator for breach of relevant standards or ethical guidelines.[23]

- The mediator might be sued in negligence or for breach of the agreement to mediate.

- The pressure experienced by the parties might affect the reputation of the mediator among potential users of their services.

---

22   Although this kind of case is yet to be brought before courts in the UK, such cases have arisen in other jurisdictions, including the US and Australia.

23   See, for example, section 5.5 Law Society Code of Practice for Civil/Commercial Mediation (in Appendix 8) which provides that mediators should not impose his/her preferred outcome on parties. Section 6.9 College of Mediators Code of Practice (also in Appendix 8) also provides that mediators should not give legal or other advice and must not predict the outcome of court or other formal proceedings. Section 4.9 CORE Solutions Group Code of Conduct (also in Appendix 8) provides that mediators should not decide or give an opinion on factual or legal issues except in the circumstances set out in the Code.

Dangers relating to the system of mediation

8.30   Some general dangers pertaining to the mediation system are:

- Bad experiences of the inappropriate use of mediator power might adversely affect the reputation of mediation in the marketplace.

- Significant inconsistencies could arise in the practice of mediation among different mediators and in different contexts.

- Users and potential users of mediation might become confused about the nature of mediation and the mediator's role.

H. Creating the balance

8.31   As indicated in the introduction to this chapter, the most difficult issue relating to the mediator's role of encouraging settlement is how interventionist or non-interventionist mediators should be. On one hand, parties in mediation usually require a settlement to their problems and that might only be forthcoming with some encouragement from the mediator (see the case illustration below). On the other hand, too much encouragement could create the problems referred to in 8.28–8.30.

> #### Case illustration: too little encouragement
>
> An experienced solicitor, Victor, recommended the choice of a particular mediator, Tony, because he was an expert in the subject matter of the dispute, had held a high position in the regional law society, and was regarded as wise and eminent in the profession. Because his client was resistant to his own recommendations on a commercial settlement, Victor thought that the right signs from a neutral mediator with the status of Tony would have the desired effect. Tony had recently completed a mediation training course and was committed to conducting the process without using his power to encourage settlement. The mediation did not produce a settlement. In a subsequent interview Victor indicated that his client had been on the brink of coming to a commercial settlement and required just a little more encouragement from the mediator. When this was not forthcoming his resistances resurfaced and he was able to justify to himself his decision to walk away without reaching agreement.

8.32   It is not easy to talk in abstract terms about the proper balance between the parties' right to self-determination and the mediator's function of encouraging them to make decisions. Much will depend on context and culture.

In relation to context, the important factors are:

- *Timing*: in terms of its likely receptiveness and effectiveness in influencing a party, encouragement of settlement should not occur before trust has been established, and therefore should come later rather than sooner in the mediation process.

- *Stage of mediation process*: which is distinct from, though related to, the timing question. There will normally be more latitude for mediators to encourage settlement in separate sessions than there will be in joint session.

■ *Attitude and circumstances* of the parties will also be an important contextual factor. If the parties jointly ask the mediator for an opinion, it is likely to be experienced as less coercive than if they have not done so. Likewise if a party has professional advisers or lay supporters present, he or she is less likely to experience pressure or coercion (at least from the mediator) than is a party without such support.

■ *Personal disposition* of a party, their educational status and emotional stability, and how as individuals they react to the various forms of encouraging settlement referred to in this chapter.

8.33   Some mediator codes of conduct attempt to provide clarity and consistency in this area.[24] For example, the Law Society's Code of Practice for Civil/Commercial Mediation requires, in section 3, mediator impartiality. The commentary to section 3 elaborates on the obligation:

> Whilst impartiality is fundamental to the role of the mediator, this does not mean that a mediator may never express a comment or view that one party may find more acceptable than another. However, the mediator must not allow his or her personal view of the fairness or otherwise of the substance of the negotiations between the parties to damage or impair his or her impartiality. The mediator must appreciate that his or her involvement in the process is inevitably likely to affect the course of the negotiations between the parties. (His or her involvement is, of course, intended to assist that process so far as possible.) This would be the case whether the mediator intervenes directly or whether he or she deals with issues indirectly, for example, through questions. Consequently, all mediator intervention needs to be conducted with sensitivity and care in order to maintain impartiality.[25]

The commentary to section 4 of the Code makes a proviso:

> The mediator and the parties should agree, as far as practicable, at the outset whether the mediator's role will be purely facilitative, or whether the mediator may at his or her discretion, provide an evaluative element based on his or her knowledge of the subject matter or legal issues involved.[26]

The Code clarifies, in section 5, that the mediator should not impose his or her prefered outcome on the parties, although the mediator may suggest solutions and help the parties to explore these.[27] The commentary to section 5 clarifies further:

> The mediator cannot be responsible for issues of justice and fairness of outcome; the parties must define their own 'fairness' of the substantive terms and criteria for agreeing terms.[28]

---

24   Most codes will at least require the mediator to maintain impartiality. See, for example, Article 2.2 the European Code of Conduct for Mediators. Appendix 8 contains a selection of codes of conduct.
25   Refer to Appendix 8 for the Code in its entirety.
26   Ibid, commentary to section 4.
27   Ibid, section 5.7.
28   Ibid, commentary to section 5.

Similarly, the ADR Group Mediation Practice and Rules provides, in section 3.2, that the mediator will not analyse a party's legal position on rights, impose a settlement on parties, or offer legal advice or act as legal adviser to any party.[29]

Codes regulating family mediators tend to be more thorough than those applying to community or commercial mediators. For example, the College of Mediators Code of Practice recognises, in section 4, that there is an expectation that family mediators should assist the parties to identify and explore options and the feasibility of those options, which may involve giving various information.[30] Whilst reaffirming that role, the EU Recommendation on Family Mediation seeks to remind mediators of the core values:

'i. the mediator is impartial between the parties;

ii. the mediator is neutral as to the outcome of the mediation process;

iii. the mediator respects the point of view of the parties and preserves the equality of their bargaining positions;

iv. the mediator has no power to impose a solution on the parties.'[31]

While a code may point to a certain underlying philosophy, it does not altogether resolve the question because of the definitional issues referred to in this chapter – the distinctions between information, opinions and advice are not self-evident.

It's all in the framing

John Haynes describes the importance of preserving the parties' rights to make outcome decisions, whilst assisting them with information or opinions, through appropriate framing.[32] For example, the following are statements from the mediator:

'You could sell the house.'

'Have you considered selling the house?'

'You may wish to consider selling the house.'

'Is selling the house one of your options?'

Haynes considers that options 1 and 2 are commands; statement 3 is information which gives the party the right to choose (although in some cases it can be received by the party as a command); and statement 4 places the option in the context of a range of options, leaving it to the party to choose, and is preferable.

8.34   There is little doubt that in practice some mediators are chosen because they have a reputation for being 'assertive' in their interventions. Likewise, a particular model of mediation might have been chosen because it allows the mediator to make a greater contribution on matters of content as opposed to

---

29   Refer to Appendix 3 for a full copy of the Procedure and Rules.
30   Refer to Appendix 8 for the Code in its entirety. See also 8.6–8.7.
31   Council of Europe Recommendation No.R(98)1 of the Committee of Ministers to Member States on Family Mediation – see Article III – in Appendix 13.
32   J. M. Haynes, 'Mediation and Therapy: An Alternative View', in 10 *Mediation Q.* 21 (1992).

matters of process. Where a mediator does not encourage settlement sufficiently in these circumstances he or she might not be doing what is required by the circumstances.[33]

At the same time, some of the methods of encouraging settlement referred to in this chapter would be regarded by many as illegitimate exercises of mediator power in many circumstances and types of cases. This suggests the need for a delicate balance between assertion and oppression, between persistence and pressure, between patience and endurance.[34] In some ways this is easier to understand in the context of mediation simulations, case studies, observation studies and other concrete mediation situations. For beginner mediators, it is recommended that they err on the side of encouraging settlement mildly rather than robustly.

I. Summary

8.35   This chapter raises the following points of particular significance:

- Great care needs to be taken in the use of key terms relevant to the topic of encouraging settlement because of the flexibility of language and the different connotations words have for different people.

- The wisdom of any attempt to encourage settlement has to be made in the context of the concrete circumstances of a mediation, including the stage it has reached, timing, party expectations, the support and resources available to the parties, and the potential dangers of this type of mediator intervention.

- While the intention and style of the mediator is a factor in evaluating the wisdom of these interventions, it will ultimately depend very much on the parties' subjective reactions to them as to whether or not they are appropriate and effective.

J. Tasks for beginner mediators

8.36   All professionals have different sources of power in the practice of their particular professions (a doctor's power is different in nature to that of a teacher). What is there inherent in the nature and process of mediation that gives particular powers to mediators? What are some of the dangers created by these powers?

8.37   Refer to the practical illustrations of ways in which mediators can encourage settlement referred to above at 8.23–8.25. Which of these interventions do you think are generally legitimate, which are illegitimate, and which would have to be assessed in the light of the particular mediation circumstances in which they were used?

8.38   Observe a video of a simulated or real mediation and make notes of the different ways in which the mediator encourages settlement as described in this chapter. Are there any ways in which he or she encourages settlement that are

---

33 See 8.30.
34 Charlton and Dewdney, *The Mediator's Handbook,* 2nd ed, 2004.

different to those referred to here? A list of mediation videos and DVDs are in section B in Appendix 10.

K. Recommended reading

Benjamin R., *The Effective Negotiation and Mediation of Conflict: Applied Theory and Practice Handbook*, 2007.

Benjamin, R. *The Guerrilla Negotiator: Effective Strategies for Reaching Agreement and the Mediation of Conflict*, 2004.

Boulle L. and Nesic M., *Mediation: Principles, Process, Practice*, Tottel Publishing, 2001, Ch 6.

Charlton R. and Dewdney M., *The Mediator's Handbook*, 2nd ed, Lawbook Co, Sydney, 2004, Ch 5.

Hammond J. H. et al, *Smart Choices: A Practical Guide to Making Better Life Decisions*, Broadway Books, New York, 2002.

LSC, *Mediation Quality Mark Standard*, 2nd ed, 2009.

Mackie K. et al, *The ADR Practice Guide: Commercial Dispute Resolution*, Tottel Publishing, 2007, at 13.9.

Pruitt D., 'Achieving Integrative Agreements' in Bazerman and Lewicki (eds), *Negotiation in Organisations*, 1983.

Raiffa H., *The Art and Science of Negotiation*, Belknap, Cambridge Mass., 2005.

Roberts M., *Mediation in Family Disputes: Principles of Practice*, Ashgate, Aldershot, 2008.

Ury, W. *The Power of a Positive No: How to Say No and Still Get to Yes*. Bantam, New York, 2007.

Wade J., 'Forever Bargaining in the Shadow of the Law' *Fourth International Mediation Conference*, Melbourne, 5–8 April 1998.

Wade J., 'Guide on Systematic Risk Analysis for Negotiators and Litigators: How to Help Clients Make Better Decisions' (2002) 13 *Bond Law Review*, 462–485 (included in Appendix 6).

Chapter 9

Variations in the Mediation Process

Cut your coat to suit your cloth

A. Introduction

9.1 There are many possible variations which can be made to the 'standard' mediation process which was described in Chapter 5, as mediation is adapted and modified to suit the circumstances in which it is being used. The variations could be required or dictated by a wide variety of circumstances: the needs of the parties, the nature of the dispute, the resources on hand, the amount of time available, the strategic judgements of the mediator and so on.

Generally, it will be the mediator who makes a discretionary decision in relation to most of these variations. However, they may also be requested by the parties and their advisers, or be demanded by the objective circumstances of the mediation. A mediator's flexibility to adopt approaches and strategies to tackle the particular circumstances is a skill requiring observation of behaviour and a broad repoirtoire of interventions.

This chapter deals with a few of the many variations that can be made to the standard mediation process.

B. Multiple meetings

9.2 Mediations can be held over one or more separate sessions conducted on different days, different months, even different years. Generally speaking mediators can, in their discretion, call adjournments after consultation with the parties. They can also call them in response to reasonable requests from the parties or their advisers for breaks and postponements in the process.

There are many reasons for the calling of adjournments. Some relate to the subjective requirements of one or both parties, such as their need for some respite from intense emotions or the need for external assistance and advice or review. Others relate to the objective requirements of the process, such as the need for further information, planning and deliberation, or a fresh mandate from relevant constituents. Double-booked venues and conflicting commitments for the parties or their advisers can lead to unplanned adjournments.

9.3   In some mediation contexts there is a policy of having multiple meetings as standard practice. This is the case, for example, in parenting disputes. Here the parties are given a break (of, say, four weeks) to enable them to consider the progress they have made, to reflect on provisional agreements, and to acquire information or make arrangements for the subsequent mediation meeting. The adjournments also serve to prevent either parent from feeling pressured into making hasty decisions. In other contexts, for example commercial mediations, adjournments are held with some reluctance, for fear that the momentum of the negotiations may be lost and the parties might move further apart during the period of interruption. In the international context, and where parties are geographically dispersed, it is often not feasible to reconvene.

9.4   Where multiple meetings are held, parties are informed about the process that will evolve,[1] and each new session usually begins with a *review* of developments since the last meeting. This allows both parties to indicate where they currently stand on important issues, what changes have occurred since the last meeting, and what new information or insight has been obtained. It also provides the opportunity to reconsider provisional agreements and here it is sometimes discovered that the 'temporary has become the permanent'.

Case illustration: making the temporary permanent

One of the advantages of multiple meetings is that they can use the factor of time to secure agreements that would otherwise be problematic to achieve. In a mediation which was scheduled to run over several sessions, the parties agreed to an interim arrangement for the four-week period between the two first meetings. This agreement was acceded to with some reluctance by both parties, and only because it did not involve a permanent commitment by them.

When the second mediation session was held the interim arrangement was reviewed, and both parties agreed to commit to it permanently and they moved on to discuss other issues. The parties had felt safe in committing to it in its temporary form and then, having satisfactorily 'road-tested' the arrangement, were able to commit to its continuation on a permanent basis.

9.5   Unfortunately the converse can also occur and after an adjournment there can be 'slippage'. One or both parties might resile from previous agreements or raise unexpected new issues in the negotiations. While this is not easy to avoid, some mediators attempt to prevent it by having personal contact with each party or their advisers during the adjournment and discussing with them the possible consequences of any slippage for which they might be responsible.

---

1   For example, F2.2 MQMS (in respect of LSC franchised mediation and those cases complying with the MQMS) requires a process to be in place during the mediation to write to the parties, at a minimum, when there is any change in planned action, or if it becomes clear that mediation is no longer appropriate, or if there is a change in mediator. This is additional to the general requirement in F2.1 to have a process in place to ensure that parties are notified of dates/venues of mediation sessions, key dates, actions to be taken and the availability of legal advice. The MQMS is included in Appendix 8.

C. Shuttle mediation

9.6   Reference was made in Chapter 5 to the concept of 'shuttle mediation'. This involves the parties being based in different physical locations, whether those be rooms, venues, cities or countries, and the mediator moving continuously between them, shuttling messages back and forth and becoming their sole avenue of communication. The system is named after the 'shuttle diplomacy' which sometimes occurs in international disputes involving nation states and political groupings. It was pointed out previously that shuttle mediation should be distinguished from a mediation in which there is a series of separate meetings, as there are practical and qualitative differences between the two.[2]

Differences in shuttle mediation

9.7   Shuttle mediation differs from a series of separate meetings in mediation in the following ways:

■ There are reasons for the parties being based in separate rooms or venues and it is understood that the full mediation will be conducted in this way unless the parties make a conscious decision to come together.

■ All the communications are conveyed through the mediator, which gives them enhanced potential control and power.

■ The usual confidentiality principle is modified to allow the mediator to convey messages between the parties.

9.8   Because of these differences, it is important that mediators should not transform a conventional mediation into shuttle mediation by default, that is, by lapsing into a prolonged series of separate sessions. There should always be a specific reason for shuttle mediation, and where the mediation does not begin in this mode the parties should be made aware of any change into shuttle and of its implications for their communications and the confidentiality principle.

When to use shuttle mediation

9.9   Mediators might consider the use of shuttle mediation in the following circumstances:

■ There are legal or safety reasons why the parties cannot be together, for example, the existence of domestic violence orders.

■ One of the parties feels intimidated or afraid or there are other high emotions which would be exacerbated by meeting in each other's presence.

■ There is a gross imbalance of bargaining power because of differences in verbal ability, size of the groups, number of advisers, and the like.[3]

■ There would be very poor communication in joint sessions because of linguistic or cultural factors.

■ The parties cannot afford for their followers to see them together, for example, in international disputes or high-profile local disputes involving political parties, minorities or ethnic groups.

---

2   See 5.60.
3   Refer to 10.3–10.10.

9.10   In these circumstances it could be the case that there will either be shuttle mediation or no mediation at all. Some commentators, however, argue that shuttle is not true mediation in that the parties do not work collaboratively on the problem, they do not learn how to negotiate with one another, and they do not have the opportunity to improve their relationship for the future. From this perspective, shuttle mediation should be used as rarely as possible.

Practical considerations

9.11   Mediators need to attend to a number of practical matters in relation to shuttle mediation. Here is a list of practical considerations for shuttle mediators, with examples of the kind of language they might use in dealing with them:

- Explain to the parties the ground rules and the practicalities of the process: 'Because this is shuttle mediation, I shall be transmitting all messages between you and the others. Please be patient when I am not with you as this kind of mediation can take some time. However, when I leave you to see the others, I shall suggest matters on which you can do some work while I am away. You will also have plenty of time for a coffee …'

- Establish a clear basis for what can be disclosed and what is to remain confidential: 'You should indicate clearly what you would like me to say to the others and what should remain confidential. This includes not only facts and figures, but also reasons and explanations both for your proposals and for your response to their proposals. Only if I know what is confidential can I avoid unwanted disclosures.'

- Be alert to the parties' sensitivities over the amount of time spent with the other side: 'I shall convey your proposals to the other side and I expect to spend about 15 minutes with them. However, in shuttle mediation it is difficult to predict exactly how much time I will spend with either of you. If I am going to be longer than expected, I shall come back and let you know.'

- Avoid losing impartiality by becoming the advocate of one or both parties: 'Now I can tell them why you are not accepting their offer, convey your counter-proposal to them, and provide the explanation and reasoning which you have just given me. However, I cannot become your advocate and persuade them to accept your proposal, just as I cannot do that to you with any of their proposals.'

- Take precautions against making mistakes in conveying the parties' messages to each another: 'Now your offer is quite a complex one, so I would like to write down the various financial amounts and times of payment that you are proposing, and then go over with you the justification for your proposal which you would like me to present to them.'

Some potential drawbacks and dangers in shuttle mediation

9.12   There are a number of potential drawbacks and dangers in shuttle mediation. The process itself has some transaction costs not found in non-shuttle mediation, for example, it could take considerably more time and it is susceptible to mistakes and misunderstandings. Communication is liable to be distorted and to focus more on substantive content and less on emotional content.

From the point of view of the parties, shuttle mediation can create dynamics not usual in non-shuttle mediation. Because they are each located in their own 'locker rooms', there is a danger that the parties will engage in bravado, fighting talk and team 'war cries', and even that they will backtrack without shame in the absence of the other side. This is because it can be easier to engage in positional bargaining, threats, bluster and other negotiation tricks when not facing the other mediating party. Shuttle mediation can also result in the parties attempting to persuade the mediator, instead of each other, and in unconsciously using the mediator as their agent to advocate their case to the other side.

9.13 Shuttle mediation also creates the potential danger of an abuse of mediator power deriving from his or her position as the sole conduit of information between the parties. This point can be illustrated by reference to the range of options which a shuttle mediator has when asked to convey an offer from one party to the other.

Case illustration

Assume that there is a shuttle mediation in an inheritance dispute relating to a deceased father–husband's will. The parties involved are the executor of the estate, the deceased's widow and his two sons. There is agreement between the relatives that reasonable provision should be made for all of them and the executor has agreed to go along with any satisfactory proposal to which they can commit. The widow wishes to make a monetary offer to her two sons through the shuttle mediator. Here the mediator has several options.

He can convey:

1. The factual offer without anything else: 'Your mother is offering you each £50,000 and one-quarter of the proceeds of the family farm when it is sold in ten years' time.'

2. The monetary offer with other information, which could be general or highly selective, explaining and justifying the offer: 'Your mother is offering you each £50,000 because that will allow you to finish your education and one-quarter of the proceeds of the family farm in ten years' time because, in the meantime, she would like to bring to fruition your father's vision of a 20,000 chicken farm producing for export.'

3. The monetary offer together with the emotional dimensions surrounding it: 'Your mother is offering you each £50,000 and one-quarter of the proceeds of the family farm when it is sold in ten years' time. She feels very upset at the strain that this dispute has put on the family, she is sad about the fact that some of your father's oft-stated wishes might not be carried out, and she is concerned that the value of the estate is diminishing while you quarrel over it. She feels that her proposal will put all this behind you and improve family relations.'

4. The monetary offer enclosed in 'gift wrap' to make it more palatable to the others: 'Now your mother is committed to coming to an agreement today, she wants that to be fair and reasonable to both of you as well as to her, and she would like to talk about family reconciliation once this is settled. She would also like you to be consulted on the development of the farm to bring to fruition your father's wishes. Her offer at the moment is …'

5. The offer, plus the mediator's intimation as to whether there might be a further offer: 'At this point in time your mother would like to make an offer. This is based on the various discussions we have had so far. It might be that with further information and negotiation her position will change. At the moment her offer is …'

Each of these approaches has advantages and disadvantages and mediators will have to make tactical judgements as to which is appropriate at different stages of the mediation proceedings.

9.14   The mediator also has considerable power in relation to the timing of offers, to 'coaching' the parties about negotiation, to getting them to anticipate possible responses to their offers, and to other features of the negotiation process referred to in this book.[4] It is conceivable, for example, that a mediator might be tempted to refuse to convey certain offers, and accompanying sentiments, because, in his or her judgement, it would be unwise to do so. For example, he or she might indicate to one side that they will get £x when the mediator knows that the other side is in fact offering the greater amount of £x + y, so that the 'excess' of £y can be disclosed later when, in the mediator's discretion, the timing is 'ripe' to do so.

9.15   These possibilities are referred to here without any approval, but in order to highlight the extensive power which mediators derive from shuttle mediation. The above strategies have considerable potential dangers if the mediator is caught out or the strategy backfires and one party or both lose trust in the mediator and faith in the process. There could also be disciplinary or legal action taken against the mediator in extreme cases.

Ways of improving shuttle mediation

9.16   Despite the drawbacks and dangers, shuttle mediation is a fact of life in many situations where mediation would not take place in any other form. Here mediators should be transparent with the parties about some of the potential problems and about ways in which they might be kept in check. They should also attend to practical matters, like keeping written notes of offers and counter-offers, or getting the parties to write these out for transmission to each other. Where shuttle mediation is an option but is not obligatory, mediators could explain to the parties the advantages of not using it unless necessary. In relation to the power of mediators and the temptations it brings, there is sometimes the option of having co-mediators conduct the shuttle process so that they keep each other honest.[5]

D.   Using more than one mediator

9.17   In co-mediation there are two or more mediators. The co-mediation process is essentially the same as that in solo mediation; the mediators' functions are similar, and the same skills and techniques are required. What is different is that there are some additional techniques, skills and behaviours which require the co-mediators' attention, and the preparation requirements are even more important to the effective conduct of the process.[6]

---

4   See Chapter 7.
5   See 9.18.
6   From a practical point of view, each mediator needs to comply with their own profession's ethical rules and to obtain their own professional indemnity cover. Refer to 12.64 and to Chapter 12 generally.

When to adopt co-mediation

9.18   The following are situations in which it might be appropriate to have more than one mediator:

■ Where additional mediator resources are needed – the 'two heads are better than one' principle – for example, in a lengthy mediation over policies in a large organisation which would require considerable mediator energy, patience and persistence; in cases where there are many stakeholders; or in cases where there is legal, financial or cultural complexity.

■ Where balance and matching are needed in respect of the gender, race, age or other attributes of the parties and the mediators – some individuals might feel uncomfortable where the mediator, other party and all the advisers are of the opposite gender[7] or of the same cultural background.

■ Where a specific professional background or experience is needed for a particular dispute, for example, an engineer in a construction dispute, a forensic accountant in a finance dispute or a social worker in a parenting dispute, with one mediator being a mediation specialist and the other a specialist in the relevant field.

■ Where there is need to stabilise the dynamics because there might be attempts at manipulation or 'triangulation', four people being a more stable number than three.

■ Where there is a need to provide experience and continuing training for new mediators.[8]

■ Where, as referred to in the previous section, there is a need to provide greater accountability, with co-mediators able to keep each other honest in their confidential and sometimes powerful role.

In addition co-mediation is only a feasible prospect where circumstances and resources allow for both the additional expense of an extra mediator and the prospect of the mediation taking a longer time.

A variant of co-mediation in the family mediation context is 'anchor mediation', where the mediator commences with one mediator on the proviso that a second mediator can be brought in, and charged for accordingly, when the circumstances require.[9]

---

7   Where a co-mediation model is adopted in family cases, the gender mix is important so that a party does not feel 'ambushed' by three people of the other sex.
8   Co-mediation should be distinguished from the practice in the UK of having a 'pupil' or 'assistant' mediator, whose time is not normally charged, although they may actively participate in the mediation, depending on the preferences and needs of the mediator and the parties, and on their subject matter or other expertise and mediation experience. The pupil model is used to give beginner mediators experience. In some cases, it is used where the pupil has particular expertise (like accounting or surveying), which is considered helpful in the particular case.
9   Law Society (England & Wales), *The Family Law Protocol*, 2nd ed 2006, para 7.4.4 at p 133 lists the circumstances when anchor mediation might be considered useful, including complexity, foreign elements, emotional neediness and disability/abuse/high conflict.

Creating a favourable environment in co-mediation

Planning and organisation

9.19   In co-mediation the presence of an additional person requires attention to seating arrangements. Usually the co-mediators will sit next to each other and apart from the parties to symbolise their 'partnership' in a mediator team. Seating arrangements should not suggest that one co-mediator is the advocate or champion of a particular party. With a round table or circular seating arrangement all persons at the mediation can be seated equidistant from one another without detracting from the co-mediators' leadership position and their status as partners in the mediator team. Subject to the qualifications mentioned in the previous section, consideration can also be given in the mediation planning stages to 'creating balance' in co-mediation teams along lines of professional qualifications, gender, age or ethnicity. In addition the co-mediators should give consideration to all the pre-mediation preparation responsibilities referred to in previous chapters. They should pay particular attention to how they will conduct the process together.

Conduct of the process

9.20   The process and stages of co-mediation are the same as those for solo mediation. However, co-mediation requires common understandings as to the different roles and functions of the co-mediators and as to the division of labour between them. This is usually more important during the early stages of the mediation when there can be a clear division of roles in the mediator's opening statement, in note taking, in attending and following during the party statements, in developing the list of issues, and in using the whiteboard or flipchart. Later in the mediation there tends to be no clear division of labour between the mediators.

9.21   Teamwork and common understandings are important ingredients of successful co-mediation.

The division and sharing of labour for co-mediators

9.22   Here is one system for dividing the mediation tasks:

- *Meeting, greeting, seating*: shared by mediators on an informal basis.

- *Mediator's opening*: clearly divided between mediators, each presenting different parts of the statement in alternating roles.

- *Party presentations*: one mediator (M1) attends and follows and the second (M2) takes notes.

- *Summaries*: given by mediator who took notes (M2).

- *Identification of common ground and listing of issues*: lead taken by other mediator (M1), but with open collaboration between mediators and with parties.

- *Writing up of issues and prioritisation*: managed by second mediator (M2), with assistance from the first, M1.

- *Separate meetings*: mediators stay together when meeting with each party.

- *Drafting*: either co-mediator can be principally involved with drafting, with the other checking the agreement against the agenda and ensuring matters of detail are accurately recorded.[10]
- *Closure*: like the mediator's opening statement, the closing statement should be clearly divided between both mediators, each presenting different parts.

Using each mediator's expertise

9.23   Where co-mediators have been chosen for their complementary expertise, each may be more active than the other at different stages of the mediation. For example, an engineer co-mediator in a construction dispute would be expected to have a more active involvement in the discussion of technical matters, while a co-mediator skilled in the mediation process would be expected to be more active in the early stages. There is no objection to these shifts in the relative ascendancy of each.

The 'non-active' mediator can still be performing a useful function in observing the parties' reactions, taking notes, considering options, and otherwise observing and analysing the negotiations. These activities can provide the basis for an appropriate contribution at a later stage in the process. In the separate meetings there might also be unequal contributions because of the mediators' respective strengths, experiences or personal attributes. Thus it might be appropriate for a male co-mediator in a family mediation to speak more in the separate meeting with the husband.[11] Co-mediators can still model respect and equality even though they are contributing in differing ways and to different degrees. However, they should not model, to the parties whose collaborative endeavours they are attempting to facilitate, a hierarchical relationship between themselves.

Avoiding bias and partiality

9.24   Where the co-mediators are selected to reflect the age, gender, class or ethnic attributes of the different parties, they should be conscious of the possibility that a particular party might perceive them as their representative or champion. Where they suspect that this is happening they should be attentive to their own body language, be observant of the other party's reactions to the proceedings, re-emphasise at appropriate points their neutral role in the mediation procedure, and confer with one another on this issue when there is an opportunity to do so.

Staying together

9.25   Co-mediation is a team effort in which the co-mediators should at all times perform their functions together and not separately. They should meet and greet the parties together, be present together throughout the joint sessions, and remain together during the separate sessions and not each meet with a different party. Co-mediators may call an adjournment so that they can meet on their own to discuss jointly progress in the mediation, to review differences in their approaches, or just to deal with their individual problems such as emotional fatigue. There is no reason not to be transparent to the parties about the reasons for calling such an adjournment wherever this is possible.

---

10   See 5.69–5.72.
11   Refer to the confidentiality issues associated with separate meetings (see 5.66).

Improving the communications in co-mediation

9.26 Co-mediators both have a responsibility to improve the communication of the parties in the various ways referred to in Chapter 6. They also need to model good communication between themselves for the benefit of the participants. This includes not interrupting one another, listening actively to what each other is saying, asking clarifying questions of each other where appropriate, and reframing each other's statements. In all these ways they are modelling for the parties the constructive communication techniques required for problem solving. Appropriate body language provides a subtle way in which co-mediators can communicate with each other, but it is also permissible to be quite transparent to the parties about communication differences between themselves. The communication techniques referred to in this book have relevance to the way in which co-mediators communicate between themselves.

Facilitating the negotiations in co-mediation

9.27 Co-mediators both have a responsibility to facilitate the negotiations of the parties in the various ways referred to in Chapter 7. They also need to model good negotiation skills between themselves for the benefit of the participants. This is particularly relevant where they have differences between themselves about the process or about the nature of their interventions. It is even more relevant where they have different views about the degree of intervention that is required. Interest-based negotiation is the behaviour which the parties need to see demonstrated by their skilled helpers. Co-mediators may have to use adjournments to discuss ways of overcoming past negotiation difficulties and avoiding them in the following sessions. However, it will often be necessary to negotiate between themselves without any interruption of the process.

9.28 The following dialogue illustrates how co-mediators might negotiate in an interest-based way over an assumed difference between them. The co-mediators are Michael and Catherine and the parties are James and Sally.

Case illustration	
Michael:	James has asked for a separate meeting with us. Shall we consider that request now?
Catherine:	Yes, as I understand it James would like some time out to consult his lawyer and to get some advice on Sally's offer.
Michael:	Yes, and it appears that Sally is interested in getting to a more advanced stage in the discussions so that these consultations will not have to be repeated. She is also concerned about the overall time question.
Catherine:	Well, we do have some time limitations. We also agreed at the beginning that Sally and James could obtain outside advice when that was necessary for them. What if we continue for about 15 minutes to keep up the momentum and then adjourn for a short period so that both James and Sally can obtain professional advice?
Michael:	Yes, that might meet the various interests.

Avoiding traps in co-mediation

9.29   Traps are preventable problems caused by mediators themselves or by the predictable difficulties inherent in the negotiation process. Some of the general traps for mediators are referred to in Chapter 10 of this book. There are some other traps which derive from the situation of having more than one mediator at the head of the table:

Good cop–bad cop routine

9.30   This involves the 'bad cop' co-mediator using his or her power forcefully and coercively, and the 'good cop' co-mediator being more empathic as a device to draw out a reticent party who perceives them as having a sympathetic ear. The problem is caused by mediators watching too much bad television. Co-mediators should avoid any impression of playing this routine as they could jeopardise the neutrality of one or both of them and be seen as manipulative and coercive (which the routine undoubtedly is).

Modelling inequality or lack of teamwork

9.31   As already indicated above, co-mediators should not model any sense of hierarchy or inequality between themselves. This requires particular attention where they have different levels of experience or expertise, and where societal inequalities based on class, gender or race are reflected in the mediator team. They should also not model any lack of teamwork when their objective is to move the parties towards collaborative problem solving themselves.

Appointing incompatible personalities

9.32   Co-mediators should not be appointed where there are serious incompatibilities in their personalities. Mediation provides the opportunity for the mediators to model constructive problem solving between themselves. It would be unnecessarily inviting trouble to create incompatible teams of co-mediators. While this does not have to involve personality testing for co-mediators (nor character references), it does require some selectivity and honesty in their appointments.

The patron syndrome

9.33   Where co-mediators have been selected to match the attributes of the parties, they should ensure that they are not perceived as the patron or champion of 'their' respective party.[12]

Preparation for co-mediation

9.34   The following questions can be regarded as important for mediators to consider in their joint preparation for a co-mediation:

---

12   See 9.24.

1. How can we ensure appropriate 'balance' in the mediation team?

2. Where it is not possible to match gender, age and other attributes, how can we reassure and encourage the mediating party who is not 'matched' (for example, a teenage party where both mediators are middle-aged)?

3. How should we divide our functions during the early part of the mediation?

4. How should we deal with differences of opinion or strategy between ourselves during the mediation?

5. How can we model equality, good communication and constructive problem solving between ourselves for the benefit of the parties?

6. How should we alert each other to problems which we think the other is causing?

7. How should we signal to each other, for example, where one of us wishes to pursue a particular topic or line of discussion?

8. How can we use each other constructively in the post-mediation debriefing?

Debriefing by co-mediators

9.35   The form and functions of mediator debriefing have been referred to in Chapter 5 above. There are two major objectives of debriefing between co-mediators.

The first is to deal with any emotional trauma which either of them is experiencing, and the second is to reflect on the skills and techniques which each mediator has demonstrated, or failed to demonstrate. In relation to the second objective, co-mediation provides at least two potential advantages when compared to solo mediation. The first is that it allows for immediate debriefing between the mediators; it can be undertaken directly after the mediation has finished where it can be more accurate and undistorted than if undertaken later with outside mentors. The second is that it can provide an objective evaluation of each mediator's performance by someone who has observed it himself or herself – it does not rely only on self-assessment, though this can be a part of the debriefing process. Unfortunately, despite this great potential, co-mediators are not always, in our experience, candid and open about each other's performance. They may require an honest broker to facilitate the debriefing process.

E.   Mediation by telephone conference

9.36   A mediation might be conducted by telephone conference in the following circumstances: where the parties are geographically distant from each other; where there is great urgency to resolve a matter; where resources do not allow for the parties to come together in the same location; where there is concern over the safety and well-being of one party; or where there is a court order which prevents them from being in each other's company. In the latter cases it might still be preferable to arrange a shuttle mediation,[13] avoiding joint meetings.

9.37   Where there is a choice between having a face-to-face mediation and a telephone mediation, it should be borne in mind that the latter has several potential disadvantages:

- It is more difficult for mediators to establish rapport and trust with the parties through telephone conversations only.

- Mediators cannot observe and react to some of the non-verbal communications of the participants, such as their body language.

- It is difficult to work with emotional content.

- Separate meetings lose their immediacy and personal touch.

- Some people find the phone intimidating.

- Visual aids cannot be used to focus the parties' attention on an agenda, diagrams, facts and figures, and so on.

- There is less scope for parties to learn conflict management skills.

- It is easier to be distracted when the meeting is not face to face.

- Technology can go wrong when it is most needed (see the illustration in the box below).

9.38   Where a telephone mediation is necessary or is chosen it would normally operate as follows.

Pre-mediation activities are the same as for face-to-face mediations, save that there is unlikely to be a preliminary conference or meeting. A date, venues for the participants and contact numbers are arranged for the mediation meeting. Confidentiality issues should be discussed with the parties, for example, if parties will make calls from work or home, how confidential will the discussions be. The possibility of interruptions should also be canvassed, for example, if a colleague were to walk in during the conference or, if a party will be calling from home, if children come in or the doorbell rings.

A conference line is set up with the carrier, with a separate line for each party and for each adviser who is not at the same location as their client (to further complicate matters). It is advisable that speaker phones are used so that hands are free for taking notes or retrieving documents, and this is a necessary arrangement where there are several persons at the same venue, for example, a client, an adviser and a witness.

The mediator follows the standard stages of mediation. Parties should be asked to identify themselves each time they speak as there can be damaging confusion over who says what – for example, Party A may think that an idea mooted by the mediator is an offer or concession from Party B.

---

13   See 9.6–9.16.

Confidentiality requires particular diligence during the mediation. If there are to be separate meetings, the safest arrangement is to disconnect the conference line and to make individual contact with each party in turn, before returning to the conference call. It is dangerous to speak with one party confidentially while the others have left their room for a consultation as it may not be apparent when the latter have returned. When it comes to finalising the agreement it is advisable to use e-mail or fax to circulate drafts while all parties are still present and not to 'leave the finalisation until later'.

9.39   Here are some additional guidelines for tele-mediations, all based on lessons from experience:

- Check time zones.

- Ensure the mediation agreement is signed before the conference call.

- Have a brief discussion with each party before the conference link up.

- Check the phone connection before the conference call.

- Recommend that the discussions should not be recorded by the parties, or at least develop a policy on this issue with the parties.

- Ask each party to disclose who is physically present with them during the mediation so that this does not complicate the situation later. Needless to say there is no guarantee that others will not also be present and be overheard.

- Give time to all participants to settle into the phone discussion.

- Because of the possibility of misunderstanding and confusion, listen harder, ask clarifying questions, and summarise more frequently.

- Ask parties to keep their opening statement short.

- Remind parties that only one person should speak at a time, and, to avoid interruptions, that they can jot down points that can be picked up later when it is their turn to speak to avoid interruptions.

- Have an agenda so that the discussion is kept on track.

- Limit air time in the case of any speaker who is monopolising.

- Be particularly diligent about noting and recording the concessions and agreements of the parties so that there is no misunderstanding on these between them.

- Beware of distractions, for example, checking e-mails or post at the same time.

- Where the mediator is in the same building as one of the parties, allow the party to leave the premises first so that there is no post-mediation contact with that party alone.

> ### Case illustration: technology hiccups
>
> In a commercial mediation conducted by telephone conference the following lessons were learned:
>
> 1. There were four separate lines, one for the two co-mediators and one for each of the three parties and their advisers. During the exploration stage one party and their adviser seemed to be silent for an extended period. Upon investigation it transpired that they had been accidentally disconnected and had missed at least six minutes of the discussions.
>
> 2. At one point the mediator made a settlement 'suggestion' without any prior identification of who was speaking. One of the parties seized on this proposal, thinking it was that of another party. It took some time to convince them that this was not so.
>
> 3. Late in the mediation it became obvious that there were frantic discussions taking place at the venue of one of the parties and significant slowing down of the process. It transpired that the party had invited four other members of its organisation into the room to confer on the impending settlement, and this incident almost caused one of the other parties to abort the mediation.
>
> 4. As the mediator left his room after the mediation he was accosted by a party who had been in the same building with the request that he should witness their copy of the agreement to 'give it more weight'.

F. Internet mediation

9.40 Besides the many other services it facilitates, the internet also provides the basis for the conduct of mediation (sometimes referred to as on-line mediation, e-mediation, on-line ADR, electronic DR and technology-mediated DR). Courts, tribunals and private dispute resolution agencies have not been slow to embrace new technology and to be innovative with the old. Computers, videos, faxes, telephones and e-mails are all used to some extent in these bodies for a range of different dispute resolution functions.[14]

9.41 Dispute resolution on the internet provides its own opportunities and challenges. One of its main attributes is that internet e-mail overcomes the tyranny of geography, and does so in a way that is quick and relatively economical. Moreover, different time zones present no problem and mediating parties can attend to their e-mails whenever convenient or appropriate. Internet mediation has the other great advantage that in legal disputes there is no need to resolve the choice of law problem as mediation does not require that determination – at least until a major problem arises and there is litigation around an internet mediation gone wrong.[15]

On-line dispute resolution can have particular benefits in certain cases. In family law cases, for example, it can be useful where a parent has moved abroad or there has

---

14 See Boulle, 'Options for Cyber-med' (1999) 1 *ADR Bulletin* 128.
15 See Alejandro E. Almaguer and Roland W. Baggott, III, 'Shaping New Legal Frontiers: Dispute Resolution for the Internet', 13 *Ohio St J on Disp Resol* 711 (1998).

been a history of violence or abuse. In public decision-making cases, public input and collaboration can be encouraged on-line. Facilitated discussions can occur on-line with stakeholders in diverse locations. In any case, where a party is in another jurisdiction, on-line dialogue offers obvious benefits.

9.42   Some of the features of internet mediation, and its potential problems, are shown in following case illustration:

Case illustration: internet mediation

The Online Ombuds Office (www.ombuds.org) is one of a number of organisations providing online dispute-resolution services (refer to Appendix 12 for others). The service has published a transcript of a dispute which was successfully mediated online; it reveals some of the opportunities and challenges of this kind of service.

Ironically, the dispute was over a copyright issue arising out of the use of the internet. The DR service was contacted by an internet enthusiast who had begun summarising local news and events and publishing the summaries on a website. He had been contacted by the local newspaper which claimed that he was in violation of their copyright and that they would institute court proceedings if he did not stop immediately. He discontinued his project and sought assistance from the DR service.

Over the next month a series of communications took place by way of e-mail, fax and phone. These were all directed through the DR service and there was no further direct contact between the disputing parties. (It was effectively a form of shuttle mediation.) As with many mediations, much of the time was spent getting the 'other party' to the table/keyboard and once this had been achieved the mediation progressed quickly.

An interesting escalation in the conflict occurred when the internet service provider (ISP), which was coincidentally used by both the newspaper and the individual, sent a document entitled *Ten Big Myths About Copyright Explained* to the individual. He thought it was instigated by the newspaper as a warning that what he was doing was wrong. It is not the first time that a party in conflict has interpreted an event in the way most detrimental to the other side. In reality the document was merely a reminder from the ISP to all its clients about the rules of copyright, which had also been sent to the newspaper. Clarification of this issue was an important factor in the ultimate resolution of the dispute.

9.43   Some interesting issues arise from this example of internet mediation:[16]

■ A transcript of the exchanges, although rare in face-to-face mediation,[17] is a product of internet mediation. It allows the course of a mediation to be followed,

---

16   For a note on this topic, see O'Hanlan and Blair, 'A Unique Jurisdiction with Unique Possibilities' at www.wvjolt.wvu.edu/wvjolt/current/issue1/articles/ohanlon/jolt.htn. See Almaguer and Baggott, 'Shaping New Legal Frontiers: Dispute Resolution for the Internet' 13 (1998) *Ohio State Journal on Dispute Resolution* 711.

17   Some standard form mediation agreements prohibit transcripts. See, for example, clause 8 CEDR Model Mediation Agreement (10th ed). Refer to Appendix 3 for a selection of model mediation agreements.

and to analyse factors such as the escalation of the dispute. The internet provides an easy and non-intrusive method of obtaining a record, subject to confidentiality requirements (referred to below).

■ New technology clearly has implications for the speed and efficiency of dispute resolution. While this relatively minor dispute took about a month to resolve, this was largely because of the difficulties in getting the newspaper to the virtual mediation table. In other situations, the ability to participate at the various parties' convenience and without the need for a fixed time, suitable venue, parking arrangements, and the like, has obvious potential benefits.

■ The question of confidentiality is always problematic with new technology. The DR service made the conventional mediator commitment to confidentiality and from the appearance of the transcript this appears to have been upheld. (Although one might wonder about the following sentence in an e-mail to the individual, 'The only tidbit I did gain from them [the newspaper] is that they are planning to have a website of some kind.') When it was made publicly available, the transcript was modified to provide anonymity to all parties, although concerns over confidentiality remain.

■ The pedantically inclined would be disturbed by the evidence in the transcript of poor spelling ('immeadiatly', 'dailey'), typographical errors, and breaches of syntax and grammar.

Special problems in cyber mediation

9.44   There are special kinds of problems presented by on-line mediation over the internet:

■ *The identity of the 'other person'.* This is always a potential problem with technologically driven mediation, creating the necessity for both security and trust. A party could secretly have another person in the room to assist them, adding their expertise to the negotiation and possibly doing the keyboarding. A nosey hacker or cyber sticky-beak could even be playing the role of one party without their, or the other's, knowledge. Passwords, encryption, trustmarks and other security developments provide some assurance on this point.

■ *The confidentiality question.* There is clearly no guarantee, even with the best precautions such as registration, passwords and encryption, that what is being said online will remain private and confidential between the parties.

■ *Communicating and dealing with emotion.* Mediation over the internet has implications for the communication process and the emotional dimensions of the negotiations, similar to those encountered in tele-mediation. Communicating over the internet is stylised and restricted and effectively diminishes the emotional dimensions of the discussion. Where it is not possible to see facial expression, hear tone of voice and observe body language, some of the most important and telling aspects of communication are taken out of the equation, and this makes it difficult to interpret what is said and to judge its sincerity. As with tele-mediation, however, having the parties at separate locations could actually assist in avoiding the intense emotional drama which might otherwise be present. In this situation, the ability to concentrate on the substantive issues in dispute may actually be facilitated by internet mediation.

- *Detraction from one of the main process values of the system.* Internet mediation may not take place in real time and there is no immediate interaction between the parties – just the blunt instrumentality of a keyboard. Thus the sense of being able to participate and the feeling of being heard, which are some of the peculiar strengths of the mediation process, are likely to be significantly reduced in this context.

- *Lowering of inhibitions.* Early research indicated that internet communication is more aggressive and less restrained by social norms,[18] affecting relationships and outcomes.

- *Rapport building is difficult.* It is easier to develop rapport via face-to-face communication.[19] In one study, trust and rapport was found to have developed via telephone contact before the on-line negotiations took place.[20]

- *Greater chance of impasse.* There is evidence that negotiation via written channels is more likely to reach impasse than negotiation face-to-face or over the telephone.[21]

- *Multi-party negotiations are more difficult.* Reaching agreements on-line is predictably more difficult as the number of parties increases. In one study, high impasse rates were found in a four-party on-line negotiation and high levels of dissatisfaction were expressed by the parties involved.[22]

- *Less preparation.* On-line communication with its time lag between conversations gives parties an excuse to be less prepared.[23]

- *'Slow-tempo' technology may make complex negotiations difficult.* In one study, complex negotiations fared better when the technology used was 'fast-tempo' (like instant messaging) rather than 'slow-tempo' (like e-mail).[24]

- *Enforcement issues.* If the parties are based in different countries, enforcement of any settlement reached could be difficult or expensive.

Thompson and Nadler also identified various biases that can affect progress in on-line negotiations:[25]

- Temporal synchronicity bias – the lack of synchronicity affects relationships and outcomes during on-line negotiations.

---

18 Sproull and Kiesler, 'Reducing Social Context Cues: Electronic Mail in Organisational Communication', in (1986) 32 *Management Science* 1492.
19 Drolet and Morris, 'Rapport in Conflict Resolution: Accounting for how face-to-face Contact Fosters Mutual Cooperation in mixed-motive Conflicts', in (2000) 36 *Journal of Experimental Social Psychology* 26.
20 Morris et al, 'Social Friction and Lubrication in e-mail Negotiations', in (2000) 6 *Group Dynamics-Theory Research and Practice* 89.
21 Valley et al, 'A Matter of Trust: Effects of Communication on the Efficiency and Distribution of Outcomes', in (1998) 34 *Journal of Economic Behaviour and Organisation* 211.
22 Kurtzburg et al, 'Multi-party E-negotiations: Agents, Alliances, and Negotiation Success', in (2005) 16 *International Journal of Conflict Management* 245.
23 van Es et al, 'Resolving Conflicts over Ethical Issues: face-to-face Versus Internet Negotiations' in (2004) 53 *Journal of Business Ethics* 165.
24 Loewensteing et al, 'At a Loss for Words: Dominating the Conversation and the Outcome in Negotiation as a Function of Intricate Arguments and Communication Media' in (2005) 98 *Organisational Behaviour and Human Decision Processes* 28.
25 Thompson and Nadler, 'Negotiating via Information Technology: Theory and Application', in (2002) 58 *Journal of Social Issues* 109.

- Burned bridge bias – as people are more prepared to use aggressive behaviour during on-line discussions than they are in face-to-face or telephone situations, disputes are more likely to escalate.

- Squeaky wheel bias – negative behaviour (like intimidation or rudeness) is more likely during on-line negotiation.

- Sinister attribution bias – due to the absence of rapport, a party may attribute sinister motives to another party, leading to poorer outcomes during on-line negotiations.

Despite these special problems, on-line mediation is increasingly available, is continually being improved and is currently being used in the UK and across Europe. For example:

- There is an on-line mediation pilot in the Small Claims Court.

- Various English law firms provide on-line mediation services.[26]

- The Mediation Room, Resolve Mediation and Consensus Mediation offer on-line mediation services.

- On-line mediation services are being used by the Commonwealth Telecommunications Organisation.

- The European Consumer Centre in England and Ireland is running a pilot on-line mediation scheme for cross border consumer disputes.

Future developments

9.45 The mere use of e-mails as a vehicle for mediation dialogue is a relatively low technology exercise. Current technology allows for mediation using a range of mechanisms, like 'listservs', chat rooms, voice technology, instant messaging, video streaming, web conferencing, and portals which contain documents allowing on-line document sharing and collaboration. All that is needed is the relevant hardware and software to support conversations between the mediator and each party individually, in order to be able to provide the joint and separate sessions encountered in face-to-face mediation.

Technological developments bring the immediacy of the telephone at a significantly reduced cost, plus the ability to exchange draft documents instantaneously. Although most services still only offer asychronous, text-based communication between parties, 'telepresence systems' simulate face-to-face meetings with mirror-image conferencing rooms at each end, CD-quality audio and high-definition panels that show parties life-size.

Virtual mediation is already available – the mediatory involvement of a person is replaced by the mediatory role of the machine. For example, E-Mediation offers software to resolve family issues without requiring any personal contact.[27] There is little doubt that artificial intelligence software will be refined to the point where it allows the computer to listen and acknowledge, define disputes mutually and neutrally, and reframe and encourage settlement.

---

26 For example, Halliwells and Brethertons.
27 See http://a2j.kentlaw.edu/a2j/system_design/Resolution/emediation.cfm - a project developed jointly in the US by Chicago-Kent College of Law, the Institute of Design and the National Center for State Courts as a way to meet the needs of self-represented litigants and provide greater access to justice.

Variations on this theme are 'assisted negotiation' sites and programmes, as in the case of SquareTrade, eBay's on-line dispute resolution service. Another are blind-bidding systems, used primarily in the case of small insurance and debt claims, involving single issue monetary claims. Parties can submit bids and if the bids fall within a certain range the programme splits the difference and the matter is settled.[28]

Adding feeling the cyber-med way

9.46   One of the obvious objections to mediation through the internet is that it lacks the inter-personal interaction which mediation claims as an advantage over other dispute-resolution processes. However, the new technologies are not so easily defeated. Electronic forms of communication have developed their own ways of expressing feelings the cyber way. This means that there is a toolbox of 'emoticons' for most occasions. Virtual worlds can also provide opportunity for expression through gestures and scripts activated by avatars. Privately created scripts can be purchased to cause an avatar to have facial expression.

Combining technologies

9.47   There are clearly no limits to the ways in which modern communication systems and information technology can be combined to provide mediation and other ADR services. A combination of telephones, e-mails and video-conferencing can provide both opportunities and challenges. Such developments, though, will also be resisted by those wishing to uphold the interpersonal nature of mediation which has always been one of its strongest attractions.

Standards

9.48   In the context of consumer disputes, concerns have been raised in Europe regarding the quality of on-line dispute resolution providers and the quality of on-line dispute resolution procedures. The Commission Recommendation on the principles applicable to bodies responsible for out-of-court settlement of consumer disputes accordingly established a number of minimum guarantees that out-of-court bodies (including on-line ADR providers) should offer users:[29]

- independence to ensure impartiality;

- transparency of procedure;

- adversarial principle – the parties have a right to be heard;

- effectiveness – access to the process without requiring legal representation;

- legality – a consumer cannot be deprived of his legal rights by participating in the process;

- liberty – a consumer cannot be deprived of the right to pursue matters through the courts;

- representation – a consumer cannot be deprived of the right to be represented or assisted in the process.

---

28   Refer to Appendix 12 for a selection of on-line dispute resolvers. See Beal, 'On-line mediation: has its time come?' in (2000) 15 *Ohio St J on Dispute Resolution* 735 and Goodman, 'The pros and cons of on-line dispute resolution: an assessment of cyber-mediation websites', in (2003) *Duke L and Tech Rev* 4 which reviews on-line products and services and the pros and cons of each.

29   Commission Recommendation of 4 April 2001.

Council Resolution of 25 May 2000 on a Community-wide network of national bodies for the extra-judicial settlement of consumer disputes aimed to overcome obstacles for consumers when seeking access to ADR across Europe. This led to the establishment of 'EEJ-Net', the European Extra-Judicial Network. There is an EEJ-Net clearing house in each EU Member State, as well as Norway and Iceland, which can route consumer complaints to a relevant alternative dispute resolution. The EEJ-Net project aims to co-ordinate the operation of various national ADR schemes in a cross-border context and to inform the consumer about the availability of appropriate ADR schemes to handle complaints.

The out-of court complaints network for financial services 'FIN-Net' links national bodies responsible for the out-of-court resolution of disputes falling under Commission Recommendation of 30 March 1998.[30] It offers consumers with problems relating to financial services (banking, insurance and investments) an out-of-court dispute resolution facility.

SOLVIT is an on-line problem solving network in which EU Member States work together to solve cross-border issues caused by the misapplication of internal market law by public authorities. The Commission was also involved in launching OCODIR (Electronic Consumer Dispute Resolution Platform).

In order to improve consumer confidence in on-line dispute resolution, trustmark programmes have evolved. For example, Web Trader is a trustmark developed by the UK Consumers' Association and is used by a consortium of consumer groups across Europe, and the programme assists users to resolve disputes with Web Trader-accredited merchants. The aim of the trustmark is to ensure that there is adherence to standards and review of the activies of on-line dispute resolution providers.

The European Committee for Standardization (CEN), the Brussels-based organisation that produces standards for products and services adopted by EU Member States, has established a committee to produce updated recommended standards for on-line dispute resolution. Some ADR organisations provide on-line mediation training as a way of ensuring quality practice in this field.[31]

G.   Hybrid processes

9.49   There are several forms of dispute resolution which involve an element of mediation, combined with other processes. These are sometimes referred to as 'hybrid' dispute-resolution systems. Some of these are informal systems, for example, a mediator might assume an advisory role in the late stages of the mediation with the consent of the parties. Others are more structured, as is typical in the case of conciliation.

Conciliation

9.50   A conciliator tends to undertake a wider range of functions than a mediator. For example, a conciliator may:

- explore formal decisions that have been made on the basis of documentation or other criteria/principles;

---

30   Recommendation 30 March 1998 on the principles applicable to the bodies responsible for out-of-court settlement of consumer disputes.
31   For example, ADR Group provide a distance training course in on-line mediation.

- facilitate or mediate disputes through discussion of the issues in order to reach agreement;
- make formal recommendations;
- consider whether some questions in dispute can be directed to other avenues, like early neutral evaluation or arbitration;
- suspend or adjourn matters, and request further information to be provided.

9.51　Accordingly, while the emphasis is on mediated decision-making, the conciliator can move beyond this function and can provide recommendations and even make binding determinations. For example, conciliators for ACAS (the Advisory Conciliation and Arbitration Service), the statutory industrial relations agency in the UK:

- explain the conciliation process to parties;
- explain the way employment tribunals operate, and what they will take into account in deciding the case;
- discuss the options open to each party, including arbitration where appropriate;
- help the parties to understand how the other side views the case, and to explore how it might be resolved without a hearing; and
- discuss proposals each party has for a settlement.[32]

Conciliation has been widely used in family law disputes in England and Wales. It is sometimes referred to as Private Law Programme Dispute Resolution, and in other cases, as 'in court mediation' (although some courts have 'in court mediation' schemes run by external independent mediators). The scope of conciliation in the family law context includes:

- conciliation appointments before the Registrar or district judge and court welfare officer (Child and Family Reporter);
- conciliation by judges if both parties are present at the Children's Appointment;
- conciliation by a court welfare officer during preparation of a children's welfare report.

Typically, these are directed dispute resolution processes, as the court officer or dispute resolver assists the parties by putting forward potential options or outcomes. There are limits to the privilege and confidentiality attaching to these processes, which is different to conventional out of court mediation.[33]

Bryson points to some potential risks where multiple roles are allocated to a single individual.[34] One is that conciliators could approach their tasks and discretions very differently from one another. Another is that conciliators might rely more on diagnostic and interpretive activities than on problem-solving and facilitative ones, leaving the impression that they are running to a predetermined script. Thus the method by which conciliators manage their multiple roles is an important factor in

---

32　ACAS has a statutory duty to conciliate after a claim has been made to the tribunal. Since 9 April 2009, it has discretion to provide conciliation in relation to matters which might become the subject of a tribunal claim. The changes herald an increased emphasis on encouraging employers and employees to resolve differences as early as possible without recourse to tribunal or other proceedings.
33　See 10.81–10.82.
34　David Bryson, 'When Wearing Different Hats: Suggestions for ADR Practice', in (1999) 1 *Dispute Resolution Bulletin* 125.

their operation. As their role becomes more 'interventionist', questions are raised as to what are the acceptable limits of their use of pressure and power. The actual exercise of the most extreme power of direction is rare, but the presence of this reserve power could subtly overshadow the management of the process and the perceptions of the parties. This creates a need for conciliators to indicate to the parties up-front what roles they have, and to signal clearly any changes in role during the course of conciliation. The way in which this can be done is illustrated below.

9.52

Changing functions: the role of signalling[35]

The importance of the opening conciliator statement

The opening statement, complementing any written or visual material sent to parties prior to the conciliation conference, should clearly explain the role of a conciliator.

Signalling transitions during process

During a conciliation meeting points of transition between roles should be clearly signalled, for example, 'My sense of the meeting so far is that you are not likely to reach agreement through discussion. As foreshadowed in my opening introduction, I now wish to move to a recommendation role ...'

Transition when exercising a formal recommendation role

If agreement cannot be reached through consensus, the conciliator signals the change of role to recommendation and gives conditions of acceptance or refusal of any recommendation proposed.

Transition when exercising a decision-making role

If agreement cannot be reached through consensus, and perhaps after attempts to get agreement by recommendation, the conciliator explains the next steps.

Transition when exercising a direction role

If appropriate, the conciliator may signal the wish to move into the role of issuing a decision. A more formal procedure ensues. A summary of the arguments in relation to the issues is given from both sides.

Med-arb and arb-med

9.53   The range of 'hybrid' processes is slowly evolving. 'Med-arb' gives the mediator a contractual power to undertake an arbitrator role and issue a binding award in the event that the mediation is not successful. There are theoretical concerns about reluctance of parties to expose their vulnerabilities to a neutral who may later become an arbitrator.[36]

---

35 Adapted from Bryson, ibid.
36 See S. Landry, 'Med-arb: Mediation with a Bite and an Effective ADR Model', in (1996) 63 *Def. Couns. J.* 263.

With 'arb-med', on the other hand, an arbitration is followed by a mediation. The arbitration typically involves a simplified process. The arbitrator makes an award in private in writing and places it in a sealed envelope, which the parties agree not to open, unless the mediation does not result in a settlement. The arbitrator then assumes the role of neutral mediator, to assist the parties to reach an agreed solution. The prospect of an arbitration award represents a risk to the parties, and accordingly provides an incentive for the parties to achieve settlement in mediation.[37] If a settlement is reached in the mediation, the award envelope is normally not opened and is destroyed. The arb-med process can produce a fast result if the arbitration is simplified and the mediation is time-limited.

Ken Feinberg, a renowned US mediator, prefers an 'adapted arb-med' type model. He first hears all sides, then prepares a written (non-binding) settlement recommedation, and ends by mediating in private meetings as a way of persuading parties to minimise their differences by reference to his recommendations.[38]

A detailed discussion of hybrid processes is beyond the scope of this book.[39]

Collaborative law

9.54   For the sake of completeness, a reference is made in the book to collaborative law. It is a process whereby lawyers and their clients agree in writing to reach a settlement without court involvement. They may use processes like mediation to resolve children and financial issues. They may also enlist other experts, like child specialists and counsellors, as part of the dispute resolution 'team'. If a resolution cannot be achieved in this way, the clients instruct other lawyers to proceed to court.[40]

H.   Time-limited mediation

9.55   In a number of contexts, the 'standard' mediation process has been adapted to cater for limitations of time and resources and the pressure of heavy case loads. In most situations this has led to the abbreviation of the mediation process, referred to as 'time limited' or even 'fast track' mediation. Time-limited examples are evolving where government departments, agencies, tribunals and courts have to deal with numerous cases involving similar fact situations. It has evolved in England for small claims cases, county court cases, community and various family law cases as briefly described in the box below.

---

37   See L. D. Connor, 'How to Combine Facilitation with Evaluation', in (1996) 14 *Alternatives High Cost Litig* 15 and Abramson, 'Protocols for International Arbitrators who Dare to Settle Cases', in (1999) *The Am. Rev. of Intl. Arb.* 1.

38   K. Feinberg, 'Mediation – A Preferred Method of Dispute Resolution', in (1989) 16 *Pepperdine L.R.* S5.

39   For more information on med-arb, refer to Onyema, 'The Use of Med-Arb in International Commercial Dispute Resolution.' In (2001) 12(3-4) *American Review of International Arbitration* 411; d'Ambrumenil, *Mediation and Arbitration for Lawyers*, Routledge-Cavendish, 1997, Chapter 8; A Burr, 'Med-Arb: A Viable Hybrid Solution?', in *Les Arbitres Internationaux* 2005; and J Lang, 'Med-arb: an English perspective', *New York State Bar Association*, 2009.

40   Refer to www.collabfamilylaw.org.uk which is under the auspices of Resolution (which was formerly, the SFLA).

Examples of time-limited mediation

HMCS Small Claims Mediation Service

The Small Claims Mediation Service is a free service, established by the HMCS, for parties in defended small claims cases. If parties agree to use the Service, the mediator makes contact with both parties to arrange an appointment. The mediation appointments are usually carried out by telephone. Where necessary, face-to-face appointments can usually be arranged. Mediation appointments generally last about an hour. If parties are unable to reach settlement at the mediation appointment, the case will be listed for a small claims hearing. The judge is not informed of the content of any discussions at mediation by the mediator. If the case is settled by mediation and the court receives notice in writing at least seven days before the hearing date, the hearing fee is refunded. Since 2008, all 23 HMCS Courts Areas in England and Wales have had full-time mediators to deal with small claims. 87% of small claims mediations in 2007/08 occurred over the phone.

Regional pilot small claims mediation schemes

In the Exeter courts small claims pilot mediation scheme, mediators who were also qualified as solicitors offered 30-minute mediation appointments to small claims litigants referred by the District Judge. In the Manchester pilot a full-time salaried mediation officer (MO) was available in court to give information and advice about mediation, and to provide free, voluntary, one hour face-to-face mediations to small claims parties. Towards the end of the pilot period he began to offer telephone mediation. The Reading pilot focused more on giving advice and information about the small claims process to unrepresented litigants, with a 'by-product' of facilitating settlement negotiations.

County court mediation

County court cases are divided into different tracks – small claims, fast track and multi-track. Mediation in fast and multi-track cases is arranged through the National Mediation Helpline. Fast-track mediations are £300 per party for three hours; and multi-track cases are £425 per party for four hours. In Scotland, the equivalent scheme, the Edinburgh Sheriff Court mediation scheme, is managed by the Edinburgh Central Citizens Advice Bureau, and is free to both parties. 67% of county court claims mediated in 2007/08 in England settled.

Community mediation

Mediation sessions in community cases usually last two to three hours, and most community mediation services are free. In 2007 an on-line Directory of UK Community Mediation was set up following the voluntary winding up of Mediation UK (the previous umbrella body for community mediation services).

In-court conciliation in child contact cases

In-court conciliation is a brief intervention, usually a one-off meeting of 30 minutes, aimed at assisting parents to negotiate child contact arrangements.

'On the spot in-court' family mediation scheme

An 'on the spot in court family mediation pilot' launched in July 2009 in the West Midlands enables local family mediation providers to work with judges to identify cases where mediation might be a suitable alternative to the court process. Families are offered the option of mediation over the court process for resolving their disputes.

9.56   Despite modifications on the conventional model of mediation, mediators in time-limited cases do not give advice, make judgements or provide solutions. There is usually some form of intake process, to ensure that suitable disputes are selected for time-limited mediation, in preference to full mediation, on the basis of specified criteria.[41] Recent evaluations of small claim mediation schemes in England have raised issues about whether 'too much emphasis is placed on expediting cases and too little on the safety of outcomes in terms of justice'.[42] Settlement rates have also tended to be lower in time-limited schemes. Settlement rates ranging from 62% to 82% have been published in the case of recent small claim schemes in the UK[43] and between 39% and 53% in the case of the Central London County Court mediation schemes over the years.[44] In addition, in the family law context, despite high settlement rates of child contact issues using time-limited conciliation, the majority of those agreements were amended down the track.[45] Studies of time-limited in-court family conciliation have also raised concerns about pressure and coercion, low satisfaction, lack of uniformity, risk issues and unsuitability of some cases for time-limited mediation.[46]

Despite the ongoing debate over the effectiveness of time-limited mediation, the HMCS Scheme has been applauded for providing a low-cost dispute resolution alternative, winning the 2008 International Crystal Scales of Justice award given by the European Commission and Council of Europe.

9.57   There is increasing pressure for time-limited or fast-track mediation in many contexts apart from small claims cases, including, for example, workplace, residential building and personal injury cases. One way of achieving this is through the use of 'standard issues' lists. Here mediators with expertise in the subject matter of the dispute, such as building or personal injuries, can begin the mediation with a list of the standard questions which would usually arise in such cases and invite

---

41 For example, in the case of the 'automatic referral to time limited mediation' scheme that first operated in the Central London County Court until 1998, Practice Direction 26b Civil Procedure Rules provided the criteria as:

'This practice direction applies to a claim if it meets all the following conditions –

(1) the small claims track is not the normal track for the claim;

(2) no party to the claim is –

    (a)   a child or protected party; or

    (b)   exempt from payment of court fees; and

(3) the court has not granted an interim injunction in the proceedings.'

('Child' and 'protected party' have the same meaning as in rule 21.1(2).)

Since the end of that pilot scheme in 1998, information about mediation has been included in all mailings sent out to parties or their solicitors from the court once a defence has been received. Small claims are no longer excluded from the scheme.

42 Jill Enterkin and Mark Sefton, *DCA Research Series 10/06* page 86, examining the schemes in Exeter, Manchester and Reading.

43 For example, 62% in the case of the Exeter small claims mediation pilot – Sue Prince, 'Institutionalising mediation? An evaluation of the Exeter Court small claims mediation pilot' in *Web Journal of Current Legal Issues*, 2007; and 82% in the case of face-to-face mediations conducted as part of the Manchester pilot – M. Doyle, *Evaluation of the Small Claims Mediation Service at Manchester county court*, September 2006.

44 Refer to H. Genn and others, *Twisting arms: court referred and court-linked mediation under judicial pressure*, Ministry of Justice Research Series 1/07, May 2007.

45 L. Trinder and K. Kellett, *The longer-term outcomes of in-court conciliation*, Ministry of Justice Series 15/07, November 2007.

46 Ibid.

the parties to add any others which they might have.[47] This serves to fast-track the problem defining stage of the mediation, though at the potential cost of full participation of the parties in this important stage.

I.   Other variations in the mediation process

Alternating venues

9.58   Occasionally the mediator, in consultation with the parties, might select different venues for different sessions of a mediation. There are three reasons for doing this.

The first is to demonstrate fairness and even-handedness to both parties, for example, by using the premises of each party, or their lawyers, in turn. The second is because a particular need can be served by changing the venue, for example, in an industrial dispute it might assist all concerned to have part of the mediation on the factory floor where the safety-related disputes actually arise, or in a retail shop leases dispute it might clarify matters if options are considered at the shopping centre where the retailer is a tenant. The third is because it is just more convenient for all concerned to change the venues, for example, in major land use mediation, which takes place over a long time period and involves multiple parties and advisers.

Variations in separate meetings

9.59   Some of these variations have been referred to already.[48] Normally, in general civil and commercial cases, legal advisers will be present at separate meetings held with their clients, but on occasions the mediator may meet separately with each party alone without their adviser (*side meetings*), or with both parties together without their lawyers (*party meetings*), or with the lawyers without the parties (*adviser meetings*). In addition, the mediator could meet separately with the experts from both sides. In each case, the mediator makes a discretionary judgement, with some degree of consultation with the parties. Sometimes, for example, it is necessary to meet with the advisers to educate them about their appropriate role in mediation or to challenge their obstruction of the mediator. In all cases the mediator's judgements should be explained and the parties reassured. Thus mediators should be sensitive about meetings between professionals alone being regarded with suspicion by the parties. Where the mediator meets with the parties alone they should be reassured that they will be able to consult their advisers before agreeing to any settlement.

Involving support persons

9.60   The flexibility of the process allows for the involvement and participation of a wide range of 'support persons' in mediation.[49] The disputing parties can bring

---

47   See 5.47.
48   See 5.56.
49   F2.3 MQMS requires family mediation services to have a process for ensuring that mediators consider whether parties have a need for information about welfare benefits suppliers, marital counselling agencies, financial advisers, child counselling services and LSC contracted family lawyers. The MQMS is included in Appendix 8.

friends, family members, work colleagues and other relevant individuals to assist them in the process by providing advice, reassurance or merely making up the numbers.[50] In some cases it may be necessary for supporters to remain outside the mediation room, because there is insufficient space or because not all parties agree to their presence. In these situations, there might have to be agreed protocols for keeping them informed of developments. In other cases, they may be in the meeting room for all or part of the mediation. Here they might be allowed to participate in all stages of the mediation, have a limited participation, or be silent observers. Mediators are required to exercise some discretionary judgements in relation to these options and to consult with the parties as is appropriate. They will want both to allow for constructive contributions from 'outsiders' and to avoid the 'cheer squad' syndrome.

All support persons should be required to sign a confidentiality undertaking before being admitted to the mediation room.[51]

Consultation with outside parties before ratifying agreement

9.61 This topic has also been referred to earlier.[52] Here the mediation process is adapted to allow the clients alone to confer with outside managers, boards, committees, lawyers or other professionals (like accountants and experts) whose approval is required or desired to make a provisional agreement final. As this approval is an issue for both parties it can be discussed openly with them in the mediation meeting. With the approval of the parties the mediator should offer his or her services to contact the ratifying body and convey to them some of the dynamics of the mediation not apparent from the drafted agreement.[53]

'Tag' mediations

9.62 Mediations do not always have the neat boundaries and identifiable participants as suggested in this book. In particular, mediations involving traditional societies might have an 'open door' policy, with different parties participating at different times. This serves the needs of consultative decision-making in which involvement and participation for all interested parties is allowed and encouraged. Sometimes mediators might have to adapt the process to these realities, even when the involvement sought is unconventional, as shown here.

---

50 In family mediations, supporters might include new partners, step-parents, grandparents and aunts/uncles.
51 Refer to Appendix 3.
52 See 5.75.
53 Ibid. In family cases, as mediation meetings are commonly conducted without lawyers or other professionals present, professionals may be invited to participate in such manner as the mediator may consider useful and appropriate and as the parties may agree. Even if the professionals are not involved during the mediation, the parties are given the opportunity to consult lawyers before finalising any binding agreement.

Case illustration

A local authority had to decide whether to introduce flood prevention measures in their area and arranged for a mediation involving a carefully considered set of participants: several government departments and representatives from the communities likely to be most affected, together with two co-mediators. The mediation was held in a community hall. After an hour of mediation a group of residents burst through the doors and announced that they wished to be involved in the mediation as their interests were not sufficiently represented. The mediating group deliberated hastily and decided to allow them to observe the proceedings and to participate through a nominated spokesperson. This protocol was followed for about an hour, with minimal participation from the spokesperson, until the group departed the hall as suddenly as they had entered it. The mediation then proceeded without them. At the end of the mediation the original participants drafted a joint statement for release to the broader community.

J. Summary

9.63   This chapter raises the following points of particular significance:

■ While there are some core procedures which should apply to all mediations, there are also many variations in the standard process which can be used to respond to peculiar circumstances and conditions.

■ New forms of technology provide innovative opportunities for the development and use of mediation, particularly where parties are separated by space or time zones and different participants, such as advisers and experts, are in different localities.

■ All the variations in the standard mediation process introduce some benefits and advantages, but they also involve some potential drawbacks and dangers which mediators need to consider before modifying the standard process.

K. Tasks for beginner mediators

9.64   You are about to represent a client in a mediation to be conducted on a shuttle basis. Write up a list of precautions which you feel should be taken to ensure:

1. that the parties do not lose trust in the mediation process when the mediator is absent from them;

2. that the mediator is accurate in conveying messages back and forth; and

3. that the mediator does not abuse the power which she will derive from being the sole source of communication between the parties.

9.65   In a co-mediation it is useful if the co-mediators can avoid any personality conflicts between themselves. Write out some of your personality traits and then generate two lists of personality traits, one listing those factors which would tend to make a co-mediator compatible with you and one which would tend to make them incompatible.

9.66 You wish to develop a business which conducts mediations over the internet. Investigate and describe ways in which information and communications technology could be used to maximise the advantages of this kind of mediation and to minimise any drawbacks.

L. Recommended reading

Almaguer and Baggott, 'Shaping New Legal Frontiers: Dispute Resolution for the Internet' 13 (1998) *Ohio State Journal on Dispute Resolution* 711.

Blackwell G., 'Online Mediation', *Canadian Lawyer Magazine*, May 2009.

Boulle L. and Nesic M., *Mediation: Principles Process Practice*, Tottel Publishing, 2001, Ch 5.

Boulle L., 'Options for Cyber-Med' (1999) 1 *ADR Bulletin* 128.

Brandon and Stodulka, '24/7 Family Dispute Resolution: Disconnection and Reconnection via the Phone Line', in (2008) 10(5) *ADR Bulletin* 84.

Bryson D., 'When Wearing Different Hats: Suggestions for ADR Practice' (1999) 1 *ADR Bulletin* 125.

Carter J., 'What's New in Telephone Mediation? A Public Sector Mediation Service Steps up to a New Level of Telephone Access for Parties in Mediation', in (2009) 11(1) *ADR Bulletin* 15.

Cole, 'Online Mediation: where we have been, where we are now and where we should be', in (2006) 38 *U Tol L Rev* 193.

Eastall and Condliffe, 'Abbreviated Mediation: Trial of a New Process' (1999) 1 *ADR Bulletin* 118.

Fairman C. M., 'Ethics and Collaborative Lawyering: Why Put Old Hats on New Heads?', *Ohio State Journal On Dispute Resolution*, 2003, 18, pp 505–528.

Gibbons et al, 'Cyber-mediation: Computer-mediated Communications Medium Massaging the Message (2002) 32 *N.M. L Rev* 27.

Gillieron, 'From face-to-face to screen-to-screen: Real Hope or True Fallacy' in (2008) 23 Ohil St J on Disp Resol 301.

Goodman, 'The Pros and Cons of Online Dispute Resolution: an Assessment of Cyber-Mediation Websites', in (2003) *Duke L & Tech Rev* 4.

Guadagnoa R. E. and Cialdini R. B., 'Persuade Him by E-mail, but see Her in Person: On-line Persuasion Revisited', in (2007) 23 *Computers in Human Behaviour* 999.

Haloush, 'Jurisdictional Dilemma in On-line Disputes: Rethinking Traditional Approaches', (2008)_42 *Int'l Law* 1129.

Haloush and Malkawi, 'Internet Characteristics and Online ADR', in (2008) 13 *Harv Neg L Rev* 327.

Haloush, 'Internet Infrastructure and Online ADR', in 25 (2008) *J Marshall J Computer & Info* 217.

Hardy S, 'Online Mediation: Internet Dispute Resolution' (1998) 9 *ADRJ* 216.

Katsh E. and Rifkin J., *Introduction to On-line Dispute Resolution*, Jossey-Bass, San Francisco, 2001.

King D., 'Internet Mediation – A Summary' (2000) 11 *ADRJ* 180.

Larson D. A., 'Online Dispute Resolution: Technology Takes a Place at the Table. *Negotiation Journal*, 2004, 20.

LSC, *Quality Mark (2010) for Family Mediation*, 2009.

Lise E. C., 'ADR and Cyberspace: The Role of Alternative Dispute Resolution in Online Commerce, Intellectual Property and Defamation', *Ohio State Journal on Dispute Resolution*, 1996, 12, p 193.

Martin, 'Keep it Online: the Hague Convention and the Need for Online ADR in International business-to-consumer E-commerce' in (2002) 20 *B.U. Int'l L.J.* 125.

Noriega and Lopez, 'Towards a platform for online mediation', at http://e-institutions. iiia.csic.es

Ponte and Cavenagh, *Cyberjustice: online dispute resolution for e-comerce*, Pearson Prentice Hall, New Jersey, 2005.

Roberts M., *Mediation in Family Disputes: Principles of Practice*, Ashgate, Aldershot, 2008.

Rogers B., 'Multiple Roles in ADR' (1999) 2 *ADR Bulletin* 8.

Rule C., *Online Dispute Resolution for Business*, Jossey-Bass, 2002.

Thompson L. and Nadler J., 'Negotiating via Information Technology: Theory and Application', in (2002) 58 *Journal of Social Issues* 109.

Victorio R. M., 'Internet Dispute Resolution (iDR): Bringing ADR into the 21st Century', *Pepperdine Dispute Resolution Law Journal*, 2000, 1, p 279.

Chapter 10

Special Issues in Mediation

A watched pot never boils

A. Introduction

10.1 This chapter deals with some of the special issues that can arise in certain mediations. Each of the issues can have important implications not only for the success of individual mediations but also for the reputation of the mediator and mediation and for broader societal interests as well. While there are no unifying themes among this array of single instances, a number of them do touch on the question of power in mediation.

As to what makes an issue 'special' is not entirely obvious. The term 'special' denotes something out of the ordinary which will be encountered in only exceptional circumstances in mediation and not as part of the routine. The term 'special' does not imply that these issues are more important than others already dealt with in this book.

10.2 There are many special issues that can arise and those dealt with here are based on relevant literature, stories about actual mediations, and the author's experiences and reflections. As usual they are raised not in order to provide any specific solutions but to consider the skills and techniques that mediators could use in dealing with them.

B. Dealing with the power issue

10.3 There is much debate over the appropriate role and responsibilities of the mediator where one party is 'more powerful' than another in a mediation. Reference has been made to the concept and nature of power in Chapter 8, with particular reference to the mediator's use of power. Here the focus is on the power relations between the mediating parties. John Wade has identified the following perceived and actual sources of power:[1]

---

1   Reprinted with the kind permission of John Wade. See also J. Wade, 'Persuasion in Negotiation and Mediation', in (2007) 10(1) *ADR Bulletin* 8.

Type of power	Example
Emotional	'You are depressed and easily rattled: I am calm.'
Risk-taking	'I am willing to take chances – with litigation, or finding an alternative supplier.'
Status quo	'I have the status quo (possession of the business, children, job); you have the burden of changing the status quo.'
Scorched earth	'I don't care what happens; I have nothing to lose; my fall-back position is to burn everything.'
Information	'I have vital information about (bank accounts; manufacturing process; customer lists; judicial hobby-horses etc) – you don't.'
Expert	'My experts have more credibility; more experience in answering difficult questions etc than yours.'
Resource	'I can spend more time and money. I will drown you in paper.'
Rights	'The law, company policy, patterns of precedent, common behaviours of decision-making, give me a stronger fall back position.'
Structural	'This dispute will be decided or enforced in X jurisdiction where the bosses/judges are accessible/cheap/honest/vigilant/independent or vice versa.'
Humiliation	'I have the moral high ground and the approval of our cultural peers. You will be ridiculed.'
Time rich	'I have nothing else to do, but to continue this dispute for the rest of my/your life. You do.'
Preparation	'I am organised, logical, equipped with graphs and summaries. You are a disorganised babbler.'
Association	'I have powerful allies/tribes (with whom you will have to trade).'
Publicity	'You fear publicity; I love any kind of publicity.'
Skeletons in the closet	'I have not told them, but what if the police, customs, your spouse, social security etc find out about X.'
Alternative fall back	'If you do not agree, then I have several alternative (suppliers, subcontractors).'
Future relationship	'If you are helpful now, I will be considerate, polite, generous in future dealings. If not (vice versa).'

10.4   There are two principal sources of concern in respect of the power relations between mediating parties. The first is whether mediation is appropriate where there is an 'imbalance of power' between them. This has been referred to earlier in the book in relation to intake and screening.[2] The second relates to the proper role of mediators where a mediation takes place in circumstances of a 'power imbalance' and is dealt with in this chapter.

---

2   See 2.14.

Some assumptions about power

10.5   As it is not possible to enter the theoretical debates on this topic, it is appropriate to state some basic assumptions on which this section is based:

■ There are *almost always* some power disparities in the resolution of disputes: they were not invented to bedevil mediation alone, and mediators should not assume too much responsibility in relation to the power inequalities in society or between the parties outside the mediation room.

■ There are many *different contexts* in which there might be disparities of power between the parties (as outlined in the table above). Some of these are self-evident: the large employer and the individual worker; the large trade union and the small employer; the professionally advised insurer and the self-represented claimant; the personally articulate party and the poorly-educated party. Other power disparities may not be self-evident, especially to outsiders such as mediators who might never understand the real power dynamics at play between the parties.

■ Power is a *complex phenomenon* and all negotiating parties have some sources of power, although they may sometimes be very slight. Power can derive from many sources, besides the obvious source of money. Summarising the table above, power could come from:

– knowledge and understanding (legal, financial, structural, emotional);

– the ability to damage or reward;

– access to authority and the media;

– rules, standards and principles and their precedent power;

– simple morality of the situation;

– reputational needs; and

– attractive alternatives to negotiating a settlement for one or other party (their BATNA).

■ Sometimes in dispute resolution the *perception of power* is more important than the objective conditions of power. Thus a party will, within limits, be at an advantage when they perceive themselves to be powerful (as illustrated in the table above), and will be at a disadvantage when they perceive the other party to be more powerful than they. In many situations both parties will have the same perceptions, namely that they are powerless or considerably less powerful than the other party.[3]

■ There is also significant *power in mediators* themselves which they can use (and abuse) in different ways and for different purposes.[4]

The extent of the mediator's responsibilities

10.6   The extent of the mediator's responsibilities in relation to the power question is a major policy issue. It can only be referred to in abbreviated form here.

---

3   As Charlton and Dewdney (*The Mediator's Handbook*, 1995, 239) point out, experienced mediators know that 'power is seldom what it seems'.
4   See 8.4.

On one hand, it is argued that mediators are intended only to conduct the mediation process fairly and impartially,[5] and they should not in their capacity as mediators assume the responsibility of redressing power imbalances which derive from circumstances outside the mediation. Power problems can rather be resolved through the use of professional advisers and support persons, through resorting to litigation and government agencies, through delay and counselling, and through other initiatives outside the mediation meeting – strikes, sabotage, sanctions and other non-mediatory actions.

On the other hand, it is said that mediators do have some responsibilities in relation to certain power imbalances and if they do nothing about them one party may be severely disadvantaged, the agreement may not last, the mediator may be sued, and the reputation of mediation may be adversely affected. Tillett considers that one of the most important functions of the mediation process is the 'empowerment' of weaker parties so that stronger parties do not prevail through might alone.[6] However, the extent of this empowerment function is not always clear.

10.7   The approach taken here is a middle of the road one. This is that mediators do have some responsibilities over the power issue but that these should revolve mainly around their control over the process of mediation. Mediators are not the advocates of the less powerful party, nor the champions of the poor and oppressed. The focus here is on practical ways in which mediators can deal with the power issue through their control of procedure. This is consistent with the Law Society's Code of Practice. In relation to general civil and commercial mediation, section 6 of the Code of Practice refers to the mediator taking reasonable steps to address the issue if power imbalances threaten to make the process unfair or unworkable. The commentary to section 6 clarifies the obligation:

> 'Power imbalances will almost invariably exist during the course of a mediation. The mediator cannot be responsible for redressing those imbalances. He or she must, however, seek to ensure that these do not cause the process to become ineffective as a result of the abuse of one party's stronger position.'[7]

Ways in which the mediator can work with power

10.8   Many aspects of the mediation process, referred to in detail in other sections of this book, have as one of their objectives the adjustment or moderation of power relations between the parties. These include:

---

5   Most mediator codes of conduct require fairness and impartiality. See, for example, Requirements E1.2 and E1.4 MQMS, section 2.3 IMI Code, Articles 2.2 and 3.2 EU Code, sections 4.1/4.3–4.4 CEDR Code, section 3 CORE Solutions Group Code, section 3 Law Society Code of Practice for Civil/ Commercial Mediation, section 3.3 Law Society Code of Practice for Family Mediation and section 4.4 College of Mediators Code of Practice (refer to Appendix 8 for codes of conduct). See also Article 7.2 UNCITRAL Conciliation Rules (included in Appendix 3).

6   *Resolving Conflict*, 2nd ed, 1999, 82.

7   The approach is also consistent with Article 3.2 EU Code of Conduct, Element (1) Stage (7) Law Society's Competencies for Civil/Commercial Mediation, section 6 Law Society Code of Practice for Family Mediation and section 4.3 College of Mediators Code of Practice. Refer to Appendix 8 for codes of conduct.

- the intake and screening procedures;

- the preliminary conference;

- the neutrality and impartiality of the mediator;

- the appropriate enforcement of the mediation guidelines;

- control over the lines of communication;

- appropriate physical, environmental and timing arrangements;

- supervision of the exchange of and access to information;

- the appropriate involvement of representatives, advocates, advisers and other professionals;

- the separate meetings with each party;

- adjournments and cooling-off periods for agreements reached at the mediation meeting.

10.9   Thus even though it might only be at a minimalist level, the mediation process itself does indirectly moderate some power differences between the parties. Beyond this minimalist level there can also be direct interventions on power issues, aimed at either the stronger party or the weaker party. Some possible approaches are summarised in the table overleaf.

Additional specific examples of dealing with the power issue are provided in Sections C–E below.

Dangers in dealing with the power balance

10.10   There are some potential dangers for mediators if they become too involved in increasing the power of the weaker party and decreasing that of the stronger:

- They might become the advocate for and protector of the weaker party, rather than helping them to obtain support from advisers, support groups, government agencies and other outside bodies.

- They might lose their impartiality because the mediator is perceived as taking sides with the weaker party and against the more powerful party.

- They might be inclined to impose their own standards and values in place of those of the parties.

- They may be in breach of their mediation contract or applicable mediation guidelines, with the adverse consequences which this might bring.[8]

---

8   Refer to provisions in note 5.

Dealing with the power issue	
Interventions for increasing the power of weaker parties	**Interventions for reducing the power of stronger parties**
The term 'empowerment' refers to ways in which mediators use their positions, skills and control of the mediation process to increase the ability of the weaker party to perform well. Some commentators suggest that it involves helping such persons or groups to use the power they already have. These interventions involve some potential deviation from the mediator's neutrality and impartiality. They require the mediator to use the procedures and strategies referred to in the previous section for the particular benefit of the weaker party.	Again, these interventions involve some potential deviation from the mediator's neutrality and impartiality. They involve the mediator creating doubt in the mind of the stronger parties over the facts, the law, the evidence and their likelihood of being successful in litigation; in pointing out the downsides, particularly in the longer term, of using their strength to overpower the weaker parties; in being the agent of reality and devil's advocate in separate sessions; and in threatening to terminate the mediation, and actually terminating it, where the proposed settlement is significantly 'outside the range'.[9]
By way of illustration, a mediator in a discrimination complaint may take particular care in ensuring that the complainant understands the nature of the process she will go through and that her story is told in full, in enforcing the mediation guidelines to avoid intimidation from the employer and their advisers, and in using the separate sessions to help her to prioritise her interests. The question of whether the mediator should 'advise' the weaker party is dealt with elsewhere in this book: see 8.9–8.11.	By way of illustration, in a mediation involving local residents and a powerful developer, the mediator might encourage the latter to make information available, to allow a wide group of representatives to negotiate on behalf of the residents, and to prevent any artificial deadlines being imposed as an intimidatory tactic by the developer.

C. Dealing with violence

10.11 A special form of the power problem arises where there has been a history of personal violence between the parties or there is ongoing violence between them. This is most pertinent in relation to domestic violence between spouses or partners,[10] but is also relevant in other situations, for example, personal violence in the workplace or within schools. The same skills and techniques relating to power imbalances have applicability here, and there are some additional policy and practical considerations.

The policy issues

10.12 The literature and policy guidelines deal extensively with the issue of when mediation should be regarded as entirely inappropriate because of the violence

---

9 See 10.24–10.28.

10 UK College of Family Mediators, *Domestic Abuse Screening Policy*, 2000b defines domestic abuse as behaviour that seeks to secure power and control for the abuser and the impact of which is to undermine the safety, security, self-esteem and autonomy of the abused person. Domestic violence contains elements of the use of any or all of physical, sexual, psychological, emotional, verbal or economic intimidation, oppression or coercion.

factor.[11] It is argued that the fear, apprehension and intimidation experienced by the abused party render them incapable of negotiating and making decisions in mediation and their problems should be dealt with elsewhere. Whatever screening and other precautions are taken in the mediation, the argument goes, it will still be a fundamentally unfair process for the victim, and possibly even a dangerous one.

10.13   Whatever the policy arguments in the literature, practising mediators are involved in a great number of cases in which there has in the past been some violence, ranging from serious to mild, and in some cases, where protection orders or injunctions are in place at the time of the mediation. These mediations usually take place in the context of scarce resources, limited dispute resolution options, and some measure of pressure to participate in mediation. In these settings, mediators seldom get to understand the true realities of the violence, nor do they obtain any follow-up in regard to mediated agreements. Here, mediation is hardly an ideal option, but it might be the only feasible one.

10.14   The approach taken in this book is that, while it is never ideal to mediate where there is a history of violence, it may be the only realistic option for parties with scarce resources who need to make practical arrangements over children and property. The focus is therefore on ways in which this reality can be best dealt with by modifying and adapting the mediation process. Fortunately, many mediation agencies (like the UK College of Family Mediators) have policies and codes which guide mediators in approaching this difficult role, and they are required to have them if they receive government funding (for example, the LSC Mediation Quality Mark Standard[12]).

Screening for violence

10.15   Pre-mediation screening for evidence of violence is one of the most important precautions in this context and has been referred to previously.[13] Screening is designed both to provide hard information on matters of violence and to create opportunities for clients to disclose their feelings and concerns about the problem. It allows the person conducting the screening to assess the victim's capacity to participate effectively in mediation and to assess the perpetrator's capacity to function appropriately.

10.16   Pre-mediation screening can have two significant outcomes. First, it allows for the identification of situations which are unsuitable for mediation, which can then be referred to another form of skilled help. This can be governed by standards of practice, codes of conduct or applicable legislation. For example:

■ The UK College of Family Mediators Domestic Abuse Screening Policy reminds mediators that screening is an ongoing requirement; that providers of family mediation services are required to have written procedures for screening; and that security and safety issues are aimed at both the participants in mediation and any significant family members.[14]

---

11   See 2.14 and Chapter 2 in general.
12   'MQMS', 2nd edition, 2009.
13   See 2.14–2.16.
14   The Policy is included in Appendix 7.

■ The UK College of Family Mediators Code of Practice requires mediators to seek to discover through a screening procedure whether or not there is fear of abuse or any other harm and whether or not it is alleged that any participant has been or is likely to be abusive towards another. Where abuse is alleged or suspected, the Code requires mediators to discuss whether any participant wishes to take part in mediation and that information about available support services should be provided. Where mediation does take place, the Code also provides that mediators must uphold throughout the principles of voluntariness of participation, fairness and safety and must conduct the process in accordance with the Code. In addition, steps must be taken to ensure the safety of all participants on arrival and departure.[15]

■ The MQMS requires LSC-franchised practices (and those complying with the MQMS) to have a screening system in place. That system has to consider the clients, the dispute and the circumstances. Evidence of operation of the system will be required on audit.[16]

■ The Law Society of England and Wales has adapted various guidelines following advice and consultation to formulate screening guidance.[17]

The EU Recommendation on Family Mediation also addresses screening. It provides that the mediator should pay particular regard to whether violence has occurred in the past or may occur in the future between the parties and the effect this may have on the parties' bargaining positions, and should consider whether in these circumstances the mediation process is appropriate.[18]

10.17   The second outcome of pre-mediation screening is that it allows for adequate preparation by the mediator where mediation is to go ahead despite a history of violence. In some settings, mediators are directly involved in the screening function, and in others it is performed by designated staff with specialised training in this area. In both contexts, mediators can plan strategies and interventions for dealing with the violence factor.

Mediator interventions in relation to violence issues

10.18   Before planning their interventions, mediators need to be able to understand and read the indicators of violence. To achieve this all mediators involved in family mediations are required to be trained on the nature of domestic violence and its consequences for both victim and perpetrator.[19]

One of the many advantages of training is that it assists mediators to recognise the indicators that one of the parties has been abused. On the part of the victim this might include continually waiting for the other to speak, glancing timidly at the perpetrator, or always trying to smooth over points of conflict; on the part of the perpetrator, it might include dominating the airways, aggressive body language,

---

15   See sections 2.3 and 4.8 of the Code (included in Appendix 8).
16   Requirement F1.1. The MQMS is included in Appendix 8.
17   Refer to *Family Law Protocol*, 2nd edition, 2006 and see 2.15 in this book.
18   Council of Europe Recommendation No. R (98) 1 of the Committee of Ministers to Member States on Family Mediation – refer to Article IV (ix): see Appendix 13.
19   See 12.4 and 12.6.

impatience or threatening tone of voice. Of course these are only indicators, and the mediator might need more information in order to understand the situation fully.

10.19 In the light of this understanding, the mediator is able to adapt and modify the mediation process to suit the circumstances. A list of practical things which mediators might do along these lines would include:

- investigating the possibility of the victim taking out a protection order before the mediation;

- organising separate arrival times and supervised waiting rooms for the parties;

- having relatively short sessions, and more than one session, so that the victim party can have time out and seek counsel and support;

- conducting separate sessions, and holding these more than once where circumstances require it;

- making strict arrangements for the victim party's safety during the mediation session;

- making use of written details of tasks which the parties are required to perform between sessions;

- considering the safety aspects of contact visits and other post-mediation meetings between the parties (with reference to neutral public venues, supervision, and so on);

- assessing the victim's comfort levels throughout the process;

- undertaking any termination of the mediation in such a way that it does not antagonise the offender towards the victim;

- ensuring that the victim is able to leave the mediation precinct first and has sufficient time to get away before the perpetrator departs;

- discussing with the victim party beforehand ways of dealing with their problems in the mediation.

Case illustration: dealing with violence symptoms in mediation

In the preparatory stages of a voluntary mediation the mediator, who was aware of a history of personal violence between the parties, conducted personal interviews with both parties. The victim, who was legally represented, was willing to take part in the mediation process jointly with the perpetrator provided her lawyer was present, but was concerned that she would become intimidated and quiet if the perpetrator raised his voice and became threatening. She would also feel nervous about asking for a separate meeting with the mediator or an adjournment to speak with her lawyer.

The mediator discussed with her options for dealing with this predicament. They agreed that as soon as she felt intimidated she would give the mediator a hand signal, and this would cause him to suggest an adjournment a few minutes later. This occurred twice in the mediation, after which the victim had developed enough confidence in the process, and in her abilities, to be able to continue through to agreement, despite the conduct of the perpetrator.

10.20 Mediators have some important responsibilities on the violence issue, but they alone cannot guarantee the safety of the victim. In relation to the responsibilities which they do have there is much more comprehensive advice available from mediation service providers and agencies operating in this area.[20]

D. Using interpreters in mediation

10.21 The need for and use of interpreters in mediation is another aspect of the power dynamic, this time created by linguistic disadvantage. Normally it is clear as to whether an interpreter should be used in mediation, namely if one or more participants are unable to understand the language in which it is conducted. However, mediators should not be too gullible on the issue. It is not unknown for parties to ask for an interpreter, despite the fact that they are conversant with the language of the mediation. The use of the interpreter is then a device for the relevant party to have time to think, and it provides the presence of a 'professional friend' in the mediation process.

10.22 Where an interpreter is necessary for the successful conduct of the mediation, the following guidelines are appropriate for mediators:

- It is clearly preferable to use professionals as interpreters, and not friends, the mediator, or one of the parties involved.

- A clear role definition is important for the interpreter, and also for the party for whose benefit they are present. Where an interpreter is being used for the first time, even if they are professionally qualified, they should be fully briefed on the nature of the mediation process and on their role in it.

- The mediator should explicitly direct the interpreter to avoid adopting a quasi-mediator role or engaging in giving advice or evaluation.

- The mediator should get the interpreter to sign a confidentiality undertaking before the mediation commences.

- The mode of interpretation should be specified and understood – this is usually consecutive as opposed to simultaneous.

- As regards seating, the interpreter should be next to the mediator, to symbolise neutrality as between the parties and the obligations of the interpreter to the process as opposed to the individual client. This also serves to maintain focus on the mediator, as opposed to another professional present at the foot of the table.

- Normally the mediator should communicate in direct speech with the interpreter translating, but may occasionally lapse into indirect speech, for example, 'Interpreter please tell X that I am going to summarise now …'.

- The mediator should intervene as soon as a dialogue ensues between the interpreter and the party for whose benefit he or she is present and get them back on track.

---

20   For further background, refer to *Re L (Contact: Domestic Violence)* [2000] 2 FLR 334 where the Court of Appeal issued guidelines; and Children Act Sub-Committee Report, *Making Contact Work*, 2002.

10.23 Where interpreters are used mediators are advised to prepare for a lengthier mediation to accommodate the additional person, longer speaking time, and inevitable difficulties arising from the role. As regards the quality of the interpreter's work, this is very difficult for a mediator to monitor. This requires the mediator to be particularly observant in relation to the reactions of the parties to see if one or both seem concerned at what is being said. However, even active listening and body language will be more problematic, given the cultural differences which operate in these situations.

E. Dealing with proposed settlements 'outside the range'

10.24 What should you do where the parties are about to settle on something which is 'outside the range' of usual settlements for a particular kind of dispute? The 'range' could involve the formal, or conventional, or usual, ways in which such disputes 'normally come out'. It could be based on court decisions, on industry norms, on community standards, or on simple commonsense ('one party should not be getting everything and the other nothing …'). It is, however, seldom a matter of scientific measurement, hence the use of the term 'range'.

Here are some examples of 'outside the range' situations:

- A self-represented claimant in a personal injury mediation is about to settle for less than he might obtain in court because he has entirely overlooked claiming damages for pain and suffering.

- A sexual harassment complainant is about to settle only for an apology, in circumstances where she would usually be awarded monetary compensation.

- A husband is entering a matrimonial property settlement in which no account is taken of his wife's pension entitlements.

10.25 The 'outside the range' problem extends to other situations in which one party is at a disadvantage, through ignorance, emotional stress, lack of advice or other considerations, which places them in a weaker situation than the other side. The question arises as to what techniques a mediator can use in the face of these imminent settlements 'outside the range'.

10.26 It is useful to start from first principles. The mediator's role is primarily to assist the parties to come to their own decisions and not to protect the interests of the weaker party. Moreover, mediators should be aware of the non-pecuniary interests, both procedural and emotional, which parties might have in settling for less than might otherwise be obtained. They may not want to come within the 'range'. Thus claimants might settle for less money than they are 'entitled' to in order to achieve finality in the dispute, to avoid the uncertainty and stress of litigation, to get a lesser amount now rather than a greater amount some time in the future, or in order to turn a corner and get on with their lives. Defendants and respondents might also agree to a commercial settlement to avoid bad publicity or to save further legal costs, despite the fact that there is virtually no prospect of their being found liable in a legal forum. It is consistent with the mediation principle of party autonomy to allow parties to give their informed consent to a settlement, despite the fact that it is 'outside the range'.

10.27   These principles suggest that one possible response is for the mediator to inform the parties about the need for independent legal advice where they are not legally represented and otherwise 'do nothing' and to allow the parties to settle on their intended terms – the *sign them up* approach. This is an extreme non-interventionist approach which might be suitable for some clients in some situations.

In other circumstances, however, the *sign them up* approach could have serious long-term consequences for one party, in particular where their 'consent' is not informed. It could also damage the reputation of mediation as a dispute resolution process. Therefore another possible response is for the mediator to adopt a strong interventionist approach of assisting such a party by advising them directly about the matter which they have overlooked or forgone. This is the *let me tell you* approach. However, this could also have problems in that the non-assisted party is likely to lose trust in the mediation process and it could lead to confusion in the marketplace about the nature of mediation.

10.28   Between these two extremes of the *sign them up* and *let me tell you* approaches, are a number of intermediate responses, each of which has some advantages and some shortcomings. Here reference will be made to the personal injury scenario referred to above, where the unrepresented claimant is Lindsay, and Henry is representing the defendant. The mediator could:

- Work systematically through the proposed agreement, checking it against the list of issues, to verify that the parties are consenting to each detail: 'Lindsay and Henry, now that you have agreement on principle on these matters let me take you through them one by one to make sure that you are entirely clear on each of them.'

- Ask the parties in joint session whether there are additional matters they would like to have dealt with in the mediation: 'Lindsay and Henry, now that you have agreement in principle on these matters, let me check with you whether there are any additional matters or issues you would like dealt with today.'

- Query the parties in joint session as to whether they would like to obtain legal advice before making final decisions: 'Henry and Lindsay, before we go any further, would either of you like an adjournment to consult other people about the settlement you are about to reach today?'

- Adjourn the mediation on the pretext that this is 'normal practice' in such matters, in the expectation that the disadvantaged party will have the opportunity to reconsider the settlement or seek legal advice: 'Well, you have nearly reached settlement, and it is my normal practice to have an adjournment at this stage, for about an hour, so that both of you can reconsider what you have agreed to and obtain advice on any matter on which you are uncertain or unclear.'

- In a separate meeting with the weaker party, the claimant, act as the agent of reality in relation to the extent to which the proposed agreement is in their best interests: 'Lindsay, you are entitled to make your own decisions here but this needs to be in your long-term interests. Once you agree to this settlement you will have no further opportunity to claim damages. I should also point out that this is a technical area of the law and many people in your position seek advice on what is best for them.'

- In a separate meeting with the stronger party, the defendant, point out the potential legal, ethical and reputational consequences of their agreeing to a settlement that disadvantages the weaker party: 'Henry, you are about to sign-off on a settlement which you know is considerably less than Lindsay would obtain in court. What if Lindsay finds out later and seeks to review it? How will that affect your company, and for that matter your professional reputation?'

- Raise the prospect of including a 'cooling-off' clause in the mediated agreement: 'Henry and Lindsay, in cases like this where one party is in the position of a consumer and the other is a big organisation, a cooling-off period can allow either of you to get out of the agreement. Is that something which might be used here?'

- Withdraw from the mediation, after explaining that the mediator is not willing to continue mediating where parties propose to settle 'outside the range': 'I'm in a difficult position here, Lindsay and Henry. While my role is not that of judge or jury, I have to be able to live with the outcome you agree on. If you insist on going ahead with an agreement which is, in my judgment, not within the bounds of reasonableness, I shall have no choice other than to terminate the mediation.'

These options become increasingly more 'interventionist' as far as the mediator is concerned. Which of them is appropriate will be a matter of judgment for the mediator in the particular circumstances of the mediation and the nature of the case and of the parties. Mediator standards and codes of conduct may provide some guidance in certain cases. For example, section 5.10 of the Law Society's Code of Practice for Family Mediation provides:

'The mediator should, if practicable, inform the parties if he or she considers that the resolutions which they are considering are likely to fall outside the parameters which a court might approve or order. If they nevertheless wish to proceed with such resolutions, they may do so. In these circumstances the mediation summary may identify any specific questions on which the mediator has indicated a need for independent legal advice. If, however, the parties are proposing a resolution which appears to the mediator to be unconscionable or fundamentally inappropriate, then the mediator should inform the parties accordingly and may terminate the mediation, and/or refer the parties to their legal advisers.'

F. Dealing with absent parties

10.29 Reference has already been made to the question of how mediators might deal with the need for formal ratification of mediated agreements by company boards, chief executives, government ministers and other outside ratifying parties.[21]

In many mediations there are also significant *absent parties*, that is, individuals who are not present at the mediation but who, without being required formally to ratify the mediated agreement, may have considerable influence over one or other party. In some cases, the existence of an absent party may be obvious to the mediator from the facts and circumstances of the case, or from an admission to this effect by a party. In other cases, the mediator might suspect the influence of an absent party from the reticence of one party or the intransigence of another.

---

21   See 5.75 and 9.61.

10.30   The following are some illustrations of *absent parties* with whom the authors have had to deal as mediators:

■ External advisers, corporate representatives and influential insiders who can affect the nature, or durability, of any agreement reached at mediation.

■ Support persons (including family members) who hold a powerful sway over the parties and their view of what is right or wrong.

■ Members of boards, committees, creditors' committees, clubs and associations to whom a mediating party will 'report back' and who may criticise, ridicule or otherwise undermine their commitment to the mediated outcome.

■ Outsiders who are directly funding one of the parties, and who has high expectations of the process.

■ New partners of former spouses in matrimonial property mediations, who are a strong influence on the mediating parties and who will themselves be affected by the outcome in the mediation.

■ Grandparents of children in parenting mediations, who have their own interests in seeing the children and who might also be used for supervised contact or as go-betweens for the parents.

10.31   Where the mediator suspects the existence of a significant absent party, or is informed about this person in a confidential separate session, he or she should work in private with the relevant party on options for dealing with the problem. Here the mediatory method is used to identify interests, priorities, options and choices for that party. Assume, for example, that there is a mediation between Mark and Phil, both employees of a private church school. There has been an allegation of sexual harassment. It becomes evident that Phil, the complainant, is concerned about how her fellow employees will react to any compromise she reaches. The mediator might say in separate session: 'Phil, you have raised this fear about your colleagues' reactions. How important is that to you, and what ways are there for dealing with it?'

10.32   If, however, the absent party is known about by both parties, the mediator can deal with the problem in joint session where he or she can explain that dealing with this outside person is a common problem for them both. In mediation terms, another issue goes up on the board or chart. In the above example it might be 'How can the school community's anticipated criticism of a settlement be dealt with?' or 'How can we prevent the school community from sabotaging the mediated agreement?' The mediator can then ask Phil and Mark for ideas on dealing with the joint problem.

10.33   In dealing with the 'external ratifier', reference was made to the need for the mediator to make contact with that person and present to them an authentic 'blood, sweat and tears' version of the mediation.[22] This will not be possible where the 'absent party' is not known to one mediating party, and may still not be easy where he or she is. However, the same principles apply and the parties might agree to the mediator having a major role in this regard. In practice, we have also found that some elaboration in the drafting of the mediated agreement, to include reasons and explanations, makes the relevant party more confident of dealing with their 'absent party'.

---

22   See 5.75.

G. Involving children in mediation

10.34 Reference has been made to the importance of involving in mediation those who, while not direct parties to the dispute themselves, are sufficiently important to warrant some inclusion in the mediation.[23] Examples of such people are senior executives in commercial mediations where middle managers were responsible for the original problem, or vehicle drivers and employers in personal injury mediations even though insurers are representing them.

Children in family mediations constitute a different category of those who might be involved in that it is their interests which are directly and intimately affected by decisions taken. While there will sometimes be a court-appointed separate legal representative to uphold the children's rights, the focus here is on the direct involvement of the children themselves.

10.35 There are various approaches to the involvement of children in mediations held to deal with disputes between their parents over residence and contact:

1. No involvement at all for the children, with the parents responsible for any communications to them about the process and its outcome.

2. Involvement of the children after the mediation has concluded, with the mediator, with or without assistance from the parents, informing them about the outcome and its practical implications for them.

3. Partial involvement of the children, in joint or separate sessions, or via indirect involvement (where children are not present at mediation), for the purpose of listening to their views about parenting arrangements, but without their having any role in the final decision-making.

4. Full involvement of the children in all stages and aspects of the mediation.

10.36 The last option is rare in practice and could only operate with older children of significant maturity, with the full consent of the parents, and with the approval of the mediator. The mediator must also be trained for that purpose and must provide appropriate facilities.[24] As with other professionals who see children, the mediator must meet requirements in respect of police checks. The first option is common in mediation practice. It is justifiable with children of tender years or where there is likely to be major confrontation between their parents. It is also supported on policy grounds by those who claim that children should not be involved in the drama of family mediations or feel the burden of choice and decision-making. However, this approach is often adopted with little consideration given to the feasibility of the second and third options in light of the children's maturity, understanding and ability to cope, and notwithstanding that family mediators are required to encourage the parties to consider their children's own wishes and feelings.

10.37 It might be entirely appropriate in some cases for the mediator to inform and educate the children about the parenting agreement and its practical implications, for example, how it might be amended in the future to take account of their changing needs. This is likely to be a more independent and objective explanation of the settlement and its practical consequences. Likewise where

---

23   See 4.19–4.20.
24   See sections 4.7.3–4.7.5 College of Mediators Code of Practice (in Appendix 8).

children are at the age where they might be consulted about their preferences they could be involved in relevant parts of the mediation, subject to safeguards and protections. Given the fact that adolescents can cause the breakdown of a carefully crafted parenting regime even before it has commenced operation, there might be good practical reasons to involve them in some way in making the arrangements. However, there is always a cautionary aspect to any involvement: children should never have adult responsibilities imposed on them and they should not feel that they are choosing between their parents.

10.38   In terms of the legislative and regulatory framework applicable in the UK:

- A child's welfare is considered of paramount importance.[25] The welfare of a child includes the wishes and feelings of the child.[26] The Family Law Act provides that the welfare, wishes and feelings of each child should be considered and that mediation must provide opportunities for the consultation of children.[27]

- The UN Convention on the Rights of the Child was ratified by the UK Government in 1991 and respects the child's right to freedom of expression and to have those opinions taken into account in any matter affecting the child.[28]

- In Scotland, the views of a child are required to be taken in account and children over 12 years of age are presumed to be able to form a view.[29]

- In *Gillick v West Norfolk & Wisbech AHA*, parental rights were considered to yield to a child's right to make his or her own decisions when a sufficient understanding and intelligence had been reached.[30]

The UK College of Family Mediators Policy on Children, Young People and Family Mediation sets out some basic guidelines, for example:

- Parents and others in mediation are encouraged to listen to any children involved.

- Children's perspectives should be taken into account in mediation.

- Mediators are encouraged to be creative in consulting with and involving children.

The College Code of Practice provides further guidance:

'4.7.3   Mediators have a special concern for the welfare of all children of the family. They must encourage participants to focus upon the needs of the children as well as upon their own and must explore the situation from the child's point of view.

4.7.4   Mediators must encourage the participants to consider children's own wishes and feelings. Where appropriate, they may discuss with the participants whether and to what extent it is proper to involve the children themselves in the mediation process in order to consult them about their wishes and feelings.

---

25   See *Re D* [1977] Fam. 158 and section 1 Children Act 1989.
26   Section 1(3) Children Act 1989.
27   Section 27(8) Family Law Act 1996.
28   Refer to Article 12 (although Articles 2, 3, 5 and 9 are also relevant).
29   Section 6 The Children (Scotland) Act 1995.
30   [1986] AC 112.

4.7.5 If, in a particular case, the mediator and participants agree that it is appropriate to consult any child directly in mediation, the mediator should be trained for that purpose, must obtain the child's consent and must provide appropriate facilities.'

The MQMS requirements in relation to franchised services (and those complying with the MQMS) are:

'F4.2 A documented procedure to ensure that, in considering whether or not children are to be directly consulted by the mediator, the mediator addresses and records on file:

- Whether, and to what extent, each child should be given the opportunity to express their wishes and feelings in mediation.

- The purpose of the consultation.

- Parental and child consent.

- The wishes and feelings of each child.'

The EU Recommendation on Family Mediation also seeks to address the issue of involvement of children in mediation. It provides that mediators should have a special concern for the welfare and best interests of the children; encourage parents to focus on the needs of children; and remind parents of their prime responsibility relating to the welfare of their children and the need for them to inform and consult their children.[31]

Some family mediation services refer to 'Direct Consultation with Children' when referring to the process, whereby mediators meet with children to hear their views and to agree with the child what they would like to have fed back to the mediation process for their parents to hear. Ultimately, as with other special issues, there are many ways in which mediators can adapt the mediation process to deal with children's needs and interests. One such option is illustrated here.

Case illustration: using children as an 'advisory panel'

Folberg and Taylor suggest the option of using the children as an 'advisory panel' to reality test a proposed parenting arrangement.[32] Here the mediator or parents seek the children's reactions before a final agreement is signed by the parents. It maintains the parents' obligation to make decisions, while taking into account the wishes of the children and allowing the children a sense of involvement in reviewing and commenting on the scheme. This part of the process can take place informally without the children coming to the mediation meeting itself. However, it is advisable that both parents be involved in a collaborative way so that any ambiguities in the agreement and queries from the children can be clarified by them together. Where there is too much antagonism between the parents the mediator should be involved, but preferably with the parents present. As with all forms of child involvement in mediation, it is possible for other trusted adults to accompany them into the mediation room and to be with them before and afterwards.

31 Council of Europe Recommendation No R (98) 1 of the Committee of Ministers to Member States on Family Mediation (refer to Article III (viii)) – see Appendix 13.
32 Folberg and Taylor *Mediation*, 1998, 182.

H.   Dealing with experts in mediation

10.39   A common feature of litigation is the involvement of experts. A frequent problem in the system is that because experts often differ fundamentally from one another dual experts become duelling experts, with a non-expert, the judge, having to decide between them.

The dual/duelling experts phenomenon is a product of the adversarial nature of the litigation process. Adversarialism entails that the parties themselves are responsible for conducting the investigation, preparation and presentation of their respective cases. The judge's traditional role is limited to that of adjudicating on the merits of the two presentations and it does not conventionally extend to establishing the truth through investigation, fact-finding and the calling of independent expert witnesses. In many cases the available remedies require the judge to give an either/ or verdict based on the evidence and arguments presented by the parties.

10.40   The adversarial system encourages each side to make the best possible case it can, to be as extreme in its presentation as is possible, and to use a range of tactics and arguments to weaken the case of the other side. Each side engages its own expert who presents reports and evidence in favour of that side's case and in contradiction of that of the other. There are three possible reasons as to why the experts give contrasting evidence:

- There may be genuine differences in their observations, evaluations and opinions as is the case in many technical areas, from the causes of industrial accidents to the long-term effects of physical injuries.

- The experts' views may be based on different versions of the facts or on partisan perceptions of events, for example, accountants may have different valuations of a business because they have been given access to different figures or are using a different basis for analysis of the same figures.

- The individuals may have been retained because they have established reputations in their areas of expertise and can be expected to behave more as advocates than as experts, for example, 'claimant' and 'defendant' doctors in personal injury disputes.

10.41   Although English civil procedure rules allow for the appointment of a single joint expert,[33] there are different ways in which ADR processes can avoid the syndrome of duelling experts. Some processes are themselves 'expert' based, for example, in case appraisal the expert gives an indicative opinion based on limited presentations of the case by each side and their experts. Although this opinion is 'non-binding' there can be cost penalties for parties who do not do as well at a subsequent trial as is indicated in the opinion. In this model, the case appraiser acts as a third independent expert who renders their opinion in the knowledge of the views of the parties' experts.

10.42   In mediation, it is the flexibility of the process that can be deployed to avoid the duelling experts syndrome. The mediator needs to diagnose the reason for the differences between the experts, in light of the three possibilities referred to above,

---

33   See CPR 35.7.

and then adapt the process in light of this diagnosis (which is always tentative). This is illustrated through three case studies in which different approaches are taken to the problem.

Duelling experts syndrome

The case of an outside engineer

There had been a number of disputes between a developer and a local authority over the years.

The developer had become accustomed to lax enforcement of development regulations over a long period of time. He had adopted an aggressive, combative style and tended to get his way with all his applications. The problems began when the local authority appointed a new manager of development who was young, enthusiastic and wanted to do things 'by the book'. A poor relationship developed between the two and there were a number of court hearings on various development applications and related matters in the court. Eventually one of the long-standing matters was brought to mediation. Progress was made on a number of issues but there was an impasse over a seemingly minor issue, namely what was the appropriate depth for sewerage pipes at a certain historical date. Each side had an expert's opinion on this matter. After discussion the parties agreed to engage an independent engineer to give an opinion which they would both accept.

There was no consensus on the identity of the expert, but they invited the President of the local chapter of the Institute of Arbitrators to nominate a suitable engineer. They further agreed on what information to provide to the expert and on what access he would have to the information. Once the technical issue had been resolved, the mediation continued on other matters.

The case of the collaborative accountants

Legal proceedings were on foot between a father and daughter over the validity of their late wife's/mother's will.

The usual legal challenges were being brought against the validity of the will and the case was set down for a court hearing. The stakes were high in that the estate had a net value of approximately £9 million, including a business. At the mediation there were some preliminary skirmishes over the validity of the will, but the focus soon shifted to the underlying issue which was the deterioration in the father–daughter relationship over the years. This was discussed for a while, after which they reverted to the distribution of assets. Now that a breakthrough had been made in the relationship, the parties briefed their accountants to work together on their respective valuations and other aspects of the businesses and properties. The accountants spent several hours together outside the mediation room and returned with virtual unanimity on all issues.

Some simple trade-offs were possible on the outstanding valuation issues and the parties were able to agree on all financial matters. While the accountants were collaborating, the parties and the mediator continued to look at relationship issues. The lawyers also played a collaborative role in their joint drafting of a complicated Heads of Agreement.

> **The case of the lawyers as 'parliamentary draftsmen'**
>
> There had been a long-standing dispute in a particular industry between the employers' association and the main union.
>
> The primary issue at the mediation concerned the meaning of a particular provision in the legislation, though there were underlying industrial relations issues arising from new technologies in the industry. The federal government initiated the mediation (and paid for it) and the relevant Minister agreed to submit to Cabinet any agreed proposal for the amendment of the legislation. This was seen as more politically expedient than the Cabinet making the decision of its own accord. Initially the lawyers acted as 'duelling experts' with conflicting views of the meaning of the copyright laws and the implications of amendment of the legislation. After several mediation meetings all present agreed that it was better for the industry to retain control of this issue rather than submit it to the vagaries of the political process. The lawyers then engaged in an extensive drafting exercise with numerous versions being provided to the parties for their consideration and refinement.
>
> A high degree of consensus was achieved, although at the cost of the original three-line clause blowing out to two and a half pages. In the end the matter did not settle because external ratifiers conspired against it. However, the lawyers' collaborative efforts remained on record as a draft model legislation for the future.

10.43   Here are other possible ways in which the problem of competing experts can be dealt with in the mediation process:

- Generally, by suggesting that the CPR 35 meeting of experts should take place at, or shortly before, the mediation so that their discussions can be fed into the mediation.

- More specifically, by requesting the experts to identify the common ground between them and to provide specific reasons for their differences, particularly where valuations are in dispute.

- By conducting a 'mini moot' in which the experts act as 'witnesses' for a short period of time so that each side, and their advisers, can hear the best case of the other. Here protocols are required to allow some questioning of the experts, without it deteriorating into cross-examination or interrogation.

- In so far as the experts' views relate to the liability question, by attempting to circumvent liability altogether by making a commercial decision on damages and other aspects of the dispute.

- By allowing the mediator to give a decision on the point of expertise, thus converting the process into med-arb, with all the advantages and shortcomings of that system.[34]

- By suggesting the appointment of a single joint expert.[35]

In this context, it is useful to refer to *Aird v Prime Meridian Limited*,[36] where the experts met and a joint statement was produced, which was then used in an

---

34   See 9.54.
35   See CPR 35.7–35.8.
36   [2006] EWHC 2338 (TCC).

unsuccessful mediation. The defendants sought leave to use the joint statement in the litigation that followed. The claimants objected, claiming the document was privileged. At first instance, the Technology and Construction Court considered that the statement was privileged. On appeal, the Court of Appeal held that where a joint statement was ordered by the court it is not privileged even though the discussions leading up to it are privileged. The document did not acquire privileged status because it was used in mediation. Although the statement in this case was prepared for the purposes of the mediation, it was stated to be pursuant to the order of the court and CPR 35.12. The Court of Appeal also stated that whilst a statement pursuant to CPR 35.12 does not attract privilege, it does not prevent the experts from producing a further document purely for the purposes of mediation and which would remain privileged.[37]

I. Dealing with professional advisers

A note on terminology

10.44 Some professional advisers such as lawyers are commonly referred to as the parties' 'representatives'. 'Representative' and 'representation' have the connotation of a professional standing in the shoes of the client, taking their place, as it were, at the negotiation table. This notion is not in keeping with the spirit of mediation at which the parties themselves are able to play a direct and active role in the process. Terms such as 'advisers', 'assistants', 'skilled helpers' and others do not have negative connotations and are preferable.

The issues for professional advisers

10.45 Some references have been made earlier in the book to the roles of lawyers in relation to the pre-mediation contact or preliminary conference, the party statements, the separate meetings and the drafting of the agreement. Here the subject of professional advisers is looked at from the mediator's side of the fence, and not from the side of the lawyer or accountant assisting a client in a mediation.[38] Generally speaking, clients and their advisers are responsible for their own participation and behaviour in mediation. However, mediators can have both proactive and reactive roles in this regard. They can, for example, educate all participants beforehand about their appropriate roles in mediation and they can intervene reactively where advisers transgress the mediation guidelines and play inappropriate roles.

10.46 Having advisers present at mediation increases the transaction costs of the process. This is because an agent's interests are never identical with those of the principal and there are more needs to accommodate. Thus professionals have a strong interest in maintaining satisfied clients, in being seen to perform their role in front of other professionals (including the mediator), in maintaining their desired reputation, and in not being sued by their own clients. There are also the many factors deriving from the complexities of the human condition which affect advisers as much as their clients: personal fears and anxieties, past (and future) relationships with other advisers, the nature of the relationship with their client, demands from

---

37 On privilege, refer to 10.82.
38 See 10.49.

colleagues and supervisors, time pressures and their own teenagers' driving habits. This makes for a complex mediation situation.

10.47   This is not, however, to suggest that professional advisers in mediation are a hindrance. On the contrary, in our experience many mediations would not have succeeded without the appropriate professional involvement of lawyers and other advisers. Lawyers can be a mediator's greatest allies. The real questions are, *what* can mediators do to shape and mould the participation of professional advisers, and *how* should they go about doing it.

10.48   To take the *how* question first, the pre-mediation contact and preliminary conference provides an early opportunity for the mediator to inform and explain to advisers what is expected of them in mediation.[39] This can be reinforced by written guidelines or protocols for advisers which can be distributed at the preliminary conference or sent out in advance of the mediation.[40] Some mediators request advisers to sign these codes as a way of reinforcing their commitment to them. More formal still are the occasional attempts to incorporate into the agreement to mediate some protocols on the behaviour of advisers and to have the advisers, as well as their clients, sign this agreement. However, there is much to be said for the less formal approach, namely that of educating, explaining and guiding the advisers.

10.49   As regards the *what* question, mediators need to educate, explain to and guide advisers on the philosophy and objectives of mediation, on the central participatory role of their clients, on the survey findings that clients appreciate mediation because it allows them to speak and to be heard, on the importance of focusing on interests as opposed to legal rights, and on other principles and values of the mediation process.[41]

As regards their role, it should be emphasised that advisers function best when they work informally, as supporters not advocates, and with less emphasis on legal rights and more on needs and interests. The assumption is that advisers who understand the nature of mediation will be less defensive about their own role, and the less defensive they are the more likely they will be to allow the mediator to conduct the process appropriately. However, this is also a somewhat optimistic approach and the ego, personality and tactics of advisers have been known to disrupt the process, notwithstanding their full understanding of mediation. Inexperienced or youthful mediators can also anticipate attempts by older and more worldly professional advisers to dominate them and subvert the process.

Case illustration: the case of the controlling barrister

A senior barrister was representing one business partner in a dispute with his fellow business partner over the division of the partnership assets. The barrister flew in to town for the mediation and in pre-mediation discussions indicated that his client could not bear to be in the same room as his partner (who, allegedly, had had an affair with his client's wife) and that the mediation should be conducted on a shuttle basis.

---

39   See 2.22–2.25.
40   See Appendix 6.
41   Refer to guidance in Appendix 6.

> The client 'confirmed' this in the presence of his barrister, and the mediation commenced with the parties in separate rooms. After two futile hours of ferrying messages, the mediator confronted the barrister and suggested a face-to-face meeting. The barrister eventually relented and the client acquiesced. After the partners had been in the same room for ten minutes, one partner moved to the whiteboard and drew a mud map of the properties being discussed. This led to an extended personal discussion between the partners about the alleged infidelity (which was denied). This resulted, albeit eight hours later, in full agreement on the division of assets. The formerly controlling barrister played a more passive, but still significant, role in the traditional mediation process.

Degrees of involvement by advisers

10.50   There are variations in relation to the degree of mediation involvement by professional advisers. In family mediations, legal advisers tend to be involved to advise on disclosure requirements and at the stage of finalising agreements and consent orders.[42] In commercial cases, legal advisers tend to be involved throughout the mediation and are proactive during mediation sessions by making presentations, assisting with bargaining and advising on settlement options.[43] Refer to the example in the box below for the potential scope of involvement by advisers.

> ### Case illustration
>
> Assume, for the purposes of the discussion in the following sections, that Dr Blood is appearing in a mediation relating to allegations of clinical negligence and he consults Ms Law, a solicitor.
>
> Ms Law could advise Dr Blood on how to represent himself in mediation and have no further involvement herself; she could attend a preliminary conference and leave her client to participate in the mediation meeting on his own; she could be present during the mediation and participate fully throughout the process; she could be present at the mediation but have only a restricted participation (for example, observe during the opening and exploration phases and participate directly thereafter); she could be physically absent from the mediation but be accessible to Dr Blood for involvement by phone, e-mail or fax; or she could join the mediation only after her client and his patient have reached agreement, in order to advise the doctor legally and to undertake the drafting of the settlement agreement. All these variations are encountered in mediation practice. Good lawyers should be comfortable about considering such options, together with their clients and the mediator, so as to suit the needs, circumstances and resources of the relevant dispute.

---

42   See 5.69–5.72 and 10.74–10.77. Parties should be informed of their right to independent legal advice. Family mediators should not discuss or correspond with a party's lawyer without the express consent of each party, and where both parties have lawyers, nothing should be said or written to the legal adviser of one, which is not also said or written to the other. Refer, for example, to section 4.5.2 College of Mediators Code of Practice (in Appendix 8).

43   Refer to the guidance in Appendix 6 on the adviser's role in general civil and commercial mediation.

10.51 Within the mediation process there is also sufficient flexibility to allow for a number of other modifications involving professional advisers:[44]

■ the mediator might see the advisers together without the clients (adviser meetings);

■ the mediator might see the clients together without the lawyers (party meetings);

■ the mediator might ask to see an individual client without his or her lawyer (side meeting);

■ the mediator might get the lawyers to meet together on their own, with a specific brief aimed at assisting the settlement process.

Asking to see prior advice

10.52 Clearly one of the major functions of lawyers in mediation is to give their clients legal advice. This is their area of expertise. In cases where a party attends mediation without their adviser, some mediators might ask to see the advice from the lawyer before the mediation commences.

In the above clinical negligence case, for example, the mediator might contact Ms Law by phone and ask her to send a summary, referring to both the strengths and weaknesses of her client's case, to the worst-case outcome should the matter proceed to trial as well as the best-case outcome, and to the costs of various specified stages of the litigation process should the matter not settle at mediation.

This arrangement not only imposes a discipline on the professional adviser, it also prevents clients like Dr Blood who do not have their advisers present at mediation from making extravagant claims to the mediator about the nature of the legal advice that has been given. Information from a lawyer would be treated as a confidential briefing paper.[45]

Seating of advisers

10.53 Reference has been made before to the great seating debate in mediation.[46] One of the reasons why mediators need to control the physical environment (and arrive early) is so that they can take charge of the seating arrangements. Many professional advisers such as Ms Law like to be seated near the mediator in a hierarchical arrangement where they are the experts 'representing' their clients. It is preferable for mediators to make the strategic decisions about seating. It is clearly more in the spirit of the mediation process and client self-determination for Dr Blood and the other party to be seated in the places of precedence near the mediator, with the professionals seated further away in their 'supportive' role. However, as in all other aspects of the process, the mediator needs to develop a hypothesis on this matter before the mediation and might have good reasons for indicating other seating arrangements.

---

44   See 5.56.
45   See 2.38.
46   See 2.32–2.33.

Documentation

10.54 Lawyers have expertise in developing and systematising relevant documentation for dispute resolution processes. Mediators can attempt to manage the lawyers' documentation functions in relation to the specific needs of the mediation.[47] In some court-encouraged mediations, the court will have made an order, in support of the mediation, requiring certain disclosure to happen before the mediation.[48] In most general civil and commercial cases, it is not unusual for lawyers to have much of the documentation necessary for litigation available at the mediation.

How essential or relevant this is, depends on the circumstances. A mediator colleague of ours makes a great show of having a file in front of him containing the court documents, correspondence, reports and other papers sent to him by the lawyers ahead of the mediation. He picks up the file, deposits it on the floor and announces to the meeting, 'Ladies and gentlemen, we may get back to this, but let's see if we can solve the problem first without it'. This is a way of emphasising that in mediation the clients' personal and commercial interests are of more importance than their legal rights. This might entail that the craftsmanship of their lawyers in providing documentary support for their legal rights has only limited significance in mediation.

Party statements

10.55 Reference has already been made to the desirability of the parties themselves making the party statements and for the professional advisers then to expand on these where necessary.[49] Again this principle might need modification, but the mediator, and not the professional advisers, should be the one to assume control over this aspect of the process. This may require some mediator assertion, but diplomacy and tact are not incompatible with such control. Again it is useful for the mediator to be educative and to normalise. She might say: 'Ms Law, in my experience mediation works best where the client makes the opening statement and the adviser is then given an opportunity to expand on it. This would allow Dr Blood to indicate what his personal concerns are here today. This is also how I normally conduct mediations. So Dr Blood, would you like to begin ...?'

Accommodating the need to be involved

10.56 One of the needs of professional advisers is for them to be seen to be involved; there is a danger in having advisers present when they do not feel fully engaged in the mediation. It can lead to problems ranging from an overt hijack of the mediation process to subtle forms of sabotage.

To avoid these consequences, mediators should ensure that there is scope for the appropriate involvement of all advisers. Thus lawyers might be asked to exchange views on legal issues and even to ask clarifying questions of the 'opposing' party, as long as this does not lead to a form of cross-examination. Legal advisers also have

---

47   See 2.13, 2.23 and 2.38.
48   See sample Commercial Court 'ADR Order' in Appendix 1.
49   See 5.16–5.17.

a significant role as negotiators, advisers and, at the drafting stage, as challengers and drafters. This involvement can be foreshadowed by the mediator from the earliest stages. Thus the mediator might say: 'Although mediation is essentially an opportunity for you to sort things out yourselves, you can always call on your lawyers for advice and support. I would also anticipate the lawyers drafting the settlement agreement and perhaps that is something they could have in mind as we move along.' In our experience, some barristers refuse to participate in drafting if they have not been sufficiently involved in the previous stages of the mediation.

Taking instructions

10.57 Lawyers in mediation often say to the mediator, 'I'd just like to take instructions from my client on this matter'. If the mediation is in joint session, this would entail a short adjournment; if it is in separate session the mediator would leave the lawyer alone with the client. When a lawyer uses this time-honoured phrase in mediation, however, it could mean one or more of the following:

■ 'I need to ask my client what they think about an offer, counter-offer, and so on, and about what they would like me to do' – the expression means what it says.

■ 'I need to advise my client on the current offer and where the negotiations might be heading' – the lawyer needs to take control.

■ 'I am not sure what to do next and need some time to reflect and consider options' – the lawyer is in trouble and needs time out.

■ 'I need to ask my client about important new information which has come up for the first time' – the lawyer is surprised by developments and needs to reconsider strategies.

■ 'I need a break and a cup of coffee' – the lawyer needs to use the amenities.

10.58 In most of these scenarios either the lawyer is 'taking instructions' with the objective of advising their client or there will be an opportunity to provide advice. The mediator should therefore inquire of a lawyer who has expressed the need to 'take instructions' what they will be advising their client: 'Mr Law, you have said that you wish to take instructions from Dr Blood, and it is my experience that in complex situations like this clients want advice from their lawyer. Can you indicate to me what you will be recommending to Dr Blood about the offer …'.

This clearly cannot be done in open session, and even if asked in the corridor the lawyer may not be forthcoming in response. However, it accords with the realities of many client–adviser relationships, namely that under the guise of 'giving instructions' clients often ask the professional what they should do. Where the mediator takes this proactive step, it gives him or her a potential opportunity to act as reality agent if the adviser is about to give extremely unrealistic or unhelpful advice.

Assisting advisers to modify their advice

10.59 Sometimes a professional adviser has given a clear statement of advice to their client, often incorporating a monetary figure, and this has been reinforced publicly in front of the other party and their adviser. For example, Ms Law may have said before the mediation, and again in the joint sessions, 'There is no basis in law for holding Dr Blood liable and the most the claimant could recover is the cost of the medical consultations.'

This public statement creates difficulties where the lawyer is required to back off this advice, because it is difficult for them to do so without losing face. Mediators can make the situation easier for the adviser by providing a pretext for them to change their advice. For example, the mediator might say 'Ms Law, now that you have heard the other side's version of the incident, which you were not aware of before, how do you see Dr Blood's position?', or 'Ms Law, now that you have seen the documentation on medical expenses, how would you suggest that we deal with the damages question?' By giving this opening to the adviser, the mediator is attempting to allow them to change their prior recommendations without losing face.

Using the advisers as quasi-mediators

10.60 In the final result, mediation-friendly advisers can be an extremely valuable resource in mediation. They can serve as quasi-mediators in many ways: in managing their clients' expectations, in keeping open the lines of communication, in acting as constructive negotiators and in serving as reality agents when they know their client is being unrealistic. It is wise mediation practice to use this potential resource to the greatest extent possible. Professionals can be either deal-makers or deal-breakers and mediators have the responsibility to aim for the former.

Case illustration: on the role of lawyers in mediation

Sometimes the question is asked, 'Is it appropriate to have lawyers in the mediation?' This closed question is unhelpful, as the roles and contributions of advisers can vary considerably. In our experience many mediations would not have been successful had it not been for the advisers, and a few others failed because of them. The better question is, 'What roles are appropriate and what kinds are inappropriate in different kinds of mediation?'

In reality, lawyers will be involved in many mediations. In general terms advisers should support all aspects of the mediation process, but there could be a whole chapter on the specific roles and interventions that are appropriate. This is becoming a specialised form of legal practice, along the lines of representing clients before commissions of inquiry, in litigation or in tribunal proceedings.

It should also be noted that in many jurisdictions there are specific obligations on lawyers in terms of statute, rules of court or professional rules of conduct to propose, or advise clients on, mediation. For example, the Solicitors' Code of Conduct 2007 requires English solicitors to have regard to, and a duty to act 'in the best interest of the client' (Rule 1), which also suggests that solicitors should consider and discuss with clients the range of ADR options available. The Code also requires solicitors to give 'the best information possible' to clients on the implications of pursuing a cause of action (Rule 2), which again suggests that relevant court procedure and other rules governing and encouraging ADR, and

> all the case law on the possibility of cost sanctions, need to be discussed with the client.
>
> Other forms of pre-mediation assistance for lawyers concern the question of appropriate timing and venue, the identity of the mediator, the relevant model of mediation, and the pre-mediation exchange of information.[50]

J. Dealing with multi-party cases

10.61 Some mediations are complicated by the wide range of issues involved, the diversity of subject matters and the large numbers of participants. There are many examples: environmental disputes, corporate mergers, workplace issues and long-standing conflicts within community organisations. Sometimes these mediations also involve broad issues of public policy, for example, in relation to council planning matters, provision of infrastructure such as mobile telephone towers, and location of controversial facilities such as prisons. These mediations are characterised by a high degree of intensity, the need for significant resources such as time, information and money, the complexity of decision-making and potential problems in the performance and enforcement of settlement agreements.

Some particular problems in dealing with multi-party cases include:

- As the number of parties increase, so does the liklihood that coalitions will form, making decision-making difficult. Members of coalitions co-operate with one another in competition with other coalitions, but they also compete against each other in terms of the allocation of benefits obtained by the coalition.

- Principled negotiation becomes problematic as groups tend to rely on common positions for their unity, making movement from positions to interests more difficult.

- Negotiation tends to be simplified through majority or unanimous decision-making rules. Majority rule fails to recognise the strength of individual preferences, whereas the unanimity rule does not encourage creativity. It is also difficult for group members to agree upon a method of voting.

- Each group (or each member of a group) considers that the others are taking extreme, or unreasonable, positions (called the 'lone moderate effect').

10.62 This topic warrants considerably more treatment than is possible here. Some relevant issues have been raised in the discussion of team negotiations.[51] It is important to bear in mind that in these situations the core principles of mediation are still relevant, they just need to be applied in a modified framework. Some matters requiring particular attention include:

- The identification of key stakeholders before the mediation meeting – who will participate in the mediation? How will participants be identified?

- Nomination of legal adviser for each team.

---

50   See also Charlton and Dewdney, *The Mediator's Handbook*, 2nd ed, 2004, Ch 13. Refer to Chapter 2.
51   See 2.18.

- Who will be the mediator? Is one mediator sufficient?

- The appropriate qualifications of the mediator, or mediators, with relevant personal attributes or professional backgrounds.

- Extensive pre-mediation preparation with different groups so as to manage expectations, secure commitment and agree on decision-making protocols.[52]

- Document exchange – is disclosure required? What should its scope be? Is there a need for expert or technical reports? Should a single expert be appointed? Is joint fact finding required?

- Consideration of important procedural matters such as mediation guidelines, speaking time, and use of separate meetings and 'shuttle diplomacy'.

- Ways of preventing, and dealing with, anticipated difficulties over resources, mandates, timing, ratification and finalisation of formal agreements.

- The need to draft a customised agreement to mediate.

- Respective roles if there is more than one mediator.

- Consideration of who not to involve in the round table discussions, such as those with long-term bitterness, and ways of preventing sabotage attempts by those excluded.

- Strict guidelines on duration of opening statements.

- The creation of a 'process control group' with representatives from each set of stakeholders, to advise the mediation on progress in the conduct of mediation.

- Method of communication with members of each team.

- Development of a broad-based reporting back system to keep external groups informed, involving the mediators where necessary.

- Decision-making methods within each team or group.

- Maintenance of list of matters agreed upon by the parties as the matter progresses.

- Extent of privacy and confidentiality, on one hand, and publicity and media statements, on the other.

- Duration of the mediation meetings.

- Ongoing monitoring of complicated agreements with continuing obligations for the parties.

10.63   Here is an example of a complex mediation in this context.

Case illustration: multi-party mediation

A mediation was required for a large number of residents of a council residential estate who had been in a state of hostility for many months. Because of the numbers involved, three mediators were appointed and they spent considerable preparation time together to design the mediation process, define their respective roles and discuss how to deal with problems arising among the mediators. A lack

---

52   Ibid.

of resources precluded lengthy pre-mediation contact with the individual parties. One mediator made the opening which was comprehensive and dealt with a wide range of queries and concerns from the participants. Each participant was allowed to make a brief opening statement and at least one concern from each was listed on flipcharts. A system of voting was used to prioritise the issues for discussion. Strict rules were imposed on speaking times to prevent domination by the angry and verbose participants. Another mediator acted as scribe and noted all concessions, agreements in principle and other matters of value mentioned by any party. The third mediator acted as 'process observer' and noted which participants were 'stabilisers' and useful catalysts for achieving settlement. No separate meetings were held as there were no identifiable factions among the participants. Agreement was reached in principle on a number of issues, and the mediators drafted this up for signature by those present. A representative group was appointed to investigate implementation of these agreements, with the option of returning to mediation if necessary.

K. Dealing with 'impossible clients'

10.64 Professionals are at times faced with the challenge of what to do with 'impossible clients'. Mediators too encounter the full gamut of challenging human behaviour. Clients can be controlling, neurotic, pedantic, intimidating, conflict-addicted and much else besides. Ironically, however, all parties in negotiations usually view themselves as cooperative and their opponents as competitive.

10.65 The book by Stone, Patton and Heen and a chapter on 'People are Different' by Spegel, Rogers and Buckley are recommended as a basis for understanding and identifying forms of 'difficult' behaviour.[53] The basic assumption in the latter is that there are significant differences in personality, values and behaviours among individuals and these differences often lead us to label the other person 'difficult', instead of just 'different'.

10.66 A common mistake in negotiations is to assume that others will respond and behave similarly to ourselves in similar circumstances, and to stereotype others according to their culture, gender, professional background and other attributes. We therefore tend to deal with people in the way in which we would like to be treated ourselves, and make unwarranted assumptions about them based on the blanket stereotypes. Spegel, Rogers and Buckley then describe some basic dimensions of observable human behaviour based on the extroversion/introversion dimensions and the people-orientation/task-orientation dimensions and discuss the significance of these factors for dispute resolution based on the Myers Briggs personality test.

10.67 All parties in mediation can be better understood if their predominant behavioural style is appreciated. Thus a 'task-oriented extrovert' will behave very differently to a 'people-oriented introvert'. Mediators too will have a predominant behavioural style and an understanding of this will also be helpful self-knowledge. Here a simple self-administered test establishes whether one is predominantly

---

53 Stone D., Patton B. and Heen S., *Difficult Conversations: How to Discuss What Matters Most*, Penguin Books, NY, 1999. Spegel, Rogers and Buckley, *Negotiation: Theory and Techniques*, 1998, Ch 7.

directing, influencing, stabilising or conscientious. Clearly this is to do no more than identify predominant behavioural patterns. All humans still remain unique and indeed display a mixture of all behavioural styles.

10.68 Of course this understanding alone will not resolve the challenge of 'impossible clients' in mediation. It will, however, allow the mediator to plan possible interventions, and even to explain to the parties something about personality types. Ultimately, mediators can modify the behaviour of only themselves and not the parties, and where the skills and techniques referred to in this book are not adequate it might be one of those rare occasions where the mediation should be terminated without agreement.

L. Dealing with costs issues

This section is not intended to provide a comprehensive overview of the law and policy relating to costs. Its aim is to highlight the practical issues that might arise in relation to costs in mediation.

Preparation on and consideration of costs

10.69 A mediator in general civil and commercial cases may ask the parties to prepare a schedule of costs incurred to the date of the mediation and an estimate of the costs of proceeding to trial. A mediator may assist the parties, especially in commercial or more complex civil cases, by providing them with a guide on the cost considerations they might usefully make before the mediation. Refer to Appendix 6 for a sample guide.

Alternatively, or additionally, the mediator may refer to costs as part of the mediator's reality testing or doubt creation functions during the mediation, and as a means of assisting the parties to move beyond impasse. The risks and implications of costs orders, issues of enforcement of costs orders and recovery of costs, and the likelihood of continuing satellite litigation over the amount of costs are matters raised by the mediator in order to reality test and create doubt. For example, in general civil and commercial cases, the mediator might discuss with each party in private:

- The principle of proportionality between amount claimed and costs that will be spent on resolution, and how the proportionality issue might be used by a court (for example, to determine the level of costs to be recovered or to impose a cap on costs).[54]

---

54   44.18–44.20 CPR provides that, in any case in which proceedings have been started, the court can impose a cap limiting the amount of future costs, including disbursements. The court can make capping orders where it considers that it is in the interests of justice to do so and there is a risk that costs will be disproportionately incurred and that risk cannot be controlled by traditional methods such as case management or detailed assessment. On an application for a cap, the court will consider whether there is an imbalance between the parties' financial positions, whether the costs of determining the cap are disproportionate, the stage of the proceedings reached and the costs which have been incurred to date. Refer also to section 23A Costs Practice Direction and to *Eli Lilly v James* [2009] EWHC 198 (QB).

- The other factors that might affect a court's discretion when awarding costs, including the manner in which the case has been conducted and the timing and reasonableness of offers.[55]

Litigation funding

10.70 Public funding of litigation has implications for settlement options, alternatives to settlement and costs recovery. For example:

- If the amount recovered as costs by a publicly funded party is less than costs payable to that party's solicitor, the shortfall is deducted from damages payable to the party, and is called 'the statutory charge'.[56] The operation of the statutory charge, and its repayment, is a practical consideration should the matter not settle at mediation.

- That the statutory charge applies to property which is recovered or preserved (even for the benefit of a third party) is an aspect which can be used to narrow the subject matter of the dispute.

- If the matter goes to trial and a funded party fails to beat a Part 36 offer, he may receive damages, plus costs, up to the date of the offer, but from those damages will be deducted the parties' costs from the date of the offer.

- The fact that a solicitor for a funded client may have to report unreasonable refusals to accept settlement, or demands that the case should be conducted unreasonably, might also be relevant in some cases.[57]

The mediator would encourage a publicly funded party to take such matters into account during mediation when considering the range of settlement options and alternatives to settlement.

Insurance will also have implications for costs. A party may have 'before' or 'after the event' insurance. These policies tend to cover a party's own solicitor's costs and disbursements whether the party wins or loses. In such cases, the insured party may have little costs pressure, and be less inclined to settle at mediation. After the event ('ATE') insured cases tend to have been asessed by insurers as strong on the merits, and insurers may be less inclined to mediate at all.[58]

Accordingly, the existence of litigation funding or insurance, and in particular the impact on costs, is discussed by mediators with parties in private session, as a way of ensuring that parties have fully assessed the implications of different options.

---

55 In *Roundstone Nurseries Ltd v Stephenson Holdings Ltd* [2009] EWHC 1431 TCC, the costs of a mediation held pre-issue in accordance with a pre-action protocol were found to be recoverable.

56 The charge does not apply if a settlement is reached in mediation.

57 Refer to LSC, *Disclosure of Information Regulations*, SI 2000/442 reg 4.

58 The CPR require the existence of ATE insurance, the level of cover, and whether premiums are staged, to be disclosed within seven days of entering into the arrangement or, if the insurance is taken out before a letter of claim, then in the letter of claim. A defendant in 'publication proceedings' (defamation, malicious falsehood or breach of confidence) who admits liability and offers to settle within a specified period after notification of an ATE premium will not incur liability for payment of the claimant's ATE insurance policy if the matter settles without court proceedings. Refer to CPR 44.3B(1), CPR 44.12B, CPR 44.15(1), Costs Practice Direction 19.4(3), Practice Direction (Pre-Action Conduct) 9.3, and Notice of Funding (Form N251).

Conditional Fee Agreements (CFAs)

10.71   The existence of a CFA is also considered in mediation when reality testing the alternatives, should the matter not settle at mediation, and regarding its effect should the matter go to trial. The uplift and insurance premium can normally be claimed against the losing party responsible for paying the costs, to the extent that the CFA terms are considered reasonable[59] and the existence of the CFA has been notified.[60] Accordingly, the level of the success fee and premium are relevant factors when the assessing costs implications of various options.[61]

In cases where the level of a lawyer's fees can be affected by the outcome in mediation, as may be the case where there is a CFA, a mediator should also be alive to the potential conflict of interest between lawyer and client. There may be circumstances where the mediator will need to remind a lawyer, or re-focus the lawyer, on the client's intrerests and the lawyer's duty to act in the client's best interests. In difficult cases, the discussions should take place in a private session between lawyer and mediator.

CFAs need to be distinguished from contingency fee agreements which are not permitted for litigation in the UK, although these arrangements may be used in 'non-contentious business', which includes tribunal work (for example, in employment tribunal cases) and claims at the Criminal Injuries Compensation Authority. In those cases, the legal representative can agree with the client to receive a percentage of the compensation recovered.

Settlement agreements and costs

10.72   It is necessary to decide, as part of any settlement reached at mediation, how the legal costs will be treated. For example, will one party pay another's costs and, if so, to what extent? Will each party bear their own costs? The parties may agree to treat legal costs differently to the mediation costs (the fees of the mediator and the expenses of the mediation). Will the costs be assessed and, if so, on what basis? Any provision in the mediation agreement about legal or mediation costs

---

59   See *Burgess v Breheny* SCCO Case No 0803560 (16 January 2009).
60   Notice of a CFA is required within seven days of entering into the agreement or, if it is entered into before a letter of claim, then in the letter of claim. Refer to CPR 44.3B(1), CPR 44.15(1), Costs Practice Direction 19.4(3), Practice Direction (Pre-Action Conduct) 9.3, and Notice of Funding (Form N251).
    Refer to cases – *Bainbridge v MAF Pipelines Ltd.* (2004) (Teesside CC 19/3/04) (unreported); *Metcalfe v Clipston* [2004] EWHC 9005 (Costs); *Hardcastle v Leeds and Holbeck Building Society* (2002) (QBD 21/10/02) (Unreported); *Choudhury v Kingston Hospital NHS Trust* (2006) (SCCO 2/5/06) (Unreported); *Cullen v Chopra* [2007] EWHC 90093 (Costs); *Montlake v Lambert* [2004] EWHC 1503 (Comm); *Connor v Birmingham City Council* (2005) (Birmingham CC 16/3/05) (Unreported); and *Supperstone v Hurst* [2008] EWHC 735 (Ch).
61   Michel Kallipetis QC observes increasing instances where the defendant has the support of an insurance company and the insurance company has refused to pay the uplift:
    This causes special problems because it is often used by insurance companies as a tactic to drive a wedge between a claimant and his lawyers. A mediator has to be particularly aware of this danger ... One method of resolving the difficulty is to persuade the insurance company to agree that the claimant's costs be subjected to assessment by a Costs Judge.
    Refer to www.kallipetis.com/documents/Costs-Of-Mediation-In-The UK.doc.

may be altered by the terms of the settlement agreement.[62] If the settlement agreement is silent, or ambiguous, the court will refer to the terms of the agreement to mediate.[63]

A mediator might find that the parties have reached agreement on the substantive issues, but reach impasse on the costs issues. It may be necessary for the mediator to encourage the lawyers to reduce their fees, or to deal with fees in a creative manner, to enable a settlement to be reached. It is also important for the mediator to ensure that each party understands the difference between costs payable to, or from, another party and those payable to each party and their own lawyer, in case there is a shortfall between what is recovered from a party and what is payable to a lawyer.[64]

Where the parties cannot agree on costs at the mediation, an assessment can be initiated.[65]

Part 36 offers

10.73　If a Part 36 offer has been made, the mediator will reality test each party's positon should the matter not settle at mediation and proceed to trial. A mediator can also explore with each party what level of offer might be made in case the mediation fails to settle.

It is useful for mediators to note that there is some unpredictability on account of the case law on Part 36 when reality testing the consequences of offers under Part 36. For example, in *Carver v BA*, the trial judge awarded the claimant a sum, which was just over the Part 36 offer made by the defendant.[66] The claimant would normally expect favourable cost consequences to follow. However, the Court of Appeal concluded that the claimant should bear both her own and the defendant's costs from the last Part 36 offer. The effect of the finding was that the claimant was treated as if she had not beaten the offer. The court considered that a reasonable litigant would not have continued to trial for the sake of the small difference. A similar finding was made in *Painting v Oxford University*, where the claimaint

---

62　In *Newcastle City Council v Paul Wieland* [2009] NSWCA 113, an Australian court (the New South Wales Court of Appeal) considered whether the phrase 'costs of the proceedings' includes the costs associated with mediation. The court considered that, where mediation takes place as part of the court procedure (as it did in that case), mediation is a 'step in the proceedings', and accordingly the costs associated with mediation were found to be 'costs of the proceedings'.

63　In *National Westminster Bank v Feeney & Feeney* [2006] EWHC 90066 (Costs), the Tomlin Order referred to costs assessment on the standard basis and the defendants argued that the costs of the mediation were included as part of the standard costs. The Agreement to Mediate provided, however, that each party should bear their own legal costs. The court found that the ambiguous provision in the Tomlin Order did not override the clear terms in the Agreement to Mediate. Many mediation agreements now provide that mediation fees and associated legal costs may be treated as costs in the case where a court is invited to rule on them, even if initially shared or borne by each party. Refer, for example, to the CEDR Model Mediation Agreement in Appendix 3.

64　Refer to the cost scenarios (which led to a range of costs and settlement difficulties in mediations) outlined by Karl Mackie and Tony Allen in 'The Costs Crisis: Mediation as a Solution?' 2009 (available at www.cedr.com).

65　Ibid, where Karl Mackie and Tony Allen argue that once mediation costs are justiciable in principle, there should be no reason why mediation fees and costs could not form the subject of 'costs-only' proceedings as to the quantum of those costs, under CPR Part 44.12A.

66　[2008] EWCA Civ 412.

beat a Part 36, but was found to have exaggerated her claim substantially, and suffered adverse cost consequences as a result.[67] Accordingly, beating a Part 36 is no guarantee of a favourable costs award. This unpredictability is a factor to be considered when reality testing with the parties.

M.   Settlement formalities

10.74   Most mediation agreements provide that agreements reached in mediation are only binding once written and signed.[68] Although it is the parties' lawyers' (or, if not represented, the parties') responsibility in general civil and commercial cases to write up the agreement, a mediator supervises the drafting, to ensure that the matters agreed are reflected in the final agreement; that the agreement is precise and specific; and that the formalities are satisfied.[69] The formalities will depend on the relevant subject matter (for example, employment, family,[70] community,[71] personal injury or commercial) and on the relevant jurisdiction.[72] The basic formalities under English law are considered below. The EU Mediation Directive requires Member States to ensure that it is possible for parties to request that an agreement reached in mediation should be made enforceable; and that an agreement can be enforceable by way of a court judgment or other authentic instrument.[73]

Basic requirements for a lawful contract

10.74A   The basic requirements for a lawful contract under English law are:

■ An intention to create legal relations – an agreement to agree is not enforceable, so that the agreement should set out all the material terms agreed between the parties. Conditional agreements are binding. Even in the family context, there is no presumption once couples separate that their agreements are legally enforceable, and an intention to create legal relations is required.[74]

---

67   [2005] EWCA Civ 161.
68   See, for example, clause 29 Law Society sample Mediation Agreement (in Appendix 3). In some cases, parties do not wish to have a legally binding outcome. In other cases, only draft heads of terms are prepared for later formalisation and finalisation by lawyers. Refer, for example, to sections 5.9–5.11 Law Society Code of Practice for Civil/Commercial Mediation. Agreements reached in community mediation matters tend to be non-binding, or self-enforcing (refer to Appendix 4 for a sample) and, in the family context, most agreements provide a memorandum of understanding which can be turned into a binding agreement by lawyers (refer to 10.77 below).
69   See, for example, section 9 CEDR Model Mediation Procedure (in Appendix 3) and Element (3) Stage (9) of the Law Society Competencies for Civil/Commercial Mediation (in Appendix 8). Article 13 UNCITRAL Conciliation Rules envisage that the mediator will be proactive when drafting (the Rules are in Appendix 3). In family, workplace and community mediations also, mediators are more proactive when drafting memoranda of understanding, statements of outcome or heads of terms.
70   See 10.77 in relation to agreements in family matters.
71   Requirement F3.1 MQMS provides that a written outcome statement is produced in community mediations listing key actions that parties are willing to take and that the outcome must be signed by all parties.
72   Refer to Appendix 4 for a sample agreement for a commercial case, an employment matter, a workplace grievance, a community matter and a family (all issues) matter.
73   Article 6, 2008/52/EC (see Appendix 13). A similar provision has made been in the EU Recommendation on Family Mediation (see Article IV) – refer to Appendix 13.
74   *Merritt v Merritt* [1970] 2 All ER 760; and N. Lowe and G. Douglas, *Bromley's Family Law*, 10th ed, Oxford University Press, 2006.

- Valuable consideration.

- Clarity and certainty of terms – there are many terms that a court will not imply into an agreement, for instance, a court will not imply into a settlement that any litigation proceedings have ended, or what is to happen in relation to past or future legal costs.[75]

- Any specific formalities required by the particular kind of contract – for example, an agreement relating to the disposal of an interest in land, maintenance agreements,[76] finance/property settlements in family cases,[77] or the settlement of employment tribunal cases.[78] In all cases, any formalities relating to tax (personal, corporate and VAT).

- Capacity to contract – children and patients under the Mental Health Acts do not have capacity to contract.

Settlement formalities

10.75   If proceedings are on foot, a decision will need to be made as to how the proceedings will end. The options are:

- consent order, or judgment, for a sum of money;[79]

- dismissal of proceedings;[80]

- stay of proceedings;

- discontinuance of the action;

- Tomlin Order – this form of consent order allows the action to be stayed on terms set out in an attached schedule, and the parties can apply to the court if the terms require effect.[81]

Potential problems

10.76   The main potential problems that can arise at the drafting stage include:

- inappropriately or inaccurately advising parties;

- a failure to comply with appropriate formalities;

---

75   See notes 53 and 54 above.
76   A maintenance agreement in writing is binding – sections 34–36 Matrimonial Causes Act.
77   Parties are encouraged to record in writing the terms, to obtain independent legal advice on those terms and to finalise their financial/property agreement via a court consent order – refer to Code of Practice of Resolution (formerly, the SFLA) and *Law Society Family Law Protocol*, 2nd ed, 2006.
78   A compromise of an employment matter has to be in writing; relate to a particular complaint which has already been made or intimated; and the employee or worker must have received independent advice from an adviser falling within one of the permitted categories of advisers.
79   See 10.77 below in relation to consent orders in family matters.
80   In the case of employment tribunal maters, a tribunal consent order dismissing the proceedings is appropriate when settlement terms have been agreed and the complaint is withdrawn. Any application filed by a party in a family matter whose claims are being dismissed should be marked 'for dismissal purposes only' (a practice accepted in the Principal Registry).
81   Refer to Appendix 4 for a sample.

- allegations that the facts surrounding the negotiations enable a party to avoid liaiblity, for example, an allegation that a party was induced to enter into the settlement by misrepresentation.[82]

The agreement to mediate might provide that the mediator accepts no responsibility for the form of any settlement reached.[83] Some agreements are expressed in wider terms, by extending to cover the whole conduct of the mediation, including settlement drafting, although the terms need to be reinforced throughout the mediation by the mediator's conduct. The precise effect of such exclusion or mediator immunity clauses are yet to be tested in the UK.[84]

Family matters

10.77 Family mediators aim to ensure that agreements reached by the parties are fully informed and freely made, and that the parties have a good understanding of the consequences of their decisions for themselves, their children and other family members.[85] When parties reach agreement in family mediation, the mediator will help them produce a written agreement, which summarises the proposals agreed, and identifies any outstanding issues.[86] The terms must be in writing when finance and property matters are involved.[87] The MQMS is specific about the written requirements, as follows:[88]

- For family mediation involving property or finance matters, a written memorandum of understanding, together with a letter confirming its meaning and effect if the document itself does not make this clear.

- For non-financial and non-property family mediation issues, a written outcome statement listing key actions signed by the parties.

- If no agreement is reached, a letter from the mediator explaining the outcome of the mediation and any further action that is to be taken by the parties or the mediator.

- If appropriate, the mediator should offer the parties in writing a future review.

The mediator will advise parties that it is desirable and in their interests to obtain independent legal advice before reaching a final agreement and will warn them of the risks and disadvantages if they decide not to do so.[89] Accordingly, the 'parenting plan', 'statement of outcome' or 'memorandum of understanding',[90] as appropriate, is normally provided to each party's independent legal adviser,[91] for

---

82 Article 3.3 EU Code of Conduct (in Appendix 8) reminds mediators to take all appropriate measures to ensure that agreements are reached through knowing and informed consent and that all parties understand the terms of the agreement.
83 For example, clause 31 Law Society sample Mediation Agreement (included in Appendix 3).
84 On mediator liability, refer to 12.57–12.58.
85 See section 6.12 College of Mediators Code of Practice (in Appendix 8).
86 Ibid, section 6.11.
87 Ibid, section 6.13.
88 Requirement F3.1.
89 Sections 6.10 and 6.17 College of Mediators Code of Practice (see Appendix 8). This provision is also included in the EU Recommendation on Family Mediation (see Article III (x)) in Appendix 13.
90 Refer to Appendix 4 for a sample memorandum of understanding on 'all issues'.
91 Requirement F3.2 MQMS provides that clients must be informed in writing of the right to independent legal advice regardless of the outcome and a blanket statement at the bottom of the memorandum or outcome statement is encouraged.

advice on whether agreements reached are appropriate[92] and for the drafting of a legally binding agreement. No financial agreement or other mediated outcome is directly binding between the parties until approved by the court as a consent order[93] or made legally binding in some other manner.[94] Where the parties have agreed interim proposals, these need to be discussed with advisers, in particular whether there are any potential difficulties, and the need to apply for any interim orders.

There are various formalities associated with consent orders, for example:

■ The need to check if the parties are required to file a Form A.

■ When undertakings are given by a party, in some courts the consent order will need to be endorsed by the solicitor that the effect of an undertaking and the consequences of breach have been explained.

■ Where a pension sharing or attachment order is required, the draft consent order will need to be sent to the pension provider for approval before lodgment to check that its terms can be implemented.

N.   Terminating mediation without agreement

10.78   In 5.73 reference was made to the principles which should guide mediators when terminating a mediation where agreement *has* been reached. In some cases, there will be *partial* agreement on some isues and no agreement on others. Where there is *no* agreement some additional principles also apply.

The main guiding principles are that, whatever the level of party frustration or disappointment, the mediator should terminate on as positive a note as possible and provide a basis for future settlement. He or she should attempt to generate a list of matters on which there is agreement and a list of issues on which agreement is still required. This will provide some sense of achievement and the mediator might highlight other achievements, such as the sharing of information, which have occurred in the mediation and have left the dispute in better shape than when the mediation started. It is also appropriate to normalise the inability to settle, in order to reduce the parties' sense of failure. The mediator might advise the parties to take their time before deciding on their next course of action, particularly if they are in a state of agitation over the current impasse. Finally, the mediator might remind them of the option of returning to mediation should circumstances change at any time in the future.

---

92   A lawyer will check, for example, if the agreement has been based on full and frank disclosure and to emphasise the dangers of a settlement without complete disclosure, especially in relation to financial matters.

93   Resolution (see Appendix 11 for contact details) provide *Precedents for Consent Orders* which are universally used and accepted and have been approved by judges.

94   See section 5.3 Law Society Code of Practice for Family Mediation.

10.79   This is a possible mediator presentation for these situations:

> Mediator: In some cases mediations do not achieve settlement for a range of reasons, and this seems to be one of those cases in which you are not going to reach full settlement today. However, you have made some progress and I have written up a list of matters on which there is agreement. Hopefully you will not have to re-open these matters again. It may also help you to have a common list of those issues on which we have yet to reach agreement so that you can work in the future from the same list. Statistically it is unlikely that this matter will reach a court hearing and you should each feel free to approach me about resuming the mediation at any time. Let me reassure you about the confidentiality of what has occurred here today and I would like to wish you both well in dealing with this in the future.

Dealing with the walk-out

10.80   Occasionally a party moves beyond idle threats and starts to walk out of the mediation. The mediator needs to think and act quickly. He or she may try to head them off before they reach the door and encourage them to stay or suggest a separate meeting. Where they have already left, the mediator might make contact once they have cooled down. Ultimately the party's right to terminate should be respected, but some mediator persistence is compatible with this principle. There is always the prospect that a walk-out is a power play designed to force concessions from the other side. These possibilities are illustrated by two kinds of walk-out:

- *The genuine walk-out* – for example, an unrepresented party had been giving some warning signals and suddenly walked out of the joint session of the mediation with the parting shot that he would see the other side in court. Four hours later there was a telephone call to the mediator from a lawyer. The client had taken legal advice, and it was recommended that he accept the last proposal on offer. The matter was settled on this basis.

- *The strategic walk-out* – for example, a legally represented couple who were business partners walked out of the mediation while the mediator was with the other party. Their lawyer suggested that the mediation continue and that if there was significant progress he would be able to contact them on their mobile phone. The other side, also represented, immediately made a major concession. After further negotiations, the couple were contacted and returned to sign-off on the settlement.

O.   Confidentiality and privilege

10.80A   This section is not intended to provide a comprehensive overview of the law and policy relating to confidentiality and privilege.[95] Its aim is to highlight the practical issues that might arise in relation to these matters in mediation.

---

95   Refer to Boulle and Nesic *MPPP* and to Mackie K. et al, *The ADR Practice Guide: Commercial Dispute Resolution*, Tottel Publishing, 2007, Ch 12 (at 12.5–12.8) for a wider review of those topics.

Confidentiality

10.81 Most mediation agreements and codes of conduct contain confidentiality clauses,[96] and English courts have indicated that confidentiality can also be implied.[97] LSC contracted mediation providers and those complying with the MQMS are required to have a confidentiality policy in place.[98] Accordingly, mediation is confidential both as between the parties and as between the parties and the mediator. There are various exceptions to confidentiality (and in some cases, mediators may also be required to report to relevant authorities and to terminate the mediation[99]). For example:[100]

- Where the information is in the public domain.

- Where the parties have released the mediator from confidentiality restrictions or have consented to disclosure.

- Where there is a court order for disclosure.

- Where there is a legal requirement to make disclosure, for example, official investigators (as in the case of HM Revenue and Customs) have powers to compel disclosure.

- Where the mediator is required by law to report to an appropriate authority.

- Where a mediator reasonably believes that there is risk of significant harm to the life or safety of a person if information is not disclosed.

- In family mediation, where a child protection issue arises, the UK College of Family Mediators Code of Practice provides (at 4.7 and 6.14) that the mediator should encourage the parties to seek help from the appropriate agency; that the mediator should report the matter to both solicitors or to Social Services or the Welfare Service of the court, as applicable, if the parties are not willing to seek help from the appropriate agency and after discussion with them (at 4.5.3); and that the mediator must also advise the parties that he is obliged to report to the relevant authorities and must withdraw from the mediation if the parties are proposing to act in a manner which is seriously detrimental to the welfare of a child (at 4.5.3).[101]

---

96 Clause 4 EU Code of Conduct, section 4 IMI Code, section 6 CORE Solutions Group Code, section 7 Law Society Code of Practice for Civil/Commercial Mediation, section 7 Law Society Code of Practice for Family Mediation, section 8 CEDR Model Mediation Procedure, clause 19 Law Society sample Mediation Agreement and clauses 5 and 6 CEDR Model Mediation Agreement. Refer to Appendices 3 and 8.

97 *Instance v Denny Bros Printing* [2000] LS Gaz R 35; and *Farm Assist Limited v Secretary of State for the Environment, Food and Rural Affairs (No 2)* [2009] EWHC 1102 (TCC).

98 Requirement F6.1 MQMS provides that the confidentiality policy must detail how confidentiality is maintained; exceptions to confidentiality; and the requirements of disclosure for audit purposes.

99 For example, refer to Article 3.3 IMI Code, section 7.2 CEDR Code of Conduct and section 5 CORE Solutions Group Code of Conduct (see Appendix 8).

100 Refer to section 8 CEDR Model Mediation Procedure, clause 3 CEDR Model Mediation Agreement, section 7 Law Society's Code of Practice for Civil/Commercial Mediators, clause 19 Law Society's Sample Mediation Agreement, section 6 CORE Solutions Group Code of Conduct for Mediators, section 4.5 College of Mediator's Code of Practice, section 4 IMI Code of Practice, article 4 EU Code of Conduct and article 14 UNCITRAL Conciliation Rules. Procedures and Agreements are in Appendix 3 and Codes of Conduct/Practice are in Appendix 8. Refer also to Rule 3 Solicitors Code of Conduct 2007 (outlining the circumstances when confidentiality may be overridden).

101 See ACAS, *Mediation: an employer's guide*, 2009; and section 8 Law Society Code of Practice for Family Mediation (in Appendix 8).

- Where a mediator becomes aware of any criminal activity, the knowledge of which might amount to collusion in a crime, or where a mediator reasonably believes that there is a serious risk of being subject to criminal proceedings if disclosure is not made (and in such cases, the relevant authority should also be notified).[102]

- Where a mediator becomes aware in a workplace, employment or other case of any breach of organisational policy which amounts to gross misconduct, the mediator may terminate the mediation and notify the relevant authorities if the breach is significant.[103]

- Publicly funded mediation files can be examined for quality assurance purposes.

Privilege

10.82 The without prejudice privilege makes oral and written statements, offers and admissions made in a genuine attempt to reach settlement of a dispute inadmissible in later proceedings relating to the same subject matter. The privilege applies to negotiations in mediation and is often sitpulated in mediation agreements and codes of conduct.[104] The privilege belongs to the parties, not the mediator, so that the mediator can be compelled to give evidence if the parties agree or if the court considers that the interests of justice require it.[105] As the privilege belongs to the parties, it cannot be waived by one alone,[106] and no adverse inference can be drawn from a party's refusal to disclose.[107] Although the EU Mediation Directive provides that Member States should ensure that mediators should not be compelled to give evidence regarding information arising out of a mediation, the Directive recognises various exceptions, including agreement of the parties and overriding public policy considerations.[108]

Issues of privilege have arisen in English case law relating to whether a party's conduct in mediation can be taken into account on the question of costs;[109] if matters which took place in mediation could be examined on the question whether a binding settlement had been reached[110] or whether a settlement should be set

---

102 See for example 4.5.4 College of Mediators Code of Practice (in Appendix 8).
103 Ibid, at 4.5.5.
104 For example, clause 21 Law Society sample Mediation Agreement, clause 5.2 CEDR Model Mediation Agreement, Article 7 ICC Rules, clauses 11.2 and 11.3 ADR Group Mediation Procedure and Rules. Refer to Appendix 3.
105 *Farm Assist case*, see note 97 above, where the question was whether the mediated settlement agreement was entered into under duress. The court concluded that the interests of justice required evidence to be given by the mediator. The court also considered that the provision in the mediation agreement whereby the parties agreed not to call the mediator applied in relation to the dispute that was mediated, and not the dispute currently before the court (ie which related to whether the settlement agreement was entered into under duress). In the event, Farm Assist's liquidator discontinued the proceedings, and the trial did not take place.
106 *Halsey v Milton Keynes NHS Trust* [2004] EWCA Civ 576; *Wethered Estates Ltd v Davies & Others* [2005] EWHC 1903; *Reed Executive v Reed Business Information* [2004] EWCA (Civ) 887; *Earl of Malmesbury v Strutt & Parker* [2008] EWHC 424 (QB); *Cumbria Waste Management and another v Baines Wilson* [2008] EWHC 786 (QB); compare, however, *Chantrey Vellacott v Convergence Group plc* [2007] EWHC 1774 (Ch).
107 *Reed Executive v Reed Business Information* [2004] EWCA (Civ) 887.
108 Article 7 (see Appendix 13).
109 See the cases at note 106 above.
110 *Brown v Rice and Patel* [2007] EWHC 625 (Ch).

aside for duress;[111] and whether an expert's report ordered by the court, and which was used in a failed mediation, was privileged by virtue of it being used in the mediation.[112] It has also been raised in family law contexts.[113]

In the family law context specifically:

■ Information regarding financial or property issues is not privileged, and can be used by either party in future court proceedings if the mediation is unsuccessful.

■ UK College of Family Mediators Code of Practice recognises that the parties can waive privilege and the law can impose an overriding obligation on the mediator to make disclosure.[114]

■ NFM Notes of Guidance stipulate that a mediator should only give evidence as a witness where subpoenaed to do so, and served with a witness summons; should withhold documentary information until supboenaed to provide it; should give factual data only; and should give information that is fair to both sides so far as is practical.

In all cases, privilege will not ordinarily apply in relation to communications indicating that a child or other person is suffering, or is likely to suffer, significant harm, or where other public policy considerations prevail, or where rules of evidence render the privilege inapplicable.[115]

P. Summary

10.83 This chapter raises the following points of particular significance:

■ As experts in conflict management and dispute resolution, mediators need to be aware of those special issues which, although they might not be relevant in many routine matters, could occur in certain situations; many of these contingencies have to do with issues of power.

■ The mediator should initially try to diagnose the special situation before developing an appropriate response; the diagnosis is always tentative and if the intervention is not appropriate will have to be modified.

■ All special situations require some modification or adaptation of the mediation process, with the mediator taking the initiative but attempting to consult the parties and advisers and secure their agreement to the changes.

---

111 *Farm Assist* case, see notes 97 and 105 above.
112 *Aird v Prime Meridien Ltd* [2006] EWHC Civ 1866
113 For example, *Re D (Minors)* [1993] 2 All ER 693, where the Court of Appeal found that statements made in conciliation could not be introduced by one of the parties in proceedings under the Children Act except in exceptional circumstances (eg – where statement indicates that harm has been, or might in future be, caused to a child).
114 See section 4.6 (in Appendix 8).
115 See for example section 7.6 Law Society Code of Practice in Family Mediation and section 7.4 Law Society Code of Practice for Civil/Commercial Mediation.

Q. Tasks for beginner mediators

10.84   Try to interview an experienced mediator or mediators about 'special issue' situations they have encountered. Draw up a list of such issues, ways in which they were dealt with in practice by the mediator, and other ways in which you think they might have been dealt with.

10.85   Consult Ch 7 of Spegel, Rogers and Buckley (*Negotiation: Theory and Techniques*, 1998), or another relevant text or website on personality testing (like Myers Briggs), and do the test. What are some of the implications of these results for your prospective role as a mediator?

10.86   Assume that you are a mediator in a case where an employee who has been unlawfully dismissed is about to settle for a fraction of the monetary compensation to which she would be legally entitled. With reference to the ways for dealing with these situations referred to in this chapter, write out a list of ways which you consider most appropriate for dealing with this scenario.

R. Recommended reading

Ancona D. and Caldwell D. F., 'Beyond Task and Maintenance: External Roles in Groups', in (1988) 13 *Group and Organisational Studies* 468.

Baker C. and Ross W., 'Mediation Control Techniques: a Test of Kolb's "orchestrator's" vs "dealmakers" Model', in (1992) 3 *International Journal of Conflict Management* 319.

Brett J., 'Negotiating Group Decisions', in (1991) 7 *Negotiation Journal* 291.

Charlton R. and Dewdney M., *A Mediator's Handbook*, 2nd ed, Lawbook Co, Sydney, 2004, Chs 13 and 14.

Fassina N. E., 'Constraining a Principal's Choice: Outcome vs Behaviour Contingent Agency Contracts in Representative Negotiations', in (2004) July *Negotiation Journal* 435.

Folberg J. and Taylor A., *Mediation – A Comprehensive Guide to Resolving Conflicts Without Litigation*, Jossey-Bass, San Francisco, 1984, Ch 7.

Kim P. H. et al, 'Power Dynamics in Negotiation', in (2005) 30(4) *Academy of Management Review* 799.

Kirby B., 'CAFCASS: Productive Conflict Management Research and the Impetus for Change', in *Family Law*, November 2006, 36.

LaFasto F. and Larson C., *When Teams Work Best*, Sage, Thousand Oaks CA, 2001.

Lowe N. and Douglas G., *Bromley's Family Law*, 10th ed, Oxford University Press, 2006.

National Audit Office, *Legal Services Commission: Legal Aid and Mediation for People involved in Family Breakdown*, NAO, London, 2007.

Roberts M., *Mediation in Family Disputes: Principles of Practice*, 3rd ed, Ashgate, 2008.

Sordo B., 'The Lawyer's Role in Mediation' (1996) 7 *ADRJ* 20.

Spegel, Rogers and Buckley, *Negotiation: Theory and Techniques*, Butterworths, Sydney, 1998, Ch 7.

Swaab R. I. et al, 'Identity Formation in Multi-party Negotiations' in (2008) 47 *British Journal of Social Psychology* 167.

Tajima M. and Fraser N. M., 'Logrolling Procedure for Multi-issue Negotiation', in (2001) 10 *Group Decision and Negotiation* 217.

Tillett G., *Resolving Conflict – A Practical Approach*, 2nd ed, Oxford UP, Melbourne, 1999, Chs 6 and 9.

Wade J., *Representing Clients in Mediation*, Bond University Dispute Resolution Centre, 2000.

Wade J., 'Strategic Interventions used by Mediators, Facilitators and Conciliators' (1994) 5 *ADRJ* 285.

Wade J., 'Tools for a Mediator's Toolbox: Reflections on Matrimonial Property Disputes' (1996) 7 *ADRJ* 193.

Yuan, Lim Lan, 'An Analysis of Intervention Techniques in Mediation' (1998) 9 *ADRJ* 196.

Chapter 11

Avoiding Mediator Traps

Forewarned is forearmed

A. Introduction

11.1   Dispute resolution is a complex phenomenon and there are many potential dangers in the mediation process. Some of these dangers are initiated by the parties and there is little that even a well-prepared mediator can do to avoid them, for example, a sudden walk-out, a physical attack, or a client dismissing their lawyer. Others are caused by external circumstances, for example, representatives of the media bursting into the mediation room or the lights failing. In these abnormal situations presence of mind is more important for the mediator than preparation or planning.

11.2   There are also potential dangers in mediation that are, at least to some degree, created by mediators, in the sense that they are the result of practices or interventions, or the lack of practices or interventions, which are attributable to the mediator and not to the parties or to external factors. These dangers are easier to avoid through planning and preparation, though presence of mind is also useful when they eventuate. They are referred to here as mediator traps.

11.3   What follows is a description of some of the traps that could be created by mediators themselves, together with potential strategies for avoiding them. As is usual, there is no single strategy which will guarantee that a trap does not eventuate and frustrate the mediation and all participating in it. There are only options and choices.

Some mediator manuals provide lists of 'dos and don'ts' for mediators. This approach has some value, though there can be resistance to learning through negatives. In a sense this chapter provides the 'don'ts' of mediation, but they are presented in a constructive fashion. Because this chapter contains some repetition from previous chapters, albeit from a different perspective, there is not the extensive cross-referencing which could be provided.

Unless otherwise indicated, the following fact scenario will be used to illustrate some of the issues raised in this chapter.

Case illustration: golf course mediation

The parties

Party A: John and Elizabeth Cavanagh

Solicitor: Not present at mediation

Party B: Penelope Coots

Solicitor: Josh Vincent

The dispute

The Cavanaghs live in a property adjoining the Paradise Golf Club of which Penelope Coots is the manager. They undertake a major landscaping and pool construction project on their land for which they require access through the golf course grounds for an extended period of time. The club grants access upon payment of a £10,000 bond, which is to be returned, with interest, once the grounds are restored to their original condition.

After completion of the work, the Cavanaghs request repayment of the bond. The manager, Ms Coots, returns £1,200 and retains the balance for tree planting and drainage works required 'to restore the grounds to their original condition'. The Cavanaghs write to the club board, which confirms the manager's decision. The Cavanaghs retain a lawyer who writes a letter of demand to the club, which in response retains its own lawyer. The Cavanaghs begin badmouthing the club publicly and seek support from neighbours who have had their own problems with the golf course in the past.

The mediation

The Cavanaghs contact the local community mediation service which obtains the agreement of the club to participate in mediation, on the proviso that their lawyer may be present. A mediator is appointed. The Cavanaghs elect not to have a legal adviser present at the mediation.

B. Unrealistic expectations

The trap

11.4   One of the themes of this book is that the mediator is a manager of client expectations.[1] The trap occurs where the mediator fails to manage client expectations from the very beginning of the mediation process, or where the mediator inadvertently increases the unrealistic expectations of the parties through word, action or omission. Clearly the mediator is not responsible for all unrealistic expectations which are found in mediation, but there are some which he or she should manage, or at least not exacerbate. An unrealistic expectation can relate to the process of mediation (the Cavanaghs think, 'The mediator will listen to my case

---

1   See 3.15–3.16.

and find in my favour') and they can relate to anticipated outcomes of the process ('We'll get back our £8,800, plus interest, immediately').

Avoidance strategies

11.5   Informing and educating the parties is the best way to deal with unrealistic expectations. This can be done in relation to both the mediation process ('John and Elizabeth, mediation is not a miracle pill, but it can assist to deal with this problem in a constructive way if you are both committed to settling …') and to the problem itself ('In my experience, John and Elizabeth, claimants who have difficulty with their facts and evidence usually have to compromise to some extent in cases such as this …'). It will always be a matter of judgment as to when and how the informing and educating should take place. The sooner it occurs in relation to the process and nature of mediation the better. In relation to the outcome of the dispute, this will depend on when the expectation first comes to the mediator's attention, how unrealistic it is, and the influence of professional advisers in creating it. This is illustrated below.

Case illustration: the trap of unrealistic expectations

In a personal injury mediation a young claimant injured in a motor vehicle accident had an expectation of receiving £600,000 in damages. The 'normal' range for this kind of injury was £200,000–£300,000. The unrealistic expectation had been generated by her barrister, who was present in the mediation and persisted with the unfounded stance on quantum.

In the negotiations the barrister operated on the basis of his 'extensive experience' and refused to justify and quantify specific heads of damages. During the separate sessions the mediator attempted to influence the barrister and there was some success, but the client whose expectations had been raised seemed inhibited by the barrister's approach, on which she was heavily reliant. There was no settlement despite the fact that the insurer was offering £275,000. With hindsight it would have been helpful for the mediator to have anticipated this problem, to have had prior contact with the barrister and to have acted as agent of reality on the issue of quantum. This would not necessarily have solved the problem, but it was the appropriate route to take in attempting to change the client's expectations.

C.   Losing impartiality

The trap

11.6   There are many ways in which mediators can forfeit their impartiality, or the appearance of impartiality. It is important to recognise that partiality is as much a matter of party perception as it is of objective behaviour, a factor which makes it more difficult for the mediator to manage and control. Irrespective of the reason for it, the loss of impartiality can lead to the collapse of one or both parties' trust, and the failure of the mediation process. Some of the ways in which the perception of partiality can arise are through the mediator:

- Not being even-handed in conducting the process (for example, consistently giving more attention to Penelope Coots and her lawyer than to the Cavanaghs).

- Arguing with one of the parties and appearing to oppose their viewpoints.

- Acting as advocate for one of the parties and representing their arguments to the other, which can happen unwittingly with unrepresented parties like the Cavanaghs.

- Interrogating and cross-examining one of the parties, for example, Penelope Coots over the nature of the remedial work required.

- Inappropriately disclosing their evaluation of and opinion on what a party is saying or their assessment of the merits of the case.[2]

The trap can also occur where mediators are not conscious of their own biases which might be detected by one or both of the parties.

Avoidance strategies

11.7   Some avoidance strategies which might succeed are:

- The mediator should be 'eternally vigilant' on the impartiality issue, particularly where he or she is an expert in the subject matter of the dispute, for example, a barrister in personal injury mediations.

- The mediator should be aware of his or her own biases where there are important value issues at stake, for example, allegations of environmental degradation or victimisation in the workplace, on which it is likely that they would have personal views.

- The mediator needs to treat the parties comparably, for example, in summarising both the Cavanaghs' and Penelope Coots's opening statements and not only that of one party, or in devoting approximately the same time to each party in separate sessions.

- The mediator could invite the parties to comment on any perceived deviation from his or her impartiality, in either joint or separate sessions – 'As indicated earlier I will be impartial, but if any of you think that this is not the case, then please let me know.'

- Where there are co-mediators, as in the golf club mediation, they could provide feedback on the impartiality concern to each other.

As with all the other avoidance strategies, it is important for the mediator to be aware of the interpersonal dynamics at play. Thus sometimes the loss of impartiality is a result of a conscious or unconscious strategy by one of the parties, as shown below.

---

2   There will be occasions when mediators have been selected for their subject-matter expertise (as often happens in commercial cases), with the view to giving the parties a steer on what might happen if the matter went to trial or, in case the mediator has industry expertise, to suggest ways in which a deal might be structured. Subject-matter expertise can range from knowledge of the relevant law, customs/practices or technology associated with the matter in dispute. This issue raises the facilitative–evaluative continuum of a mediator's functions, as to which refer to Chapters 1, 5 and 8.

Losing impartiality – the triangulation problem

11.8   Haynes refers to the fact that many mediating parties try to win the mediator over to their side. They try to befriend the mediator in the hope that the mediator will befriend them. Haynes uses the term *triangulation* to refer to this phenomenon.

> Triangulation is an attempt by a negotiator to put the mediator in a position of supporting him or her. Every triangulation strategy is dangerous to the mediator. If the mediator responds in the terms the negotiator is looking for, the mediator will alienate the other negotiator. If the mediator tries to check the triangulator, the mediator is likely to alienate him or her. I usually use a reframing strategy to change the meaning or direction of the triangulation attempt.[3]

D.   Dominating the process

The trap

11.9   Many survey studies have shown that one of the aspects of mediation evaluated favourably by clients is the direct participation which it allows them in the process of resolving their dispute and the control they experience in respect of the outcome of that process. These benefits are derived from a faithful adherence, to the extent that this is possible, to the different stages and elements of the mediation process. Mediators can fall into the trap of undermining these potential benefits by:

- Talking too often and for too long, and generally dominating the airways.

- Interrupting the parties too much, particularly in the early stages of the process.

- Failing to listen and cutting parties off in mid sentence.

- Cross-examining the parties and pointing out inconsistencies in what they have said.

- Not allowing the parties to tell their own story in their own time and manner and thereby preventing important information from being disclosed.

- Using closed, leading and interrogatory questions to constrict the parties' contributions.

- Assuming a narrow notion of what is relevant in the mediation, for example, by restricting discussion to matters covered by the statements of case.

- Making assumptions about the parties' priorities.

Avoidance strategies

11.10   Here are some of the factors which mediators might consider in order to avoid dominating the process:

---

3   Refer to Haynes, *Mediating Divorce,* 1983, 39.

- Using open and clarifying questions, particularly in the early stages of the process: 'Penelope, how did you understand the original agreement and the responsibilities of each side?'

- Practising active listening as a major ingredient in successful mediation: 'So Elizabeth, it sounds as though you were angered and stressed by the club's attitude?'

- Inviting the parties to indicate to the mediator if they feel they are unable to speak their mind and are not being heard: 'Now, do you all feel you have had your say and been heard on the drainage question?'

- Checking with the parties in separate sessions about how they are experiencing the process: 'Elizabeth and John, how do you feel the negotiations are going for you?'

- Using language and terminology which allows the parties to understand and 'own' the mediation process and avoiding the technical and arcane.

Avoiding technical language

11.11 An indirect way of dominating the process is for the mediator to use technical language or jargon which is not understood by one or more parties. This is tempting in cases where technical issues are in question, such as in medical negligence or building or computing disputes ('intermittent claudication' and 'paroxysmal nocturnal dyspnoea', or, 'RSJs' and 'cost-plus contract', or 'gigabytes' and 'ISPs' – simple and self-evident to insiders, gobbledegook to outsiders). Likewise, professional jargon ('taking it on spec' or 'party and party costs') or trade usage ('an ambit claim' or 'a conjunctional sale') is problematic when parties external to the relevant occupation or trade are present.

Mediation has its own jargon, first instilled during training courses. It is best left to seminars and learned papers, unless it can be easily explained for the uninitiated. Thus terms such as 'caucus' (for separate meeting), 'the bottom triangle', 'conditional linked bargaining' and 'reframing to interests' should best be avoided – unless you are mediating between two mediators.

11.12 Mediator domination through the use of this kind of terminology could lead to loss of face for a party where they have to make inquiries and to a loss of understanding for a party when they do not. Rather than mediators being the cause of this problem, it is incumbent on them to resolve it when it arises through the technique of 'mediator vulnerability'. Thus where, in the golf club mediation, Josh Vincent or Penelope Coots uses a legal technical term which is not understood by the Cavanaghs, the mediator should ask for clarification on behalf of himself or herself so that John and Elizabeth can benefit from it without having to appear ignorant themselves.

E. Losing control of the process

The trap

11.13 This is the converse of the previous trap. Mediators must provide a reasonable measure of structure and control for the mediating parties. While they may share some of their control with their clients, for example, over whether there should be an adjournment or whether advisers can be present, they should also retain ultimate control over the process, particularly on the important procedural issues. Control is lost where mediators allow:

■ the parties to break the ground rules consistently without the mediator attempting to intervene in any way – Penelope talks over John whenever he speaks;

■ professional advisers to subvert the process and revert to their accustomed 'comfort zone' of operation;[4]

■ a party to manipulate the process, for example, by imposing unilateral time limits or causing disruptions, having multiple adjournments, and the like – Elizabeth insists on taking mobile phone calls during the mediation;

■ outsiders to be present and to become involved in the mediation in a fashion that is not constructive for the progress of the negotiations – John invites a large group of neighbours to come into the mediation room to support his case.

Avoidance strategies

11.14 As with many of the avoidance strategies, sound commonsense suggests that mediators should be attentive to the control factor from the earliest stages. This involves a balancing act between appropriate control, on one hand, and inappropriate authoritarianism, on the other. Thus, each of the following strategies requires some basic judgement and diplomacy in their execution:

■ Prior education of the parties about the importance of structure in effective dispute resolution: 'Now Penelope, John and Elizabeth, it is important to deal with these issues in an orderly way and I can help you to have that structure during the mediation.'

■ Early assertion of the mediator's authoritative role on questions of process: 'Now you've all asked me to act as mediator for you so I would suggest that you follow the guidelines as regards speaking in order.'

■ Positive reinforcement of compliance with the mediator's requests and directions: 'Thank you for being patient and not interrupting, Penelope, while the Cavanaghs were speaking, now would you like to give me your opening statement?'

■ Appropriate enforcement by the mediator of the mediation guidelines: 'You did agree at the beginning that there should be no denigration of one another, which there has been, and I would like to suggest that you all recommit to that agreement.'

■ Using the separate meetings to reassert control and warn about the consequences of continued lack of orderliness: 'Elizabeth and John, you have had difficulty in listening to Penelope's case and have interrupted her continually. If this continues there is a possibility that she and Josh will walk out. Can we reduce the likelihood of a walk-out which will be in no-one's interests?'.

---

4   See 11.15.

- Securing renewed commitment to the guidelines where they have been consistently breached: 'You have all had difficulty in keeping to the speaking guidelines, so I am going to restate them now and ask you to give your commitment to them for the next phase of the mediation.'

The trap of allowing professional advisers to dominate the process

11.15 In some mediations professional advisers play an indispensable role in its success, and in others their involvement is highly problematic and leads to failure.[5] Generally speaking, advisers are a problem where their own interests diverge from those of their clients, and the former are allowed to surface and dominate in the mediation. Some of those interests can be restated here:

- The professional interest of being seen to act as the zealous promoter of their client's cause and not being called into question by the client.

- The reputational interest of being known as a tough negotiator.

- The competitive interest of needing to win and not showing weakness towards or making concessions to the other professionals present.

- The accountability interest of being able to render a flattering report to outside partners, supervisors and colleagues.

11.16 Dealing with professionals involves a further delicate balance for mediators: they cannot allow advisers and their interests to dominate, but if they deal with the problem undiplomatically the advisers may become defensive and even more problematic. Thus the timing of interventions, and the factor of who is present when they are made, are important matters to consider. Some ways of avoiding the trap are:

- prior education of professional advisers about their appropriate role in mediation;

- making advisers signatories to a protocol of conduct for the mediation: see Appendix 6;

- using adviser meetings to speak to advisers about the nature and consequences of their dominating behaviour;

- making mild intimations about unprofessional conduct or professional misconduct.

F. Ignoring emotions

The trap

11.17 There is a danger in mediators ignoring the emotional factors which arise in mediation. It has been shown that most forms of mediation do not involve a therapeutic relationship between the mediator and the parties. Nevertheless the process allows for the expression, acknowledgment and validation of deeply felt

---

5   See 10.44–10.60.

emotions more than do some other forms of dispute resolution.[6] Where mediators attempt to force the parties into a 'cool, rational and objective' discussion of their problems, there is a danger that they will not be ready or willing to move towards a settlement, or that a settlement will come undone at a later stage. The complete disregard of emotions could also result in the parties finding the process alienating and unsatisfying.

11.18 Conversely, mediators should avoid the trap of identifying with one side emotionally, for example, with the weaker party or with one whom the justice of the situation seems to favour. Particularly where there are significant imbalances of power, mediators need to maintain an objective stance to avoid falling into this version of the trap.

Avoidance strategies

11.19 The standard mediation process is designed to prevent intense emotional feelings from being disregarded and to deal with them in appropriate ways. More specifically, the mediator is able to:

- Facilitate wide-ranging communication by the parties on matters of concern to them, whether or not they are within 'the pleadings': 'Elizabeth, tell us how the incident has affected you personally over the past six months.'

- Encourage some ventilation of emotion in joint or separate sessions: 'John, it sounds as though your treatment by the club made you frustrated and angry. Would you like to tell us about that?'

- Acknowledge the parties' deeply held feelings: 'So Penelope, it sounds as though this has been a very stressful and damaging episode for you and the board.'

- Validate some implicit feelings: 'It's not unusual for parties in mediation to feel apprehensive about conceding too much to the other side.'

Mediators can anticipate the kinds of emotions that are likely to be present in an approaching mediation and plan ways of dealing with them. They should also be conscious of their own reactions to emotion and deal with these appropriately.

G. Moving to solutions too quickly

The trap

11.20 This book has emphasised the importance in dispute resolution of first defining the dispute comprehensively in terms of underlying needs and interests before moving into possible solutions.[7] This is because where mediators allow parties to move too quickly into solutions there is a danger that they will focus only on monetary or material factors and ignore matters of procedural or emotional significance. There is also a danger that the parties will move too quickly into incremental positional bargaining and fail to close the final gap, or that they will reach a settlement that does not exploit all the potential value at the negotiation table.

---

6   See 3.30–3.37.
7   See 4.30–4.35.

313

If the mediator allows the parties to move too quickly into solutions it also does not allow for convergent, as opposed to divergent, problem solving thinking. Furthermore, it tends to discourage the disclosure of the information that might be influential in reaching a settlement.

Avoidance strategies

11.21   Here are some of the factors which mediators might consider in order to avoid falling into the trap of allowing the parties to move too quickly into solutions:

- Being transparent with the parties about the advantages of discussing the general circumstances of the dispute before dealing with the money or other 'hard' solutions: 'In my experience it would help to talk a little about how this incident arose and what effects it had on each of you in order to get a fuller perspective on the problem, before we discuss the question of money.'

- Asking each party to explain how they approach the question of monetary figures before they actually make a dollar offer or counter-offer: 'John, you've acknowledged that you should not receive the full bond back. Before you mention the figure you do want, explain to Penelope and Josh how you have gone about quantifying this amount.'

- Seeking agreement on matters of principle, before moving into the financial details: 'Let's see if there is agreement on the following matters before discussing the money: you'd all like to settle the matter today, Elizabeth and John, you agree that you can't recover the full amount you deposited with the club, and Penelope and Josh, you agree that you need to itemise the expenses which you have incurred in restoring the grounds. Are we all agreed in principle on those matters?'

- Coaching the parties in separate sessions on how to package deals so that the money is not the only point of focus: 'John and Elizabeth, you are about to ask for some money, but perhaps you could first tell Penelope, as you've told me, that you are prepared to stop badmouthing the club, to stop any further agitation by the neighbours, and to consider this dispute settled once and for all. This may make them more receptive to your figure.'

Delaying the money moves

11.22   In a mediation involving a claim by a lender against a valuer for alleged negligence in drawing up a valuation of security property, the valuer denied liability but was prepared to offer a small monetary amount in order to reach a financial settlement. The claimant had some legal and evidential difficulties on the liability question and had financial pressures which demanded a commercial settlement. In order to keep the parties from moving too quickly into the figures, the mediator requested the valuer's lawyer to explain how they were approaching the monetary settlement, which he did in terms of risk assessment and costs recovery. The claimant was asked to respond along the same lines, and although this highlighted substantial differences in approach between the two parties it did provide a theoretical point of reference when they bargained on the money. The monetary negotiations were successful, despite the fact that the claimant accepted only 15% of what he had lost. Had there not been the 'philosophical initiation', the deal on the money may have been difficult to attain.

H. Pushing the parties

The trap

11.23   This trap involves the mediator expressing judgements and personal views on what is important for resolving the dispute or on how it should be resolved and otherwise pursuing his or her own agenda in the mediation.[8] It includes the situation in which the parties have provided their own list of issues and the mediator insists that the mediation should also deal with other matters that they themselves have not raised ('You cannot finalise these neighbour disputes without discussing how to deal with such problems in the future'). Likewise the mediator might insist that a particular issue, for example, the question of interest to be paid or the drafting of a confidentiality undertaking, be dealt with in accordance with his or her preferred approach to the matter.

11.24   There are several reasons why there is a trap in pushing the parties to the mediator's preferred approach or outcome:

- The mediator can only view the dispute from an objective 'rights-based' perspective and not from the subjective 'interests-based' perspectives of the parties.

- The mediator may only have a restricted knowledge of the facts, the law, and other relevant factors, and may push towards an 'incorrect' outcome.

- At least one party may become more intransigent where the mediator's view appears to favour them.

- At least one party may lose trust in the mediator if they would not stand to benefit from the expressed view.

- The mediator may base his or her view, in part, on information disclosed during the confidential separate sessions.

- It may confuse clients who did not expect such interventions from a mediator, and it may result in confusion in the marketplace over the nature of mediation.

- The mediator may breach a code of conduct or ethical standard and be sued for negligence.

- The mediator may no longer be 'mediating' and may thereby lose a statutory immunity.

11.25   This trap is particularly problematic where both parties request the mediator to provide an opinion or make a recommendation. While this expressed consent will obviate some of the problems referred to above, it might create difficulties of its own. Thus one party, or conceivably both parties, may, in asking for the mediator to express a view, be influenced by what they perceived to be the mediator's support for them in a separate session. If this is the case, they will be at least surprised and possibly disappointed about the actual opinion expressed or recommendation made by the mediator.

---

8   See 8.5–8.15.

Avoidance strategies

11.26　It is more difficult for some categories of mediators to avoid the 'pushing the parties' trap than it is for others. Mediators with high levels of expertise in the subject matter of the dispute will be more likely to push to their preferred position than those selected because of their skills in the process of mediation. Regardless of these variables, the following strategies will minimise the worst dangers of this trap:

- Defining from the earliest stages of the mediation the nature of the mediator's role, and reinforcing this definition in the minds of the parties wherever necessary: 'I am not here to make any decisions for you, or to advise you on the law, or to recommend outcomes for you. I am here to assist you in other ways ...'.

- Deflecting requests for advice or opinions in terms of the stated mediator role: 'You've asked my advice on what are reasonable deductions from the bond but, as I've indicated, that is not my role. What ideas do you have on that issue?'

- Identifying the concern or interests underlying any request for this kind of mediator intervention and attempting to address those motivating factors: 'Elizabeth and John, from what you've just asked you seem to be uncertain over your legal rights. Does this mean you'd like to consider ways of dealing with that uncertainty?'

- Avoiding the seductive nature of the power conferred by shuttle mediation (see below).

Distorting the parties' views during shuttle mediation

11.27　It has been indicated already in this book that mediators acquire immense potential power during shuttle mediation by virtue of their control over the communications between the parties.[9] This power can be used to push unsuspecting parties to the mediator's preferred outcome. As the holding and conduct of shuttle mediation is largely within the mediator's control, the abuse of this power is a trap which mediators can avoid by:

- delaying the holding of separate meetings until discussions are advanced, and avoiding lapsing into shuttle through default rather than by design;

- checking with the parties what is and what is not to be conveyed back and forth between them;

- reducing the parties' offers to writing, and considering how strategically to relay the information, before conveying it to the other side;

- bringing the parties back together if the reasons for adopting shuttle no longer exist or are no longer fruitful;

- continually reflecting on how they are performing their shuttle role, and where possible, conferring with their assistant on this point.

9　See 9.6–9.16.

I. Assuming a differing professional role

The trap

11.28 All occupations and professional practices have boundary problems between what they can legitimately do and what is in the province of others. There is a difficult boundary problem in mediation where the mediator feels required to play the role of adviser, advocate, counsellor or lawyer. This is a particular problem where only one party has professional advice or other skilled assistance in the mediation, although the trap could still be present where both parties are professionally advised. As usual there are semantic issues in relation to the differences between the legitimate functions of mediators and those of lawyers, counsellors or other professionals.

For example, where it appears to a mediator that a child is suffering or is likely to suffer significant harm, the mediator must advise participants to seek help from the appropriate agency (and is obliged to report the matter irrespecitve of whether or not the parties seek that help). Where finance and property issues are involved in a family matter, the parties must be informed of the nature and extent of the financial disclosure required; the nature and finality of the court orders that might be made; and the broad principles of law applicable to the matter in dispute. Family mediators must inform parties that it is desirable for them to seek independent legal advice before reaching a final agreement and warn them of the risks of failing to do so.[10]

It is nevertheless possible to envisage some functions which would not be regarded as part of mediators' roles. Thus, some mediators might be inclined to advise John and Elizabeth legally about their situation, and in other situations they might attempt to counsel a grieving party. The mediator is more likely to be drawn into playing the role of the absent professional where there are separate sessions.

11.29 There are many problems associated with the transgression of professional boundaries. Essentially they revolve around what parties expect, and can legitimately expect, when they come to a mediation. Despite all the debate over the exact contours of the mediator's role, there are clear transgressions which should not occur. Thus in the golf club mediation, the co-mediators should not counsel the claimants over their loss and grief, or advise them on their legal position, or calculate the legitimate deductions that could be made by the club. Such interventions could create confusion among clients, loss of trust in mediation, and subsequent problems for mediators.

Avoidance strategies

11.30 Some avoidance strategies which might be successful are:

- Providing as clear a definition as possible of the mediator's role before the mediation, in the agreement to mediate, and during the mediator's opening statement: 'Our role today is not to give you legal advice, to act as therapists or counsellors, or to assess and quantify the alleged damages.'

---

10   See 8.6–8.7 and Chapter 8 generally.

- Discussing in separate meetings the implications of not having professional advisers present: 'John and Elizabeth, you have decided not to have advisers here and I cannot give you legal advice, how is that affecting your participation in the mediation?'

- Exploring options for the obtaining of professional advice when the parties are not represented: 'It seems clear that you need to be advised on the liability question, how can we modify the mediation process to make that possible for you?'

- Exploring other professional help if that is called for in the case: 'It seems that a plumber's report on the drainage issues could help to progress matters ...'

- Pointing out the difficulties and possible negative consequences for the parties of the mediator transgressing professional boundaries: 'The problem with my giving you a view on the reasonable deductions which could be made from the bond are that I do not have all the facts at my disposal, I might get it wrong, and it might affect the long-term viability of the agreement you make.'

J.   Being unprepared

The trap

11.31   Implicit in many of the above traps is a lack of preparation by the mediator. Being unprepared is also a trap of its own. Mediators need to be prepared on the specific features of the case in which they are involved, including the nature of the dispute, the possible causes of conflict, potential mediator interventions and ways of dealing with predictable problems. They also need to be prepared in a more generalised way in relation to theories of conflict, negotiation dynamics, communication requirements, dealing with impasses and emotions, and on the other skills and techniques required in mediation. In many cases there will be no occasion for specific preparation as the mediator receives no prior knowledge of the case, and only the generalised preparation is possible. Being unprepared in either sense is one of the most preventable of the mediator-generated problems.

Avoidance strategies

11.32   The main avoidance strategy to being unprepared is an obvious truism: prepare. Throughout this book there are indications of how mediators should prepare for their task, and of the factors on which they should be prepared. Where circumstances and resources allow, specific preparation can be done before a mediation commences, for example, by obtaining necessary information and having appropriate contact with the parties. Where circumstances and resources do not allow for systematic prior preparation, a snatched conversation in the corridor with parties and advisers will have to suffice for the impending mediation. In all situations, mediators can improve their generalised preparation, for example, by revising their understanding of basic frameworks of conflict and negotiation, with particular reference to the predictable problems which can occur. This should be an ongoing process: systematic reflection on yesterday's mediation constitutes a form of preparation for that of tomorrow.

K. Allowing the agreement to be left undocumented

The trap

11.33 It is now common practice for agreements to mediate to stipulate that no decision made in mediation will be final and binding until reduced to writing.[11] Whether this condition applies or not, the problem of leaving the agreement hanging in the air can still arise where the parties feel drained and exhausted and they would rather go home than write up their terms of settlement. The trap results in the parties either forgetting what they have agreed upon, or returning to adversarial combat the next day despite having reached agreement. In either case the efforts of the mediating parties could be rendered futile.

Avoidance strategies

11.34 Mediators can avoid the trap of leaving agreements undocumented by:

- reinforcing throughout the mediation the requirement that agreements be reduced to writing in order to make them binding: 'Penelope, John and Elizabeth, you have agreed on what additional work is required on the course grounds, and that will be binding once we have reduced it to writing';

- maintaining lists of matters agreed on by the parties to assist the parties in the drafting process;

- recommending abbreviated memoranda of understanding or heads of agreement, for later redrafting into a fuller agreement;

- working off standard form agreements or using modern technology such as laptop computers to shorten the required drafting time;

- allowing clients time out from the mediation while professional advisers, or the mediator, undertake the drafting exercise.

L. Ignoring external parties

The trap

11.35 Reference has been made to the problems of the 'external ratifier', whose formal approval is required for any mediation agreement, and the 'absent party', who is not directly involved in the mediation but who could destabilise any agreement after the event. While it may be opportune in terms of reaching agreement to ignore these persons in the short term, failure to take account of them can result in the long-term viability of the mediated agreement being jeopardised. This is one of the predictable potential problems in any mediation which mediators can take steps to prevent.

---

11   See, for example, paragraph 9 CEDR Model Mediation Agreement (10th ed) in Appendix 3. In some contexts, such as family mediation, agreements reached in mediation are not binding until reviewed by lawyers and turned into a legally binding agreement or consent order. On drafting and settlement formalities, see 5.69–5.72 and 10.74–10.77.

Avoidance strategies

11.36   The following avoidance strategies may be successful:

- Before commencement of the mediation, checking with the parties about the existence of stakeholders whose approval is, formally or informally, a required factor for success: 'Penelope, what sort of formal and informal ratification will you require for any mediated agreement?'

- Keeping a note of any reference by the parties to significant external individuals or bodies and referring to them at appropriate times: 'John, you have referred several times to the neighbouring Simpsons, what will their interests be in the mediated outcome?'

- Checking with the parties in separate meetings whether there are any ratifiers or absent parties who have not yet been identified: 'Elizabeth, are there any other people who will be insistent on knowing from you how this matter settled, and will that cause you any problems?'

- Emphasising to the parties that the existence of a ratifier or absent party is a problem which both of them need to address: 'John and Elizabeth, you have heard Penelope say that she requires board approval for this agreement and I think it would be helpful if we all discussed that requirement.'

- Developing options with the parties for dealing with the ratification issue, with consideration of the mediator being involved: 'What are the options for persuading the board to endorse this agreement, and would my services be useful in this regard?'

M.   Summary

11.37   This chapter raises the following points of particular significance:

- Mediators can be responsible for a number of self-induced traps and these can be prevented, avoided or minimised through preparation, planning and more preparation.

- Many of the traps are a result of the mediator's own interests in a mediated settlement and in a reputation for settling disputes through mediation; they cause short-term expedient thinking which is not to the long-term benefit of the parties.

- Avoidance of the traps entails specific preparation in the light of the peculiar circumstances of individual mediations, and generic preparation through education and training, reflecting on experience, and reading skills books.

N.   Tasks for beginner mediators

11.38   Select an area with which you have some familiarity or expertise, for example, studying a discipline, a hobby, playing a particular sport, or working as a professional. Draw up a list of some of the traps which, through experience, you have learned to avoid in this area of activity. What do you think might be some of the counterpart traps for mediators?

11.39   Write up a guide for professional advisers who will participate in mediations which you conduct, defining their role, the preferred approach to their tasks, their rights and responsibilities, and the attitude and demeanour expected of them. Ask a lawyer you know or a colleague to comment on the guide.

11.40   Prepare a set of lists, tables or mind maps which set out important features and principles of conflict and negotiation and make these into manageable and accessible cards for use on trains, planes and cranes as memory aids for your mediation practice.

O.   Recommended reading

Benjamin R., *The Effective Negotiation and Mediation of Conflict: Applied Theory and Practice Handbook*, 2007.

Boulle L. and Nesic M., *Mediation: Principles Process Practice*, Tottel Publishing, 2001, Chs 4, 5 and 6.

Charlton R. and Dewdney M., *The Mediator's Handbook*, 2nd ed, Lawbook Co, Sydney, 2004, Chs 13 and 14.

Hanger I., 'Eight Pitfalls Observed in Mediation' (1995) 6 *Queensland ADR Review* 8.

Haynes J., 'Avoiding Traps Mediators Set Themselves' (1986) 2 *Negotiation Journal* 187–194.

Haynes J. and Haynes G., *Mediating Divorce: Casebook of Strategies for Successful Family Negotiations*, John Wiley and Son/Jossey-Bass, San Francisco, 1989, Ch 5.

Menkel-Meadow C., Love L. P. and Schneider A. K., *Mediation: Practice, Policy and Ethics*, Aspen Publishers, 2006.

Tillett G., *Resolving Conflict – A Practical Approach*, 2nd ed, Oxford University Press, Melbourne, 1999, Ch 10.

Chapter 12

Developing a Practice and Practising Mediation

Rome was not built in a day

A. Introduction

12.1   Few mediators in private practice would complain about an increase in demand for their services. Historically, mediation has been a supply-driven system and there is considerably greater availability of mediators than there is demand for their services. One of the puzzling paradoxes about mediation is that, while it is such a 'good thing' for the right clients and the appropriate disputes, there is relatively little spontaneous demand from paying clients for mediation services. For a range of complex reasons the 'need' for mediation does not translate into a demand for the service. It is probably fair to say that mediation is only flourishing where it is encouraged by statute, rules of court or judges; where it is supported by government departments, agencies, tribunals, companies or lawyers; where it is a term in a contract; or where it is provided on a subsidised basis or at little cost to users.

12.2   This chapter deals with various ways of attempting to establish a mediation practice and with some of the issues involved in practising mediation. There are no clear career paths for mediators in general civil and commercial cases, and no guaranteed methods for prospective mediators to secure work (just as there are no guarantees for existing practitioners). An investment has to be made, and the nature, size and timing of the returns on that investment are very uncertain.

B. Developing mediator credentials

12.3   As indicated earlier there are three elements in the development of any new occupational practice, whether it be in the law, accounting, counselling or mediating: *knowledge* about the particular activity; development of *skills and techniques* in the relevant areas; and *attitudes* towards standards and ethical requirements.[1]

---

1   See 1.6.

There are different ways in which these three elements are developed by those interested in embarking on a mediation career. These methods are explored in this chapter.[2]

Training

12.4   Some universities, mediation organisations and dispute resolution service providers conduct introductory or basic mediation training courses. Some also provide forms of intermediate or advanced training, or specialist training (for example, in commercial mediation or family mediation). The basic courses range in duration between three and the equivalent of ten days. The main focus in training courses is on the mediation process and on the skills and techniques associated with the system. In some cases there is competency assessment of the skills, and in others only attendance certificates are provided to participants. Continuing, in-service and audit training is available for practising mediators, and is required by some service providers and some codes of mediator conduct. A sample of mediator training in the general civil and commercial, workplace, family and community areas in England is provided in the box below.[3]

Sample mediator training programmes[4]
General civil and commercial mediator training[5]

CEDR

- A five-day programme

- Days 1 and 2 – skills and process with practical exercises and case studies

- Day 3 – practice and coaching day

- Days 4 and 5 – assessment via simulated mediations

ADR Group

- A 40-hour programme

- Module 1 is preparation via cd-rom/distance learning

- Module 2 is the foundation programme involving a three-day core competency intensive with assessment via simulated mediation

---

2   Article 4 of the EU Mediation Directive (included in Appendix 13) encourages the development of codes of conduct for mediators and for organisations providing mediation services, as well as other effective quality control mechanisms concerning the provision of mediation services, including the training of mediators.
3   Refer also to Appendix 8 for a sample of training and accreditation schemes.
4   Refer to the Civil Mediation Council website (www.cmcregistered.org) for approved mediation providers. Most providers offer a range of mediation training programmes, including those leading to accreditation.
5   For a list of course providers approved by the Law Society for the purpose of its Civil and Commercial Mediation Accreditation Scheme, refer to the Law Society's Accreditation for Civil/Commercial Mediation included in Appendix 8.

CIArb

- Module 1 is a five-day programme including practice, role play and coaching.
- Module 2 is mediation accreditation assessment

Family mediator training[6]

ADR Group and FMA

Foundation Training – an eight-day course leading to Family Mediation Council and Legal Services Commission recognised family mediator foundation training

Advanced Family Mediator Training

Professional Practice Consultancy (PPC) Foundation Training – a two-day course recognised by the Family Mediation Council and Legal Services Commission leading to qualification as a Professional Practice Consultant

PPC Updates – one-day courses recognised by the Family Mediation Council aimed at providing networking, debates and CPD for Professional Practice Consultants

Employment/workplace mediator training[7]

Various courses provide specialist components to equip delegates with the knowledge and skills they need to deal effectively with employment disputes and to operate within the new legislative frameworks. For example:

CMP Resolutions

A six-day course split into two sets of three dates, leading to accreditation.

ACAS

ACAS provides a wide range of training on topics that are relevant to mediators across disciplines, although the training is aimed at those who deal with workplace and employment issues. A sample of their training programmes is listed below. The ACAS workplace mediation programme is five days, leading to accreditation, and is aimed at those who will become internal mediators at their workplace.

Conflict management
Dispute resolution
Negotiating skills
Mediation
Certificate in Internal Workplace Mediation
Bullying and harassment

---

6   Refer to section 5 of the College of Mediators Code of Practice (included in Appendix 8).
7   Ibid.

Discrimination
Equal pay
Disability discrimination
Equality and diversity

People management
Discipline and grievance
Handling difficult conversations
Induction
Investigations
Managing change
Performance management
Skills for supervisors
Staff surveillance

Community mediator training[8]

The College of Mediators checklist of areas to be covered by approved community mediation courses includes:

■ Mediator self-awareness and development

■ Understanding the process and developing mediation skills

■ Various themes (eg confidentiality, discrimination, co-mediation)

■ Assessment through role play

The MQMS requires mediators to devise training plans (covering organisational, managerial and mediation competence as necessary) and to retain a record of training attended.[9]

Academic qualifications

12.5   Some tertiary institutions now provide academic qualifications in mediation and other dispute-resolution subjects. These comprise mainly diplomas, offered at a postgraduate level of study, and masters degrees with mediation and dispute resolution as substantial components. With respect to undergraduate degrees, negotiation, mediation and ADR tend to be electives or a component of other subjects.

Accreditation

12.6   'Accreditation' refers to the formal recognition of a mediator's qualifications and experience as a basis for the entitlement to practise. Accreditation is generally not necessary for mediation practice and untrained or unqualified individuals can hang out their shingles in the hope of attracting clients. However, many courts,

---

8   Refer to section 5 of the College of Mediators Code of Practice (included in Appendix 8).
9   Requirements D2.3 and D2.4 MQMS. The MQMS is included in Appendix 8.

government departments, community organisations and private service providers have systems of 'accreditation' or other recognition in place, with differing requirements for intending practitioners.

For example:

- The CMC (Civil Mediation Council) provides standards for ADR service providers, and has proposed to introduce standards for individual mediators.[10]

- Family mediaton providers are approved by the Family Mediation Council.

- Mediators who wish to mediate publicly funded cases are required to produce an LSC (Legal Services Commission) practice portfolio, which can lead to a nationally recognised qualification. Mediation services that are contracted with the LSC must comply with the Mediation Quality Mark developed by the LSC,[11] which sets a standard for issues such as providing clear information to clients, mediator accreditation,[12] professional practice supervision and suitable premises.[13]

- The Law Society of England and Wales has developed criteria for accreditation of solicitor mediators and membership on its Family and Civil/Commercial Mediation Panels.[14]

- The College of Mediators has requirements for professional membership,[15] professional practice consultancy (PPC)[16] and CPD[17] of family, workplace and community mediators. The College was initially set up to educate the public about family mediation; to maintain high standards of conduct, training and practice; and to provide details of registered mediators.

Many mediation service providers also have their own 'accreditation' systems. For example, in relation to commercial mediators:

- CEDR requires assessment via simulated mediations and various written assessment for its accreditation. Accreditation provides membership to CEDR Exchange (a network for the development of knowledge and skills), Peer Practice sessions (an opportunity to practise new techniques) and various CPD programmes.

---

10 These draft standards are included in Appendix 8 – the CMC's AGM in 2009 resolved to conduct further consultation on the draft.
11 Refer to Appendix 3 to the MQMS which contains the Quality Mark Agreement.
12 Refer to Requirement D5.1 MQMS.
13 MQMS had its first revision (since the Standard was introduced in 2002) in 2009 and is included in Appendix 8. For further information on publicly funded mediation and mediation services, refer to the LSC website, www.legalservices.gov.uk/civil/family/mediation.
14 From 1 July 2009, the Law Society took over from the SRA responsibility for the Family and Civil/Commercial Mediation Accreditation Schemes and Panels. Appendix 8 contains the Criteria for membership on the Civil/Commercial Panel, which includes, for General Membership, mediation training (a minimum of 24 hours over three days), mediation practice (a minimum of four mediations), written summaries of mediations, self-reflection summaries, CPD (a minimum of 16 hours) and mediation education/promotion (a maximum of 12 hours).
15 Section 5.2 College of Mediators Code of Practice.
16 Section 5.3 College of Mediators Code of Practice. Refer to Appendix 1 of the Code for a summary of the PPC requirements for family, workplace and community mediators. In summary, the requirements are for a minimum of two hours one-to-one PPC in the year to application. The College publishes a PPC Requirements Policy (reproduced in Appendix 7).
17 Section 5.4 College of Mediators Code of Practice. Refer to Appendix 1 of the Code for the CPD requirements for family, workplace and community mediators. In summary, the requirements are for at least ten CPD points in the year to application.

- ADR Group requires assessment via simulated mediations and a Module which focuses on practice issues. Once accredited, mediators can join ADR Net and participate in CPD programmes.

- CIArb have a two-day accreditation module, after which successful candidates become CIArb accredited mediators and are eligible to apply to be a Member of the CIArb.

12.7   Refer to Appendix 8 for sample training and accreditation schemes in England.

Developing experience

12.8   A major challenge for prospective mediators is obtaining practical experience, either after education and training or concurrently with it. Training, qualifications and 'accreditation' do not in themselves guarantee practical experience. They are necessary but not sufficient conditions for starting a practice. The difficulty is caused by the limited societal demand for mediator services, the restricted number of programmes that provide opportunities for experience, and the large number of prospective mediators in search of mediating practice.

Experience as a volunteer

12.9   In most countries there is a queue of beginner mediators wishing to undertake unpaid work in voluntary mediation services provided by government funded and community organisations or programmes. Some professional associations also have pro bono mediation schemes for those wishing to develop experience as a volunteer mediator.

Experience in community-type services

12.10   There is some assurance of developing experience in community mediation programmes.

Experience through pupillage, assistantships and co-mediation

12.11   Another way of developing experience is as a pupil or assisant to another mediator, a kind of apprenticeship, or mentoring, arrangement. This is easier to achieve through organised programmes than through approaches to private mediators.

Co-mediation is typically undertaken by experienced mediators and differs from acting as pupil or assistant mediator. Co-mediation is discussed in further detail in Chapter 9.

Experience through observation and simulation

12.12   Some mediators may, subject to the parties' consent, permit you to observe them in practice and while this is not a substitute for direct experience it does provide greater familiarity with the process, skills and techniques you will be using. Experience in simulated mediations is also useful, provided that volunteers can be found to role-play the clients, but there are the shortcomings inevitable in the fact that it is not the 'real thing'.

Experience through panels

12.13 Mediators can also apply for appointment to mediator panels (which tend to operate as part of court-annexed mediation schemes in England). While panels have differing criteria for appointment, all require some form of skills training and other experience. Membership of these panels normally leads to at least some mediation experience, though actual referrals may be limited and sporadic.

Reflective practice

12.14 Where beginner mediators are able to gain practical experience, they are advised to follow the principles of reflective practice in order to develop their skills and expertise. This involves learning from experience through self-debriefing, mutual debriefing with a co-mediator[18] or another mediator, performance appraisals[19] or supervisory debriefing with an experienced external mediator.[20] Other ways of developing the benefits of reflective practice are to undertake follow-up surveys of those who have attended the mediation, including both clients and professional advisers.[21] These 'audit' activities provide both an 'objective' appraisal of what mediators are doing well and what they could be doing differently, as well as subjective evaluations of effectiveness from clients and their advisers.[22] In all cases it is advisable to focus on qualitative as well as quantitative indicators of effectiveness.[23]

Kolb highlighted the need for debriefing and reflection in mediation practice at all levels of experience as a way of addressing the 'inordinately stressful' and 'emotionally draining' nature of what mediators do, and as a way of preventing high attrition rates and 'burnout'. The mediators interviewed by Kolb identified the need to be patient, to slow down and reflect, and highlighted the difficulties created by the ambiguities of the mediator role.[24]

---

18 The co-mediation model is evolving for workplace issues and allows for informal evaluation of the process, ongoing improvement of internal grievance processes and preserves confidentiality.

19 MQMS requires annual performance appraisals for all staff of LSC franchises: Requirement D2.2.

20 In family mediation, supervision (or professional practice consultancy, 'PPC') is recognised in the standards of the UK College of Family Mediators (2000a and 2003) and in the MQMS. Refer to Requirements for PPC published by the College of Mediators (see Appendix 7). Refer to MQMS Requirements D3.1 (the position of supervisor), D3.2 (supervision skills) and D4.1–4.3 (how supervision works). Many in-house mediators dealing with workplace issues will have a debrief with the 'mediation co-ordinator' or HR manager, whilst ensuring that confidentiality is strictly preserved.

21 Appendix 7 contains various debriefing forms for mediators and for the parties and their lawyers. Refer also to section 3.4 IMI Code (refer to Appendix 8) and IMI's Feedback Request Form.

22 Refer to Requirements G2.1 and G2.2 MQMS.

23 Refer to survey results of experienced mediators in Australia, outlining the most frequently used interventions, observations on behaviours which jam negotiations, helpful behaviour from advisers, and learning points from mediation practice: Dispute Resolution Centre, 'How mediators assess behaviours in mediation', in (2005) 7(8) *ADR Bulletin* 145.

24 Kolb, *When Talk Works: Profiles of Mediators*, Jossey-Bass, San Francisco, 1994.

Kolb's findings are similar to findings by the Accord Group in Australia, who surveyed their mediators and found, amongst many things, the degree of mental exhaustion amongst mediators arising from expectations that they will be counsellors, psychologists, referees, moderators, philanthropists and 'squabble stoppers'.[25] Forums for reflection, discussion and swapping 'war stories' were identified as being helpful to allay the difficulties being experienced by mediators.

A survey of experienced mediators by the Bond Dispute Resolution Centre in Australia also identified the breadth of learning that is possible from reflection. The results are included in Appendix 7.

Developing mediation experience informally

12.15 Where there are limited options for gaining experience in formal mediation, it is still possible to do so informally. In many situations outside formal mediations there will be opportunities to apply some of the process and many of the skills and techniques. Here are some of the many areas in which this is possible:

- chairing meetings of businesses and voluntary associations;
- holding planning meetings for partners and associates;
- conducting hearings in disciplinary tribunals;
- teaching in small group seminars;
- managing grievances in employment situations and complaints from customers;
- dealing with aggrieved shareholders or other passionate and committed people;
- dealing with crowds in emergency or crisis situations.

There are many other possibilities (like family meetings and parent–teacher interviews).

Networking

12.16 Prospective mediators can also develop their awareness and understanding of the process by engaging in networking activities. This could involve joining mediation associations, attending and speaking at dispute-resolution conferences, joining mediation interest groups or reading groups, making contacts on the internet, developing a web page, writing for the local press, and speaking to voluntary associations and service organisations. Some of these activities overlap with the marketing initiatives, referred to later in this chapter, which mediators are advised to undertake.

---

25 B. Keys, 'No Mediator is an Island: a Mediator Supports others, but who Supports the Mediator?' in (2006) 8(10) *ADR Bulletin* 204.

C. Infrastructure and resources

12.17 At the same time that prospective mediators are developing their credentials, they need to develop, obtain or acquire access to resources, as summarised below.

Premises and equipment

12.18 While King Arthur (if he existed) did not attend a mediation workshop, his round table (if that existed) was inspired by the principles of equality and proximity for all knights, including himself. This precedent can be followed by modern mediators of more modest title. They require access to a meeting room to house the round or other-shaped mediation table, and to one or more additional rooms for the separate sessions.[26] Other appropriate amenities include whiteboards or flipcharts, communication facilities, refreshments and comfort stations, and the other necessities of modern life. While it is expensive to have dedicated premises, mediators can explore various hired premises that have the appropriate facilities. Meeting rooms at law firms, client premises, hotels and conference venues are also possibilities.

Business planning and resource development

12.19 As with any other business endeavour, a business plan is a useful starting point for mediators. The plan can usefully cover:[27]

- areas of qualification, expertise and speciality;

- detail of services to be provided;

- how these services will be provided (and what will be needed for delivery of the services, in terms of premises, IT, insurance, resources etc);

- target 'client' groups and subject matter areas;

- finance plan/budgeting issues;

- SWOT (strengths, weaknesses, opportunities and threats).

12.20 Mediators also need to develop their own resources, or at least have access to relevant resources.[28] Many of these have been alluded to in the discussion of the mediation process and the mediator's functions in earlier parts of the book. Thus they require information brochures on mediation, standard form letters, videos, CD-ROMs and DVDs which demonstrate the process in action and access to some of the documentation referred to in the following paragraph. They should also maintain a file of references from satisfied clients, and results of client satisfaction surveys, for marketing purposes and for responding to prospective clients.

---

26 Refer to requirement C4 MQMS.
27 A business plan covering these matters is required by the MQMS: refer to Requirement A1.1. The business plan is reviewed at least every six months: Requirement A1.2 MQMS.
28 See Requirements D4.4 and D4.5 MQMS.

Some mediators develop 'client libraries' as resources for mediating parties. These should preferably be housed in dedicated rooms and provide brochures, books, videos, audio tapes, CD-ROMs, DVDs and related resources through which clients can inform and educate themselves about mediation. Essentially the client library is an educational centre and it also serves as a marketing tool for prospective clients.[29]

The National Mediation Helpline provides information, resources and advice on mediation in the UK. The Service was launched by the DCA (Department for Constitutional Affairs) in conjunction with the CMC (Civil Mediation Council).[30]

Appendix 10 contains a list of useful mediation books, other resources, videos, DVDs and podcasts.

Standard documentation

12.21 Prospective mediators require a range of standard documentation. This includes:

- Factsheets or brochures with information on the nature and benefits of mediation, for dispatch to those inquiring about mediation services: see Appendix 2.

- A standard agreement to mediate: see Appendix 3.

- Rules for the procedure or conduct of mediation: see Appendix 3.

- Protocols of behaviour for lawyers and other professional advisers: see Appendix 2.

- Confidentiality undertakings for witnesses and others who have not signed the agreement to mediate: see Appendix 3.

- Standardised settlement agreements in electronic form on laptop computers which can be adapted and individualised for specific mediated settlements: see Appendix 4.

The brochures or information sheets can be sent to those individuals and institutions which might make referrals to mediation, with the intention that they be kept on file or displayed in reception rooms. The other forms of documentation can be retained by the mediator for use when needed.

Referral network

12.22 At times mediators will regard it as necessary, or will feel obliged, to make referrals of their own clients to lawyers, counsellors or other skilled helpers and a referral network should be developed for this purpose. Likewise a list of government departments, such as legal services commissions, child support agencies and welfare bodies, is also useful to have at hand for those clients with needs for their respective services. It may also be necessary to refer a matter to a public sector mediation service, such as a LSC franchise, for reasons of cost or required expertise.

---

29   See Mosten, *The Complete Guide to Mediation*, 1997, 79–80.
30   See www.nationalmediationhelpline.com.

Needless to say, referral networks can operate reciprocally and those to whom mediators make referrals may become sources of referrals as well.[31]

Appendix 11 contains a list of mediation organisations in the UK, across Europe and internationally.

Business entity

12.23   Many mediators practise through the same business entity which provides their other professional services, such as a law partnership or accountancy firm. Mediators also operate out of barristers' chambers. They could also practise as sole traders or in partnerships with other mediators, and as corporate structures. The MQMS prescribes the organisational structure for LSC franchises, including requirements relating to staff structure,[32] key roles,[33] management committees[34] and membership of relevant bodies.[35]

D.   Marketing mediation

12.24   Marketing involves the education of the public and potential consumers as to the nature and form of mediation with a view to increasing demand for the service. There is already some generic marketing of mediation by governments, courts and agencies which portray it to the public as a credible and attractive form of dispute resolution.[36] This generic publicity provides a foundation for the marketing of specific mediation services.

Life cycles

12.25   Tom Altobelli, refers to the following four stages in the mediation product life cycle:[37]

- Stage 1 – Introduction
- Stage 2 – Growth
- Stage 3 – Maturity
- Stage 4 – Decline

In terms of these categories, mediation in the UK has entered a growth stage. Altobelli refers to a different product life cycle from a mediation *consumer's* perspective:

---

31   See 12.44–12.49.
32   Requirement C1.1 MQMS.
33   Requirement C1.2 MQMS.
34   Requirement C1.3 MQMS.
35   Requirement C1.4 MQMS.
36   Article 9 of the EU Mediation Directive (included in Appendix 13) encourages Member States to provide to the public, by any means which they consider appropriate, and in particular on the Internet, information on how to contact mediators and organisations providing mediation services.
37   Tom Altobelli, 'Are you Getting Enough? Marketing Mediation' (1999) 1(9) *ADR Bulletin* 113.

- Stage 1 – Awareness
- Stage 2 – Interest
- Stage 3 – Evaluation
- Stage 4 – Trial
- Stage 5 – Adoption

Potential mediation consumers in the UK are moving into the awareness and interest stages. Altobelli advocates 'educating the consumer' as the basis of any mediation marketing plan.

Mediation as a product

12.26 How mediation is classified as a product has a bearing on the appropriateness of marketing strategies. The system is a *service* as opposed to *goods*, in the sense that it is intangible and cannot be owned and transferred. This creates different market realities for mediation in comparison with tangible goods such as cars, cat food or widgets. The differences are depicted in the following table by Zeithaml and Bitner:[38]

Goods such as widgets	Services such as mediation	Resulting implications for services
Tangible	Intangible	Services cannot be inventoried.
		Services cannot be patented.
		Services cannot be readily displayed or communicated.
		Pricing is difficult.
Standardised	Heterogeneous	Service delivery and customer satisfaction depend on employee actions.
		Service quality depends on many uncontrollable factors.
		No sure knowledge that the service delivered matches what was planned and promoted.
Production separate from consumption	Simultaneous production and consumption	Customers participate in and affect the transaction.
		Customers affect each other.
		Employees affect the service outcome.
		Decentralisation may be essential.
		Mass production is difficult.
Non-perishable	Perishable	It is difficult to synchronise supply and demand with services.
		Services cannot be returned or resold.

---

38 *Services Marketing*, 1996, 19.

From this table we note that mediation is a perishable product, such as advocacy and electricity, which cannot be stored for use when demand increases, and no two mediators offer identical services, given the significance of the identity, personality and style of each mediator in the delivery of mediation services.

12.27 These features of services have implications for mediation marketing. Consistency of service quality is a problem for all private mediators in that the horror stories about Mediator X (the other guy) could have market repercussions for Mediator Y (me). Likewise it is not easy to achieve significant economies of scale through centralisation, as it is with goods such shoes or food, which means that mediation has to be marketed on a relatively decentralised basis.

As Seawright points out, however, ideas and concepts can be and are regularly marketed, as is done by political parties and public interest groups such as the anti-smoking lobby.[39] The same can be done with mediation.

The marketing mix for mediation

12.28 The concept of marketing is understood here as comprising 'individual and organisational activities that facilitate and expedite satisfying exchange relationships in a dynamic environment through the creation, distribution, promotion and pricing of goods, services and ideas'.[40] In the 1960s McCarthy developed the concept of the 'marketing mix' as the essence of successful marketing and this is still a basic marketing concept. It is popularised in terms of the 'four Ps', namely product, price, promotion and place (or distribution).

12.29 *Product* refers to the service which mediators provide, that is, how they respond and provide solutions to clients' needs. In relation to the resolution of disputes, the product of mediation has unique claims in relation to client involvement, creative outcomes, cost and time effectiveness, and its other well-known attributes. While mediators provide an intangible service, the product can be referred to tangibly in terms of the value that they can add. The product needs to be identified in terms of its distinctive characteristics, and to be distinguished from its competitor services such as litigation, arbitration, counselling or self-help.

12.30 *Price* places a figure on the value which mediators add. The factors which go into pricing include the cost of production and the value which the client is prepared to pay for the service. Discount pricing may be used to stimulate short-term referrals but cannot be a long-term proposition; most mediators in private practice are there to earn a living and not to provide subsidised charity. Remuneration is normally based on an hourly fee for preparation and mediation time and reasonable expenses incurred, with some provision for sliding scales to take into account clients' abilities, or lack thereof, to pay. Market mechanisms tend to sort out pricing structures for private mediators, though full-time mediators attached to courts and agencies are salaried employees whose remuneration is less directly related to the market. Most private mediators charge as much as the market will bear. In England, they earn between £50 an hour (in the case of certain time-limited mediation schemes) and £5,000 a day or more (in the case of commercial mediations). In most cases the parties share the costs of mediation equally. Excess

---

39   *Marketing of Mediation as a New Professional Service,* 1997.
40   Pride and Ferell, *Marketing Concepts and Strategies,* 8th ed, 1993, 4.

supply of mediation services over demand can put downward pressure on the fees that private mediators can charge.

12.31 *Promotion* consists of personal marketing, publicity and advertising. Where the product has unique qualities it does its own promotion. Mediators gain publicity through involvement in conferences, professional seminars, presentations to community groups, media exposure and educational activities. Brochures can be cost-effective, though less immediate and 'credible' than other forms of advertising. Some mediators appear on lists held at courts, on mediator panel lists, or in directories.[41] Modern forms of technology such as the internet and web pages are used by service providers and, increasingly, individual mediators.

12.32 *Place* refers to distribution, which in the case of a service such as mediation highlights the factor of accessibility, rather than physical location. While many professions have traditionally sat behind half-closed doors waiting for clients to arrive, this is now changing and we are entering an age where professionals are going to their clients. As Folberg and Taylor point out, mediation does not require a special setting, so the 'Have Process, Will Travel' philosophy can apply.[42] Mobile phones, laptop computers and e-mail facilities render physical location less important than it would otherwise be and mediators can conduct business from any manner of premises. Crisis intervention mediation, in particular, will require the process to be conducted on the factory floor, the airport control room, or other relevant venue.

12.33 In marketing terms what is required is a *matching* process, that is, a strategic and managerial process of ensuring that the marketing mix is appropriate for the circumstances. This leads to consideration of other relevant marketing factors.

Other marketing factors

Market forces

12.34 Important considerations in any mediation marketing are the external market forces which provide both opportunities and threats for private providers. Market forces comprise factors such as the relevant regulatory framework, economic realities, the extent of competition and substitute products, the trends and activities in rival professions and services, and consumer loyalty. Apart from family and LSC-franchised mediation, there is relatively little direct regulation of mediators in England, although there is some indirect regulation through their other professional associations, for example, the Law Society. This lack of regulation entails that 'rival' professions can move into the mediation market with institutional backing and the support of their professional associations. Mediation is coming into the marketplace during a time of considerable flux in the traditional professions, involving harsh competition, blurring of professional boundaries and consumer activism. This creates more demanding market forces than in earlier and gentler times.

---

41 Mediators who are members of the Law Society's Family or Civil/Commercial Mediator Panel can use a Panel logo (refer to the Law Society's website for information regarding its Panels and the restrictions regarding use of Panel logos) and LSC franchises can use an LSC Quality Mark logo (refer to Appendix 2 to the MQMS for logo guidance).

42 Folberg and Taylor, *Mediation: A Comprehensive Guide to Resolving Conflicts without Litigation*, 1984, 296.

Market segmentation

12.35   This refers to the process of dividing the market into segments according to similarity of needs. The characteristics of individuals and organisations in the various groups give them relatively similar product needs. As Seawright points out, the market for mediation could initially be divided into two broad areas: the dispute resolution area, on one hand, and the broader conflict management area, on the other.[43] The needs of potential consumers will be different in these two areas. Further segmentation of the dispute resolution area can occur in terms of substantive areas of dispute, such as industrial, personal injuries, building and international matters. Another important form of segmentation is between the repeat users of mediation services, such as governments, insurers and large corporations, and those who might use it only once in a lifetime, such as one-off claimants. The purpose of market segmentation is to identify segments in which the individual mediator might have a competitive edge and to allow them to focus their marketing in those areas.

Market specialisation

12.36   Mediation lends itself to considerable specialisation, for example, in complaints handling, workplace disputes, family law matters, or environmental and planning disputes. In some countries there are mediators who specialise in only disputes within churches; all faiths, denominations and believers are accepted, provided they have a mediatable dispute. Emerging technologies in the information technology field attract specialist mediators. Mediators can market themselves as generalists, for example, Independent Mediation Services Pty Ltd, or as specialising in certain kinds of disputes, for example, XYZ Employment Mediation Service. Despite its relative newness as an occupation, mediation does not easily accommodate the generalist mediator – the specialisation of the age affects this service as well.

Managing impressions

12.37   As King indicates, marketing is not simply selling or advertising, though these are important tools of marketing.[44] It is more a process of managing impressions, that is, creating the image of a service and a service provider which will satisfy client needs in a particular area. Technical excellence alone will not develop mediation practice unless in the minds of the clients there is good service in matters such as communication, responsiveness, turnaround time, and the like. Needless to say, the gap between impressions and reality cannot be too large – at least not in the long term.

Individual marketing responsibility

12.38   While individual private mediators will derive some benefit from the 'generic' promotion of mediation and the activities of high-profile mediators, much of the responsibility for marketing will fall on their own shoulders. They will have to

---

43   *Marketing of Mediation as a New Professional Service*, 1997, 19.
44   *Professional Practice Management*, 1995, 298.

undertake extensive marketing and promotion of their services in order to develop a reasonable practice. Some of the marketing can be aimed at potential users of mediation services, and some at those who might make referrals to mediation, such as lawyers, social workers, government agencies, courts and the police.

12.39 Private mediators will need to make marketing decisions about three factors, namely *concept, model* and *brand*. As regards concept, Bush and Folger identify four main accounts of the mediation movement:[45]

- the *satisfaction* story, focusing on interests, mutual problem solving and self-determination for the parties;

- the *social justice* story, focusing on means of organising individuals around common interests and building stronger community ties and structure;

- the *transformation* story, focusing on mediation's capacity to transform the character of individual disputants and society as a whole; and

- the *oppression* story, focusing on the production of outcomes that are unjust or unfair or unreasonable for weaker parties, or for parties not present in the mediation.

12.40 In the context of private mediation practice, the prevailing concept being marketed is the *satisfaction* story, where satisfaction is measured in terms of cost, time, effectiveness, privacy and other attractive features of the process. Which of these features will be the most attractive, or more attractive than the others, will vary considerably. In some situations private mediation may be competing with a free or subsidised dispute-resolution service provided publicly by tribunals or government agencies, in which case the privacy of the process may be its attractive feature. In others, prospective clients might be more attracted by mediation's potential for preserving existing business relationships where there are no alternative commercial options available to them. Generally, however, individual satisfaction is the prevailing *concept* in the current promotion of mediation (and in this book).

12.41 As regards the *model,* reference was made in Chapter 1 to the *settlement,* the *facilitative,* the *therapeutic* and the *evaluative* models of mediation. These terms mean little to an uninformed public, and only a little more to informed consumers, but over time it will be important to move away from the notion that there is only a single model of mediation service. Repeat consumers, and their discerning advisers, will come to differentiate among the models and to be selective about their choices. There is anecdotal evidence that they are already doing that. Just as patients needing health assistance seek out specific forms of intervention, such as surgery, homeopathy, reflexology or vegetarianism, and then more specific forms within these categories, so this trend will emerge even within the formerly narrow confines of mediation.

12.42 Then there is the question of *brand*. While there are some attempts to provide uniformity in the context of government funded services, with one 'brand' of mediation, this is not the case in private practice where the service is closely identified with the provider. This has always been a feature of professional services, despite some contemporary pressures towards standardisation. As Mosten points

---

45 Bush and Folger, *The Promise of Mediation: Responding to Conflict through Empowerment and Recognition,* 1994, 20.

out,[46] as consumers are increasing their comparison shopping (tyre kicking) it is important for mediators in general civil and commercial cases to advertise their individual styles (brands) of mediation to prospective clients and referral sources. As mediation normally has so direct a human interface, much of the brand aspect has to do with the mediator's personality, interpersonal skills, professional background and life experience. There is again only anecdotal evidence of consumer preferences here, but it would appear that the demand in private practice is for 'A' the mediator, and not for a mediator who happens to be called 'A'.

12.43 Thus *concept*, *model* and *brand* are all of relevance when it comes to the marketing of private mediation services. While individual mediators are potential beneficiaries of the generic marketing of the *concept* of mediation, they will have to market specific *models* and their own *brands* of the service.

E. Securing referrals

12.44 A sign of marketing effectiveness will be the development of mediation referrals from regular sources, and a network of referral sources will provide an opportunity for further marketing. Referrals are the lifeblood of a mediation practice, but developing referral networks is not easy. The traditional professions, government agencies, and other potential sources of referrals need not only to be targeted, but also to be educated about mediation and its advantages for clients, and its benefits for referrers.

Self-referrals

12.45 Self-referral refers to prospective clients of mediation bringing their dispute directly to a mediator. There is unlikely to be much scope for self-referrals to private mediation in the near future, partly for reasons of the 'reluctant user' syndrome and partly because of the fact that it takes 'two to tango' in getting to the mediation table – you cannot come to the negotiation dance without the other side agreeing to be your partner. However, some self-referrals may come from mediation clients satisfied with prior services, from existing clients who have used the mediator in other professional capacities, and as a result of word-of-mouth references. Direct self-referrals can also be encouraged through advertising.

Referral networks

12.46 Mediators in private practice need to develop existing networks and create new ones. Despite their ubiquitous modesty, mediators are in a sense the specialists and not the general practitioners of dispute resolution practice. Little work will come directly off the street. Potential mediation clients will usually make primary contact with counsellors, lawyers, medical professionals, accountants, Citizens Advice Bureaux, welfare services, other government departments and other institutions. These are the generalists in dispute resolution and they all need to be educated about the appropriateness of mediation as a 'specialist' referral option.

---

46   *The Complete Guide to Mediation*, 1997, p 348.

They are the groups to which mediators should direct some of their marketing. But whatever the level of understanding, referrals in this area are likely to be no different to referrals in other services where they are based on personal knowledge of the practitioner, previous experience, or high reputation. Printed brochures and long lunches are a poor substitute for these attributes. Reciprocal referrals among practitioners are a possibility with all professional services, but they require more organisation in the case of mediation because of its dependence on two consenting clients.

Structured sources of referral

12.47   Structured referrals are the ideal arrangement, but it is not easy for private service providers to have structured referrals from public departments or other such sources. Examples include the structured referral of mediations from enquiries made to the National Mediation Helpline and referrals in accordance with the MQMS.[47]

Ease of referrals

12.48   Folberg and Taylor suggest that, after educating clients, ease of referrals is one of the most significant factors in attracting mediation work.[48] By this they mean the ability of interested parties to contact the mediator and the mediator's ability to deal with queries and follow-ups. This requires mediator accessibility by phone, e-mail and letter, and prompt responses to inquiries. Having the standard information sheets and other documentation at hand, and placing relevant information in the prospective referrers' offices, are important factors in facilitating the ease of referrals.[49]

A warning on referrals (the 'dumping phenomenon')

12.49   There is an ancient tradition among professionals to refer their failures or hopeless cases to other professionals or to other disciplines. Mediation is at times a target for this dumping phenomenon. A danger signal is when a referring lawyer says to the mediator, 'Do I have an interesting case for you?' While mediators can have their own screening mechanisms to assess suitability for mediation,[50] it also makes sense to secure some preliminary screening from referrers. Such referrers may require some education and training so that they can conduct this screening themselves. For mediators this may be a worthwhile long-term investment in avoiding the dumping phenomenon.

---

47   Refer to Requirement B1.2 MQMS on referrals and to Requirement B1.3 MQMS on referrals record keeping.
48   Folberg and Taylor, *Mediation: A Comprehensive Guide to Resolving Conflicts without Litigation*, 1988, 307.
49   See 12.21.
50   See 2.10–2.14.

F. Standards and ethics

Codes of conduct

12.50 Some mediators are subject to codes of conduct, standards of competence or ethical guidelines, or all of these. These normally operate in respect of those mediators who work for family, workplace or community mediation services, tribunals and government departments, or who are subject to statutory or other regulation (as in the case of LSC mediation franchises) or who are members of professional associations which have standards for their members when they are practising as mediators (as with the Law Society). These also apply to mediators who are put forward by private mediation services providers (like CEDR, ADR Group, CIArb and CORE Solutions Group). Other mediators are not subject to any of these formal requirements. There is thus an array of different standards and ethical regimes.

The EU Mediation Directive encourages Member States to develop codes of conduct for mediators and mediation service providers, as well as other quality-control mechanisms.[51] An attempt to set an international standard is being undertaken by IMI, the International Mediation Institute.[52] The CMC, the Civil Mediation Council, has set English standards for mediation services providers[53] and has recently proposed a draft code of conduct for individual mediators. The Law Society of England and Wales has designed standard documentation for solicitors when they act as mediators. The UK College of Family Mediators sets and monitors standards of training and practice for family mediators. It is a national membership body which solely fulfils a regulatory function. The LSC's Mediation Quality Mark (MQMS) was developed in 2002 and revised in 2009. Mediators who do publicly funded mediation have to comply with the MQMS.[54] Appendix 8 contains a selection of codes of conduct and standards for mediators.

Complaints

12.51 Most mediation service providers provide a mechanism in case there are complaints against their mediators.[55] The Law Society provides a mechanism for complaints against mediators on the Society's Mediation Panels. The CMC provides members of the CMC with access to a complaints-resolution service whereby either a member, or a client of a member, who has exhausted the member's own complaints process, can refer the matter to the CMC for resolution (through mediation).[56] The IMI has a Professional Conduct Assessment Procedure.[57] The MQMS requires a complaints procedure compliant with the Family Mediation

---

51 Article 4 (the Directive is included in Appendix 13).
52 See its website, www.imimediation.org.
53 See its website, www.civilmediation.org.
54 For example, to have arrangements for ensuring voluntary participation in mediation; to identify violence, abuse or harm to children; and to provide information about the availability of independent legal advice.
55 See, for example, section 8 of the CEDR Code of Conduct for Mediators (which is included in Appendix 8); section 10 of the CEDR Model Mediation Procedure (10th ed) (which is included in Appendix 3); and the CEDR Complaints Procedure (which is in Appendix 9).
56 See its website, www.civilmediation.org, section on Members' Complaints Resolution Service.
57 Refer to section 5 IMI Code (included in Appendix 8).

Council's Code of Conduct.[58] Appendix 9 includes a selection of complaints-handling schemes.[59]

Content of codes of conduct

12.52 In relation to the functions and competencies of mediators, codes tend to refer to:

- the mediator's role in conducting and managing the process;[60]

- the mediator's role in gathering and using information;[61]

- the mediator's role in defining the dispute;[62]

- the mediator's functions in assisting the parties to communicate and negotiate, via the opening statements, by identifying options and encouraging problem-solving;[63]

- the mediator's role in providing information to the parties;[64]

- the decision-making role of the mediator, where this is relevant;[65]

- the mediator's functions in relation to the termination or concluding of the mediation;[66]

- various limitations on the mediator's ability to express opinions, advise, recommend or otherwise influence outcomes.[67]

12.53 In relation to ethical standards and requirements, codes tend to refer to:

- the mediator's obligation to be available and competent;[68]

- the mediator's obligation to be neutral and independent;[69]

---

58 Requirements G1.1. and G1.2 MQMS (included in Appendix 8).
59 Including CMC, CEDR, CORE Solutions Group, NMI, IMI and College of Mediators.
60 For example, section 3.1 IMI Code, Article 3.1 EU Code, section 4 Law Society Code of Practice for Civil/Commercial Mediation, section 4 Law Society Code of Practice for Family Mediation, section 5 CEDR Code and section 4 CORE Solutions Group Code (these documents are included in Appendix 8).
61 For example, section 6.3 College of Mediators Code of Practice (which is included in Appendix 8). Refer also to Element 2 (Stage 6) of the Competencies for Civil/Commercial Mediation which is Annex A to the Law Society's Accreditation for Civil/Commercial Mediation (which is also included in Appendix 8).
62 For example, section 4.2 Law Society Code of Practice for Family Mediation (which is in Appendix 8).
63 For example, refer to Element 2 (Stage 7) of the Competencies for Civil/Commercial Mediation which is Annex A to the Law Society's Accreditation for Civil/Commercial Mediation (which is included in Appendix 8).
64 For example, sections 5.7 and 5.8 Law Society Code of Practice for Family Mediation, sections 6.4/6.6–6.7 and 6.9 College of Mediators Code of Practice, and Requirement F5.3 MQMS. These documents are included in Appendix 8.
65 For example, section 4.9 CORE Solutions Group Code (included in Appendix 8).
66 For example, section 7.2 CEDR Code and section 5 CORE Solutions Group Code (which are included in Appendix 8). Refer also to Element 3 (Stage 9) of the Competencies for Civil/Commercial Mediation which is Annex A to the Law Society's Accreditation for Civil/Commercial Mediation (which is also included in Appendix 8).
67 For example, section 5 Law Society Code of Practice for Civil/Commercial Mediation and Section 5.5 Law Society Code of Practice for Family Mediation (refer to Appendix 8).
68 For example, Article 1.1 EU Code of Conduct, section 2.1 CEDR Code, sections 2.1–2.2 CORE Solutions Group Code and section 2.1 IMI Code (refer to Appendix 8). Refer also to Article 7.1 UNCITRAL Conciliation Rules (in Appendix 3).
69 For example, section 2.2 IMI Code, section 3 Law Society Code of Practice for Civil/Commercial Mediation and section 4.2 College of Mediators Code of Practice (refer to Appendix 8).

- the obligation to disclose (throughout the mediation) any factors which might create a conflict of interest;[70]

- the requirement to act fairly and impartially as between the parties;[71]

- the duty to ensure effective participation by the parties;[72]

- the requirement not to disclose, either within or outside the mediation, any information provided to the mediator in confidence;[73]

- to duty to disclose information as required by law, order of a court, or as provided by the terms of the agreement to mediate;[74]

- the avoidance of coercion, undue influence or the provision of legal advice in order to induce a settlement;[75]

- various obligations relating to the disclosure and payment of fees;[76]

- the mediator's obligation to promote and advertise mediation services accurately and informatively;[77]

- non-discrimination in the provision of services;[78]

- record keeping;[79]

- where relevant, making parties aware of the need for independent legal advice.[80]

---

70 For example, Requirements E1.2 and E1.4 MQMS, section 2.3 IMI Code, Articles 2.1 and 3.2 EU Code, sections 4.1/4.3–4.4 CEDR Code, section 3 CORE Solutions Group Code, section 3 Law Society Code of Practice for Civil/Commercial Mediation, section 3.3 Law Society Code of Practice for Family Mediation and section 4.4 College of Mediators Code of Practice (refer to Appendix 8). See also Article 7.2 UNCITRAL Conciliation Rules (included in Appendix 3).
71 For example, section 2.2 IMI Code, Article 2.2 EU Code, section 4.1 CEDR Code, section 3 Law Society Code of Practice for Family Mediation and section 4.3 College of Mediators Code of Practice (refer to Appendix 8).
72 For example, Articles 3.1–3.2 EU Code, section 4.8 College of Mediators Code of Practice and section 6 Law Society Code of Practice for Family Mediation (refer to Appendix 8).
73 For example, Article 4 EU Code and Requirement F6.1 MQMS (included in Appendix 8).
74 For example, Requirement F6.1 MQMS, section 4 IMI Code, section 6 CORE Solutions Group Code, section 7 Law Society Code of Practice for Civil/Commercial Mediation, section 7 Law Society Code of Practice for Family Mediation and sections 4.5 and 6.5 College of Mediators Code of Practice. Refer to Appendix 8 for these documents.
75 For example, clause 3.2 ADR Group Mediation Procedure and Rules (included in Appendix 3).
76 For example, Requirements F5.1–5.2 MQMS, Article 1.3 EU Code, section 3.1 CEDR Code, section 7 CORE Solutions Group Code and section 3.5 IMI Code (refer to Appendix 8).
77 For example, Requirement A2.1 MQMS, Article 1.4 EU Code, section 9 Law Society Code of Practice for Civil/Commercial Mediation, section 10 Law Society Code of Practice for Family Mediation and section 9 CORE Solutions Group Code (refer to Appendix 8). Refer also to Rule 7 Solicitors Code of Conduct. A2.1 MQMS requires franchised mediation practices to complete LSC's Directory questionnaire and to promote their services by other likely points of public contact, although leafleting and cold-calling the public are not encouraged.
78 For example, Requirements A3.1–3.2 MQMS (which is included in Appendix 8).
79 For example, Requirement E1.5 MQMS (included in Appendix 8) lists the minimum information that should be recorded on LSC franchise files during or after each mediation session:
    - who attended each session;
    - agreement of both parties to mediation and any appropriate ground rules;
    - information relevant to the mediation;
    - relevant issues and proposals of each party;
    - relevant options identified during the mediation session;
    - any action to be taken by either party or the mediator;
    - the outcome of the session and the issues for any further session.
80 For example, see Requirements F1.3 and F3.2 MQMS, sections 5.4/5.11–5.12 Law Society Code of Practice for Family Mediation and section 6.10 and 6.17 College of Mediators Code of Practice (refer to Appendix 8). See also, for example, clause 5.2 ADR Group Mediation Procedure and Rules (including in Appendix 3).

12.54 In many cases, though, tackling ethical issues will require considerable reflection, rather than 'looking up the answer' in a code of conduct. Ethical issues often require a balancing act between the provisions of mediation agreements and codes of conduct and self-determination. For example, the question of how evaluative a mediator should be arises often in the context of commercial mediation. Too little may disappoint the parties and their lawyers; and too much may result in overstepping the mark, by giving advice or annoying the parties and their advisers.

Where there are no applicable standards documents, mediators are still subject to legal redress in relation to negligence, breach of contract or breach of fiduciary duty, or to relevant legislation relating to deceptive and misleading conduct and other consumer remedies. These forms of liability are not easy to establish,[81] and the issue of laibility is briefly outlined below.

G. Other regulatory issues

This section is not intended to cover all the law, theory or policy applicable to competition and money laundering issues. It is intended to provide an overview of some of the practical issues arising in so far as these relate to the practice of mediation.

Competition law

12.55 A party entering into an agreement which offends the EU competition rules may face fines and the agreement by set aside. Alarm bells might start ringing for mediators if a proposed settlement:

- covers more than one EU Member State;
- the parties control a large share of a particular market;
- the agreement seeks to grant exclusive rights over an EU territory;
- the agreement contains a price-fixing mechanism; a commitment not to compete; restrictions on the amount of trade; or restrictions on the customer base that can be targeted.

In such cases, the mediator should raise concerns with the parties in private; encourage them to receive legal advice; and may also encourage a cooling-off period in any proposed settlement. Although the mediator cannot advise the parties on competition law issues, the mediator has some responsibility for ensuring the durability of the settlement reached in mediation. In addition, if a party is not legally represented, the mediator may run the risk that that party will accuse the mediator of having negligently allowed or encouraged the parties to enter into an unlawful agreement.

---

81   See Boulle and Nesic, *MPPP*, 2001, 512–523.

Money laundering

12.56   The Proceeds of Crime Act 2002 and the Money Laundering Regulations in England make it an offence to enter into, or become concerned in, an arrangement which the person concerned knows or suspects facilitates the acquisition, use, retention or control of criminal property.[82] In various circumstances, suspicions have to be reported to the authorities, and it is a separate offence to 'tip off' those involved.[83]

Mediators need to make sure that they know who the parties to the mediation are and that their identity has been established by those representing them. The mediator also needs to consider the underlying dispute to ensure that it is what it is represented to be, and not a sham. A mediator should not assume that the parties' lawyers will consider the money laundering implications of any proposed settlement.[84] Anyone involved in the making of an agreement that facilitates money laundering could become involved in an investigation or prosecution.[85]

Although these circumstances will be rare in mediation, a mediator should be familiar with the reporting obligations,[86] the duty not to tip off and the related provisions in most mediation agreements that allow the mediator to terminate the mediation.[87]

H.   Mediator liability

12.57   As mediators are normally signatories to the mediation agreement, they can be liable for breach of the agreement. A mediator could also face a negligence claim.[88] Professionals when acting as mediators remain liable for breaches of their own professional codes of conduct.

---

82   Refer to POCA 2002, ss 327–329.
83   There is a defence to money laundering offences if an 'authorised disclosure' is made under POCA 2002, s 338.
84   In relation to family mediation, refer to the College of Mediators Guidance 2006c.
85   *Bowman v Fels* [2005] EWCA Civ 226 excludes certain activities from the scope of the arrangements offence (POCA 2002, s 328). These include 'litigation from the issue of proceedings and the securing of injunctive relief or a freezing order up to its final disposal by judgement'. Law Society guidance considers that the exception extends to consensual resolution of issues in a litigious context and ADR, so that those involved in ADR are not involved in s 328 arrangements and do not need to make authorised disclosures (refer to Law Society, *Guidance on Money Laundering Issues*, 2006).
86   Even if ADR might fall outside the ambit of the POCA offences, the property itself remains 'criminal property' for the purpose of POCA 2002, s 340 and any dealings with it after any settlement may require reporting (refer to Law Society, *Guidance on Money Laundering Issues*, 2006).
87   For example, section 3.3 IMI Code, 4.5.4 College of Mediators Code of Practice, sections 7.1–7.2 CEDR Code and section 5 CORE Solutions Group Code (refer to Appendix 8). Refer also, for example, to section 9 CEDR Model Mediation Procedure and clause 9 ADR Group Mediation Procedure and Rules (included in Appendix 3).
88   Refer to the Australian case, *Tapoohi v Lewenberg and others* [2003] VSC 379 for an outline of the likely considerations where negligence is claimed against a mediator.

A mediator can reduce risks by not giving the parties legal advice (actually or inadvertently) and by not drafting the settlement agreement or heads of terms. Compliance with mediator standards, codes of conduct and the terms of the mediation agreement will also reduce the riks that the mediator's conduct might fall below the acceptable standard. Ultimately, in cases of negligence claims against mediators, proving causation and damage are difficult, as it would have to be established that it was the conduct of the mediator, and not the actions of the parties or their lawyers, that caused, or contributed, to the loss. A mediator can reduce the risks by ensuring that the partes are either legally represented at the mediation or have the chance to obtain inependent legal advice if legal representation is not available at the mediation.

12.58 Most mediation procedures and agreements contain mediator immunity clauses, which attempt to exclude the mediator's liability for negligence, breach of contract and other civil wrongs.[89] Such a clause would not operate against third parties who had not signed the mediation agreement. Exclusion clauses are construed narrowly and are open to attack, depending on the circumstances, under unfair contract terms legislation. Such clauses need to be drafted carefully and clearly to aim to cover the consequences of negligence.

Mediators will sometimes also add clauses into the settlement agreement as additional potential protection, for example:

- a clause that the parties accept that the mediator has no liability for accidental or uninentional advisory roles undertaken during the mediation;

- a clause confirming that the parties and their lawyers have read and signed the agreement and that each signatory has entered into it freely and without duress, having first consulted with their legal advisers;

- a clause that the signatories release the mediator from responsibility arising from the drafting of the settlement agreement.

In some cases, mediators will continue to help the parties to reach resolution after a failed mediation. In such cases, it is sensible to ensure that the mediation agreement makes it clear that the exclusion of liability clause will continue to apply to the mediator's later activities. If the mediator takes a different role after a failed mediation, as an arbitrator or case appraiser for example, a separate agreement that governs this process, with its own exclusion clause, should be entered into.

Mediators should hold insurance (see futher below) in case they are not protected by an exclusion clause in the mediation or settlement agreement.[90]

---

89 For example, clause 4 CEDR Model Mediation Agreement, clauses 31–32 Law Society sample Mediation Agreement and Article 7.5 ICC ADR Rules (refer to Appendix 3).
90 In the New Zealand case, *McCosh v Williams* [2003] NZCA 192, the Court of Appeal indicated that, had the mediator been negligent, he would not have been protected by the exclusion clause in the mediation agreement as he had taken himself outside the scope of the agreement by assisting the parties after a failed mediation by making a determination.

I. New frontiers – growth options for mediation services

12.59 All modern professions[91] are under pressure to develop new services, to provide more services to existing clients, and to provide existing and new services to new clients. Effective mediation marketing has the potential for attracting new clients, retaining existing and new clients, and persuading clients to use more of the particular service. It is sometimes overlooked that mediation has potential application in many situations, for example, in the negotiation of contracts, in drafting regulations and in dispute prevention. Some of the largest corporate mergers have been facilitated by a mediator and the scope for this form of *transactional mediation* is significant.

12.60 The following Ansof matrix suggests how new services or new opportunities could be considered in an overall marketing plan for mediation.[92]

	Existing products/services	New products/services
Existing markets	*Market penetration*	*Product/service development*
	Repeat business from first time clients	New products/services, such as med-arb, advisory mediation
	Increased frequency of mediation use by existing clients	New image for existing products, such as transformative potential of mediation
New markets	*Market development*	*Diversification*
	Industry groups requiring industry-wide dispute resolution schemes	Dispute system design for industries with no dispute resolution systems
	Segmented growth in areas of grievance-handling, complaints	Conflict-management services, including dispute prevention

J. Other practicalities of practice

Following up on referrers

12.61 It is good business sense for mediators to send notes of appreciation to those who have referred clients to them for mediation, advising that the mediation has been completed. Mediators can also make contact with the other, non-referring professionals whose clients were involved in the mediation as an indirect way of marketing their services for the future. These professionals can be informally surveyed about their clients' satisfaction levels.

---

91 For a discussion about whether mediation is a profession, and the criteria for a profession, refer to D. Ardagh, 'Is Mediation now a Profession?' in (2009) 10(8) *ADR Bulletin* 167.
92 See Seawright, *Marketing of Mediation as a New Professional Service*, 1997, 22.

Performance review

12.62 In relation to practices complying with the MQMS, the Standards (included in Appendix 8) provide a structure for review, including:

- client feedback;[93]
- file reviews;[94]
- individual performance review and feedback;[95]
- review of the service;[96]
- capacity review;[97]
- financial review;[98]
- overall quality review;[99]
- complaints procedure.[100]

In all other cases, client surveys have been referred to earlier as an aspect of reflective practice. Individual surveys provide feedback on specific cases, and collectively surveys can provide statistically significant indicators of various aspects of client attitudes and mediator performance. Longitudinal surveys can trace subsequent attitudes of clients, as well as the longer term viability of mediated agreements.

For sample survey forms, refer to Appendix 7. ACAS provides the following guide questions for employers in relation to internal workplace mediations:[101]

> Were you satisfied with the process?
>
> Were you satisfied with the outcome?
>
> Would you use mediation again?
>
> How skilful was the mediator? How did they help to facilitate an agreement?
>
> Was the case suited to mediation? And why?
>
> Did the mediation have any unintended consequences?

---

93   Requirement G2.1 MQMS – the feedback must cover whether the service was approachable and friendly; whether the client was kept informed; whether the information was explained sufficiently; and whether matters were managed competently and in a timely fashion.
94   Requirements E2.1–2.6 MQMS – the review can be of files or of mediation sessions as these occur. The reviews are carried out by independent mediators. A record of each review needs to record any adverse findings in relation to quality, actions and adherence to organisational procedures.
95   Requirement D2.2 MQMS – annual appraisals are required of all staff.
96   Requirement C2.1 MQMS – the items to be monitored include number of clients, hours of mediation, number of mediations and proportion of clients from target areas.
97   Requirement C2.2 MQMS – performance information is used to check the service's capacity and cross-checked against the business plan to ensure that it remains on track.
98   Requirements C3.2–3.3 MQMS – financial information must be reviewed every six months and accounts certified or audited every 18 months.
99   Requirements G3.1–3.3 and Appendix 1 MQMS.
100 Requirement G1.2 MQMS – the complaints procedure must indicate the definition of complaint, how complaints are reviewed and who is responsible for complaints handling. The procedure must comply with the Family Mediation Councils Code of Conduct.
101 ACAS, *Mediation: guide for employers*, 2009, p 30.

How long did the process take from beginning to end?

How long did the mediation itself take?

Has mediation improved the working environment?

To what extent have resolutions reached at the time lasted?

Have you any suggestions about how the process could be improved?

What costs were involved?

Getting paid

12.63   Some mediators ask for an advance payment (which may be held in a trust account) for, say, four hours or one day of mediation. If the mediation runs for less than the time paid for, the balance is returned to the clients. Others request only a deposit so that the financial entry barrier is not too high. Yet others bill clients after the mediation on an hours-incurred basis or a daily rate (usually a sliding scale dependent on the amount of the claim).[102]

It is always difficult to give clients a costs estimate when billing is costed on a time basis. Most mediations finish within eight hours, many within a shorter period. Complex legal, financial or technical issues can prolong the process beyond those times, as can difficult emotional and relationship issues between the parties, or simply the presence of multiple parties and advisers. However, commodity pricing is often demanded by clients and it is certainly less difficult to stipulate a fixed fee for mediation than it is for traditional legal services.

A mediation referred through a mediation service provider will usually also incur that provider's administration charges.

Professional indemnity insurance

12.64   Professional indemnity insurance is required by most mediator standards and codes of practice.[103] Where mediation is mandated by statute or court rules, mediators operating under those schemes usually enjoy some form of immunity.(as in the case of ACAS mediators). Some professionals, such as lawyers, are covered by their existing professional indemnity insurance policy,[104] provided their mediation work is carried out in their capacity as a member of their firm.[105] Other mediators can obtain professional indemnity insurance commercially from the normal industry sources. Some mediation organisations have block insurance for their mediators.

---

102 For an example, refer to In Place of Strife Mediation Terms and Business and Fee Guidelines in Appendix 3.

103 For example, section 6 CEDR Code of Conduct, section 8 CORE Solutions Group Code of Conduct, section 5.5 College of Mediators Code and Requirement C3.5 MQMS. Refer to Appendix 8.

104 For example, section 8 Law Society Code of Practice for Civil/Commercial Mediation and section 9 Law Society Code of Practice for Family Mediation (refer to Appendix 8).

105 A solicitor who practises as a mediator outside his or her legal practice must have regard to Rule 21 Solicitors' Code of Conduct 2007.

Combining practice with teaching

12.65   Many practising mediators conduct mediation seminars and training workshops. This educational activity serves three purposes: it maintains and develops their theoretical understanding in the field; it provides opportunities for networking and marketing their services; and it supplements their income. While in some industries those who 'can't do teach others to do', in mediation it is not possible to conduct training workshops without being a practitioner. The mediation discipline requires both scholar-practitioners and practitioner-scholars.

K.   Conclusion

12.66   As with any other venture, the larger and wiser the investment in mediation, the greater the likely return. The investment comprises the costs of training, materials, association memberships, conference attendances and marketing, and the opportunity costs which all of these entail. As with other investments, there are no guaranteed returns and some risk assessment is required.

As Folberg and Taylor point out, private practice can be financially risky and stressful, and 'mixed practices' where private work is, at least initially, a supplement to other work, including public sector mediation, might be a more realistic option.[106]

The most important thing is to keep your 'day job' while developing a mediation practice.

L.   Summary

12.67   This chapter raises the following points of particular significance:

- There is more resistance in the consumer market to the use of mediation than might be expected, given the high satisfaction ratings from those who use it. This resistance requires prospective mediators to engage in planning and marketing activities to develop and maintain their practice.

- Marketing initiatives should be focused on the organisations and individuals that are likely sources of referral to mediators, and should take account of new areas in which both conventional mediation and adaptations thereof might be adopted by clients.

- Even where prospective mediators find it difficult to obtain practice in mediation, they can still apply some aspects of the process, and many of the skills and techniques of the mediation, in many areas of professional and personal life.

---

106 Folberg and Taylor, *Mediation: A Comprehensive Guide to Resolving Conflicts without Litigation*, 1988, 293.

M.   Tasks for beginner mediators

12.68   Peruse a few daily newspapers and use news articles, editorials, job advertisements and other sources to develop a list of potential areas in which mediation might be applied. What modifications would be needed to make mediation suitable in each situation and how might it be marketed and to whom?

12.69   Write a proposal to an educational institution, voluntary association or other organisation in which you point out the advantages of developing a mediation system for relevant disputes facing the organisation and suggest ways in which you might be able to contribute to the system. Ask a knowledgeable person to comment on your proposal.

12.70   Examine current advertising and marketing campaigns for mediation and other dispute resolution services in the press, Yellow Pages, television, websites and other relevant places. Which *models* and *brands* of dispute resolution are being marketed and what messages are being provided about the nature of these processes?

N.   Recommended reading

Ardagh D., 'Is Mediation now a Profession?' in (2009) 10(8) *ADR Bulletin* 167.

Altobelli T., 'Are you Getting Enough? Marketing Mediation' (1999) 1(9) *ADR Bulletin* 113.

Bush R. and Folger J., *The Promise of Mediation: Responding to Conflict through Empowerment and Recognition*, Jossey-Bass, San Francisco, 1994.

Cloke K., *The Crossroads of Conflict: A Journey Into the Heart of Dispute Resolution*, Janis Publications Inc., 2006.

Folberg J. and Taylor A., *Mediation: A Comprehensive Guide to Resolving Disputes without Litigation*, Jossey-Bass, San Francisco, 1984, Chs 11 and 12.

Goldberg S. B., 'The Secrets of Successful Mediators', in (2005) 21(3) *Negotiation Journal* 365.

Haynes J. and Charlesworth S., *The Fundamentals of Family Mediation*, Federation Press, Sydney, 1996, Ch 8.

Hoffman D. A., 'The Future of ADR Practice: 3 Hopes, 3 Fears and 3 Predictions', in (2006) 22(4) *Negotiation Journal* 467.

Justice T. and Jamieson D., *The Facilitator's Fieldbook: Step-by-Step Procedures, Checklists and Guidelines*. AMACOM, 2006.

King P., *Professional Practice Management*, LBC Information Services, Sydney, 1995, Ch 20.

Keys B., 'No Mediator is an Island: a Mediator Supports others, but who Supports the Mediator?' in (2006) 8(10) *ADR Bulletin* 204.

Kolb, *When Talk Works: Profiles of Mediators*, Jossey-Bass, San Francisco, 1994.

Krivis J. and Lucks N., *How to Make Money as a Mediator: 30 Top Mediators Share Secrets to Building a Successful Practice*, Jossey-Bass, San Francisco, 2006.

Kurtzburg T. R. et al, Multi-party E-negotiations: Agents, Alliances and Negotiation Success', in (2005) 16 *International Journal of Conflict Management* 245.

Legal Services Commission (LSC), *Quality Mark (2010) for Family Mediation*, 2009.

Lenski T., *Making Mediation Your Day Job: How to Market Your ADR Business Using Mediation Principles You Already Know*. iUniverse Inc, 2008.

Pride W. and Ferrell O., *Marketing: Concepts and Strategies*, 8th ed, Houghton Mifflin, Boston, 1993, Ch 4.

MacDonald M., *Marketing Plans,* 3rd ed, Butterworth-Heinemann, Oxford, 1995, Chs 1, 2, 3 and 13.

McIlwrath M., 'Can Mediation Evolve into a Global Profession?', in (2009) 11(1) *ADR Bulletin* 12.

Mosten F., *The Complete Guide to Mediation*, American Bar Association, Chicago, 1997, Chs 5 and 21.

Mosten F. S., *Mediation Career Guide: A Strategic Approach to Building a Successful Practice*, Jossey-Bass, San Francisco, 2001.

Patrick J., *Equal Opportunities and Anti-Discriminatory Practice*, in Liebmann M. (ed), *Community and Neighbourhood Mediation*, Cavendish Publishing, London, 1998.

Picker B., *Mediation Practice Guide: A Handbook for Resolving Business Disputes*, American Bar Association, 2004.

Roberts M., *Mediation in Family Disputes: Principles of Practice*, 3rd ed, Ashgate, Aldershot, 2008.

Seawright J., *Marketing of Mediation as a New Professional Service*, unpublished postgraduate diploma paper, Bond University, 1997.

Sheehy B. and Palanovics N., 'E-negotiations: Rapport Building, Anonymity and Attribution', in (2006) 17 *Australasian Dispute Resolution Journal* 221.

Stein D. and Stein C., *Legal Practice in the 90s*, LBC Information Services, Sydney, 1994, Chs 2 and 4.

Zeithaml V. and Bitner M., *Services Marketing*, McGraw-Hill, New York, 1996.

Chapter 13

European Comparisons

One generation plants the trees; another gets the shade

A. Official EU efforts

13.1   The discussion paper on ADR, published by the EU Commission in 2002, sought to tackle quality issues and the relationship between ADR and the courts across Member States. The Code of Conduct for Mediators was approved in 2004[1] and the Directive on Mediation was adopted in 2008.[2] The Directive calls on Member States to encourage recourse to mediation, the development of mediation procedures and the publication of codes of conduct to ensure quality mediation services. The Council of Europe Recommendation on Family Mediation encourages Member States to promote family mediation.[3] Although this book has focused on developments across the UK, this chapter provides a brief overview of the growth of mediation across Europe.

B. Austria

13.2   The Civil Law Mediation Act[4] governs mediation in cases which fall under the jurisdiction of the ordinary civil courts. The Act has established the 'registered mediator'. A list is kept of mediators who meet the required qualifications. For registration, mediators must be over 28 years of age; have a professional qualification; be trustworthy; and hold professional indemnity insurance. The Act imposes on registered mediators obligations of fairness, equal treatment, impartiality and confidentiality. Registered mediators cannot be called as witnesses in subsequent judicial proceedings arising out of the matter mediated. Registered mediators can be prosecuted for breaches of confidentiality. Mediation under the Act interrupts the statutory and other time limits. Except in the case of family matters, there is no general provison for legal aid for mediation.[5]

---

1   Refer to Chapter 12 and Appendix 8.
2   Refer to Appendix 13.
3   Recommendation No. R(98)1 – refer to Appendix 13.
4   Zivilrechts-Mediations-Gesetz 2004.
5   For mediation enquiries relating to Austria, reference can be made to the mediation organisations in Austria and to the international organisations listed in Appendix 11.

C. Belgium

13.3   The Belgian Law on Mediation[6] provides for voluntary mediation (which is not linked to existing court proceedings) and court-instigated mediation. These mediations suspend the running of the limitation period; the status of a court order can be conferred on any agreement reached in such mediations; and these mediations are conducted by accredited mediators. Accredited mediators are required by the Law to be competent; have relevant training and experience; be independent and impartial; and that they have not been subject to any sanctions that are incompatible with mediation practice. The Law provides that mediation is privileged; that the mediator cannot be called to give evidence in any civil or administrative proceeding regarding the facts that came to his attention during mediation; and that the mediator is bound by the duty of professional secrecy under the Belgian Criminal Code.[7]

D. Finland

13.4   The Code of Procedure requires courts in civil matters to establish whether a matter can be resolved amicably. Judges conduct these mediations and can make proposals for settlement. Where a matter is not settled by mediation, the judge presiding over the trial is not the same person as the judge acting as mediator. Matters disclosed before a judge during the mediation are not invoked before the trial court. Arbitration is the preferred ADR method in the case of family matters. The Consumer Complaints Board makes recommendations to assist parties to resolve consumer disputes. There are specific mediation procedures in criminal matters.[8]

E. France

13.5   The New Code of Civil Procedure allows judges, with the parties' consent, to appoint a mediator to assist the parties to resolve the case. The Code specifies that the mediator so appointed should have appropriate qualifications, training and experience, and be independent. The mediator is required to report to the court if the parties have or have not resolved the matter. The court can approve any agreement reached in mediation. Declarations made in mediation cannot be used in later proceedings without the consent of the parties.[9]

---

6   Dated 21 February 2005 and came into effect on 30 September 2005. It added Part 7 into the Belgian Judicial Code, headed 'Mediation'.

7   Refer also to the Cepani (Belgium) Mediation Rules in Appendix 3 and their Code of Conduct in Appendix 8. Mediation enquiries relating to Belgium can be made to the mediation organisations in Belgium and to the international organisations listed in Appendix 11.

8   Mediation enquiries relating to Finland can be made to the international mediation organisations listed in Appendix 11.

9   For an overview of developments in mediation training and accreditation in France, refer to J Bonafe-Schmitt, 'Global Trends in Mediation Training and Accreditation – the Case of France', in (2009) 11(3) *ADR Bulletin* 47. Mediation enquiries relating to France can be made to the mediation organisations in France and to the international organisations in Appendix 11.

F. Germany

13.6   Conciliation Boards in Germany deal with the amicable resolution of consumer conflicts. The Social Security Code provides for mediation in family matters. Private mediation is used in both commercial and family cases. The Code of Civil Procedure provides for mandatory conciliation in certain cases.[10] In all cases, judges keep amicable settlement under review, whether by judicial settlement or voluntary referral to mediation.[11] There is currently no uniform professional background for those carrying out ADR activities in Germany. Professionals, like lawyers, who conduct mediation, are subject to their professional rules of conduct and regulations. Settlements can be directly enforced provide these are concluded as so-called lawyers' settlements in accordance with the German Civil Code.[12]

G. Greece

13.7   There is a history of conciliation in Greece.[13] Cases within the jurisdiction of a multi-member Court of First Instance are now subject to pre-trial settlement procedures.[14] Such settlement procedures may be assisted by a third party acting as mediator. Lawyers have to attend. Mediation confidentiality and privilege are protected.[15] Agreements can be ratified by the court and enforced as a judgment. Family and probate cases are excluded from pre-trial ADR.[16] Although out of court settlement has been encouraged by the Civil Procedure Code since 1995, take-up has been slow, and arbitration still appears to be the most widely used form of ADR. The training and accreditation of mediators commenced in 2008, co-ordinated by the Hellenic Mediation Association and the Chartered Institute of Arbitrators in London.[17] This is likely to provide impetus for greater take-up of mediation in Greece.

H. Hungary

13.8   In accordance with Act LV 2002 on Mediation, the Minister of Justice maintains a register of mediators, who are expected to have a higher degree, at least five years experience in the respective field, and no prior criminal record. The Ministry has power to conduct inspections to control mediator operations. The law prohibits mediators from handling a case where there is a conflict of interest. Unless otherwise prescribed by law, mediators must maintain the confidentiality of the mediation process. The law also prescribes the information that the parties must be given by mediators before the start of mediation, including the basic principles

---

10   Introductory Law of the Code of Civil Procedure Section 15a.
11   Section 278 Civil Procedure Code.
12   Section 796a Civil Procedure Code. Mediation enquiries relating to Germany can be made to the mediation organisations in Germany and to the international organisations listed in Appendix 11.
13   Articles 208–214A Code of Civil Procedure.
14   Law 2479/97.
15   Article 214A Civil Code and Article 6 Law 2479/97.
16   Article 6 Law 2479/97.
17   Refer to Appendix 8 for the Hellenic Mediation Association Mediation Rules and Regulations, whose contact details are in Appendix 11.

of mediation, the process, its costs and confidentiality. Mediators are required to record any agreements reached at mediation.[18]

I. Italy

13.9   There has been a long history of judicial conciliation in Italy, especially in labour, agricultural and family matters. Mediation was officially introduced into the legal system in Italy in 2003.[19] A Register of Mediators and a mandatory fee system for public mediation organisations has been introduced in the meantime.[20]

Mediation organisations are required to keep a record of each mediation for three years. Retired judges, university professors in law or economics and lawyers or accountants with at least 15 years' professional experience can become registered mediators. Mediation training can be considered in lieu of some of the professional experience requirement. The law provides that mediations are confidential and privileged. A settlement reached at mediation is recorded as minutes and signed by the parties and the mediator, and then filed with the court. If a mediation is unsuccessful, parties can request the mediator to provide a recommendation for settlement.

Reforms to corporate law provided that, if a mediation is successful, and the mediated agreement is approved by the court (a mere formality), it becomes directly enforceable by execution, specific performance and even registration of title to land.

Where an agreement is not reached in mediation, the reasons for failure are recorded by the mediator and may be taken into account when determining how the costs should be allocated. In addition, as a general rule for all types of civil proceedings, the court can, in making its decisions, rely on the declarations and behaviour of the parties during the proceedings and during any attempt to settle the case. In the case of successful mediations, the settlement is exempted from registration tax (of up to €25,000).

Most recently, Law 1082 has obliged lawyers to suggest that their clients should attempt mediation before commencing proceedings.[21]

J. Netherlands

13.10   From 2005 all courts dealing with specific administrative and civil cases (including family matters) have had mediation referral facilities. Mediation does not influence the limitation periods. An agreement reached in mediation can be confirmed in a notorial act, which makes it enforceable as a judgment. If the

---

18 Mediation enquiries relating to Hungary can be made to the international mediation organisations listed in Appendix 11.
19 LD 5/2003.
20 Law 2463. For further information, refer to G. De Palo and V. Alvisi, 'Mediation in Italy: Toward a Professional Practice', in (2009) 11(2) *ADR Bulletin* 37.
21 Mediation enquiries relating to Italy can be made to the mediation organisations in Italy and to the international organisations listed in Appendix 11.

mediation has been referred by a judge, the agreement reached can be confirmed in a judgment by the court in accordance with the Dutch Civil Code.[22]

K. Poland

13.11 Mediation has evolved in various contexts in Poland:

- Mediation is compulsory in the case of collective disputes. A list of mediators is retained by the Minister of Employment and Social Policy. Failure to reach agreement authorises strike action.

- Mediation in criminal matters is regulated by the Code of Criminal Procedure.

- Mediation is available in civil law disputes between consumers and businesses.

- Mediation can also occur in proceedings before the Court of Arbitration in disputes relating to property rights of international and domestic nature. The Court maintains a list of mediators. The mediator can make recommendations for settlement. An agreement is recorded and signed by the parties and the mediator. A judgment can be issued pursuant to any agreement reached.[23]

L. Portugal

13.12 Judicial conciliation is enshrined in the Code of Civil Procedure. Mediation is mainly used for small claims, family and consumer matters.[24] Although judges tend to recommend referral to mediation in family matters, the parties have to agree. The Family Mediation Office provides a free public mediation service in family matters. Mediation at the small claims courts is charged at a small fixed fee. Legal aid is available where mediation is referred from courts. Recourse to mediation does not affect statutory or other time limits. Agreements reached at mediation are ratified by a court and has the status of a decision made by the court in accordance with the Civil Procedure Act. The Ministry of Justice has collaborated with a law school in Portugal to develop an e-justice centre, aimed at providing mediation services for commercial disputes.[25]

M. Scotland

13.13 The Sheriff Courts in Scotland have been running mediation pilots for a number of years. Judges may suggest mediation. The parties must agree to referral. Employment-related cases constitute a large proportion of cases that are mediated. There are also a number of community mediation schemes operating in Scotland. These are funded by the Scottish Government. The Scottish Community Mediation

---

22 Refer to Appendix 3 for the NMI (Netherlands Mediation Institute) Mediation Rules and to Appendix 8 for the NMI Code of Conduct. Mediation enquiries relating to the Netherlands can be made to the mediation organisations in the Netherlands and to the international organisations listed in Appendix 11.

23 Mediation enquiries relating to Poland can be made to the mediation organisations in Poland and to the international organisations listed in Appendix 11.

24 For example, Portuguese Law 78/2001.

25 The Faculty of Law at Lisbon New University was involved – see www.ejusticecenter.mj.pt/.

Network provides a forum for further development of this area. Family Mediation Scotland and Relate provide family mediation services in Scotland. Child-related cases and 'all issues' cases (which include financial claims) are mediated using their services.

Lord Gill's review of civil justice in Scotland may encourage the further take-up of mediation.[26]

N. Slovakia

3.14   A mediation law was introduced in Slovakia in 2004. The Association of Mediators of Slovakia has been established. Pilot mediation programmes have operated in district courts. Mediation does not affect statutory or other time limits. Agreements reached in mediation can be judicially enforced if it is drawn up in the form of a notarial act or is endorsed in court by an arbitration body.[27]

O. Slovenia

3.15   Court-related mediation is available in civil, family and commercial matters in accordance with the Civil Procedure Acts. Non-governmental bodies provide mediation for neighbour, tenant, school, employment and consumer disputes. Courts can stay proceedings so that an attempt at mediation can be made. Court procedural rules protect confidentiality and provide that mediations are privileged. Court-related mediation is usually free of charge (except that the parties pay for the costs of any legal representation used by them). Mediation does not affect any statutory or other time limits. Agreements concluded as court settlements can be enforced as judgments.[28]

P. Spain

3.16   Judicial conciliation is regulated by the Code of Civil Procedure. Although costs sanctions for failure to engage in conciliation is not provided for in the Code, courts have a discretion regarding costs and may refuse to award costs to a winning party if there has been any bad faith. In Spain it is possible, for example, for a party to seek to adduce a document or evidence obtained in negotiations in court proceedings. Although private mediation agreements, and various institutional mediation rules, provide for confidentiality and privilege, the enforceability of such provisions in Spain is not absolute.

---

26 For a recent overview of developments in Scotland, refer to J. Sturrock, 'Civil and Commercial Mediation – a Scottish Perspective', in *International Bar Association – Practice Division*, October 2009, 23.

27 Mediation enquiries relating to Slovakia can be made to the international mediation organisations listed in Appendix 11.

28 Mediation enquiries relating to Slovenia can be made to the mediation organisations in Slovenia and to the international organisations listed in Appendix 11.

If a mediated settlement is not complied with, although it can be enforced as a contract, it cannot be enforced directly, unless the parties have previously submitted the dispute to the court and the agreement has been approved by the court.

As considerable costs are payable up front when litigating in Spain, these costs provide some incentive for the development of private mediation in Spain. Mediation is used in family, labour and consumer cases. It is uncertain whether certain matters, like company or insolvency matters, can be mediated. Interest in arbitration has increased, particularly since the new Arbitration Act in 2003, which has simplified the regulation of arbitration.

The Department of Justice of Catalonia is developing a White Book on mediation, containing research on the state of mediation and other alternative dispute resolution in Catalonia.[29]

Q. Sweden

3.17   Mediation is commonly used in Sweden in the case of employment, tenancy, rental, copyright and family matters.

The Swedish Code of Judicial Procedure provides for conciliation and mediation. It is the court that takes the initiative in conciliation talks between the parties. The judge presides over the conciliation. If mediation is considered more appropriate than conciliation, the court can appoint an external mediator. Although judicial conciliation is free, the parties bear the costs of external mediation if they agree to proceed with it.

The National Mediation Office has been set up to provide mediation for disputes between employers and employees over wage negotiations and terms of employment and for disputes where a company has refused to sign a collective agreement.[30]

R. Switzerland

3.18   Some of the Cantons in Switzerland have passed civil procedure laws containing mediation provisions. It is expected that, in 2010, all civil procedure laws will be unified and will provide for mediation as an alternative to judicial conciliation.

Civil and criminal mediation currently exists as part of the Geneva Law on Criminal Procedure and the Geneva Law on Civil Procedure. Mediation is available prior to issue of a claim, as well as during its progress in court. The law provides for confidentiality of mediation; the independence, neutrality and impartiality of the

---

29 Mediation enquiries relating to Spain can be made to the mediation organisations in Spain and to the international organisations listed in Appendix 11.
30 Mediation enquiries relating to Sweden can be made to the mediation organisations in Sweden and to the international organisations listed in Appendix 11.

mediator; and that limitation and other time periods are not suspended during mediation. A settlement reached in mediation can be ratified as a court or arbitration award.[31]

S.   Summary

13.19   Although arbitration, complaints boards/omubdsmen and judicial conciliation has had a long history across Europe, over the last five to ten years mediation has evolved in many European countries, spanning a range of civil litigation courts. Many European countries have also introduced requirements for the registration of mediators where cases are being referred to mediation by courts.

T.   Tasks for beginner mediators

13.20   Identify what are the main differences between 'judicial mediation' (as practised by judges in many European countries) and private mediation (even where it is encouraged or referred by a court).

13.21   Identify instances where Member States have implemented the EU Mediation Directive.

U.   Recommended reading

Abramson H., Chew, P. and Nolan-Haley J., *International Conflict Resolution: Consensual ADR Processes*, West, 2005.

Alexander N. (ed), *Global Trends in Mediation*, Kluwer Law International, The Hague, 2006.

Bonafe-Schmitt J., 'Global Trends in Mediation Training and Accreditation – the Case of France', in (2009) 11(3) *ADR Bulletin* 47.

Carroll, E., Mackie, K. and Hurd, L. *International Mediation: The Art of Business Diplomacy* (2nd Ed), Kluwer Law International, 2006.

CPR Institute New York, ADR Podcast Program, www.cpradr.org

De Palo G. and Alvisi V., 'Mediation in Italy: Toward a Professional Practice', in (2009) 11(2) *ADR Bulletin* 37.

EU Directive 2008/52/EC on Certain Aspects of Mediation in Civil and Commercial Matters (see Appendix 13).

EU Recommendation on Family Mediation (see Appendix 13).

European Code of Conduct for Mediators (see Appendix 13).

McCabe, J. *Uniformity in ADR: Thoughts on the Uniform Arbitration Act and Uniform Mediation Act*, Pepperdine Dispute Resolution Law Journal, 2002, 3, p 317.

---

31   Refer to Appendix 3 for the Swiss Chamber of Commerce Mediation Rules. Mediation enquiries relating to Switzerland can be made to the mediation organisations in Switzerland and to the international organisations listed in Appendix 11.

Merrills, J. G., *International Dispute Settlement*, Cambridge University Press, Cambridge, 2005.

Ministry of Justice Netherlands, *Paths to Justice in the Netherlands*, www.wodc.nl/images/obl219_sum_tcm11-5431.pdf (English version).

Sanders, P. *The Work of UNCITRAL on Arbitration and Conciliation*, Kluwer Law International, London/The Hague, 2004.

Steger D. P., *Peace Through Trade: Building the World Trade Organization*, Cameron May Ltd, London, 2004.

Appendix 1

Court documentation

A.   Sample ADR Directions

Practice Direction to CPR 29
Paragraph 4.10:

Where the court is to give directions on its own initiative without holding a case management conference…, its general approach will be:

…..

(9) in such cases as the Court thinks appropriate, the Court may give directions requiring the parties to consider ADR. Such directions may be, for example, in the following terms:

'The parties shall by [date] consider whether the case is capable of resolution by ADR. If any party considers that the case is unsuitable for resolution by ADR, that party shall be prepared to justify that decision at the conclusion of the trial, should the judge consider that such means of resolution were appropriate, when he is considering the appropriate costs order to make.

The party considering the case unsuitable for ADR shall, not less than 28 days before the commencement of the trial, file with the court a witness statement without prejudice save as to costs, giving reasons upon which they rely for saying that the case was unsuitable.'

B.   Commercial Court 'ADR Order'[1]

THE ADMIRALTY & COMMERCIAL COURTS GUIDE 2006
Appendix 7

Draft ADR Order

1. On or before [*] the parties shall exchange lists of 3 neutral individuals who are available to conduct ADR procedures in this case prior to [*]. Each party may [in addition] [in the alternative] provide a list identifying the constitution of one or more panels of neutral individuals who are available to conduct ADR procedures in this case prior to [*].

2. On or before [*] the parties shall in good faith endeavour to agree a neutral individual or panel from the lists so exchanged and provided.

3. Failing such agreement by [*] the Case Management Conference will be restored to enable the Court to facilitate agreement on a neutral individual or panel.

4. The parties shall take such serious steps as they may be advised to resolve their disputes by ADR procedures before the neutral individual or panel so chosen by no later than [*].

5. If the case is not finally settled, the parties shall inform the Court by letter prior to [disclosure of documents/exchange of witness statements/exchange of experts' reports] what steps towards ADR have been taken and (without prejudice to matters of privilege) why such steps have failed. If the parties have failed to initiate ADR procedures the Case Management Conference is to be restored for further consideration of the case.

6. [Costs].

C.   Master Ungley 'ADR Order'[2]

The parties shall by [date] consider whether the case is capable of resolution by ADR. If any party considers that the case is unsuitable for ADR, that party shall be prepared to justify that decision at the conclusion of the trial, should the judge consider that such means of resolution were appropriate, when he is considering the appropriate costs order to make. The party considering the case unsuitable for ADR shall, not less than 28 days before the commencement of the trial, file with the court a witness statement without prejudice save as to costs, giving reasons upon which they rely for saying that the case was unsuitable.

---

1   © Her Majesty's Court Service.
2   © Her Majesty's Court Service.

D. 'FORM E' Financial Statement
   (used in family cases)

FINANCIAL
STATEMENT
OF

In the

*[County Court]
*[Principal Registry of the Family Division]**

Case No. *Always quote this*	
Petitioner's Solicitor's reference	
Respondent's Solicitor's reference	

*Husband/*Wife/*Civil partner

(delete as appropriate)

Between

	and	

Who is the *husband/*wife/*civil partner
*Petitioner/*Respondent in the
*divorce/*dissolution suit
Applicant in this matter

Who is the *husband/*wife/*civil partner
*Petitioner/*Respondent in the
*divorce/*dissolution suit
Respondent in this matter

Please fill in this form fully and accurately. Where any box is not applicable, write 'N/A'.

You have a duty to the court to give a full, frank and clear disclosure of all your financial and other relevant circumstances.

A failure to give full and accurate disclosure may result in any order the court makes being set aside.

If you are found to have been deliberately untruthful, criminal proceedings for perjury may be taken against you.

You must attach documents to the form where they are specifically sought and you may attach other documents where it is necessary to explain or clarify any of the information that you give.

Essential documents that must accompany this statement are detailed in the form.

If there is not enough room on the form for any particular piece of information, you may continue on an attached sheet of paper.

If you are in any doubt about how to complete any part of this form you should seek legal advice.

This Statement must be sworn before a solicitor, a commissioner for oaths or an Officer of the Court or, if abroad, a notary or duly authorised official, before it is filed with the Court or sent to the other party (see last page).

This statement is filed by

Name and address of solicitor

Appendix 1   Court documentation

1   General information

1.1   Full name

	Day	Month	Year				Day	Month	Year
1.2 Date of birth					**1.3 Date of the marriage/ civil partnership**				

1.4   Occupation

	Day	Month	Year	
1.5 Date of the separation				Tick here • if not applicable

1.6 Date of the	Petition			Decree nisi/Decree of judicial separation Conditional order/ Separation order			Decree absolute/ Final order (if applicable)		
	Day	Month	Year	Day	Month	Year	Day	Month	Year

1.7 If you have subsequently married or formed a civil partnership, or will do so, state the date	Day	Month	Year

1.8   Are you co-habiting?   • Yes   • No

1.9   Do you intend to co-habit within the next six months?   • Yes   • No

1.10 Details of any children of the family	Full names	Date of birth			With whom does the child live?
		Day	Month	Year	

1.11 Details of the state of health of yourself and the children if you think this should be taken into account.	Yourself	Children

1.12   Details of the present and proposed future educational arrangements for the children.

Present arrangements	Future arrangements

1.13   Details of any child support maintenance calculation or any maintenance order or agreement made in respect of any children of the family. If no calculation, order or agreement has been made, give an estimate of the liability of the non-resident parent in respect of the children of the family under the Child Support Act 1991.

1.14   If this application is to vary an order, attach a copy of the order and give details of the part that is to be varied and the changes sought. You may need to continue on a separate sheet.

1.15   Details of any other court cases between you and your spouse/civil partner, whether in relation to money, property, children or anything else.

Case No.	Court

1.16   Your present residence and the occupants of it and on what terms you occupy it
(e.g. tenant, owner-occupier).

Address	Occupants	Terms of occupation

Appendix 1   Court documentation

2 Financial Details   *Part 1   Real Property and Personal Assets*

2.1 Complete this section in respect of the family home (the last family home occupied by you and your spouse/civil partner) if it remains unsold.

Documentation required for attachment to this section:

a) A copy of any valuation of the property obtained within the last six months. If you cannot provide this document, please give your own realistic estimate of the current market value

b) A recent mortgage statement confirming the sum outstanding on each mortgage

Property name and address	
Land Registry title number	
Mortgage company name(s) and address(es) and account number(s)	
Type of mortgage	
Details of who owns the property and the extent of your legal and beneficial interest in it (i.e. state if it is owned by you solely or jointly owned with your spouse/civil partner or with others)	
If you consider that the legal ownership as recorded at the Land Registry does not reflect the true position, state why	
Current market value of the property	
Balance outstanding on any mortgage(s)	
If a sale at this stage would result in penalties payable under the mortgage, state the amount	
Estimate the cost of sale of the property	
Total equity in the property (i.e. market value less outstanding mortgage(s), penalties if any and the costs of sale)	

TOTAL value of your interest in the family home: Total A

2.2 **Details of your interest in any other property, land or buildings. Complete one page for each property you have an interest in.**

Documentation required for attachment to this section:
a) A copy of any valuation of the property obtained in the last six months. If you cannot provide this document, please give your own realistic estimate of the current market value
b) A recent mortgage statement confirming the sum outstanding on each mortgage

Property name and address	
Land Registry title number	
Mortgage company name(s) and address(es) and account number(s)	
Type of mortgage	
Details of who owns the property and the extent of your legal and beneficial interest in it (i.e. state if it is owned by you solely or jointly owned with your spouse/civil partner or with others)	
If you consider that the legal ownership as recorded at the Land Registry does not reflect the true position, state why	
Current market value of the property	
Balance outstanding on any mortgage(s)	
If a sale at this stage would result in penalties payable under the mortgage, state the amount	
Estimate the cost of sale of the property	
Total equity in the property (i.e. market value less outstanding mortgage(s) penalties if any and the cost of sale	
Total value of your interest in this property	

TOTAL value of your interest in ALL other property: Total B [ ]

2.3   **Details of all personal bank, building society and National Savings Accounts that you hold or have held at any time in the last twelve months and which are or were either in your own name or in which you have or have had any interest. This applies whether any such account is in credit or in debit. For joint accounts give your interest and the name of the other account holder. If the account is overdrawn, show a minus figure.**

Documentation required for attachment to this section:
For each account listed, all statements covering the last 12 months.

Name of bank or building society including branch name	Type of account *(e.g. current)*	Account number	Name of other account holder *(if applicable)*	Balance at the date of this statement	Total current value of your interest
			TOTAL value of your interest in ALL accounts: (C1)		

2.4   **Details of all investments, including shares, PEPs, ISAs, TESSAs, National Savings Investments (other than already shown above), bonds, stocks, unit trusts, investment trusts, gilts and other quoted securities that you hold or have an interest in. (Do not include dividend income as this will be dealt with separately later on.)**

Documentation required for attachment to this section:
Latest statement or dividend counterfoil relating to each investment.

Name	Type of Investment	Size of Holding	Current value	Name of any other account holder *(if applicable)*	Total current value of your interest
			TOTAL value of your interest in ALL holdings: (C2)		

...

2.5   **Details of all life insurance policies including endowment policies that you hold or have an interest in. Include those that do not have a surrender value. Complete one page for each policy.**

Documentation required for attachment to this section:

A surrender valuation of each policy that has a surrender value

Name of company			
Policy type			
Policy number			
If policy is assigned, state in whose favour and amount of charge			
Name any other owner and the extent of your interest in the policy			
Maturity date *(if applicable)*	Day	Month	Year
Current surrender value *(if applicable)*			
If policy includes life insurance, the amount of the insurance and the name of the person whose life is insured.			
Total current surrender value of your interest in this policy			

TOTAL value of your interest in ALL policies: (C3)	

2.6   **Details of all monies that are OWED TO YOU. Do not include sums owed in director's or partnership accounts which should be included at section 2.11.**

Brief description of money owed and by whom	Balance outstanding	Total current value of your interest

TOTAL value of your interest in ALL debts owed to you: (C4)	

2.7 Details of all cash sums held in excess of £500. You must state where it is held and the currency it is held in.

Where held	Amount	Currency	Total current value of your interest

| | | | TOTAL value of your interest in ALL your cash sums: (C5) | |

2.8 Details of personal belongings individually worth more than £500.

INCLUDE
- Cars (gross value)
- Collections, pictures and jewellery
- Furniture and house contents

Brief description of item	Total current value of your interest

| TOTAL value of your interest in ALL personal belongings: (C6) | |

Add together all the figures in boxes C1 to C6 to give the TOTAL current value of your interest in personal assets: TOTAL C

2 Financial Details *Part 2 Capital: Liabilities and Capital Gains Tax*

2.9 Details of any liabilities you have.

EXCLUDE liabilities already shown such as:
* Mortgages
* Any overdrawn bank, building society or National Savings accounts

INCLUDE:
* Money owed on credit cards and store cards
* Bank loans
* Hire purchase agreements

List all credit and store cards held including those with nil or positive balance. Where the liability is not solely your own, give the name(s) of the account holder(s) and the amount of your share of the liability.

Liability	Name(s) of other account holder(s) *(if applicable)*	Total liability	Total current value of your interest in the liability
TOTAL value of your interest in ALL liabilities: (D1)			

2.10 If any Capital Gains Tax would be payable on the disposal now of any of your real property or personal assets, give your estimate of the tax liability.

Asset	Total Capital Gains Tax liability
TOTAL value of ALL your potential Capital Gains Tax liabilities: (D2)	
Add together D1 and D2 to give the TOTAL value of your liabilities: TOTAL D	

373

2 Financial Details   *Part 3 Capital: Business assets and directorships*

2.11 Details of all your business interests. Complete one page for each business you have an interest in.

Documentation required for attachment to this section:

a)   Copies of business accounts for the last two financial years

b)   Any documentation, if available at this stage, upon which you have based your estimate of the current value of your interest in this business, for example a letter from an accountant or a formal valuation.

It is not essential to obtain a formal valuation at this stage

Name of the business	
Briefly describe the nature of the business	

You are
e.g. Sole trader
    Partner in a partnership with others
    Shareholder in a limited company	

If you are a partner or a shareholder, state the extent of your interest in the business **(i.e. partnership share or the extent of your shareholding compared to the overall shares issued)**	
State when your next set of accounts will be available	
If any of the figures in the last accounts are not an accurate reflection of the current position, state why. **For example, if there has been a material change since the last accounts, or if the valuations of the assets are not a true reflection of their value (e.g. because property or other assets have not been re-valued in recent years or because they are shown at a book value)**	
Total amount of any sums owed to you by the business by way of a director's loan account, partnership capital or current accounts or the like. Identify where these appear in the business accounts	
Your estimate of the current value of your business interest. Explain briefly the basis upon which you have reached that figure	
Your estimate of any Capital Gains Tax that would be payable if you were to dispose of your business now	
Net value of your interest in this business after any Capital Gains Tax liability	

Total value of ALL your interests in business assets: TOTAL E

2.12   List any directorships you hold or have held in the last 12 months (other than those already disclosed in section 2.11).

375

2 Financial Details   *Part 4 Capital: Pensions*

2.13 Give details of all your pension rights. Complete a separate page for each pension.

EXCLUDE:
* Basic State Pension

INCLUDE (complete a separate page for each one):
* Additional State Pension (SERPS and State Second Pension (S2P))
* Free Standing Additional Voluntary Contribution Schemes (FSAVC) separate from the scheme of your employer
* Membership of ALL pension plans or schemes

Documentation required for attachment to this section:

a) A recent statement showing the cash equivalent transfer value (CETV) provided by the trustees or managers of each pension arrangement (or, in the case of the additional state pension, a valuation of these rights).

b) If any valuation is not available, give the estimated date when it will be available and attach a copy of your letter to the pension company or administrators from whom the information was sought and/or state the date on which an application for a State Earnings Related Pension Scheme was submitted to the Department of Work and Pensions.

Name and address of pension arrangement	
Your National Insurance Number	
Number of pension arrangement or reference number	
Type of scheme e.g. occupational or personal, final salary, money purchase, additional state pension or other (if other, please give details)	
Date the CETV was calculated	
Is the pension in payment or drawdown or deferment? *(Please answer Yes or No)*	
State the cash equivalent transfer value (CETV) quotation, or in the additional state pension, the valuation of those rights	
If the arrangement is an occupational pension arrangement that is paying reduced CETVs, please quote what the CETV would have been if not reduced. If this is not possible, please indicate if the CETV quoted is a reduced CETV	
TOTAL value of ALL your pension assets: TOTAL F	

2 Financial Details   *Part 5 Capital: Other assets*

2.14 Give details of any other assets not listed in Parts 1 to 4 above.

INCLUDE (the following list is not exhaustive):
- Any personal or business assets not yet disclosed
- Unrealisable assets
- Share option schemes, stating the estimated net sale proceeds of the shares if the options were capable of exercise now, and whether Capital Gains Tax or income tax would be payable
- Business expansion schemes
- Futures
- Commodities
- Trust interests (including interests under a discretionary trust), stating your estimate of the value of the interest and when it is likely to become realisable. If you say it will never be realisable, or has no value, give your reasons.
- Any asset that is likely to be received in the foreseeable future
- Any asset held on your behalf by a third party
- Any asset not disclosed elsewhere on this form even if held outside England and Wales

You are reminded of your obligation to disclose all your financial assets and interests of ANY nature.

Type of asset	Value	Total net value of your interest
TOTAL value of ALL your other assets: TOTAL G		

2 Financial Details *Part 6 Income: Earned income from employment*

2.15 Details of earned income from employment. Complete one page for each employment.

Documentation required for attachment to this section:
a) P60 for the last financial year (you should have received this from your employer shortly after the last 5th April)
b) Your last three payslips
c) Your last Form P11D if you have been issued with one

Name and address of your employer	
Job title and brief details of the type of work you do	
Hours worked per week in this employment	
How long have you been with this employer?	
Explain the basis of your income i.e. state whether it is based on an annual salary or an hourly rate of pay and whether it includes commissions or bonuses	
Gross income for the last financial year as shown on your P60	
Net income for the last financial year i.e. gross income less income tax and national insurance	
Average net income for the last three months i.e. total income less income tax and national insurance divided by three	
Briefly explain any other entries on the attached payslips other than basic income, income tax and national insurance	
If the payslips attached for the last three months are not an accurate reflection of your normal income briefly explain why	
Details and value of any bonuses or other occasional payments that you receive from this employment not otherwise already shown, including the basis upon which they are paid	
Details of any benefits in kind, perks or other remuneration received from this employer in the last year (e.g. provision of a car, payment of travel, accommodation, meal expenses, etc.)	
Your estimate of your net income from this employment for the next 12 months. If this differs significantly from your current income explain why in box 4.1.2	

Estimated TOTAL of ALL net earned income from
employment for the next 12 months: **TOTAL H**

2 Financial Details *Part 7 Income: Income from self-employment or partnership*

2.16 You will have already given details of your business and provided the last two years accounts at section 2.11. Complete this section giving details of your income from your business. Complete one page for each business.

Documentation required for attachment to this section:

a) A copy of your last tax assessment or, if that is not available, a letter from your accountant confirming your tax liability

b) If net income from the last financial year and estimated net income for the next 12 months is significantly different, a copy of management accounts for the period since your last account

Name of the business	
Date to which your last accounts were completed	
Your share of gross business profit from the last completed accounts	
Income tax and national insurance payable on your share of gross business profit above	
Net income for that year (using the two figures directly above, gross business profit less income tax and national insurance payable)	
Details and value of any benefits in kind, perks or other remuneration received from this business in the last year e.g. provision of a car, payment of travel, accommodation, meal expenses, etc	
Amount of any regular monthly or other drawings that you take from this business	
If the estimated figure directly below is different from the net income as at the end date of the last completed accounts, briefly explain the reason(s)	
Your estimate of your net annual income for the next 12 months	

Estimated TOTAL of ALL net income from self-employment or partnership for the next 12 months: TOTAL I [ ]

2 Financial Details   *Part 8 Income: Income from investments*
e.g. dividends, interest or rental income

2.17 Details of income received in the last financial year (the year ended last 5th April), and your estimate of your income for the current financial year. Indicate whether the income was paid gross or net of income tax. You are not required to calculate any tax payable that may arise.

Nature of income and the asset from which it derived	Paid gross or net	Income received in the last financial year	Estimated income for the next 12 months

Estimated TOTAL investment income for the next 12 months: TOTAL J

380

2 Financial Details   *Part 9 Income: Income from state benefits (including state pension and child benefit)*

2.18 Details of all state benefits that you are currently receiving.

Name of benefit	Amount paid	Frequency of payment	Estimated income for the next 12 months

Estimated TOTAL benefit income for the next 12 months: TOTAL K

381

2 Financial Details   *Part 10 Income: Any other income*

2.19 Details of any other income not disclosed above.

INCLUDE:
- Any source from which income has been received during the last 12 months (even if it has now ceased)
- Any source from which income is likely to be received during the next 12 months

You are reminded of your obligation to give full disclosure of your financial circumstances.

Nature of income	Paid gross or net	Income received in the last financial year	Estimated income for the next 12 months

Estimated TOTAL other income for the next 12 months: TOTAL L

2 Financial Details *Summaries*

2.20 Summary of your capital (Parts 1 to 5)

Description	Reference of the section on this statement	Value
Current value of your interest in the family home	**A**	
Current value of your interest in all other property	**B**	
Current value of your interest in personal assets	**C**	
Current value of your liabilities	**D**	
Current value of your interest in business assets	**E**	
Current value of your pension assets	**F**	
Current value of all your other assets	**G**	
TOTAL value of your assets (Totals A to G less D):		

2.21 Summary of your estimated income for the next 12 months (Parts 6 to 10)

Description	Reference of the section on this statement	Value
Estimated net total of income from employment	**H**	
Estimated net total of income from self-employment or partnership	**I**	
Estimated net total of investment income	**J**	
Estimated state benefit receipts	**K**	
Estimated net total of all other income	**L**	
Estimated TOTAL income for the next 12 months (Totals H to L):		

383

3 Financial Requirements   *Part 1   Income needs*

3.1   Income needs for yourself and any children living with you or provided for by you. ALL figures should be annual, monthly or weekly (state which). You must not use a combination of these periods. State your current income needs and, if these are likely to change in the near future, explain the anticipated change and give an estimate of the future cost.

The income needs below are: *(delete those not applicable)*	Weekly	Monthly	Annual

I anticipate my income needs are going to change because

3.1.1 Income needs for yourself.

INCLUDE:
- All income needs for yourself
- Income needs for any children living with you or provided for by you only if these form part of your total income needs (e.g. housing, fuel, car expenses, holidays, etc)

Item	Current cost	Estimated future cost
SUB-TOTAL your income needs:		

3.1.2 Income needs for children living with you or provided for by you.

INCLUDE:
- Only those income needs that are different to those of your household shown above

Item	Current cost	Estimated future cost
SUB-TOTAL children's income needs:		
TOTAL of ALL income needs:		

384

3 Financial Requirements   *Part 2   Capital needs*

3.2 Set out below the reasonable future capital needs for yourself and for any children living with you or provided for by you.

3.2.1 Capital needs for yourself

INCLUDE:

* All capital needs for yourself
* Capital needs for any children living with you or provided for by you only if these form part of your total capital needs (e.g. housing, cars, etc)

Item	Cost
SUB-TO TAL your capital needs:	

3.2.2 Capital needs for children living with you or provided for by you.

INCLUDE:

* Only those capital needs that are different to those of your household shown above.

Item	Cost
SUB-TO TAL your children's capital needs:	
TO TAL of ALL capital needs:	

4   Other Information

4.1   Details of any significant changes in your assets or income.

At both sections 4.1.1 and 4.1.2, INCLUDE:

- All assets held both within and outside England and Wales
- The disposal of any asset.

4.1.1   Significant changes in assets or income during the LAST 12 months.

4.1.2   Significant changes in assets or income likely to occur during the NEXT 12 months.

4.2   Brief details of the standard of living enjoyed by you and your spouse/civil partner during the marriage/civil partnership.

4.3   Are there any particular contributions to the family property and assets or outgoings, or to family life, or the welfare of the family that have been made by you, your partner or anyone else that you think should be taken into account? If there are any such items, briefly describe the contribution and state the amount, when it was made and by whom.

INCLUDE:
* Contributions already made
* Contributions that will be made in the foreseeable future.

4.4   Bad behaviour or conduct by the other party will only be taken into account in very exceptional circumstances when deciding how assets should be shared after divorce/dissolution. If you feel it should be taken into account in your case, identify the nature of the behaviour or conduct below.

4.5   Give details of any other circumstances that you consider could significantly affect the extent of the financial provision to be made by or for you or any child of the family.

INCLUDE (the following list is not exhaustive):
* Earning capacity
* Disability
* Inheritance prospects
* Redundancy
* Retirement
* Any plans to marry, form a civil partnership or cohabit
* Any contingent liabilities.

387

Appendix 1   Court documentation

4.6   If you have subsequently married or formed a civil partnership (or intend to) or are living with another person (or intend to), give brief details, so far as they are known to you, or his or her income, assets and liabilities.

Annual Income		Assets and Liabilities	
Nature of income	Value (if known, state whether gross or net)	Item	Value (if known)
Total income:		**Total assets/liabilities:**	

388

5   Order Sought

5.1   If you are able at this stage, specify what kind of orders you are asking the court to make. Even if you cannot be specific at this stage, if you are able to do so, indicate:

   a)   If the family home is still owned, whether you are asking for it to be transferred to yourself or your spouse/civil partner or whether you are saying it should be sold

   b)   Whether you consider this is a case for continuing spousal maintenance/maintenance for your civil partner

or whether you see the case as being appropriate for a "clean break".   *(A 'clean break' means a settlement or order which provides amongst other things, that neither you nor your spouse/civil partner will have any further claim against the income or capital of the other party. A 'clean break' does not terminate the responsibility of a parent to a child.)*

   c)   Whether you are seeking a pension sharing or pension attachment order

   d)   If you are seeking a transfer or settlement of any property or assets, identify the property or assets in question.

5.2   If you are seeking a variation of an ante-nuptial or post-nuptial settlement or a relevant settlement made during, or in anticipation of, a civil partnership, identify the settlement, by whom it was made, its trustees and beneficiaries and state why you allege it is a settlement which the court can vary

5.3   If you are seeking an avoidance of disposition order, or if you have already applied for such an order, identify the property to which the disposition relates and the person or body in whose favour the disposition is alleged to have been made.

Sworn confirmation of the information

I [   ]   *(the above named Applicant/Respondent)*

of [   ]   MAKE OATH and confirm that the information given above is a full, frank, clear and accurate disclosure of my financial and other relevant circumstances.

Sworn by the above named

at [   ]   )
)
)
)
)
)

this   day of   )   ....

Before me, ...

A Solicitor, commissioner for oaths, an Officer of the Court, appointed by the Judge to take affidavits, a notary or duly authorised official.

Address all communications to the Court Manager of the Court and quote the case number. If you do not quote this number, your correspondence may be returned.

SCHEDULE OF DOCUMENTS TO ACCOMPANY FORM E

The following list shows the documents you must attach to your Form E if applicable. You may attach other documents where it is necessary to explain or clarify any of the information that you give in the Form E.

Form E paragraph	Document	Please tick		
		Attached	**N/A**	**To follow**
1.14	Application to vary an order: if applicable, attach a copy of the relevant order.			
2.1	Matrimonial home valuation: a copy of any valuation relating to the matrimonial home that has been obtained in the last six months.			
2.1	Matrimonial home mortgage(s): a recent mortgage statement in respect of each mortgage on the matrimonial home confirming the amount outstanding.			
2.2	Any other property: a copy of any valuation relating to each other property disclosed that has been obtained in the last six months.			
2.2	Any other property: a recent mortgage statement in respect of each mortgage on each other property disclosed confirming the amount outstanding.			
2.3	Personal bank, building society and National Savings accounts: copies of statements for the last 12 months for each account that has been held in the last twelve months, either in your own name or in which you have or have had any interest.			
2.4	Other investments: the latest statement or dividend counterfoil relating to each investment as disclosed in paragraph 2.4.			
2.5	Life insurance (including endowment) policies: a surrender valuation for each policy that has a surrender value as disclosed under paragraph 2.5.			
2.11	Business interests: a copy of the business accounts for the last two financial years for each business interest disclosed.			
2.11	Business interests: any documentation that is available to confirm the estimate of the current value of the business, for example, a letter from an accountant or formal valuation if that has			
2.13	Pension rights: a recent statement showing the cash equivalent transfer value (CETV) provided by the trustees or managers of each pension arrangement that you have disclosed (or, in the case of the additional state pension, a valuation of these rights). If not yet available,			
2.15	Employment income: your P60 for the last financial year in respect of each employment that you have.			
2.15	Employment income: your last three payslips in respect of each employment that you have.			
2.15	Employment income: your last form P11D if you have been issued with one.			
2.16	Self-employment or partnership income: a copy of your last tax assessment or if that is not available, a letter from your accountant confirming your tax liability.			
2.16	Self-employment or partnership income: if net income from the last financial year and the estimated income for the next twelve months is significantly different, a copy of the management accounts for the period since your last accounts.			
Relevant Form E paragraph	**Description of other documents attached:**			

Case No.

In the

* Delete as appropriate

*[High/County Court]
*[Principal Registry of the Family Division]

In the marriage/Civil Partnership between

who is the husband/wife/civil partner

and

who is the husband/wife/civil partner

Financial statement on behalf of

who is the husband/wife/civil partner and the
Petitioner/Respondent in the divorce/dissolution suit

This statement is filed by

who are solicitors for the husband/wife/civil partner

392

Appendix 2

Standard Forms for Mediation Practice

A. Family Mediation Screening/Assessment

College of Mediators Domestic Abuse Screening Policy[1]

---

1   This document is reproduced with the kind permission of the College of Mediators. The College website is a regularly updated source of information and resources so for the most up to date material please visit www.collegeofmediators.co.uk.

DOMESTIC ABUSE SCREENING POLICY

A   **Principles to be adopted by the College of Mediators on Domestic Abuse Screening**

1.   There must be a screening policy for domestic abuse which screening must take place prior to and throughout the mediation process.

2.   There must be a policy on violence and abuse in the work place.

3.   These policies must be in writing

4.   There must be written procedures setting out the requirements for the implementation of these policies.

B   **Policy on Screening for Domestic Abuse**

1.   Each participant must make a fully informed and voluntary decision to enter mediation. This requires that each participant is sufficiently informed and has sufficient time to make the decision to attempt mediation after all safety issues have been fully considered.

2.   Safety issues must include not only the participants in mediation but also any children and any other significant member of the family of either party.

3.   Assessment for Domestic Abuse and/or Child Protection is a continuing requirement which lasts throughout the whole of the mediation process.

4.   Implementation of this policy requires a written procedure for safe and effective screening for domestic abuse.

C   **Definition of Domestic Abuse**

Domestic abuse is behavior that seeks to secure power and control for the abuser and the impact of which is to undermine the safety, security self-esteem and autonomy of the abused person. Domestic violence contains elements of the use of any or all of physical, sexual, psychological, emotional, verbal or economic intimidation, oppression or coercion.

COLLEGE OF MEDIATORS – DOMESTIC ABUSE SCREENING POLICY – 18 May 99

The most important factors in domestic abuse are:

- The impact of the behavior as experienced by each/any of the individuals involved.

- That it is viewed from the perspective of the recipient of the abuse/abused person.

D   Principles of Screening for Domestic Abuse

    1.1   Mediators must routinely screen for domestic abuse before a decision is taken to proceed with mediation.

    1.2   Screening must take place separately with each participant.

    1.3   In reaching a decision about whether to proceed, priority should be given to the individual's perception of abuse over any judgement about levels of severity or types of abuse.

    1.4   If in doubt about the appropriateness of mediation the mediator could consult with his/her supervisor and if doubt still remains, must not proceed.

2.   Separate screening for domestic abuse must be carried out in circumstances that allow free, frank and safe discussion of the issues of domestic abuse to take place and a fully informed choice to be made by the participants as to whether or not to proceed to mediation.

3.   Mediators must adopt clear, written procedures to screen all clients and to record all decisions about the appropriateness of mediation and termination if domestic abuse or child protection issues have been identified. If mediation is appropriate, procedures to ensure client protection, child protection and mediator safety must be implemented and recorded in writing.

4.   Whether or not domestic abuse emerges as an issue at an initial screening, continued screening must take place throughout mediation and a written record made of all such screening.

5.   In cases where the abused person has made an informed choice to mediate, the mediator's responsibility is to ensure that appropriate arrangements are agreed which so far as possible guarantee that relevant safety issues are addressed and reviewed. Such issues will include for example the exploration of safety matters, implications for children, safe termination, voluntariness and informed consent.

6.   If mediation does not proceed, mediation must be terminated safely, other alternatives to mediation explored, and appropriate advice and referral possibilities should be considered, if possible.

B. Workplace Mediation Screening/Assessment

CMP Resolutions 'Ready to Resolve Questionnaire'[2]

Ready to Resolve Mediation Questionnaire

Please answer all questions!

Section 1: Legislation

		Yes	No
1	Are you aware of the new dispute resolution legislation as introduced by BERR?	○	○
2	Are you aware mediation is being advocated and encouraged?	○	○
3	Have you made any changes to your dispute resolution processes in light of the legislation?	○	○
4	Have your sought any external guidance with regards to compliance with the new legislation?	○	○

If the answer to 4 is yes go to question 5 otherwise go to question 6

		Yes	No
5	Was this via a government agency - i.e. ACAS or BERR?	○	○
6	Do you have plans to make changes/further changes to ensure compliance?	○	○

Section 2: Mediation Experience

1   Have you ever used a mediator in your organisation?   ○ Yes   ○ No   **If 'No' go to Section 3**

2   How many times has mediation been used in the last 12 months?   ○ 0   ○ 1-5   ○ 6-10   ○ 11-15   ○ 16+

3   Did you use an internal or external mediator?   ○ Internal   ○ External   ○ Both   ○ N/A

4   Was the mediator a trained specialist?   ○ Yes   ○ No   ○ N/A

Questions 5 - 9 Please rate your mediation experience.   Not at all   Poor   Satisfied Exceptional

5	How satisfied were you with the process of mediation?	◉	◉	◉	◉
6	How satisfied were you with the feedback from the mediation?	◉	◉	◉	◉
7	How satisfied were you with the mediators?	◉	◉	◉	◉
8	How satisfied were you with the outcome of the mediation(s)?	◉	◉	◉	◉
9	How satisfied were you with mediation as a dispute resolution tool?	◉	◉	◉	◉

Section 3: Organisational Commitment

a   Policy and Practice

Is mediation included within any of your policies?   ◉ Yes   ◉ No

If yes please tick which

1   Grievance Policy   ☐

2   Dignity at Work Policy   ☐

3   Performance Management Policy   ☐

4   Equality and Diversity Policy   ☐

5   Bullying and Harrassment Policy   ☐

6   Other please state   [   ]

b   Internal Emphasis

1   Is mediation given equal emphasis as your formal resolution processes?   ◉ Yes   ◉ No   ◉ Don't Know

2   Do you have a process for accessing mediation services if required?   ◉ Yes   ◉ No   ◉ Don't Know

3   Do you have a defined and allocated budget for mediation?   ◉ Yes   ◉ No   ◉ Don't Know

4   Are there published guidelines for the identification of cases suitable for mediation?   ◉ Yes   ◉ No   ◉ Don't Know

5   Have you calculated / identified the potential numbers of mediation cases?   ◉ Yes   ◉ No   ◉ Don't Know

6   Has a business case been produced for the utilization of mediation versus formal solutions?   ◉ Yes   ◉ No   ◉ Don't Know

c   Stakeholder Support

		No Support	Neutral Support	Partial Support	Full Support	Don't Know
1	How much would you rate the support of mediation from the following key stakeholders in your organisation?					
	a Managing Director / CEO	◉	◉	◉	◉	◉
	b Board of Directors	◉	◉	◉	◉	◉
	c Senior Management	◉	◉	◉	◉	◉
	d Finance Director	◉	◉	◉	◉	◉

e HR Director
f Trade Unions
g Diversity Representative Groups
h Legal Staff

2 How supportive of mediation as an effective dispute resolution process is your organisation generally?

Section 4: Communication, Awareness and Support

a Communication
How are employees made aware of their rights, responsibilities and options regarding mediation?

1 Hard copies of policy documents — Yes No Don't know
2 Electronic copies of policy documents — Yes No Don't know
3 Flyers or leaflets on mediation — Yes No Don't know
4 Intranet information Provision — Yes No Don't know
5 Workshops or seminars — Yes No Don't know
6 Briefings — Yes No Don't know
7 Newsletters — Yes No Don't know
8 Other please state

b Awareness
1 How informed are your staff about the process of mediation? — Not at all Poorly Aware Fully Informed

c Support
Who is available to provide support and guidance about mediation to employees?

1 HR — Yes No Don't know
2 Trade Unions — Yes No Don't know
3 Designated Support or Contact Officers — Yes No Don't know
4 Employee Assistance Programme — Yes No Don't know
5 Advice and support line — Yes No Don't know
6 Briefed Line Managers — Yes No Don't know
7 Other please state

d Support Staff
Are support staff:
1 Well informed about mediation? — Yes No Don't know

2 Well Trained? ⦿ Yes ⦿ No ⦿ Don't know

3 Regularly Updated about mediation? ⦿ Yes ⦿ No ⦿ Don't know

4 Accessible? ⦿ Yes ⦿ No ⦿ Don't know

5 Trusted? ⦿ Yes ⦿ No ⦿ Don't know

e   Mediation Deployment

1 Is there a designated person responsible for the initiation of a mediation process? ⦿ Yes ⦿ No ⦿ Don't know

2 Are suitable locations / venues for mediation identified and available? ⦿ Yes ⦿ No ⦿ Don't know

3 Do you have standard documentation about mediation available for all parties? ⦿ Yes ⦿ No ⦿ Don't know

4 Do you have a process for evaluating the mediation process? ⦿ Yes ⦿ No ⦿ Don't know

Section 5: Performance

a   Quality Assurance

Please complete on the basis of your mediation experience.

1 Do your mediators operate under a clear code of conduct? ⦿ Yes ⦿ No ⦿ Don't know

2 Is there a clear statement on Equality and Diversity ⦿ Yes ⦿ No ⦿ Don't know

3 Is there a formal complaints procedure within the mediation policy? ⦿ Yes ⦿ No ⦿ Don't know

4 Do your mediators hold the Certificate in Mediation Skills qualification? ⦿ Yes ⦿ No ⦿ Don't know

4a If yes please state which accrediting body it is certified by ⦿ OCR ⦿ OCN

4b If no please state what type of mediation training has been used.

5 Is a mediator always accessible when required? ⦿ Yes ⦿ No ⦿ Don't know

6 Do you have a formal assessment process for the mediators competence and or performance? ⦿ Yes ⦿ No ⦿ Don't know

7 How satisfied are you in the performance of internal mediators? Not at all ⦿ Poor ⦿ Satisfied ⦿ Exceptional ⦿

b   Overall Mediation Performance

How confident are you that: No confidence   Limited Confidence   Confident   Totally Confident

1 Mediations are conducted promptly without undue delay ⦿ ⦿ ⦿ ⦿

2 Parties are informed of their rights and options ⦿ ⦿ ⦿ ⦿

3 Communication is clear and accurate ⦿ ⦿ ⦿ ⦿

4 Mediators are overtly and demonstrably impartial ⦿ ⦿ ⦿ ⦿

5 Mediators can deal at senior management level   ◉   ◉   ◉   ◉

6 Mediators can handle complex cases   ◉   ◉   ◉   ◉

7 Mediators can handle multi-party disputes   ◉   ◉   ◉   ◉

8 Mediators can handle diversity and equality issues   ◉   ◉   ◉   ◉

9 Mediations will remain confidential   ◉   ◉   ◉   ◉

Section 6: Summary

Do you feel that your organisation could be doing more to utilise mediation?   ◉ Yes ◉ No

Do you feel that you understand the elements and process of mediation?   ◉ Yes ◉ No

Were you considering developing your mediation capability prior to the legislation?   ◉ Yes ◉ No

C. Covering letters

(i) Sample covering letter (used in general civil or commercial cases)[3]

Dear [ ]

Re: Information about mediation

Thank you for your recent telephone inquiries about mediation and the services which I provide.

As promised, I am sending you some information on the mediation process in the form of commonly asked questions and answers. The same information is being sent to the other parties involved in this matter.

Please take time to consider this information and to discuss it with your advisers, if any. You or your adviser are welcome to contact me at any time should you have any further queries.

If you wish to go ahead with the mediation, please let me know. As soon as all parties have agreed to participate in the mediation, I shall send you my usual Agreement to Mediate, Guidelines on Preparing for Mediation and fee agreement.

You can contact me as follows: phone [ ], mobile [ ], fax [ ] and email [ ].

If I do not hear from you before, I shall contact you in about two weeks to find out whether or not you would like to go ahead with the mediation.

Yours sincerely

---

3   For mediations conducted in accordance with the LSC Mediation Quality Mark (typically, family, community and some workplace mediations), refer to Requirement 1.2 of the MQMS (which is included in Appendix 8) for the information about mediation required to be relayed to a party before the mediation. Refer also to Chapter 2.

(ii) CORE Solutions Group example (used in less formal contexts, like workplace matters)[4]

This is an example of the type of letter which Core Solutions Group send out in employment, workplace or other situations where the formality of an agreement to mediate is not appropriate.

[Date]

Dear [ ]

I am looking forward to meeting you on [date]. I understand that this has been a difficult matter for you and I very much hope that you will be able to make good use of the day to find constructive and positive ways to go forward. I know also from what [x] has told me that each of you is keen to move forward. This letter is simply to supplement what [x] already mentioned to you.

The venue will be [y]. I will be in touch with you to discuss a starting time which is convenient, but I would expect to start as soon after 9am as possible.

On the day itself, I would hope to meet with each of you individually and privately to discuss with you the issues which have caused and others concern. To allow this to happen, we will each have a separate room where these private meetings can take place. If it seems appropriate for us to do so, we may at some stage all meet together – but we shall decide if that is appropriate on the day itself. The important point is that this is a completely flexible process and you are under no pressure to do or say – or agree to – anything with which you are not comfortable. I do wish to emphasise the confidentiality both of the whole process itself and of all the individual conversations that we have.

Clearly, we hope to come up with satisfactory ways forward. [x] has asked that any outcome be relayed to him so that he can help everyone to take matters forward as they have been agreed. This does seem sensible – however, I shall pass nothing on without permission to do so from all those involved. [x] has said that he and others can be available at the end of a telephone during the day to discuss with us any proposals or strategies which may emerge so that we can be sure that these can be implemented and supported.

It would help me if you could let me have a short summary of the issues and concerns as you see them. This will help me to gain a greater understanding of what this is all about.

Please rest assured that I shall not make any judgments based on this summary and look forward to hearing from you directly on the day of the mediation the details of how you feel, what your concerns are and what possible solutions there might be. The summary can be sent to me at the address in this letter. To help you in this, I enclose a preparation sheet with questions, some of which I hope may be helpful. We shall discuss this further on the day.

---

4   This document is reproduced with permission from the Guide to Mediation Services published by Core Solutions Group. Core Solutions Group is Scotland's pre-eminent provider of mediation services to business, organisations and the professions in Scotland (www.core-solutions.com)

I should emphasise, as a formality, that the meeting will not prejudice your legal rights or your employment rights in the event that we do not reach a satisfactory outcome and you may withdraw from the meeting at any stage if you are not happy with what is happening. I would also be pleased if you would agree that you may not call me as a witness or involve me in any other way in any proceedings which might follow in connection with the matters we discuss. Again, as a matter of formality, I need to ask you to confirm that neither Core Mediation nor I will be liable to you for anything I may do or not do in connection with my role as mediator. I have to address these mattes for professional indemnity insurance purposes.

I hope that this helps to summarise the arrangements for this process. May I ask you to acknowledge receipt of this letter, your commitment to trying to resolve the issues and your agreement that the process is a confidential one, by signing the copy of this letter which is enclosed? Your signature will also confirm your agreement with the other matters covered in this letter.

I would like to be able to have a brief conversation with you prior to the meeting itself. I wonder if I could ask you to give me a telephone number and convenient times at which I might contact you prior to the meeting? Perhaps you could give me this information when you return the copy of this letter?

Situations like this are very often the source of worry and anxiety. Having the opportunity to talk about them and to look forward and find constructive solutions can make a huge difference. I have been involved in a number of similar matters and have found that the mediation process can be very rewarding. In my experience, parties very frequently find creative and satisfactory ways to leave difficulties behind them and to move forward positively. I very much hope that this will be the outcome of our meeting.

Yours sincerely

[Name]

Telephone No:

E-mail:

I acknowledge that I have received this letter and that I agree with all that is set out in this letter:

Signed:

Name:

Date:

Telephone number:

D. Information about the mediator

(i) Sample mediator resume

[Mediator's name]

Qualifications and Current Positions
>
> BA (1980), LLB (1982)
> Accredited Mediator, CEDR
> Solicitor, England & Wales
> Partner, Rudd & Rudd, London
> Mediation panellist for [ ]

Mediation Experience

Conducted approximately 40 mediations from 2005 to date.
Experience in general commercial, organisational and environmental disputes.

Other Relevant Experience

Consultant to state and local governments on dispute resolution
Member, Law Society ADR Committee
Author of three articles on mediation and dispute resolution
Served as role play coach in mediator training workshops
Acted as assessor in Schools Conflict Resolution and Mediation Competition

Contact

Postal:	[ ]
Telephone:	[ ]
Fax:	[ ]
Email:	[ ]

(ii) Generic mediator profile[5]

NMI (Netherlands Mediation Institute)
Professional profile of a mediator[6]

Description of services provided by a mediator

A mediator assists as an independent expert in a process which is aimed at two or more parties through negotiations reaching a joint solution to a dispute dividing them, on the basis of the provisions laid down in the NMI Mediation Rules and

---

5   The sample is from a jurisdiction (Netherlands), where mediators are certified. Although the document is used in the Netherlands, and refers specifically to mediations conducted under the NMI procedures/rules, it has been included here to provide a useful template which can be adapted to suit the circumstances of any case as a way of explaining the qualities of mediators and what they do.

6   Reproduced with the kind permission of the Nederlands Mediation Instituut – NMI. For further information please visit www.nmi-mediation.nl.

the NMI Code of Conduct for Mediators, or declared at least equivalent by the Mediator Quality Assurance Committee.

Within the framework of the certification of mediators, the following shall apply for the assessing of the services provided by a mediator:

- the services consist in assisting in a process which is aimed at two or more parties through negotiations reaching a joint solution to a dispute dividing them;

- the mediator must have made it clear in advance that he/she provides this assistance as a mediator;

- the frame of reference for the process is provided by the NMI Contract, the NMI Mediation Rules and the NMI Code of Conduct, including the complaints scheme and disciplinary rules, or another frame of reference at least equivalent thereto.

Qualities of mediators

A mediator must be capable of conducting mediations independently. For this, the mediator must have sufficient experience, personal qualities, knowledge, personal interactive and other skills, and a professional attitude.

Experience

The mediator must have sufficient life, social and work experience to be able to adequately comprehend the nature of the conflict dividing the parties.

Personal qualities

- Composure.
- Flexibility.
- Creativity.
- Positive attitude.
- Ability to handle stress and conflicts and to render these controllable.

Knowledge

- Patterns in communications between people who have a dispute with one another.
- The concept of conflict mediation.
- Different negotiation methods, such as the Harvard method.
- The conditions (with respect to the parties and the mediator him/herself) which must have been met before mediation can be commenced.

Skills

General skills

The ability:

– to make the areas of common interest and/or responsibilities transparent for the parties and to highlight the differences in their perceptions;

– to determine and/or identify the agenda and/or the 'hidden agenda';

– to help the parties negotiate effectively and to overcome deadlocks;

– to recognise abuse of the mediation;

– to recognise information which must be treated as confidential, even if this has not been explicitly said to be confidential;

– to ensure a balanced handling of the dispute in such a way that each party is given equal opportunity to participate in the mediation;

– to recognise when and when not to intervene in the negotiation process between the parties;

– to speed up the mediation process and to keep it going.

Technical skills

The ability:

– to explain, discuss and conclude a mediation agreement;

– to record and report on the matters discussed at mediation sessions;

– to draw up or give instructions for the drawing up of a settlement agreement.

Understanding commercial matters, analytical powers

The ability:

– to monitor the underlying principles of the mediation;

– to deploy understanding and knowledge of commercial matters, and insofar as relevant branch-related knowledge;

– to render complex problems controllable and to identify and make part problems transparent.

Interactive skills

The ability:

– to show respect for the parties and to ensure that the parties show respect for each other;

– to ensure that common courtesy is observed;

– to treat all parties as equals.

Professional attitude

The ability:

- to consciously confine oneself to assisting the mediation process;

- to remain aware of the limits of mediation;

- to refrain from knowingly cooperating in the abuse of the mediation procedure;

- to withdraw from the mediation as soon as the limits of professional ethics are transgressed;

- to remain neutral.

- to draw the appropriate line between being involved in the mediation and not becoming involved in the dispute.

- to remain open to 'feedback' concerning one's own performance as mediator eg – through assessment while carrying out one's duties by the (temporary) presence of another mediator or another person designated for that purpose.

- to keep the costs of the mediation procedure for the clients as low as possible.

- to commit oneself never to perform any act that could bring mediation into disrepute.

E. Information about mediation (used in general civil or commercial cases)[7]

What is mediation?

Mediation is a process in which an outside person assists two or more people or organisations in dispute to communicate, to negotiate and to make mutually satisfactory decisions on the disputes between them. It is a form of 'assisted decision-making'.

What are the events leading up to mediation?

Every mediation process is different, but normally a mediation involves the following initial steps:

■ The mediator is approached by one person or organisation with a request for information or mediation assistance.

■ The mediator contacts the other persons or organisations involved and asks if they are willing to consider mediation.

■ The mediator sends to each person or group information about mediation and about the mediator, and a mediation contract for the parties to complete. Sometimes the mediator requests written background information on the dispute.

■ The mediator makes contact with each individual or organisation to explain the process and to assess the suitability of the dispute for mediation. This may involve telephone contact or personal meetings in which the mediator prepares each side for the mediation.

■ A time and place, suitable for all persons, is arranged for the mediation meeting.

What happens in the mediation meeting?

The mediator welcomes each person and explains the mediation process. He or she first asks each person to talk in turn about their principal concerns.

The mediator clarifies the parties' concerns and translates them into issues for discussion. The issues are written up and listed in order of priority. The mediator then defines the areas where the parties are in agreement or disagreement, and provides a structure for the discussions. Each party is asked to give their views and explain their perceptions to the other on each issue, and together the parties explore options for resolving the points of difference. Thereby an agreement is pieced together, like a jigsaw.

---

7   This guidance note can be adapted to suit the nature of the case, the agreements reached with the parties/the lawyers about the process, whether standard mediation procedures/rules will be used, whether a formal mediation agreement will be entered into and the mediator's ways of working/ charging etc.

Who can be present and how confidential is it?

Advisers, supporters, witnesses and other persons can be present at the mediation if the parties both agree, and if those attending sign a confidentiality undertaking.

The parties can agree on what will be said publicly about the mediation. Neither party can lead evidence in court about what was said in the mediation, nor produce in court documents prepared for the mediation.

What is the legal status of agreements reached at mediation?

This depends on the wishes of the parties. The parties and their advisers, with assistance from the mediator, will record the outcome in a Heads of Agreement document which contains both matters which have been agreed and the issues, if any, which are still to be settled. The parties can redraft the agreement into a legally binding document after receiving advice from their lawyers or other professional advisers.

What if I feel uncomfortable in the mediation?

It is a normal part of the mediation process for the mediator to meet separately with each party on a confidential basis. You can also ask to speak to the mediator alone or you can ask for the mediation session to be adjourned if you have the need. You can always express any concerns openly in the mediation and the mediator will try to deal with them there and then.

Some of the mediator's tasks are to create a favourable environment for dispute resolution, to assist each side to negotiate, and to minimise intimidation or other causes of anxiety in the parties.

What does it cost?

Mediators charge at an agreed hourly rate for preparation, for actual meeting time, and for other expenses, if any, such as travel. Many mediations are complete after 8–10 hours of work.

What happens afterwards?

One aim of mediation is to model a method of working through disputes so that the parties can solve their own disputes in the future. Mediated agreements often contain a dispute resolution clause in terms of which the parties commit themselves, in the event of a breach of the agreement, to come back to mediation before initiation of court proceedings.

Appendix 3

Mediation Procedures and Agreements

A. Model Mediation Procedures

(i) CEDR Model Mediation Procedure (used in general civil and commercial cases)[1]

1. What is mediation?

Mediation is a flexible process conducted confidentially in which a neutral person actively assists the parties in working towards a negotiated agreement of a dispute or difference, with the parties in ultimate control of the decision to settle and the terms of resolution.

The principal features of mediation are that it:

- involves a neutral third party to facilitate negotiations;
- is quick to set up and is inexpensive, without prejudice and confidential;
- involves party representatives with sufficient authority to settle;
- is flexible, with no set procedure, enabling the process to be designed and managed by the Mediator to suit the parties, in consultation with them;
- enables the parties to devise solutions which are not possible in an adjudicative process such as litigation or arbitration, and which may benefit all the parties, particularly if there is the possibility of a continuing relationship between them;
- can be used in both domestic and cross-border disputes, two-party and multi-party disputes, and whether or not litigation or arbitration has been commenced.

Many commercial and government contracts now require parties to use mediation in accordance with CEDR's Model Procedure. While mediation is essentially flexible, the Model Procedure set out in this document, taken with the CEDR Solve Mediation Agreement, will give sufficient certainty to enable the process to be set up and used.

If settlement terms cannot be agreed at a mediation, the parties are free to revert to litigation or arbitration.

---

1   Reproduced with the kind permission of CEDR. Please visit www.cedr.com to check for latest version of this document as these documents are updated and existing versions can become out of date.

2.   Referral to mediation

Referral of a dispute to a mediator or to CEDR Solve for mediation may be as a result of:

- voluntary referral by all parties;
- referral by one party who asks CEDR Solve to secure the involvement of other parties into a mediation;
- responding to a Pre-action Protocol, the Civil Procedure Rules 1998, a Court Order or a recommendation by a judge before trial or appeal;
- the provisions of a clause in a commercial or government contract requiring the use of mediation as a step in the parties' agreed dispute resolution process.

3.   Choosing the mediator

Parties may choose their own mediator directly, or may ask CEDR Solve to nominate one or more persons to act as mediator for a dispute in accordance with the wishes of the parties or any relevant Court Order (a copy of which must be supplied to CEDR Solve by the parties as soon as possible after CEDR Solve has been instructed). If the parties require it, more than one mediator can be appointed to work as co-mediators, or the parties can agree on an independent neutral expert to advise the mediator on technical matters.

CEDR Solve will only nominate or appoint a mediator who, in their view, possesses the relevant skills and experience to mediate the dispute for the parties effectively, and who will comply with the CEDR Solve Code of Conduct for Third Party Neutrals ('the Code'). Any nominated mediator will be required to confirm immediately to CEDR Solve if there is any matter which might prevent the nominated mediator from complying with the Code in relation to the mediation of the dispute, such as a conflict of interest. CEDR Solve will then notify the parties of any such matter immediately it is disclosed to them.

If required by either the parties or the Court, or under the published terms of any CEDR Solve dispute resolution scheme, CEDR Solve will appoint a mediator to be used in relation to a dispute, subject always to that mediator not being prevented from complying with the Code in relation to the mediation of that dispute.

The parties may be asked by CEDR Solve to approve the appointment by them of an assistant mediator (who will be a CEDR Accredited Mediator) or an observer to attend a mediation at no cost to the parties, provided that they too comply with the Code in respect of the mediation of that dispute. The identity of any assistant mediator or observer proposed to attend the mediation will be made known in advance of the mediation to the parties, who are free to object to any such nomination or decline any such appointment. The mediator's signature of the mediation agreement binds any assistant mediator or observer to its terms.

4.   Preparation for the mediation

Depending on the CEDR Solve service selected by the parties, either CEDR Solve or the mediator when agreed or appointed, will make the necessary arrangements for the mediation as required or agreed by the parties or under the terms of any scheme, including:

- drafting the agreement, submitting it for approval by the parties and preparing the final form for signature, incorporating any agreed amendments;

- facilitating agreement as to the date, venue and start time for the mediation;

- organising exchange of case summaries and document bundles between the parties and the mediator;

- setting up any pre-mediation meetings agreed by the parties and the mediator.

The parties will:

- agree the appointment of the mediator or a process to select or appoint the mediator;

- agree with CEDR Solve the date, venue and start time for the mediation;

- pay CEDR Solve's fees and expenses as agreed under CEDR Solve's Terms and Conditions of business;

- each prepare and exchange a case summary in respect of their approach to the dispute at the mediation and endeavour to agree with all other parties what documents are needed for the mediation;

- send to the mediator (direct or through CEDR Solve) a copy of their case summary and two copies of the document bundles no less than two weeks before the date set for the mediation, making clear whether case summaries have or have not yet been exchanged, whether or not and when CEDR Solve is to effect exchange, and whether all or any part of any case summary or documentation is intended to be confidential for the mediator only;

- notify the mediator direct or through CEDR Solve of the names and roles of all those attending the mediation on their behalf, so that CEDR Solve can inform all Parties and the mediator in advance of the mediation;

- ensure that a lead negotiator with full authority to settle the dispute (or not) attends the mediation to sign the mediation agreement;

- alternatively notify the mediator, CEDR Solve and (unless very good reason exists to the contrary) the other parties of any limitation on authority to settle, for instance lack of legal capacity, or the need for ministerial committee or board ratification, in which case the lead negotiator will need to have power to recommend acceptance of any settlement. Late disclosure of limited authority to settle can call into question that party's good faith involvement in the mediation process, and have detrimental effects on the prospects of success of any mediation.

The mediator will:

- ensure at all times that the Code is complied with in respect of the mediation of the dispute, reporting any conflict of interest or other relevant matter, if any, to CEDR Solve and (subject to any question of confidentiality or privilege) the parties immediately it emerges;

- attend any pre-mediation meetings on terms and agenda agreed by the parties;

- read each case summary and document bundle submitted in advance of the mediation by the parties;
- make contact with a representative of each of the parties before the mediation to assist in preparation for the mediation.

5.   Documentation

Documentation intended to be treated as confidential by the mediator or CEDR Solve (such as a counsel's opinion, an undisclosed expert report, a draft proof of evidence or a confidential briefing for the mediator) must be clearly marked as such, and will not be circulated further without express authority.

One of the advantages of mediation is that its success is not dependent on exhaustive disclosure of documents. Bundles can usually be relatively limited in size, containing only key documents, and case summaries can be quite brief, and can to advantage be prepared jointly by the parties. The parties can ask CEDR Solve to effect simultaneous exchange of case summaries if required.

While documents brought into existence for the purpose of the mediation, such as case summaries, are clearly privileged from later production in those or other proceedings, the fact that a document which is otherwise disclosable in proceedings is produced for the first time during the mediation does not normally confer privileged status on it. The parties must take legal advice on such matters if they arise.

6.   The mediation agreement

The agreement to mediate provides the essential legal basis for the mediation. Its signatories (the parties to the dispute, the mediator and CEDR Solve) all agree by signing it that the mediation is to be conducted consistent with both this CEDR Solve Model Procedure and the Code.

A draft mediation agreement will be sent for approval to the parties as part of the preparation process for the mediation, and any proposed amendments can then be discussed and inserted if agreed. The mediation agreement will normally be signed at the beginning of the mediation day on behalf of each of the parties and the mediator, having been pre-signed on behalf of CEDR Solve. In any pre-mediation contact with the parties, CEDR Solve staff and any CEDR mediator once appointed will observe its terms as to confidentiality, even though the agreement has not yet been signed.

7.   The mediation

It is normal for each of the parties to have a private room for confidential consultations on their own and with the mediator during the mediation. There should also be a further room large enough for all parties to meet with the mediator jointly.

The mediator will chair and take responsibility for determining the procedure at the mediation, in consultation with the parties.

The likely procedure will comprise:

- preliminary meetings with each of the parties when they arrive at the venue;

- a joint meeting of all attending the mediation, at which each of the parties will normally be invited to make an oral presentation;

- a mix of further private meetings and joint meetings (which may involve all or some of each party's team), as proposed by the mediator and agreed by the parties.

Professional advisers, particularly lawyers, can and usually do attend the mediation. Such advisers play an important role in the exchange of information and opinion on fact, evidence and law; in supporting their clients (particularly individuals) in the negotiations; in advising clients on the implications of settlement; and in drawing up the settlement agreement and any consent order.

Although the agreement provides that no verbatim recording or transcript will be made of the whole mediation by the parties or the mediator, they can make their own private notes which will be undisclosable to anyone else, including in any subsequent litigation or arbitration.

Mediations can last beyond a normal working day and it is important that the key people present for each of the parties remain present or at worst available by telephone for so long as the mediation continues. Any time constraints should be reported to CEDR Solve or the mediator as soon as known, as any unexpected departure can be detrimental to the progress of the mediation and perceived as disrespectful by other parties.

8.   Confidentiality in relation to the mediation

The CEDR Solve standard agreement provides that what happens at the mediation is to be treated as confidential by the parties, the mediator and CEDR Solve, including the fact and terms of settlement. However, the fact that the mediation is to take place or has taken place is not normally made confidential, as either or both of the parties may wish to claim credit for agreeing to engage in the process. If it is desired to make the fact that the mediation is taking place confidential also, the agreement can be amended.

Apart from where the parties agree in writing to consent to disclosure of what would normally be confidential, there may be rare circumstances in which the confidentiality of the mediation process cannot be preserved, such as where:

- the mediator or any party or their representative is required by law to make disclosure;

- the mediator reasonably considers that there is a serious risk of significant harm to the life or safety of any person if the information in question is not disclosed; or

- the mediator reasonably considers that there is a serious risk of being personally subject to criminal proceedings unless the information in question is disclosed.

Such questions might arise in relation to duties under the Proceeds of Crime Act 2002 or related legislation or under any other legislation. Legal representatives (who may themselves be under a comparable duty of disclosure in their own capacity) must take full responsibility for advising their clients of the implications of disclosure in relation to any such matters at a mediation.

9.   Conclusion of the Mediation

The mediation may end in a number of ways:

- by settlement of the dispute in whole or part, when all agreed matters must be written down and signed by the parties to be binding;
- by one or more parties leaving the mediation before settlement is achieved;
- by an agreed adjournment for such time and on such terms as the parties and the mediator agree;
- by withdrawal of the mediator in accordance with the mandatory and optional circumstances set out in the Code.

The mediator will facilitate the drawing up of any settlement agreement, though the drafting is normally done by the lawyers representing each of the parties. Where proceedings *have not* been started in respect of the dispute, the settlement agreement will (if so intended and drafted) be a contract enforceable by legal action. Where proceedings *have* been issued in relation to the dispute, it is normal for a Consent Order to be agreed either at or after the mediation and later lodged to end the proceedings on the terms agreed.

Where the mediation does not end in complete settlement, the Mediator may make contact with the parties thereafter to see whether further progress might be possible. Many disputes which do not settle at the mediation settle later, usually as a result of what occurred or was learned at the mediation.

CEDR Solve endeavours to make contact with all the parties after every mediation to obtain their feedback on both the process itself and, in particular, the mediator. Any feedback obtained regarding the mediator will be given in full to the mediator as part of the mediator's continuing learning and development.

10.   Complaint

Any formal complaint about CEDR Solve or any mediator nominated by CEDR Solve should follow the procedure set out on the CEDR website at www.cedr.com.

(ii)   ADR Group Mediation Procedure & Rules (used in general civil and commercial cases)[2]

ADR Group mediations are governed by the following procedure ('The Mediation Procedure') as amended by ADR Group from time to time. It will be taken that the parties have agreed that the mediation shall be conducted in accordance with the Mediation Procedure.

---

2   Reproduced with the kind permission of the ADR Group. For further information please visit their website at www.adrgroup.com

1. Mediation Procedure

1.1 The parties to the dispute or negotiation in question will attempt to settle by mediation. Representatives of the parties including, if desired, their advisers (legal representatives) and the mediator will attend the mediation session.

1.2 The representatives (Legal or otherwise) of the parties must have the necessary authority to settle the dispute. If a party is a natural person, that person must attend the mediation session. If a party is not a natural person it must be represented at the mediation session by an officer or employee with full authority to make binding agreements settling the dispute. If that person comes with 'limited' authority, that is, authority up to a certain amount, he or she must disclose this information to the mediator prior to the mediation.

1.3 Any and all communications relating to, and at, the mediation are private & confidential and will be without prejudice.

1.4 Upon request ADR Group will provide to the parties, details of recommended mediators drawn from its panel of mediators (ADR Net Limited). Consideration will be given to the nature of the dispute, the complexity, the location and the experience required. If the parties are unable to agree to the appointment of a mediator, ADR Group will appoint a mediator if requested to do so.

2. Mediation Agreement

2.1 The parties sign an agreement ('Agreement to Mediate') at the start of the mediation. This agreement governs the relationship between the parties before, during and after the mediation.

2.2 Each party, in signing the Agreement to Mediate, will be deemed to be agreeing on behalf of both itself and all such other persons to be bound by the confidentiality provisions of the Mediation Procedure.

3. The Mediator

3.1 The Mediator will:

Attend any meetings with any or all of the parties preceding the mediation, if requested to do so, or if the mediator decides it is appropriate

Prior to the commencement of the mediation read and familiarize him/herself with each party's Position Statement and any documents provided in accordance with paragraph 6.1

Determine the procedure

Assist the parties in drawing up any written settlement agreement

Abide by the terms and conditions of the Mediation Procedure, the Agreement to Mediate and ADR Group's Code of Conduct

3.2 The Mediator will not:

Analyse an party's legal position or rights

Impose a settlement on the parties

Offer legal advice or act as legal adviser to any party

417

3.3 The parties and mediator acknowledge that the mediator is an independent contractor and is not appointed as an agent or employee of any of the parties or ADR Group. Neither the mediator nor a member of his or her firm or business will act, or have acted, as a professional adviser, or in any other capacity, for any of the parties individually in connection with the dispute either before, during the currency of the mediation or at any time thereafter.

4. Mediation Agreement

4.1 ADR Group will in consultation with the parties and the mediator, make the necessary arrangements for the mediation including, as appropriate:

Recommend mediators with regard to, inter alia, nature of the dispute, degree of complexity, location of parties etc and drawing up the Agreement to Mediate

Liaise between the parties to agree suitable date and venue

Assist the parties in preparing their Position Statement (see paragraph 6) and supporting documentation

Discuss or meet with any or all of the parties or their representatives (and the mediator if appropriate), either together or separately, on any matter pursuant to the proposed mediation

General administration in relation to the mediation

5. Representation

5.1 Parties do not require legal representation to attend the mediation.

5.2 Where a party is un-represented, ADR Group encourages such party to obtain independent legal advice prior to the mediation.

5.3 Each party is require to notify ADR Group and other parties involved in the mediation of the names of those people intended to be present on its behalf at the mediation.

6. Position Statements and Documentation

6.1 Each party will be required to prepare and deliver to the mediator, seven (7) days prior to the mediation, a concise summary ('Position Statement') of the case in dispute. Together with this statement should be copies of documents referred to in the Position Statement and those which parties will be seeking to refer to during the mediation.

6.2 ADR Group do not impose any obligation on the parties to exchange Position Statements, but parties are free to agree to the simultaneous exchange of the Position Statements, if so agreed or if considered appropriate.

6.3 The Position Statement is private and confidential and will not be disclosed (by the mediator) to any other third party unless expressly authorised to do so. ADR Group will provide to the parties a guide to position statement preparation.

6.4 Parties are encouraged to prepare and agree a joint bundle of documents where appropriate.

7. The Mediation

7.1 No formal record or transcript of the mediation will be made.

7.2 The mediation session is for the purpose of attempting to achieve a negotiated settlement and all information provided during the mediation session is without prejudice and will be inadmissible in any litigation or arbitration of the dispute. Evidence, which is otherwise admissible, shall not be rendered inadmissible as a result of its use in the mediation session.

7.3 If the parties are unable to reach a settlement during the mediation, the mediator may, if requested to do so, facilitate further negotiation after the mediation session itself has ended.

8. Settlement Agreement

8.1 Any settlement reached in the mediation will not be legally binding until it has been recorded in writing and signed by, or on behalf of, the parties.

9. Termination

9.1 Any of the parties may withdraw from the mediation at any time and shall immediately inform the mediator and the other representatives either orally or in writing. The mediation will terminate when:

A party voluntarily withdraws from the mediation or

A written settlement agreement is concluded or

The mediator elects, in his / her sole discretion, that continuing the mediation is unlikely to result in a settlement or

The mediator decides that he / she should retire for any of the reasons set our in the Code of Practice.

10. Settlement Agreement

10.1 Where the dispute has been referred to mediation by the Court or where the Court has ordered that the parties consider mediation, and the mediation does not achieve settlement, the current litigation or arbitration in relation to the dispute may be commenced or continued, notwithstanding the mediation, unless the parties agree otherwise.

11. Settlement Agreement

11.1 Every person involved in the mediation will keep confidential and not use for any collateral or ulterior purpose:

The fact that the mediation is to take place or has taken place and

All information, (whether given orally or in writing or otherwise), produced for, or arising pursuant to, the mediation including the settlement agreement (if any) arising out of it except if so far as is necessary to implement and enforce any such settlement agreement.

Not withstanding the above it would be prudent of the parties to include an express confidentiality clause (if so desired) in any settlement agreement.

11.2 All documents or other information produced for, or arising in relation to the mediation will be privileged and not admissible as evidence or discoverable in any litigation or arbitration connected with the dispute (see paragraph 11.1 above). This does not apply to any information, which would in any event have been admissible or discloseable in such proceedings.

11.3 The parties will not subpoena or otherwise require the mediator, ADR Group (or any employee, consultant, director or representative of ADR Group) or any other person attending the mediation under the auspices of ADR Group to testify or produce records, notes or any other information or material whatsoever in any future or continuing proceedings.

12. Mediation Costs

12.1 It is usual that the costs of the mediation are borne equally between the parties.

12.2 Payment of these costs will be made to ADR Group in accordance with its fee schedule and terms and conditions of business (as amended from time to time).

12.3 Each party attending the mediation is to bear its own costs and expenses of its participation in the mediation (including legal representative costs) and unless agreed otherwise, such costs will be costs in the cause.

13. Waiver of Liability

13.1 Neither the mediator nor ADR Group shall be liable to the parties for any act or omission in connection with the services provided by them in, or in relation to, the mediation, unless the act or omission is fraudulent or involves willful misconduct.

14. Human Rights

14.1 The referral of a dispute to mediation does not affect any rights that may exist under Article 6 or the European Convention of Human Rights. Should the dispute not settle through the process of mediation, the parties' right to a fair trial shall remain unaffected.

(iii) ICC ADR Rules (used in commercial cases)[3]

ADR RULES OF THE INTERNATIONAL CHAMBER OF COMMERCE

In force as from 1 July 2001

Preamble

Amicable settlement is a desirable solution for business disputes and differences. It can occur before or during the litigation or arbitration of a dispute and can often be facilitated through the aid of a third party (the 'Neutral') acting in accordance with simple rules. The parties can agree to submit to such rules in their underlying contract or at any other time.

The International Chamber of Commerce ('ICC') sets out these amicable dispute resolution rules, entitled the ICC ADR Rules (the 'Rules'), which permit the parties to agree upon whatever settlement technique they believe to be appropriate to help them settle their dispute. In the absence of an agreement of the parties on a settlement technique, mediation shall be the settlement technique used under the Rules. The Guide to ICC ADR, which does not form part of the Rules, provides an explanation of the Rules and of various settlement techniques which can be used pursuant to the Rules.

Article 1
Scope of the ICC ADR Rules

All business disputes, whether or not of an international character, may be referred to ADR proceedings pursuant to these Rules. The provisions of these Rules may be modified by agreement of all of the parties, subject to the approval of ICC.

Article 2
Commencement of the ADR Proceedings

A   Where there is an agreement to refer to the Rules

1
Where there is an agreement between the parties to refer their dispute to the ICC ADR Rules, any party or parties wishing to commence ADR proceedings pursuant to the Rules shall send to ICC a written Request for ADR, which shall include:

a)   the names, addresses, telephone and facsimile numbers and e-mail addresses of the parties to the dispute and their authorized representatives, if any;

b)   a description of the dispute including, if possible, an assessment of its value;

---

3   Reproduced with the kind permission of the ICC. The text reproduced here is valid at the time of publication of this book. For a full set of the Rules please visit www.iccwbo.org/uploadedFiles/Court/ Arbitration/other/adr_rules.pdf. As amendments may from time to time be made to the text, readers are referred to www.iccadr.org for the latest version and for more information on this ICC dispute resolution service. The text is also available in the ICC Dispute Resolution Library at www.iccdrl.com.

c) any joint designation by all of the parties of a Neutral or any agreement of all of the parties upon the qualifications of a Neutral to be appointed by ICC where no joint designation has been made;

d) a copy of any written agreement under which the Request for ADR is made; and

e) the registration fee of the ADR proceedings, as set out in the Appendix hereto.

2

Where the Request for ADR is not filed jointly by all of the parties, the party or parties filing the Request shall simultaneously send the Request to the other party or parties. Such Request may include any proposal regarding the qualifications of a Neutral or any proposal of one or more Neutrals to be designated by all of the parties. Thereafter, all of the parties may jointly designate a Neutral or may agree upon the qualifications of a Neutral to be appointed by ICC. In either case, the parties shall promptly notify ICC thereof.

3

ICC shall promptly acknowledge receipt of the Request for ADR in writing to the parties.

B Where there is no agreement to refer to the Rules

1

Where there is no agreement between the parties to refer their dispute to the ICC ADR Rules, any party or parties wishing to commence ADR proceedings pursuant to the Rules shall send to ICC a written Request for ADR, which shall include:

a) the names, addresses, telephone and facsimile numbers and e-mail addresses of the parties to the dispute and their authorized representatives, if any;

b) a description of the dispute including, if possible, an assessment of its value; and

c) the registration fee of the ADR proceedings, as set out in the Appendix hereto.

The Request for ADR may also include any proposal regarding the qualifications of a Neutral or any proposal of one or more Neutrals to be designated by all of the parties.

2

ICC shall promptly inform the other party or parties in writing of the Request for ADR. Such party or parties shall be asked to inform ICC in writing, within 15 days of receipt of the Request for ADR, as to whether they agree or decline to participate in the ADR proceedings. In the former case, they may provide any proposal regarding the qualifications of a Neutral and may propose one or more Neutrals to be designated by the parties. Thereafter, all of the parties may jointly designate a Neutral or may agree upon the qualifications of a Neutral to be appointed by ICC. In either case, the parties shall promptly notify ICC thereof.

In the absence of any reply within such 15-day period, or in the case of a negative reply, the Request for ADR shall be deemed to have been declined and ADR proceedings shall not be commenced. ICC shall promptly so inform in writing the party or parties which filed the Request for ADR.

Article 3
Selection of the Neutral

1
Where all of the parties have jointly designated a Neutral, ICC shall take note of that designation, and such person, upon notifying ICC of his or her agreement to serve, shall act as the Neutral in the ADR proceedings. Where a Neutral has not been designated by all of the parties, or where the designated Neutral does not agree to serve, ICC shall promptly appoint a Neutral, either through an ICC National Committee or otherwise, and notify the parties thereof. ICC shall make all reasonable efforts to appoint a Neutral having the qualifications, if any, which have been agreed upon by all of the parties.

2
Every prospective Neutral shall promptly provide ICC with a curriculum vitae and a statement of independence, both duly signed and dated. The prospective Neutral shall disclose to ICC in the statement of independence any facts or circumstances which might be of such a nature as to call into question his or her independence in the eyes of the parties. ICC shall provide such information to the parties in writing.

3
If any party objects to the Neutral appointed by ICC and notifies ICC and the other party or parties thereof in writing, stating the reasons for such objection, within 15 days of receipt of notification of the appointment, ICC shall promptly appoint another Neutral.

4
Upon agreement of all of the parties, the parties may designate more than one Neutral or request ICC to appoint more than one Neutral, in accordance with the provisions of these Rules. In appropriate circumstances, ICC may propose the appointment of more than one Neutral to the parties.

Article 4
Fees and Costs

1
The party or parties filing a Request for ADR shall include with the Request a non-refundable registration fee, as set out in the Appendix hereto. No Request for ADR shall be processed unless accompanied by the requisite payment.

2
Following the receipt of a Request for ADR, ICC shall request the parties to pay a deposit in an amount likely to cover the administrative expenses of ICC and the fees and expenses of the Neutral for the ADR proceedings, as set out in the Appendix hereto. The ADR proceedings shall not go forward until payment of such deposit has been received by ICC.

3

In any case where ICC considers that the deposit is not likely to cover the total costs of the ADR proceedings, the amount of such deposit may be subject to readjustment. ICC may stay the ADR proceedings until the corresponding payments are made by the parties.

4

Upon termination of the ADR proceedings, ICC shall settle the total costs of the proceedings and shall, as the case may be, reimburse the parties for any excess payment or bill the parties for any balance required pursuant to these Rules.

5

All above deposits and costs shall be borne in equal shares by the parties, unless they agree otherwise in writing. However, any party shall be free to pay the unpaid balance of such deposits and costs should another party fail to pay its share.

6

A party's other expenditure shall remain the responsibility of that party.

Article 5
Conduct of the ADR Procedure

1

The Neutral and the parties shall promptly discuss, and seek to reach agreement upon, the settlement technique to be used, and shall discuss the specific ADR procedure to be followed.

2

In the absence of an agreement of the parties on the settlement technique to be used, mediation shall be used.

3

The Neutral shall conduct the procedure in such manner as the Neutral sees fit. In all cases the Neutral shall be guided by the principles of fairness and impartiality and by the wishes of the parties.

4

In the absence of an agreement of the parties, the Neutral shall determine the language or languages of the proceedings and the place of any meetings to be held.

5

Each party shall cooperate in good faith with the Neutral.

Article 6
Termination of the ADR Proceedings

1

ADR proceedings which have been commenced pursuant to these Rules shall terminate upon the earlier of:

a)   the signing by the parties of a settlement agreement;

b)   the notification in writing to the Neutral by one or more parties, at any time after the discussion referred to in Article 5(1) has occurred, of a decision no longer to pursue the ADR proceedings;

c)   the completion of the procedure established pursuant to Article 5 and the notification in writing thereof by the Neutral to the parties;

d)   the notification in writing by the Neutral to the parties that the ADR proceedings will not, in the Neutral's opinion, resolve the dispute between the parties;

e)   the expiration of any time limit set for the ADR proceedings, if not extended by all of the parties, such expiration to be notified in writing by the Neutral to the parties;

f)   the notification in writing by ICC to the parties and the Neutral, not less than 15 days after the due date for any payment by one or more parties pursuant to these Rules, stating that such payment has not been made; or

g)   the notification in writing by ICC to the parties stating, in the judgment of ICC, that there has been a failure to designate a Neutral or that it has not been reasonably possible to appoint a Neutral.

2

The Neutral, upon any termination of the ADR proceedings pursuant to Article 6(1), (a)–(e), shall promptly notify ICC of the termination of the ADR proceedings and shall provide ICC with a copy of any notification referred to in Article 6(1), (b)–(e). In all cases ICC shall confirm in writing the termination of the ADR proceedings to the parties and the Neutral, if a Neutral has already been designated or appointed.

Article 7
General Provisions

1

In the absence of any agreement of the parties to the contrary and unless prohibited by applicable law, the ADR proceedings, including their outcome, are private and confidential. Any settlement agreement between the parties shall similarly be kept confidential except that a party shall have the right to disclose it to the extent that such disclosure is required by applicable law or necessary for purposes of its implementation or enforcement.

2

Unless required to do so by applicable law and in the absence of any agreement of the parties to the contrary, a party shall not in any manner produce as evidence in any judicial, arbitration or similar proceedings:

a)   any documents, statements or communications which are submitted by another party or by the Neutral in the ADR proceedings, unless they can be obtained independently by the party seeking to produce them in the judicial, arbitration or similar proceedings;

b)   any views expressed or suggestions made by any party within the ADR proceedings with regard to the possible settlement of the dispute;

c)   any admissions made by another party within the ADR proceedings;

d)   any views or proposals put forward by the Neutral; or

e)   the fact that any party had indicated within the ADR proceedings that it was ready to accept a proposal for a settlement.

3
Unless all of the parties agree otherwise in writing, a Neutral shall not act nor shall have acted in any judicial, arbitration or similar proceedings relating to the dispute which is or was the subject of the ADR proceedings, whether as a judge, as an arbitrator, as an expert or as a representative or advisor of a party.

4
The Neutral, unless required by applicable law or unless all of the parties agree otherwise in writing, shall not give testimony in any judicial, arbitration or similar proceedings concerning any aspect of the ADR proceedings.

5
Neither the Neutral, nor ICC and its employees, nor the ICC National Committees shall be liable to any person for any act or omission in connection with the ADR proceedings.

APPENDIX
SCHEDULE OF ADR COSTS

A
The party or parties filing a Request for ADR shall include with the Request a non-refundable registration fee of US$1,500 to cover the costs of processing the Request for ADR. No Request for ADR shall be processed unless accompanied by the requisite payment.

B
The administrative expenses of ICC for the ADR proceedings shall be fixed at ICC's discretion depending on the tasks carried out by ICC. Such administrative expenses shall not exceed the maximum sum of US$10,000.

C
The fees of the Neutral shall be calculated on the basis of the time reasonably spent by the Neutral in the ADR

proceedings, at an hourly rate fixed for such proceedings by ICC in consultation with the Neutral and the parties. Such hourly rate shall be reasonable in amount and shall be determined in light of the complexity of the dispute and any other relevant circumstances. The amount of reasonable expenses of the Neutral shall be fixed by ICC.

D
Amounts paid to the Neutral do not include any possible value added taxes (VAT) or other taxes or charges and imposts applicable to the Neutral's fees. Parties have a duty to pay any such taxes or charges; however, the recovery of any such taxes or charges is a matter solely between the Neutral and the parties.

(iv) NMI Mediation Rules[4]

Netherlands Mediation Institute
NMI MEDIATION RULES 2008

Article 1 – Definitions

In these Rules the following terms have the following meaning:

a.   Issue: the issue described in the Mediation Agreement.

b.   Certifying institution: the institution which issues certificates of professional competence to Mediators on the basis of a certification schedule recognized or accepted by the NMI.

c.   Mediation: procedure in which the Parties make an effort to resolve their Issue under the supervision of a Mediator in accordance with the Rules.

d.   Mediation Agreement: the written agreement in which the Parties agree to endeavour to resolve the Issue through Mediation, and instruct the Mediator to act as Mediator in respect of the Issue and the Mediator accepts this instruction.

e.   Mediator: the person who conducts the Mediation and who is listed in the Register.

f.   The NMI: the Foundation 'Stichting Nederlands Mediation Instituut', having its registered office in Rotterdam.

g.   Party/Parties: the parties who wish to resolve the Issue through Mediation.

h.   Register: the Register of Mediators kept by the NMI.

i.   The Rules: these Rules.

j.   Secretariat: the Secretariat of the NMI.

Article 2 – Appointment of the Mediator

2.1.   The Parties shall themselves appoint a mediator.

2.2.   If the Parties wish to be assisted by the NMI in selecting a Mediator, they must file a written request thereto with the Secretariat. This request must contain the names, (e-mail) addresses, telephone and fax numbers of the Parties and their representatives, if any, as well as a general description of the Issue.

2.3.   Upon receipt of the request, the Secretariat will send to the Parties:

a.   a list with the names of the Mediators who, on the basis of the description of the Issue and/or the relevant criteria stated by the Parties, are considered eligible;

4   Reproduced with the kind permission of the Nederlands Mediation Instituut – NMI. For further information please visit www.nmi-mediation.nl

        b.   a copy of the Rules and a copy of the Code of Conduct for NMI registered Mediators;

        c.   an invoice for administrative charges.

2.4   The Parties will together select a Mediator from the aforementioned list. The Parties may then contact the Mediator directly. If the Parties do not wish to contact the Mediator directly, they must inform the Secretariat in writing which Mediator they have selected. Upon receipt of this letter the Secretariat will inform the Mediator concerned of the request and of his having been selected, so that the Mediator may then contact the Parties.

2.5   If the Parties fail to jointly agree on the selection of a Mediator, they (or either one of them) may request the Secretariat to make a written proposal for a Mediator who may be appointed by the Parties.

2.6.   On acceptance of the instruction the Mediator will draw up a Mediation Agreement. The Parties and the Mediator will then sign the Mediation Agreement.

Article 3 – Commencement of Mediation

3.1   The Mediation will commence as soon as the Mediation Agreement has been signed by the Parties and the Mediator, unless a different time is agreed in the Mediation Agreement.

Article 4 – Activities of the Mediator and process supervision

1.1.   The activities of the Mediator relate to the Mediation sessions, but may also comprise other activities such as reporting, contacts with the Parties (either electronically, in writing or by telephone), studying papers, contacts with third parties, and drawing up agreements, all this from the commencement of the Mediation onwards.

1.2.   The Mediator shall decide, after having consulted the Parties, on the manner in which the Mediation will be conducted.

1.3.   The Mediator may communicate with the Parties separately and confidentially.

1.4.   The Parties and the Mediator shall do their best to ensure that the Mediation proceeds in an expeditious manner.

Article 5 – Voluntariness

5.1.   The Mediation shall take place on the basis of voluntariness of the Parties. Each Party, as well as the Mediator, may put an end to the Mediation at any time.

5.2.   Agreements in the interim shall bind the Parties only insofar as the Parties explicitly lay down the binding nature of these agreements in a signed agreement. They shall not be bound by the positions adopted or proposals made by them or by the Mediator during the Mediation. The Parties shall be bound only by what has been laid down in the agreement referred to in article 10.1 and signed by them.

Article 6 – Privacy

6.1.   No person shall be present at the Mediation other than the Mediator and the Parties, or their representatives and/or advisers, if any. For the involvement of other persons in the Mediation, the consent of the Parties shall be required. If the Mediator wishes, he may cause himself to be assisted clerically at the Mediation by a person designated by him for that purpose. In such event the Mediator shall ensure that all persons involved in the Mediation sign a declaration of confidentially.

6.2.   If either Party causes himself to be represented during the Mediation, his representative must be authorized to perform all (legal) acts that are necessary for the Mediation, including the entering into an agreement as referred to in article 10.1. If the Mediator so requests, a written power of attorney must be produced showing the authority of the representative.

Article 7 – Confidentiality

7.1   The Parties undertake not to disclose to any third party – including courts and arbitrators – any information concerning the progress of the Mediation, the positions adopted, proposals made or the information supplied thereat by those present at the Mediation, either verbally or in writing, and either directly or indirectly.

7.2   The Parties undertake not to reveal, quote from, refer to, paraphrase or in any other way invoke as against any third party – including judges and arbitrators – any documents, if such documents have been revealed, shown or otherwise made public, shown or otherwise disclosed during or in connection with the Mediation by any person involved in the Mediation. This obligation shall not apply if and insofar as the person in question already himself had or could have had this information at his disposal independently of the Mediation. By documents as referred to in this article shall also be meant: the Mediation Agreement, notes or minutes drawn up by the Parties or by the Mediator within the framework of the Mediation, the agreement referred to in article 10.1 insofar as the Parties have agreed in accordance with article 10.3 that this agreement shall remain confidential, as well as other data carriers, such as audiotapes, videotapes, photographs and digital files in whatever form.

7.3   The provisions of articles 7.1 and 7.2 shall also apply in respect of the Mediator.

7.4   The Parties herewith waive the right to, at law or otherwise, use anything that has transpired during the Mediation in evidence against each other and/or against the NMI, (former) board members of the NMI or persons employed with or otherwise involved with the NMI, examine or cause each other, the Mediator or other persons involved in the Mediation to be examined as a witness or otherwise regarding information supplied and/or recorded during or in connection with the Mediation, or regarding the contents of the agreement as referred to in article 10.1, all this to be construed in the widest sense of the word. The Parties shall be deemed to have concluded an agreement as to burden of proof for that purpose.

7.5   All information supplied to the Mediator by either Party in the absence of the other Party, shall be treated by the Mediator as confidential, unless and insofar as the Party in question has explicitly given its consent to the disclosure of that information during the Mediation.

7.6   The provisions of articles 7.1 to 7.5 shall not apply in the case of:

   a.   information concerning criminal acts in respect of which there exists a statutory obligation to report or a statutory right to report,

   b.   information concerning the threat of a crime,

   c.   complaints, disciplinary or liability proceedings against the Mediator. In such event the Mediator shall be released from his obligation to observe confidentiality insofar as may be necessary in order to defend himself against the claims and/or make a claim under his professional liability insurance,

   d.   a request from the Certifying Institution to the Mediator to produce anonymized information evidencing conduct of practice if the Certifying Institution undertakes to observe confidentiality.

Article 8 – End of the Mediation

8.1.   The Mediation shall end:

   a.   by the signing by the Parties of the agreement referred to in article 10.1;

   b.   by a written statement from the Mediator to the Parties stating that the Mediation has ended;

   c.   by a written statement from either Party to the other Party or Parties and to the Mediator stating that it withdraws from the Mediation.

8.2.   Termination of the Mediation shall leave the obligations of confidentiality and payment of the Parties under the Mediation Agreement intact.

Article 9 – Other proceedings

9.1.   Any legal or similar proceedings already pending on commencement of the Mediation regarding the Issue or parts thereof – with the exception of steps to safeguard rights – shall be stayed by the Parties for the duration of the Mediation.

9.2.   The Parties undertake for the duration of the Mediation not to institute any proceedings as referred to in article 9.1 against each other, with the exception of steps to safeguard rights.

9.3.   If a Party takes steps to safeguard rights, or institutes proceedings other than those referred to in article 9.1, that Party shall be obliged to notify this to the Mediator and to the other Party or Parties within 24 hours after having taken such steps or after having instituted such proceedings.

Article 10 – Recording of the outcome of the Mediation

10.1.   The Mediator shall see to it that the agreements made by the Parties are properly recorded in an agreement, by or with the aid of an expert third party. The Parties themselves, with the exception of the Mediator, shall remain responsible for the contents of the agreement. The Parties shall have the right to call in the advice of an external expert.

10.2.   The Mediator shall not be liable for the contents of the agreement concluded by the Parties nor for any damage that may arise from the same.

10.3.   The Parties shall jointly decide and record in writing to what extent the contents of the agreement to be concluded shall remain confidential. The contents of the concluded agreement may in any case be submitted to a court if this is necessary in order to claim compliance with the agreement.

Article 11 – Limitation of liability

Any liability of the Mediator in case of damage caused by any act or omission of the Mediator in the Mediation, shall be limited to at most the amount that in the case in question is paid by his professional liability insurer, plus the amount of the excess which under the contract of insurance is for the account of the Mediator in the case in question. Except for intentional act or gross negligence on the part of the Mediator, the Parties undertake to hold the Mediator harmless and indemnify him in respect of all claims that a third party may institute as against the Mediator at any time and which are related to acts or omissions of the Mediator during the Mediation.

Article 12 – Rules of conduct and complaints

The Mediator shall be bound by the Rules of Conduct for NMI registered Mediators adopted by the Board of the NMI and shall be subject to the NMI complaints scheme and disciplinary rules in accordance with the Rules of the foundation 'Stichting Tuchtrechtspraak Mediators'. A Party may lodge a complaint with the NMI within twelve months from the termination of the Mediation in accordance with the NMI Complaints Scheme at that time in force.

Article 13 – Cases not provided for by these Rules

In all cases not provided for by these Rules the Mediator shall decide. In doing so the Mediator shall act in accordance with the purport of these Rules.

Article 14 – Amendments to the Rules and/or deviations from the Rules

1.1   If and insofar as the Parties wish to deviate from the NMI Mediation Rules, this shall be possible only by means of an agreement in writing with the explicit consent of the Mediator.

1.2   The NMI shall have the power to amend the Rules at any time. Such amendments shall not affect Mediations that are already ongoing at that time. The version of the Rules in force at the time of the commencement of such ongoing Mediations shall apply to such Mediations.

Article 15 – Applicable law

These Rules shall be governed by Dutch law.

The same shall apply in respect of the agreement referred to in article 10.1.

(v) Cepani Belgium Mediation Rules[5]

SECTION IV
MEDIATION

PRELIMINARY PROVISIONS

Article 1 Scope

Section IV shall apply if one or more parties wish to settle their disputes through mediation according to the CEPANI rules. It is not required that the parties have agreed in advance on a mediation agreement. Mediation means a process, whether referred to by the expression mediation, conciliation or any expression of similar import, whereby parties request a third person (the mediator) to assist them in their attempt to reach an amicable settlement of their dispute arising out of, or relating to, a contractual or other legal relationship. The mediator does not have the authority to impose upon the parties a solution to the dispute.

Article 2 Confidentiality

1. The mediator, the parties and their counsel, shall be bound by a duty of strict confidentiality.

2. Under no circumstances may any mention be made in arbitral or judicial proceedings of anything which has been done, said or written with a view to obtaining a settlement that eventually is not achieved.

COMMENCEMENT OF THE PROCEEDINGS

Article 3 Request for mediation

A party wishing to have recourse to mediation under the CEPANI rules shall submit its Request for Mediation to the Secretariat.

The Request for Mediation shall contain, *inter alia*, the following information:

a)   name, first name and the name in full, description, address, telephone and fax numbers, e-mail addresses and VAT-number, if any, of each of the parties;

b)   a recital of the nature and circumstances of the dispute giving rise to the claim;

c)   a statement of the relief sought, a summary of the grounds for the claim, and, if possible, a financial estimate of the amount of the claim;

d)   any comments as to the seat of the mediation, the language of the mediation and the applicable rules of law.

e)   The proof of payment of the registration costs as determined under article 2 of annex I.II.

---

5   Reproduced with the kind permission of CEPANI. For further information on CEPANI and their documents please visit www.cepani.be.

Together with the Request, Claimant shall provide copies of all agreements, in particular the mediation agreement, the correspondence between the parties and other relevant documents.

The Request for mediation and the documents annexed thereto shall be supplied in a number of copies sufficient to provide one copy for each party, one copy for the mediator and one copy for the Secretariat.

Article 4 Answer to the Request for Mediation

1. If the request is complete following article 3 the Secretariat shall inform Respondent of the Request for Mediation as soon as possible, and grant him a period of fifteen days to accept or reject the Request to take part in the attempt to mediate.

2. If no positive answer is given within that the said time limit, the Request for Mediation shall be considered void. The Secretariat shall immediately inform Claimant accordingly.

If Respondent accepts to take part in the mediation, the date on which he informs the Secretariat thereof shall be deemed to be the date of commencement of the mediation. The Secretariat shall confirm this date to the parties.

3. This time limit may be extended pursuant to a reasoned request of Respondent, or on its own motion, by the Secretariat.

Article 5 Effect of the mediation agreement

When the parties agree to resort to CEPANI for mediation, they thereby submit to the Rules, including the annexes, in effect on the date of commencement of the mediation proceedings, unless they have agreed to submit to the Rules in effect on the date of their mediation agreement.

Article 6 Written notifications or communications and time limits

1. The Request for Mediation, the Answer to the Request for Mediation, all pleadings, the appointment of the mediator shall be valid if they are made by delivery against receipt, by registered mail, courier, fax or any other means of telecommunication that proves their dispatch. All other notifications and communications made pursuant to these Rules may be made by any other form of written communication.

If a party is represented by counsel, all notifications or communications shall be made to the latter, unless that party requests otherwise. All notifications or communications shall be valid if dispatched to the last address of the party, as notified either by the party in question or by the other party.

2. A notification or communication, made in accordance with paragraph 1, shall be deemed to have been made when it is received or should have been received by the party itself, by its representative or its counsel.

3. Periods of time specified in the present Rules, shall start to run on the day following the date a notification or communication is deemed to have been made in accordance with paragraph 1. If the last day of the relevant period of time granted is an official holiday or a non-business day in the country where the notification or communication has to be made, the period of time shall expire at the end of the first following business day.

A notice or communication shall be treated as having been sent timely if it is dispatched in accordance with paragraph 1 prior to, or on the date of, the expiry of the time limit.

THE MEDIATIOR

Article 7 General provisions

1. Only those persons who are independent of the parties and of their counsel and who comply with the rules of good conduct set out in Schedule II, may serve as mediator in mediations organized by CEPANI.

2. The Appointments Committee or the Chairman shall appoint the mediator. The parties may nominate the mediator by mutual consent, subject to the approval of the Appointments Committee or the Chairman.

3. The mediator who was appointed or whose nomination has been approved, shall sign a statement of independence and disclose in writing to the Secretariat any facts or circumstances which might be of such a nature to call into question the mediator's independence in the eyes of the parties. The Secretariat shall provide such information to the parties in writing and fix a time limit for any comments from them.

4. The mediator shall immediately disclose in writing to the Secretariat and to the parties any facts or circumstances of a similar nature as those mentioned in paragraph 3 which may arise during the mediation.

5. The decisions of the Appointments Committee or the Chairman as to the appointment or replacement of the mediator shall be final. These decisions do not have to state the reasons for the decision.

6. By accepting to serve, every mediator undertakes to carry out his responsibilities until the end in accordance with these Rules.

7. Unless otherwise agreed by the parties, the mediator shall not act as an arbitrator, representative or counsel of a party in arbitral or judicial proceedings relating to the dispute which was the subject of mediation.

Article 8 Appointment of the mediator

The Appointments Committee or the Chairman appoints the mediator after the payment by the parties, or by one of them, of the advance on mediation costs in accordance with the provisions of Article 17. It will thereby take into account more particularly the availability, the qualifications and the ability of the mediator to conduct the mediation in accordance with these Rules.

Article 9 Replacement of the mediator

1. In the event of the mediator's death, accepted withdrawal, resignation, or if there is a cause preventing him from fulfilling his duties, or upon request of all parties, the mediator shall be replaced.

2. The mediator shall also be replaced when the Appointments Committee or the Chairman finds that the mediator is prevented *de jure* or *de* facto from fulfilling his duties in accordance with these Rules or within the allotted time limits.

In such event, the Appointments Committee or the Chairman shall decide on the matter after having invited the mediator and the parties to comment in writing to the Secretariat within the time limit allotted by the latter. Such comments shall be communicated to the parties and to the mediator.

THE MEDIATION

Article 10 Transmission of the file to the mediator

Provided that the advance on mediation costs has been fully paid, the Secretariat shall transmit the file to the mediator as soon as the latter has been appointed or his nomination approved.

Article 11 Language of the mediation

1. The language of the mediation shall be determined by mutual agreement between the parties. Failing such an agreement, the language or languages of the mediation shall be determined by the mediator, due regard being given to the circumstances of the case and, in particular, to the language of the contract.

2. The mediator shall have full authority to decide which of the parties shall bear the translation costs, if any, and to what extent.

Article 12 Seat of the mediation

1. The Appointments Committee or the Chairman shall determine the seat of the mediation, unless the parties have agreed otherwise.

2. Unless otherwise agreed by the parties and after having consulted with them, the mediator may decide to hold the hearings and meetings at any other location that he considers appropriate.

Article 13 Examination of the case

1. The mediator is free to organize the mediation as he sees fit.

2. As quickly as possible after its appointment the mediator shall set time limits for the parties to present their arguments.

3. After having received the arguments of the parties, the mediator shall examine the case and submit a mediation proposal to the parties.

4. The hearings shall not be public. Save with the approval of the mediator and the parties, persons not involved in the proceedings shall not be admitted.

5. The parties shall appear in person or through duly authorized representatives or counsel.

SETTLEMENT AND END OF THE MEDIATION

Article 14 Settlement

1. Should the mediation lead to a settlement, the agreement shall be set forth in writing and signed by the parties. This document sets out the precise undertakings of each of the parties.

2. Subsequently, the mediator shall record in a set of minutes the fact that the parties have reached an agreement. The said minutes shall be signed by the mediator and by the parties. A copy of the minutes shall be sent to the Secretariat

3. In the event that the mediation fails to bring about a settlement, the mediator shall record this fact in the minutes, which he shall sign and immediately notify to the Secretariat

Article 15 End of the mediation

1. When an agreement is reached, the mediation shall end when the parties and the mediator sign the minutes stating that an agreement has been reached.

2. If no agreement is reached, the mediation shall end as soon as the mediator notifies to the Secretariat the minutes stating that no agreement has been reached.

3. Should one of the parties fail to appear in the proceedings after having been duly summoned, the mediation shall end as soon as the mediator informs the Secretariat in writing of this fact.

4. At any time, either party may refuse to continue the mediation. In such event, the mediation ends when written notification of that party's refusal is sent to the mediator, if already appointed, and to the Secretariat.

5. The mediator may also decide that there is no further justification for continuing with the mediation. In such event, the mediation ends as soon as the mediator informs the Secretariat in writing of this fact.

MEDIATION COSTS

Article 16 Nature and amount of the mediation costs

1. The mediation costs shall include the fees and expenses of the mediator, as well as the administrative expenses of the Secretariat. They shall be fixed by the Secretariat on the basis of the amount of the principal claim and of the counterclaim, according

to the Scale of Mediation Costs in effect on the date of the commencement of the mediation proceedings.

2. Other costs and expenses relating to the mediation, such as the expenses incurred by a party, are not included in the mediation costs and are borne by this party.

3. The Secretariat may fix the mediation costs at a higher or lower figure than that which would result from the application of the Scale of Mediation Costs, should this be deemed necessary due to the exceptional circumstances of the case.

4. If the amount in dispute is not specified, totally or partially, the Secretariat, may determine, taking into account all available information, the amount in dispute on the basis of which the mediation costs will be calculated.

5. The Secretariat may adjust the amount of the mediation costs at any time during the proceedings if the circumstances of the case or if new claims reveal that the scope of the dispute is greater than originally considered.

Article 17 Advance on mediation costs

1. The advance required to cover the mediation costs, as determined in accordance with Article 16, paragraph 1, shall be paid to CEPANI prior to the appointment or the approval of the nomination of the mediator by the Appointments Committee or the Chairman.

2. Further advance payments may be required if and when any adjustments are made to the mediation costs in the course of the proceedings.

3. The advance on mediation costs, as well as the additional advance on mediation costs, shall be payable in equal shares by Claimant and Respondent. However, any party shall be free to pay the whole of the advance on mediation costs should the other party fail to pay its share.

4. When the advance on mediation costs exceeds €50.000,00 a bank guarantee may be posted to cover such payment.

5. When a request for an additional advance on mediation costs has not been complied with, and after consultation with the mediator, the Secretariat may direct the mediator to suspend his work and set a time limit, which must be not less than fifteen days, on the expiry of which the relevant claims or counterclaims on the basis of which the additional advance was calculated shall be considered as withdrawn. A party shall not be prevented on the ground of such a withdrawal from reintroducing the same claim or counterclaim at a later date in another proceeding.

Article 18 Decision on mediation costs

1. The mediation costs shall be finally fixed by the Secretariat.

2. Unless otherwise agreed, the parties shall each bear one half of the costs of the mediation.

3. The minutes which state that the parties have reached an agreement, set forth the mediation costs, as determined by the Secretariat, and set out the agreement between the parties, if any, on the allocation of the mediation costs.

(vi) Swiss Chamber of Commerce Mediation Rules[6]

SWISS RULES OF COMMERCIAL MEDIATION OF THE SWISS CHAMBERS OF COMMERCE AND INDUSTRY

**April 2007
(reprinted 2008)**

I. Introductory Rules

Article 1 – Scope of application

1. The Swiss Rules of Commercial Mediation (hereinafter 'The Rules') shall govern any mediation proceedings where the parties have agreed, whether by a prior contractual agreement or after a problem or a dispute has arisen, to refer their dispute to mediation under these Rules.

2. Unless the parties have agreed otherwise, these Rules shall apply as in force at the date when the Chambers received the request for mediation.

Article 2 – Filing of the request for mediation

1. Any party or parties wishing to have recourse to mediation under the Swiss Rules of Commercial Mediation of the Swiss Chambers of Commerce shall submit a request to one of the Swiss Chambers of Commerce listed in Appendix A of these Rules.

2. The request shall include:

a)   the names, addresses, telephone and fax numbers and e-mail addresses of the parties and their counsel if any;

b)   a copy of the agreement to mediate (unless the requesting party is filing a request according to Article 5 of these Rules);

c)   a short description of the dispute and, if applicable, an estimate of the amount in dispute;

d)   a joint designation of the mediator or, failing an agreement, a description as to any qualifications required;

e)   any comments on the language of the proceedings;

f)   the payment of the registration fee, as required by article 28(a) of these Rules and the Schedule for Mediation Costs included in these Rules (Appendix B of these rules), to the account of the Chamber to which the request for mediation is submitted as listed in Appendix A ;

3. The request and the enclosed documents shall be submitted in as many copies as there are parties, as well as one copy per mediator and one copy for the Chambers.

---

6   Reproduced with the kind permission of the Swiss Chamber's Court of Arbitration and Mediation. For further information please visit www.sccam.org.

4. The party (or parties) requesting mediation shall pay the registration fee provided for by the Schedule in force, pursuant to Appendix B of these Rules. The request shall be registered by the Chambers upon receipt of the registration fee.

5. The request for mediation, together with any existing agreement to mediate, shall be submitted in German, French, Italian or English. Failing that, the Chambers shall set a time-limit to the requesting party or parties to submit a translation into one of these languages. If the translation is submitted within said time-limit, the request for mediation is deemed to have been validly submitted at the date when the initial version was received by the Chambers. Any attachments or exhibits may be submitted in their original language.

Article 3 – Where the parties have agreed to the application of these Rules

1. Where the parties have agreed to the application of these Rules and a request for mediation has been submitted, the Chambers shall determine whether the mediator designated by the parties may be confirmed and shall proceed as provided for by article 9 of these Rules. Where the parties have not jointly designated a mediator, the Chambers shall proceed as provided for by article 8 of these Rules.

2. Where the request for mediation was submitted by one party, the Chambers, after receipt of the registration fee, shall provide a copy of the request to the other party or parties and grant a 15-day time-limit for the joint designation of the mediator.

3. If no positive answer is received by the Chamber or if the parties fail to jointly designate the mediator, the Chambers shall appoint the mediator.

Article 4 – Where the parties have agreed to mediate their dispute without specifying these Rules

1. Where the parties have agreed to refer their dispute to mediation, but without specifying these Rules, the Chambers shall, upon receipt of a request for mediation submitted by one party and of the registration fee, provide the other party or parties with a copy of the request and of the documents, and set a 15-day time-limit to the parties to agree on the application of these Rules and to designate a mediator.

2. In cases where all the parties agree to refer their dispute to the Swiss Rules of Commercial Mediation of the Swiss Chambers of Commerce, the mediation proceedings are governed by these Rules. The mediation proceedings are deemed to commence on the date on which the Chambers received the written consent to mediation signed by all the parties.

3. If no answer is received within the time-limit or in case of an explicit refusal by any party to refer the dispute to these Rules, the request for mediation is deemed to be rejected and the mediation proceedings shall not commence. The Chambers shall promptly inform the requesting party in writing and close the file. The registration fee is not refundable.

Article 5 – The parties have no prior agreement to mediate

1. Where there is no prior agreement in favour of mediation, a party to a dispute may request the Chambers to invite the other party or parties to agree to accept mediation under these Rules.

2. The requesting party shall submit to the Chambers a request for mediation which shall contain the elements provided for in article 2 of these Rules.

3. Upon receipt of the registration fee, the Chambers shall inform the other party or parties and invite them to agree to refer the dispute to mediation under these Rules. A 15-day time-limit is granted to the other party or parties to decide to accept mediation and to designate the mediator.

4. Upon agreement by all the parties, the mediation proceedings are submitted to these Rules. The mediation proceedings are deemed to commence on the date on which the Chambers received the written consent to mediation signed by all the parties.

5. If no answer is received within the time-limit or in case of an explicit refusal by any party to refer the dispute to these Rules, the request for mediation is deemed to be rejected and the mediation proceedings shall not commence. The Chambers shall promptly inform the requesting party in writing and close the file. The registration fee is not refundable.

Article 6 – Arbitration agreement

If the parties do not completely resolve the dispute by mediation and they are bound by an agreement to arbitrate referring to the Swiss Rules of International Arbitration of the Swiss Chambers of Commerce or to the domestic arbitration Rules of one of the Chambers, the Chambers, upon receipt of the Notice of Arbitration, shall proceed as provided for by the applicable arbitration Rules.

II. Selection of Mediator(s)

Article 7 – Number of mediators

1. Unless the parties agree otherwise or the Chambers recommend otherwise, a single mediator shall be appointed.

2. Where there is more than one mediator, the mediators are selected in accordance with the parties' joint wishes. In general, where the mediators are selected successively, the first mediator is consulted for the selection of the other mediator(s).

Article 8 – Designation of a mediator by the parties

1. The parties may jointly designate a mediator when the request for mediation is filed. Where the mediator designated by the parties cannot be confirmed by the

Chambers or refuses his/her designation, the Chambers shall grant a 15-day time-limit to the parties for the joint designation of a new mediator.

2. Where the parties did not jointly designate a mediator in the request for mediation or failed to jointly designate a mediator within the time-limit set by the Chambers, the Chambers shall submit to the parties a list of at least three names of mediators suggested after considering the nature of the dispute and the qualifications required. The parties shall be invited, within a short time-limit set by the Chambers, to designate a mediator from among those on the list. Failing an agreement by the parties within the time-limit set forth, the Chambers shall appoint the mediator from among the suggested names.

3. If, within five days of the receipt of the Chambers' notice of appointment, a party objects to the appointment in writing stating reasons that are considered appropriate by the Chambers, the Chambers may promptly appoint another mediator.

Article 9 – Confirmation of mediators by the Chambers

1. All joint designations of mediator(s) by the parties are subject to confirmation by the Chambers, upon which the appointment shall become effective. The Chambers have no obligation to give reasons when they do not confirm a mediator.

2. In order to be in a position to decide on the confirmation, the Chambers shall request from the prospective mediator(s) his/her agreement to serve, his/her curriculum vitae, his/her statement of independence duly dated and signed, and his/her adherence to the European Code of Conduct for Mediators (Article 13). The statement of independence shall contain, if applicable, disclosure of information in conformity with Article 12, paragraph 2 of these Rules.

Article 10 – Replacement of the mediator

If the mediator is no longer in a position to fulfil his/her duties or is no longer accepted by the parties, the Chambers shall, upon joint request of the parties, proceed as provided for in Article 8 of these Rules.

Article 11 – Transmission of the file to the mediator

After his/her confirmation or appointment, the Chambers transmit the file to the mediator. They shall invite the mediator to promptly convene the parties to a joint preliminary session.

III. Qualifications and Role of the Mediator

Article 12 – Independence, neutrality and impartiality of the mediator

1. The mediator shall be and remain at all times impartial, neutral and independent from the parties.

2. Prior to his/her confirmation or appointment by the Chambers, the prospective mediator shall disclose any circumstances known to him/her that may likely give rise to justifiable doubts as to his/her impartiality, neutrality or independence towards the parties.

3. If, in the course of the mediation, the mediator discovers the existence of any circumstances likely to affect his/her impartiality or independence towards the parties, he/she informs the parties. Upon their consent, the mediator continues to serve. If the parties disagree, the mediator stays the mediation and informs the Chambers, which shall proceed to replace the mediator.

Article 13 – Code of Conduct

Anyone who accepts to act as mediator under the Swiss Rules of Commercial Mediation shall undertake in writing to comply with the European Code of Conduct for Mediators attached to these Rules.

Article 14 – Role of the mediator

1. The mediator helps the parties in their attempt to reach an acceptable and satisfactory resolution of their dispute. He/she has no authority to impose a settlement on the parties.

2. The mediator and the parties shall be guided by fairness and respect.

IV. Procedural Rules

Article 15 – Conduct of the proceedings

1. The mediation shall be conducted in the manner agreed to by the parties. Failing such an agreement, the mediator shall conduct the mediation proceedings as he/she considers appropriate, taking into account the circumstances of the case, the wishes expressed by the parties, and the need for a prompt settlement of the dispute.

2. With the parties' agreement, the mediator determines the place of the meetings, the language of the mediation, the possibility of separate caucuses (Article 15, paragraph 3), the timetable, if any, the submissions of written pleadings and documents, if any, and equal attendance by other persons. The mediator may ask the parties to sign a mediation agreement.

3. The mediator may, if he/she considers appropriate, hear the parties separately. Any information given in such separate sessions (caucuses) is confidential and will not be revealed to the other party without prior consent.

4. Whenever necessary, the mediator may, provided the parties agree and assume the expenses, seek expert advice concerning technical aspects of the dispute.

5. The mediator may end the mediation whenever, in his/her opinion, further efforts would not contribute to a resolution of the dispute between the parties. The mediator may then suggest other dispute resolution tools to the parties, including:

a)   an expert determination of one or more particular issues of the dispute;

b)   the submission of last offers;

c)   arbitration.

Article 16 – Seat of the mediation

Unless otherwise agreed by the parties, the seat of the mediation is at the place of the Chamber where the request was submitted, although meetings may be held elsewhere.

Article 17 – Applicable law

1. Unless otherwise agreed by the parties, mediation is subject to Swiss law.

2. The relationship between the Chambers and any person intervening in the mediation proceedings (parties, mediator(s), expert(s), etc.) is subject to Swiss law.

Article 18 – Confidentiality

1. Mediation is confidential at all times. Any observation, statement or proposition made before the mediator or by him/herself cannot be used later, even in case of litigation or arbitration, unless there is a written agreement of all the parties.

2. The sessions are private. The parties may, with the consent of the mediator, agree that other persons attend the sessions.

Article 19 – Representation

The parties shall appear in person to all mediation sessions or through duly authorized and empowered representatives, whose names and addresses shall be communicated in writing to the mediator, to the other parties and to the Chambers. The parties may also be assisted by counsel of their choice.

V. Termination of the mediation

Article 20 – End of mediation

1. A mediation under these Rules shall be deemed to have ended:

a)   upon the signing by all parties of a settlement agreement putting an end to the dispute;

b)   at any time, by notification in writing by a party or the parties to the mediator and to the Chambers of its/their decision to end the mediation;

c)   upon expiration of any termination time-limit set by the parties and the mediator for the resolution of the dispute, if not extended by all the parties;

d)   in case of non-payment, by the parties, of the advance on costs according to the enclosed Schedule of costs.

2. At the end of the mediation, the mediator shall promptly inform the Chamber in writing that the mediation proceedings are terminated. He/she shall indicate the date of the termination and whether it resulted in a full or partial settlement.

3. The Chambers shall confirm in writing to the parties and to the mediator the end of the mediation proceedings.

4. The mediator shall destroy any document or brief in his/her possession 90 days after the end of the mediation unless he/she is involved in subsequent proceedings as envisaged in Article 22 of these Rules.

Article 21 – The settlement agreement

Unless otherwise agreed to by the parties in writing, no settlement is reached until it has been made in writing and signed by the relevant parties.

Article 22 – Subsequent proceedings

1. Unless the parties expressly agree otherwise, the mediator cannot act as arbitrator, judge, expert, or as representative or advisor of one party in any subsequent proceedings initiated against one of the parties to the mediation after the commencement of the mediation.

2. If the parties decide to designate the mediator as arbitrator, judge or expert in any subsequent arbitral proceedings, the latter may take into account information received during the course of the mediation.

VI. Mediation and Arbitration

Article 23 – Recourse to arbitration

1. In international mediations, the parties may jointly agree in writing at any time during the course of their mediation to refer their dispute or any part of their dispute to an Arbitral Tribunal under the Swiss Rules of International Arbitration of the Swiss Chambers of Commerce for resolution by arbitration. Either party may then initiate arbitration proceedings under those Rules, including the provisions for an Expedited Procedure under article 42 of those Rules, by submitting a notice of arbitration as provided for by Article 3 of those Rules. If the parties settle the dispute during the arbitral proceedings, article 34 of those Rules shall be applicable for the rendering of an award on agreed terms.

2. In domestic mediations, the parties may jointly agree in writing at any time during the course of their mediation to refer their dispute or any part of their dispute, to the domestic arbitration Rules of one of the Chambers for resolution by arbitration.

Either party may then initiate arbitration proceedings under those Rules, including an expedited or fast-track procedure as may be provided for by those Rules, by submitting a request or notice of arbitration as provided for by those domestic Rules. If the parties settle the dispute during the arbitral proceedings, the domestic Rules shall govern, where applicable, the procedure for the rendering of an award on agreed terms.

Article 24 – Mediation during the course of arbitral proceedings

1. In all arbitral proceedings pending before the Chambers where mediation appears to be worth trying, whether in whole or in part, the Chambers or the arbitrator(s) may suggest to the parties to amicably resolve their dispute, or a certain part of it, by having recourse to a mediator.

2. If the parties agree to accept mediation under these Rules, the Chambers shall, upon receipt of a request for mediation filed in accordance with Article 2 of these Rules and upon receipt of the registration fee, proceed with the selection of the mediator in accordance with Chapter II of these Rules.

VII. Exclusion of Liability

Article 25 – Exclusion of liability

1. None of the Chambers or their staff, mediator(s), or appointed experts shall be liable for any act or omission in connection with any mediation proceedings conducted under these Rules, save where their act or omission is shown to constitute deliberate wrongdoing or extremely serious negligence.

2. After the settlement of the dispute or the end of the mediation, neither the Chambers nor the mediator(s) or the appointed experts shall be under any obligation to make statements to any person or tribunal about any matter concerning the mediation, nor shall a party seek to make any of these persons a witness in any legal or other proceedings arising out of the mediation.

VIII. Costs

Article 26 – Rates

The expenses and fees of mediation are set pursuant to the Schedule of costs (Appendix B to these Rules) in force at the time of the filing of the request for mediation.

Article 27 – Apportionment of the costs

1. Unless otherwise agreed by the parties, all mediation costs shall be equally split amongst the parties. The parties are jointly and severally responsible for the payment of all the mediation fees and costs.

2. The personal expenses incurred by one party in relation with the mediation (for example legal fees, hotel, travel, etc.) are borne by this party and are not included in the costs of the mediation.

Article 28 – The Chambers' fees

The fees due to the Chambers pursuant to the Schedule for the mediation costs according to Appendix B of these Rules include:

a)   registration fee paid by the requesting party or parties when filing the request for mediation;

b)   administrative fees calculated as a percentage of the mediator's fees. These fees are due to the Chambers by the mediator.

Article 29 – The mediators' fees

Unless otherwise agreed by the parties, the mediators' fees are calculated on the basis of an hourly rate, or if applicable a daily rate, set out in the Schedule for mediation costs (Appendix B of these Rules).

Article 30 – Advance payment for costs

1. At any time during the proceedings, the mediator may request each party to deposit an equal amount (unless otherwise agreed) as advance payment towards the costs of the mediation.

2. The mediator shall provide a copy of such request for information to the Chambers

3. If the required deposits are not paid in full by the parties within a specified time-limit, the mediator may stay the proceedings or inform the Chambers in writing that the mediation is terminated.

Article 31 – Statement of costs

1. Upon termination of the mediation, the mediator provides an invoice for his/her fees and costs to the parties and the Chambers.

2. The mediator shall include the expenses incurred in the course of the proceedings, the number of hours or days spent by the mediator, the hourly or daily rate and any advances paid by the parties. He/she shall also mention the amount of any administrative fees which are due to the Chambers.

3. Any excess payment shall be reimbursed to the parties in proportion to their payments.

Appendix A :   Addresses of the Chambers of Commerce

[   ]

Appendix B: Schedule for the Costs of Mediation

1. Chambers' Fees

1.1. When submitting a request for mediation, the requesting parties shall each pay CHF 300 for the Chambers' registration fee.

1.2. Where the request for mediation is submitted by one party, this party pays CHF 600 for the Chambers' registration fee.

1.3. The Chambers shall not proceed unless and until the registration fee is fully paid.

1.4. The registration fee is not refundable.

1.5. The Chambers receive administrative fees of 10 % calculated on the basis of the fees set by the mediator. These fees are paid by the mediator to the Chambers at the end of the proceedings.

2. Mediators' fees

2.1 The hourly rate shall in principle be between CHF 200 and CHF 500, of which 10% is for the Chambers' administrative fees.

2.2 The daily rate shall in principle be between CHF 1'500 and CHF 2'500, of which 10% is for the Chambers' administrative fees.

2.3 The parties and the mediator may agree on other rates. The 10% for the Chambers' administrative fees cannot be changed.

(vii) Hellenic Mediation Association Mediation Rules & Regulations[7]

HELLENIC MEDIATION & ARBITRATION CENTRE

MEDIATION /RULES

ARTICLE 1

SCOPE OF APPLICATION

These Rules shall govern the mediation procedure conducted under the supervision of the Hellenic Mediation and Arbitration Centre (hereinafter called the "Centre"), seated in Athens, belongs to the Greek Association of "Societés Anonymes" and Limited Liability Companies and was founded by the 30.03.2006 decision of its AGM. The parties resorting to the Centre should abide by its rules.

ARTICLE 2

DEFINITIONS

1. Mediation

Mediation is the procedure through which two or more [different] parties of a commercial dispute are facilitated by one or more persons in order to accomplish a consensual settlement of their dispute. Mediation is founded on the principles of good faith, equal treatment of the parties and confidentiality.

2. Submitting a dispute to mediation

Submission of a dispute to mediation is the agreement of the parties to refer to mediation the dispute that has occurred or will occur from their relation. This agreement may have the form of a mediation clause in a contract before or after the occurrence of the dispute.

3. Mediator

The Mediator is the unbiased and impartial third party who facilitates the consensus settlement of the conflict. The Mediator should be certified and appointed by the Centre in order to act as such.

Mediators are appointed after a decision of the Board of Directors of the Centre following a proposal of two of its members. This appointment is valid for two years with the potential of renewal according to the above procedure. These provisions also apply to assistants and trainees.

ASSOCIATION OF S.A. AND L.TD. COMPANIES
PANEPISTIMIOU 16 & AMERIKIS (2ⁿᵈ floor) · GR 106 72 ATHENS · T: +30 210 36 20 274 +30 210 36 36 326 · F: +30 210 36 26 610 · e mail: sae@hol.gr

7 Reproduced with the kind permission of the Hellenic Mediation and Arbitration Centre. For further information please visit www.hellenic-mediation.gr.

4. Documents

Any kind of information imprint is considered to be a document.

ARTICLE 3

INITIATING RECOURSE TO MEDIATION

1. Initiating Recourse

The party who wishes to initiate mediation shall give a notice of mediation in writing to the Centre. This notice includes the necessary contact details of the parties or/and their representatives and a brief description of the dispute. If it is necessary, the Centre approaches the other party and seeks its consent. The consent of the parties for the initiation and the progress of the mediation process is always required.

2. Mediation agreement

The Centre furnishes to the parties the Agreement of Submission of the Dispute to Mediation and negotiates the terms with them. When the content of the Agreement is established, it is then engrossed by the Centre and the parties receive a copy to sign.

The Agreement of Submission of the Dispute to Mediation is furnished signed by the parties at least fifteen days before the fixed day for the commencement of the mediation main procedure. The Agreement of the Submission of the Dispute to Mediation is also signed by the Centre, the Mediator and the trainee or the assistant that might be present in the discussions.

3. Appointment of the Mediator

The Mediator is appointed by the Centre on the basis of his particular experience and specific knowledge of the legal and technical frame of the subject matter in dispute. The final appointment of the mediator depends on the condition that there are no objections expressed by the parties.

Only one mediator is appointed, unless otherwise agreed.

After agreement of the parties, other persons (such as assistants or trainees) may assist the mediator. These persons are bound by the current Regulation and are obliged to abide by the applicable Code of Conduct in force.

ASSOCIATION OF S.A. AND L.TD. COMPANIES
PANEPISTIMIOU 16 & AMERIKIS (2nd floor) · GR 106 72 ATHENS · T: +30 210 36 20 274 +30 210 36 36 326 · F: +30 210 36 26 610 · e-mail: sae@hol.gr

450

4. Impartiality of the Mediator

The Mediator should be impartial and unbiased. The mediator should acknowledge to the parties and to the Centre any fact that might affect his impartiality. <u>If such fact is ascertained at stage of the mediation procedure, the parties, with the consultation of the Centre, decide for the exemption of the Mediator. Nevertheless, the parties may allow the mediator to proceed with his task, provided they have expressly agreed on that in writing.</u> Alternatively, another mediator is appointed in replacement of the exempted.

5. Collection of facts

The case file of the dispute is furnished to the mediator and according to the nature of the dispute it should include information such as the following:
   i. the history and a summary of the dispute
   ii. the documents in which the summary is referred to and other facts the parties
      wish to mention during the mediation procedure
   iii. a copy of demands/claims of the parties to the court or to arbitration
   iv. the subject matters in dispute

6. Representation of the parties and participation to the meeting

   The [different] parties are present and participate in the procedure or appoint a representative with an exclusive authorisation to handle the subject matter in dispute.
   The parties may be present with their lawyer, or other consultant of their choice, but they have the obligation to inform the Centre in writing for their actions before the date of the mediation meeting.

7. Place and date of mediation

   The Centre in cooperation with the Mediator determines the details of the meetings to be held (day, time, place etc).
   The mediation is held either in the Centre or in a regional annex of the Centre or in any other setting that is deemed to be appropriate and is proposed by the parties or the Mediator, with the consent of the Centre.

8. Preliminary meeting

If the Mediator considers that it is necessary, a preliminary meeting is being held with the parties and/or their representatives aiming, <u>especially</u>:
   i)   to inform them about/of the rules of mediation
   ii) to provide the necessary directions
   iii) to determine the place where the mediation is going to take place and the work
      timetable.
   iv) to deal with any other relevant matter.

ASSOCIATION OF S.A. 8ND L.TD. COMPANIES
PANEPISTIMIOU 16 & AMERIKIS (2ⁿᵈ floor) · GR 106 72 ATHENS · T: +30 210 36 20 274 · +30 210 36 36 326 · F: +30 210 36 26 610 · e-mail: sae@hol.gr

ARTICLE 4

THE MAIN PROCEDURE OF MEDIATION

1. The competence of the Centre

The Centre supervises the mediation procedure. More specifically, it assists in the selection of the appropriate place and time and generally in every matter relevant to the procedure.

2. The role of the Mediator

The Mediator is bound by the Centre's Code (however, until its configuration, the Mediator is bound by the European Code of Conduct) for Mediators, which can be found in annex 1.

The parties acknowledge that neither the Mediation Centre nor the Mediator offer legal advice or act as legal consultants to the parties.

3. Holding Mediation

The Mediator chairs the meetings, allows the parties to speak, addresses questions and generally leads the discussion. The Mediator decides on the performing of the Mediation in joint or separate meetings of the parties or/and their representatives, or/and their consultants and of any other persons present at the meeting.

When needed, the Mediator requests the opinion of an expert for the technical aspects of the dispute, if the parties agree to this and undertake the expenses of such an opinion.

4. Confidentiality

The Mediation meetings are confidential. Apart from the parties and their representatives other persons may attend the meetings only with permission of the parties and the consent of the Mediator.

5. Recording

During the mediation process no minutes are taken.
If the parties do not object to the presence of an employee of the Centre during the Mediation process, this employee may, under the directions of the Mediator, keep the minutes or take notes or any other material that shall be used in the process.

6. Adjournment and repetition of Mediation

The Mediator may adjourn Mediation, so that s/he will allow the parties to examine/prepare specific claims, to demand any information, or for any other reason, if

ASSOCIATION OF S.A. 4ND L.TD. COMPANIES
PANEPISTIMIOU 16 & AMERIKIS (2nd floor) · GR 106 72 ATHENS · T: +30 210 36 20 274 · +30 210 36 36 326 · F: +30 210 36 26 610 · e-mail: sae@hol.gr

452

he considers it necessary in order to carry on with the procedure. The Mediation is repeated with the consensus of the parties in writing.

ARTICLE 5

CLOSURE OF THE MEDIATION PROCEDURE

1. Closure of Mediation

The Mediation is terminated when:
  i.   a consensus agreement in writing is formulated and signed in order to achieve the resolution of the dispute.
  ii. the Mediator drafts a report of failure of Mediation
  iii. the Mediator or one of the parties or the Centre states in writing to all the persons involved to Mediation that the Mediation procedure cannot proceed with the appropriate tranquility and impartiality
  iv. a party is withdrawn from the Mediation or states in writing that the Mediation has closed without having the obligation to expose a particular reason
  v.   the Mediator, exercising his discretion, can withdraw from Mediation by giving a statement in writing to the Centre

In every case, the Mediator informs the Centre in writing of the completion of his task and reports whether the procedure has terminated successfully or not.

2. Successful closure of mediation- The resolution of the dispute with a consensus agreement

No agreement is legally binding until it is stipulated in a document and signed by all the parties, and **each one of them receives a confirmed copy.**
The execution of the agreement may be realized, depending on the case, either by document drafted by a notary public or by court compromise.

3. Mediator's proposal for the resolution of the dispute

If no agreement is accomplished between the parties, each party may request from the Mediator to formulate an **opinion** in writing for the resolution of the dispute. The Mediator is no obliged to this action.

4. Confidentiality and secrecy of information

Every communication among the parties or the parties and the Mediator, the documents and the meetings during the Mediation procedure are private and confidential.

The Mediator as well as any other person that provides services for Mediation, is covered by professional confidentiality, as he is deemed to be a technical advisor (article

ASSOCIATION OF S.A. ΑND LTD. COMPANIES
PANEPISTIMIOU 16 & AMERIKIS (2nd floor) · GR 106 72 ATHENS · T: +30 210 36 20 274 · +30 210 36 36 326 · F: +30 210 36 26 610 · e-mail: sae@hol.gr

453

212 of the Greek Civil Procedure Code) of the parties in the case concerning the dispute occurs.

It is particularly forbidden to disclose information that concerns:

i. application of one of the parties to recourse to Mediation or the intention of one of the parties to participate in the Mediation,
ii. opinions that are expressed or the indications that are made by one of the parties submitted to Mediation,
iii. statements or confessions avowed by one of the parties during Mediation·
iv. suggestions made by the Mediator;
v. the statement of intention of one of the parties to accept the proposal for settlement of the dispute that is formulated by the Mediator;
vi. every document that has been formulated exclusively for the purposes of Mediation

Facts, documents and other of proof accepted as a proof probative evidence which could produce in support of a claim or statement in an arbitral, judicial or other procedure do not rendered inadmissible from their use or appearance in Mediation.

The Centre preserves the right to use certain elements, such as the subject matter of the dispute, the result of mediation, the total amount that is estimated to have been economized with this kind of procedure, etc, aiming at the collection of statistical facts and the formulation of informative publications, strictly under the condition of preserving the anonymity of the relative parties.

From the above are exempted:
a. information that is broadly known to everyone or easily accessible to the public;
b. information or facts for the disclosure of which the parties agree;
c. information or facts to the extent that they are necessary for the application or the execution of the settlement agreement that results directly from the Mediation
d. information that reasons of public order impose their disclosure (especially in order to guarantee the protection of children),
e. information that their disclosure will trigger, in Mediator's opinion, great danger of major damage to someone's life or security if this information is not disclosed;
f. information that if it is disclosed they contain in Mediator's opinion, great danger of his personal involvement in illegal activities.

In case that the Mediation fails and a discussion of the dispute follows in front of a tribunal, the Mediator, his assistant or the trainee **is impeded from being examined as witnesses or being appointed as experts or technical advisors or to participate** in the hearing of the case under any kind of position (article 214 of the Greek Civil Procedure Code).

ASSOCIATION OF S.A. &ND L.TD. COMPANIES
PANEPISTIMIOU 16 & AMERIKIS (2nd floor) · GR 106 72 ATHENS · T: +30 210 36 20 274 · +30 210 36 36 326 · F: +30 210 36 26 610 · e-mail: sae@hol.gr

5. Destruction of written evidence

After the end of the Mediation procedure, either an agreement or not is accomplished, the Mediator returns all the documents to the parties and destroys all the kept minutes and all his notes in front of the representative of the Centre drawing a relevant protocol of delivery and destruction.

The Centre holds the original of the settlement agreement and furnishes a confirmed copy to each party. Every written agreement such as the above is maintained for five (5) years and then it is destroyed.

ARTICLE 6

PAYMENT AND OTHER EXPENDITURE

The payment of the Centre and the payment of the Mediator and his assistant are pre-determined, with regard to the case, according to the table of payments that consists an annex of the current Regulation.

The payment of the Mediator includes the study of the case file and its preparation, the contacts (e-mails, phone calls) and the meetings with the parties. In case of especially complicated disputes and, particularly, when the parties provide a great amount of documentation, an additional payment is imposed for the preparation. The same apply also for the payment of the trainee to the above situations.

Emergency expenses that occur during the procedure after a demand of the parties encumber them equally e.g. transportation, food, hiring another place for meetings, translation fees etc).

The payments of the Centre and of the Mediator, as well as the rest of the expenses of the procedure burden equally the parties, even if one of them before the closure of the mediation. The payments and the additional expenses are paid through the Centre.

An advance payment should be paid to the Centre, as it is determined to the attached table of payments so that a Mediator is appointed.

ARTICLE 7

GENERAL PROVISIONS

1. Interpretation of the Rules

The right to interpret these Rules belongs to the Centre.

2. Critical time for the application of the Rules

The mediation is governed by the Regulation and the table of payments which are in force on the day that the application for Mediation is submitted to the Centre.

ASSOCIATION OF S.A. AND L.TD. COMPANIES
PANEPISTIMIOU 16 & AMERIKIS (2ⁿᵈ floor) · GR 106 72 ATHENS · T: +30 210 36 20 274 · +30 210 36 36 326 · F: +30 210 36 26 610 · e-mail: sae@hol.gr

455

3. Exclusion of Liability

Neither the Centre nor the Mediator (or his assistant) are liable for everything committed or omitted in relation to the procedure of Mediation, unless this action or omission was committed in full awareness that consists a violation of duty or was done in bad faith.

The Centre is not liable for any act or omission of the Mediator in violation of his duty.

4. Violation of rules- Resignation from rights

If during Mediation a party becomes aware of the violation of the above rules, but continues without expressing his reservations or without acknowledging his disagreement, this party is deemed to have resigned from the right to invoke this violation.

5. Applicable law [Exclusive jurisdiction of the Greek courts]

Greek law is applicable to Mediation, without taking into consideration the place of meeting and the applicable substantive law of this dispute.

[Greek courts have exclusive jurisdiction to rule any dispute that may occur due to or in combination with Mediation]

6. Language

The discussion and all the documents of the Mediation procedure shall be in the Greek language, unless agreed otherwise by the parties and the Mediator.

7. Duration

The Mediation shall not last more than two months from the date of the appointment of the Mediator. The duration may be prolonged by the Centre with the agreement of the Mediator and all the parties.

8. Reserved rights

Tactic trial or arbitration in relation with the dispute is not prevented from starting or continuing in spite of Mediation.

The submission of the dispute to Mediation does not affect the rights that are protected by the Article 6 of the Human Convention on Human Rights. If the dispute is not settled by Mediation, the parties preserve intact their rights to a fair trial.

ASSOCIATION OF S.A. AND LTD. COMPANIES

PANEPISTIMIOU 16 & AMERIKIS (2ⁿᵈ floor) · GR 106 72 ATHENS · T: +30 210 36 20 274 · +30 210 36 36 326 · F: +30 210 36 26 610 · e-mail: sae@hol.gr

(viii) UNCITRAL Conciliation Rules[8]

APPLICATION OF THE RULES

Article 1

(1) These Rules apply to conciliation of disputes arising out of or relating to a contractual or other legal relationship where the parties seeking an amicable settlement of their dispute have agreed that the UNCITRAL Conciliation Rules apply.

(2) The parties may agree to exclude or vary any of these Rules at any time.

(3) Where any of these Rules is in conflict with a provision of law from which the parties cannot derogate, that provision prevails.

COMMENCEMENT OF CONCILIATION PROCEEDINGS

Article 2

(1) The party initiating conciliation sends to the other party a written invitation to conciliate under these Rules, briefly identifying the subject of the dispute.

(2) Conciliation proceedings commence when the other party accepts the invitation to conciliate. If the acceptance is made orally, it is advisable that it be confirmed in writing.

(3) If the other party rejects the invitation, there will be no conciliation proceedings.

(4) If the party initiating conciliation does not receive a reply within thirty days from the date on which he sends the invitation, or within such other period of time as specified in the invitation, he may elect to treat this as a rejection of the invitation to conciliate. If he so elects, he informs the other party accordingly.

NUMBER OF CONCILIATORS

Article 3

There shall be one conciliator unless the parties agree that there shall be two or three conciliators. Where there is more than one conciliator, they ought, as a general rule, to act jointly.

---

8   Reproduced with the kind permission of UNCITRAL. For further information please visit www.uncitral. org.

APPOINTMENT OF CONCILIATORS

Article 4

(1)

(a) In conciliation proceedings with one conciliator, the parties shall endeavour to reach agreement on the name of a sole conciliator;

(b) In conciliation proceedings with two conciliators, each party appoints one conciliator;

(c) In conciliation proceedings with three conciliators, each party appoints one conciliator.

The parties shall endeavour to reach agreement on the name of the third conciliator.

(2) Parties may enlist the assistance of an appropriate institution or person in connexion with the appointment of conciliators. In particular:

(a) A party may request such an institution or person to recommend the names of suitable individuals to act as conciliator; or

(b) The parties may agree that the appointment of one or more conciliators be made directly by such an institution or person.

In recommending or appointing individuals to act as conciliator, the institution or person shall have regard to such considerations as are likely to secure the appointment of an independent and impartial conciliator and, with respect to a sole or third conciliator, shall take into account the advisability of appointing a conciliator of a nationality other than the nationalities of the parties.

SUBMISSION OF STATEMENTS TO CONCILIATOR

Article 5

(1) The conciliator, upon his appointment, requests each party to submit to him a brief written statement describing the general nature of the dispute and the points at issue. Each party sends a copy of his statement to the other party.

(2) The conciliator may request each party to submit to him a further written statement of his position and the facts and grounds in support thereof, supplemented by any documents and other evidence that such party deems appropriate. The party sends a copy of his statement to the other party.

(3) At any stage of the conciliation proceedings the conciliator may request a party to submit to him such additional information as he deems appropriate.

REPRESENTATION AND ASSISTANCE

Article 6

The parties may be represented or assisted by persons of their choice. The names and addresses of such persons are to be communicated in writing to the other party and to the conciliator; such communication is to specify whether the appointment is made for purposes of representation or of assistance.

ROLE OF CONCILIATOR

Article 7

(1) The conciliator assists the parties in an independent and impartial manner in their attempt to reach an amicable settlement of their dispute.

(2) The conciliator will be guided by principles of objectivity, fairness and justice, giving consideration to, among other things, the rights and obligations of the parties, the usages of the trade concerned and the circumstances surrounding the dispute, including any previous business practices between the parties.

(3) The conciliator may conduct the conciliation proceedings in such a manner as he considers appropriate, taking into account the circumstances of the case, the wishes the parties may express, including any request by a party that the conciliator hear oral statements, and the need for a speedy settlement of the dispute.

(4) The conciliator may, at any stage of the conciliation proceedings, make proposals for a settlement of the dispute. Such proposals need not be in writing and need not be accompanied by a statement of the reasons therefor.

ADMINISTRATIVE ASSISTANCE

Article 8

In order to facilitate the conduct of the conciliation proceedings, the parties, or the conciliator with the consent of the parties, may arrange for administrative assistance by a suitable institution or person.

COMMUNICATION BETWEEN CONCILIATOR AND PARTIES

Article 9

(1) The conciliator may invite the parties to meet with him or may communicate with them orally or in writing. He may meet or communicate with the parties together or with each of them separately.

(2) Unless the parties have agreed upon the place where meetings with the conciliator are to be held, such place will be determined by the conciliator, after consultation with the parties, having regard to the circumstances of the conciliation proceedings.

DISCLOSURE OF INFORMATION

Article 10

When the conciliator receives factual information concerning the dispute from a party, he discloses the substance of that information to the other party in order that the other party may have the opportunity to present any explanation which he considers appropriate. However, when a party gives any information to the conciliator subject to a specific condition that it be kept confidential, the conciliator does not disclose that information to the other party.

CO-OPERATION OF PARTIES WITH CONCILIATOR

Article 11

The parties will in good faith co-operate with the conciliator and, in particular, will endeavour to comply with requests by the conciliator to submit written materials, provide evidence and attend meetings.

SUGGESTIONS BY PARTIES FOR SETTLEMENT OF DISPUTE

Article 12

Each party may, on his own initiative or at the invitation of the conciliator, submit to the conciliator suggestions for the settlement of the dispute.

SETTLEMENT AGREEMENT

Article 13

(1) When it appears to the conciliator that there exist elements of a settlement which would be acceptable to the parties, he formulates the terms of a possible settlement and submits them to the parties for their observations. After receiving the observations of the parties, the conciliator may reformulate the terms of a possible settlement in the light of such observations.

(2) If the parties reach agreement on a settlement of the dispute, they draw up and sign a written settlement agreement. If requested by the parties, the conciliator draws up, or assists the parties in drawing up, the settlement agreement.

(3) The parties by signing the settlement agreement put an end to the dispute and are bound by the agreement.

CONFIDENTIALITY

Article 14

The conciliator and the parties must keep confidential all matters relating to the conciliation proceedings. Confidentiality extends also the settlement agreement, except where its disclosure is necessary for purposes of implementation and enforcement.

TERMINATION OF CONCILIATION PROCEEDINGS

Article 15

The conciliation proceedings are terminated:

(*a*) By the signing of the settlement agreement by the parties, on the date of the agreement; or

(*b*) By a written declaration of the conciliator, after consultation with the parties, to the effect that further efforts at conciliation are no longer justified, on the date of the declaration; or

(*c*) By a written declaration of the parties addressed to the conciliator to the effect that the conciliation proceedings are terminated, on the date of the declaration; or

(*d*) By a written declaration of a party to the other party and the conciliator, if appointed, to the effect that the conciliation proceedings are terminated, on the date of the declaration.

RESORT TO ARBITRAL OR JUDICIAL PROCEEDINGS

Article 16

The parties undertake not to initiate, during the conciliation proceedings, any arbitral or judicial proceedings in respect of a dispute that is the subject of the conciliation proceedings, except that a party may initiate arbitral or judicial proceedings where, in his opinion, such proceedings are necessary for preserving his rights.

COSTS

Article 17

(1) Upon termination of the conciliation proceedings, the conciliator fixes the costs of the conciliation and gives written notice thereof to the parties. The term 'costs' includes only:

(*a*) The fee of the conciliator which shall be reasonable in amount;

(*b*) The travel and other expenses of the conciliator;

(*c*) The travel and other expenses of witnesses requested by the conciliator with the consent of the parties;

(*d*) The cost of any expert advice requested by the conciliator with the consent of the parties;

(*e*) The cost of any assistance provided pursuant to articles 4, paragraph (2)(*b*), and 8 of these Rules.

(2) The costs, as defined above, are borne equally by the parties unless the settlement agreement provides for a different apportionment. All other expenses incurred by a party are borne by that party.

DEPOSITS

Article 18

(1) The conciliator, upon his appointment, may request each party to deposit an equal amount as an advance for the costs referred to in article 17, paragraph (1) which he expects will be incurred.

(2) During the course of the conciliation proceedings the conciliator may request supplementary deposits in an equal amount from each party.

(3) If the required deposits under paragraphs (1) and (2) of this article are not paid in full by both parties within thirty days, the conciliator may suspend the proceedings or may make a written declaration of termination to the parties, effective on the date of that declaration.

(4) Upon termination of the conciliation proceedings, the conciliator renders an accounting to the parties of the deposits received and returns any unexpended balance to the parties.

ROLE OF CONCILIATOR IN OTHER PROCEEDINGS

Article 19

The parties and the conciliator undertake that the conciliator will not act as an arbitrator or as a representative or counsel of a party in any arbitral or judicial proceedings in respect of a dispute that is the subject of the conciliation proceedings. The parties also undertake that they will not present the conciliator as a witness in any such proceedings.

ADMISSIBILITY OF EVIDENCE IN OTHER PROCEEDINGS

Article 20

The parties undertake not to rely on or introduce as evidence in arbitral or judicial proceedings, whether or not such proceedings relate to the dispute that is the subject of the conciliation proceedings;

(a) Views expressed or suggestions made by the other party in respect of a possible settlement of the dispute;

(b) Admissions made by the other party in the course of the conciliation proceedings;

(c) Proposals made by the conciliator;

(d) The fact that the other party had indicated his willingness to accept a proposal for settlement made by the conciliator.

(ix) CMAP Mediation Rules

 FOREWORD

Conflict management is an important strategic matter for enterprises, which they cannot afford to leave to chance.

Until recently enterprises dealt with their commercial disputes almost exclusively in the national courts, with the risks and restrictions that this entailed, and which often led to unsatisfactory outcomes for business managers.

Any dispute, no matter its nature, weakens an entity and its business relationships. It affects its profitability and performance and, if an outcome is not rapidly reached, it can even affect its future development prospects or continued existence.

Today, an company can decide to resort to an economical and rapid means of resolving disputes, outside of the courthouse, by resorting to "Alternative Dispute Resolution (ADR)" as it is called in common law countries, or "Modes Alternatifs de Règlement des Conflits (MARC)" as it is called in France.

Mediation and arbitration are the two main procedures that are offered by CMAP to settle disputes. This guide is primarily dedicated to these two forms of dispute resolution.

Mediation is an amicable dispute resolution process. It provides a shield of confidentiality and trust, which allows entities to negotiate and explore by themselves a mutually acceptable solution to their dispute. The mediator orchestrates these exchanges, without becoming involved in the substance of the dispute, leaving the parties entirely free to decide the outcome to their dispute.

Arbitration is a contentious and private means of dispute resolution. It enables the establishment of judicial proceedings, identical to those conducted before national courts, in a confidential setting. The arbitrators, who are selected for their competence and their availability, ensure rapid access to justice by means of a flexible process.

The award rendered by a sole arbitrator or an arbitral panel is equivalent to a judgment that is binding on the parties.

These two procedures can be complementary and used in succession (e.g. mediation followed by arbitration if the parties did not reach an amicable settlement; or arbitration, which once started may be suspended to try mediation) or at the same time (simultaneous Med-Arb).

7

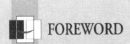 **FOREWORD**

CMAP has also designed other procedures, called "New Solutions", that are explained in another specific guide. These innovative procedures seek to offer enterprises with tools to prevent litigation from occurring, through the early intervention of skilled and neutral third parties, who are mandated to provide an independent legal evaluation, an amicable technical expert opinion, or to provide rapid decisions. Finally, an online recommendation service allows access to a neutral third party via a secure computer network system.

The purpose of these two guides, which revisit and explain the entire range of rules provided by CMAP, is to allow companies, at any moment, whether from the moment that the symptoms of a conflict first appear or after several years of litigation, to engage in an efficient and customized dispute resolution process, with managed deadlines and costs, using CMAP's know-how in this field.

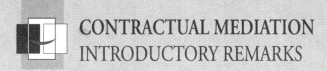

CONTRACTUAL MEDIATION
INTRODUCTORY REMARKS

The purpose of this guide is to familiarise company managers and their advisors, lawyers and chartered accountants, as well as legal managers with mediation so that they may appreciate its advantages, understand how it differs from arbitration, and thus more readily have recourse to mediation as a means of resolving their disputes.

CMAP Rules of Mediation contribute to:

– helping companies to learn about and understand mediation;

– creating a climate favourable to mediation by using qualified mediators selected by the Centre who mutually benefit from each other's experience;

– providing companies with a simple and often inexpensive method of reconciling their differences, in an environment conducive to dialogue and guaranteed by professionalism.

As a preliminary observation, it should be recalled that the fundamental difference between mediation and arbitration is that the purpose of mediation is to bring about reconciliation between parties through the intervention of a third party and not to settle the dispute by imposing a binding decision, as is it the case of arbitration.

Mediation as put in place by CMAP is an amicable process for the resolution of disputes. Its object is to assist the parties in reaching the optimal negotiated solution or, at least, a solution which is acceptable by all of the parties. In this context, it is necessary to highlight that the mediator is neither judge nor arbitrator but rather a catalyst whose objective is to facilitate negotiation between the parties in order to help them find a solution to their dispute. In principle, (s)he gives an opinion only when unanimously requested to do so.

The agreement reached by the parties at the end of mediation may be the subject of a written settlement agreement if the parties so wish. This has the advantage of rendering the agreement res judicata, i.e. conferring upon it, between the parties, similar status and effect to a final court judgement.

11

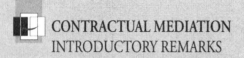

CONTRACTUAL MEDIATION
INTRODUCTORY REMARKS

Lastly, unless otherwise agreed by the parties beforehand, the failure of the mediation does not automatically result in arbitration. Mediation is not intrinsically linked to arbitration.

The characteristics of CMAP mediation are as follows:

• The response to a need
Promoting a mediation process for resolving business disputes responds to a need which is increasingly felt. Parties to a business relationship wish to find, even before a conflict develops, a neutral venue in which to examine and discuss their respective interests, in the presence of a third party. Appropriate solutions, which in many cases could not otherwise have been adopted, allow the parties to continue their business relationship.

• A very open access
The Chamber of Commerce and Industry of Paris is committed to promoting recourse to mediation. For this reason, **mediation can be initiated not only upon the joint request of the parties but also in response to a desire expressed by one of the parties, in which case CMAP proposes to the other party that the process be set in motion.** But, by its very nature, mediation cannot, of course, be imposed on the parties.

• A flexible, rapid and confidential process
The mediator's task is to assist the parties to seek, with loyalty and due regard for their respective interests, a conciliatory solution to the dispute between them. The mediator may perform his task as he sees fit. Since no particular restrictions are placed on the mediator or the parties with regard to the conduct of the mediation proceedings, the mediator and the parties do not find themselves in a context constrained by formalities. However, **the mediator must complete her/his task within a two-month time limit,** unless an extension is requested by both parties.

Lastly, the confidential nature of the mediation process is clearly highlighted in the Rules: no statement or proposal made before or by the mediator may be subsequently used, notably in arbitral or judicial proceedings.

• Impartial and qualified mediators
CMAP Rules of Mediation aim both at respecting the parties' freedom, without which the mediation cannot attain its desired object, and at giving full latitude to the mediator to assist the parties throughout the process. However, it is necessary to recall that the legitimacy of the mediator relies wholly on the confidence placed in her/him by the parties. This is the reason for which

CMAP calls for mediators who are trained in the technicalities of mediation and whose professional competence and negotiation skills are recognised.

• Mediation costs
To permit all companies an easy access to this amicable means of dispute resolution, the Paris Chamber of Commerce wants that CMAP guarantees to the companies a manageable cost of its mediation services as part of the Chamber of Commerce's mission of public service.

A distinction is thus made between **disputes involving a sum of more or less than 15.000 euros.** For disputes involving a sum in dispute of less than €15.000, the cost of opening the file as well as the fees of the mediator are fixed, while an hourly rate applies to mediations with an amount in dispute of more than €15.000. This distinction ensures that disputes of lesser financial significance but of otherwise significant importance for companies are dealt with efficiently and inexpensively.

Further, a distinction is made between mediations initiated after the dispute has developed and mediations initiated under a clause set forth in the contract between the parties.

Thus, **in the absence of a mediation clause, the fee for opening the file is met by the party who retains CMAP.** The fees of the mediator are then shared between the parties as agreed between them, the matter of the allocation of costs being one of the issues to be discussed by the mediator and the parties during the course of the mediation. However, **failing agreement between the parties with respect to the costs, the costs remain the responsibility of the party who originally retained CMAP for the mediation.**

In the case of a joint retainer of CMAP, the costs of the mediation are, in principle, shared equally by the parties.

13

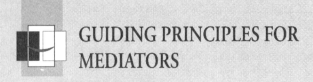

GUIDING PRINCIPLES FOR MEDIATORS

• Role of the Mediator

Article 7 of the Rules of Mediation provides that: " The mediator helps the parties to find a negotiated outcome to their dispute. (S)he has full discretion as to the methods by which (s)he performs her/his task, subject to obligations of loyalty and respect of the interests of each of the parties. If (s)he considers it useful, (s)he may hear the parties separately, if they have agreed to this. "

The mediator has no authority other than that arising out of the confidence placed in her/him by the parties.

The mediator is neither a judge nor an arbitrator. His/her role is to seek with the parties a negotiated solution by bringing together their points of view.

The mediator undertakes to respect CMAP Rules of Mediation, in particular with respect to time limits.

• The Mediator and the Parties

As soon as possible after accepting his/her appointment, the mediator contacts the parties to organise his/her mission.

(S)he obtains the agreement of the parties, if (s)he considers it appropriate, to meet separately with them. In such a case, the mediator undertakes to respect the principle of equality between the parties.

The mediator analyses with each party its position with respect to the dispute and makes sure that each party fully understands the position of the other party or parties.

To accomplish this, (s)he may suggest ideas to resolve the issues, but in no circumstances may (s)he attempt to impose any terms of settlement, particularly on a party which is clearly in a weak position. In her/his approach, the mediator must not only be guided by principles of fairness but also take into account the parties' expectations with regard to the agreements entered into by them.

© CMAP-2006

15

GUIDING PRINCIPLES FOR MEDIATORS

If her/his mission is successful, the mediator invites the parties to formalise their agreement by signing a written settlement agreement. Since the mediator is not a party to that document, (s)he does not sign it.

However, upon the request of the parties, (s)he may affix his/her signature to the settlement agreement to attest to the agreement reached. In such case, her/his signature is preceded by the words "in the presence of X, mediator designated by CMAP."

• Secrecy and Confidentiality

The mediator is bound by a duty of secrecy regarding the dispute entrusted to her/him, both with regard to its existence and to all other aspects of the mediation.

The mediator's duty of secrecy is general, absolute, and unlimited in time. The mediator may be released from it only under the conditions prescribed by law.

The mediator is prohibited from having any professional relationship with any of the parties during the year following the end of her/his mission.

The mediator's mission ends when a settlement agreement is signed or when the failure of the mediation is recorded. From that date onward, the mediator cannot intervene in any capacity whatsoever in connection with the dispute or its resolution, except upon the request of all the parties and after giving notice thereof to the General Secretariat of CMAP.

MEDIATION RULES

ARTICLE 1: INITIATION OF MEDIATION PROCEEDINGS

1.1 Mediation proceedings are initiated upon the request of the parties, where they have so agreed at the outset of the dispute, or upon the request of one party, where the parties have so agreed under the terms of their contract.

1.2 Mediation proceedings may also be initiated :
   (a) at the request of one party who wishes the Centre to propose mediation proceedings and where the other party is not opposed to it,
   (b) or, alternatively, where the Centre receives a request for arbitration and considers that mediation may be proposed to the parties, subject to their acceptance of it.

1.3 Any mediation which is entrusted to CMAP entails acceptance by the parties of the present Rules.

ARTICLE 2: REQUEST FOR MEDIATION

2.1 The Centre is seized with a matter at the request of the parties or one of them, upon receipt of a request for mediation that contains:
   - the legal particulars or company details and the addresses of the parties;
   - a brief description of the nature and circumstances of the dispute; and
   - their respective positions or the position of the party requesting mediation.

2.2 The request for mediation is not registered unless it is accompanied by payment of the administrative fees for opening the matter calculated in accordance with the scale of fees in effect, as provided by Article 8 hereof. Under no circumstances is this sum refundable.

2.3 Where mediation proceedings are suggested by the Centre of its own initiative (under Article 1 paragraph 2b of CMAP's Mediation Rules and Article 19 of CMAP's Arbitration Rules), the request for arbitration shall serve as request for mediation. It entails payment of the initial fees in accordance with the preceding paragraph, which will be set off against the sum paid at the time of the registration of the arbitration request.

17

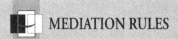 MEDIATION RULES

ARTICLE 3: INFORMING THE OTHER PARTY

3.1 **Where a mediation clause already exists:**
When the Centre is seized by a party who invokes an existing conciliation or mediation clause in the contract subject of the dispute, it shall inform the other party of the initiation of mediation proceedings. The Centre shall send these Rules to the other party and allow it fifteen (15) days from receipt of CMAP's letter to provide its comments.

3.2 **In the absence of a mediation clause:**
As soon as the request is registered, the Centre shall so inform the other party and invite it to participate in mediation proceedings. It shall send these Rules to the other party and allow it fifteen (15) days from receipt of CMAP's letter to reply to the Centre.

ARTICLE 4: RESPONSE TO THE REQUEST

4.1 **Where a mediation clause already exists:**
As soon as the comments of the other party have been received, or once the time limit defined in Article 3.1 above has expired, the General Secretariat of the Centre shall submit the case to CMAP's Accreditation and Appointments Committee so that a mediator may be designated.

4.2 **In the absence of a mediation clause:**
If the other party so agrees, the General Secretariat submits the case to CMAP's Accreditation and Appointments Committee so that a mediator may be designated. If the other party explicitly refuses to participate in mediation proceedings or fails to respond once the time limit defined in Article 3.2 above has expired, the Centre shall so advise the party who submitted the request for mediation and close the file, without refunding the administrative fees paid for opening the matter.

ARTICLE 5: APPOINTMENT OF THE MEDIATOR

5.1 As soon as the parties have agreed to participate in mediation proceedings or when the contract between them contains a clause referring to these Rules, the Accreditation and Appointments Committee shall appoint a mediator, who shall be selected according to the nature of the dispute or, as the case may be, based on a suggestion from the parties.

5.2 CMAP may propose to the parties that a trainee mediator attend the mediation sessions. The trainee mediator will then be bound by the same obligation of confidentiality as the appointed mediator.

ARTICLE 6: INDEPENDENCE, NEUTRALITY AND IMPARTIALITY OF THE MEDIATOR

6.1 The mediator must be impartial, neutral and independent of the parties. In appropriate cases, (s)he must disclose to the parties and to CMAP's General Secretariat any circumstances which might affect her/his independence and/or impartiality in the eyes of the parties. In such case, (s)he may be confirmed or maintained as mediator only after a decision by the Accreditation and Appointments Committee and with the written consent of all the parties.

6.2 The mediator appointed by the Committee shall sign a statement of independence.

6.3 Should (s)he come to the view, during the course of the mediation process, that there exists any factor liable to call into question her/his independence, (s)he shall so inform the parties. The mediator shall continue her/his task if the parties so agree in writing. Otherwise (s)he shall stay the mediation proceedings. The Accreditation and Appointments Committee shall then proceed to appoint a replacement mediator.

ARTICLE 7: THE MEDIATOR'S ROLE AND THE CONDUCT OF MEDIATION PROCEEDINGS

7.1 The mediator helps the parties to find a negotiated outcome to their dispute. (S)he has full discretion as to the methods by which (s)he performs her/his task, subject to obligations of loyalty and respect of the interests of each of the parties. If (s)he considers it useful, (s)he may hear the parties separately, if they have agreed to this. In this case, (s)he tries to ensure equal balance of treatment between all the parties and the respect of the confidentiality of the procedure (cf. paragraph 4 below).

7.2 In the case of contractual mediation, at the beginning of mediation proceedings, the mediator has the parties sign an agreement apportioning the expenses and fees of the mediation between them.

19

◪ MEDIATION RULES

7.3 Where a mediation clause exists, if one of the parties refuses to attend a meeting organised by the mediator, an end of mission report is submitted to the Centre by the mediator. Similarly, the mediator also submits a report in the event that the mediation ends without the parties having reached an agreement. CMAP's General Secretariat then closes the file and so informs the parties.

7.4 The mediator and the parties are held to the strictest obligation of confidentiality for everything that relates to the mediation: no finding, statement, or proposal made by or before the mediator may be used subsequently, even in court proceedings, except in cases where all parties have formally agreed to this.

7.5 The duration of the mediation shall not exceed two months starting from the appointment of the mediator by the Centre. This period may be extended by CMAP or by the judge that ordered the mediation, with the agreement of the mediator and all the parties, the Centre being entitled to terminate the mediation proceedings on the expiry of a period of six months from the date of appointment of the mediator, without refunding the administrative fees.

7.6 If it appears to the mediator that the mediation process will not result in an agreement, (s)he may terminate her/his mission. Equally, and at any time, either party is free to bring the mediation proceedings to a close.

7.7 Should the mediator consider that (s)he is unable to pursue her/his mission, (s)he shall stay the mediation proceedings. (S)he shall promptly give notice thereof to CMAP's General Secretariat. The CMAP's Accreditation and Appointments Committee shall then proceed to appoint a replacement mediator as soon as possible, if the parties so request.

7.8 In the hypothesis provided for at Article 1, paragraph b, the parties may at any time request that the mediation proceedings be terminated and, where appropriate, that arbitration proceedings be started.

7.9 The mediator may not be appointed as an arbitrator or participate in any capacity whatsoever in any ongoing proceedings, except upon the written request of all the parties.

7.10 The agreement reached as a result of mediation proceedings shall be written up in a document that is signed by the parties.

7.11 In the case of an international dispute, the parties may ask the mediator if (s)he is willing to be appointed by the Centre as an arbitrator in order to deliver an award by consent. If the mediator so agrees, CMAP starts arbitration proceedings. In addition to the fees and expenses due for the mediation, shall be added half of the fees and expenses, in accordance with the minimum fee for the range of the sum in dispute, that would be incurred shall an arbitration be commenced, as defined in the scale appended to the Arbitration Rules in effect at the time proceedings were originally initiated with the Centre. Once any sums due for this arbitration procedure have been paid, the Accreditation and Appointments Committee is requested to validate the appointment of the arbitrator. The award is delivered in accordance with CMAP's Arbitration Rules.

ARTICLE 8: MEDIATION FEES AND EXPENSES

8.1 The fees and expenses of the mediation shall be set, as appropriate, in accordance with the fixed or sliding scale annexed to these Rules that are in effect at the date CMAP receives the request for mediation.

8.2 During the course of mediation proceedings that are not covered by the fixed scale, the Centre may request an additional upfront advance against final fees and expenses.

8.3 In the case of a clause designating CMAP, and unless the parties agree otherwise, the fees and expenses shall be borne equally by the parties. In the absence of a contractual clause designating CMAP and of an agreement on the sharing of mediation costs, the fees and expenses shall be borne by the applicant.

8.4 If an arbitration follows, no filing fee for opening the matter, other than the fee already paid in respect of the mediation, is due by the parties.

ARTICLE 9: INTERPRETATION OF RULES - APPLICABLE RULES

9.1 CMAP shall have sole jurisdiction to interpret these Rules.

9.2 A request for mediation shall be processed in accordance with the Rules and scale of fees and expenses in effect on the date of receipt of the request.

21

ARBITRATION
INTRODUCTORY REMARKS

Promoting recourse to arbitration by all companies by virtue of its flexibility, promoting a procedure which is adapted to the nature of each dispute, these are the objectives that CMAP has set itself.

• Dynamic Rules
Flexibility and speed, the advantages of arbitration which led to its development, find full expression in CMAP Rules of Arbitration. From the moment the Centre is retained, and even before the appointment of the arbitral tribunal, CMAP creates an environment which is conducive to dialogue and encourages the parties to reach a negotiated agreement by first proposing that the parties proceed to mediation (article 19 of CMAP Rules of Arbitration).

Furthermore, arbitrators are given a broad discretion to tailor the arbitration to the needs of the disputes submitted to them, by adapting the procedure to the specific issues and difficulties of the case.

Another original feature of CMAP Rules of Arbitration is the rapidity of the proceedings: in addition to short time limits, the arbitrators are constantly encouraged to proceed rapidly. The intentional absence of formalism in the procedure, in particular, permits the preliminary procedures to be hastened.

A fast-track procedure has also been established and proves particularly useful for disputes which do not require complex preliminary inquiries. This procedure can be used either at the request of the parties or, in circumstances where the arbitral tribunal considers it appropriate, in view of the nature of the dispute. One of the main features of the fast-track procedure is that the arbitrator may decide the case within three months, possibly on the sole basis of the documents submitted by the parties, or after a single exchange of pleadings, or after hearing the parties.

At last, the parties may have recourse to the **Established Arbitral Tribunal** of CMAP. Composed of prominent arbitration specialists, coming from varied professional horizons (lawyers, magistrates, law professors, CEOs, etc.), which ensures its plurality of competence, the Established Arbitral Tribunal offers the possibility to hasten the proceedings even more. In particular, the parties **do not waste time appointing the sole arbitrator or** the arbitral **tribunal in its entirety,** the Established Arbitral Tribunal being ready to proceed immediately at the request of the parties.

© CMAP-2006   25

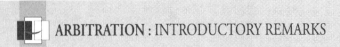

ARBITRATION : INTRODUCTORY REMARKS

• Rules Suitable for a Wide Range of Disputes

Because the procedure is relatively simple and rapid and because the pace of the proceedings varies according to the nature or size of the dispute, the Rules have proved suitable for a wide range of cases.

Before the case is referred to the arbitral tribunal, each party remains free to apply to any competent judicial authority for conservation and/or interim measures.

• High Quality Arbitral Proceedings

While the rules governing the proceedings are determined by the arbitral tribunal - subject to the agreement of the parties - this freedom is restricted by the obligation to respect the principles inherent in the proper administration of justice and by the provisions of CMAP Arbitration Rules. Thus, for example, in accordance with the right of each party to be heard, which is a principle of public order, each party must be informed of the other party's claims and the documents produced in support thereof.

Nothing, however, prevents the arbitral tribunal from exploring speedy methods of communication, provided the arbitral tribunal ensures that each party is afforded the opportunity to present its case.

CMAP and the Approval and Appointments Committee have an important role to play in overseeing the arbitral proceedings and in ensuring that they progress smoothly.

• Independent, Impartial and Qualified Arbitrators

The arbitrator must be independent from the parties. (S)he must be impartial and respectful of the confidentiality of his/her task, both during the arbitration and after the handing down of the award.

CMAP obtains the assistance of arbitrators whose morality and professional qualities are recognised. CMAP arbitrators come from diverse professional backgrounds: practitioners in law, business and finance, former judges, university professors, company managers, engineers, etc.

Moreover, they possess practical and technical knowledge which ensures that they have a perfect understanding of the business sector in which the dispute takes place.

Upon request, names of arbitrators can be communicated to the parties. In all cases, a sole arbitrator or the chairman of an arbitral tribunal is to be appointed by the Approval and Appointments Committee and, where appropriate, the appointment is made upon the proposal of the parties or arbitrators nominated by the parties.

• Arbitration Costs
The costs of the arbitration include the arbitrator's fees and the administrative expenses. They are borne by the parties in the proportion indicated in the award. Their amount is fixed according to the scale in force found at page 47.

27

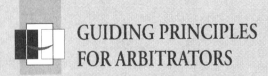

GUIDING PRINCIPLES FOR ARBITRATORS

Any person likely to be appointed by CMAP, or by one of the parties, is requested to read carefully the following rules, and to sign and return a copy to the Centre.

By signing the rules, a copy of which is to be kept by its signatory, (s)he undertakes to respect and apply, strictly, the rules, which constitute CMAP's arbitration rules.

Each signatory recognises that he has been informed that the violation of any of the provisions of the arbitration rules will result in her/his personal liability and furthermore her/his removal from CMAP's list of arbitrators.

ARTICLE 1 : INDEPENDENCE AND IMPARTIALITY

A CMAP arbitrator shall act as an independent and impartial judge.

1/ Before agreeing to be appointed, the prospective arbitrator shall :
- declare to CMAP any possible past and present relationship with one or several of the parties, their lawyers or the other arbitrators ;
- reveal, in writing, to CMAP and to all the parties any circumstances which might affect her/his independence or impartiality in the eyes of the parties.

2/ The arbitrator shall, furthermore, reveal in writing, to CMAP and to the parties, any of the circumstances referred to in paragraph 1 above that occurs after her/his appointment.

3/ As soon as (s)he is aware that (s)he is a propspective, as well as during the proceedings, (s)he undertakes not to enter into any form of relationship with the parties, except for the needs of the arbitration, in which case (s)he will always afford all the parties the opportunity to be heard.

4/ When he sits in an arbitral tribunal, the arbitrator who was appointed by one of the parties and whose appointment then received validation by the Accreditation and Appointments Committee, is prohibited from acting as the representative of the said party or considering that (s)he is acting in such capacity.

© CMAP-2006   29

GUIDING PRINCIPLES FOR ARBITRATORS

5/ The arbitrator shall not receive any compensation or benefit from any of the parties or from a person having an interest in the resolution of the dispute, such prohibition, however, to be without prejudice to her/his candidacy for appointment as an arbitrator in a further matter.

ARTICLE 2 : AVAILABILITY

Any arbitrator who accepts to act as an arbitrator on a tribunal where the arbitration rules of CMAP apply, shall carry out her/his mission until the dispute for which (s)he was appointed is finally resolved.

In accepting the mission, the arbitrator commits to respect the arbitration calendar or arbitration proceedings and to render the award on the scheduled date.

He shall undertake, even if acting in the framework of a panel of several arbitrators, to accomplish, in totality, the mission as contemplated personally, the arbitrators having no flexibility to share or delegate their tasks.

ARTICLE 3 : ABILITY

The arbitrator shall accept her/his mission only if her/his abilities are sufficient to enable her/him to perform the task for which her/him is appointed in conformity with the expectations of the parties, and to fully perform and complete her/his mission.

ARTICLE 4 : CONFIDENTIALITY

The arbitrator shall not reveal to anyone neither the existence of the dispute, nor the content of the arbitration proceedings.

Once the award has been rendered, the arbitrator shall respect this same obligation of secrecy and, in the case where (s)he is a member of a tribunal consisting of several arbitrators, (s)he shall respect the absolute secrecy of the deliberations, including with the party who has appointed her/him.

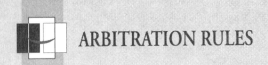

ARBITRATION RULES

ADHERENCE TO THE RULES

ARTICLE 1: ADHERENCE

The parties shall be bound by the provisions of the current Rules either by signing an arbitration agreement which contains a clause nominating the Centre as the arbitration institution or by voluntary adherence to these Rules, or in cases where the Centre is appointed by a state court.

COMMENCEMENT OF ARBITRAL PROCEEDINGS

ARTICLE 2: REQUEST FOR ARBITRATION

2.1 CMAP is seized either by a unilateral request for arbitration, or by a joint request by the parties, which indicates:
- the particulars or business name and address of the claimant(s) and, where appropriate, the name(s) and address(es) of its or their counsel
- the particulars or business name and address of the defendant(s) and, where appropriate, the name(s) and address(es) of its or their counsel;
- a brief description of the nature and circumstances of the dispute;
- the claims and applications; and
- where both parties have agreed that the dispute is to be referred to three arbitrators, the name of the arbitrator nominated by the claimant(s)

2.2 The supporting documents shall be submitted in three or more copies together with a schedule enumerating the documents.

2.3 The Request shall not be registered unless it is accompanied by payment of the filing fee as fixed by the scale in force at the time of filing.

© CMAP-2006   31

 **ARBITRATION RULES**

2.4 A request for arbitration of an international character requires at least one of the parties to be French unless both parties, being of foreign nationality, agree otherwise. The supporting documents to be used in the procedure shall be supplied in their original language, with a French translation if CMAP or the arbitral tribunal so requests, the cost of such translation to be agreed by the parties and with the Centre.

ARTICLE 3: ANSWER TO THE REQUEST

3.1 Once the request has been registered, CMAP shall send a copy of the request and the documents annexed thereto to the defendant(s) by registered post accompanied by a request for advice of delivery. This notification shall grant the defendant one month to respond.

3.2 The response addressed to the Centre by registered post with advice of delivery must, in cases where three arbitrators will be nominated, indicate the name of the arbitrator chosen by the defendant.

3.3 This response shall contain any potential counter-claims and must be accompanied by at least three copies of the documents the defendant intends to produce in reliance upon its claim, with a schedule enumerating the documents relied upon.

3.4 When the arbitration has an international character and subject to the provisions of article 2 paragraph 5 of the present Rules, the response shall be made in French, unless the parties agree otherwise, within a time limit of one month, and accompanied by a translation into another language if the Centre or the arbitral tribunal so request. Similarly, throughout the proceedings, the documents relied upon by the defendant must be supplied in their language of origin accompanied by a translation if the Centre or the arbitral tribunal so requests.

3.5 Upon receipt of the response, the Centre shall communicate it to the claimant by registered post accompanied by a request for advice of delivery.

ARTICLE 4: FAILURE TO REPLY

After the time limit defined in Article 3, paragraph 1, the General Secretariat of CMAP checks that the notification specified has been received by the defendant and:

1/ in the case of an arbitration clause that does not appoint CMAP, so informs the applicant and closes the file; the administrative expenses are non-refundable.

2/ in the case of an arbitration clause that appoints CMAP as responsible for organising arbitral proceedings, initiates the arbitration procedure in accordance with the provisions outlined below, notifying each step of the procedure to the defaulting party.

ARTICLE 5: JURISDICTION

Should the appointment of the Centre or the jurisdiction of the arbitral tribunal be challenged, before the arbitral tribunal has been formed, the Accreditation and Appointments Committee shall consider prima facie whether arbitration proceedings can be initiated.

ARTICLE 6: ASSISTANCE AND REPRESENTATION OF THE PARTIES

6.1 Each party may be assisted by any person of its choice.

6.2 Each party may arrange to be represented at the arbitral proceedings by a person empowered by it for such purpose.

ARTICLE 7: ADVANCE ON COSTS AND TRANSMISSION OF THE FILE TO THE ARBITRAL TRIBUNAL

7.1 As soon as CMAP has received the parties' respective claims and applications, or upon expiry of the time-limit specified in Article 3 paragraph 1 hereof, or in the event of a joint request, CMAP shall request all the parties to pay an equal amount as an advance on fees and expenses calculated in accordance with the scale in force and payable within the time limit fixed by the Centre.

© CMAP-2006

33

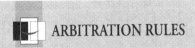 **ARBITRATION RULES**

7.2 CMAP shall transmit the file to the arbitral tribunal only once the required advances on costs have been paid in full. Should one of the parties fail to pay its share, another party may pay it instead, or, in lieu thereof, post a bank guarantee acceptable to CMAP.

7.3 Upon failure to pay the costs, after expiry of the time limit and without an offer from a party to meet the costs of the other party (cf. the preceding paragraph), the Centre shall have the right to consider the arbitral procedure as having lapsed. It shall so inform the parties, the administrative fees remaining non-refundable.

7.4 Where the share of the advance owed by the defaulting party is paid by another party, the latter may request that the Accreditation and Appointments Committee revise and fix the total amount of the advance on the basis of its application alone.

7.5 In the latter case, the arbitral tribunal is seized only with respect to the application of the party who met the costs of its opponent, after notifying the defaulting party by registered letter with a request for advice of delivery.

7.6 The defaulting party can seize the arbitral tribunal with a counter-claim only after having effected payment of the costs payable by it.

7.7 If, in the course of the arbitration, additional claims are put forward by the parties, the Accreditation and Appointments Committee may call for an additional advance on costs upon the request of the arbitral tribunal, which payment is subject to the rules provided for in paragraphs 2, 3 and 4 of the current article. Failing payment within the time limit set, the additional claims are considered to have never been made.

MEASURES OF CONSERVATION
AND INTERIM MEASURES

ARTICLE 8: MEASURES OF CONSERVATION AND INTERIM MEASURES

After the file has been transmitted to it, the arbitral tribunal shall have jurisdiction to make orders of conservation and interim measures, unless by their nature they should be ordered by another authority.

THE CONSTITUTION OF THE ARBITRAL TRIBUNAL

ARTICLE 9: NUMBER OF ARBITRATORS

Subject to any previous or current agreement of the parties with respect to the number of arbitrators, the Accreditation and Appointments Committee shall decide how many arbitrators will compose the arbitral tribunal. There must always be an uneven number of arbitrators.

ARTICLE 10: APPOINTMENT OF ARBITRATORS

10.1 The sole arbitrator or the chairman of the arbitral tribunal, or, in the case of multi-party arbitration, the arbitral tribunal in its entirety, shall be appointed by the Accreditation and Appointments Committee. Where appropriate, the appointment shall be made upon a proposal of the parties or of the arbitrators nominated by the parties. If the arbitration is of an international character, the sole arbitrator or the chairman of the arbitral tribunal shall, unless otherwise agreed by the parties, be of a nationality other than those of the parties and shall be chosen after consulting with the French National Committee of the International Chamber of Commerce.

10.2 Where an arbitrator must be proposed by a party, CMAP shall set the said party a time limit for so doing. If the party fails to reply, the appointment shall be made by the Accreditation and Appointments Committee.

10.3 All appointments made by the parties shall be subject to confirmation by the Accreditation and Appointments Committee.

© CMAP-2006   35

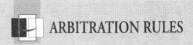 **ARBITRATION RULES**

ARTICLE 11: ESTABLISHED ARBITRAL TRIBUNAL

11.1 The Centre also provides an Established Arbitral Tribunal which is available to parties who wish to resort to it.

11.2 The Established Arbitral Tribunal is made up of three appointed arbitrators and three alternate arbitrators. They are appointed by the Accreditation and Appointments Committee for a two year tenure which cannot be renewed without a hiatus. If an arbitrator has already been appointed (s)he will continue the mission to its conclusion even if this means working beyond the appointed two years.

11.3 The Established Arbitral Tribunal sits as a college made up of three arbitrators. If one or more of the arbitrators who have tenure is unable to continue or is challenged the Accreditation and Appointments Committee designates a substitute or substitutes from amongst the alternate arbitrators.

11.4 The arbitrators of the Established Arbitral Tribunal designate one of their member to act as chairman for each of their proceedings.

11.5 With the agreement of the parties, the Established Arbitral Tribunal may be made up of a single arbitrator chosen by the Accreditation and Appointments Committee from amongst the arbitrators who have tenure and alternate arbitrators.

11.6 The parties may opt for the Established Arbitral Tribunal when contacting the Centre with a joint request for arbitration.

11.7 All the other provisions of the Arbitration Rules that are not inconsistent with this Article apply to proceedings before the Established Arbitral Tribunal.

ARTICLE 12: INDEPENDENCE AND IMPARTIALITY OF ARBITRATORS

12.1 The arbitrators shall be independent. They must inform the parties and the Accreditation and Appointments Committee of any circumstances which might affect their independence or their impartiality in the eyes of the parties.

12.2 In such case, they may be confirmed or maintained as arbitrators only after a decision by the Accreditation and Appointments Committee, after the opinion of the parties has been taken into consideration.

12.3 The arbitrators shall act impartially in the exercise of their functions.

ARTICLE 13: CHALLENGE TO ARBITRATORS

13.1 Any party wishing to challenge an arbitrator, for circumstances occurring or coming to light after the arbitrator's appointment, shall immediately and in any case within no more than fifteen (15) days of the occurrence or revelation of the particular circumstances on which the challenge is based, submit a reasoned application to the Accreditation and Appointments Committee. After affording each party the opportunity to be heard, the Accreditation and Appointments Committee shall rule on the application by handing down a decision which does not contain reasons and which shall not be subject to appeal.

13.2 The arbitral proceedings shall be suspended during such inquiries.

13.3 Once the award has been notified to the General Secretariat, in accordance with Article 24, paragraph 3, no challenge of arbitrators is admissible.

ARTICLE 14: REPLACEMENT OF ARBITRATORS

14.1 The arbitrator shall undertake to carry out her/his mission to its completion.

14.2 Any arbitrator who is unable to continue or who is removed following a challenge shall be replaced according to the same procedure applying at the time of her/his appointment. The arbitration period shall be suspended from the occurrence or revelation of the event constituting the ground for replacement until the new arbitrator accepts her/his mission.

14.3 The arbitral tribunal so constituted shall decide whether and to what extent the arbitral proceedings are to be resumed.

© CMAP-2006

 ARBITRATION RULES

THE ARBITRAL PROCEEDINGS

ARTICLE 15: PLACE AND LANGUAGE OF THE ARBITRATION

15.1 Unless otherwise agreed by the parties, the arbitration shall take place in Paris, where the award shall be rendered, but this shall not preclude the arbitral tribunal from gathering at any other location.

15.2 In an international arbitration, the language of the arbitration shall be chosen by the parties. By default, the language to be used shall be set by the arbitral tribunal. French or English will be used until another language has been agreed upon.

ARTICLE 16: APPLICABLE RULES

16.1 When the arbitral tribunal has been formed, CMAP shall send to each of its members a copy of the parties' claims and applications as well as of the supporting documents.

16.2 The arbitral tribunal shall then organise the proceedings in whatever form it sees fit, according to the nature of the case and taking into account any arrangements agreed on by the parties.

16.3 The arbitration proceedings are governed by the arrangements agreed between the arbitral tribunal and the parties or, in the absence of such agreement, by the provisions of these Rules. Any points not covered by these arrangements will be governed by French law as defined by the New Code of Civil Procedure.

16.4 Unless otherwise agreed by the parties and the arbitral tribunal, the arbitration proceedings shall be confidential and the hearings shall not be not public.

ARTICLE 17: PROCEDURAL ORDERS

The arbitral tribunal, or its chairman if authorised to do so by the other arbitrators, may make orders to determine all procedural issues. Such orders are not liable to appeal.

ARTICLE 18: NOTICES AND WRITTEN SUBMISSIONS

18.1 All written statements, files, correspondence, and supporting documents must be communicated simultaneously to all the parties, to their counsel, and to each member of the arbitral tribunal.

18.2 All notices shall be validly given if sent to the parties at the address indicated by them or, upon request, to their representatives. Any change of address must be notified to CMAP by registered post accompanied by a request for advice of delivery.

18.3 Notices addressed to the members of the arbitral tribunal are to be sent to the CMAP's head office.

SETTLEMENT OF DISPUTES BY AGREEMENT

ARTICLE 19: MEDIATION

19.1 A mediation process may be proposed to the parties either by the Centre prior to the appointment of the arbitral tribunal or by the tribunal itself once it has been appointed.

19.2 If the parties accept that a mediation should be initiated, it shall be immediately organised according to CMAP Mediation Rules, the arbitration process being merely suspended.

19.3 If the mediation does not result in an agreement which settles the dispute, the arbitration proceedings shall be resumed, upon the request of the most diligent party and in conformity with the provisions of the present Rules.

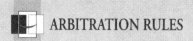 **ARBITRATION RULES**

FAST-TRACK PROCEDURE

ARTICLE 20: IMPLEMENTATION OF THE FAST-TRACK ARBITRATION PROCEDURE

20.1 A fast-track procedure shall be implemented if one of the parties so requests and the other party consents thereto or if the parties have agreed in advance and, if the arbitral tribunal considers that the nature of the dispute permits it.

20.2 The arbitral tribunal shall organise the fast-track procedure and, in particular, shall prescribe the time limits, so as to allow an award to be delivered within three months of the transmission of the file to it by CMAP. If the parties so propose or accept, the arbitral tribunal may decide the case solely on the basis of the documents submitted by the parties, without hearing them.

20.3 The reduced time limit for delivery of the award may be extended in exceptional circumstances by the Accreditation and Appointments Committee.

AWARD

ARTICLE 21: TIME LIMITS

21.1 The award shall be rendered by the arbitral tribunal as soon as possible, having regard to the nature of the dispute. In all cases, it must be delivered within six months from the date the file was transmitted to the arbitral tribunal by CMAP, in accordance with Article 7, paragraph 2 of these Rules.

21.2 This time limit may be extended by the Accreditation and Appointments Committee if it decides that it is necessary to do so or at the request of the parties and of the arbitral tribunal.

ARTICLE 22: RULES APPLYING TO THE MERITS OF THE DISPUTE AND APPEAL

22.1 The arbitral tribunal shall decide the dispute in accordance with rules of law, unless the parties have granted to it the power to act as amiable compositeur.

22.2 The award may not be appealed except, in the case of internal arbitration, where the parties have agreed otherwise in writing.

ARTICLE 23: PARTIAL OR INTERIM AWARDS

23.1 If it considers it appropriate, the arbitral tribunal may make partial or interim awards. Similarly, at the request of one of the parties or on its own motion, the arbitral tribunal may make any order relating to the collection of evidence or the appointment of an expert to investigate technical matters.

23.2 The arbitral tribunal may itself carry out any investigations it deems necessary, including where this may require visiting other locations.

23.3 It may decide to hear witnesses, experts appointed by the parties, or any other person or persons which one of the parties requests be heard or which it decides to hear of its own initiative.

23.4 The arbitral tribunal, when it deems this necessary, may appoint one or more experts, define their mission which must afford each party an opportunity to be heard and receive their report.

23.5 Any difficulties arising during the expert proceedings that cannot be settled by the expert or the parties shall be submitted to the arbitral tribunal.

23.6 Under all these circumstances, the deadline for delivering the award is postponed to allow for the time required to carry out the measure plus an additional period of two months.

41

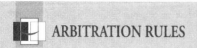 **ARBITRATION RULES**

ARTICLE 24: FORM AND CONTENT OF THE AWARDS

24.1 All awards shall be given by majority decision of the arbitrators on the arbitral tribunal who shall also state the reasons upon which they are based.

24.2 In accordance with the draft award which has been sent to it by the arbitral tribunal, the Accreditation and Appointments Committee shall indicate the amount of the arbitration fees and expenses which shall be charged to the parties in the proportion fixed by the arbitral tribunal in the award.

24.3 The award, dated and signed by the arbitrators or, where appropriate, referring to one of the arbitrator's refusal to sign it, shall be transmitted to the General Secretariat of CMAP with one copy for each of the parties plus an original which will be conserved in the Centre's archives.

ARTICLE 25: NOTIFICATION OF AWARDS TO PARTIES

25.1 After full payment of the arbitration fees, CMAP shall notify the parties of the award, by registered post accompanied by a request for advice of delivery, and send a copy to their counsels. Certified copies can subsequently be sent by the Centre but only to the parties or their beneficiaries.

25.2 If one of the parties fail to pay the outstanding balance of its share of the fees and expenses, another party may pay it instead in order to enable the Centre to notify the award.

25.3 The award shall be confidential. However, it may be published with the agreement of all the parties to the proceedings and the arbitral tribunal.

ARTICLE 26: AWARD BY CONSENT

Should the parties reach a settlement agreement during the course of the arbitral proceedings, they can request the arbitral tribunal's consent to record it in an award.

ARTICLE 27: CORRECTION, OMISSION TO RULE AND INTERPRETATION

27.1 The arbitral tribunal may, of its own initiative or on the application of a party, correct any material errors or omissions of the award.

27.2 If one of the parties so requests, the arbitral tribunal may supplement the award if it has omitted to rule on a claim which came within its jurisdiction or proceed to the interpretation of the award.

27.3 Any application to correct a material error or an omission or to interpret shall be addressed to the Centre by registered post accompanied by a request for advice of delivery, which shall refer the application to the arbitral tribunal. However, such applications are admissible only if the arbitral tribunal can be reconvened or the application can be referred to the sole arbitrator and only if they are submitted within one year of service of the sentence on the parties.

27.4 If the arbitral tribunal cannot be reconvened or if the application cannot be referred to the sole arbitrator, the Accreditation and Appointments Committee designates, as appropriate, a new tribunal or a new arbitrator, in accordance with the provisions of Article 10 above.

27.5 The parties shall have the opportunity to be heard with respect to all of the above procedures.

27.6 The arbitral tribunal shall make its ruling within the shortest amount of time possible and the ruling shall state the reasons upon which it is based.

ARTICLE 28: ENFORCEMENT OF THE AWARD

By agreeing to submit to arbitration under these Rules, the parties undertake to execute the award without delay.

43

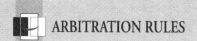 ARBITRATION RULES

APPLICATION OF RULES

ARTICLE 29: INTERPRETATION AND RULES IN FORCE

CMAP alone shall have jurisdiction to interpret these Rules. The arbitration shall be subject to the Rules and the scale in force on the day CMAP is seized of the file.

SCALE OF FEES AND EXPENSES UNDER CMAP RULES OF MEDIATION *

 Contractual Mediation**

NATIONAL MEDIATION

Amount in dispute less than € 15 000 – Fixed rate	
Case Filing expenses (1)	€ 200
Mediator's fees (2)	€ 500

Amount in dispute exceeds € 15 000	
Case Filing expenses (1)	
- joint initiation of mediation proceedings	€ 200 per party
- individual initiation of mediation proceedings	€ 200 x number of parties
Administrative expenses and	€ 300 per hour
Mediator's fees (3) (4) (5)	

INTERNATIONAL MEDIATION

Case Filing expenses (1)	
- joint initiation of mediation proceedings	€ 250 per party
- individual initiation of mediation proceedings	€ 250 x number of parties
Administrative expenses and	€ 400 per hour
Mediator's fees (3) (4) (5)	

 Court-annexed Mediation***

Administrative expenses and Mediator's fees	€ 300 per hour

---

* Tax-exclusive scale applicable from 14 June 2005.

** A 20% night rate increase will apply as well to mediator's fees and to administrative expenses in case a mediation would last after 9 PM.

*** However, if (s)he deems it appropriate, the magistrate may propose that CMAP applies a fixed rate fee to cover the mediator's fees and administrative expenses.

(1) The amount of the filing fee will, in any case, be withheld by CMAP: it is not refundable, whether or not mediation proceedings are initiated (cf. Article 4 of the Mediation Rules).

(2) Payable as soon as mediation proceedings are initiated.

(3) An amount of € 1200 for national mediation and € 1600 in the framework of international mediation are payable by each party to cover mediator's and other related fees, which expenses will not, in any case, be refundable by CMAP, whatever the duration of the proceedings.

(4) Other expenses not included: transport, accommodation expenses of mediator, etc.

(5) The mediator's fees include studying the case, holding mediation meetings and communicating (by phone or by email) with the parties.

46   © CMAP-2006

SCALE OF FEES AND EXPENSES UNDER
CMAP RULES OF ARBITRATION*

■ Arbitration costs** shall include a fixed-rate filing fee which shall be deducted from the administrative expenses and arbitrators' fees calculated according to the following scale:

Case Filing fee: € 500

Sum in dispute by slice	CMAP	Fees of one arbitrator***	
	Administrative expenses	Minimum	Maximum
1: Up to € 50 000	€ 500	no minimum	€ 6 000
2: from € 50 001 to € 250 000	€ 2 500	€ 4 000	€ 12 000
3: from € 250 001 to € 500 000	€ 3 500	€ 6 000	€ 18 000
4: from € 500 001 to € 1 000 000	€ 5 000	€ 9 000	€ 25 000
5: from € 1 000 001 to € 5 000 000	€ 9 000	€ 15 000	€ 40 000
6: from € 5 000 001 to € 10 000 000	€ 12 000	€ 20 000	€ 50 000
7: from € 10 000 001 to € 30 000 000	€ 15 000	€ 25 000	€ 60 000
8: from € 30 000 001 to € 50 000 000	€ 20 000	€ 30 000	€ 80 000
9: over € 50 000 001	€ 30 000	€ 35 000	estimate provided on demand

*   Tax-exclusive scale applicable from 14 June 2005.

**   Should an expert be appointed, the expert's fees shall be in addition to the arbitration costs.

*** Where there are three arbitrators, these figures are to be multiplied by 3 and, unless otherwise directed by the arbitrators, the Accreditation and Appointments Committee shall apportion the total amount of the arbitration fees as follows: 40% for the Chairman of the arbitral Tribunal and 30% for each of the arbitrators.

47

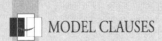 MODEL CLAUSES

Upon entering into a contract, the various parties may agree to settle their disputes by means of mediation and/or arbitration under CMAP Rules. The following clauses are proposed (select appropriate option):

 Option 1: Mediation and Arbitration

All disputes arising out of or in connection with the validity, interpretation, performance, non-performance or termination of this Contract shall be submitted to the Mediation Rules and, in the event that no settlement is thereby reached, to CMAP (Centre for Mediation and Arbitration of Paris, Paris Chamber of Commerce and Industry) Arbitration Rules to which the parties undertake to adhere.

 Option 2: Mediation Only

All disputes arising out of or in connection with the validity, interpretation, performance, non-performance or termination of this Contract shall be submitted to mediation in accordance to CMAP (Centre for Mediation and Arbitration of Paris, Paris Chamber of Commerce and Industry) Mediation Rules to which the parties undertake to adhere.

 Option 3: Arbitration Only

All disputes arising out of or in connection with the validity, interpretation, performance, non-performance or termination of this Contract shall be submitted to arbitration under CMAP (Centre for Mediation and Arbitration of Paris, Paris Chamber of Commerce and Industry) Arbitration Rules to which the parties undertake to adhere.

B. Sample Agreements to Mediate

(i) CEDR Model Mediation Agreement (used in general civil and commercial cases)[9]

THIS AGREEMENT   dated   **IS MADE BETWEEN**

Party A

....*of* ....

Party B

....*of* ....

(together referred to as
'the Parties')

The Mediator

....*of* ....

(a term which includes any agreed **Assistant Mediator**)

and

CEDR Solve of IDRC, 70 Fleet Street, London EC4Y 1EU

in relation to a mediation to be held

on ....

at ....

('the Mediation')

concerning a dispute between the Parties in relation to

....

....

('the Dispute')

IT IS AGREED by those signing this Agreement THAT:

The Mediation

1   The Parties agree to attempt in good faith to settle the Dispute at the Mediation. All signing this Agreement agree that the Mediation will be conducted in accordance with its terms and consistent with the CEDR Solve Model Mediation Procedure and the CEDR Code of Conduct for Mediators current at the date of this Agreement.

Authority and status

2   The person signing this Agreement on behalf of each Party warrants having authority to bind that Party and all other persons present on that Party's behalf at the Mediation to observe the terms of this Agreement, and also having authority to bind that Party to the terms of any settlement.

3   The Mediator is an independent contractor and not an agent of CEDR Solve, and neither the Mediator nor CEDR Solve is an agent for any of the Parties in relation to the Dispute or this Agreement.

4   Neither the Mediator nor CEDR Solve shall be liable to the Parties for any act or omission in relation to the Mediation unless the act or omission is proved to have been fraudulent or involved wilful misconduct.

Confidentiality and without prejudice status

5   Every person involved in the Mediation:

1.1   will keep confidential all information arising out of or in connection with the Mediation, including the fact and terms of any settlement, but not including the fact that the Mediation is to take place or has taken place or where disclosure is required by law to implement or to enforce terms of settlement; and

5.2   acknowledges that all such information passing between the Parties, the Mediator and CEDR Solve, however communicated, is agreed to be without prejudice to any Party's legal position and may not be produced as evidence or disclosed to any judge, arbitrator or other decision-maker in any legal or other formal process, except where otherwise disclosable in law.

6   Where a Party privately discloses to the Mediator any information in confidence before, during or after the Mediation, the Mediator will not disclose that information to any other Party or person without the consent of the Party disclosing it, unless required by law to make disclosure.

7   The Parties will not call the Mediator or any employee or consultant of CEDR Solve as a witness, nor require them to produce in evidence any records or notes relating to the Mediation, in any litigation, arbitration or other formal process arising from or in connection with the Dispute and the Mediation; nor will the Mediator nor any CEDR Solve employee or consultant act or agree to act as a witness, expert, arbitrator or consultant in any such process.

8   No verbatim recording or transcript of the Mediation will be made in any form.

Settlement formalities

9   No terms of settlement reached at the Mediation will be legally binding until set out in writing and signed by or on behalf of each of the Parties.

Fees and costs of the Mediation

10   The Parties will be responsible for the fees and expenses of CEDR Solve and the Mediator (*'the Mediation Fees'*) in accordance with CEDR Solve's Terms and Conditions of Business current at the date of this Agreement.

11   Unless otherwise agreed by the Parties and CEDR Solve in writing, each Party agrees to share the Mediation Fees equally and also to bear its own legal and other costs and expenses of preparing for and attending the Mediation (*'each Party's Legal Costs'*) prior to the Mediation. However, each Party further agrees that any court or tribunal may treat both the Mediation Fees and each Party's Legal Costs as costs in the case in relation to any litigation or arbitration where that court or tribunal has power to assess or make orders as to costs, whether or not the Mediation results in settlement of the Dispute.

Legal status and effect of the Mediation

12   Any contemplated or existing litigation or arbitration in relation to the Dispute may be started or continued despite the Mediation, unless the Parties agree or a Court orders otherwise.

13   This Agreement is governed by the law of [England and Wales] and the courts of [England and Wales] shall have exclusive jurisdiction to decide any matters arising out of or in connection with this Agreement and the Mediation.

14   The referral of the dispute to the Mediation does not affect any rights that exist under Article 6 of the European Convention of Human Rights, and if the Dispute does not settle through the Mediation, the Parties' right to a fair trial remains unaffected.

Changes to this Agreement

15   All agreed changes to this Agreement and/or the Model Procedure are set out as follows:

Signed

Party A _____

Party B _____

Mediator _____

CEDR Solve _____

(ii)   In Place of Strife MediationTerms of Business and Fee Guidelines[10]

Mediation Fee Guidelines and Terms of Business

Our aim is to provide the services of experienced mediators cost effectively and proportionately.

These guidelines indicate the basic rate at which we are able to provide a mediator. However fees will be individually quoted in each case and will reflect the mediator selection and other factors. Please call our case managers to discuss your case and they will do all they can to find the right mediator at the right price.

Amount of claim §	Arrangement fee*	Mediation fee (daily rate)
Up to £50,000	£300	£1,500
£50,000 to £150,000	£300	£2,700
£150,000 to £300,000	£300	£3,100
£300,000 to £700,000	£300	£3,500
£700,000 to £1m	£300	£3,900
£1m to £5m	£300	£4,200
£5m upwards	£300	£5,000

§ including any counter-claim
* increased by £150 for each party over two parties involved in the mediation

■ The fee is the total amount to be shared between the parties.

■ Three hours preparation included.

■ No extra mediation charges (unless mediator is required to stay after 7pm).

■ Concessionary rates considered where there is need.

■ Venue selection and booking service free of any administration charge.

Terms and Conditions

1. Fees and expenses, plus VAT, are shared equally between the parties unless In Place of Strife is informed otherwise.

2. Fees do not include agreed expenses such as room hire, catering, and the mediator's travelling costs, all of which can be estimated at the time mediation fees are quoted.

3. The day rate is quoted inclusive of up to three hours preparation time. Preparation time spent by the mediator in excess of three hours will be charged at 12.5% of the daily rate per hour.

4. In Place of Strife reserves the right to make a charge at 12.5% of the daily rate per hour for time spent at the mediation after 7pm or in subsequently continuing to mediate by telephone or by attendance in person.

---

10   Reproduced by kind permission of In Place of Strife, The Mediation Chambers.

5. Where a party is represented by solicitors, our invoice will be addressed to those solicitors, who must accept liability for agreed charges and expenses.

Payment:

6. The arrangement fee and the mediation fee (based on number of days booked) and estimated expenses are payable one week in advance of the mediation.

7. A final balancing invoice or credit note, if applicable, will be issued and become payable immediately following the mediation.

8. Interest will be chargeable on amounts overdue at 15% pa.

Cancellation:

9. Where a cancellation is made after the mediation date has been agreed but more than a week ahead of that date, the cancellation charge is the arrangement fee shared between the parties.

10. Where a cancellation is made within one week of the mediation date, 50% of agreed fees will be payable.

11. Where a cancellation is made within 48 hours of the mediation date (excluding Saturday, Sunday and public holidays), the full agreed fees will be payable.

12. All agreed expenses incurred by In Place of Strife and the cost of any preparation time by the mediator will be payable in full.

(iii) Law Society (England & Wales) Sample Mediation Agreement (used in general civil and commercial cases) [11]

This **agreement** is made on _____ 200__

Between:

of

and:

of

(each a 'party' and together 'the parties')

and:

of

(the 'mediator')

and:

of

(the 'co-mediator', and together 'the mediator')

and:

of

(the 'pupil mediator', and together 'the mediator')

Recitals

A. Disputes have arisen between the parties ('the disputes') as briefly described in schedule 1 to this agreement.

B. The parties have requested the mediator, and the mediator has agreed, on the terms and conditions of this agreement to assist the parties to resolve, if possible, the disputes.

---

11   @ The Law Society 2009, Reproduced by permission.

Agreement

Appointment of the mediator

1. The parties appoint the mediator, and the mediator accepts the appointment, to mediate the disputes ('the mediation') in accordance with the terms of this agreement.

2. The parties will share equally and will be liable together and separately to the mediator for the mediator's fees and all the other costs of the mediation, as described in schedule 2 to this agreement. The timing of payment of those fees and other costs are also set out in schedule 2 to this agreement.

3. If the mediation does not result in an agreement to resolve the disputes, the costs of the mediation, including costs of advisers retained under clauses 7 or 14, will be costs in the cause, that is, paid by the party who loses the action to the party who wins the action, if an order for costs is made in that party's favour.

Role of the mediator

4. The mediator will be neutral and impartial. The mediator will assist the parties to isolate the issues, develop and explore options for resolution of these issues and, if possible, achieve expeditious resolution of the disputes by agreement between them.

5. The mediator makes no representation that any such agreement between the parties will equate with any result which might be achieved by a contested trial of the disputes or any part of them.

6. The mediator will not make decisions for a party or impose a solution on the parties. If the parties request, and the mediator agrees, the mediator may, if the parties reach impasse, provide the parties with a non-binding recommendation based on the mediator's own knowledge of the subject matter and law.

7. The mediator will not obtain from any independent person advice or an opinion as to any aspect of the disputes, unless the parties agree in writing and then only from such person agreed by the parties. The cost of the advice or opinion will be paid in accordance with clauses 2 and 3 and schedule 2 of this agreement.

8. The mediator acknowledges that, prior to commencement of the mediation, the mediator has disclosed to the parties any prior dealings that the mediator has had with any of the parties and any interest that the mediator has in the disputes.

9. If in the course of the mediation the mediator becomes aware of any circumstances that might reasonably be considered to affect the mediator's capacity to act impartially the mediator will immediately inform the parties of those circumstances. The parties will then decide whether the mediation will continue with that mediator, or with a new mediator appointed by the parties. In the absence of agreement by the parties, the new mediator will be appointed by

[_____   _____].

Co-operation

10. Each party must use its best endeavours to comply with reasonable requests made by the mediator to promote the efficient and expeditious resolution of the disputes. If either party does not do so, the mediator may terminate the mediation.

Authority & representation

11. In the absence of consent by the other parties and the mediator, if a party is a natural person, that party must attend the mediation. If a party is not a natural person or is not present in person, it must be represented at the mediation by a person with knowledge of the relevant issues and with authority to settle within any range that can reasonably be anticipated and to make agreements binding on that party in settling the disputes.

12. Without limiting the responsibility of the parties under clause 11, if any party has any limitation on their authority to settle, this must be disclosed to the mediator before the commencement of the mediation.

13. Each party may have one or more persons, including legally qualified persons, to assist and advise them at the mediation.

Conduct of the mediation

14. The mediation, including all preliminary steps, shall be conducted in such manner as the mediator considers appropriate having due regard to the nature and circumstances of the disputes, the agreed goal of an efficient and expeditious resolution of the disputes and the view of each party as to the conduct of the mediation.

15. Without limiting the mediator's powers under clause 14, the mediator may give directions as to

(a) the exchange of brief written outlines of the issues raised by the disputes and a supporting bundle of documents which are relevant to those issues

(b) providing the mediator prior to the mediation with any such outlines and documents, and any further information or documents that the mediator may request following perusal of the outlines and supporting documents and

(c) preliminary conferences, by phone or meeting, prior to the mediation.

Communication between the mediator and a party

16. The mediator may meet as frequently as the mediator deems appropriate with the parties together or with a party alone.

17. The mediator may communicate with a party or the parties orally and/or in writing.

18. Except as the parties may otherwise agree in writing, anything said or done by any person at the mediation is said or done without prejudice and no party shall be entitled to call evidence of anything said or done by any person at the mediation.

Confidential information

19. Information, whether oral or written, disclosed to the mediator in private will be treated as confidential by the Mediator unless

(a) the party making the disclosure states otherwise

(b) the law imposes an obligation of disclosure, or

(c) the mediator believes believe that the life or safety of any person is or may be at serious risk

20. The parties and the mediator agree in relation to all confidential information disclosed to them during the mediation, including the preliminary steps

(a) to keep that information confidential

(b) not to disclose that information except to a party or a representative of that party participating in the mediation or if compelled by law to do so, and

(c) not to use that information for a purpose other than the mediation.

Each representative in signing this agreement is deemed to be agreeing to this provision on behalf of the party he/she represents and all other persons present on behalf of that party at the mediation.

Privilege

21. The parties and the mediator agree that, subject to clause 31, all documents or statements produced, used or made in the mediation, not otherwise available or known or subject to other obligations of discovery, will be privileged and will not be disclosed in or relied upon or be the subject of a summons to give evidence or to produce documents in any arbitral or judicial proceeding in respect of the disputes.

Subsequent proceedings

22. The mediator will not accept an appointment in relation to any arbitral or judicial proceeding relating to the disputes or any of them.

23. No party will take action to cause the mediator to breach clause 22.

24. No party will summons the mediator to give evidence or to produce documents in any arbitral or judicial proceeding in respect of the disputes.

Termination

25. If a party does not wish to continue the mediation, the mediator must terminate the mediation in so far as it relates to that party and may terminate the mediation as regards all the parties.

26. The mediator may terminate the mediation if

(a) after consultation with the parties, the mediator feels unable to assist the parties to achieve resolution of the disputes

(b) the mediator receives, from a source outside the mediation, confidential information relevant to the disputes or any party

(c) the mediator receives confidential information relevant to a client during the mediation

(d) the mediator considers it appropriate for any other reason, which the mediator may decline to give to the parties

27. The mediation will be terminated upon execution of a settlement agreement in respect of the disputes.

28. Termination of the mediation does not terminate the operation of clauses 18–33.

Settlement

29. Unless otherwise agreed by the parties, a settlement reached at the mediation will need to be written down and signed by the parties or their representatives in order to be binding on the parties. If the mediation has been ordered by a court the parties will advise the court of the outcome of the mediation if required by the court rules to do so.

Enforcement

30. In the event that one or more of the disputes is or are settled, as the case may be, either party may

(a) enforce the terms of the settlement agreement by judicial proceedings, and

(b) in such proceedings adduce evidence of and incidental to the settlement agreement (other than matters which are privileged by reason of clauses 18–20).

Indemnity and exclusion of liability

31. The mediator will not be liable to a party, except in the case of fraud by the mediator, for any act or omission (whether negligent or misleading or otherwise) in the performance or purported performance of the mediator's obligations under this agreement.

32. The parties together and separately indemnify the mediator against all claims, except in the case of fraud by the mediator, arising out of or in any way connected

with any act or omission by the mediator in the performance or purported performance of the mediator's obligations under this agreement.

Governing law and jurisdiction

33. This agreement is governed by, and is construed and takes effect in accordance with, English law. Unless otherwise specified in any settlement agreement, the courts of England will have exclusive jurisdiction to settle any claim, dispute or matter of difference that may arise out of or in connection with the mediation.

Schedule 1 – Description of the disputes

_____

_____

_____

_____

_____

_____

_____

_____

Schedule 1 – Costs of the mediation

[   ]

Signed:

_____

On behalf of [party] Print name

_____

On behalf of [party] Print name

_____

On behalf of [mediator] Print name

[Co-mediator]

[Pupil mediator]

(iv)   Resolution Model Agreement to Mediate[12]

Agreement to Mediate

BASIC PRINCIPLES AND TERMS OF MEDIATION

The following are the terms on which this mediation is undertaken. At the first joint mediation meeting you will be asked to sign this document as an indication of your commitment to the process and of your agreement to the terms set out below.

This Agreement is made between me xxxx ('the Mediator') and AA and BB

Mediation Organisation and Code of Practice

1   I undertake this mediation as a member of Resolution (formerly the Solicitors Family Law Association). In doing so I am guided and bound by the Codes of Practice approved by the Solicitors Regulation Authority.

Mediator's professional capacity and functions

2.   I am a family mediator [*and solicitor*] and undertake this mediation as part of my practice at [*insert name of firm or as appropriate*]. When working as a mediator, I do not advise or represent parties but instead I work in an impartial way to help you arrive at your own decisions. I do not give legal or any other advice to you, jointly or individually or make judgments about your individual or joint situation. I can, however, provide legal or other information on an even handed basis, to assist you both for example in understanding the applicable principles of law and the way those principles are generally applied.

3.   My role is to assist you both to consider possible ways of resolving any issues that you may have or of making future arrangements for yourselves and any children. I will help you both to explore the options available to you, with a view to your reaching a resolution that you both consider appropriate to your circumstances. That may not necessarily be the same conclusion that might be arrived at by the court. If practicable I will tell you if I consider that your proposed terms are likely to fall outside of the parameters that a court might approve.

4.   I will not tell you what you should do or comment about what your 'best interests' are or might be. The choices and decisions are yours. It is possible and often very helpful for you to have advice from your solicitor during the mediation process in order to make informed decisions and so that your respective advisers are kept informed as to progress. I may help you to consider when legal advice outside the meeting is appropriate.

No conflict of interests

5.   Mediation cannot take place if I have prior knowledge of the situation through a previous involvement as a solicitor, counsellor or in any other professional role. If any other conflict, potential conflict or perceived conflict of interest arises or emerges, I will not continue to act as mediator.

---

12   Reproduced with the kind permission of Resolution (www.resolution.org.uk). Resolution was formerly the SFLA

Confidentiality and privilege

6. I will treat all matters in the mediation as confidential, except as otherwise agreed, and subject to the terms of this Agreement, in particular Paragraphs 10, 11 and 12. I ask you to agree that the mediation and any summaries may be reviewed on a strictly confidential basis by a Professional Practice Consultant/Supervisor and/or other appointee of my mediation organisation and that anonymised details about your case may be used for mediation training purposes.

7. Information, written or oral, which either of you may provide to me will not ordinarily be maintained confidentially as between yourselves, except any address or telephone number either of you ask me to keep private, or otherwise as you may both agree with me.

8. All financial information is provided on an 'open' basis, which means that it can be used in court. This may be in support of a consent application made by either of you or in contested proceedings. Such disclosure will assist your individual legal adviser and will avoid information having to be provided twice over. This reinforces the importance of full and accurate disclosure, as your individual legal or financial adviser before advising you on any settlement terms will need to check with you as to the completeness and accuracy of all information received.

9. However, communications about possible options, proposals and terms of financial settlement are conducted on a 'without prejudice' basis, so cannot be referred to in court. Also, an evidential privilege will ordinarily be claimed for all attempts to resolve issues in the mediation including those relating to children. Where an evidential privilege exists, it can only be waived by agreement. You both agree not to call me (and/or any co mediator if applicable) to give evidence in court, nor will you seek to have any of my or our notes brought into evidence.

10. These provisions for confidentiality and privilege will not apply if it appears that a child or other person is suffering or likely to suffer significant harm. In this event, I would normally, as far as practicable and appropriate, seek to discuss the action to be taken with both of you before taking any action to contact the appropriate authority/ies in line with the Mediation Code(s) of Practice under which I work. These provisions are also subject to any overriding obligations of disclosure imposed by law.

11. (*check the following against your firm's policy or as appropriate*) These provisions for confidentiality and privilege will also not apply if information is communicated to me with the intention of furthering a criminal purpose. I am required by law to comply with the Proceeds of Crime Act 2002 ('the Act'), The Terrorism Act 2000, the Serious Organised Crime and Police Act 2005 and Money Laundering Regulations 2003 and 2007 and all other regulations made under the Act ('the Regulations'). The Act may cover your partner's conduct as well as your own. It also covers overseas conduct, which, although lawful outside of the UK, may be or would have been unlawful if committed in the UK. First, the Regulations require me to carry out proper client identification procedures (see below) and to keep the information about identification up to date. Furthermore, if I become aware in the course of acting for you as a mediator, that you have engaged or may engage in any criminal conduct, I am obliged to report that knowledge or suspicion to the Serious Organised

Crime Agency (SOCA) and by entering into this agreement, you authorise me to make such reports to SOCA as are appropriate under the Regulations.

12. In order to comply with the obligations as to client identification, I should be grateful if each of you could supply us with a photocopy of your passport (photograph page) or driving licence, together with an original utility or credit card bill showing your current address which is not less than three months old.

Financial and other information

13. You both undertake to provide complete and accurate disclosure of all your financial circumstances, with supporting documents where necessary. I will try to help you to identify what information and documents would help the resolution of any issues, and to consider how best these may be obtained.

14. I do not verify the completeness and accuracy of the information you provide but if required, I can help you to consider the ways in which you may make such enquiries or obtain such verification. I will ask you to sign and date a statement in the Open Financial Statement confirming that you have made a full disclosure. If it should emerge that full disclosure has not been made, any agreements flowing from the proposals reached in mediation based on materially incomplete information could in some cases be set aside and the issues re opened.

Professional advice and qualified nature of agreements

15. Any significant decisions arrived at in mediation (including any settlement proposals) will not ordinarily be turned into a binding agreement until you have each had the opportunity to seek advice on them from your separate legal advisers. However, decisions on matters that are not materially significant to your respective positions or to the substantive outcome, may be entered into as binding agreements without legal advice. If during the course of the mediation it would be helpful for me to draw up an Interim Summary on a without prejudice basis to record interim decisions on minor matters or options/proposals discussed, I would do so. Such a document would be privileged and could not be produced in evidence to a court.

16. Mediation meetings are commonly conducted without lawyers present. However, your legal advisers may, by agreement between you both and me, participate in the mediation process in any useful and appropriate way.

17. I may help you to consider the desirability of seeking assistance from other professionals such as accountants, expert valuers or others, or from counsellors or therapists.

Summaries and recording of agreements

18.1   During the course of the mediation, usually once financial disclosure is complete, I will ordinarily draw up:-

- ■ **An Open Financial Statement/Summary** of your financial circumstances which will be on the record (and could be used in evidence in a court if need be).

510

18.2   At the end of the mediation (or earlier if appropriate), I will also ordinarily draw up:

- A privileged summary called a **Memorandum of Understanding** of your mutually acceptable proposals for the settlement of matters discussed in the mediation, outlining the context in which those proposals have been reached. This is a without prejudice document.

In the event of this mediation being conducted under the Legal Services Commission's publicly funded scheme, I may instead draw up an **Outcome Statement** confirming the terms of the outcome of the mediation.

These documents are generally provided to enable you both to obtain separate and independent legal and/or other advice before entering into a legally binding agreement. You will need such independent advice to assess how the proposed settlement terms may affect your own individual position.

19.   Your solicitors will usually undertake the formal recording of any agreements that may be reached after you have each been able to seek their advice, including for example the drawing up of any Separation Agreement or draft court consent order.

Complaints and Compliance

20.   I hope that I will work with you as a mediator in a manner fully satisfactory to you both. Any concern you may have as to my practice or the service provided by me should be referred to me in the first instance. If I am unable to resolve this with you directly or otherwise, any complaint you have, will be considered through my firm's complaints procedure, and thereafter if it is still unresolved you may refer your complaint to Resolution for consideration in accordance with their complaints procedure. Please let me know if you would like a copy of the Complaints and Compliance Rules and I would be happy to provide this to you.

Termination of mediation

21.   Under the Code(s) of Practice to which I subscribe, I will be concerned to ensure that each of you enter into the mediation process able to discuss and plan freely together and without risk of threat or harm. I ask that you inform me if there are concerns for you about your ability to negotiate freely.

22.   Either of you may terminate the mediation at any stage. I may also terminate the process if I do not think it appropriate or helpful to continue. In either such event, I will if required provide information as to other options available to you.

Mediation fees

23.   My fees, payable at the end of each session or as otherwise arranged, are £x per hour plus VAT (ie £1 ½ x + VAT for a 1 ½ hour session). I will usually ask for an amount on account of costs at the start of a mediation case of between £750 and £1000. Depending on the issues, 3 to 5 sessions of 1½ hours each are commonly

required, but more or less may be needed. Once you have arranged dates for future mediation sessions, if these are cancelled, a cancellation charge may be required.

24.   The hourly rate also applies for any work that may be required between sessions for example in drafting documents or in reviewing financial disclosure but I do not normally charge separately for routine telephone calls or letters. Depending on the degree of complexity, it usually takes around 2 hours to prepare the summaries, with a cost of around £2x plus VAT, shared between you. Sometimes less or more time is needed.

25.   If your issues are particularly complicated or you require interim documentation for consultation with your personal adviser/s, the cost will be negotiated separately and in consultation with you both. I will provide you with cost estimates wherever practicable to assist your planning of likely costs.

26.   If you do not agree to the contrary these costs are shared equally between you so you are each responsible for paying half. You are also responsible for meeting the costs in full of any individual mediation preparation sessions.

Mutual commitment

27.   I will do my best to help you both. I ask you both to give your commitment to the mediation process and to co operate as fully as possible in looking for workable solutions.

Terms of Business

28.   The terms of business letter which has already been sent to you is incorporated into this Agreement.

Dated the   day of   200

....

[INSERT NAME]
Family Mediator

We agree to the above terms which we have read and understood:

....

....

Signed   Signed

Date: Date:

© Resolution 2008

(v) NMI Model Mediation Agreement[13]

Model Mediation Agreement

(This model is intended for a mediation between two parties. If more than two parties are involved in the mediation, the preamble, the wording of articles 6.1 and 8.3, and the signing of the agreement must be altered accordingly.)

THE UNDERSIGNED:

...., Mediator,

and the Parties:

A: ....

herein represented by:

....

and

B: ....

herein represented by:

....

HEREBY AGREE AS FOLLOWS:

Article 1 – Mediation

1.1 The Parties and the Mediator mutually undertake to use their best endeavours in attempting to resolve the dispute between the Parties described in article 2 through Mediation in accordance with the Rules of the Foundation 'Stichting Nederlands Mediation Instituut' (hereinafter called the Rules) as worded on the date of this Agreement.

1.2 The Parties and the Mediator mutually undertake to abide by the Rules.

1.3 The person mentioned in the heading of this Agreement who is listed in the NMI Register of Mediators, shall act as the Mediator.

---

13 Reproduced with the kind permission of the Nederlands Mediation Institut – NMI. For further information please visit www.nmi-mediation.nl.

Article 2 – Concise description of the dispute

....

Article 3 – Voluntariness

The Mediation shall be conducted on a voluntary basis. Each Party and the Mediator shall be free to terminate the Mediation at any time.

Article 4 – Confidentiality

4.1 Insofar as this Agreement in conjunction with the Rules imposes the obligation of confidentiality upon the Parties, this Agreement shall also be deemed to be an agreement concerning the distribution of the onus of proof, as referred to in the Law. (Section 7:900, subsection 3, of the [*Dutch*] Civil Code, in conjunction with section 153 of the [*Dutch*] Code of Civil Procedure).

4.2 The Mediator shall ensure that the obligation of confidentiality as described in the Rules is also undertaken by all third parties involved in or informed concerning the Mediation by the Mediator, as referred to in article 7.

Article 5 – Special obligations of the Parties

Besides the provisions laid down in the Rules, the Parties also undertake both vis-à-vis the Mediator and vis-à-vis each other:

– to refrain from any act or omission that could seriously interfere with or obstruct the Mediation;

– to be prepared to listen to each other's arguments and to search for compromises.

Article 6 – Representation

6.1   During the Mediation procedure each Party shall be present either in person or represented by a person designated by it.

(WHERE APPLICABLE:)

Party A is represented by:

....

Party B is represented by:

....

6.2 Each Party warrants that its representative is legally empowered to on its behalf perform all legal acts that may be necessary within the framework of the Mediation, including the entering into a settlement agreement as referred to in article 9.1, and that the representative will maintain confidentiality as prescribed in the Rules.

6.3 A written power of attorney must be produced at the request of the Mediator, showing the representative's aforementioned authority.

Article 7 – Third parties

7.1 For secretarial support the Mediator may avail himself of the assistance of a person to be designated by him for that purpose.

7.2 With the consent of the Parties the Mediator may admit others to the Mediation or involve others in the Mediation, including Auxiliary Persons within the meaning of the Rules.

Article 8 – Fees, costs and expenses

8.1 The Mediator shall charge a fee amounting to € ……….. (in words) per hour, increased by the statutory value added tax.

8.2 The Parties shall be obliged, irrespective of the progress and outcome of the Mediation, to pay the fee charged by the Mediator and to reimburse all expenses incurred by the Mediator. The Parties shall also bear all direct and indirect costs attaching to the Mediation, such as accommodation rentals, telephone, fax and travelling expenses, postage, fees and expenses of third parties involved in the Mediation pursuant to article 7, increased by the statutory value added tax.

8.3 The fees, costs and expenses referred to in article 8.2 shall be borne by the Parties according to the following ratio: Party A: … % ; Party B: … %

8.4 Each Party shall bear its own costs and expenses.

Article 9 – Settlement agreement, interim agreements

9.1 Any amicable resolution of the dispute reached by means of the Mediation shall be recorded in writing in a settlement agreement to be concluded for that purpose between the Parties.

9.2 Any agreements made between the Parties during the course of the Mediation shall be binding upon them only insofar as these have been recorded and agreed by them in writing. In such a written agreement the Parties may stipulate that any such agreements shall not be binding upon them if and as soon as the Mediation is terminated without the concluding of a settlement agreement as referred to in the preceding paragraph.

Article 10 – Disputes

10.1   In case of any dispute arising out of any agreement as referred to in article 9 or any further agreements based thereon, the Parties shall attempt to resolve these in the first instance by means of Mediation in accordance with the Rules as worded on the date of commencement of the Mediation.

10.2   If the resolution of a dispute as referred to in article 10.1 by means of Mediation has proved to be impossible, such dispute shall be settled by:

(WHEN DRAWING UP THE AGREEMENT / CONDITIONS CHOOSE A OR B:)

(A)

arbitration in accordance with the relevant rules of

................(fill in the name and location of the arbitration institute) as these are worded on the date of the request for arbitration by the most diligent Party.

(B)

the competent court in

....

Article 11 – Applicable law

This agreement shall be exclusively governed by [Dutch law].

Agreed upon and drawn up in ...plicate and signed

at .... on . ...

The Mediator:

....

Party A: Party B:

....

(.....................................)   (.....................................)

C.   Confidentiality Agreement for a general civil or commercial case[14]

Name: ....

As the condition of my being present or participating in this mediation, I agree that I will unless otherwise compelled by law preserve total confidentiality in relation to the course of proceedings in this mediation and in relation to any exchanges that may come to my knowledge whether oral or documentary concerning the Dispute passing between any of the Parties and the Mediator or between any two or more of the Parties during the course of the mediation.

Signed: ....

In the presence of ....

Dated: ....

---

14   This agreement is for sample purposes only. Legal advice is required in each case.

Appendix 4

Mediated Settlement Agreements

A. Sample settlement agreement (for a general civil or commercial case)[1]

DATE

DATE OF AGREEMENT [   ]

OR

DATE OF DEED [   ]

PARTIES

(1) [ABC Limited] (Company number [12345]) whose registered office is at [specify address] ('[ABC Limited]')

(2) John Smith of [add address] ('[John Smith]')

each a 'party' and together 'the Parties'

RECITALS[2]

A.   [Provide a description of the dispute] ('the Dispute').

B.   [Outline the reference to mediation and refer to the mediator/s ('the Mediator/s')].

C.   In the mediation the parties settled their differences in relation to the Dispute and wish to record the terms of settlement, on a binding basis, in this Agreement.

---

1   This agreement is for sample purposes only. It will need to be adapted to suit the requirements of the particular case. Legal advice should also be obtained in each case.

2   The recitals are a descriptive introduction to the operative provisions which follow. Obligations set out in recitals will not form part of the agreement and will therefore not be enforceable under the terms of the agreement.

OPERATIVE CLAUSE

IT IS AGREED:

INTERPRETATION

1. In this agreement, unless the context otherwise requires, the following words and expressions have the following meanings:

[...]

RIGHTS AND OBLIGATIONS[3]

2. Upon signature by the Parties, this Agreement shall immediately be fully and effectively binding on them by way of a complete and final settlement of the Dispute and all claims that any of them [and any subsidiaries of the Parties] may have against one another in relation to the Dispute. [A Tomlin Order and/ or any other court order shall be obtained by consent to give effect to these terms][4] OR [An Award shall be obtained by consent to give effect to these terms][5].

3. This Agreement supersedes all previous agreements between the Parties in respect of the matters which are the subject of the mediation.[6]

4. The terms of settlement agreed between the Parties are [as follows:] OR [set out in the Schedule attached to this Agreement and are signed by the Parties] OR [set out in the draft Consent [Order][Award] with Schedule attached to this Agreement and are signed by the Parties][7].

5. [In the event of any dispute or difference arising in relation to any aspect of the settlement, or the implementation or performance of its terms, the parties agree that, before taking any formal contentious step, they will first attempt to resolve the dispute or difference by negotiation. If that fails, they agree to refer the matter to further mediation by the Mediator [or specify name of mediator] in accordance with the [ ] Mediation Rules. If the matter remains unresolved within [4] weeks of such referral to mediation, either party shall be free to take such action in such forum as it may see fit. These provisions shall not, however, preclude either party from taking any injunctive or other interim legal proceedings considered necessary for the urgent protection of a party's rights.]

6. [The Parties will each pay their own legal costs in relation to the mediation, and will share the costs of the mediation in the manner provided in the Mediation Agreement entered into between them].

---

3   This is the main body of the agreement where the obligations and entitlements of the parties are set out. The clauses that follow are samples only and will need to be adapted to suit the particular circumstances.
4   Not necessary if no court proceedings are on foot.
5   Not necessary if no arbitration proceedings are on foot.
6   Not necessary if there are no previous agreements.
7   This clause provides various options for recording the terms of settlement.

7. [The action will be stayed and the Parties will consent to the Order in the terms of the attached Order.] OR [The action will be discontinued with [no order as to costs].[8]

8. The Parties will keep confidential and not use for any collateral or ulterior purpose the terms of this Agreement except as required by law [and so far as necessary to implement and enforce any of its terms].

9. Each signatory to this Agreement has entered into it freely and without duress, having first consulted with professionals of their choice. Except in the case of fraud, each signatory hereby releases the Mediator and [insert name of services provider if applicable] from any liability of any kind whatsoever arising out of, or in connection with, the Mediator's appointment or the mediation, including the drafting of this Agreement; and the signatories jointly and severally indemnify, and will keep indemnified, the Mediator and [insert name of services provider if applicable] for and against any claim for negligence arising out of or in connection with the Mediator's appointment or the mediation, including the drafting of this Agreement.

GENERAL PROVISIONS[9]

10. This Agreement shall be governed by, and be construed and take effect in accordance with, [English] law.

11. Subject to clause 5 above, the Courts of England and Wales shall have exclusive jurisdiction to settle any claim, dispute or matter of difference arising out of, or in connection with, this Agreement.[10]

SCHEDULE

SIGNATURE/EXECUTION[11]

SIGNED by
[SIGNATORY]

OR

SIGNED and
delivered as a
deed by
[SIGNATORY]

OR

---

8   Not necessary if no court or arbitration procedures are on foot. In relation to the second option, specify what is to happen in relation to the costs of the action/arbitration ('no order as to costs' is used in the sample). In addition, ensure consistency between clause (6) and clause (7) on the issue of costs.
9   Include any mechanical provisions designed to ensure that the agreement functions correctly.
10 This clause is not usually necessary if the parties are located in the UK and the subject matter of the agreement relates to the UK.
11 Ensure correct formality for the case in question.

SIGNED and
delivered as a
deed by
[COMPANY]
acting by two
directors or by
one director and
the secretary:

Director
Signature   :
Name   :

Director/Secretary
Signature   :
Name   :

B.   Sample employment compromise agreement

Refer to the ACAS website (www.acas.org.uk) for general information on COT3 agreements. A sample compromise agreement is available from the Personnel, Employment Advice and Conciliation Service website (www.lvsc.org.uk/peace).

C.   Sample workplace/grievance agreement

WORKPLACE MEDIATION AGREEMENT[12]

Mediation dates: [   ]

Mediator: [   ]

Organisation: Shirt and Co.

Parties: Jenny Jones and Tom Button

Jenny and Tom both agreed at the close of the mediation to record the agreements they reached during the mediation.

REMEMBER:

- The fact of the mediation and the discussions in the mediation are confidential and without prejudice.

---

12   Reprinted with the kind permission of Felicity Steadman. This document is for sample purposes only. The names, details and circumstances used are fictitious and merely illustrative. Each agreement has to be adapted to suit the particular circumstances.

- The purpose of the mediation was to enable you to establish and maintain an effective working relationship to make it possible for you to work together without friction in the future
- The purpose of this agreement is a reminder of the agreements you reached as a result of the work you both put in during the mediation

1. Acknowledgments of feelings:

Jenny and Tom each had a chance to say how they felt about their experience of the grievance procedure. They each acknowledged how the other had felt. In particular Tom acknowledged the stress Jenny had experienced as the accused in the process; Jenny acknowledged Tom's difficulty raising the grievance as a new employee.

2. Communication styles:

Jenny and Tom acknowledged that their communication styles had played a part in the difficulties they had experienced in their relationship. Both agreed to be more open-minded, considerate and diplomatic with one another, and to choose their words carefully when communicating with one another. They also both committed themselves to foster an open communication style, to raise concerns as they arise, to try to see things from the other's point of view and to be mindful of the impact of their communication style.

3. Building a consistent relationship:

Jenny and Tom both acknowledged that they are committed to building an effective working relationship. To do this they agreed to do the following:
- Put the past difficulties in their relationship, including particular examples of these difficulties, behind them without bearing grudges, and to focus on the future.
- Communicate with one another consistently and reciprocate communication. This communication includes greeting one another and having conversations in and outside meetings, as well as routinely writing in e-mails etc all briefs, instructions, requests, feedback and key discussion or decision points clearly to record progress and minimise misunderstandings.
- Accept and be tolerant of different styles of communicating and different needs in the way they relate to one another, speak to one another in a calm and diplomatic fashion, managing emotions effectively.
- Be open to feedback about behaviours that cause difficulties so that they each learn from and develop a greater understanding of one another. Being open to feedback might include acknowledging that the other perceives behaviour by one of them as aggressive.
- Recognise that it will take time to develop a more effective working relationship and be tolerant of this uncertainty.

4. The working relationship:

Jenny and Tom are committed to work together collaboratively and will be respectful of each other's roles and responsibilities within the team. In particular they acknowledge and respect each other's responsibilities as agreed at the recent team meeting. Should a difference of opinion occur during the development of one of these projects Tom and Jenny agree to discuss and try to resolve such differences in a professional and productive manner. Occasionally where this is not possible the issue should be referred to the team leader.

5. Implementation:

Both Jenny and Tom agree to make a concerted effort to implement the spirit and the undertakings set out in this agreement. In the event that difficulties arise between them or that they think that part or all of the agreement is not working they may approach Ian, for his assistance in resolving the difficulty. In any event they will meet with Ian in six to eight weeks to monitor the efficacy of the agreements reached between them in the mediation. Ian may decide to refer them back to mediation for this monitoring process to take place.

Jenny and Tom may share this agreement and the background to the grievance and mediation process with Jane and David, but it will otherwise remain confidential.

Signed by Jenny   Signed by Tom

D. Sample family dispute memorandum of understanding

MEMORANDUM OF UNDERSTANDING[13]

Without prejudice

Miles Flurry and Katherine (Kate) Jane Flurry have been in mediation with [Name] regarding various matrimonial issues. They have had six mediation meetings, during which they have examined their respective financial and personal circumstances, and have been looking at proposals for their financial settlement. They have also had regard to the position as it affects their children, Oliver (aged 8) and Tamsin (aged 5).

This memorandum is furnished on an evidentially privileged and 'without prejudice' basis. It is intended to help Miles and Kate to consider and obtain advice on the current proposals and does not record or create a binding agreement. An agreement will only come into being should they both decide to commit themselves to it, and they execute an appropriate formal document, after having each had an opportunity to take independent legal advice.

Background circumstances

Miles is a director and shareholder in the company Manifest Occult Publications Limited which publishes fantasy and occult books. He has expressed concern about the future of this specialist field of publishing, but accepts that for the foreseeable future, the company is likely to continue to be profitable. Kate is a full-time primary school teacher. She is currently being considered as deputy-head of her school.

Miles and Kate are both living at 33 Aspinall Road, London N3, but are conducting their lives separately. They wished to separate and used the mediation to discuss how they could do so in an orderly way and on terms that they could both accept.

Kate and Miles had a number of factors in mind in formulating their proposals. They were concerned to ensure that any arrangements they might reach in the mediation would be best for Oliver and Tamsin and would provide them with the necessary security. They wanted to achieve a 'clean break' settlement but recognised the difficulties in doing this. They wanted the settlement terms to feel fair to themselves and to one another.

Settlement discussions and proposals

The following are the matters discussed in the mediation, including the proposals which Kate and Miles find mutually acceptable:

---

13 Reproduced with the kind permission of Henry Brown and Resolution (formerly the SFLA). This document is for sample purposes only. The names, details and circumstances used are fictitious and merely illustrative. Each memorandum has to be adapted to suit the particular circumstances.

Future of the relationship

1. Miles and Kate have resolved to separate. This will be achieved in practice when they sell their property at 33 Aspinall Road, London N3, and can buy separate homes.

2. They have accepted that their marriage has broken down and that a divorce is now inevitable. They do not regard this as urgent, though both wish to have this properly formalised in the ordinary course.

Recording the proposed terms

4. Miles and Kate will record their settlement terms in a Deed of Separation, or in whatever way they may be advised by their solicitors; and they will implement such terms. They realise that until a court order is obtained, there is a possibility that either of them might seek to vary any such terms and that the court retains the power (if it considers it appropriate) to re-open matters. However, neither of them has any present intention to seek to vary the terms, and barring anything wholly unforeseen that might materially change the position, neither would expect or wish to do so in the future.

Arrangements for Oliver and Tamsin

5. Both Kate and Miles have expressed their concerns for the needs and interests of Oliver and Tamsin. They wish to maintain a good relationship with one another in the children's interests, and propose to arrange their separation, housing and future contact and communications generally in such a way that this is achieved.

6. Detailed practical arrangements concerning Oliver and Tamsin, including decision making, communications and other matters still need to be discussed and agreed. Kate and Miles have, however, arrived at a broad understanding as to how they will approach these aspects:

    6.1   Oliver and Tamsin will continue to reside with Kate when she moves into her new home.

    6.2   Kate and Miles will establish a framework for Oliver and Tamsin to spend time with Miles.

    6.3   The kind of pattern that Miles and Kate have in mind will be something like Miles spending time with Oliver and Tamsin for a weekend every fortnight. Provisionally, the idea is that he will fetch them on Friday evening and bring them back on Sunday evening; but the details remain to be discussed. Miles will also speak to them freely on the phone between weekend visits, and may visit them if he is in the area. However, he will always check in advance whether interim visits will be convenient for them and for Kate. He will also arrange to have them with him for part of the holiday periods.

Kate and Miles both recognise that Oliver and Tamsin need a good relationship with them both. They want to support one another in achieving this.

6.3 Once the pattern is in place, both Kate and Miles accept that there will need to be flexibility. They will try to establish a mechanism for making changes without unduly inconveniencing the children or one another.

6.4 They have in mind to liaise with one another about Oliver and Tamsin as necessary, and where practicable to deal jointly with matters such as schooling, health needs and the like. They will try to devise a way to ensure that these communications take place, and how each will deal with emergencies in case they cannot contact the other.

6.5 The detailed arrangements concerning these matters have been deferred, partly because of time constraints and partly because both Miles and Kate will find it easier to discuss these matters more usefully when they have actually separated and have established themselves in their separate homes. Meanwhile they are satisfied that these broad principles will be able to guide them in their discussions. If necessary, they will arrange further mediation to deal with any difficulties, should they arise.

Sale of 33 Aspinall Road and division of proceeds

7. The house at 33 Aspinall Road is to be marketed immediately at an asking price of £620,000. Any genuine offer of £600,000 or more will be acceptable. (A tentative offer of that sum has already been received.) If that level cannot be achieved within three months, Kate and Miles will consider accepting less, as advised by their agents, Creative Sales (who are being given an initial three months sole agency).

   Contracts will not, however, be exchanged on any sale or separate purchases until agreement between Kate and Miles has been reached and formalised.

8. The mortgage redemption, costs of sale and provision for both parties to move to their new homes are set out in the schedule provided by Miles and Kate. Provisionally, this is expected to total approximately £160,000. It is proposed that the net proceeds of sale will be paid to Kate absolutely, in settlement of all her capital claims against Miles. Assuming a price of £600,000, such net proceeds will be about £440,000. If there is any surplus over £440,000 this will be shared as to 67% (Kate): 33% (Miles).

9. Kate intends to use the proceeds of sale of 33 Aspinall Road to buy a house for herself and the children for about £400,000. She will pay all costs of purchase and any other expenses out of her capital. It is not her intention to have a mortgage. She has seen a house in the nearby area, which will enable her to remain in the same catchment area for the school. The asking price is £410,000, but it requires £15-20,000 of work to be done to it. She believes that it (or something similar) will be suitable.

10. Miles has made an offer of £265,000 on a flat for himself, which has been accepted, subject to contract. He will be using his capital towards this, and intends to borrow about £175,000 by way of mortgage.

11. If Kate and Miles wish to proceed with the sale of 33 Aspinall Road and the purchase of new homes for themselves, then they are aware that certain steps will be necessary before any binding legal commitments are made on the sale and purchases.

    11.1 Both Miles and Kate intend to obtain specific advice from their respective solicitors on the agreement they are proposing to enter into between themselves, to satisfy themselves about doing so.

    11.2 They propose to sign a written agreement on an open basis, in terms approved by their respective solicitors.

    11.3 If a comprehensive settlement is not yet reached, they know that an interim agreement should be entered into on an open basis. It will be expressed to be without prejudice to any further adjustment that might need to be made in the context of any overall resolution of the financial issues and to both of their rights generally. It will also be without prejudice to any argument that either of them may wish to pursue in any subsequent proceedings if matters are not settled by agreement. Its intention would be expressed as being to facilitate their separation, to be taken into account in any final resolution of the matter. The terms of the interim agreement would need to be agreed between the solicitors.

12. If final terms of settlement are now reached and approved by Miles and Kate after having been advised by their respective solicitors, then an interim agreement would not be necessary. In that event, all terms can be incorporated into a final agreement as advised by the respective solicitors (for example, in a Deed of Separation or in minutes of order if proceedings are envisaged).

Maintenance for Oliver and Tamsin

13. Miles proposes to pay Kate the sum of £900 per month as maintenance for each of Oliver and Tamsin, with effect from the first day of the month following completion of the sale of 33 Aspinall Road. That would be acceptable to Kate. This will continue until each child attains the age of 18 years or completes full-time schooling, whichever is the later, or further agreement or order. This offer is being considered within the context of Kate's income needs generally. It is not being considered within the provisions of the Child Maintenance and other Payments Act. Kate and Miles have declined to have CSA calculations informally made, but may revert to this if they wish.

Maintenance considerations for Kate

14. In consideration of the imbalance of payment of the proceeds of sale of 33 Aspinall Road in favour of Kate, Miles wished to be relieved of any further maintenance obligation towards Kate personally. He accordingly proposed

that the settlement terms should constitute a 'clean break', with Kate having no claims at all against him. The implications and effect of a 'clean break' were considered and discussed.

Having regard to her other financial resources, Kate was willing to consider these proposals, and to accept the capital imbalance and the maintenance figure of £1800 per month for the children, in return for receiving no personal maintenance. However, she did not feel able to agree to waive her right to maintenance permanently, in case anything should arise while the children were still young, which might preclude her from working. She therefore proposed that Miles's offer would be acceptable if instead of an immediate clean break, he was willing to pay her a nominal sum of £1 per year in order to reserve her rights.

Considerable time was spent in trying to find a solution to this issue. Ultimately, both agreed to consider the following formula:

14.1   The above terms would be acceptable, with a nominal maintenance payment of £1 per annum to Kate, on the basis of the further matters set out below.

14.2   It would be recorded that a substantial capital imbalance had been paid in consideration of Kate's personal maintenance being waived, and that although she was reserving her rights, that would only be against an unforeseen and serious problem arising, which could not be met in any other way. Maintenance would not be sought to meet any day-to-day difficulties that Kate might experience in managing on her income. (Both parties acknowledged that it would be difficult to know which way the court would exercise its discretion if the issue ever had to be dealt with by the court.)

14.3   If and to the extent that Kate sought any future maintenance, either directly for herself or attributable to her within a CSA context, she would agree to credit Miles with a corresponding capital sum by way of an interest in her property, subject to a maximum of £50,000. She would hold that by way of a Declaration of Trust. (It was understood that this provision might not necessarily be legally enforceable.)

14.4   Attempts would be made to cover Kate by way of sickness and if possible redundancy insurance for a period of 10 years. By that time, Oliver would attain his majority and Tamsin would be 15 years of age. Miles would contribute 50% of the premiums for the duration of this period (subject to these not being 'loaded' in any way, otherwise 50% of the unloaded level).

14.5   Kate's claims for personal maintenance would be dismissed 10 years from the date of an Agreement being formalised on this settlement. She would not be entitled to apply for this term to be extended.

Division of assets

15. Miles and Kate will each retain their own motor car and other personal possessions. They will share the contents of 33 Aspinall Road, according to their respective needs, which they expect to be able to resolve without assistance. Broadly, they envisage that Kate will have all bedroom furniture for herself, Oliver and Tamsin, and that the remaining furniture will be divided approximately 3:1 in Kate's favour. If they have any difficulty in resolving this, they will arrange a further mediation meeting.

16. Miles will pay Kate's Visa and personal debts in full as listed in her financial statement.

17. Subject to the above, Kate and Miles will each retain as their sole property all assets respectively in their own name or under their individual control.

Full settlement of all capital claims

18. Subject to the above terms, Kate makes no further claim on Miles's assets, nor Miles on Kate's. This is a full and final settlement of all capital claims that either of them may have against the other, however arising. All capital claims are to be reciprocally dismissed in any court proceedings to be brought in due course. All claims under the Inheritance (Provision for Family and Dependants) Act 1975 are similarly to be dismissed as and when Kate's maintenance claims are extinguished: meanwhile will be reserved. The implications of that Act were briefly discussed, but Kate and Miles will discuss and consider these further with their solicitors.

Dealing with future issues

19. Miles and Kate have resolved to try to deal in a reasonable way with any issues that may arise in the future, whether to do with Oliver and Tamsin, or of a financial nature, so far as the latter aspect has been reserved. If they have any problems about doing so personally, they intend to revert to mediation.

Miles and Kate will now wish to consult their respective solicitors for advice on these proposals. If, having received advice, they wish to enter into an agreement to settle all issues, the solicitors will prepare the necessary documents. Alternatively, the solicitors may assist with the preparation of interim documents (in discussion with me if so agreed) to enable the house sale and purchases to proceed in the meanwhile.

If after seeing solicitors Miles and Kate wish to discuss matters further, then further mediation meeting(s) can be arranged for that purpose (attended by the solicitors as well, if that is considered helpful and necessary).

E.   Sample community dispute agreement[14]

PARTIES

Bill Smith
Syd Brown

TERMS OF AGREEMENT

Because Bill and Syd had difficulties as neighbours they made use of mediation to deal with their problems and reach the following agreements:

1.   Syd and Bill agree that they wish to resolve all matters discussed by them at the mediation.

2.   Bill agrees not to use his power tools before 7.00 am Monday–Saturday, and only between the hours of 3.00 pm and 6.00 pm on Sundays.

3.   Syd undertakes to complete the unfinished fence between the two properties within two months of this agreement, using treated pine of 1.2 m in height.

4.   Within seven days of Syd providing him with the invoice, Bill will pay Syd 40 per cent of the cost of the fence timber and the other costs of the fencing will be borne by Syd.

5.   Both parties agree to discuss future problems directly with each other before involving neighbours and other outside persons.

6.   Syd and Bill agree to treat each other with mutual respect in the future.

7.   Syd and Bill confirm that the mediator has advised them to obtain independent legal advice.

Signed *Bill Smith*   Signed *Syd Brown*

                                                                                            [date   ]

---

14   This agreement is a sample only and will need to be adapted to suit the requirements of each case. The names and other details are fictitious and merely illustrative.

F.   Sample Tomlin Order[15]

CONSENT/TOMLIN ORDER

[ACTION HEADING]

[PARTIES]

CONSENT ORDER

UPON THE APPLICATION of the parties

AND UPON the parties having agreed to the terms set forth in the Schedule hereto

BY CONSENT

IT IS ORDERED:

(1) That all further proceedings in this action be stayed upon the terms set out in the [Schedule][Settlement Agreement between the parties dated....], except for the purpose of carrying such terms into effect.

(2) That each party shall have permission to apply to the Court as to carrying such terms into effect.

(3) That [there shall be no order as to costs] [each party shall bear its own costs].

Dated this [ ] day of [ ] 2[ ]

Signed:

[Name]   [Name]
Solicitors   Solicitors

For and on behalf of the Claimant   **For and on behalf of the Defendant**

---

15   This is a sample only. Legal advice is required in every case. For sample consent orders in family cases, refer to Resolution, *Precedents for Consent Orders* (Resolution's contact details are in Appendix 12).

Appendix 5

Mediator Practice Tools

A. Conflict analysis sheet

Who are the parties to the conflict	
History to the conflict	- Chronology?
Attitudes of parties towards settlement	
Positions of each party	
Interests of each party	- Aims? - Priorities? - Third parties?
Causes of conflict	- Data issues? - Relationship blocks? - Power imbalances? - Value differences? - Differences on merits/rights?

Risks for each party	
	- Weaknesses?
	- Costs?
	- Non-money factors (time, reputation and lost opportunities)?
Alternatives	
	- BATNA?
	- WATNA?
	- RATNA?
Options	
	- Goals/objectives?
	- Deal breakers? Or Minimum terms?
	- Applicable customs?
	- Objective criteria?
Mediator interventions	
	- People – who needs to attend?
	- Info – what info is required?
	- Process – what is required to make the most effective use of the mediation attempt?
	- Preparation – what is required to prepare the parties most effectively?

B.   Checklist for mediator's opening statement[1]

Preliminaries

The preliminaries consist of the 'housekeeping' matters. While they may seem perfunctory, they are not trivial and you should not underestimate their importance.

---

1   Adapted from Chapter 4 in L. Boulle, M. Colatrella & A. Picchioni, *Mediation – Skills and Techniques*, Lexis Nexis Matthew Bender, 2008.

- Mediators should begin with a welcome and introductions. Do not assume that everyone knows each other, especially in commercial disputes where companies may send representatives who were not involved in the disputed transaction, or where lawyers may have never met. Whether first names or last names are used is a matter of a mediator's personal style, the relationship of the parties and the particular culture in which you are mediating. This said, many mediators prefer to use first names to emphasise the informality of the mediation process.

- Next, the mediator should introduce himself or herself. Some mediators also like to provide a 'credibility statement,' which is a short explanation of the mediator's experience or training. This helps to generate confidence in the mediator's ability to successfully assist the parties. Whether and to what extent you provide a credibility statement will depend on how well the participants know you and how much interaction you have had with them in pre-mediation activities. Where some or all of the parties do not know you well, it is almost always good to provide a brief comment about your relevant experience or training. This is just one small way of building the trust and confidence that is so crucial for you to be effective in the mediation.

- Other important preliminary matters to address are duration of the mediation, attendance by all necessary parties, and authority to settle.

Explaining the Nature of Mediation

For mediation to be effective the participants must understand the nature of the process and the roles and responsibilities of everyone involved.

- First, the mediator should explain that mediation is a 'voluntary' procedure, to the extent that the parties decide whether they wish to resolve the matter or not. Even when a court compels parties to participate in mediation, the parties' decision to reach a mutually acceptable agreement is entirely their choice. The mediator has no authority to impose a solution on the parties in the way a judge or arbitrator would.

- Second, the mediator should explain that he or she is impartial and neutral concerning the parties and the dispute.

- Finally, the mediator may want to address his or her particular mediation style and philosophy, to the extent that it is strategically appropriate to share this information with the parties.

Explaining the Mediation Process

The mediator's opening statement should also explain to the parties the particular process that will be followed. Providing this information helps to reduce any anxieties participants may feel about how the mediation will be conducted.

- Most mediators describe the mediation process at a fairly high level of generality during the opening statement. Participants, especially if mediation is new to them, can be easily overwhelmed with too much information.

- Mediators should also indicate if and how they will use separate meetings during the mediation. Explaining your policy regarding separate meetings in the opening statement establishes an expectation that such meetings are a normal part of the process. If the use of separate meetings is not explained at the beginning of the mediation, when one is called for the first time, parties might make some mistaken, unhelpful assumptions about why the meeting is being held.

Explaining the Guidelines

Although mediation is an informal process, there are a few practical guidelines or table manners that participants should be asked to follow to foster a productive environment. The following are some of the guidelines that most mediators include as part of the opening statement.

- **One Person Speaks at a Time**

  Parties cannot communicate effectively if they are speaking over each other, which is a common and predictable occurrence during mediation.

- **No Personal Attacks**

  Personal attacks, such as name-calling, sarcasm and belittling undermine the mediation process.

- **Anyone Can Take a Break at Anytime for Any Reason**

- **No Binding Agreement Until Reduced to Writing and Signed by the Parties**

  This rule also helps to prevent misunderstandings among the participants over the terms of the agreement. Oral agreements are often inexact and ambiguous. The rule also promotes open discussion as the parties are not committing until agreements are reduced to writing and signed.

- **Confidentiality Obligations**

  Parties will be more willing to share information, interests, and concerns and evaluate the relative merits of their positions more objectively, if such information subsequently could not be used against them if the matter is not resolved in mediation. There are of course exceptions to confidentiality. Mediators typically explain confidentiality to the parties in more general terms during the mediation. Rarely will a mediator venture into any detail about the exceptions to the general confidentiality rules in the opening statement unless he or she believes that they may have some particular relevance to the dispute.

- **Commitment to Comply**

  To increase the likelihood of compliance with mediation guidelines, the mediator should obtain an explicit commitment from the parties to follow them.

Commitment to Begin the Mediation

Gaining a commitment from the parties to begin the mediation assists the parties in making the necessary transition from listener to active participants in the mediation process. It also provides general motivation to parties to live up to their promise of actively participating in the mediation.

C.   Negotiation preparation checklist

Parties	Interests	Alternatives	Objective Criteria	Options/ Solutions

D.   Table of reframing examples

Party's negative term	Mediator's replacement term
He's telling lies.	So you see the facts differently?
It's all her fault.	So you had different expectations?
I have my rights.	So you wish to exercise your options?
I want residence of the children.	So we need to discuss parenting arrangements?
I have a serious grievance against them.	So this is a situation you're not comfortable with?
He abused me verbally.	So you felt his language was inappropriate?
His repair work was shoddy.	So he did not work according to specifications?
I can't stand it when...	You feel uncomfortable with...
She totally ignored me.	There was inadequate consultation?
We had no room to move.	So you felt that you had limited options?
I think he was stealing.	So some funds could not be accounted for?
I'll destroy you in court.	So litigation is a possible option?

Guidelines for Lawyers Representing Clients in Mediation

A. Decision tree for finding the right mediator

IMI (International Mediation Institute) Guide[1]

---

1   Reproduced with the kind permission of the International Mediation Institute (IMI). For further information and to download IMI documents free of charge please visit www.IMImediation.org.

Finding the Right Mediator | Before you start |

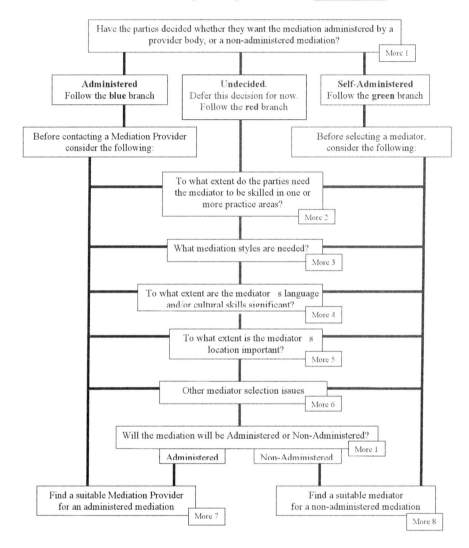

Have the parties decided whether they want the mediation administered by a provider body, or a non-administered mediation?

More 1

| **Administered** Follow the **blue** branch | **Undecided.** Defer this decision for now. Follow the **red** branch | **Self-Administered** Follow the **green** branch |

Before contacting a Mediation Provider consider the following:

Before selecting a mediator, consider the following:

To what extent do the parties need the mediator to be skilled in one or more practice areas?

More 2

What mediation styles are needed?

More 3

To what extent are the mediator's language and/or cultural skills significant?

More 4

To what extent is the mediator's location important?

More 5

Other mediator selection issues

More 6

Will the mediation will be Administered or Non-Administered?

More 1

| Administered | Non-Administered |

Find a suitable Mediation Provider for an administered mediation

More 7

Find a suitable mediator for a non-administered mediation

More 8

Before you start

About this Decision Tree

Congratulations! You are considering mediation. Statistics throughout the world convincingly establish that mediation has at least an 80% chance of successfully leading the parties to an agreement, including situations where the parties are deadlocked. Few other processes have a success rate that high.

To maximize the chances of a successful outcome   just like anything else   preparation is essential, and that is the purpose of this Decision Tree. It has been designed to provide objective and impartial guidance to users of mediation services on what to bear in mind when appointing a mediator. It has been prepared with the benefit of comments and suggestions from members of the IMI **Independent Standards Commission** and others.

Because mediation is a consensual, selecting the right mediator and the right process is often the first thing parties find themselves agreeing on, often after a long history of disagreement. To the maximum extent possible, engage the other party or parties in this process. If all parties apply similar considerations when selecting a mediator a joint choice will be easier to make.

Because mediation is not just consensual but also flexible, the process can be moulded to the parties needs. Choices that the parties need to make include all the branches on the Decision Tree.

One point of clarification before you start. The Tree refers to   Mediation Providers   . These are organizations and institutions that provide a mediation service to users. That service can vary widely in scope and contact but generally includes helping with the selection of a mediator and often case management support. IMI is not a provider   IMI does not have a panel of mediators, nor does it offer case management support. What it does do is run an open portal that enables users to find competent mediators, review their Profiles with feedback from prior Users in the form of a Feedback Digest, and provide impartial information about mediation. But IMI does not compete in the market for mediation services, and is not a   Provider   .

Like any tree, this is a living thing. Feedback, ideas and proposals for improving the Decision Tree are welcomed from users, professional advisers, mediators, providers, educators and others. Just click **contact us**

More 1

Have the parties decided whether they want the mediation administered by a provider, or a self-administered mediation?

This is a useful first question, but it does not necessarily have to be decided immediately. In both administered and non-administered mediations, part of the service you should expect is that the process will be flexible and adapted to the parties   specific needs. The provider institution or the mediator should be able to assist you in this.

If the dispute relates to a contract, there may be a mediation clause in it that specifies how a mediator will be chosen and specify a particular Mediation Provider that may offer a list of suitable mediators, recommend a mediator, or help to make the choice for the parties. The mediation clause may also provide that the mediation will be administered by, and under a mediation agreement and code of conduct of a Mediation Provider. However, mediation is a flexible and consensual process - if the parties think these contractual rules are inappropriate, they are usually at liberty to agree to approach mediation differently.

Alternatively, a referral body, like a Court or other authority, may direct or suggest how a mediator can or will be chosen. This may be important if the parties need a settlement to be formally recognized by the Court.

Or there may be no contract with a mediation clause, and no referral body. The choice of mediator, and whether to use a Mediation Provider, may be entirely up to the parties. Some parties and professional advisers have developed internal mechanisms for mediator selection based in past experience and other criteria. Or there may be no guidance at all.

Administered and Non-Administered mediations

In administered mediations:

* A professional Mediation Provider manages all or part of the administration and case management aspects so that these can be separated from the dispute.
* Often the provider body operates under a set of rules or offers a mediation agreement that governs how the mediation is set up and conducted, confidentiality issues, impartiality of the mediator, the application of time/cost constraints, etc.
* The provider can select or recommend a suitable mediator to the parties, which can avoid the risk of the parties not agreeing in the choice of a mediator.
* A Provider usually charges an administration fee and may set the mediator   s fee and specify how these costs will be paid (eg shared equally by the parties).
* Parties can usually discuss case management issues/choice of mediator with the Mediation Provider either together or independently. While providers (but this also applies to mediators in self-administered mediations) can not force parties to agree to anything, their neutrality can help ease communication between the parties and ensure all participants understand the process constructively.

Administered mediations can be particularly valuable where there are strong communication barriers between the parties, or where one or more of the parties is reluctant to mediate or to co-operate in a mediation, though these issues can also be overcome by mediators in non-administered processes.

<u>In non-administered mediations:</u>

*	No provider or third party case management is involved, or if involved, merely helps the parties choose a suitable mediator but does not provide other case management services.
*	The parties select the mediator themselves and agree with the mediator what rules, agreement to mediate and process will apply. Many mediators have model mediation agreements and rules that can apply or be adapted to the parties needs.
*	The mediator performs case management tasks or shares them with the parties.
*	Administration costs, if any, are usually part of the mediator s fee.
*	The parties have more control, and also more issues that need to be addressed.

One factor that may affect this issue is whether any deadlines apply. Must the parties try to arrive at a settlement within a given time frame, or are there any financial constraints on how or when the mediation should take place? In some situations, there may be a requirement that a mediation must occur in a certain manner, or using only mediators from a named panel or Provider, otherwise the settlement may not be legally enforceable. Identifying whether deadlines, budgetary constraints, and any legal requirements apply can impact on the selection and engagement of a mediator and whether an administered or non-administered process can or should be chosen.

More 2

To what extent do the parties need the mediator to be skilled in one or more practice areas?

It is said that *No dispute is ever about what it s about* Very often, the drivers of a dispute are several issues or motives, and sometimes the formalities of the dispute are merely superficial, while the real dispute (and therefore the key to a true resolution) may be centred in something not captured in the legal framing or technical complexities.

Mediators are not empowered to judge the merits of a dispute   they are not judges or arbitrators. Their role is to help the parties come to an agreement, usually by getting to the roots of their problems. So two of the key questions in selecting a mediator are:

Will we benefit from having a mediator who is familiar with the substantive issues that are most likely to arise in the settlement negotiation?

Or will others at the table supply such specific expertise as is needed?

If you need a more evaluative mediator (see 3) the importance of familiarity with the specific legal and/or substantive issues governing the dispute may be more important than if the outcome is likely to require the generation of new options or improving relationships for the future.

Remember, when you engage a mediator you are buying that person s skill to mediate. Not every mediator necessarily has substantive experience in all the practice areas your dispute presents. So, you may need to weigh (a) the mediator s process skills, against (b) the legal and substantive experience of the mediator in the issues in dispute.

Where both process and substantive expertise are needed, one option may be to consider co-mediation. For example, where a dispute arises over the future of a construction joint venture, and the need arises to change key elements of the venture, you may consider that you need a construction mediator and also an accountant. Or, if the matter involves intellectual property, patent litigation, or technical or arcane subject matter, you may want an intellectual property/patent/software specialist **as well as** a skilled mediator. Selecting co-mediators that work well together may have an additional cost impact but may greatly streamline the negotiation and help the parties reach a more rounded outcome more quickly. Another option may be to engage a neutral expert with competency in specific technical areas even if that person is not a mediator.

More 3

What mediation style do you need?
Facilitative, Evaluative, Transformative

Often too little thought is given to the mediation styles that mediators practice. It is important for users of mediation services to select a mediator with a style or number of styles that meet the needs of their specific case — right both for all the parties involved and for the situation that needs to be resolved. But, as in the choice of any professional service, you first need to identify your likely needs and then ensure your choice of a professional meets those needs.

Essentially, there are three main — and rather different — mediation styles: Facilitative, Evaluative and Transformative. For a concise review of what practice styles and skills are involved in each style, see: [http://imimediation.org/?cID=188&cType=document]

Although a facilitative style is commonly regarded as the most mainstream form of mediation, it is not unusual in a mediated dispute that evaluative and/or transformative competencies are applied by the mediator at different moments and in differing measures. Many mediators shift easily from one style to another according to the needs of the situation. But some facilitative mediators prefer not to be evaluative unless they are specifically asked by the parties.

If the most important tasks are to overcome communication blockages, identify hidden obstacles, and develop options for mutual gain to help the parties think creatively and enable an agreement to be reached, the parties probably need a facilitative mediator.

If the parties perceive that there will be a need for the mediator to break deadlocks by giving non-binding opinions, asking hard questions, making comments about the facts and the law of the case, guiding the parties in other more directive ways, or helping set guidelines for a settlement based on objective norms (such as Industry standards, law, etc), they will need a mediator who is able to be evaluative.

If the goal is not to resolve a specific dispute but rather improve the parties relationship, and if that relationship is important for the future, then a transformative mediator will focus more on helping the parties communicate and work together than on resolving short term conflicts. Among other applications for transformative mediation in business contexts are relations among: competitors or members of an Industry, joint venture partners and the regulated and regulators/government agencies.

It helps if the parties discuss these issues before narrowing the search for a mediator or a Mediation Provider and then discuss the styles needed with short-listed mediators. Agreements to mediate can also reflect style issues — for example the inclusion of a paragraph confirming the parties expectation that the mediator will be asked to give a non-binding view or evaluation if a deadlock is reached.

More 4

To what extent are the mediator s language or cultural skills significant?

There may be more to this question than is initially apparent.

Clearly, a mediator needs to communicate effectively with all parties and their representatives. Where the parties do not share the same mother tongue, it may be useful consider a mediator who can mediate successfully in the parties natural languages.

It is most important to ensure, however, that the parties can effectively communicate with one-another and with the mediator, and that understanding is facilitated. Using co-mediators, each with different language and cultural skills, may be one way forward. Another approach is use of interpreters; if they are independent of the parties they can be considered aides to the mediator, and therefore have an important neutral role.

In addition to language capability, consider the mediator s cultural acceptability to all the parties, including the mediator s ability to engage effectively with the parties. Where there are language issues, there are also likely to be cultural issues, but there can be strong cultural differences among parties having the same mother tongue.

Where there is a diversity of cultural backgrounds among the parties, a mediator or Mediation Provider that shares only one party s cultural values and credentials may not be trusted or accepted by the other party. Consider expressing a willingness to select a mediator or Provider perceived as sharing the other party s cultural background, or a mediator very familiar with both cultures, or propose using one from a third culture who is skilled in negotiating cross-culturally, or an international institution or provider. Again, co-mediators can be a solution. In situations where the other party shows reluctance to engage in mediation, these approaches can be a way to help them feel more comfortable with the process.

Above all, ensure that the mediator is sensitive to cultural diversity and has the capacity to understand the differences involved and implied by cultural dynamics.

Mediation relies for its effectiveness on all parties trusting the mediator. It is part of the mediator s job to earn that trust.

More 5

To what extent is the mediator s location important?

The mediator s location may be important, but often not as critical as many assume.

Travel costs may be involved, but these are often small in relation to the amount in dispute and the sums that will be spent if there is no settlement. The other party may be suspicious if you select a mediator in your locality (unless the other party is also in the same locality).

It is generally wise to consider the location of the mediator as a practical issue when reviewing a shortlist of mediators, some of whom are local and some not, rather than as a prevailing consideration at the outset. If the parties want a mediator to join them in their locale, or in some other place, keep in mind that some mediators charge travel expenses and travel time. This may, or may not, be a factor in choosing a mediator.

A neutral venue can be an important consideration, reflecting the neutrality of the process. Selecting an outside mediator and/or a neutral venue can be particularly helpful where parties are from different locations or where there is a high level of hostility, or where an obvious power imbalance exists.

In online mediations, location of the mediator is far less relevant, but other considerations may then apply   such as availability (eg in light of time zones) and their skills in mediating online.

More 6

Other key mediator selection issues

Mediator Profiles

Study mediator Profiles and compare them. Focus on impartial feedback from prior users and peers. Follow up on links they offer. Use search engines for more information.

Costs

Costs of mediating are invariably a fraction of litigating. Nevertheless, the costs need to be understood and accepted. Mediation Providers often quote costs on a scale of charges which may include the costs charged by their mediators. In larger cases, the costs may be negotiable. Some mediators charge hourly rates, some charge day rates, and some charge for preparation and traveling time while others do not. In international disputes, travel costs can be significant, but can also be estimated in advance.

The total costs of a mediation are usually split equally between the parties. Some parties (such as repeat users of mediation like insurers) may agree to pay more than an equal split. Any legal fees are usually carried by each party. These arrangements can be confirmed before the mediation (eg in an agreement to mediate), or varied afterwards, in a settlement agreement.

Code of Conduct

Trust underpins the mediation process. If the parties do not trust a mediator s integrity in terms of competence, diligence, neutrality, independence, impartiality, fairness and the ability to respect confidences, mediation is unlikely to succeed. When choosing mediators, confirm from the providing organizations (or if you are choosing the mediator directly, confirm with the mediators) whether they adhere to a Code of Professional Conduct and ask to see copies.

References

Follow up any references. Do not probe for answers than may entail party-confidential information but general questions are usually regarded as perfectly proper.

Research

Conduct further research, perhaps jointly with the other party. Not all competent mediators have chosen to be IMI Certified, so consider the complete panels of Mediation Providers and professional organizations. If the mediator or provider cannot give you access to prior user feedback in an anonymous form, you need to find other ways to know more about the mediator s actual performance in prior cases and other indicators of the mediator s competency and suitability.

More 7

Find an appropriate Mediation Provider

First, identify exactly which services the parties need from a Mediation Provider. This will help compare various provider bodies to determine what services each offers and whether they coincide with the parties   needs. Feel free to discuss these needs, and the respective costs involved, with Providers   they will help you make the necessary decisions.

If you have already identified one or more potentially suitable mediators, and if they are on a Provider   s panel, consider using that provider to administer your mediation.

IMI is impartial, and does not recommend any providers. Many are not exactly comparable because of variations in the services they provide, their geographic reach and the distinctive needs of different cases. Links to a number of Mediation Providers are given on the IMI web portal as an informational aid to users. Providers and other panels having members who are IMI Certified may be linked on the IMI web portal, as may certain international institutions and professional organizations.

More 8

Find a Suitable Mediator

The IMI search engine is a useful place to start your search for a mediator   whether the parties decide to use a provider body or not. IMI has no financial stake in the decision. Neither the mediator nor any provider body pay a case fee to IMI. Only mediators who have established their competency in the opinion of prior users and peers are able to be IMI Certified   the parties   focus in selecting a mediator is therefore likely to be less related to competency and more directed to the suitability of the mediator for the issues facing the parties.

On the suitability level, you may narrow your search, as appropriate, by practice area, location, language skills and mediation style. Save, print and read the full Profiles of your selection. Modify the selection criteria to capture details on other mediators.

Read the Feedback Digest embedded in each IMI Certified Mediator s Profile. It is an independently-prepared summary of feedback provided by prior users on each mediator s performance. Consider speaking to some of those listed as referees.

Once you have made a shortlist, consider involving the other party in the selection process. Choice of mediator/provider should be a joint choice. Invite them to go through the same process in case they find other suitable mediators that should be considered. Refer them to this Decision Tree and express interest in their choices.

The parties should feel free to contact individual mediators remaining in their selection. That direct contact should help you come to a final selection.

Where more than two parties are involved in the dispute, consider asking the shortlist of mediators whether they have experience of mediating with multiple parties, and whether a provider body was involved in those cases. The administrative and case management issues can be more challenging in multi-party mediations.

Although mediators work hard, control over the negotiation remains firmly with the parties and the outcome is theirs, not the mediator s. In any mediation, choosing the most suitable mediator is vital.

B. Lawyers' functions and notes for lawyers/advisers

(i) General overview

Before the mediation meeting

- To educate their clients about the nature of mediation and its procedures.

- To prepare their clients for participating in the mediation process.

- To prepare necessary documents, reports and other materials necessary for successful mediation.

- To give clients realistic and clear estimates about the expenses and likely cost recoveries of other dispute resolution processes, including litigation, and to refer to both best- and worst-case outcomes.

- To advise their clients on relevant legal issues, including the Agreement to Mediate (Appendix 3).

During the mediation meeting

- To allow the mediator to conduct the process and to provide support to the mediator where appropriate.

- To permit and encourage their clients to participate fully and directly in the process.

- To assist clients to focus on their real personal and commercial interests as opposed to their legal rights.

- To assist clients to communicate accurately and comprehensively and to negotiate constructively and productively.

- To provide to their clients, legal information and advice, where appropriate, on their rights and duties.

- To give ongoing realistic predictions about likely outcomes in court or other non-mediation processes and their relative advantages or disadvantages.

- To assisting in the drafting of agreements and the formalisation of the mediation in appropriate ways.

After the mediation meeting

- To undertake any activities required for the formalisation or ratification of the mediated agreement and to liaise with other lawyers where necessary.

- To reassure clients who have second thoughts and to inform them about the options of dealing with problems in the implementation of the agreement, including through return to mediation.

- To maintain the confidentiality of the mediation meeting.

For exercise in forums other than mediation

- Acting as the adversarial advocate of their clients' legal rights.

- Cross-examining the other client or clients.

- Raising technical procedural points or insisting on formality.

- Engaging in other adversarial or combative strategies.

(ii) CORE Solutions Group

Mediation Notes for Lawyers and other Advisers[2]

These notes are offered to assist you to advise and represent your client effectively in mediation. They are not designed to help you achieve any particular outcome nor to suggest that the mediator will be affected by any particular approach.

- Prepare well in advance. Representing a client in mediation is a challenging role. At different times, you may act as advocate, adviser and counsel to your client. Think about how you might prepare yourself and your client for these roles. How will you help your client to negotiate effectively and to listen to and respond to the other side?

- Ask yourself and your client what you actually wish to achieve – and why. What are your objectives? What are the options for resolution? It is sometimes helpful to prepare a list of possible outcomes and to identify priorities, with an explanation of what each would mean to your client in terms of time, money and future relationships. What proposals might you make, remembering that, in negotiations, non-monetary matters are often as important as those with monetary value?

- Gather all the relevant documentation and sift out the crucial facts. What will matter in the discussions which are designed to achieve a resolution? What are the real issues in the case? What are your client's true interests? What concerns does the client have? What factors are relevant other those in the documents or court papers? It is usually necessary to ensure that you have a clear understanding of your client's financial situation.

- Ensure that all relevant material, figures and supporting documentation is easily accessible on the mediation day. Consider what documents you may wish to agree with the other party or parties to mediation as being useful to the process.

- Consider strengths and weaknesses on both sides. What are the risks and benefits of different routes? For example, if the case does not resolve in the mediation, what will happen? It is often helpful to consider your Best Alternative to a Negotiated Agreement (BATNA) and the Worst Alternative to a Negotiated Agreement (WATNA). These set benchmarks against which to assess any proposals.

- Consider the other side's situation and what a satisfactory outcome might look like to the other side. Try to obtain an understanding of their likely position and

---

2   This document is reproduced with permission from the Guide to Mediation Services published by Core Solutions Group. Core Solutions Group is Scotland's pre-eminent provider of mediation services to business, organisations and the professions in Scotland. www.core-solutions.com.

concerns. Consider what concessions you might make and list each in order, with consideration of what each concession might mean in terms of time, money and future relationships.

■ Mediation offers a unique opportunity to explain your client's approach to the other side. Consider what the other side may need to know or may not fully understand. Consider how best to present your client's situation. What will make most impact on the other party, in a constructive way? What might help to break deadlock? What proposals might you make? Similarly, mediation is an opportunity for your client to ask questions and to gain a better understanding of the issues in dispute – and to hear from the other side. What more do you need to know? What questions do you wish to ask?

■ In the opening phase of the mediation day, there may be an opportunity to present a statement of your client's position in an opening joint meeting. Who will do this? You or the client? Or both? What do you wish to include in any statement and how will you and the client present your position? What language will you use? What effect do you wish to have on others in the room? How will you help to achieve an environment in which a solution can be found?

■ Before and subsequently, you and the client will probably have meetings in private with the mediator. What can you usefully discuss and reveal in these, confidential, meetings? What will help the mediator the parties to resolve the matter?

■ Ensure that your client has authority to reach a conclusion. If your client does not have direct authority to resolve the matter, then ensure that there will be ready access to a person with authority to do so.

Appendix

The mediator may often ask parties to prepare in advance or at the beginning of the mediation day by addressing some specific questions. These may include the following:

■ What are your overall objectives?

■ What in particular are you seeking to achieve?

■ What is in dispute? What do parties have in common?

■ What are your strengths? What are your weaknesses?

■ What are your needs? What are your concerns?

■ What might the other party's needs be? Their concerns?

■ What do you think the other side need to hear from you? What might you say to the other side?

■ If you do not reach agreement, what are the alternatives?

■ What costs have you incurred to date? If you do not reach agreement, what costs will you incur in future?

■ If you do not reach agreement, what other consequences will there be? For you? For the other party?

■ What are the options for resolving this matter?

- How will you assess any proposals put by the other party?
- What proposals might you make?

(iii) ADR Group notes on 'preparing your case for mediation'[3]

The mediation involves facilitated discussion of the issues in a case not a presentation of evidence as occurs in a trial or arbitration. Preparation is therefore much easier as it is not necessary to organise witnesses, evidence or produce trial bundles and there are no formal preliminaries.

This document is intended for both lawyers and clients and is broken into three sections to help better prepare for a mediation session. This is not intended to be definitive guide and some of the information will not be relevant in all circumstances, however, if you have considered all points then you should be in a prime position to get the most out of the mediation session.

1. General Preparation for Presenting your Case at Mediation

This document outlines the questions you need to consider before the mediation and strategies you can adopt on the day to assist in reaching a positive conclusion. This document will also help you prepare a Comprehensive Position Statement and useful Confidential Checklist that you retain and refer to during the mediation.

2. Position Statement

The only pre-written work that should be carried out is the preparation of a Position Statement. It is usually prepared for the mediator's eyes only although in some cases parties do agree to the mutual exchange of this document. The Position Statement is simply an overview of the facts, issues and interests of the case (and each party) to enable the mediator to understand the dispute ahead of the mediation. It is certainly not intended to be an all encompassing document and should be kept as short as possible (we would recommend no more than 4 pages).

3. Confidential Checklist

In order for mediation to be successful you need to have discussed and considered with your client everything about the strengths and weaknesses of the case as well as the pros and cons of settling early. This can either be kept private or disclosed to the mediator if you think it would help the process. Effective management of parties' expectations can greatly assist the chance of settlement.

Key examples of information that should be considered are:

- Cost implications
- Litigation risks
- Time restraints
- Settlement expectations

---

3   Reproduced with the kind permission of the ADR Group. For further information please visit their website at www.adrgroup.com.

1. General preparation for presenting your case at mediation

The following points are designed to help you prepare your case and present it on the day.

Know your case

The more familiar you are with the issues of the case and the interests of those involved, the better you will be able to effectively present it. Prior to the sessions you should have considered the following:

- Do you have all the information necessary to evaluate the case – for example do you have all the necessary expert evidence to support your claim?

- Know the facts and witnesses involved in the case. Whilst they will probably not be required at the mediation it is likely that you will be discussing them.

- Identify and analyse the key issues.

- List the strengths and weaknesses of your case. If possible do the same for your opponent. This can be a useful tool to help the mediator develop tough questions for them.

- Consider and confirm who will be attending. Make sure all those with authority to settle will be there. Confirm the same from the other side.

Develop a settlement strategy

If you have not developed a settlement strategy then resolving the dispute on the day will be more difficult. There are a number of key considerations that you should review to establish what your settlement parameters are and whether they are reasonable.

- Determine your position on liability and damages. What issues or information may cause you to change your mind?

- Develop a negotiation plan including where you want to settle and how you plan to get there.

- Consider the language and terminology you use on the day. For instance, avoid basing your offer on the age of the case ('I never offer that much this early…'). Phrases such as this in an opening session can have a hugely detrimental effect on the whole session.

- Plan to offer or demand what you will eventually be prepared to settle for.

Authority – who should attend the mediation session?

The aim of mediation is to reach and conclude settlement on the day. If the people with the authority to close the deal are not in attendance then this may well jeopardise the settlement. It is thus important that all parties come to mediation with sufficient authority to settle, and not just their legal advisors.

Roles and level of participation

It is important to decide in advance of the session who is going to lead discussions. Often when clients are represented by legal advisors it is the lawyer who takes the lead. However depending on the nature of the case and the personalities of the individuals it may be more prudent and have greater impact if the client were to lead or support the conversations. The most important context for this is the opening statement.

Opening statement

The mediator will commence the session by going over the ground rules for the mediation, explaining the process and timing. Your will then be given an opportunity to make a short opening statement (usually 10-15 minutes) explaining your position. As this is your opportunity to talk directly to the other side, you need to be prepared and organised. Once you have agreed who should deliver your statement, you may want to consider the following:

■ Introduction of yourself and/or your client/legal representative, and confirmation that it is your or your client's wish to work towards settlement

■ An overview of the facts as you see it. If the other side went first then indicate any agreement or disagreement with their statement

■ Your analysis of the issues (e.g. on liability and damages)

During your presentation be realistic. While you obviously want to present your case in the most favourable way by emphasising your strengths, do not ignore your weaknesses. If for instance you have already factored any of these weaknesses into a previous offer, it will add credence to the rest of your case and your rationale for being at the mediation to mention this. It is also useful in the opening phase to avoid specific settlement figures and emotive language. Saying something like, 'I will settle for £50,000 and not a penny less' is likely to cause the other side to become very reactive to the process and they are then likely to spend the rest of the session thinking up why you are not going to get that sum, rather than actively listening to the facts as you see them.

Other points for consideration

■ Review the mediation procedures so you know what to expect

■ Schedule sufficient time for the mediation

■ Take your files and sufficient copies of any documents you plan to refer to

■ Charts, summaries and chronologies can help to make points, however, be mindful about when you give them out as you will want people to listen to you rather than read through them.

■ Complete the confidential checklist before you go

2. Preparing the position statement

Before a mediation, the mediator will want to know some details about the case. They will not want or need to know about every single aspect, however gaining an insight into the facts, the issues and the interests of those involved will be key in helping to make the mediation progress effectively.

This document is a guide / checklist to help you to prepare your Position Statement. If you are unclear as to whether something is relevant and should be included, please discuss the matter with the mediator or with one of ADR Group's mediation advisers.

General

- The parties' name
- Solicitor's details
- Names and titles / positions of the attendees
- Date and location of the mediation

Case Summary

- Describe concisely the background to the case ensuring that the issues of liability and quantum are clearly set out. A list of the issues and/or a chronology of the key events is often helpful to the mediator
- What are the key issues?
- What are the unique features that the mediator ought to be aware of?
- Have any negotiations taken place?
- Have there been any without prejudice offers?
- Have there been any admissions or changes since the close of pleadings?
- What do you / does your client hope to achieve by the end of the mediation?

Your Opponent's Position

- Please provide a short synopsis of what you believe your opponent's position to be
- What do you think they hope to achieve at the end of the mediation?

Documents

- There are no formal rules of disclosure and the mediator only requires, prior to the mediation, sight of those documents that will enable him/her to formulate an understanding of the case and the respective issues involved
- If there is a fundamental aspect to the claim which can only be explained by way of a document then please enclose this with the Position Statement
- If a document is to be relied upon at the mediation, please make sure that it is available on the day
- Where legal proceedings have commenced please annex copies of the key pleadings, particularly the claim, defence and counter-claim

Parties and Attendees

- Name all the people who will be attending the mediation and explain in what capacity
- Ensure that the nominated person with full authority to settle attends the mediation

■ Whilst it is not always relevant for all witness to attend (remember the mediator does not assess witnesses of fact) it may be helpful to provide a summary of any witness evidence if it is intended that this is material information that will be considered during the mediation

Costs

■ Litigation and cost risk implications need to be fully considered and discussed with your client in advance of the mediation.

■ What are your client's costs to date? If possible ensure that a full costs schedule is prepared in advance of the mediation which can be referred to on the day of the mediation.

■ What are your client's estimated costs to trial? Is your client covered by any legal expense insurance or are they paying privately?

■ Do you know what the other sides legal expense position is? Can you estimate their costs to date or what their costs to trial may be?

Mediation

■ What does your client seek from the mediation?

■ What are their expectations for the day?

Any Other Business

■ Are there any other aspects, 'red-herrings' or issues you consider the mediator should be aware of?

3. Confidential checklists

In order for mediation to be successful you need to have discussed and considered with your client everything about the strengths and weaknesses of the case as well as the pos and cons of settling early. This can either be kept private or disclosed to the mediator if you think it would help the process. Key examples of information that should be considered are: cost implications, litigation risks, time restraints and mediation expectations.

Confidential Checklist – Your case

List your evidence – Witnesses, documents, reports, statements etc.
1.
2.
3.

List damages:
1.
2.
3.

List your legal arguments concerning liability and damages:

Liability:
1.
2.
3.

Damages:
1.
2.
3.

List your strengths and weaknesses and any mitigating circumstances:

Strengths:
1.
2.
3.

Weaknesses:
1.
2.

Calculate your settlement range:

1. Would like to get

2. Would accept

3. Bottom line

4. Walkaway point

How did you value the case? What elements are included e.g. special damages etc.

What is your best alternative to no agreement? (BATNA)

What is the worst outcome to no agreement? (WATNA)

How much will it cost to go to trial? £

How long will it take?

What are your chances of winning in court? %

What do the other side consider as their chance? %

What questions / line of argument do you want the mediator to put to the other side?

Confidential Checklist – The other side's case

List their key issues:
1.
2.
3.

List their evidence:
1.
2.
3.

Guess their probable arguments regarding:

Liability:
1.
2.
3.

Damages:
1.
2.
3.

List their strengths and weaknesses:

Strengths:
1.
2.
3.

Weaknesses:
1.
2.
3.

Consider / guess the basis of their demands/offer:

How else may they have valued their demand / offer?

(iv) Guide on systematic risk analysis for negotiators and litigators[4]

Systematic Risk Analysis for Negotiators and Litigators: How to Help Clients Make Better Decisions.[5]

Professor John Wade[6]

Outline

This article will set out:

- What is a written risk analysis

- Reasons why such a document is essential for any negotiator, or for any disputant who is considering ending negotiations, or undertaking 'litigotiation'

- Reasons why such documents currently appear to be uncommon in many legal cultures

- Examples of the use of risk analysis prior to negotiation and mediation

- Precedent forms to assist a client or lawyer to prepare a risk analysis

What is a risk analysis?

A risk analysis is a list of known or guessed (benefits and) detriments which could flow from a particular decision. In business language, it is a 'cost-benefit analysis', with particular precision about the 'costs'. In other terminology, it is a listing of the 'pros' and 'cons' of a particular course of action.

One ideal form of a risk analysis includes:

- Writing

- In familiar language, diagrams and figures

- A short summary in one page if possible

- Evolving in several successive versions as more information becomes available to clarify the risks

---

4   Reproduced with the kind permission of Professor John Wade, Bond University Law School, Australia (john_wade@bond.edu.au).

5   The topics in this paper are not new. They are dealt with extensively in literature on decision-making and 'counselling'. However, professional practice anecdotally does not live up to the wisdom in this literature. The anonymous case studies used in this article have occurred in a variety of jurisdictions, and details have been altered to prevent identification of the parties involved. An earlier version of this paper appears in (2002) 13 *Bond Law Review*, 462-485.

6   Director of Dispute Resolution Centre, School of Law, Bond University, Gold Coast Queensland, Australia 4213; email john_wade@bond.edu.au; website http://www.bond.edu.au/law/centres/index. Consultant, Hopgood Ganim, Lawyers, Brisbane.

- Outcomes expressed in 'good day – bad day' ranges where precision is not possible

- Inclusion of personal, legal, social and business risks

Litigation lawyers and their clients are constantly making conscious or subconscious risk-analyses when making decisions whether to begin negotiation, what settlement offers to make, when to suspend negotiations, when to file a formal claim with what strategies to pursue a claim.[7]

CASE STUDY – When to switch from Negotiation to Litigious Levers?

A married couple were negotiating about the division of an Australian business and cash held in the USA valued at $6 million. The husband had contingent debts which, if they ever become payable by him, would eat up all of those assets held in his name. At mediation, the parties negotiated along two different tracks: first in classical positional bargaining, to pay the wife out in cash and houses; or alternatively, to rewrite the disorganised accounts of the family businesses over time, pay out any realised debts, and divide the residue 60/40 to the wife. They agreed twice on the latter course in complex written agreements, which the husband breached immediately. The Husband suffered from attention deficit disorder and had a history of marihuana use.

The repeated breach of the mediated agreements convinced the wife that a complex co-operative solution was not likely to be effective. Accordingly, the wife's lawyer successfully sought interlocutory injunctions to freeze expenditure in the husband's business and seize his passport. These imposed inconveniences led to a phone call from the husband's lawyer, some hasty positional bargaining, and an immediate payout and indemnities to the wife.

Introduction

One of the benefits of being a mediator is that a mediator voyeuristically observes negotiation behaviour – of both disputants and sometimes their legal representatives.[8]

In this role as observer, a mediator sees outstanding, journeyman and incompetent negotiators. A recent survey of forty of the most-employed commercial mediators in Australia recorded the following four most commonly observed unhelpful negotiation or problem solving behaviour by lawyers. That is, lawyers sometimes became part of the problem, rather than part of a solution for clients. The statistical incidence of these behaviours was not measured – only that it was 'often'.

---

7   See D. Binder, P. Bergman, S. Price, *Lawyers as Counsellors* (St Paul: West 1991) esp. chs 1, 19, 21 (identifying consequences of various alternatives before making a decision). On this general topic of risk analysis, see now *Law, Probability and Risk – A Journal of Reasoning Under Uncertainty* (Oxford University Press, 2002).

8   C. Menkel-Meadow, 'Lawyer Negotiations: Theories and Realities – What We Learn from Mediation' (1993) 56 *Modern L. Rev.* 361; J. Lande, 'How Will Lawyering and Mediation Practices Transform Each Other?' (1997) 24 *Florida State U. L. Rev.* 839; J.H. Wade, 'Lawyers and Mediators: What Each Needs to Learn From and About Each Other' (1991) 2 *Aust. Dispute Res. J.* 159.

' A lawyer who has given wildly optimistic advice
Concentration on legal questions and missing commercial interests
Lawyers who themselves have become antagonistic/emotionally involved
"Entrapment" – disputants have invested too much in the conflict '[9]

One of the essential prerequisites to wise decision-making is to know what alternatives are available, and what are the costs and risks attached to each alternative. It is indeed foolish to negotiate without first carefully cataloguing alternatives and risks.[10]

In the jargon of negotiation, every wise negotiator should attempt to set out in writing his/her WATNA, BATNA and PATNA **before** the negotiations begin.[11]

'While success in negotiation is affected by how one plays the game, the most important step for success in negotiation is how one gets ready for the game...

Although time constraints and work pressures may make it difficult to set aside the time to plan adequately, the problem is that for many of us planning is simply boring and tedious, easily put off in favour of getting into the action quickly.'[12]

The writer's experience as a mediator is that:

■ lawyers often describe the trilogy of legal risks (delay, cost, uncertainty of judicial decision) only, and omit personal and business consequences

■ lawyers often use vague language such as 'danger', 'no guarantees'; 'who knows what a judge will do'

■ clients have selective deafness even when risks are described orally

■ lawyers rarely set out risks in precise, one-page written form – but rather use long rambling opinions, or just anecdotal conversations.

This kind of preparation makes it impossible for the client and lawyer to negotiate confidently, or to make a wise life and business decision.

Written Risk Analysis – Why So Important?

Set out below are some of the reasons why it can be argued that a written risk analysis is essential for every client who contemplates or insists upon starting or ending negotiations, or upon a litigation or 'litigiotiation' path. This will be followed by a list of reasons why such clear documentation of risks attached to continuing a conflict is apparently rare for most lawyers.

It is essential to have a written analysis of the risks which may flow from a failure to settle a conflict because:

---

9   J.H. Wade, *Representing Clients at Mediation and Negotiation* (Bond University Dispute Resolution Centre, 2000), p 180.
10   J.S. Hammond, R.L. Keeney and H. Raiffa, *Smart Choices – A Practical Guide to Making Better Decisions* (Boston: Harvard Business School Press, 1999).
11   R. Fisher and W. Ury, *Getting to Yes* (Boston: Mass: Houghton Muffin, 1991).
     WATNA – Worst Alternative to a Negotiated Agreement; BATNA – Best Alternative to a Negotiated Agreement; PATNA – Probable Alternative to a Negotiated Agreement).
12   R.J. Lewicki, D.M. Saunders and J.W. Minton, *Negotiation* (New York: Irwin McGraw Hill, 2000), p 52.

(1) One decision-making adage is 'garbage in, garbage out'. If risks are not progressively defined and listed, clients and lawyers (or other advisers) will make decisions to end or continue negotiation based upon false data and assumptions.

(2) It is definitely not sufficient for clients to 'give instructions' to end negotiations, or to commence on the litigation pathway. Clients must give 'informed consent'. Informed consent requires:

(i)   the capacity to consider, reflect and decide
(ii)   appropriate education and understanding of alternative courses of action
(iii) appropriate education and understanding of specific legal, personal and commercial risks attached to each alternative.

(3) All decision-making processes are fraught with psychological tendencies towards error particularly if the decision is made at a time of conflict.[13]

Our error-prone capacities as humans have been categorised as 'psychological traps' or 'cognitive biases' under such labels as:

- **ANCHORING** TRAP: over-relying on first thoughts

- **SUNK-COST** TRAP (ENTRAPMENT): protecting earlier choices

- Mythical **FIXED-PIE** Beliefs

- **STATUS QUO** TRAP: keeping on keeping on

- **CONFIRMING EVIDENCE** TRAP: seeing what you want to see

- **FRAMING** TRAP: triggering a premature answer with the wrong question

- **EASILY AVAILABLE INFORMATION** TRAP: 'What an impressive chart!'

- **WINNER'S CURSE**: 'Perhaps we could have done better?'

- **OVERCONFIDENCE** TRAP: being too sure of your knowledge and ability

- **BASE-RATE** TRAP (the law of small numbers): neglecting relevant information

- **SELF-SERVING BIAS**: environment versus personality

- **IGNORING OTHERS' INTERESTS AND PERCEPTIONS**: 'Let's get down to business'

- **REACTIVE DEVALUATION**: ridiculing 'opposition's' ideas and behaviour[14]

Litigation lawyers can readily identify the names of their own clients and of other lawyers (and sometimes self?) who fit into each of these psychological traps.

---

13   *Smart Choices* supra note 2; J.Z. Rubin, D.G. Pruitt & S. Kim, *Social Conflict: Escalation Stalemate and Settlement*, 2nd ed. (New York: McGraw Hill, 1994); M.H. Bazerman and M.A. Neale, *Negotiating Rationally* (NY: Free Press, 1992); R. Hastie and R. Dawes, *Rational Choice in an Uncertain World* (NY: Sage, 2001).

14   *Smart Choices* supra 4, Ch.10. See also G Goodpaster 'Rational Decision-Making in Problem-Solving Negotiation: Compromise, Interest, Valuation and Cognitive Error' (1993) 8 *Ohio St. J. on Dispute Res.* 299: R Korobkin and C Guthrie, 'Psychology, Economics and Settlement: A New Look at the Role of the Lawyer' (1997) 76 *Texas Law Rev* 77; S Plous, *The Psychology of Judgment and Decision Making* (New York: McGraw-Hill, 1993); R J Lewicki, B Barry, D M Saunders, J W Minton, *Negotiation* (New York: McGraw-Hill) 2003, Ch. 5.

If there are already so many subconscious factors pushing us as (conflicted) decision-makers towards error, why add the conscious omission of 'considering' predictable risks?

CASE STUDY – The Sunk-Cost and the Overconfidence Trap

For an excellent case study of apparent failure to undertake a risk-analysis, see J. Vidal, *McLibel – Burger Culture on Trial* (New York: New Press, 1997). McDonalds conducted 313 days of libel litigation against two demonstrators who had helped to distribute pamphlets in London which detailed alleged misconduct by the hamburger chain. McDonalds (at least!), over-relied on first thoughts, kept on keeping on, engaged in group think, misunderstood the nature of 'power', was overconfident, and protected early (bad) choices! Their educational mistakes are now eternally recorded in a website (McSpotlight), book, legend, a video and a musical stage play. McDonalds had partial 'success' in the libel judgment at the price of eight years of international ridicule. McDonalds never collected their multi-million dollars of legal costs and lost time and opportunity costs; much less the tiny judgment against the two unemployed demonstrators. Additionally, the trial judge found that a number of statements in the pamphlets were true.

This is yet another sober example of where it is professional negligence for a lawyer to predict to a client that 'you will win this case'. In the writer's experience, using the word 'win' without express, immediate and written qualification amounts to professional negligence. Clients are not experienced enough to understand the limited meaning of that emotive 'win' word, or the nature of pyrrhic victories.

---

(4) Lawyers, like other skilled helpers, are wise to engage in professional self-protection. When a chosen process turns out to be disappointing for a client, then those clients may refuse to pay fees, claim damages for negligent advice, bad-mouth the skilled helper, and/or make reports to professional disciplinary committees. Doctors, computer suppliers, manufacturers and lawyers increasingly document a list of risks attached to any chosen process or service as a means of documentary (rather than verbal) defence against a raging client.

(5) A verbal risk analysis is hardly worth the paper it is not written on. This is because all clients hear only a small proportion of what an adviser says; clients hear selectively; the adviser is at risk in a subsequent memory-battle on what was actually said; and without clear writing, the client will convey inaccurate messages about risks to key constituents, relatives and bosses. These 'outsiders' need accurate information in order to influence the visible disputants towards a wise decision.

(6) There are some studies which suggest that customers are far less satisfied with litigation lawyers than litigation lawyers believe.[15] That is, as litigation lawyers,

---

15   Eg J. Lande, 'Failing Faith in Litigation? A Survey of Business Lawyers' and Executives' Opinions' (1998) 3 *Harvard Neg. L. Rev.* 1; P. McDonald (ed) *Settling Up* (Sydney: Prentice-Hall, 1986) Ch 13; ALRC, *Managing Justice – A Review of the Federal Civil Justice System* Report No 89, 1999, pp 78-88; *Studer v Boettcher* [2000] NSWCA 263 (24 November, 2000) 63 (Fitzgerald JA).

we live in a state of delusion about the level of satisfaction of our customers, particularly once a dispute 'goes to court'

This suggests that one response may be for lawyers to continue to search for creative ways to deliver the familiar but awkward double message. That is, lower client expectations about the possible benefits of continued conflict/litigation/war; and yet emphasise that sometimes aggression, stone-walling or litigation ('non-settlement') may be necessary pain.[16]

(7)   A written risk analysis can make a client and lawyer powerful during negotiations. Bluffing, lying and pontification are reduced. A client can state 'We have completed a detailed 16-point risk analysis and tried to assign percentage chances and monetary values to each risk. That list is confidential, but most items on it would already be known to you (for example A, B, C...). We assume/hope that you have a similar written analysis'; 'Can you suggest some risk we have omitted if we do not reach a settlement today'; 'If our current risk analysis is approximately correct, we believe we know what is the worst that could happen outside this negotiation, and will not be able to go above/below that figure/outcome'; 'If we are wrong, we would be glad for you to give us more information so that we can make a better decision' etc.

(8)   (Legal) professionals live in a climate which demands transparency, multi-skilling and accountability.

To be employable and retain customers we need to be traditional dobermans and drafters; but also wise diplomats, doubt creators and decision-makers.

Apparent Reluctance to Prepare a Written Risk Analysis

If there are so many reasons in favour of writing one or more risk analyses for any client who cannot 'settle' a conflict, why are these documents apparently so rare in most legal circles? No doubt there are some individual lawyers and corners of legal culture who regularly use detailed written risk-analyses of 'no-settlement' (or at least no early settlement). What follows are some possible reasons for rarity (none of which, in the writer's opinion, is particularly convincing).[17]

(1)   **Habit.** Creation of such a document has not been part of the systems in law firms, or the habits of many lawyers.

(2)   **No Training.** Lawyers have not been trained to prepare risk-analyses routinely and have few role models to learn from. By way of contrast, risk analysis and decision-making courses appear to be a normal part of the curriculum in university business schools.

(3)   **Expense.** To prepare an initial risk analysis, and then subsequent amended versions as new information emerges, is yet another expense for a client. A client may be more willing to spend a limited conflict budget on discovering

---

16   Eg See J.H. Wade, 'Don't Waste Money on Negotiation or Mediation, This Conflict Needs a Judge' (2000) 18 *Mediation Quarterly* 259. Apart from potential benefits to *individuals* from litigation, there are sometimes important *social* benefits – see D. Luban, 'Settlements and the Erosion of the Public Realm' (1995) 83 *Georgetown L.J.* 2619.
Compare the awkward double message delivered daily by medical doctors 'Drugs or surgery may have some benefits but ....'

17   Analogous discussions can be found in abundant medical literature which addresses the ideal and tensions of patients giving 'informed consent' to medical interventions; eg. K. Cox, *Doctor and Patient: Exploring Clinical Thinking* (Sydney: Uni of NSW Press, 2000).

weaknesses in the opposition's arguments, rather than carefully systematising his/her own weaknesses and risks.

(4) **Repetitive client education.** Educating inexperienced clients about the harsh realities of conflict and of the legal system is often an exhausting and expensive process.[18]

Lawyers sometimes lecture and debate with inexperienced disputants for months in an attempt to dispel the myths which surround the litigotiation system. Robert Benjamin has observed that inexperienced litigants sometimes allow the myths of justice, truth, rationality and finality to influence their decision in favour of a litigation path.[19]

Some lawyers may too readily cease this demanding education of clients who do not want to hear.

(5) **Unnecessary scare-mongering.** A comprehensive listing of the risks of conflict or litigation may unnecessarily scare some clients. They may react to a three-page list and be unable to see that the vast majority of these risks are inapplicable or statistically unlikely. For example, a list of risks which result from driving a car would be so long and dramatic that some readers would unnecessarily abandon driving forever. The medical profession struggles with this factor whenever legislation requires a comprehensive catalogue of possible side-effects of new drugs or surgery.[20]

(6) **Loss of a Client.** Following from the previous factor, some lawyers need money. They fear the loss of a client if the client hears 'negative' comments from the lawyer.

Accordingly, they sell the client too readily what (s)he wants, rather than what may be needed.

(7) **Client is 'not ready' to hear.** Following the previous two factors, some people in conflict have suffered profound losses – loss of farm, business, reputation, mobility, self-respect, spouse, health, or hope for the future. These losses send them into a normal cycle of grief which may be manifested by shock, denial, bargaining with God, depression or anger.[21]

People in the early stages of grief (which may last for years) are 'not ready to hear' difficult truths about conflict. Skilled helpers may wait until the aggrieved client emotionally 'moves on' before attempting any detailed risk analysis.

(8) **Irrational Nature of Human Decision-Making.** A more permanent version of the emotional rollercoaster is the theory that human beings are frequently irrational, and that we have and will always make a 'number' of important decisions based upon irrational factors and feelings.[22]

---

18 A. Sarat and W. Felstiner, *Divorce Lawyers and Their Clients* (New York: OUP, 1995); D. Binder, P. Bergman & S. Price, *Lawyers as Counsellors* (1991).

19 R. Benjamin, 'Negotiation and Evil: The Sources of Religious and Moral Resistance to the Settlement of Conflicts' (1998) 15 *Mediation Q* 245.

20 M. Weir, *Complementary Medicine: Ethics and Law* (Brisbane: Prometheus, 2000) pp 93-101; *Rogers v Whitaker* (1992) 109 ALR 625; *Chappel v Hart* (1998) 156 ALR 517 (It is professional negligence if a patient consents to a medical procedure without also consenting to even remotely possible side effects.)

21 See E. Kubler-Ross, *On Death and Dying* (Macmillan, 1969).

22 Eg D. Kagan, *On the Origins of War* (Doubleday, 1995); J. Keegan. *A History of Warfare* (New York: Vintage, 1993).

Many anecdotes about war and litigation indicate unequivocal stupidity on the part of the instigators, or promulgators. The decision to 'fight' had little or no possible benefit for any one.[23]

What persuasive effect will a systematic and rational risk-analysis have on such irrationality? Probably none.

Nevertheless, one side benefit of the cognitive and written exercise may be to help protect a warrior lawyer (or soldier) from subsequent allegations of failure to advise competently.

This theory about the irrational nature of (some) decision-making, guarantees long term employment for lawyers, arms-dealers and soldiers, whether as aggressors or defenders.

(9)   **Avoid Creation of Dangerous Documents.** Some lawyers rightly fear that a documented list of risks will be 'leaked' to the opposition. A letter, e-mail or fax can be copied by a disgruntled employee, accidently lost, stolen by a surveillance team, or left visible on a table during negotiations or mediation.

However, the benefits of clarifying decision-making processes can usually be balanced with the risks of losing 'sensitive' information to the 'opposition'.

(10)   **'Woops … Before this Escalates Further, Can we Consider …'** During an emergency or crisis consultation with a lawyer, there is a predictable tendency to focus on the crisis, and only to consider the systematic risks of ongoing conflict *later*, rather than *earlier*. Lawyers are then sometimes reluctant to deliver later news of risks to an entrenched client who can (rightly?) retort – 'Why did you not tell me this earlier before I spent x dollars….?'; 'Are you losing your nerve in this fight?'

Lawyers sometimes rely upon mediators, judges or other expert lawyers to deliver tactfully the belated risk analysis ('bad news') in these cases.

(11)   **Avoid Premature Advice.** Many advisers are wary of giving any advice about risks before more alleged facts and evidence are collected. Of course, all relevant facts are never known before, during or after a trial. Some lawyers wait until the door of the court when a few more facts fall into place – such as the identity of the judge, illness of lawyers or witnesses, documents produced under subpoena – before giving a first or revised risk analysis.

Anecdotally, the writer in the role of mediator has found one small but dangerous group of lawyers who allegedly 'represent' inexperienced litigants. These lawyers file claims in the 'insult' zone, and then refuse to give good day-bad day ranges and risks to their naïve clients, using the repetitive excuse, 'we don't have all the facts yet'.

The deferral of at least a *preliminary* risk analysis is a dangerous habit as ironically the process of collecting facts and evidence usually escalates conflict. Working towards creating a *comprehensive* risk analysis is itself a risk.

(12)   **Fear of inaccuracy.** Some lawyers seem to avoid writing out any list of 'no-settlement' risks for a client for fear of understating or overstating the dangers. This is a form of perceived self-protection. 'Put nothing in writing and you can never be proved to be wrong.'

---

23   Eg J. Vidal, *McLibel: Burger Culture on Trial* (London: Macmillan, 1997). Every litigation lawyer has a catalogue of stories about 'insane' claims or litigation.

(13) **Standardised Risk List.** The logical converse of the previous point is that some lawyers, like doctors, are unwilling to prepare pro forma precedents which set out 68 standard risks of a business continuing with unresolved conflict or commencing litigation. Such a standard form may contain 'truth', but will rarely be read by a client, does not lead to 'informed' client consent, and may give the client the impression that the lawyer lacks competence as a warrior and negotiator: or is trying to avoid responsibility for minimising some of these risks.

Nevertheless, such forms may become increasingly common in lawyers' offices, as they are in medical surgeries, and on manufacturer's labels.

(14) **Avoid public denigration of courts.** A risk analysis will necessarily itemise in detail the accident prone nature of the court system. The criticism of Western court systems is abundant and public – slow, uncertain, error-prone, expensive, stressed judges, judges ignorant of clients' lives and businesses, tactical gamesmanship by lawyers, client loss of control, translation of conflict into narrow legal and monetised categories, repetitive adjournments, process by attrition etc. etc.[24]

These repetitive and publicised critiques of courts are well known by litigation lawyers. Their own anecdotal vitriol towards courts usually far exceeds the surveyed and published dissatisfaction.

However, many lawyers remain wary about cataloguing court and judicial failings in writing for clients. These documents will inevitably get back to the judges. Some sensitive judges may be offended and the lawyer may alienate an ally needed at a later urgent hearing.[25]

Thus lawyers tend to tell stories to clients about the accident prone nature of the judicial system, rather than record these tales of woe in writing.[26]

(15) **I'm a lawyer, not a counsellor.** Some lawyers take the approach that they will advise only on 'legal' risks, not about personal, community or business risks. Thus they readily state that litigation is delayed, uncertain and expensive (a 'lottery').

---

24 Australian Law Reform Commission, *Managing Justice – A Review of the Federal Civil Justice System* Report No. 89; 1999 pp 69–97.

25 One mediator colleague tactfully hands a large-print copy of the following *judicial* quote to overconfident lawyers and disputants
    '[I]t is often impossible to predict the outcome of litigation with a high degree of confidence. Disagreements on the law occur even in the High Court. An apparently strong case can be lost if evidence is not accepted, and it is often difficult to forecast how a witness will act in the witness-box. Many steps in the curial process involve value judgments, discretionary decisions and other subjective determinations which are inherently unpredictable. Even well-organized, efficient courts cannot routinely produce quick decisions, and appeals further delay finality. Factors personal to a client and any inequality between the client and other parties to the dispute are also potentially material. Litigation is highly stressful for most people and notoriously expensive. An obligation on a litigant to pay the costs of another party in addition to his or her own costs can be financially ruinous. Further, time spent by parties and witnesses in connection with litigation cannot be devoted to other, productive activities. Consideration of a range of competing factors such as these can reasonably lead rational people to different conclusions concerning the best course to follow.' *Studer v Boetcher* [2000] NSWCA 263 (24 November, 2000) [63] (Fitzgerald JA).

26 Eg A. Sarat & W. Felstiner, *Divorce Lawyers and Their Clients* (New York: OUP 1995). (Tape recordings of family lawyers speaking to clients reveal constant oral warnings about the arbitrary and chaotic nature of the court system.)

However they do not investigate the client's life, goals and business in detail or set out how ongoing (litigious) conflict may impact those 'non-legal' areas – eg. newspaper publicity, perceived employee incompetence, loss of work references, lost opportunities to compete, diversion from work, deterioration in health, exposure of personal or trade secrets, humiliation in a witness box etc. Such 'commercial' analyses are often left to the client or other more expert advisers.

This artificial division between legal and non-legal effects of conflict is conceptually flawed and professionally dangerous.[27]

Medical doctors have particularly been criticised for an analogous tendency to say, 'I am an expert in disease; I do not discuss illness'. By way of contrast, patients want consideration of their whole life and life goals; not just the 'curing' of a technical disease.[28] It is not acceptable for a surgeon to say 'I am an expert cutter; the psychological, economic and injury risks attached to surgery are not my business'.

The writer anecdotally meets some lawyers who give a 'legal' risk analysis based on their own expertise and research; and then switch to a brainstorming process with the client to create a second 'commercial' or 'personal' risk analysis.

(16) **Hired a doberman.** There are several variations on the previous reason for certain lawyers being reluctant to provide a written risk analysis. For example, some lawyers say that they have been hired in a specialist role as an aggressor, hired gun, bad cop or doberman. They have not been hired as a diplomat or as a wise decision-maker. It would be patronising to a client to assume uninvited (and non-expert) roles.

This interpretation continues by saying that all the lawyer's intellectual and emotional energy must be directed at discovering 'weaknesses' and doubts in the opposition's position – not listing risks in his/her own client's chosen course of action. No doubting dobermans required.

There is no doubt that some lawyers who have adopted this interpretation of their 'bad cop' role, have found long term employment. Others have not.

(17) **Wise elder and god-professional.** One interpretation of the professional-client contract is that the submissive client brings his/her problem to the wise expert for the expert to provide a solution.[29]

The client wants this contract and wants the expert to make judgments on his/her behalf. The client does not want to be bothered with lists of doubts, risks, options or alternatives. It is clear that there remains a class of clients who still want (at least initially) this god-professional contract, and will shop around until they find the right fixit doctor, dentist, builder or lawyer.

Given market forces some of these god-professionals will be successful. However, particularly as lawyers, they live in increasingly mine-infested territory.[30]

---

27   Eg J.H. Wade, 'Forever Bargaining in the Shadow of the Law – Who Sells Solid Shadows? (1998) 12 *Aust. J. of Fam. L.* 256.
28   Eg K. Cox, *Doctor and Patient: Exploring Clinical Thinking* (Sydney: Uni of NSW Press, 2000).
29   D. Schon, *The Reflective Practitioner; How Professionals Think in Action* (Harper Collins, 1983).
30   Eg M. Behm, 'A Risk Perspective of Managing a Mediated Matter' (1999) December *Proctor* (Queensland) 27.

(18) **Belated Risk Analyses by Third Parties.** The preceding catalogue suggests reasons why many lawyers do not undertake a systematic and comprehensive written risk analysis early, if ever, for their clients. Accordingly, it sometimes becomes the belated task of a mediator, business adviser or barrister to undertake this task in an attempt to create clarity, and to assist a disputant make a wise decision in the face of inevitable uncertainty. A barrister and a mediator will usually also attempt to protect the initial lawyer from any criticism for failure to prepare such a document earlier – eg. 'I'm sure that your lawyer will have told you all of this already'; 'All I am doing is helping you create a list of the many things your lawyer has told you in the past'; 'Your lawyer has helpfully analysed the legal advantages and dangers, now can you help me understand the commercial dangers if this dispute goes on endlessly?'; 'Many of these risks have only become apparent recently and you must now re-evaluate in the light of this new information'; 'Litigation is like war, clients commonly plunge into it in a moment of passion; as the emotions subside, it comes time to evaluate' etc etc.

One of the major reasons that lawyers employ mediators is to 'beat up' a client who is not listening to the lawyer's repetitive written and oral warnings about continuation of conflict or litigation. What follows is an example of a colloquial questionnaire form of risk analysis given to all team members prior to a mediation.

CASE STUDY – Example Risk Analysis for Jammed Negotiations[31]

(Typical service provider – customer 'contractual' dispute)

A cotton factory owner contracted with an expert factory designer and builder to renovate sections of his mill for $2million. When the renovations were complete, the owner was disappointed as the promised rate of production did not eventuate until three months thereafter. (The new machinery often did not work during the first three months – the factory experienced repetitive 'down-time'.) Accordingly the factory owner withheld the last payment of $250,000 to the renovator. Incensed, the renovator commenced court action in one state (the state of the contract) to recover the last instalment. Predictably, the factory owner cross-claimed, in the state where the factory was actually constructed, for three months of diminished profits, being around $1million. The entrenched parties and lawyers were required to attend mandatory mediation.

The 'legal issues' distilled by the mediator during telephone preparation with lawyers and clients were as follows:

POSSIBLE FACTUAL AND 'LEGAL' QUESTIONS/ISSUES??

FACT   1. How many minutes of down-time occurred during the relevant period?   ☐

FACT   2. What combination of factors caused each down-time?   ☐

---

31 J.H. Wade, *Representing Clients at Mediation and Negotiation* (Bond University Dispute Resolution Centre, 2000), pp 62-66.

FACT/ EVIDENCE	3. What expert evidence is available/credible to argue (2)?	
FACT	4. Which particular down-time minutes were arguably 'normal' incidents of an overhaul? (eg. compared to other mills around Australia)	
LAW	5. Who has the joint or individual responsibility to remedy each particular stoppage? In what time frame?	
FACT	6. What steps were taken by whom to remedy each down-time?	
LAW	7. At what minute does each particular down-time become a possible/probable breach of contract?	
LAW & FACT	8. How should 'loss' be measured for those minutes of down-time in breach?	

On the day of the joint mediation meeting (which involved two teams with 5 members each), the mediator met with each team and gave each of the members the following risk-analysis. Each team member was asked to fill in the form and then discuss each risk with fellow team-members.

Business Risk Analysis for Each Participant in each Team

(1) How far will I and my employees be able to concentrate on new projects over the next x years of conflict? $

(2) How many days of worktime will I and my employees lose over the next x years preparing for this dispute? $

(3) Do I/they have anything better to do? $

(4) How much money, best to worst, will I spend on

  • Lawyers $

  • Duelling witnesses $

  • Duelling experts $

  • Travel
    Over the next x years? $

(5) How much money, best to worst, will be spent on *procedural* issues (eg. which court), before we even focus on historic analysis? $

(6) What damage, if any, might flow in my business community by a public hearing during which we each label the other:
 	
   • Impetuous
   • Deceptive
   • Incompetent, etc.
	$

(7) If war continues for x years and bitterness escalates, how far (if at all) can each of us lose customers from bad-mouthing by the other?	$
(8) What are the chances that a judge will understand my industry and how it operates?	
(9) What are the chances that a judge will believe 100% of my version of 'the facts'?	
(10) During years of conflict, what are the chances that a judge will attribute 'fault' 100% to one side, and zero to the other?	
(11) What dynamics will emerge when my colleagues are subpoenaed and cross-examined?	
(12) What pressures will x years of conflict put on our families?	
(13) After x years of historic research, will perceived facts and dynamics be any different at the door-of-the-court? (if so, how)	Yes No Maybe
(14) Will x years of argument effectively convince either of us that the other is legally or morally 'right'? (back to question 13)	Yes No Maybe
(15) What are the risks of miscommunication by using letters and legal documents over the next x years?	
(16) If one of us in incensed by the trial judge, what chances of an appeal and recycling risks (1)-(14)?	
(17) Other risks???	

ATTEMPT TO PUT BEST/WORST MONETARY VALUES ON EACH OF THESE RISKS FOR YOU. THEN ADD UP BEST/WORST TOTALS.

The dispute settled at the mediation after 8 hours of sometimes tense communication. One of the many factors (as told to the mediator by a legal representative) which removed barriers to settlement was that the written exercise and team discussion refocussed the teams on risk management, long term interests beyond just money, moral and legal rights.

TERMS OF THE SETTLEMENT (drafted in detail at the mediation)

(1) Mutually drafted press release for Trade Newspaper about re-establishment of excellent working relationship between parties.

(2) Signed contract for renovation of another factory.

(3) Claim for lost profits abandoned.

(4) Payment to renovator of $75,000; plus a further $25,000 for an earlier outstanding debt.

(5) Agreement to include in any future contracts a security clause for instalment payments.

(6) Establishment of emergency trouble-shooting phone numbers if/when conflicts arose in the future.

Precedent Risk Analysis[32]

What follows are two example forms of risk analysis which can be used or adapted. Many variations on this are possible – though writing, lists and multiple specific categories (as compared to oral, literary and generalised risks – 'you may lose'; 'there are no guarantees'; 'it depends who is believed') are essential.

Anecdotally, many (legal) representatives tell mediators that they have 'advised the client about the risks'. However, when mediators ask clients in private about the risks of not settling, the client has heard selectively or not at all, or the client speaks in vague generalities about the high cost of litigation, or unpredictable nature of the behaviour of judges or other decision-makers.

The following are examples of another way of trying to analyse and communicate ranges of risk.

---

32 J.H. Wade, *Representing Clients at Mediation and Negotiation* (Bond University Dispute Resolution Centre, 2000), pp 59-61.

Example 1

Client Information Sheet – **Risk Analysis**

NAME _____

Normal transaction costs of filing a formal court claim and proceeding to the door of the court (or occasionally even to the Umpire) 3/ 7	Applicable to me	Estimated $ value Best to worst	Applicable to other disputants	Estimated $ value Best to worst
1. ....Years of personal stress and uncertainty				
2. ....Years of stress of family members				
3. ....Years of stress on others and my work associates				
4. ....Weeks of absenteeism from work				
5. ....Weeks of lost employee time preparing for court				
6. ....Years of lost concentration and focus at work				
7. Life/business on hold for ....years				
8. Inability to 'get on with life' for ....years				
9. Embarrassment and loss of good will when relatives/friends/ business associates are subpoenaed to court				
10. Negative publicity in press or business circles				
11. My lawyer's fees				
12. My accountant's fees				
13. My expert witness's fees				

14. Possible costs order against me				
15. Interest lost on money received later rather than sooner				
16. Loss of control over my life to professionals				
17. Post litigation recriminations against courts, experts and lawyers				
18. Loss of value by court ordered sale/ appointment of receiver etc				
19. Lost future goodwill with and 'pay backs' by opponents				
20. Cost and repeat of all previous factors if there is an appeal				
Other?				
Other?				
Other?				
ESTIMATED TOTAL of Transaction Costs (best to worst)*		$	No.	$
Date _____				
Signed _____ (client)				

NB: These are only rough estimates. All these figures will fluctuate up or down as the conflict develops and as more factors emerge.

* The best-worst transaction cost estimates should be deducted from best to worst BENEFITS of LATE SETTLEMENT (or umpired decision).

Example 2 – Risk Analysis

In a recent family property mediation, the wife drew up the following more specific list of risk attached to ongoing conflict. She ranked the importance of each risk by number, and placed the list on her refrigerator for reflection between sessions.

RISKS ATTACHED TO ONGOING CONFLICT?

	Rank 0-5 0 = unsure 1= small concern 5= big concern
1. 2-3 years of uncertainty.	
2. 2-3 years of sniping; lawyers letters; miscommunication.	
3. Risk of semi-public documents bad-mouthing each other **Long term family albums and memories.**	
4. Long term sense of bitterness. The lawyers say that 'I had to say those things about you'.	
5. Public gossip for 2-3 years.	
6. Strain on families, grief for boys.	
7. **Inability** to **plan**; or **spend** own $ for 2-3 years; or to **travel**; or **start business.**	
8. Loss of control of life to '**experts**'.	
9. $ paid to **lawyers** and **experts** – 2% of the estate.	
10. **Spotlight** on your **super** fund with detailed affidavits for **tax** department to **examine**.	
11. Judges **ignorant** of your businesses; random decision-making.	
12. '**Same**' **settlement** forced on you at door-of-court in 2 years' time.	
13. **Injury, illness** or **death** before **solution** emerges	
14. Other?	

Life-Goals Analysis – A Useful Flip-Side of a Risk Analysis

One of the interesting ongoing activities of lawyers, mediators and counsellors who are involved in conflict management, is to swap stories and research on 'interventions' used successfully or unsuccessfully with clients.[33]

---

33   Eg G Egan, *The Skilled Helper* 5th ed (California: Brooks/Cole, 1994); L Boulle, *Mediation – Skills and Techniques* (Australia: Butterworths, 2001); J H Wade, 'Strategic Interventions Used by Mediators, Facilitators and Conciliators' (1994) 5 *Aust Dispute Res J* 292; J H Wade 'Tools From a Mediator's Toolbox: Reflections on Matrimonial Property Disputes' (1996) 7 *Aust Dispute Res J* 93.

A 'life-goals analysis' is a short (preferably one page) written list of a person's short and long term business, health, financial and emotional goals. The goals are specified by a client, with careful listening and some prompting from a skilled helper, whether mediator, lawyer or counsellor. The writer frequently uses these documents in the capacity of either lawyer or mediator; either early in a consultation, or late when negotiations have jammed.

A 'life goals analysis' may be more suitable in some situations than a 'risk-analysis'. These two analyses are the same except each list is expressed in different language. The former emphasises the glass half full, while the latter may sometimes seem to be referring to the glass half empty.

This switch may find some justification from several psychological studies[34] which suggest that most (not all) people are 'risk averse'. Therefore, any list should express positively what has already been *gained* by the current offer, not how far the current offer is short of a 'target' or perceived 'entitlement'. This persuasive negotiation or decision-making language may seem obvious, but the writer rarely sees these linguistic transitions being systematically used by lawyers or clients in mediations or negotiations. The linguistic transition from a 'risk analysis' to a 'life goal' is illustrated by the chart below:

Risks if Conflict Continues	Life Goals?	This Offer?
1. Another 2-3 years of delay.	1. To get on with life	1
2. Subpoenas and stress for business partners and family.	2. To minimise stress for colleagues	1
3. Legal costs of between $30 000 – $40 000.	3. To minimise legal costs	1
4. Lose control of life and decision-making to lawyers.	4. To regain control of my life	1
5. Delay making a decision to expand a business	5. To diversify my business	1
6. Lose interest on cash for 2 years	6. Receive and invest cash now	1
7. etc	7. etc	

To repeat, a number of studies indicate that changing language towards the language in the right column emphasises current gains. Additionally language, brevity and visuals influence perception, and the majority of people being risk averse, will decide to 'hang on' to the existing offer made 'late' in negotiations when it is expressed as gains.

Of course, such knowledge of psychology and language, (if it is correct!) potentially places considerable power in the hands of negotiators and mediators when working with less experienced negotiators.

---

34   R H Mnookin, 'Why Negotiations Fail: An Exploration of Barriers to the Resolution of Conflict' (1993) 8 *Ohio St J Dispute Res* 235; and references in footnote 7, and Goodpaster, footnote 8.

In the tool box of interventions, the writer (as mediator) regularly converts a risk analysis into a one page 'life-goal chart' either during separate preparation with each individual disputant, and/or at the last gap in the negotiations, when one or all disputants have become focussed on 'what I have already lost' during the course of the negotiations.[35]

This mediator (and negotiator) intervention commonly has the following steps in a private meeting, the mediator –

(i)   Acknowledges the client's sense of frustration that (s)he feels (s)he is 'giving away too much'.

(ii)   Confirms that the mediator's (and lawyer's) job is to help the client make a wise decision in the face of uncertainty, and to reduce the possibility of future client regrets. If it is a wise decision, then the client should 'end' the round of negotiations, and continue the conflict.

(iii) Asks the client to brainstorm on a whiteboard a list of life goals (in the client's reframed words); and prompts the client about other possibilities to add to the list. Predictably, a list of multiple life goals emerges (one life goal may be 'To be paid $1 million dollars!') Set out below is an example of the type of list that commonly emerges in family property disputes.

LIFE GOALS?	THIS OFFER??
■ To get on with life	☐
■ To open a new business	☐
■ To invest money	☐
■ To stop paying lawyers	☐
■ To stay healthy	☐
■ To minimise contact with 'x'	☐
■ To reduce stress on colleagues	☐
■ To take a holiday	☐
■ To focus on my work	☐
■ To avoid becoming bitter	☐
■ To regain 'control' of my life	☐
■ To settle 'in the range'	☐
■ To reduce risks of paybacks	☐
■ To receive [$540,000]	☐
■ Other??	☐

---

35   See J H Wade 'The Last Gap in Negotiations – Why is it Important? How can it be crossed?' (1995) 6 *Aust Dispute Res J* 93

(iv)   Asks the client to work down the list and tick (or check) the boxes if a life goal is achieved by the current offer. Other boxes are marked with a question mark. Standardly, the client decides that more than 90% of his/her life goals are contained in the current offer! This is a visual surprise.

(v)   Immediately copies the whiteboard 'life goals' and ticks chart to a single hand printed sheet of paper and gives this to the client to ponder in silence.

(vi)   Asks the client whether (s)he would   like to continue the negotiation immediately, or take a break to consider the current offer, or immediately meet to call off the jammed negotiations for a time.

(vii) Gives advice that many clients like to take a break of several days, stick the life-goals sheet on their refrigerator for quiet contemplation and discussion with influential friends or family[36] and phone the mediator back between 7-9pm on a specified day with a process decision – accept the offer, adjourn or resume an agreed process.

(viii) Tells the other disputant(s) in a separate meeting what process is happening and perhaps repeats a similar confidential 'life goals' analysis.

(ix)   The majority of clients have opted for the refrigerator break, and over 80% have phoned the mediator back on the assigned day with a speech to the effect 'In the light of the life goals we listed (and a few more...), and discussions I've had with ..., I have decided to cut my losses etc and to accept the offer that was "finally" made.'

Obviously, there are many interesting dynamics occurring during the course of this particular intervention extracted from the conflict managers' toolbox.

Conclusion

This article has set out briefly:

- a description of a risk analysis

- reasons why such documents are essential for professional advisers and their clients in conflict

- some hypothesised reasons why written risk analyses are uncommon in many legal practices

- examples and precedents of risk analyses

- the use of a 'life goals' list, as a positive flip-side of a risk analysis

The writer's hope is that the evolving written risk analysis will become a routine document in the offices of professional conflict managers – particularly lawyers and mediators (and armed services!).

In my opinion the problems attached to such documents are, usually outweighed by the clarity they provide for conflicted clients who are attempting to make wise decisions in the face of ongoing uncertainty.

---

36   It is a constant challenge to lawyers, mediators, managers and diplomats how to include influential 'outsiders' or 'tribal members' constructively in negotiations. See J Johnson and L Campbell *Impasses of Divorce* (New York: Free Press, 1988) Ch 2, 'Unholy Alliances and Tribal Warfare'.

Risk Analysis Exercise A

You are a legal representative or mediator. The manager of a huge shopping mall comes to see you and asks for your advice as a recent attempt to negotiate with a tenant has been unsuccessful. The manager is puzzled at the tenant's unreasonable behaviour as all the legal rights and power seem to be on the landlord's side.

The lessee is a specialist retailer in the lessor's shopping mall. The lessee alleges that its recent downturn in profits has been caused by repair work done by the lessor to the pavement outside the lessee's shop. Allegedly, this repair work diverted customers walking in the mall. The lessee has had a history of conflict with the lessor's managers and has now left the mall and terminated his lease. He is now unemployed. The lessee initially claimed $100,000 damages and the lessor offered nothing. The lessor has clear documentary evidence to show that the three shops adjoining the lessee's shop actually had increases in profits during the repair work.

The lessee's manager is the brother-in-law of the founder of the franchise of similar stores that exist across the country.

The Retail Shop Leases Tribunal ordered the disputants to mandatory mediation. They had one quick meeting where the lessee reduced his offer to $50,000; and the lessor increased her offer to $5,000.

Prepare a two-column risk analysis if a settlement is not reached.

(i)   Use a whiteboard or a large sheet of paper and draw up two columns of possible risks – one for the landlord and one for the tenant, if the dispute does not settle.

(ii) Then in the light of that analysis, advise the manager of possible procedural options.

RISKS IF SETTLEMENT DOES NOT OCCUR 'EARLY'			
FOR SHOPPING MALL	$ VALUE	FOR FORMER LESSEE	$ VALUE
1.		1.	
2.		2.	
3.		3.	
4.		4.	
5.		5.	
6.		6.	
7.		7.	
8.		8.	
9.		9.	
10.		10.	

EXERCISE B – RISK ANALYSIS AND LIFE GOALS ANALYSIS

A husband and wife, both Chinese, separate. She is 36 years, he is 45 years of age. There are no children of their eleven year marriage. He has an income of over $400,000 per year and visible assets of about $800,000. She runs an importing shop which does not make any money, and has assets of about $300,000. They are in conflict about property distribution (under an equitable property distribution law).

The husband is a distinguished doctor and is revered by the Chinese community. He has many supporters and relatives who attend court and ridicule the wife. He has paid his lawyer's bills in advance. The wife has been somewhat isolated by her own community, and does not have sufficient money to pay her lawyers. She is indecisive, vengeful and emotional.

Several attempts to organise culturally appropriate mediations have failed, partly because the husband's lawyers and tribe are convinced that they will 'win' in court. There are cross allegations of missing assets, inherited assets and of forgery of the wife's signature on a mortgage. The negotiations are emotional, escalated, and positional.

At the last round of negotiations, the parties are only $40,000 apart. The wife wants $180,000 cash and the husband has offered $140,000. (The legal costs for *each* party will be well over $100,000 if the case proceeds to trial.)

Choose one of the disputants, either husband or wife, and write out in parallel columns in point form (i) a risk analysis; and (ii) convert each point into a life goals' analysis for the person you have chosen.

Then, in the light of the risks and life goals, write out your advice to your chosen client (a full court hearing is scheduled in 8 weeks' time).

RISK FOR .... IF CONFLICT CONTINUES	LIFE GOALS OF ....
1.	
2.	
3.	
4.	
5.	
6.	
7.	
8.	
9.	
10.	
11.	
12.	
Advice	

APPENDIX C

Critiques of litigation and adjudication

- Results uncertain
- Legal costs higher than outcomes
- Hearings and judgments delayed
- Judges stressed; impatient
- Judges do not understand complex evidence
- Legal categories hide real conflicts
- Legal remedies unimaginative
- Inaccessible to poor and middle class
- Rarely 'finalises' conflict
- Results depend on expert's skill
- Involves constant deceit, ambush, tricks
- Process is convoluted
- Disadvantageous to 'one-shotters'
- Disputants lose control
- Disputants suffer hidden costs of trauma, absence from work, etc
- Myths of justice, rationality and finality hide realities
- Lawyers have few incentives to settle early
- Judges tend to split difference
- DIY litigants confuse and clog courts
- Constant procedural reforms
- Case management multiplies hurdles
- Damaging publicity
- Perceived or actually incompetent lawyers or 'experts'

C.   Guide for preparing costs information

SAMPLE GUIDE FOR CLAIMANT

CLIENT'S COSTS

1. Client's legal costs to date of mediation

2. Client's estimated future legal costs

3. Client's total legal costs

4. Estimate of client's non-legal costs

to date

future

Total estimated non-legal costs to hearing

OTHER PARTY'S COSTS

5. Other party's estimated legal costs

to date

future

Other party's total estimated legal costs

6. Other party's estimated non-legal costs

- to date

- future

Other party's total estimated non-legal costs

VALUE OF CLIENT'S CLAIM

7. Value of Claim to date (inc interest)

Total value of Claim to date

8. Value of Claim if case proceeds to hearing
(inc interest)

Estimated Total value of claim

VALUE OF ANY COUNTER-CLAIM

9. Value of any Counter-claim to date (inc interest)

Total value of any Counter-claim to date

10. Estimated value of any Counter-claim at hearing
(inc interest)

Estimated total value of any Counter-claim

POSSIBLE OUTCOMES

11. Prospects of success

On each issue

On counter-claim

On beating a Part 36 offer (if any)

Cost implications of each of the above

12. BATNA (best alternative to negotiated agreement)

Claim

Less irrecoverable legal costs

Less non-legal costs

13. Client's WATNA (worst alternative to negotiated agreement)

Own costs (legal and non-legal)

Other (relevant) parties' claims

Less irrecoverable legal costs of other (relevant) parties

14. Offers to date

Claimant:

    Date

    Principal

    Interest

    Costs

Total

Defendant/Respondent:

    Date

    Principal

    Interest

    Costs

Total

15. Compare BATNA with offers

Appendix 7

Mediation and Mediator Evaluation

A. Mediator experience, self-assessment and debrief forms

(i) General self-assessment form

Names of clients:

....

....

Date and venue of mediation:

....

....

Referral source:

....

....

Nature and sources of conflict:

....

....

Escalation/de-escalation factors:

....

....

Pre-mediation conference:

....

....

Participants at mediation and their roles:

....

....

Major issues, agenda items, hidden agendas:

....

....

The following went well:

....

....

With hindsight the following could have been done better:

....

....

How clients/advisers assessed the process:

....

....

One lesson learned for future:

....

....

Issues to debrief with mentor:

....

....

(ii) Law Society (England & Wales) sample experience, self-assessment and feedback forms[1]

Annex E – Sample mediation experience summaries
E1 – Sample mediation summary
E2 – Sample personal debrief summary
E3 – Sample summary of debrief of another mediator
E4 – Sample meeting summary
E5 – Sample review of feedback summary

Annex E1 – Sample mediation summary

Part 1
1. Your name

---

2. Date of the mediation
3. Indicate whether actual or mock mediation
4. Your role in the mediation
5. Other participants and their roles
6. Brief description of the dispute
7. Result of the mediation
8. Outline the pre-mediation activities and preparation
9. Indicate whether you had any post-mediation involvement

Part 2
Refer to the relevant Law Society competencies for civil/commercial mediators when completing this part.

1. Outline what went well in the mediation
2. Outline what you could have done differently or better in the mediation
3. Outline your learning points

Part 3
Make a note of the duration of this summary

Annex E2 – Sample personal debrief summary

Part 1
1. Your name
2. Name of the mediator who debriefed you
3. Date of the mediation being debriefed
4. Your role in the mediation
5. Brief description of the dispute
6. Result of the mediation

Part 2
Refer to the relevant Law Society competencies for civil/commercial mediation when completing this part.

1. Provide a description of the mediation (from start to finish)
2. Outline what went well in the mediation
3. Outline what could you have done better or differently in the mediation
4. Outline the other mediator's feedback, input, advice or suggestions to you on debrief
5. Outline your learning points from the debrief

Part 3
Make a note of the duration of the debrief and summary

Annex E3 – Sample summary of debrief of another mediator

Part 1

1. Your name
2. Name of mediator being debriefed
3. Date of the mediation being debriefed
4. Role in the mediation of the person being debriefed
5. Brief description of the dispute

6. Result of the mediation

Part 2
Refer to the relevant Law Society competencies for civil/commercial mediation when completing this part.

1. Provide a description of the mediation (from start to finish)
2. Outline what went well in the mediation
3. Outline what did not go well in the mediation
4. Outline your feedback, input, advice or suggestions in the debrief
5. Outline your learning points from the debrief

Part 3
Make a note of the duration of the debrief and summary

Annex E4 – Sample meeting summary

Part 1

1. Your name
2. Date of meeting
3. Brief description of what was discussed

Part 2
Refer to the relevant Law Society competencies for civil/commercial mediators when completing this part.

1. Outline what you learnt in the meeting
2. Outline how the meeting made you reconsider your attitudes to mediation, style of mediating, or previous mediation experiences

Part 3
Make a note of the duration of the meeting and summary

Annex E5 – Sample review of feedback summary

If you include in your application a copy of the written feedback you have received (along the lines of the form set out in appendix E to the criteria and guidance notes), you do not need to complete Parts 1 and 2 of this summary.

Part 1

1. Your name
2. Date of the mediation
3. Indicate the role played in the mediation by the provider of the feedback
4. Indicate whether the mediation was court-ordered, agreed by the parties, recommended by the lawyers (if any) or occurred for some other reason (please specify)
5. Indicate the result of the mediation

Part 2

1. Outline what the provider of the feedback considered went well in the mediation

2. Outline what the provider of the feedback considered did not go well in the mediation
3. Provide an outline of any suggestions for improvement given by the provider of the feedback

Part 3

Refer to the relevant Law Society competencies for civil/commercial mediators when answering this part. Outline the learning points from the feedback.

Part 4

Make a note of the duration of the feedback (if oral) and review and summary of the feedback.

B.   For party or adviser

(i) General sample

In order to assess and improve our mediation services, we would like to receive your comments about the performance of your Mediator.

Please complete this form and return it to the [ABC Mediation Service, PO Box [ ]].

Mediation date:
....

Mediator's name:
....

Your name/name of
lawyer:...

Was the mediation: (please tick)

Encouraged by court/tribunal ☐

Agreed by the parties ☐

Recommended by legal advisers ☐

Other (please specify) ☐

Type of Dispute: (please tick)

Banking/finance ☐

Building/construction ☐

Partnership/joint venture   ☐

Planning/local government   ☐

Insurance   ☐

Estates/wills   ☐

Professional malpractice/negligence   ☐

Intellectual property/IT   ☐

Contractual   ☐

Corporate   ☐

Industrial Relations/workplace   ☐

Other (please specify)   ☐

To what extent did the dispute settle at Mediation?

Fully ☐   Partially ☐   Not at all ☐

Have you previously used:

ABC Mediation Service	Yes	No
Other Mediation Services	Yes	No
Your Mediator	Yes	No

The performance of your Mediator (please circle your response)

                      Poorly/extremely well   Other comments

Explained nature of
mediation and answered
your queries

                      1. 2. 3. 4. 5   ....

Helped me prepare for
mediation

                      1. 2. 3. 4. 5   ....

Explained the mediation
process
                            1. 2. 3. 4. 5   ....

Identified relevant issues   1. 2. 3. 4. 5   ....

Understood your side of
the dispute
                            1. 2. 3. 4. 5   ....

Helped the parties
generate options
                            1. 2. 3. 4. 5   ....

Made communication
easier
                            1. 2. 3. 4. 5   ....

Kept the process on track   1. 2. 3. 4. 5   ....

Helped reach a good result

                            1. 2. 3. 4. 5   ....

Please name one thing the Mediator did particularly well:

....

....

What would you have preferred the Mediator to do differently:

....

....

Would you recommend to others:

(Please give reasons)

Mediation   Yes   No
....

The Venue   Yes   No
....

Your Mediator   Yes   No
....

Other comments or evaluations:

....

....

....

(ii) Law Society (England & Wales) sample mediator feedback form[2]

Annex D – Sample mediator feedback form

Name of mediator/co-mediator

_____

Date of mediation:

_____

Please complete this form and return to the mediator by fax on

_____

or post back in the self-addressed and stamped envelope provided.

The information you supply will ensure that the quality of mediation services are reviewed and improved.

1. Please tick the box which describes your role in the mediation:
- lawyer
- party

2. Was the mediation:
- ordered by a court
- agreed by the parties
- recommended by lawyers (if any)
- other (please specify)

_____

3. To what extent did the dispute settle at mediation?
- fully
- partially
- not at all

4. What did the mediator do well?

_____

_____

_____

_____

_____

_____

5. In relation to the activities below, please comment briefly on the mediator's performance. If the activity does not apply, please tick in the N/A column.

Activity	Comment	N/A
Answering any queries you had ahead of the mediation		
Making practical arrangements for the mediation		
Explaining and entering into the mediation agreement		
Explaining the mediation process		
Explaining the essential features of mediation eg – confidentiality		

Activity	Comment	N/A
Building rapport with you and putting you at ease		
Listening		
If agreement was reached, assisting you to record it		

6. Overall, are you satisfied with the mediation? Why?

_____

_____

_____

_____

_____

_____

C.   For supervisors

Requirements for Providers of PPC (Professional Practice Consultancy) – College of Mediators[3]

---

3   This document is reproduced with the kind permission of the College of Mediators. The College website is a regularly updated source of information and resources so for the most up to date material please visit www.collegeofmediators.co.uk.

College of Mediators

Requirements for providers of professional practice consultancy
– and guidelines to the requirements
for professional practice consultancy.

*Approved by the College Board of Governors April 2003,
effective from 1 June 2003*

1. General requirements

1.1   Professional practice consultancy must comprise the following three components:

  1.1.1   professional accountability, involving quality control of professional standards

  1.2.2   a professional development function, involving training and continuing professional education

  1.3.3   support, for a stressful and difficult occupation

1.2   Providers must ensure that consultants are members of the College's professional practice consultants' register.

1.3   All providers must have an equal opportunities policy approved by the College

1.4   All providers must have a Complaints and Disciplinary procedure approved by the College.

2   Professional Practice Consultancy

2.1   Mediators must receive professional practice consultancy from a professional practice consultant approved by the College.

  2.1.1   the minimum required annual consultancy after training is either 4 hours individual consultancy (Associates)/2 hours (members) or 10% (Associates)/5% (Members) of time spent in face to face mediation, whichever is the greater, subject to a maximum of 12 hours.

  2.1.2   1 hour for both Associates and Members must be on an individual, one to one, face to face basis.

2.1.3 Consultancy must be maintained even if the mediator is not practising.

2.1.4 Access to emergency consultancy must be available as and when required. Such emergency practice consultancy (e.g. where there may be issues of child protection or risk of harm) may be sought and/or provided by the use of a range of media including telephone, telephone or video conferencing or other means. Such consultancy must always ensure proper and adequate data protection and protection of client confidentiality. Where emergency consultation is carried out by remote means the mediator must ensure that prompt arrangements are made to meet with a Consultant and to provide any and all written or other reporting or recording of them matter

2.2 Consultants must conform to the following specifications:

2.2.1 There must be written contracts for consultancy detailing all the standards set out below with a joint expectation of commitment by both mediator and consultant

2.2.2 there must be evidence that consultants conform to an Equal Opportunities Perspective:

a) Consultants will possess knowledge, experience and skills in anti-discriminatory practice
b) Consultants must promote anti-discriminatory practice and not condone discriminatory practice
c) training of Consultants will include an anti-discriminatory perspective.

2.2.3 Consultants will seek for evidence and assist the development of:

a) the acquisition of core family mediation skills and knowledge
b) the application of core family mediation skills and knowledge
c) the understanding of family mediation principles and values
d) the ability to cope with a range of family mediation issues
e) professional development
f)   the positive use of consultancy

2.2.4 Consultants will either belong to an approved organisation or otherwise be approved as a Consultant by the College. They will:

a) be Members of the College PPC Register
b) have received approved training in consultancy of family mediation
c) maintain a minimum level of practice consistent with retaining membership of the College PPC Register.

2.2.5 Professional Practice Consultancy **must** consist of:

a) individual consultancy on a one to one basis
b) monitoring by sampling of records kept by the mediator. (Mediators must ensure prior information and notification to clients regarding sampling and that the permission of clients is given and recorded

authorising access to records of the purpose of professional practice consultancy)

2.2.6   The Consultant helps the mediator deal with the following:

a)   Professional mediation practice
b)   Ethics
c)   Procedures

These are primary areas of accountability. The Consultant must assist the mediator in developing an action plan in addressing any of these areas that need attention and must follow up to see how it has been implemented and to review it if necessary.

A crucial area of professional accountability is for the Consultant to identify poor mediation practice and to help remedy it, or for if that fails, report it to the mediator's family mediation organisation.

3.   The requirements for the Professional Practice Consultants' Register

3.1   For *entry* onto the PPC register consultants must:

3.1.1   Be a member of the College;

3.1.2   Be proposed for the Register by an approved organisation or be otherwise approved as a consultant by the College.

3.1.3   Have received approved training in the professional practice consultancy of family mediators.

3.2   for *re-registration* onto the PPC register consultants must meet the requirements for re-registration specified by the College.

<u>GUIDELINES ON THE REQUIREMENTS FOR PROFESSIONAL PRACTICE CONSULTANCY</u>

1   Whilst 1 hour of professional practice consultancy for both Associates and Members must be on an individual, one to one, face to face basis, the remaining hours may be by a range of methods including pair working with the PPC, or group consultation (led by the Professional Practice Consultant) or by direct observation of practice (by the PPC).

2   The range of methods may also include an element of telephone or video conferencing or by other means provided this does not comprise the greater part of the required levels of professional practice consultancy laid down by the

College standard. (Such consultancy must always ensure proper and adequate data protection and protection of client confidentiality) Consultancy by this range of media must not replace the required minimum of one hour of face to face, one to one consultation.

3   Professional practice Consultancy may consist of

   a)   direct observation of mediation practice before recommendation for membership of the register on the basis of competence. (Observation of practice is a particularly valuable means of fulfilling the quality control function of the PPC. It shows directly how the mediator manages the mediation session and allows the quality of management to be assessed. It is a simple and effective way of demonstrating and recording the quality of practice independently and objectively and feed- back can also take place immediately after the session. All the necessary safeguards need to be in place e.g. free and fully informed consent, the suitability of the premises, confidentiality, and the positioning and recording arrangements relating to the observer.)
   b)   group consultancy which must be led by a Professional Practice Consultant is recommended in addition
   c)   consultancy of pair working by a College approved professional practice consultant.
   d)   consumer feedback

4   The Consultant's duties of professional accountability apply for both Associates and Members to the following:

   a)   whatever the mediator discusses or tells the Consultant
   b)   documents (e.g. Memorandum of Understanding) submitted by the mediator to the Consultant. (The Consultant should ensure the clients permission has been given and recorded for access to files, records, and documents pertinent to the mediation.)
   c)   Information established by the Consultant from proactive inquiry of the mediator, which should include some element of file checking or sampling
   d)   any appropriate follow-up enquiries by the Consultant of the mediator.

5   Although the Consultant relies on what the individual mediator tells him or her, the Consultant should also:

   a)   adopt a proactive role in making reasonable and appropriate enquiries of the mediator about the mediator's practice
   b)   where necessary, follow these enquiries through by further enquiry subsequently to ensure continuing good standards of professional mediation practice.
   c)   review the mediator's documents with a careful and critical eye, raise and deal with any issues from same
   d)   ensure that the mediator/s for whom they provide consultation are aware that the Consultant's role is to help and support the mediator's practice, to be a professional resource and to act in a quasi-supervisory fashion to provide assurances for the public that there are quality and other controls over the practice of mediation.

D.   **Mediator Learning Points**[4]

- Patience

- Listening skills

- To see two sides to the dispute.

- Never take at face value the position put by the lawyers.

- Ensure parties have ample opportunity to outline their views on evidence, despite what may appear to be overwhelming evidence to the contrary.

- Importance of breaks.

- Deflect personal questions from family law parties (eg – how many children do you have?).

- Importance of frequent reframing and summaries to encourage progress.

- Ability to manage difficult behaviour.

- To tell parties important things about the legal process without giving legal advice.

- Get in the right frame of mind before mediation.

- Don't despair when interest-based bargaining turns positional – it will!

- Try to have parties focus on preparation.

- Get parties to perform risk analysis.

- Use of pre-mediation session for coaching parties on negotiation.

- Empathy.

- Be less directive.

- Create spreadsheets, cycles etc on whiteboard and notice how the parties focus and contribute more.

- Acknowledge client's emotions.

- Do better and more preparation.

- Congratulate parties with progress made.

- People like to be heard – not rushed.

- What is hidden is often the most important factor in the dispute.

- Don't insist on offers and counter-offers too quickly.

---

4   Reproduced with the kind permission of the Bond Dispute Resolution Centre. A survey of experienced mediators conducted by the Centre in 2005 identified what the mediators had learned over the last year of their practice which had made them better mediators. The full results of the survey are published in (2005) 7(8) *ADR Bulletin* 149.

Appendix 8

Ethical Standards and Accreditation

A Codes of Conduct

(i) Law Society (England and Wales) Code of Practice for Civil/ Commercial Mediation[1]

Annex B – The Law Society Code of Practice for civil and commercial mediation

Introduction

The Law Society requires that all solicitors offering civil/commercial mediation comply with this code. This code is designed to deal with the fundamentals of civil/commercial mediation. It is not intended that it should cover every situation that may arise. The concept of not giving advice to the parties, individually or collectively, when acting as a mediator, permeates this entire code.

Section 1 – Objectives of civil/commercial mediation

Civil/commercial mediation is a process in which:

1.1 two or more parties in dispute;

1.2 whether or not they are legally represented;

1.3 and at any time, whether or not there are or have been legal proceedings;

1.4 agree to the appointment of a neutral third party (the mediator);

1.5 who is impartial;

1.6 who has no authority to make any decisions with regard to their issues;

1.7 which may relate to all or any part of a dispute of a civil or commercial nature;

1.8 but who helps them reach their own decisions;

1.9 by negotiation;

1.10 without adjudication.

---

1   © The Law Society 2009. Reproduced by permission.

605

Commentary

The code is aimed at those undertaking civil/commercial mediations on a commercial basis, although it may be observed equally by those undertaking civil/commercial mediations on a pro bono basis. Whilst the mediation may deal, typically, with the whole of any dispute, the parties may, should they so choose, deal with only one aspect of a dispute, for example, liability or quantum. Whilst the majority of mediations are undertaken by a sole mediator, there may be occasions where two or more mediators co-mediate the dispute. In those circumstances, the solicitor mediator should be aware that the co-mediator may need to comply with his or her own ethical rules and will need to obtain his or her own insurance cover. The mediator must not give legal advice to the parties individually or collectively. The mediator may, however, provide legal information to the parties to assist them in understanding the principles of law applicable to their circumstances and the way in which those principles are generally applied. In the context of the code, adjudication means the formal determination by a third party. It does not preclude the mediator, at his or her discretion and with the consent of the parties, from expressing an opinion or from providing some elements of non-binding evaluation in those models of mediation that are not purely facilitative but also evaluative. The mediator should not, however, advise parties in the sense of asserting what their rights are and recommending how those rights should be translated into settlement terms.

Section 2 – Qualification and appointment of mediator

2.1 Every mediator must comply with the criteria and requirements for mediators stipulated from time to time by the Law Society, including those relating to training, consultancy, accreditation and regulation.

2.2 Save where appointed by or through the court, a mediator may only accept appointment if both or all parties to the mediation so request, or agree.

2.3 Whether a mediator is appointed by the parties or through the court or any other agency, he or she may only continue to act as such so long as both or all parties to the mediation wish him or her to do so. If any party does not wish to continue with the mediation, the mediator must discontinue the process as regards that party and may discontinue the process as regards all parties. Also, if the mediator considers that it would be inappropriate to continue the mediation, the mediator shall bring it to an end, and may, subject to the terms of the mediation agreement, decline to give reasons.

Commentary

This section should be read in conjunction with paragraph 4.1.

Section 3 – Conflicts of interest, confidential information and the impartiality of the mediator

3.1 The impartiality of the mediator is a fundamental principle of mediation.

3.2 Impartiality means that:

3.2.1 the mediator does not have any significant personal interest in the outcome of the mediation;

3.2.2 the mediator will conduct the process fairly and even-handedly, and will not favour any party over another.

3.3 Save as set out in 3.2 above, a mediator with an insignificant personal interest in the outcome of the mediation may act if, and only if, full disclosure is made to all of the parties as soon as it is known, and they consent.

3.4 The mediator must not act, or, having started to do so, continue to act:

3.4.1 in relation to issues on which he or she or a member of his or her firm has at any time acted for any party;

3.4.2 if any circumstances exist which may constitute an actual or potential conflict of interest;

3.4.3 if the mediator or a member of his or her firm has acted for any of the parties in issues not relating to the mediation, unless that has been disclosed to the parties as soon as it is known, and they consent.

3.5 Where a mediator has acted as such in relation to a dispute, neither he or she nor any member of his or her firm may act subsequently for any party in relation to the subject matter of the mediation.

Commentary

Whilst impartiality is fundamental to the role of the mediator, this does not mean that a mediator may never express a comment or view that one party may find more acceptable than another. However, the mediator must not allow his or her personal view of the fairness or otherwise of the substance of the negotiations between the parties to damage or impair his or her impartiality. The mediator must appreciate that his or her involvement in the process is inevitably likely to affect the course of the negotiations between the parties. (His or her involvement is, of course, intended to assist that process so far as possible.) This would be the case whether the mediator intervenes directly or whether he or she deals with issues indirectly, for example, through questions. Consequently all mediator intervention needs to be conducted with sensitivity and care in order to maintain impartiality. There may be circumstances where the mediator may have some personal interest in the outcome of the mediation (for example, he or she has a very small shareholding in a company which is a party to the mediation). In those circumstances, and where the mediator feels able to act impartially, he or she must disclose full details of his or her interest to the parties immediately, inviting them to decide whether or not the mediator should continue to act. The mediator should decline to act if he or she feels he or she will be prejudiced (for example, he or she knows one of the parties socially), or in circumstances where either party may perceive there to be a prejudice. It is important not only that the mediator should be neutral, but also that he or she should be perceived by the parties to be so. The mediator must therefore take particular care to avoid conflicts of interest, whether actual or potential, real or perceived.

Whilst a mediator may not undertake cases in respect of which his or her firm has already provided legal advice to one of the parties, the mediator would not be precluded from acting as such in respect of unrelated issues involving a party for whom his or her firm has previously acted, provided that, before undertaking the mediation, the mediator discloses this fact to the parties and the parties consent to the mediation. It is usual in mediation for the parties to agree that the mediator should treat as confidential information which he or she acquires during the course of private meetings; almost invariably such information will be relevant to the dispute and it is unlikely that it will give rise to a conflict situation as described in Rule 3.06 of the Solicitors Code of Conduct).

However, if either:

■ the mediator acquires confidential information relevant to the dispute or to any of the parties involved in the mediation from another source (for example, from another client, partner, colleague or firm), whether before or during the mediation, or

■ the mediator acquires confidential information relevant to another client of his or her firm, during the mediation a conflict of interest as defined in Rule 3 of the Solicitors Code of Conduct would exist, necessitating the mediator's withdrawal from the mediation.

If the mediator is in any doubt on any possible conflict of interest or confidentiality point, the mediator should contact Professional Ethics for further advice.

Section 4 – Mediation procedures

4.1 The mediator must ensure that the parties agree the terms and conditions regulating the mediation before dealing with the substantive issues. This should be in a written agreement which should reflect the main principles of this code. Such agreement should also contain the terms of remuneration of the mediator.

4.2 The procedure for the conduct of the mediation is a matter for the decision of the mediator. Insofar as the mediator establishes an agenda of matters to be covered in the mediation, the mediator should be guided by the needs, wishes and priorities of the parties in doing so.

4.3 In establishing any procedures for the conduct of the mediation, the mediator must be guided by a commitment to procedural fairness and a high quality of process.

Commentary

This section should be read with section 5 and its commentary. The mediator is the manager of the process and should manage the mediation, at his or her discretion, with the object of meeting as best as possible the wishes of the parties. The mediator and the parties should agree, as far as practicable, at the outset whether the mediator's role will be purely facilitative, or whether the mediator may at his or her discretion, provide an evaluative element based on his or her knowledge of the subject matter or legal issues involved. The role of the mediator, whether facilitative or evaluative, may change during the course of the mediation by agreement of the parties.

Section 5 – The decision-making process

5.1 The primary aim of mediation is to help the parties to arrive at their own decisions regarding the disputed issues.

5.2 The parties should be helped to reach such resolution of such issues which they feel are appropriate to their particular circumstances. Such resolution may not necessarily be the same as that which may be arrived at in the event of adjudication by the court. That allows the parties to explore and agree upon a wider range of options for settlement than might otherwise be the case.

5.3 The mediator may meet the parties individually and/or together. Solicitors, barristers or other professional advisers acting for the individual parties may, but need not necessarily, participate in the mediation process if the parties so wish. Such solicitors and/or advisers may take part in discussions and meetings, with or without the parties, and in any other communication and representation, in such manner as the mediator may consider useful and appropriate.

5.4 Parties are free to consult with their individual professional advisers as the mediation progresses. The mediator may make suggestions to the parties as to the appropriateness of seeking further assistance from professional advisers such as lawyers, accountants, expert valuers or others.

5.5 The mediator must not seek to impose his or her preferred outcome on the parties.

5.6 The mediator shall be free to make management decisions with regard to the conduct of the mediation process.

5.7 The mediator may suggest possible solutions and help the parties to explore these, where he or she thinks that this would be helpful to them.

5.8 The mediator must recognise that the parties can reach decisions on any issue at any stage of a mediation.

5.9 Agreements reached in mediation fall into three categories:

5.9.1   non-binding agreements;

5.9.2   binding agreements (which would be enforceable by a court);

5.9.3   binding agreements enshrined in a court or arbitration order.

The mediator should ascertain how the parties wish their agreement to be treated. Where the parties do not wish to have a legally binding solution (for example, where they have resolved personal rather than legal issues), their wishes should be respected.

5.10 At the end of the mediation or at any interim stage, the mediator and/or the parties or their representatives may prepare a written memorandum or summary of any agreements reached by the parties, which may, where considered by the mediator to be appropriate, comprise draft heads of such agreements for formalisation by the legal advisers acting for the parties.

5.11 If the parties wish to consult their respective individual legal advisers before entering into any binding agreement, then any terms which they may provisionally propose as the basis for resolution will not be binding on them until they have each had an opportunity of taking advice from such advisers and have thereafter agreed, in writing, to be bound.

5.12 Mediation does not provide for the disclosure and inspection of documents in the same way or to the same extent as required by court rules. The parties may voluntarily agree to provide such documentation, or any lesser form of disclosure considered by them to be sufficient. This should be considered in advance of the mediation. The mediator may indicate any particular documents that he or she considers should be brought to the mediation.

5.13 The mediator may assist the parties, so far as appropriate and practicable, to identify what information and documents will help the resolution of any issue(s), and how best such information and documents may be obtained. However, the mediator has no obligation to make independent enquiries or undertake verification in relation to any information or documents sought or provided in the mediation.

5.14 If, in cases where one or more parties is unrepresented at the mediation and the parties are proposing a resolution which appears to the mediator to be unconscionable, having regard to the circumstances, then the mediator must inform the parties accordingly and may terminate the mediation and/or refer the parties to their legal advisers.

Commentary

The mediator is the manager of the process. It is important that, where possible, a flexible approach is adopted by the mediator. He or she may suggest the introduction into the process of professional, technical, and/or business advisers to the parties to assist in such a manner as agreed between the parties. It is for the parties to decide whether they wish to be represented in mediation, but for the mediator to decide how the process is managed. Some mediation organisations suggest that, at the request of the parties and with his or her consent, the mediator may provide a non-binding written recommendation on terms of settlement. This is rarely used and then, usually, as a last resort at the end of the mediation. This would not be precluded by paragraph 5.5. Whenever possible, the mediator should consider with the parties, in advance of the mediation, what documents should be made available and, where appropriate, how verification in relation to documents or information sought, should be obtained. It must be recognised, however, that there will be circumstances where this is not possible in advance of the meeting, in which circumstances, in the interests of fairness, consideration should be given to adjourning the mediation for further enquiries or for such verification to be obtained. It is quite common and proper in the context of mediation for the parties to disclose information and documents on a confidential basis to the mediator only. This section should be read in conjunction with section 7 which deals with the confidentiality and privilege surrounding mediation. Whilst the mediator must permit the parties, if they so wish, to adjourn a mediation to seek advice from their professional advisers once a resolution has been proposed and agreed in principle, caution should be exercised in recommending this, since this may have the effect of losing the momentum of the mediation and, in some cases, the resolution proposed. The mediator is concerned with fairness of process.

The mediator cannot be responsible for issues of justice and fairness of outcome; the parties must define their own 'fairness' of the substantive terms and criteria for agreeing terms. However, the mediator must be able to dissociate him or herself from the proposed resolutions in certain extreme circumstances, as indicated in paragraph 5.14. When deciding whether to terminate the mediation pursuant to paragraph 5.14, them mediator must consider all of the circumstances of the dispute and the mediation process itself. It is important to distinguish those who are represented at the mediation from those who are not; in the former situation, the mediator is entitled to rely on the fact that the party has reached a decision based on legal advice given to him or her by his or her legal representative and should not seek to look behind that decision; in the latter case, in extreme circumstances, the mediator must be able to distance him or herself from the resolution proposed. In those circumstances, the mediator may wish to suggest that the parties seek legal advice before proceeding further in the mediation.

Section 6 – Dealing with power imbalances

6.1 The mediator should be alive to power imbalances existing between the parties. If such imbalances seem likely to cause the mediation process to become unfair or ineffective, the mediator must take reasonable steps to try to prevent this.

6.2 The mediator must seek, in particular, to prevent abusive or intimidating behaviour by any of the parties.

6.3 If the mediator believes that, because of power imbalances, the mediation would not be able to be fairly and effectively conducted, he or she may discuss this with the parties, recognising that the mediation may have to be brought to an end and/or the parties referred to their lawyers.

Commentary

Power imbalances will almost inevitably exist and will shift during the course of a mediation. The mediator cannot be responsible for redressing those imbalances. He or she must, however, seek to ensure that these do not cause the process to become ineffective as a result of the abuse of one party's stronger position. The likelihood of abuse occurring will diminish where the parties are legally represented in the mediation.

Section 7 – Confidentiality and privilege

7.1 Before the mediation commences, the parties should agree in writing as to the provisions concerning confidentiality and privilege that will apply to the mediation process itself and any resultant mediation agreement, save as otherwise agreed in the mediation settlement agreement.

7.2 The mediator must maintain confidentiality in relation to all matters dealt with in the mediation. The mediator may disclose:

7.2.1   matters which the parties and the mediator agree may be disclosed;

7.2.2   matters which are already public;

7.2.3   matters which the mediator considers appropriate where he or she believes that the life or safety of any person is or may be at serious risk;

7.2.4   matters where the law imposes an overriding obligation of disclosure on the Mediator.

In any such event the mediator should, where appropriate, try to agree with the party furnishing such information as to how disclosure shall be made.

7.3 Subject to paragraph 7.2 above, where the mediator meets the parties separately and obtains information from any party which is confidential to that party, the mediator must maintain the confidentiality of that information from all other parties, except to the extent that the mediator has been authorised to disclose any such information.

7.4 Mediators should note that the mediation privilege will not ordinarily apply in relation to communications indicating that any person is suffering or likely to suffer serious bodily harm, or where other public policy considerations prevail, or where for any other reason, the rules of evidence render privilege inapplicable.

7.5 The mediator should remind the parties that (unless the mediation agreement provides otherwise) the confidentiality and privilege attaching to the mediation process may not extend to the provisions of any settlement agreement which results. The mediator should suggest to the parties that they consider the extent to which they wish the terms of the resulting settlement to be disclosable – and to provide accordingly in the agreement itself.

Commentary

Prior to commencement of mediation, the mediator should obtain agreement from the parties that no party should be permitted to refer, in any proceedings that may subsequently take place, to any such privileged discussions and negotiations, or require the mediator to do so; nor should any party have access to any of the mediator's notes, or call any mediator as a witness in any proceedings, save where the parties agree that this is not appropriate. The mediator should remind the parties that (unless the mediation agreement provides otherwise) the confidentiality and privilege attaching to the mediation process may not extend to the provisions of any settlement agreement which results. The mediator should suggest to the parties that they consider the extent to which they wish the terms of the resulting settlement to be disclosable, bearing in mind that they may have some overriding obligation of disclosure to a third party – and to provide accordingly in the agreement itself.

There are circumstances in which, even though the parties do not co-operate, there is an overriding duty of disclosure. In these circumstances general public policy prevails and the duty of disclosure would apply to all mediators, not merely solicitors. Mediators must have regard to the circumstances when confidentiality may be overridden, as set out in Rule 3 of the Solicitors Code of Conduct 2007. If in doubt, mediators should contact Professional Ethics. Ordinarily, the mediator should suggest to the parties that they expressly agree that all discussions and negotiations during the mediation will be regarded as evidentially privileged and conducted on a 'without prejudice' basis.

Section 8 – Professional indemnity cover

8.1 All solicitor mediators must carry professional indemnity cover in respect of their acting as mediators.

8.1.1 Solicitors who practise as mediators will be covered by the Solicitors' Indemnity Fund in respect of their acting as a mediator, provided they are doing so in their capacity as a member of their firm.

8.1.2 If a solicitor is acting as a mediator as a separate activity outside his or her legal practice, separate indemnity insurance must be obtained.

Commentary

Solicitors who mediate outside their practices as members of mediation organisations may be covered by block insurance provided by those organisations. If not, they must make their own arrangements for appropriate cover. A solicitor practising as a mediator outside his or her legal practice must have regard to rule 21 of the Solicitors' Code of Conduct 2007.

Section 9 – Promotion of mediation

9.1 Solicitor mediators may promote their practice as such, but must always do so in a professional, truthful and dignified way. They may reflect their qualification as a mediator and their membership of any other relevant mediation organisation.

9.2 Solicitor mediators must comply with Rule 7 of the Solicitors Code of Conduct.

(ii) Law Society (England and Wales) Code of Practice for Family Mediation2

Members of the Law Society's Family Mediation Accreditation Scheme must agree to be bound by this code.

Introduction

The Solicitors Code of Conduct July 2007 contains the general principles and rules regarding solicitors' practice, including alternative dispute resolution.

This code is designed to deal with the fundamentals of family mediation. It is not intended that it should cover every situation that may arise.

The concept of not giving advice to the parties, individually or collectively, when acting as a mediator permeates this entire code.

---

2   © The Law Society 2009. Reproduced by permission.

Section 1 – objectives of family mediation

Family mediation is a process in which:

1.1   a couple or any other family members

1.2   whether or not they are legally represented

1.3   and at any time, whether or not there are or have been legal proceedings

1.4   agree to the appointment of a neutral third party (the mediator)

1.5   who is impartial

1.6   who has no authority to make any decisions with regard to their issues

1.7   which may relate to separation, divorce, children's issues, property and financial questions or any other issues they may raise

1.8   but who helps them reach their own informed decisions

1.9   by negotiation

1.10 without adjudication.

Section 2 – qualifications and appointment of mediator

2.1   Every mediator shall have regard to the criteria and requirements for mediators stipulated from time to time by the Law Society, including those relating to training, consultancy, accreditation and regulation.

2.2   Save where appointed by or through the court, a mediator may only accept appointment if both or all parties to the mediation so request, or agree.

2.3   Whether a mediator is appointed by the parties or through the court or any other agency, he or she may only continue to act as such so long as both or all parties to the mediation wish him or her to do so. If any party does not wish to continue with the mediation, the mediator must discontinue the process. Also, if the mediator considers that it would be inappropriate to continue the mediation, the mediator shall bring it to an end, and may decline to give reasons.

Section 3 – conflicts of interest and impartiality of mediator

3.1   The impartiality of the mediator is a fundamental principle of mediation.

3.2   Impartiality means that:

3.2.1   the mediator does not have any significant personal interest in the outcome of the mediation

3.2.2   a mediator with any personal interest in the outcome of the mediation may act if, and only if, full disclosure is made to all of the parties as soon as it is known and they consent

3.2.3   the mediator will conduct the process fairly and even-handedly, and will not favour any party over another.

3.3   The mediator must not act or, having started to do so, continue to act:

3.3.1   in relation to issues on which he or she or a member of his or her firm has at any time acted for any party

    3.3.2   if any circumstances exist which may constitute an actual or potential conflict of interest

    3.3.3   if the mediator or a member of his or her firm has acted for any of the parties in issues not relating to the mediation, unless that has been disclosed to the parties as soon as it is known and they consent.

3.4 Where a mediator has acted as such in relation to a dispute, neither he nor she nor any member of his or her firm may act for any party in relation to the subject matter of the mediation.

Section 4 – mediation procedures

4.1 The mediator must ensure that the parties agree the terms and conditions regulating the mediation before dealing with the substantive issues. This should ordinarily be in a written agreement which should reflect the main principles of this code. Such agreement should also contain the terms of remuneration of the mediator.

4.2 The procedure for the conduct of the mediation is a matter for the decision of the mediator. Insofar as the mediator establishes an agenda of matters to be covered in the mediation, the mediator should be guided by the needs, wishes and priorities of the parties in doing so.

4.3 In establishing any procedures for the conduct of the mediation, the mediator must be guided by a commitment to procedural fairness, the fostering of mutual respect between the parties and a high quality of process.

Section 5 – the decision-making process

5.1   The primary aim of family mediation is to help the parties to arrive at their own decisions regarding their issues, on an informed basis with an understanding, so far as reasonably practicable, of the implications and consequences of such decisions for themselves and any children concerned.

5.2   The parties may reach decisions on any issue at any stage of the mediation.

5.3   Subject to paragraph 5.4, decisions arrived at in family mediation should not be binding on the parties until they have had the opportunity to seek advice on those decisions from their own legal representatives.

5.4   The parties must be offered the opportunity to obtain legal advice before any decision can be turned into a binding agreement on any issue which appears to the mediator or to either party to be of significance to the position of one or both parties.

5.5   The mediator must not seek to impose his or her preferred outcome on the parties and should try to avoid becoming personally identified with any particular outcome.

5.6   The mediator shall, however, be free to make management decisions with regard to the conduct of the mediation process, and may suggest possible solutions and help the parties to explore these, where he or she thinks that this would be helpful to them.

5.7   The mediator should assist the parties, so far as appropriate and practicable, to identify what information and documents would help the resolution of any issue(s), and how best such information and documents may be obtained.

However, the mediator has no obligation to make independent enquiries or undertake verification in relation to any information or documents sought or provided in the mediation. If necessary, consideration may be given in the mediation to the ways in which the parties may make such enquiries or obtain such verification.

5.8 Family mediation does not provide for the disclosure and discovery of documents in the same way or to the same extent as required by court rules. The mediator may indicate any particular documents that he or she considers each party should furnish.

5.9 Parties should be helped to reach such resolution of such issues which they feel are appropriate to their particular circumstances. Such resolutions may not necessarily be the same as those which may be arrived at in the event of an adjudication by the court.

5.10 The mediator should, if practicable, inform the parties if he or she considers that the resolutions which they are considering are likely to fall outside the parameters which a court might approve or order. If they nevertheless wish to proceed with such resolutions, they may do so. In these circumstances the mediation summary may identify any specific questions on which the mediator has indicated a need for independent legal advice. If, however, the parties are proposing a resolution which appears to the mediator to be unconscionable or fundamentally inappropriate, then the mediator should inform the parties accordingly and may terminate the mediation, and/or refer the parties to their legal advisers.

5.11 Parties may consult with their own solicitors as the mediation progresses, and shall be given the opportunity to do so before reaching any binding agreement on their substantive issues. Where appropriate, the mediator may assist the parties to consider the desirability of their jointly or individually seeking further assistance during the course of the mediation process from professional advisers such as lawyers, accountants, expert valuers or others, or from counsellors or therapists. The mediator may also assist the parties by providing relevant lists of names.

5.12 Mediation meetings are commonly conducted without lawyers present. However, solicitors or counsel acting for the individual parties may be invited to participate in the mediation process, and in any communications, in such manner as the mediator may consider useful and appropriate, and as the parties may agree.

Section 6 – dealing with power imbalances

6.1 The mediator should be alive to the likelihood of power imbalances existing between the parties. These may relate to various different aspects including, for example, behaviour which is controlling, abusive or manipulative, finance; children and family, status, communication and other skills, possession of information, the withholding of cooperation, and many other kinds of power.

6.2 If power imbalances seem likely to cause the mediation process to become unfair or ineffective, the mediator must take appropriate steps to try to prevent this.

6.3 The mediator must ensure that the parties take part in mediation willingly and without fear of violence or harm. Additionally, the mediator must seek to prevent manipulative, threatening or intimidating behaviour by either party.

6.4 If the mediator believes that power imbalances cannot be redressed adequately and that in consequence the mediation will not be able to be fairly and effectively conducted, he or she may discuss this with the parties, but in any event must bring the mediation to an end as soon as practicable.

Section 7 – confidentiality and privilege

7.1 The mediator must maintain confidentiality in relation to all matters dealt with in the mediation. The mediator may disclose:

7.1.1   matters which the parties and the mediator agree may be disclosed

7.1.2   matters which the mediator considers appropriate where he or she believes that any child or any other person affected by the mediation is suffering or likely to suffer significant harm (and in such case, the mediator should, so far as practicable and appropriate, discuss with the parties the way in which such disclosure is to take place), or

7.1.3   matters where the law imposes an overriding obligation of disclosure on the mediator.

7.2 Any information or correspondence provided by any party should be shared openly with both and not withheld, except any address or telephone number and except as the parties may otherwise agree.

7.3 All information material to financial issues must be provided on an open basis, so that it can be referred to in court, either in support of an application made with the consent of the parties or in contested proceedings.

7.4 However, discussions about possible terms of settlement should be conducted on the 'without prejudice' basis; and in any event a mediation privilege should ordinarily be claimed for them, so that parties may explore their options freely.

7.5 The mediator must discuss arrangements about confidentiality with the parties before holding separate meetings or caucuses. It may be agreed that the mediator will either:

7.5.1   report back to the parties as to the substance of the separate meetings, or

7.5.2   maintain separate confidences: provided that if separate confidences are to be maintained, they must not include any material fact which would be open if discussed in a joint meeting.

7.6 The mediation privilege will not ordinarily apply in relation to communications indicating that a child or other person affected by the mediation is suffering, or likely to suffer, significant harm, or where other public policy considerations prevail, or where for any other reason the rules of evidence render privilege inapplicable.

Section 8 – families and children

8.1   Mediators shall have regard at all times to the provisions of Part I of the Family Law Act 1996.

8.2 In working with the parties, the mediator should also have regard to the needs and interests of the children of the family.

8.2.1   When it appears to the mediator that a child is suffering, or is likely to suffer, significant harm, the mediator should consider with the parties what steps should be taken outside mediation to remedy the situation. But in exceptional circumstances where there is serious risk of harm to any person the mediator may decide not to inform the parties.

8.2.2   Where it is necessary to protect the child from significant harm, the mediator must in any event contact an appropriate agency or take such steps outside the mediation as may be appropriate.

8.3 Occasionally children might be directly involved in mediation. The mediator should consider whether and when children may be directly involved in mediation. The mediator should not ordinarily invite children to be directly involved in the mediation unless specifically trained to do so and alive to the issues such as confidentiality and the dynamics inherent in doing so.

Section 9 – professional indemnity cover

9.1 All solicitor mediators must carry professional indemnity cover in respect of their acting as mediators.

9.1.1   Solicitors who practise as mediators will be covered by appropriate indemnity insurance in respect of their acting as a mediator, provided they are doing so in their capacity as a member of their firm.

9.1.2   f a solicitor is acting as a mediator as a separate activity outside his or her legal practice, separate indemnity insurance must be obtained.

Section 10 – promotion of mediation

10.1 Solicitor mediators may promote their practice as such, but must always do so in a professional, truthful and dignified way. They may reflect their qualification as a mediator and their membership of any other relevant mediation organisation.

10.2 Solicitor mediators should have regard to the requirements in relation to publicity, as stipulated in the Solicitors Code of Conduct, rule 7.

Section 11 – Family Law Act 1996, section 27 (Legal Aid Act 1988, section 13b)

Every mediator must have arrangements designed to ensure:

11.1 that parties participate in mediation only if willing and not influenced by fears of violence or other harm

11.2   that cases where either party may be influenced by fears of violence or other harm are identified as soon as possible

11.3   that the possibility of reconciliation is kept under review throughout mediation, and

11.4 that each party is informed about the availability of independent legal advice.

(iii) CEDR Solve Code of Conduct for Neutrals[3]

April 2008

1 Introduction

This Code of Conduct ('the Code') applies to any person who acts as a Mediator or other neutral third party ('the Neutral') in any dispute resolution procedure ('the Process') conducted under the auspices of the Centre for Effective Dispute Resolution ('CEDR Solve') in relation to an attempt to resolve a dispute or difference ('the Dispute') between all the parties ('the Parties') to the Dispute under the terms of a written agreement signed by the Parties the Neutral and CEDR Solve ('the Process Agreement') to seek resolution of the Dispute.

2 Competence and availability

The Neutral assures the Parties that he or she:

2.1 possesses the necessary competence and knowledge about the Process to deal with the Dispute, based on proper training and updating of education and practice in the necessary skills; and

2.2 has sufficient time to prepare properly for and conduct the Process expeditiously and efficiently.

3 Fees and expenses

The Neutral undertakes:

3.1 to make clear either directly to the Parties or through CEDR Solve the basis for charging fees and expenses as between CEDR Solve and the Parties for the conduct of the Process before the Process starts; and

3.2 not to prolong the Process unnecessarily where there is, in the Neutral's opinion, no reasonable likelihood of progress being made towards settlement of the Dispute through the Process.

4 Independence and neutrality

The Neutral:

4.1 will at all times act, and endeavour to be seen to act fairly, independently and with complete impartiality towards the Parties in the Process, without any bias in favour of, or discrimination against, any of the Parties;

4.2 will ensure that the Parties and their representatives all have adequate opportunities to be involved in the Process;

---

3   Reproduced with the kind permission of CEDR. Please visit www.cedr.com to check for latest version of this document as these documents are updated and existing versions can become out of date.

4.3 will disclose to the Parties any matter of which the Neutral is or at any time becomes aware which could be regarded as being or creating a conflict of interest (whether apparent, potential or real) in relation to the Dispute or any of the Parties involved in the Process, and, having done so, will not act or continue to act as Neutral in relation to the Dispute unless the Parties specifically acknowledge such disclosure and agree to the Neutral's continuing to act in the Process: such matters include but are not limited to:

- any personal or business relationship with any of the Parties;

- any financial or other interest in the outcome of the Mediation;

- having acted (either personally or through the Neutral's own firm or business) in any capacity other than as a Neutral in another Process for any of the Parties;

- being in prior possession of any confidential information about any of the Parties or about the subject-matter of the Dispute (but excluding any confidential information given to the Neutral by one of the Parties while acting as Neutral in relation to the Dispute);

- any such matters involving a close member of the Neutral's family.

4.4 will not (nor will any member of the Neutral's own firm or business or close family) act for any of the Parties individually in relation to the Dispute either while acting as Neutral or at any time thereafter, without the written consent of all the Parties.

5 Conduct of the Process

The Neutral will observe all the terms of the Process Agreement (especially as regards confidentiality) and will conduct the Process consistent with any relevant CEDR Model Procedure.

6 Professional Indemnity Insurance

The Neutral will take out professional indemnity insurance in an adequate amount with a responsible insurer against such risks as may arise in the performance of the Neutral's duties in relation to the Dispute before acting as a Neutral.

7 Withdrawing from any Process

7.1 The Neutral will withdraw from the Process and cease to act as such in relation to the Dispute if the Neutral:

- is requested to do so by one of the Parties, except where the Parties have agreed to a procedure involving a binding decision by the Neutral to conclude the Mediation;

- would be in breach of the Code if continuing to act as the Neutral; or

- is required by one or more of the Parties to act or refrain from acting in a

- way which would be in material breach of the Code or in breach of the law.

7.2 The Neutral may withdraw from the Process at the Neutral's own discretion and after such consultation with the Parties as the Neutral deems necessary and appropriate (and always subject to the Neutral's obligations as to confidentiality) if:

- any of the Parties is acting in material breach of the Process Agreement;

- any of the Parties is acting in an unconscionable or criminal manner;

- the Neutral decides that continuing the Process is unlikely to result in a settlement;

- any of the Parties alleges that the Neutral is in material breach of the Code.

8 Complaints

The Neutral will respond to, and co-operate with, any complaints procedure initiated by a party through CEDR Solve in relation to the Process in which the Neutral acted, including attending (without charging a fee or claiming any expenses for attending) any meeting convened by CEDR Solve as part of that complaints procedure.

(iv) CORE Solutions Group Code of Conduct for Mediators [4]

1. Introduction

All Mediators appointed by Core Mediation shall comply with this Code and with the terms of the agreement between the parties to take part in mediation (the Agreement to Mediate).

2. Competence and Appointment of the Mediator

2.1 The Mediator shall be competent and knowledgeable in the process of mediation. The Mediator shall have undertaken proper training and shall undertake continuous education and practice in mediation skills.

2.2 The Mediator shall satisfy himself or herself as to his or her competence to conduct mediation before accepting appointment as a mediator and, upon request, shall disclose information concerning his or her background and experience to the parties.

3. Conflict of Interest and Impartiality

3.1 The Mediator shall be independent of any party to the dispute or difference, shall have no interest in the outcome and shall at all times act courteously, impartially and fairly, without discriminating on any grounds.

---

4   This document is reproduced with permission from the Guide to Mediation Services published by Core Solutions Group. Core Solutions Group is Scotland's pre-eminent provider of mediation services to business, organisations and the professions in Scotland (www.core-solutions.com).

3.2 In the event of the Mediator becoming aware of a conflict of interest or possible conflict of interest of any kind or of any circumstances occurring which give rise to reasonable doubts about the Mediator's impartiality or independence, the Mediator shall immediately disclose this to all the parties in writing. The Mediator shall then only continue to act if all the parties to the dispute acknowledge the disclosure and agree in writing to the Mediator continuing to act as Mediator and if the Mediator is satisfied that he or she may properly do so.

3.3 An individual shall not be appointed as Mediator in a dispute or other difference if a firm or company with whom the individual is connected has acted in any capacity for any of the parties in the dispute or difference in connection with that dispute or difference.

3.4 The Mediator shall not act in any capacity for any of the parties in connection with the dispute or difference which is the subject of mediation. The Mediator will not accept an appointment in relation to any arbitral or judicial proceedings relating to the dispute or difference.

4. The Role of the Mediator and the Mediation Process

4.1 The Mediator shall prepare adequately for the mediation, including reading the parties' summaries and any supporting documents.

4.2 The Mediator shall satisfy himself or herself that the parties understand the characteristics of the mediation process and the role of the Mediator and the parties in it.

4.3 The Mediator shall ensure, prior to commencement of mediation, that the parties have understood and expressly agreed the terms and conditions of the Agreement to Mediate, including in particular obligations of confidentiality imposed on the Mediator and on the parties. The Agreement to Mediate shall, unless agreed otherwise, be drawn up in writing. The Mediator shall ensure that the Agreement to Mediate is signed by all participating in the mediation, unless the parties agree otherwise.

4.4 The Mediator shall ensure that the parties are aware that they may withdraw from mediation at any time without giving any reason.

4.5 The Mediator shall conduct the proceedings in an appropriate manner, taking into account all the circumstances of the matter, including the wishes, needs and priorities of the parties. The parties shall be free to agree with the Mediator, by reference to a set of rules or otherwise, on the manner in which mediation is to be conducted.

4.6 The Mediator shall ensure that all parties have adequate opportunities to be involved in the process. The Mediator, in discussion with the parties, may at any time elect to meet the parties and/or their advisers separately or together.

4.7 The Mediator shall take all appropriate steps to ensure that the parties understand the terms of any agreement reached by them.

4.8 The Mediator may, upon request of the parties and within the limits of his or her competence, inform the parties as to how they may formalise and enforce any agreement they reach.

4.9 Subject to the exception which follows, the Mediator shall not decide or give an opinion on the factual or legal issues in the dispute or difference. In exceptional circumstances, the parties may ask the Mediator to express a view or to make non-binding written recommendations on the resolution of the dispute or difference. The Mediator shall not be obliged to comply with such a request or any other request to vary his or her role as independent facilitator of the process of mediation. The Mediator may do so if the Mediator considers that he or she is competent to do so and that to do so would assist in the resolution of the dispute or difference.

5. Withdrawal of Mediator

The Mediator shall withdraw from mediation if requested to do so by any of the parties, or if the Mediator considers that it is necessary to do so. In particular, the Mediator may withdraw from mediation at the Mediator's own discretion, without giving any reason, if the Mediator considers that a) any of the parties is acting or has acted in breach of the Agreement to Mediate or in an improper, illegal or criminal manner, (b) the Mediator is required to do so by law, or (c) continuing mediation is unlikely to result in resolution.

6. Confidentiality

The Mediator shall keep confidential and not disclose to any third party for any purpose:

(a) the fact that mediation may take place, is to take place or has taken place between the parties;

(b) any information given to the Mediator, whether orally or in writing, at any stage in mediation, including that given by parties in confidence. (All papers submitted by parties to the Mediator and notes made by the mediator will be destroyed as soon as possible and not later than 8 weeks after the mediation process concludes);

(c) the Resolution Agreement (if any) arising out of mediation;

   unless:

   (i)   the parties consent to disclosure;

   (ii)   disclosure is necessary to implement and enforce the Resolution Agreement;

   (iii) the Mediator is required by law to make disclosure or report to an appropriate authority;

   (iv)   the Mediator reasonably considers that there is serious risk of significant harm to the life or safety of any person if the Mediator does not make such a disclosure;

   (v)   the Mediator requires assistance in confidence from any senior officer of Core Mediation on any ethical or other serious question arising out of mediation;

(vi)   the Mediator is engaged on a confidential basis in Core Mediation's process of reviewing the performance of, and maintaining professional standards among, its mediators.

(vii)   any action is brought by a party against Core Mediation or the Mediator in relation to the mediation and disclosure is necessary for them to defend the action.

7. Fees

Unless otherwise agreed, Core Mediation shall agree with the parties, before the commencement of the mediation process, the fees and expenses which will be charged for mediation or, alternatively, the basis on which fees and expenses will be charged.

Core Mediation will collect fees and expenses from the parties and reimburse the mediator.

8. Insurance

Prior to conducting mediation, the Mediator shall take out professional indemnity insurance in an adequate amount with a responsible insurer.

9. Advertising and Solicitation

Advertising and any other communication with the public concerning the services offered or regarding the education, training and expertise of the mediator shall be honest and professional.

(v) College of Mediators Code of Practice for Mediators[5]

1 DEFINITIONS

1.1 This Code of Practice applies to all mediation conducted or offered by mediators who are standard or recognised members of the College of Mediators.

1.2 Mediation is a process in which an impartial third person assists those involved in conflict to communicate better with one another and reach their own agreed and informed decisions concerning some, or all, of the issues in dispute.

1.3 This Code applies whether or not there are or have been legal proceedings between any of the participants and whether or not any, or all of them, are legally represented.

---

5   This document is reproduced with the kind permission of the College of Mediators. The College website is a regularly updated source of information and resources so for the most up to date material please visit www.collegeofmediators.co.uk.

1.4 In this Code, 'mediation' means the mediation to which this Code applies. 'Mediator' means any person offering such mediation. 'Participant' means any individual taking part in it. The 'College' means the 'College of Mediators'.

2 AIMS AND OBJECTIVES

2.1 Mediation aims to assist participants to reach the decisions which they consider appropriate to their own particular circumstances.

2.2 Mediation also aims to assist participants to communicate with one another now and in the future and to reduce the scope or intensity of dispute and conflict.

2.3 Mediators should have regard to the ethics of mediation in that it should be carried out in a way that:

- minimises distress to the participants and any others involved;
- promotes as good a relationship between the participants and any others involved as possible;
- removes or diminishes any risk of abuse to any of the participants or others involved, and
- avoids unnecessary cost to the participants.

In relation to family mediation

2.4 By virtue of the Children (Scotland) Act 1995, family mediators in Scotland are required to have regard to the principles contained in Part 1 of that Act on Parental Responsibilities and Rights.

2.5 By virtue of the Family Law Act 1996, family mediators in England and Wales are required to have regard to the general principles set out in section 1 of that Act when exercising functions under or in consequence of it.

2.6 By virtue of the Children (Northern Ireland) Order 1995, family mediators in Northern Ireland are required to have regard to the general principles contained in Part 2, Article 3 regarding the paramountcy of a child's welfare and Article 5 regarding Parental Responsibility.

3 SCOPE OF MEDIATION

3.1 Mediation may cover any issue in dispute which the parties have freely agreed it would be helpful to resolve and which the mediator considers suitable for mediation.

4 GENERAL PRINCIPLES

4.1 Voluntary Participation

Participation in mediation is always voluntary. Any participant or mediator is free to withdraw at any time. If a mediator believes that any participant is unable or unwilling to participate freely and fully in the process, the mediator may raise the issue with the participants and may suspend or terminate mediation. The mediator may suggest that the participants obtain such other professional services as are appropriate.

4.2 Neutrality

Mediators must at all times remain neutral as to the outcome of mediation. They must not seek to move the participants towards an outcome which the mediator prefers, whether by attempting to predict the outcome of court or formal proceedings or otherwise.

There is an expectation that mediators will help participants to identify and explore the options available to them and the feasibility of those options. This may involve giving initial information in a neutral way, which participants may research further outside of the mediation process.

4.3 Impartiality

4.3.1 Mediators must at all times remain impartial as between the participants. They must conduct the process in a fair and even-handed way.

4.3.2 Mediators must seek to prevent manipulative, threatening or intimidating behaviour by any participant. Mediators must conduct the process in such a way as to redress, as far as possible, any imbalance in power between the participants. If any behaviour seems likely to render mediation unfair or ineffective, the mediator must take appropriate steps to prevent this, terminating mediation if necessary.

4.4 Independence and Conflicts of Interest

4.4.1 Mediators must not have any personal interest in the outcome of the mediation.

4.4.2 Mediators must not mediate in any case in which they have acquired or may acquire relevant information in any private or other professional capacity.

4.4.3 Mediators who have acquired information in the capacity of mediator in any particular case must not act for any participant in any professional or other capacity in relation to the subject matter of the mediation.

4.4.4 Mediators must distinguish their roles as mediators from any other professional role in which they may act and must make sure that they make this clear to the parties.

4.5 Confidentiality

4.5.1 Subject to paragraphs 4.5.3 mediators must not disclose any information about, or obtained in the course of a mediation to anyone, without the express consent of each participant.

4.5.2 Mediators must not discuss or correspond with any participant's legal adviser without the express consent of each participant. Where both participants have legal advisers, nothing must be said or written to the legal adviser of one, which is not also said or written to the legal adviser of the other(s), unless at the specific request of both participants.

4.5.3 Where a mediator suspects that a person is in danger of significant harm, or it appears necessary so that a specific allegation that a child has suffered significant harm may be properly investigated, mediators must ensure that the relevant authority is notified.

4.5.4 Where a mediator becomes aware of any criminal activity, the knowledge of which would be classified as collusion in a crime, the mediator must terminate the mediation. If the crime involves the risk of significant harm the mediator must ensure that the relevant authority is notified.

In relation to workplace mediation:

4.5.5 Where a mediator becomes aware of any breach of organisational policy which might be classified as gross misconduct, the mediator must terminate the mediation. Where the breach is significant the mediator must ensure that those with relevant authority are notified.

4.6 Privilege and Legal Proceedings

4.6.1 Subject to paragraphs 4.6.2, all discussions and negotiations in mediation must be conducted on a legally privileged basis. Participants must agree that discussions and negotiations in mediation are not to be referred to in any legal or other formal proceedings, and that the mediator cannot be required to give evidence or produce any notes or recordings made in the course of the mediation, unless all participants agree to waive the privilege or the law imposes an overriding obligation upon the mediator.

In relation to family mediation

4.6.2 Participants must, however, agree that any factual disclosure made with a view to resolving any issue relating to their property or finances may be disclosed in legal proceedings.

4.7 Welfare of Children

4.7.1 Where it appears to a mediator that any child is suffering or likely to suffer significant harm, the mediator must advise participants to seek help from the appropriate agency. The mediator must also advise participants that whether or not they seek that help, the mediator will be obliged to report the matter in accordance with paragraph 4.5.3.

4.7.2 Where it appears to a mediator that the participants are acting or proposing to act in a manner likely to be seriously detrimental to the welfare of any child the mediator may withdraw from mediation. The reason for doing so must be outlined in any summary which may be available to any participants' legal advisers or relevant authority as described in paragraph 4.5.3.

In relation to mediation concerning children:

4.7.3 Mediators have a special concern for the welfare of all children of the family. They must encourage participants to focus upon the needs of the children as well as upon their own and must explore the situation from the child's point of view.

4.7.4 Mediators must encourage the participants to consider children's own wishes and feelings. Where appropriate, they may discuss with the participants whether and to what extent it is proper to involve the children themselves in the mediation process in order to consult them about their wishes and feelings.

4.7.5 If, in a particular case, the mediator and participants agree that it is appropriate to consult any child directly in mediation, the mediator should be trained for that purpose, must obtain the child's consent and must provide appropriate facilities.

4.8 Abuse, Bullying and Harassment

4.8.1 In all cases, mediators must seek to discover through a screening procedure whether or not there is fear of abuse or any other harm and whether or not it is alleged that any participant has been or is likely to be abusive towards another. Where abuse is alleged or suspected mediators must discuss whether any participant wishes to take part in mediation and information about available support services should be provided.

4.8.2 Where mediation does take place, mediators must uphold throughout the principles of voluntariness of participation, fairness and safety and must conduct the process in accordance with this section. In addition, steps must be taken to ensure the safety of all participants on arrival and departure.

5 QUALIFICATIONS AND TRAINING

5.1 Mediators must have successfully completed such training as is approved by the College to qualify them to mediate upon those matters upon which they offer mediation.

5.2 Mediators must be a standard or recognised member of the College. They must therefore have successfully demonstrated personal aptitude for mediation through an approved training and subsequent experience (standard member) and of specific experience and competence to mediate (recognised member).

5.3 Mediators must satisfy the College that they have made satisfactory arrangements for regular professional practice consultancy or supervision in relation to their mediation practice with a supervisor or consultant who is a member of, or who has been approved by, the College. The current requirements are listed in Appendix A.

5.4 Mediators must agree to maintain and improve their skills through the acquisition of a set number of continuing professional development points each year. The current requirements are listed in Appendix A.

5.5 Mediators must not mediate upon any case unless they are covered by professional indemnity insurance.

5.6 Mediators must abide by the complaints and disciplinary procedures and the ethical and equality requirements as laid down by the College.

5.7 Mediators who are members of the College must adhere to this Code of Practice.

6 CONDUCT OF MEDIATION

6.1 Participants must be clearly advised at the outset of the nature and purpose of mediation and of how it differs from other services. Each participant must be supplied with written information covering the main points and given an opportunity to ask questions about it.

6.2 The terms upon which mediation is to be undertaken should be agreed in advance. Where an agreement is in writing, such agreement must include the basis upon which any fees are to be charged and should, if practicable, indicate the anticipated length of the mediation. Where participants are legally advised, they must be advised to notify any legal advisers acting for them of the appointment of a mediator.

6.3 Mediators must assist participants to define the issues, identify areas of agreement, clarify areas of disagreement, explore the options and seek to reach agreement upon them.

6.4 Mediators must seek to ensure that participants make decisions with sufficient information and knowledge. They must inform participants of the need to give full and frank disclosure of all material relevant to the issue(s) being mediated and to assist them where necessary in identifying the relevant information and requesting any supporting documentation.

6.5 Mediators must not guarantee that any communication from one participant will be kept secret from the other(s), except that they may always agree not to disclose one participant's address or telephone number to the other(s). They may see participants separately, if both agree, but if any relevant information emerges which one participant is not willing to have disclosed to the other(s), mediators must consider whether or not it is appropriate to continue with mediation.

6.6 Mediators must ensure that each participant is given the opportunity to make further enquiries about the information disclosed by any other participant and to seek further information and documentation when required. Mediators must promote the participants' equal understanding of such information before any final agreement is reached

6.7 Mediators must make it clear that they do not themselves make further enquires to verify the information provided by any participant; that each participant may seek independent legal advice as to the adequacy of the information disclosed before reaching a decision and that in any court or formal proceedings a sworn affidavit, written statement or oral evidence may be required.

6.8 Mediators must, where appropriate, inform participants of the benefits of seeking the expertise of other relevant professionals.

6.9 Mediators must inform participants about the court or other formal proceedings which are available and the procedures applicable to these. They must not give legal or other advice. They must not predict the outcome of court or formal proceedings in such a way as to indicate or influence the participants towards the outcome preferred by the mediators.

6.10 Mediators must inform participants of the advantages of seeking independent legal advice whenever this appears desirable during the course of a mediation.

6.11 Whenever appropriate or requested by the participants, mediators must prepare a written summary of the factual outcome of the mediation.

6.12 Mediators must ensure that agreements reached by participants are fully informed and freely made. Participants must have as good an understanding as is practicable of the consequences of their decisions for themselves and relevant others.

In relation to family mediation:

6.13 The terms upon which mediation is to be undertaken should, preferably, be in writing and must be in writing where finance and property issues are involved.

6.14 Participants must be informed of the extent of the disclosure which will be required, particularly in cases relating to their property and finances, of the nature and limits of the principles of confidentiality and privilege and of the family mediators' special concern for the welfare of the children of the family.

6.15 Family mediators must keep the possibility of reconciliation under review throughout the mediation.

6.16 Where finance and property issues are involved participants must be informed of the nature and extent of the financial disclosure which would be required; the nature and finality of the court orders which might be made; and the broad principles of law applicable to the matter in dispute.

6.17 Family mediators must advise participants that it is desirable and in their own interests to seek independent legal advice before reaching any final agreement and warn them of the risks and disadvantages if they decide not to do so.

APPENDIX A

SUPERVISION AND CONTINUING PROFESSIONAL DEVELOPMENT REQUIREMENTS AS AT DECEMBER 2008

Family mediators

Professional Practice Consultancy

Standard and recognised members must have had a minimum of two hours one-to-one professional practice consultancy in the year to application. This must be with a professional practice consultant who is a member of, or approved by, the College.

Continuing professional development

Standard and recognised members must have gained at least 10 continuing professional development (CPD) points in the year to application. At least five of these must be gained through attending training with an approved CPD provider[1] (category A) and the balance may be through PPC approved self directed learning[2] (category B).

Workplace mediators

Professional Practice Consultancy/supervision

Standard and recognised members must have had a minimum of two hours one-to-one practice consultancy/supervision in the year to application. Whilst formal mechanisms for College recognition of non-family practice consultants/supervisors are being developed the College's requirement for PPCs/supervisors in non-family mediation are at least three years experience in mediation and continued supervised mediation practice.

Continuing professional development

Whilst the College is developing CPD recognition structures for workplace mediation standard and recognised members should be able to demonstrate that they have undertaken at least 10 hours ongoing training each year which may include attendance on courses or self directed learning[2].

Community mediators

Supervision

Standard and recognised members must have had a minimum of two hours one-to-one practice consultancy/supervision in the year to application. Whilst formal mechanisms for College recognition of non-family practice consultants/supervisors are being developed the College's requirement for PPCs/supervisors in non-family mediation are at least three years experience in mediation and continued supervised mediation practice.

Continuing professional development

Whilst the College is developing CPD recognition structures for community mediation standard and recognised members should be able to demonstrate that they have undertaken at least 10 hours ongoing training each year which may include attendance on courses or self directed learning[2].

Notes:
1.   Details of the College CPD scheme are available on the website. To register as an approved CPD provider please contact the College.
2.   Self directed learning includes training with non-College approved providers, group practice review/ supervision, relevant academic study, self directed reading, relevant project work.

(vi) Civil Mediation Council – Draft Code of Good Practice for Mediators 2009

Introduction

i. This is the Civil Mediation Council (CMC)'s Code of Good Practice for Mediators 2009 ('the Code') which is designed to supplement the CMC Registered Mediator Scheme ('the Scheme'). The Code has been developed in cooperation with the Ministry of Justice, the Department for Business Enterprise and Regulatory Reform, the ADR Committee of the Civil Justice Council, the legal professions, as well as the CMC Board Members.

(ii. The 2009 Code of Good Practice was adopted by the CMC's EGM on DTBC 2009 and come into force on DTBC 2009.)[6]

iii. The Code will be reviewed annually by the CMC in the light of its research programme, consultation, and feedback. Suggestions for amendments and additions are welcomed from users and practitioners and should be sent to the CMC Secretary (secretary@civilmediation.org).

Code of Good Practice for Mediators

A Mediator who follows Good Practice will:

(1)   Accept appointments only when they have sufficient time to prepare for, conduct, and if necessary, follow up the mediation.

(2)   Conduct mediations under the principle of party self-determination, by facilitation.

(3)   Conduct mediations impartially as between participants and as regards outcome.

---

6   The EGM resolved that further consultation should take place on this draft.

(4)   Before (and if necessary during) mediation disclose any actual or potential conflicts of interest which could reasonably be seen to affect the mediator's impartiality.

(5)   Explain the process to the participants before the mediation begins including how information disclosed to the mediator in private sessions (caucus) will be treated.

(6)   Ensure that all mediations are conducted under a signed Mediation Agreement.

(7)   Maintain the confidentiality of all communications made to the mediator by those involved in the mediation process, unless otherwise agreed to by them or required by law, and promote understanding among the participants regarding the extent to which they shall maintain confidentiality of information obtained in mediation.

(8)   Ensure that confidentiality is maintained in the storage before mediation and disposal after mediation of mediation records, notes, and files.

(9)   Not be influenced by a desire to maintain or increase their personal settlement rate.

(10) Not knowingly misrepresent any facts or matter in the course of mediation.

(11) Have an efficient system of personal practice administration.

(12) Have access to an effective complaints resolution system.

(13) Have effective arrangements for ensuring mentoring and/or peer review and an effective system for obtaining and reviewing feedback.

(14) Be insured to cover errors, omissions, and negligence: the CMC recommends a minimum of £1 million of such insurance or a higher level as appropriate.

(15) Be sensitive to diversity, equality, and anti-discrimination issues.

(16) Follow a published Code of Conduct.

(17) When sufficiently experienced, and where the parties willingly permit, offer opportunities to newly-trained mediators to observe his/her mediations.

(vii) NMI (Netherlands) Code of Conduct[7]

Code of Conduct for NMI registered Mediators

Where reference is made in this Code of Conduct to the term 'Rules', this shall mean the NMI Mediation Rules. The terms used in this Code of Conduct are in conformity with those used in the NMI Mediation Rules.

Article 1 – General

1.   Mediators shall at all times conduct themselves in a manner that is not prejudicial to confidence in the NMI and in Mediation as a process for resolving disputes.

2.   Mediators shall abide by the Rules.

---

7   Reproduced with the kind permission of the Nederlands Mediation Instituut – NMI. For further information please visit www.nmi-mediation.nl.

Article 2 – Independence and impartiality

1. Mediators shall not accept an appointment if they have any direct or indirect personal interest in the outcome of the Mediation.

2. Mediators shall refrain from acting in a dispute in which they have previously advised any of the Parties. The foregoing shall not apply if the Mediator has made his position clear to all the Parties and the Parties nevertheless request him to act as Mediator.

3. Mediators have the responsibility to clearly inform all the Parties of the existence of any relationship that they or any of their associates or partners have or have had with any of the Parties.

4. Mediators shall withdraw from the Mediation if in their opinion the Code of Conduct and/or the Rules are not or cannot be observed.

5. In the performance of their duties Mediators shall not be guided by any interests beyond those relating to the Mediation.

6. Mediators shall act with complete independence and impartiality. Mediators shall not express their views on a dispute or any part thereof except upon the explicit joint request thereto of the Parties.

Article 3 – Mediation Agreement

Prior to the commencement of the Mediation Mediators shall enter into a Mediation Agreement with all the Parties and explain to them the Mediation process, the contents of the Mediation Agreement and the Rules.

Article 4 – Mediation process

1. Mediators shall conduct the Mediation with the necessary speed.

2. Mediators shall request the Parties to provide such information as may be necessary for sound decision-making.

3. Mediators shall ensure a balanced handling of the Dispute and shall insofar as possible see to it that the Parties are given equal opportunity to participate in the Mediation.

Article 5 – Confidentiality

1. Mediators shall not involve any third party in the Mediation and shall not disclose any information to any third party, except with the consent of the Parties.

2. Mediators shall impose an obligation of confidentiality in writing upon any third party they may involve in or inform concerning the Mediation.

Article 6 – Fees

1. Mediators shall make an agreement with the Parties concerning their fees and shall record such agreement in the Mediation Agreement.

2.   Mediators shall determine their fees solely on an hourly basis and irrespective of the outcome of the Mediation.

3.   Mediators shall present a clearly itemized bill of costs showing the work done and the relevant fee structure. Mediators shall keep a record of their activities and produce such record upon request.

4.   Mediators may make the commencement or progress of their work conditional upon the Parties furnishing security for the payment of their bills of costs.

Article 7 – Collegiality

1.   When taking over a Mediation from another Mediator Mediators must inform their predecessors concerning this.

2.   If a Mediator is replaced, the new Mediator shall not commence work until the bills of costs of his predecessor and any Auxiliary Persons involved up to that time have been paid in full.

3.   Such Mediator may nevertheless commence work once he has received written permission from the Board of the NMI.

4.   If a Mediator is replaced by another Mediator, the former shall have the duty, if so requested by the Parties, to fully inform his successor, with the exception of information furnished in the course of Separate Talks, unless in respect of such information it was agreed that it could be disclosed to the other Party.

Article 8 – Disciplinary rules

Mediators shall be subject to disciplinary rules in accordance with the Rules of the Foundation 'Stichting Tuchtrechtspraak Mediators' in force in respect of Mediators.

(viii) Cepani (Belgium) Rules of Good Conduct[8]

III. 2.1.d.1. Rules of good conduct

1. The Chairman and Secretary-General of CEPANI, their associates and employees, shall not participate in any proceedings conducted under the CEPANI rules, either as an arbitrator, chairman of the mini-trial committee, mediator, expert, third person appointed to adapt contracts, or counsel.

2. In accepting his appointment by CEPANI, the arbitrator, chairman of the mini-trial committee, mediator, expert or third person shall agree to apply strictly the CEPANI rules and to collaborate loyally with the Secretariat. He shall regularly inform the Secretariat of his work in progress.

3. The prospective arbitrator, chairman of the mini-trial committee, mediator, expert or third person shall accept his appointment only if he is independent of the parties and of their counsel. If any event should subsequently occur that is likely to

---

8   Reproduced with the kind permission of CEPANI. For further information on CEPANI and their documents please visit www.cepani.be.

call into question this independence in his own mind or in the minds of the parties, he shall immediately inform the Secretariat which will then inform the parties. After having considered the parties' comments, the Appointments Committee or the Chairman of CEPANI shall decide on his possible replacement. It or he shall make the decision alone and shall not disclose the reasons.

4. An arbitrator appointed upon the proposal of one of the parties shall neither represent nor act as that party's agent.

5. Once nominated by CEPANI, the arbitrator appointed upon the proposal of a party undertakes to have no further relation with that party, nor with its counsel, in the course of the arbitration. Any contact with this party shall take place through the chairman of the arbitral tribunal or with his explicit permission.

6. In the course of the arbitration proceedings, the arbitrator, chairman of the mini-trial committee, mediator, expert or third person shall, in all circumstances, show the utmost impartiality, and shall refrain from any deeds or words that might be perceived by a party as bias, especially when asking questions at the hearings.

7. If the circumstances so permit, the arbitrator may, with due regard to paragraph 6 here above, ask the parties to seek an amicable settlement and, with the explicit permission of the Secretariat and of the parties, to suspend the proceedings for whatever period of time is necessary.

8. By accepting his appointment by CEPANI, the arbitrator undertakes to ensure that the Award is rendered as diligently as possible. This means, namely, that he shall request an extension of the time limit, provided by the CEPANI Rules, only if necessary or with the explicit agreement of the parties.

9. The arbitrator, chairman of the mini-trial committee, mediator, expert or third person shall obey the rules of strict confidentiality in each case attributed to him by the Secretariat.

10. Awards may only be published anonymously and with the explicit approval of the parties. The Secretariat shall be informed thereof beforehand.

11. The signature of the Award by a member of an Arbitral Tribunal of three arbitrators does not imply that that arbitrator agrees with the content of the award.

(ix) IMI (International Mediation Institute) Code of Professional Conduct[9]

IMI CODE OF PROFESSIONAL CONDUCT

Those who trust to chance, must abide by the results of chance

President John Calvin Coolidge

Trust underpins the mediation process. If the parties do not trust a mediator's integrity in terms of competence diligence, neutrality, independence, impartiality, fairness and the ability to respect confidences, mediation is unlikely to succeed.

The IMI Code of Professional Conduct ('the Code') provides users of mediation services with a concise statement of the ethical standards they can expect from Mediators who choose to adopt its terms and sets standards that they can be expected to meet.

Users who believe the standards established in this Code have not been met may activate the *IMI Professional Conduct Assessment Process.*

IMI Certified Mediators are required to make known to users which code of conduct governs their professional mediation practice. They are not required to select this Code provided they have subscribed to a code, and that they indicate this to users.

DEFINITIONS

For the purposes of this Code, Mediation is defined as a process where two or more parties appoint a third-party neutral ('Mediator') to help them in a non-binding dialog to resolve a dispute and/or to conclude the terms of an agreement.

An IMI Certified Mediator (also called a Mediator in this Code) is one:

- whose competency in the practice of mediation has been certified by IMI, and

- who is authorized by IMI to use IMI's name and logo, and

- whose Profile is included on the IMI web portal at: www.IMImediation.org.

1. MEDIATOR APPOINTMENT

1.1   Entitlement to use the title 'IMI Certified Mediator' and the IMI logo

In the event that an IMI Certified Mediator fails to maintain IMI's requirements for certification, or no longer qualifies as an IMI Certified Mediator, use of the title IMI Certified Mediator and use of IMI's name and logo will end, and the Mediator's Profile will no longer be included on the IMI web portal.

---

9   Reproduced with the kind permission of the International Mediation Institute (IMI). For further information and to download IMI documents free of charge please visit www.IMImediation.org.

1.2 Promotion of Mediators' services

Subject to applicable laws and to regulations governing professional practice, Mediators will present and promote their practice in a truthful way. They may quote freely from, and link to, their Profile on the IMI web portal and they are free to replicate that Profile, or extracts from it, for their own professional purposes.

1.3 Appointment

Before the mediation begins, Mediators will advise the parties (eg by way of directing them to the Mediator's Profile on the IMI web portal, or in the mediation agreement):

- about their relevant background and experience

- which code of conduct the Mediator will observe

- which process will apply in the unlikely event of a party believing the Mediator has not met the standards of the stated code of conduct

- that at the end of the process they will be invited to offer written feedback on the process and on the Mediator's role, and

- whether they hold a current professional indemnity liability insurance policy covering their professional practice as a Mediator.

2.   DILIGENCE, INDEPENDENCE, NEUTRALITY, IMPARTIALITY

2.1   Diligence

Mediators may accept an assignment to act as Mediator in any situation where they feel competent to serve in that capacity.

2.2 Independence, Neutrality and Impartiality

2.2.1 Mediators will not accept an appointment without first disclosing anything within their knowledge that may, or may be seen to, materially affect their independence neutrality or impartiality. This duty to disclose is a continuing obligation throughout the mediation process.

2.2.2 The existence of circumstances potentially affecting, or appearing to affect, a Mediator's independence, neutrality or impartiality will not automatically imply unfitness to act as a mediator provided these circumstances have been fully disclosed and addressed to the satisfaction of the parties and the Mediator.

2.2.3 Mediators will always act in an independent, neutral and impartial way. They shall act in an unbiased manner, treating all parties with fairness, quality and respect. If at any time a Mediator feels unable to conduct the process in an independent, neutral and impartial manner, (s)he will express that concern and will offer to withdraw from the mediation. Such circumstances include:

- financial or personal interests in the outcome of the mediation

638

- existing past or future financial, business or professional relationship with any of the parties or their representatives about which the Mediator is aware.

- other potential source of bias or prejudice concerning a person or institution which may affect that Mediator's independence, neutrality or impartiality or reasonably create an appearance of partiality or bias.

2.3 Conflicts of Interest

2.3.1   Mediators will conduct reasonable inquiries to determine if any interests, conflicts of interests or potential biases may exist. They will have a continuing duty to disclose any interests, conflicts of interests or potential biases that may become apparent during the mediation process.

2.3.2   Following any such disclosures, a Mediator will decline to participate as a mediator in a particular case if any of the parties raises an objection, unless a contract or applicable law or Court Order nevertheless requires the Mediator's participation. Even then, if a Mediator personally believes that the matters disclosed would inhibit their actual impartiality, the Mediator should withdraw as the mediator.

2.3.3   After accepting appointment, and until the mediation process ends, Mediators will not enter into financial, business, professional, family or social relationships or acquire financial or personal interests that are likely to affect or might reasonably create the appearance of conflict of interest, partiality or bias, without making a prior disclosure to all the parties and gaining their consent.

2.3.4   Within 12 months following the end of a mediation, Mediators will not represent in an advisory capacity any party to a mediation in the same or a substantially related matter, unless all parties to the mediation expressly consent to that representation after full disclosure. Acting as a neutral in other dispute resolution proceedings (eg as a mediator or arbitrator) that may involve some or all of the parties will not be considered a *representation in an advisory capacity* for the purposes of this clause.

2.3.5   At no time following the end of a mediation will Mediators adduce evidence or testify on behalf of one of the parties in making or defending a claim against another party to the same mediation where they have acquired confidential information from the other party, unless all that information is no longer confidential or unless the party protected by the confidentiality gives consent.

3.   MEDIATION PROCESS

3.1   Procedure

Mediators will satisfy themselves that the parties to the mediation and their advisers understand the characteristics of the mediation process, their roles as parties and advisers, and the role of a mediator. The Mediator will ensure that before the mediation begins, the parties have understood and agreed the terms and conditions which will govern the mediation including those relating to obligations of confidentiality on the Mediator and on the parties. It is best practice for those terms to be contained in a written Mediation Agreement unless the parties or the circumstances dictate otherwise.

3.2 Fairness and Integrity of the process

3.2.1   Mediators will explain the mediation process to the parties and their advisers, and be satisfied that that they consent to the process being used and to the Mediator selected (unless applicable law, court rules or contract require use of a particular process and/or mediator). Mediators will ensure that, if there are to be any pre-mediation private communications with the Mediator, all parties are aware they will have equal opportunity to raise issues.

3.2.2   Mediators will conduct the process with fairness to all parties and will take particular care to ensure that all parties have adequate opportunities to be heard, to be involved in the process and to have the opportunity to seek and obtain legal or other counsel before finalizing any resolution.

3.2.3   Mediators will take reasonable steps to prevent any misconduct that might invalidate an agreement reached at a mediation or create or aggravate a hostile environment. Mediators will also be satisfied that the parties have reached agreement of their own volition and knowingly consent to any resolution.

3.3 Termination of the process

3.3.1   The Mediator will ensure the parties understand that they may withdraw from the mediation at any time by informing the Mediator and all other parties without being required to give any justification for doing so.

3.3.2   Mediators may withdraw from a mediation if a negotiation among the parties assumes a character that to the Mediator appears unconscionable or illegal.

3.4 Feedback

Unless inappropriate in the circumstances, Mediators will, at the conclusion of a mediation, invite the parties and advisers and any co-mediators or assistant mediators, to complete an IMI Feedback Request Form and return it to the Reviewer indicated by the Mediator in his/her IMI Profile to assist in the preparation of the Mediator's Feedback Digest.

3.5 Fees

3.5.1   Mediators will, before accepting appointment, agree with the parties how their fees and expenses will be calculated, and how they will be paid by the parties (and if shared between the parties, in what proportions). Mediators who withdraw from a case will return to the parties any fees already paid relating to the period following withdrawal.

3.5.2   Mediators will not suggest to the parties that their remuneration should be based on or related to the outcome of the mediation.

4. CONFIDENTIALITY

4.1.1   Mediators will keep confidential all information acquired in the course of serving as a mediator in a mediation unless:

- compelled to make a disclosure by law, by a Court of Law or by some governmental agency having appropriate authority and jurisdiction or

- required under paragraph 5.1, in which event the recipients of the confidential information shall themselves be bound to maintain the confidentiality, or

- the specific information comes into the public domain (otherwise than as a result of a disclosure by the Mediator), or

- the parties release the Mediator from the confidentiality restriction, or

- necessary to defend the Mediator from any proceedings or charges for which (s)he risks incurring any liability.

4.1.2   The Mediator may, however, disclose having previously served as a mediator in a mediation involving one or more of the parties, provided none of the details of that case are disclosed.

4.2   Mediators will discuss confidentiality with the parties before or at the beginning of the mediation and obtain their consent to any communication or practice by the Mediator that involves the disclosure of confidential information.

4.3   Mediators may use or disclose confidential information obtained during a mediation when, and to the extent that, they believe it to be necessary to prevent death or serious physical harm or damage from arising or believe an illegal act may realistically arise. Before using or disclosing such information, if not otherwise required to be disclosed by law, Mediators must, if they consider it appropriate, make a good faith effort to persuade the party and/or the party's counsel or other advisers, to act in such a way that would remedy the situation.

5.   Professional Conduct Issues and Complaints

5.1   An IMI Certified Mediator may consult his/her *Reviewer* about any professional or ethical dilemmas.

5.2   Where an IMI Certified Mediator is subject to the Code, a party to a mediation who believes there has been a lack of compliance with this Code may activate the *IMI Professional Conduct Assessment process.*

Adherence to this Code does not replace or qualify any legislation or rules regulating individual professions or any more extensive rules of conduct which may apply in specific circumstances

This Code of Professional Conduct may be adopted by any IMI Certified Mediator irrespective of nationality or professional background. This Code is inspired by and based on:
  (1) The Model Rule for the Lawyer as a Third Party Neutral of the CPR-Georgetown Commission on Ethics & Standards in ADR (2002)
  (2) Code of Conduct for Mediators of the UIA Forum of Mediation Centres (2003)
  (3) European Code of Conduct for Mediators of the European Commission (2004)
  (4) Model Standards of Conduct for Mediators (2005) adopted by AAA, ABA and ACR
  (5) Ethical Guidelines for Mediators of the Law Council of Australia (2006)
  (6) JAMS Mediators Ethical Guidelines
  (7) The Guidelines for the appointment of mediators, confidentiality and termination of the Chartered Institute of Arbitrators.

(x) EU Code of Conduct[10]

EUROPEAN CODE OF CONDUCT FOR MEDIATORS

This code of conduct sets out a number of principles to which individual mediators can voluntarily decide to commit, under their own responsibility. It may be used by mediators involved in all kinds of mediation in civil and commercial matters.

Organisations providing mediation services may also make such a commitment, by asking mediators acting under the auspices of their organisation to respect the code of conduct. Organisations may make available information on the measures, such as training, evaluation and monitoring, they are taking to support the respect of the code by individual mediators.

For the purposes of the code of conduct, mediation is defined as any structured process, however named or referred to, whereby two or more parties to a dispute attempt by themselves, on a voluntary basis, to reach an agreement on the settlement of their dispute with the assistance of a third person – hereinafter 'the mediator'.

Adherence to the code of conduct is without prejudice to national legislation or rules regulating individual professions.

Organisations providing mediation services may wish to develop more detailed codes adapted to their specific context or the types of mediation services they offer, as well as to specific areas such as family mediation or consumer mediation.

European Code of Conduct for Mediators

1. COMPETENCE, APPOINTMENT AND FEES OF MEDIATORS AND PROMOTION OF THEIR SERVICES

1.1 Competence

Mediators must be competent and knowledgeable in the process of mediation. Relevant factors shall include proper training and continuous updating of their education and practice in mediation skills, having regard to any relevant standards or accreditation schemes.

1.2 Appointment

Mediators must confer with the parties regarding suitable dates on which the mediation may take place. Mediators must verify that they have the appropriate background and competence to conduct the mediation in a given case before accepting the appointment. Upon request, they must disclose information concerning their background and experience to the parties.

---

10   *Source*: European Code of Conduct for Mediators, ec.europa.eu, © European Communities, 1995–2009.

1.3 Fees

Where not already provided, mediators must always supply the parties with complete information as to the mode of remuneration which they intend to apply. They must not agree to act in a mediation before the principles of their remuneration have been accepted by all parties concerned.

1.4 Promotion of mediators' services

Mediators may promote their practice provided that they do so in a professional, truthful and dignified way.

2. INDEPENDENCE AND IMPARTIALITY

2.1 Independence

If there are any circumstances that may, or may be seen to, affect a mediator's independence or give rise to a conflict of interests, the mediator must disclose those circumstances to the parties before acting or continuing to act.

Such circumstances shall include

– any personal or business relationship with one or more of the parties,

– any financial or other interest, direct or indirect, in the outcome of the mediation;

– the mediator, or a member of his firm, having acted in any capacity other than mediator for one or more of the parties.

In such cases the mediator may only agree to act or continue to act if he is certain of being able to carry out the mediation in full independence in order to ensure complete impartiality and the parties explicitly consent.

The duty to disclose is a continuing obligation throughout the process of mediation.

2.2 Impartiality

The mediator must at all times act, and endeavour to be seen to act, with impartiality towards the parties and be committed to serve all parties equally with respect to the process of mediation.

3. THE MEDIATION AGREEMENT, PROCESS AND SETTLEMENT

3.1 Procedure

The mediator must ensure that the parties to the mediation understand the characteristics of the mediation process and the role of the mediator and the parties in it.

The mediator must in particular ensure that prior to commencement of the mediation the parties have understood and expressly agreed the terms and conditions of the mediation agreement including any applicable provisions relating to obligations of confidentiality on the mediator and on the parties.

The mediation agreement may, upon request of the parties, be drawn up in writing.

The mediator must conduct the proceedings in an appropriate manner, taking into account the circumstances of the case, including possible imbalances of power and any wishes the parties may express, the rule of law and the need for a prompt settlement of the dispute. The parties may agree with the mediator on the manner in which the mediation is to be conducted, by reference to a set of rules or otherwise.

The mediator may hear the parties separately, if he deems it useful.

3.2 Fairness of the process

The mediator must ensure that all parties have adequate opportunities to be involved in the process.

The mediator must inform the parties, and may terminate the mediation, if:

- a settlement is being reached that for the mediator appears unenforceable or illegal, having regard to the circumstances of the case and the competence of the mediator for making such an assessment, or

- the mediator considers that continuing the mediation is unlikely to result in a settlement.

3.3 The end of the process

The mediator shall take all appropriate measures to ensure that any agreement is reached by all parties through knowing and informed consent, and that all parties understand the terms of the agreement.

The parties may withdraw from the mediation at any time without giving any justification.

The mediator must, upon request of the parties and within the limits of his competence, inform the parties as to how they may formalise the agreement and the possibilities for making the agreement enforceable.

4. CONFIDENTIALITY

The mediator must keep confidential all information, arising out of or in connection with the mediation, including the fact that the mediation is to take place or has taken place, unless compelled by law or grounds of public policy to disclose it. Any information disclosed in confidence to mediators by one of the parties must not be disclosed to the other parties without permission, unless compelled by law.

B   Accreditation Schemes

(i)   CEDR Accreditation[11]

1.1 Become a mediator

Our <u>Mediator Skills Training</u> is a five-day programme of comprehensive tuition in mediation skills. Participants are trained in the skills required for effective mediation of commercial disputes and assessed for CEDR Accreditation, the international benchmark of mediation excellence.

On the final two days of the five-day course participants are rigorously assessed by <u>CEDR faculty members</u>, themselves practising mediators, and around 70 per cent achieve accreditation.

What you will learn

Under the expert guidance of leading mediator trainers you will learn how to:

- settle disputes effectively – in days rather than months saving vital management time

- add value to commercial disputes – by finding commercial solutions to commercial problems

- manage the mediation process and facilitate advanced negotiation

- advise others on the features and uses of other effective dispute resolution techniques

- transform the way you communicate.

No specific qualifications or experience are needed to undertake the Mediator Skills Training course and participants from a variety of professions and backgrounds attend the open courses.

Accreditation

As a developing field, there are no statutory qualifications required to mediate. However, the market dictates that most mediators who get work have some form of accreditation. CEDR is widely acknowledged as the leading commercial mediation trainer, although there are others. CEDR was the first to establish a <u>Continuing Professional Development scheme</u> for mediators. Other organisations specialise in family and community mediation.

Achieving accreditation is no guarantee of receiving work as a mediator. Mediation is no different from any other emerging profession in that there is no fast track or guaranteed route to securing work. Persistence and dedication are important traits of practising mediators and successful mediators tend to spend a good deal of time developing the market before they receive referrals in that market.

---

11   Reproduced with the kind permission of CEDR. Please visit www.cedr.com to check for latest version of this document as these documents are updated and existing versions can become out of date.

Accredited mediators are eligible to participate in CEDR's Continuing Professional Development (CPD) scheme, which provides a framework for individual development and operates through The CEDR Exchange, a network for individuals. Mediators achieving CEDR accreditation are recognised in the UK and internationally as offering a service of quality and integrity.

Mediation providers and associations of mediators

Once a mediator is accredited, mediator appointments can come from linking up with a mediation provider or association of mediators. There are a number of regional mediator groups and associations.

CEDR accreditation is widely recognised by other mediation providers.

CEDR Solve mediators

Accreditation with CEDR is no guarantee of mediation appointments from CEDR Solve. Where practicable, CEDR Solve offers clients the services of an assistant mediator. Participants in CEDR's CPD scheme may be invited to continue their development through experience by undertaking an assistant mediator appointment. All mediators, both assistant and lead mediators go through a rigorous system of performance monitoring that includes client and peer feedback.

Mediations referred to CEDR Solve, CEDR's dispute resolution service, are conducted by a group of mediators selected for their outstanding ability. This ability will have initially been demonstrated during assistant mediator appointments or by some other verifiable track record of excellence.

Client satisfaction is of primary concern at CEDR Solve and therefore feedback is sought after every mediation. Mediators must consistently receive positive feedback if they are to continue to work on CEDR Solve mediations and they are also expected to maintain an ongoing level of continuing professional training and development.

(ii) ADR Group Accreditation[12]

This 40-hour programme provides detailed and comprehensive tuition for professionals seeking to acquire core mediation skills. Completing and passing ADRg's Civil and Commercial Mediator Foundation Programme will enable you to become a fully accredited mediator meeting European standards in mediation.

Becoming a mediator

Commercial mediation is a well established profession in the US and is becoming ever more popular here in the UK. Training to become a mediator enables both individuals and companies to offer an enhanced range of dispute resolution services, with the majority of mediators practising mediation as part of a portfolio career.

---

12   Reproduced with the kind permission of the ADR Group. For further information please visit their website at www.adrgroup.com.

Benefits of training with ADRg

Aligning yourself to the right organisation is key. As the longest running dispute resolution company in the UK, ADRg has developed an enviable reputation for professionalism, diversity and quality.

Quality assurance

One of the founding members of the Civil Mediation Council, ADR Group has earned a reputation of excellence in the field of mediation. With ISO 9002 accreditation and ongoing quality review processes, we are widely acknowledged as one of two leading providers of professional mediator training and development in the UK.

Proven results

ADR Group is accredited by the Civil Mediation Council and all our training programmes are approved by the Law Society of England and Wales and the Bar Council. Our courses have continually evolved in association with distinguished experts to ensure that they reflect the latest thinking and practice in the field of alternative dispute resolution.

Time efficient

Our foundation programme is organised to be complete and effective, with minimal disruption to your working schedule by requiring only three days of intensive training.

Prestigious accreditation

Following successful completion of the course, you will be awarded with the title of an ADR Group Accredited Mediator, with recognition from the Law Society and the Bar Council of England and Wales.

Opportunity to practice mediation through ADR Net

Once accredited, delegates have the opportunity to join ADR Net and participate in ADR Group mediation referrals. To become an ADR Net panel mediator, members are required to undertake additional observation assessments.

ADR Net membership

ADR Net is a nationwide panel of accredited mediators. Unlike other ADR companies, all commercial mediations introduced through ADR Group are then referred directly to our members. Being an ADR Net panel mediator provides the opportunity for you to be put forward for ADR Group mediation referrals. Your appointment as a mediator will depend on a number of factors including experience, speciality and the preferences of the mediation participants.

Other ADR Net membership benefits include continuing professional development opportunities, discounts on training and mediation networking events. ADRg hold regular regional meetings to discuss ways in which all members can promote and develop the use of ADR to the business community. Our regional meetings also provide great networking opportunities for members as well as useful discussion forums. In addition to this we also hold an Annual Conference which is not only attended by members but also by high profile judges and politicians involved in legal reform. You can either join our network as a firm (corporate), an individual or an associate.

Who should attend?

The Civil and Commercial Mediator Foundation Training Programme is essential for any professional wanting to practice as a mediator. The skills obtained form part of an essential management tool-kit for:

- Professionals with responsibility for resolving disputes
- Legal professionals – Private Practice Solicitors,
- In-house Legal Directors and Counsel, Barristers etc.
- Professional advisers e.g. accountants, architects, healthcare and other
- professionals
- HR managers, union representatives and policy advisers

ADRg also offers Employment and Workplace Mediation Skills Training for senior executives and key decision makers, HR professionals, supply chain managers and complaints handlers and customer services representatives.

Course Objectives

The course aims to help you to:

- Understand the role mediation plays in the business and legal community
- Develop advanced facilitation skills to promote communication between parties
- Acquire competencies to distinguish issues from interests and develop commercial solutions
- Enhance listening, probing and evaluation skills

Course Outcomes

On successful completion of the course you will become an ADR Group Accredited Civil and Commercial Mediator and able to practice mediations with the appropriate level of skill, professionalism and confidence.

Attendance accrues 40 hours of Law Society and Bar Council of England and Wales continuing professional development (CPD).

Programme content

Module 1 – Preparation – distance learning CD-ROM on history, theory and basic dispute recognition

(12 hours)

The initial phase gives you an insight into the history and theory of mediation. The CD takes you through specific tutorials and case studies together with 6 exercises which must be submitted to ADRg prior to attending Module 2.

Module 2 – Foundation – three-day core mediator competency

(28 hours)

This intensive module involves tutoring in mediation's core competencies; planning & organisation, process management, communication skills, facilitation and creative problem solving. Delegates will be involved in role-playing mediation sessions, group discussions and practical exercises in order to practice the skills being learned. The use of video provides opportunity for maximum feedback. Delegate assessment will be conducted throughout the course and will conclude with a final video recorded assessment of a role-play on day 3 in which delegates will be required to demonstrate the practical application of skills and core mediator competencies. The video recording will be retained for external moderation. On successful completion of modules 1 & 2 you will become an ADR Group Accredited Civil and Commercial Mediator.

Module 3 – Becoming an ADR Net Panel Member

Once accredited, delegates have the opportunity to join ADR Net and participate in ADR Group mediation referrals. To become an ADR Net panel mediator, members are required to undertake additional observation assessments.

Course Pre-requisites

The ADRg Civil and Commercial Mediation Foundation Training Programme is designed for individuals affiliated with a professional body. In order to fully engage in the role-play aspect of the course participants require a strong command of the English language. If you have any concerns in this regard, please call us to discuss further prior to booking. There are no other particular course prerequisites other than a willingness to engage in shared learning through role-plays and interactive exercises. Knowledge of law is helpful but not essential.

Continuing Professional Development (CPD)

Attendance of the ADRg Civil and Commercial Mediation Foundation Programme, Modules 1 and 2 accrues 40 hours Law Society and Bar Council CPD.

(iii) Law Society (England & Wales) Accreditation for Civil and Commercial Mediation[13]

Criteria and guidance notes[14]

Education and Training Unit

Version 1

Introduction

The Civil and Commercial Mediation Accreditation Scheme covers mediations arising from all types of civil/commercial disputes. Whilst scheme members may have expertise in certain kinds of civil/commercial disputes, it is expected that they are able to demonstrate awareness and knowledge of general dispute resolution and mediation skills and issues. The scheme aims to:

- ensure that the legal profession and the public can easily identify Law Society approved civil/commercial mediators;

- satisfy users and potential users of mediation services that mediators on the scheme have been trained in accordance with the **training standards for civil/commercial mediation;**

- satisfy users and potential users of mediation services that practitioner members on the scheme have sufficient mediation experience to act as lead mediators;

- certify that scheme members have either practised as solicitors or Fellows of the Institute of Legal Executives for three years or have demonstrated exceptional circumstances which allow a waiver of this requirement;

- acknowledge that scheme members are required to hold professional indemnity insurance when mediating (see the Solicitors Indemnity Insurance Rules 2007);

- confirm that scheme members are required to mediate in accordance with the **competencies for civil/commercial mediators** (see Annex A) and to comply with the **Law Society's Code of Practice for civil/commercial mediation** (see Annex B);

- confirm that each scheme member has an ethical obligation not to act for a party to a mediation in which they were a mediator in the same case, and to disclose any prior involvement with or interest in any party to a mediation in which they are asked to mediate.

Overall, the scheme aims to provide a good quality service for the delivery of civil/commercial mediation.

Types of membership

There are two types of membership are available.

---

13   © The Law Society 2009. Reproduced by kind permission..
14   Refer to the Law Society website (www.accreditation.Law Society.org.uk) for the criteria in the case of family mediation.

General membership

General membership is a one-off membership for two years. General members are expected to gain mediation experience and apply for practitioner membership by the end of the two years.

Practitioner membership

Practitioner membership is for an initial period of three years, after which the member is expected to apply for re-accreditation for further terms of five years each. Practitioner membership may be achieved by one of two routes.

- The **development route** is open to those who have achieved general membership and are able to demonstrate compliance with the mediation experience and other standards for the scheme by the end of their two-year membership.

- The **direct route** is available you are already trained and experienced in civil/commercial mediation, and are able to demonstrate compliance with the criteria and standards for the scheme.

Eligibility criteria
Who is eligible to apply?

You can apply if:

- You have practised as a solicitor for at least three years and have held a practicing certificate throughout that period. You must hold a current, unconditional practicing certificate throughout your membership.

- You have been a Fellow of the Institute of Legal Executives (FILEX) for at least three years, and held Fellowship of the Institute throughout that period. If you are a FILEX you must be employed by a solicitor throughout your membership.

What are the eligibility criteria for each route to membership?

General membership

1 You must provide evidence of completion, and an understanding of the content, of a Law Society approved civil/commercial mediation training course. If the course you have done is not one of our approved courses, you may still apply. However, you must include a copy of the course programme, syllabus and course papers to enable the course to be assessed against the **training standards**.

2 You must comply with the **competencies for civil/commercial mediators** attached in Annex A.

3 You must agree to be bound by the **Law Society Code of Practice for civil/commercial mediators** attached in Annex B.

4 You must understand that if you do not apply to become a practitioner member by the end of your two year general membership your membership will be terminated,

unless there are exceptional circumstances. You can apply for an extension before the end of the two-year general membership, providing that there are clear reasons why you are unable to achieve practitioner status. You should also detail what steps you have taken towards practitioner membership. An extension, if granted, will be for a maximum of two years. Applications for extensions will be considered on a case by case basis.

5 You must agree to attain a minimum total of 16 hours continuing professional development on civil/commercial mediation issues during your two-year general membership.

6 You also need to provide details of two referees (see References below).

Practitioner membership – development route eligibility criteria

1 You must have been accepted as a general member of the Civil and Commercial Mediation Accreditation Scheme.

2 You must demonstrate that you have satisfied the mediation experience criteria.

3 You must provide evidence that you have attained a minimum total of 16 hours continuing professional development on civil/commercial mediation issues during your general membership.

4 You must comply with the **competencies for civil/commercial mediators** attached in Annex A.

5 You must agree to be bound by the **Law Society Code of Practice for civil/ commercial mediators** attached in Annex B.

6 You must understand that, if you do not apply for re-accreditation by the end of the initial three-year practitioner membership period, your membership will be terminated unless there are exceptional circumstances. Details of the re-accreditation process will be sent to you at least two months prior to the end of your membership. If you cannot comply with the re-accreditation criteria you must apply for an extension by providing clear reasons in writing, of why you are unable to apply for re-accreditation, and details of the steps you have taken towards re-accreditation. If granted, an extension will be for a maximum of one year. Applications for extensions will be considered on a case by case basis.

7 You must agree to attain a minimum total of 24 hours continuing professional development on civil/commercial mediation issues during your initial three-year practitioner membership.

Practitioner membership – direct route eligibility criteria

1 You must demonstrate that you have dispute resolution knowledge.

2 You must provide evidence of completion, and an understanding of the content, of an Law Society approved civil/commercial mediation training course. If the course you have done is not one of our approved courses, you may still apply.

However, you must include a copy of the course programme, syllabus and course papers to enable the course to be assessed against the **training standards**.

3 You must demonstrate that you have satisfied the mediation experience criteria or comparable criteria of a mediation organisation of which you are a member.

4 You must comply with the **competencies for civil/commercial mediators** (see Annex A).

5 You must agree to be bound by the **Law Society Code of Practice for civil/ commercial mediators** in Annex B.

6 You must understand that, if you do not apply for re-accreditation by the end of the initial three-year practitioner membership, you will cease to be a member unless there are exceptional circumstances. Details of the reselection process will be sent to you at least two months prior to the end of your membership. If you cannot comply with the reaccreditation criteria you must apply for an extension by providing clear reasons in writing, of why you are unable to apply for re-accreditation and details of the steps you have taken towards re-accreditation. If granted, an extension will be for a maximum of one year. Applications for extensions will be considered on a case by case basis.

What level of experience do I need to demonstrate?

Practitioner membership

When you apply, you will be expected to have a minimum of 90 hours of mediation experience over the two years preceding the date of the application (subject to any extensions) including:

1 Experience in at least four civil/commercial mediations comprising a minimum total of 30 hours. The mediations can be actual or mock mediations. Your experience can be as lead mediator, co-mediator, pupil/assistant mediator, legal representative or client, **provided** that it is gained in at least two actual civil/ commercial mediations, with at least 14 hours as lead mediator, co-mediator or pupil/assistant mediator. General members are encouraged to act as pupil/assistant mediators before acting as lead mediators.

2 A 200-500 word summary of each civil/commercial actual or mock mediation experienced. This should provide a summary of the dispute, the pre-mediation activities, the result, any difficulties experienced, and the learning points from the mediation, with particular reference to the **competencies for civil/commercial mediators** (see

Annex A). The sample summary in Annex E1 can be used. This activity should account for a minimum total of four hours.

3 A minimum total of four hours spent on self-reflection activities, which can be evidenced in any of the following ways:

■ A personal debrief with another mediator (whether individually or in a group) following an actual mediation as a lead, co-mediator or pupil/assistant mediator only. You should provide a summary of the personal reflection points, with particular reference to the **competencies for civil/commercial mediators** (see Annex A), which came out of the debrief (use the sample personal debrief summary **in** Annex E2).

- Debriefing another mediator. You should provide a summary outlining the discussions, with particular reference to any learning points relating to the **competencies for civil/commercial mediators** attached in Annex A (use the sample debrief summary in Annex E3).

- Attending a meeting or forum of mediators and making a summary of the discussions, with particular reference to any learning points relating to the **competencies for civil/commercial mediators** attached in Annex A (use the sample meeting summary in Annex E4).

- A summary of the personal reflection points, with particular reference to the **competencies for civil/commercial mediators** (see Annex A), which follow receipt of feedback after an actual mediation as a lead mediator or co-mediator only. Feedback can be received orally (and written up using Annex E5) or in writing. Feedback forms can be provided to the parties (see Annex D for a sample) or, if a party is legally represented, to the party's legal representative after an actual mediation as a lead mediator or co-mediator only. Alternatively, if an actual mediation is administered by a mediation organisation and they follow up mediations with feedback forms, the applicant may refer to their forms. You may include with the summary a copy of written feedback received. You should provide a 200-500 word summary for any of the above methods.

4 Continuing professional development of a minimum total of 16 hours relating to civil/commercial mediation issues, for example:

- communication and listening skills
- negotiation skills and problem-solving
- ethics in mediation
- sector-specific mediation training, for example, construction or clinical negligence mediation
- offers to settle
- settlement agreements

and keep a training record.

5 You may make up any remaining mediation experience requirements through further time spent on any of the activities listed in 1 – 3 above and/or any of the following activities:

- attending mediation courses
- writing, lecturing or providing training courses on mediation
- private study of mediation (eg – reading relevant articles, journals or books: a mediation reading list can be found at page 10)
- promoting mediation, for example, by producing client mediation newsletters or seminars.

Time spent on these activities should account for no more than a total of 12 hours.

General membership applicants will apply for practitioner status through the development route, and are advised to keep a log of their mediation experience activities. A suggested form of log follows.

Activity and requirement

Mediation training

Minimum 24 hours over three days approved by the Law Society or satisfies the Law Society's training standards.

How to record: collate details of the course, its content and duration, and of the provider. Also make a note of any assessment procedures and the result.

Mediation practice

Minimum four (minimum total 30 hours) actual/mock mediations as lead mediator/ co-mediator/assistant or pupil mediator/legal representative or client, **provided** that minimum two actual cases (minimum total 14 hours) as lead mediator, co-mediator or pupil/assistant mediator.

How to record: keep a list of the mediations, together with details of dates and duration, with a note of the capacity in which the applicant was involved.

Written summaries

200-500 word summary for each mediation. Minimum total of four hours on this activity.

How to record: each summary should outline the dispute, pre-mediation activities, mediation result, any difficulties and the learning points in the mediation.

Self-reflection

Can be evidenced by:

- personal debrief after an actual mediation as lead mediator, co-mediator or pupil/assistant mediator
- debriefing another mediator
- attending a meeting or forum of mediators
- review of feedback after an actual mediation as a lead mediator or comediator

Together with a 200–500 word summary to record the reflection.

Minimum total of four hours on these activities.

How to record: record the event, its date and duration, and make a 200-500 word note of the discussions and your personal reflection points.

CPD

Minimum total of 16 hours.

How to record: list the date, activity and duration, together with any comments.

Mediation education/promotion

Maximum total of 12 hours.

How to record: record the activity, its date and duration, with any comments.

How we will deal with your application

Your application will be subject to the general application procedures described in the Professional Accreditation Schemes booklet. There are additional assessment processes that are specific to the Civil and Commercial Mediation Accreditation Scheme.

References

When you make you application, you must provide details of two referees who have knowledge of, and can comment on, your character and knowledge of law and practice. At least one of the referees must also be able to comment on your ability to mediate civil/commercial disputes. For example, someone that has observed you in mediation training or in a mock mediation or someone who has received feedback on your performance in mediation training or in a mock mediation. Referees should not be partners in, or employees of, your firm. The Law Society reserves the right to obtain references from other sources if considered necessary or desirable.

- As a scheme member, you may receive work as a lead mediator, co-mediator and pupil/assistant mediators via mediation organisations or direct. In either case, you must hold professional indemnity insurance which covers mediation (please see the undertakings / codes of practice section later in this booklet).

- Where you receive work direct, it is a condition of membership that you will provide ahead of a mediation to each party or, where a party is legally represented, to their legal representative:

  - an outline of your experience (together with mediation training and mediation experience), how mediation fees and expenses will be charged, and the codes of practice or conduct you adhere to

  - a sample mediation agreement (see Annex C)

Following a mediation, you may send a sample feedback form (see Annex D) to the parties or, where a party is legally represented, to the legal representative, for self-reflection purposes.

Compulsory training

You must have completed a mediation training course, which either:

- has been approved for the purpose of the Civil and Commercial Mediation Accreditation Scheme by the Law Society (see page 9 below for a list of any approved training courses), or

- is a course comprising not less than 24 contact hours over at least three days and satisfying the **training standards for civil/commercial mediation**. A copy of the course programme, syllabus and course papers should be included with the application form, to enable the course to be assessed against the **training standards for civil/commercial mediation.**

You will also be required to demonstrate understanding of the content covered by the mediation training course. You can do this by providing evidence of satisfactory completion of assessment or attainment of accreditation following the mediation training course attended. Alternatively you can do this by satisfactorily answering a series of questions covering the main topics in the **training standards for civil/ commercial mediation**.

Approved course providers

ADR Chambers UK
1 Ropemaker Street
City Point
London
www.adrchambers.co.uk
adr@adrchambers.co.uk
T – 0845 072 0111
F – 0845 072 0112
EC2Y 9HT
T – 0117 946 7180
F – 0117 946 7181

ADR Group
Mediation Foundation Training
Course*
Grove House
Grove Road
Redland
Bristol
www.adrgroup.co.uk
info@adrgroup.co.uk
BS6 6UN
T – 0117 946 7180
F – 0117 946 7181

ADR Group
Mediator Conversion Course
Grove House
Grove Road
Redland
Bristol
www.adrgroup.co.uk
info@adrgroup.co.uk
BS6 6UN
T – 0207 536 6000
F – 0207 536 6001

CEDR
Mediator Skills Training Course
International Dispute Resolution
Centre
70 Fleet Street
London
www.cedr.co.uk
info@cedr.co.uk
EC4Y 1EU
T – 0121 355 0900
F – 0121 355 5517

Central Law Training
Wrens Court
52-54 Victoria Road
Sutton Coldfield
www.clt.co.uk
Birmingham B72 1SX

Regents College School of
Psychotherapy and Counselling
School of Psychotherapy and
Counselling
Regent's College,
F – 0207 487 7446
www.spc.ac.uk
spc@regents.ac.uk
Regent's Park
Inner Circle
London NW1 4NS

Chartered Institute of Arbitrators,
International Centre for Arbitration
and Mediation,
12 Bloomsbury Square,
London, WC1A 2LP
www.ciarb.org

Please note: The scheme criteria also specify that applicants should complete a course of three days' duration. The ADR Group course has been a three-day course since June 2001. Prior to that date, it was a two-day course. For scheme applicants who completed the ADR

Group course prior to June 2001, the following options are available:

- completion of ADR Group's CD ROM course, or

- completion of ADR Group's one-day advanced pupilage course, or

- attendance at a one-day mediation course (or various courses comprising a total of one day or eight hours) offered by another civil/commercial mediation provider, or

■ in exceptional cases, mediation experience gained in the meantime may constitute a waiver (each application for waiver will be assessed on a case-by-case basis).

Annex A – Competencies for civil and commercial mediators

There are different ways of dividing mediation into stages. The approach adopted below is intended to facilitate considering the process in its component parts. In practice, these stages will not necessarily occur in the same order as below, nor will every stage be present in every case. Mediators need to be able to adopt a flexible approach, to meet the needs of a particular mediation.

Element 1: Before mediation

Mediators will be aware of the processes for engaging the parties in the mediation forum, obtaining the commitment of the parties to mediation, establishing the parties' agreement to the items for discussion and the ground rules of the mediation (including the voluntary nature of the process) and for conducting the necessary preliminary communications and preparation for the mediation, using a variety of methods.

Stage 1: Engaging the parties in the mediation forum

This stage is the 'intake' or 'point of entry' phase. Although mediation has not yet commenced, this may be regarded as a specific stage in the process because it is the point at which the parties have to consider and agree the forum in which they are to operate.

Mediators will:

1a   Understand and be able to explain to the parties

   ● the basic principles of mediation, emphasising its voluntary nature

   ● the difference between facilitative and evaluative mediation (and agree with the parties which form they wish to use)

   ● the relationship between mediation and the traditional litigation process

   ● the binding nature of an agreement reached in mediation and confirmed in writing

b   Be aware at this stage, that parties coming from different legal and/or business cultures may have differing expectations of ADR in general and mediation in particular.

c   Recognise and be able to explain to the parties the importance of maintaining impartiality and non-directiveness and of avoiding discussion with either party on the merits of the matter.

d   Be aware of any contrary indications to mediation and be able to act appropriately.

e   Be able to give objective information about the relative merits of mediation as against other ways of proceeding and to help the parties choose the procedure best suited to their circumstances.

Stage 2: Obtaining commitment and agreeing mediation rules

Mediators will be able to obtain the commitment of the parties to mediation, and their acceptance of its terms and rules. Mediation will ordinarily be conducted in accordance with the agreed terms set out in the mediation agreement, the 'ground rules' set by the mediator for the particular mediation, the Law Society's code of practice and the code of practice, or rules of the mediation organisation offering the process. Signing a *written* agreement to mediate is both practical (to record the basis for the mediation) and symbolic (to commit to the process of seeking an agreed resolution). The Law Society's sample mediation agreement may be used.

Mediators will:

2a   Be familiar with the Law Society's Code of Practice which contains elements of the practical, theoretical and ethical base underlying the mediation process, including, in particular, the principles of confidentiality and privilege.

b   Understand the importance of making available to the parties an appropriate agreement to mediate.

c   Recognise that an agreement to mediate requires the parties to give their commitment to the process. It should explain the process, and deal with matters such as confidentiality (and when this might not apply), privilege, the mediator's role, payment (where applicable) and other practical and ethical matters. It should not conflict with the code of practice.

d   understand the importance of giving the parties an opportunity to discuss the agreement with the mediator and raise any queries, and will recognise the different ways in and times at which this may be achieved.

e   Understand the importance of inviting the parties to sign the agreement to mediate at the commencement of mediation and will be able to deal effectively with any reservations which the parties may have about making that commitment.

Stage 3: Preliminary communications and preparation

Mediators will understand the preliminary matters to be attended to before a mediator meets the parties, including matters for the parties to deal with, and matters (usually procedural) for decision by the mediator.

Mediators will:

3a   Understand the different methods of communicating effectively with the parties to obtain relevant background details, information and documents, including the case summary.

b   Understand the importance of obtaining the case summary and be able to explain its relevance, structure and essential content to the parties and/or their legal representatives.

c   Understand how to use the background information and documents to assess whether there are any issues requiring attention *before* commencement of the mediation which must be acquired and whether they indicate a likelihood of power imbalances.

d   Appreciate the importance of establishing rapport with the parties and be able to do so.

e   Be aware of when co-mediation or a pupil/assistant mediator may be appropriate and how to engage the services of that person.

Element 2: During the substantive mediation

Mediators will be able to demonstrate an understanding of the importance of the venue and arrangements for receiving the parties including the provision of suitable facilities. Mediators will be able to demonstrate an understanding of the importance and purpose of the first meeting with the parties which is likely to include the following elements:

■   how to establish both the presenting issues and those which are underlying or submerged

■   how to establish an agenda

■   how to prioritise issues

Stage 4: Establishing the venue and meeting the parties

Mediators will be able to make proper arrangements for receiving the parties and for setting up the room(s) where the mediation will be conducted, and to provide the necessary facilities for the mediation. When first meeting the parties, there are preliminary matters to be covered before the mediation process properly gets underway.

Mediators will:

4a   understand the need for sensitivity in making reception arrangements.

b   understand the importance of making appropriate practical arrangements for the conduct of the mediation itself, for example, seating, arranging separate soundproof rooms, equipment and refreshments.

c   understand how to put the parties at their ease and help create an environment in which they feel able to discuss matters candidly with the mediator, for example, by appropriate use of first names.

d   be able to explain the mediation agreement to the parties and deal with their queries before it is signed.

Stage 5: Establishing the issues and setting the agenda

The documents and case summary provided by each party will give some information about the issues. This can be enlarged upon or clarified when the parties explain the issues to the mediator at a joint opening session. The mediator will commonly invite each of the parties (or their representatives) to make an opening statement, highlighting what they regard as the key issues. The mediator may summarise or ask some preliminary questions at the conclusion of each statement. The mediator may then establish an agenda in collaboration with the parties.

Mediators will:

5a   be aware of the different approaches to dealing with discrepancies or matters which might be embarrassing to the parties

b   be aware of how to manage the opening session of the mediation including when it is appropriate to ask questions, what can be learned from the reaction of the parties and how to manage interruptions

c   recognise the appropriateness, or otherwise, of opening statements and of controlling the length of such statements.

d   be aware that one way of deciding on the approach for the conduct of the mediation is by setting an agenda, in collaboration with the parties, either formally or informally.

Stage 6: Information gathering

The mediator obtains information from the parties in different ways. First, preliminary (usually, basic) information will be provided when the request for mediation is made. Then, after the mediator has been appointed, it will be usual for the parties to furnish a case summary to the mediator and to one another. This will usually be accompanied by a bundle of documents, which ideally will be a single, agreed bundle. This will not be comprehensive disclosure, (as in litigation) but a selection of papers directly relevant to the issues in the dispute. Where the case is already subject to litigation or arbitration, the bundle will probably include statements of case, expert reports, orders and other court documents. Documents which are relevant to the mediation but have not yet been disclosed or are confidential can be provided to the mediator under cover of a note explaining that those documents are provided for the mediator's information only. Consequently, by the time the mediator first meets the parties, he or she should already have a good picture of the issues. However, it should not be assumed that these are necessarily the only, or indeed, the real issues between the parties. Some mediators may ask for supplementary information or documents before the mediation starts. In most models of commercial/civil mediation, parties are asked to present their case briefly at the outset to the mediator and to one another in a joint opening session. The main purpose of this exercise is to enable the mediator to ensure that he or she has understood each party's case and the issues correctly, and to obtain any necessary amplification. It may also help to establish whether the *parties* have a true perspective of each other's concerns. Information is also obtained as the mediation progresses. This may occur in joint session, but more usually it will occur during the separate sessions which the mediator has with the parties. Consequently, additional information may well be received on a confidential basis, not to be shared with the other party, except with the express authority of the giver of the information. In all forms of mediation, the mediator will establish further relevant information by careful listening and observation, by picking up signals that either party may give as to underlying concerns and possible solutions, and by sensitive questioning.

Mediators will:

6a   understand the different kinds of information: including factual, technical (eg about valuations, tax or legal implications), or underlying (eg about aspirations, wants and needs).

b   be aware of and know how and when to apply as appropriate, the different questioning skills needed to obtain further or amplification of information

Stage 7: Managing and facilitating discussions and negotiations

This is the main stage of the mediation process. It involves the mediator in helping the parties to explore options jointly and/or in private meetings, and to negotiate the resolution of their dispute. This requires the mediator to act both as manager of the process, keeping control of it, and as a facilitator of negotiations and communications. These roles demand various attributes and skills from the mediator, which can be both learned and developed.

During this stage the mediator will continue to listen effectively to the parties, watching for signals that may provide clues for creating settlement options. The mediator will try to encourage a problem-solving mode, but will understand that parties commonly continue to negotiate in a competitive mode. By the use of summarising, acknowledging, mutualising, reframing and normalising the mediator will help to create conditions in which the parties may feel heard and may find it easier to shift their positions. The mediator will facilitate negotiations between the parties. This is commonly done by conducting separate meetings with the parties. The mediator will use these private meetings to explore their respective concerns, aspirations, interests and possible options for settlement. The mediator will try to establish potential settlement terms from each party, recognising that they do not necessarily reveal their 'bottom lines' at this stage. In any event, the mediator should discourage the putting forward of 'bottom lines' which tend to be artificial and to inhibit movement. During this phase, the mediator will try to win the trust of each party, so as to gain a full understanding of the issues, both as initially presented and underlying, and to carry proposals effectively to the other party. An element of 'shuttle' mediation will usually be required. Other types of meeting may help. For example, the mediator may meet the parties without their lawyers, or vice versa, or may meet other professional advisors such as accountants. The mediator may re-convene a joint session or convene working groups consisting of any combination of clients, lawyers and other professional advisers, as appropriate. The mediator will adopt a flexible and creative approach to seeking settlement terms, within the bounds of ethical propriety and practical efficacy.

Mediators will:

7a   often be familiar with a competitive bargaining approach to negotiation. Some may be less familiar with a problem-solving approach, which encourages exploration of the expectations, needs and interests of the parties. Mediators will be aware of the value and limitations of each of these approaches and will be able to deploy them as necessary.

b   recognise the importance of controlling the pace of the mediation, having regard to available time and to the requirements of the process and of each party.

c   know how to help the parties, in joint or separate meetings, to identify, explore, develop and narrow options for dealing with issues. These options may be generated by either party, or by the mediator.

d   recognise when it is appropriate (and how to hold) joint meetings with the parties and when to conduct private meetings, who to see first and for how long, and how to shuttle effectively.

e   recognise the importance of helping each party to test the reality of the available options and of their respective ideas and aspirations. This involves examining the implications of such options and ideas.

f   recognise the importance of and know how to use a variety of communication skills in dealing with each party. This may include summarising what they have said; giving the parties credit for their comments, views, concerns and their shifts and concessions; helping to give parties to appreciate that they share similar views or concerns, albeit from different angles ('mutualising'1); giving an appropriate indication to a party or parties that they have been heard and understood by the mediator or the other party ('acknowledging'); helping parties to realise the normalcy of their situation or feelings in order to help reduce undue anxiety, tension, or pessimism ('normalising'3); and summarising and/or rewording their statements effectively ('reframing')

g   recognise the importance of asking effective and appropriate questions

h   be able to act appropriately when parties express feelings, sometimes strongly, recognising the need to prevent such expressions from destroying the mediation process

i   recognise the likelihood of power imbalances and will understand and insofar as appropriate and applicable, be able to manage and deal with these effectively, ensuring that neither party is permitted to abuse the process

j   recognise the importance of not giving advice or attempting to predict the outcome of the case if it were to be litigated, unless the parties have agreed in advance that s/he *should* do so. Mediators will also be able to identify other professionals who might assist the parties

k   recognise the importance of encouraging those parties who are not legally represented in the mediation, to consult their own legal advisers and when it would be appropriate to do so

l understand the appropriateness of negotiation techniques which assist the parties to move forward in a problem-solving rather than an adversarial mode

Stage 8: Employing impasse strategies

An impasse arises during the mediation when parties are stuck on some point that prevents them from moving forward. An impasse strategy helps the mediator to break the deadlock and to allow the parties to revert to their negotiations.

Mediators will:

8 recognise an impasse, understand how it is caused and be able to deal appropriately with each impasse as it arises.

Element 3: The end of mediation and afterwards

Mediators will be aware of the variety of reasons for mediations ending, the process for the termination of the mediation by the mediator and further steps, which may involve the mediator after the mediation has terminated. Mediators will also be aware of the effect upon the parties' legal position of both a successful mediation (ie a mediation resulting in a settlement agreement) and a mediation which terminates temporarily or permanently, *without* agreement being reached.

Stage 9: Concluding mediation and recording the outcome

This is the final stage. Mediation may end for various reasons, for example because parties have resolved their issues or because they find they cannot do so and need a different process such as negotiation between solicitors or adjudication by the court. Mediation may be discontinued as inappropriate, for example, where a party appears to be unable to continue to mediate, or where a party is abusing the process. In some of these events, a written memorandum of some sort may be necessary or advisable. Certainly it is likely to be essential where the parties have resolved their issues and wish to have a record of their agreement. In that event, the mediator, and/or the parties and their lawyers, would prepare a record of the agreed terms which, when signed by the parties, becomes binding upon them.

Mediators will:

9a recognise when it is inappropriate to continue the mediation, having particular regard to ethical principles set out in codes of practice, and should be able to bring the mediation to an end effectively.

b be familiar with relevant codes of practice regulating mediation are what the codes provide as to when a mediation should not be continued, eg where one party abuses the process and makes it ineffective.

c recognise when it may be appropriate to suspend the mediation (for example, to allow parties to address certain issues before returning to mediation).

d recognise when and how to bring negotiations to a close.

e ensure that all parties have the same understanding of the settlement and their obligations under it.

f ensure that all issues in dispute are included in the settlement, or, if not, the mechanism for dealing with outstanding issues.

g recognise when it is appropriate to draft a memorandum of agreement, partial agreement, and where appropriate, of issues outstanding. If the parties are not legally represented, mediators will be able to draft a binding agreement for the parties.

h recognise the importance of explaining before the commencement of the mediation the consequences of both a successful and an unsuccessful outcome; and of reminding the parties of the consequences at appropriate points during the process.

i check that parties have considered the tax implication of agreement (personal, corporate and VAT).

Stage 10: Post-termination

After the mediation has concluded and the mediator has given a copy of the agreement or other memorandum to the parties, that would ordinarily end the mediator's function. It is, however, possible for certain matters to be reserved to the mediator, or for further meetings with the mediator to be required.

Mediators will:

10a   recognise when it may be appropriate for the parties to mediate in the future on settlement terms or on continuing aspects.

b   recognise when, although the formal mediation session has come to an end, prospects for settlement remain and it may be appropriate for the mediator to be proactive in promoting on-going discussion between the parties.

c   recognise when the parties may require assistance in order to implement the settlement terms, and how to offer such assistance without providing advice.

Annex A – Law Society code of practice for family mediation

Members of the Law Society's Family Mediation Accreditation Scheme must agree to be bound by this code.

Introduction

The Solicitors Code of Conduct July 2007 contains the general principles and rules regarding solicitors' practice, including alternative dispute resolution.

This code is designed to deal with the fundamentals of family mediation. It is not intended that it should cover every situation that may arise.

The concept of not giving advice to the parties, individually or collectively, when acting as a mediator permeates this entire code.

Section 1 – objectives of family mediation

Family mediation is a process in which:

1.1   a couple or any other family members

1.2   whether or not they are legally represented

1.3   and at any time, whether or not there are or have been legal proceedings

1.4   agree to the appointment of a neutral third party (the mediator)

1.5   who is impartial

1.6   who has no authority to make any decisions with regard to their issues

1.7   which may relate to separation, divorce, children's issues, property and financial questions or any other issues they may raise

1.8   but who helps them reach their own informed decisions

1.9   by negotiation

1.10   without adjudication.

Section 2 – qualifications and appointment of mediator

2.1   Every mediator shall have regard to the criteria and requirements for mediators stipulated from time to time by the Law Society, including those relating to training, consultancy, accreditation and regulation.

2.2   Save where appointed by or through the court, a mediator may only accept appointment if both or all parties to the mediation so request, or agree.

2.3   Whether a mediator is appointed by the parties or through the court or any other agency, he or she may only continue to act as such so long as both or all parties to the mediation wish him or her to do so. If any party does not wish to continue with the mediation, the mediator must discontinue the process. Also, if the mediator considers that it would be inappropriate to continue the mediation, the mediator shall bring it to an end, and may decline to give reasons.

Section 3 – conflicts of interest and impartiality of mediator

3.1   The impartiality of the mediator is a fundamental principle of mediation.

3.2   Impartiality means that:

    3.2.1   the mediator does not have any significant personal interest in the outcome of the mediation

    3.2.2   a mediator with any personal interest in the outcome of the mediation may act if, and only if, full disclosure is made to all of the parties as soon as it is known and they consent

    3.2.3   the mediator will conduct the process fairly and even-handedly, and will not favour any party over another.

3.3   The mediator must not act or, having started to do so, continue to act:

    3.3.1   in relation to issues on which he or she or a member of his or her firm has at any time acted for any party

    3.3.2   if any circumstances exist which may constitute an actual or potential conflict of interest

    3.3.3   if the mediator or a member of his or her firm has acted for any of the parties in issues not relating to the mediation, unless that has been disclosed to the parties as soon as it is known and they consent.

3.4   Where a mediator has acted as such in relation to a dispute, neither he nor she nor any member of his or her firm may act for any party in relation to the subject matter of the mediation.

Section 4 – mediation procedures

4.1   The mediator must ensure that the parties agree the terms and conditions regulating the mediation before dealing with the substantive issues. This should ordinarily be in a written agreement which should reflect the main principles of this code. Such agreement should also contain the terms of remuneration of the mediator.

4.2   The procedure for the conduct of the mediation is a matter for the decision of the mediator. Insofar as the mediator establishes an agenda of matters to be covered in the mediation, the mediator should be guided by the needs, wishes and priorities of the parties in doing so.

4.3   In establishing any procedures for the conduct of the mediation, the mediator must be guided by a commitment to procedural fairness, the fostering of mutual respect between the parties and a high quality of process.

Section 5 – the decision-making process

5.1   The primary aim of family mediation is to help the parties to arrive at their own decisions regarding their issues, on an informed basis with an understanding, so far as reasonably practicable, of the implications and consequences of such decisions for themselves and any children concerned.

5.2   The parties may reach decisions on any issue at any stage of the mediation.

5.3   Subject to paragraph 5.4, decisions arrived at in family mediation should not be binding on the parties until they have had the opportunity to seek advice on those decisions from their own legal representatives.

5.4   The parties must be offered the opportunity to obtain legal advice before any decision can be turned into a binding agreement on any issue which appears to the mediator or to either party to be of significance to the position of one or both parties.

5.5   The mediator must not seek to impose his or her preferred outcome on the parties and should try to avoid becoming personally identified with any particular outcome.

5.6   The mediator shall, however, be free to make management decisions with regard to the conduct of the mediation process, and may suggest possible solutions and help the parties to explore these, where he or she thinks that this would be helpful to them.

5.7   The mediator should assist the parties, so far as appropriate and practicable, to identify what information and documents would help the resolution of any issue(s), and how best such information and documents may be obtained. However, the mediator has no obligation to make independent enquiries or undertake verification in relation to any information or documents sought or provided in the mediation. If necessary, consideration may be given in the mediation to the ways in which the parties may make such enquiries or obtain such verification.

5.8   Family mediation does not provide for the disclosure and discovery of documents in the same way or to the same extent as required by court rules. The mediator may indicate any particular documents that he or she considers each party should furnish.

5.9   Parties should be helped to reach such resolution of such issues which they feel are appropriate to their particular circumstances. Such resolutions may not necessarily be the same as those which may be arrived at in the event of an adjudication by the court.

5.10   The mediator should, if practicable, inform the parties if he or she considers that the resolutions which they are considering are likely to fall outside the parameters which a court might approve or order. If they nevertheless wish to proceed with such resolutions, they may do so. In these circumstances the mediation summary may identify any specific questions on which the mediator has indicated a need for independent legal advice. If, however, the parties are proposing a resolution which appears to the mediator to be unconscionable or fundamentally inappropriate, then the mediator should inform the parties accordingly and may terminate the mediation, and/or refer the parties to their legal advisers.

5.11   Parties may consult with their own solicitors as the mediation progresses, and shall be given the opportunity to do so before reaching any binding agreement on their substantive issues. Where appropriate, the mediator may assist the parties to consider the desirability of their jointly or individually seeking further assistance during the course of the mediation process from professional advisers such as lawyers, accountants, expert valuers or others, or from counsellors or therapists. The mediator may also assist the parties by providing relevant lists of names.

5.12   Mediation meetings are commonly conducted without lawyers present. However, solicitors or counsel acting for the individual parties may be invited to participate in the mediation process, and in any communications, in such manner as the mediator may consider useful and appropriate, and as the parties may agree.

Section 6 – dealing with power imbalances

6.1   The mediator should be alive to the likelihood of power imbalances existing between the parties. These may relate to various different aspects including, for example, behaviour which is controlling, abusive or manipulative, finance; children and family, status, communication and other skills, possession of information, the withholding of cooperation, and many other kinds of power.

6.2   If power imbalances seem likely to cause the mediation process to become unfair or ineffective, the mediator must take appropriate steps to try to prevent this.

6.3   The mediator must ensure that the parties take part in mediation willingly and without fear of violence or harm. Additionally, the mediator must seek to prevent manipulative, threatening or intimidating behaviour by either party.

6.4   If the mediator believes that power imbalances cannot be redressed adequately and that in consequence the mediation will not be able to be fairly and effectively conducted, he or she may discuss this with the parties, but in any event must bring the mediation to an end as soon as practicable.

Section 7 – confidentiality and privilege

7.1   The mediator must maintain confidentiality in relation to all matters dealt with in the mediation. The mediator may disclose:

    7.1.1   matters which the parties and the mediator agree may be disclosed

    7.1.2   matters which the mediator considers appropriate where he or she believes that any child or any other person affected by the mediation is suffering or likely to suffer significant harm (and in such case, the mediator should, so far as practicable and appropriate, discuss with the parties the way in which such disclosure is to take place), or

    7.1.3   matters where the law imposes an overriding obligation of disclosure on the mediator.

7.2   Any information or correspondence provided by any party should be shared openly with both and not withheld, except any address or telephone number and except as the parties may otherwise agree.

7.3   All information material to financial issues must be provided on an open basis, so that it can be referred to in court, either in support of an application made with the consent of the parties or in contested proceedings.

7.4   However, discussions about possible terms of settlement should be conducted on the 'without prejudice' basis; and in any event a mediation privilege should ordinarily be claimed for them, so that parties may explore their options freely.

7.5   The mediator must discuss arrangements about confidentiality with the parties before holding separate meetings or caucuses. It may be agreed that the mediator will either:

    7.5.1   report back to the parties as to the substance of the separate meetings, or

    7.5.2   maintain separate confidences: provided that if separate confidences are to be maintained, they must not include any material fact which would be open if discussed in a joint meeting.

7.6   The mediation privilege will not ordinarily apply in relation to communications indicating that a child or other person affected by the mediation is suffering, or likely to suffer, significant harm, or where other public policy considerations prevail, or where for any other reason the rules of evidence render privilege inapplicable.

Section 8 – families and children

8.1   Mediators shall have regard at all times to the provisions of Part I of the Family Law Act 1996.

8.2   In working with the parties, the mediator should also have regard to the needs and interests of the children of the family.

8.2.1   When it appears to the mediator that a child is suffering, or is likely to suffer, significant harm, the mediator should consider with the parties what steps should be taken outside mediation to remedy the situation. But in exceptional circumstances where there is serious risk of harm to any person the mediator may decide not to inform the parties.

8.2.2 Where it is necessary to protect the child from significant harm, the mediator must in any event contact an appropriate agency or take such steps outside the mediation as may be appropriate.

8.3   Occasionally children might be directly involved in mediation. The mediator should consider whether and when children may be directly involved in mediation. The mediator should not ordinarily invite children to be directly involved in the mediation unless specifically trained to do so and alive to the issues such as confidentiality and the dynamics inherent in doing so.

Section 9 – professional indemnity cover

9.1   All solicitor mediators must carry professional indemnity cover in respect of their acting as mediators.

   9.1.1   Solicitors who practise as mediators will be covered by appropriate indemnity insurance in respect of their acting as a mediator, provided they are doing so in their capacity as a member of their firm.

   9.1.2   If a solicitor is acting as a mediator as a separate activity outside his or her legal practice, separate indemnity insurance must be obtained.

Section 10 – promotion of mediation

10.1   Solicitor mediators may promote their practice as such, but must always do so in a professional, truthful and dignified way. They may reflect their qualification as a mediator and their membership of any other relevant mediation organisation.

10.2   Solicitor mediators should have regard to the requirements in relation to publicity, as stipulated in the Solicitors Code of Conduct, rule 7.

Section 11 – Family Law Act 1996, section 27 (Legal Aid Act 1988, section 13b)

Every mediator must have arrangements designed to ensure:

11.1   that parties participate in mediation only if willing and not influenced by fears of violence or other harm

11.2   that cases where either party may be influenced by fears of violence or other harm are identified as soon as possible

11.3   that the possibility of reconciliation is kept under review throughout mediation, and

11.4   that each party is informed about the availability of independent legal advice.

(iv) LSC (publicly funded) Mediation Quality Mark Standard[15]

Mediation

Quality Mark

Standard

Second edition
September 2009

---

15 © The Legal Services Commission 2002, 2009. Reproduced with the kind permission of the Legal Services Commission. For further information please visit their website at www.legalservices.gov.uk.

Contents page

1

1.3   Quality Mark Framework (pg7)
Foreword

This is the first revision of the Quality Mark standard for Mediation (MQM) since its launch in 2002. The revision is intended to keep the standard up to date and in line with the other Quality Mark standards.

The prime purpose of the MQM is to ensure that mediation services are well organised and managed and provide a competent service. To this end, the focus of this standard is on the individual competence of mediators and on client care – a milestone in Quality Mark development.

I hope that you find the revised MQM, continue to be a standard that helps organisations ensure they are well run, profitable, and provide clients with an excellent value for money, high quality service.

Patrick Reeve
Director, Strategic Development
Legal Services Commission

2

The Quality Mark

1. The Quality Mark is a quality standard for legal information, advice and specialist legal services. It comprises a set of standards designed to ensure that a service is well run and has its own quality control mechanisms that assure the quality of the information or advice the service provides.

2. There are three essential elements to the scheme:

    •   The specification of standards of quality assurance

    •   The independent audit of the standard to ensure that standards are being achieved and maintained

    •   Continuous improvement in the service offered by suppliers of legal services to their clients.

3. The Specialist level of this standard is described in this document.

1.1   The Community Legal Service (CLS)

Membership of the Community Legal Service (CLS) is achieved following certification to any one of the Quality Mark standards.

The CLS, launched in April 2000, aims to improve access for the public to quality information, advice and legal services through local networks of quality-assured services supported by co-ordinated funding, based on an assessment of local need.

The CLS Legal Adviser Directory provides information on Quality Marked suppliers in England and Wales, including the level of service and categories of work they provide. The Directory is accessible via the internet on www.communitylegaladvice.org.uk and via the Community Legal Advice national helpline **0845 345 4 345**. Community Legal Advice is designed to help the most vulnerable in society tackle their problems by providing free information, help and advice direct to the public on a range of common legal issues. Providers of legal services who have been awarded the Quality Mark are entitled to order for display any of the series of free printed legal information leaflets produced by Community Legal Advice.

1.2   CLS/CDS Logos

There are separate logos for the CLS and CDS, which Quality Mark holders may use according to guidance published separately (see Appendix 1).

3

1.3   Quality Mark Framework

The standards cover seven key quality areas, known as the Quality Mark Framework:

- **Access to Service:** Planning the service, making others aware of the service and non-discrimination

- **Seamless Service:** Signposting and referral to other agencies

- **Running the Organisation:** The roles and responsibilities of key staff, and financial management

- **People Management:** Equal opportunities for staff, training and development, supervision and supervisors' standards

- **Running the Service**: Case management, independent review of files and feedback to caseworkers

- **Meeting Clients' Needs:** Providing information to clients, confidentiality, privacy and fair treatment, and maintaining quality where someone else delivers part of the service

- **Commitment to Quality:** Complaints, other user feedback and maintaining quality procedures.

1.4   Benefits of Achieving the Quality Mark

The experience of Quality Mark holders since 2002 has shown that the implementation of formal management and administration systems, as required by the standard, brings numerous benefits in terms of increased efficiency and improved use of resources. These benefits include:

- **Improved risk management:** Effective risk management can reduce the likelihood of insurance claims being brought against the organisation. Some of the areas identified by insurers and underwriters as being the main causes of claims against organisations are addressed by the Quality Mark, which encourages:

    o   Increased management responsibility

    o   Diary control

    o   Conducting conflict of interest checks

    o   Effective supervision of staff

    o   Provision of comprehensive information about cost and other case matters including client care and complaints. For solicitors this is also covered Code of Conduct Rule 2.

- **Improved client care:** Where effective client care and supervision procedures are in place, the risk of complaints from clients, including those reaching the Legal Complaints Service and umbrella bodies, is greatly reduced. A large number of complaints from clients are due to misunderstandings caused by insufficient or incorrect information provided by the solicitor or adviser

4

- **Efficient management practices and reduced costs:** Having effective management systems leads to a reduction in administrative failures, preventing wasted costs and poor service to clients

- **Effective deployment of resources:** Where effective staff supervision, training, assessment and support are provided, staff motivation and morale are improved, and each staff member is able to contribute to the running of the organisation to the best of their ability

- **Increased client confidence:** Holding a recognised quality assurance standard demonstrates a commitment to the provision of quality services

- **Funder confidence:** Funders, including the LSC, currently require or may require in the future, certification to the Quality Mark to ensure that the services they fund meet minimum competence standards.

5

This page has been left blank intentionally

6

A ACCESS TO SERVICE

One aim of the Community Legal Service (CLS) is to improve access to services, which *offer help in preventing or settling or otherwise resolving disputes*, and to base the delivery of services on local needs and priorities. Members of the CLS should be aware of the environment in which they operate, and develop their services to meet the needs of their community.

Requirement A1	Business Planning
Purpose:	To ensure that members of the local/target community have access to mediation services that have been developed taking into account the day-to-day problems that the community may encounter, and the barriers that they may face in seeking mediation.
Requirement A2	Promoting Your Service
Purpose:	To ensure that members of the community can access services by finding out what services are available and how to make contact with the relevant organisation. The same information is also required for signposting and referral purposes, allowing organisations to access one another's services as necessary.
Requirement A3	Equality of Access
Purpose:	To ensure that in planning and delivering the service, organisations do not discriminate (directly or indirectly) in their choice of clients on unreasonable and unlawful grounds.

7

Quality Mark Standard for Mediation

A1 Business Planning

Requirements:

A1.	Your business plan
1	

A1.	A current business plan is available that sets out, in detail for the current year, and in
1	outline for the following two years, the key objectives of the organisation.

Definitions:

(These qualify the requirements and are mandatory where the word "must" appears)

A1.1   Your business plan

- A copy of the plan (or a summary of the main aims and objectives of the service) **must** be available to all members of staff, as appropriate, and to Quality Mark auditors (when requested).

Plan content

- The plan (which may be a number of related documents or a single plan) **must**:
  - o Be relevant to your own organisation's aims and objectives.
  - o Include details about how each objective is going to be achieved.
  - o Have been developed having regard to the following information (to which you can demonstrate that you have access; see guidance):
    - ▪ Description of the client group(s) to be served – i.e. the actual market you intend to target.
    - ▪ Details of services to be delivered, as well as details for any additional or enhanced services planned (e.g. what is to be offered, to whom, on what basis, and from when).
    - ▪ Details of opening hours and access arrangements – i.e. How you deliver services and whether you offer facilities to aid access (e.g. hospital or home visits, and access arrangements for people with disabilities).
    - ▪ A summary of mediators' areas of expertise and any (as appropriate) professional/legal qualification(s).   This includes mediator specialisms in victim/offender or other applications of mediation that are applicable to the service.
    - ▪ A finance plan/budget – The monetary impact, in broad terms, of the planned service on income and expenditure (and any capital investment), i.e. an analysis that shows how you can afford to deliver the planned services (including steps to secure funding or to generate investment capital if necessary).
    - ▪ A SWOT analysis – Covering assumptions you have made and taken into account when planning your services (e.g. IT provision, interest rates, other available services), and including reference to any available needs

---

8

680

assessment/community profile.

- For the plan to be "current" it **must** include all the changes required as a result of the most recent review (see A1.2), plus details of any issue likely to have a significant impact on delivery of the planned service.

- *Note* that to demonstrate compliance with the requirement, you will either need to provide the auditor with access to your plans (current and old) and any background information, or provide other suitable evidence (see guidance).

A1 Business Planning

Requirements:

A1.2	Reviewing your business plan

A1.2	The current business plan is reviewed, at least every six months, and a record of that review is kept until the next audit, as a minimum.

Definitions:

(These qualify the requirements and are mandatory where the word "must" appears)

A1.2	Reviewing your business plan
	• Specific projects or action proposals **must** be reviewed (against actual performance) at least every six months, while background information about the organisation, opportunities for development and client feedback, **must** be reviewed at least annually.
	• The evidence of the review **must** be available to the auditor, and you **must** be able to demonstrate that action has been taken (or there is a timetable for impending action) wherever required changes to the plan have been identified.

9

Appendix 8   Ethical Standards and Accreditation

Quality Mark Standard for Mediation

A2 Promoting Your Service

Requirements:

A2.1	**Providing service information**

A2.1	Details are provided to clients and members of the public about the type of work you do, and you take action to amend this and other information you distribute, where there is any change that has an impact on access and/or the services offered.

Definitions:

(These qualify the requirements and are mandatory where the word "must" appears)

A2.1   Providing service information

- You **must** complete the Community Legal Advice questionnaires LSC's Directory questionnaire (provided by Resource Information Services; (RIS) giving relevant details about the service you offer. If you wish your details to be displayed on the Community Legal Advice Directory.

- *Note* that you should additionally consider promoting your services by providing your details to other likely points of public contact (see guidance), although also note that leafleting and cold-calling the general public are not encouraged.

- A change in the service you offer that has an "impact on access and/or the services offered" would include changes to opening hours or cessation of a certain service. In these circumstances you **must** be able to demonstrate that action has been taken to amend the relevant information at the earliest opportunity.

- *Note* that it is not a requirement for you to retrieve any information that has already been distributed, although it is good practice for you to do so wherever possible.

10

682

A3: Equality of Access

Requirements:

A3.1   Non-discrimination in the provision of services

A3.1   A written non-discrimination policy is in place and available to all staff covering the provision of services to clients, which precludes discrimination on the grounds of race, colour, ethnic or national origins, sex, marital status or sexual orientation, disability, age or religion or belief.

A3.2   Targeting a specific client group

A3.2   Where organisational principles or charter provide for the service to be offered only to a specific client group, this is detailed in the business plan (A1.1) and reflected in your signposting and referral procedures (B1.2).

■   **Definitions:**

The definitions below qualify the requirement and are mandatory where the word "must" appears.

Where the sentence or paragraph begins with the word "Note", it contains information to help you (see also the separate Guidance document) and is not mandatory.

A3.1   Non-discrimination in the provision of services

- "Provision of services" **must** cover both the planning of services, and decisions about whether or not to accept clients. In respect of the latter, it **must** also outline the action to be taken if any breaches occur.

- *Note* that this policy is only part of the equal opportunities framework required by the Quality Mark; a single document may cover all areas (see also D1.3 and F5.1).

- *Note* that you may adopt an existing model policy, but may need to include additional information or procedures in order to meet the Quality Mark minimum requirements (see Guidance).

11

A3.2 Targeting a specific client group

- Where your organisational principles or charter require you to offer services to a specific group, your procedure (at B1.2) **must** specify the arrangements for explaining your approach to all those who are not in the target client group(s) and for signposting and/or referring them to alternative providers.

- The arrangements you have for people who are not in your target client group **must** be understood by all members of staff who may need to signpost (or possibly refer) them, and be practised whenever the need arises.

This page has been left blank intentionally.

13

685

Quality Mark Standard for Mediation

B SEAMLESS SERVICE

Where a member of the Community Legal Service (CLS) cannot provide the particular service needed by the client, they must inform the client and direct them to an alternative service provider, where available.

Requirement B1	Signposting and Referral
Purpose:	To enable individuals to receive the right help at the earliest opportunity, and to ensure that, if the mediation service being offered is not appropriate for the client, a procedure for signposting or referral is operated that assists them to find another more suitable service. To review the use of signposting and referral in order to make improvements, where appropriate, to the service your organisation offers.

B1 Signposting and Referral

Requirements:

B1.1	Staff knowledge about when to use signposting and referral
B1.1	Members of staff know when to use signposting and referral, with clear information given verbally, or in writing, about the mediation service being offered.

Definitions:

(These qualify the requirements and are mandatory where the word "must" appears)

B1.1   Staff knowledge about when to use signposting and referral

- Staff **must** be able to demonstrate how they identify when to signpost and when to refer. See notes below and guidance for examples.

- *Note* that the need for signposting will usually arise when the individual first provides information about the type of legal problem they have, and you realise they require a service that your organisation cannot provide. Often this will be when they make their first contact with you to seek help, though sometimes it may become apparent only after an initial diagnostic interview/appointment. *Note* also that although it is not a requirement for you to decide which alternative provider they should see or to offer assistance in making arrangements for them, you are likely to consider this appropriate in certain circumstances (see guidance).

- *Note* that the requirement for referral arises only where you have an established client relationship in a current matter. Good referral practice means that you will usually identify the need for, and make, a referral before you reach the point where you cannot offer further help. *Note* also that in case of referrals (unlike signposting), you are expected to make arrangements for the client to see someone from the new organisation, and you will need to meet minimum requirements (see B1.2 below) about information provided to both the client and the new organisation.

B1 Signposting and Referral

Requirements:

B1.2   A procedure for conducting signposting and referral

B1.2   A procedure and process for conducting signposting and referral exist, and are in effective operation.

15

- **Definitions:**

The definitions below qualify the requirement and are mandatory where the word "must" appears.

Where the sentence or paragraph begins with the word "Note", it contains information to help you (see also the separate Guidance document) and is not mandatory.

B1.2   A procedure for conducting signposting and referral

Signposting

- For signposting - your procedure **must** confirm that, as a minimum, you will signpost any individual whom your organisation is unable to help. Signposting means that you **must** do at least *one* of the following:

- Provide access to details of other Quality Mark holders through the CLS Legal Adviser Directory (**www.communitylegaladvice.org.uk** or   national helpline number **0845 345 4 345**) and offer of assistance to guide them through it.

- Provide a list of local (or specialist) organisations that you have produced by area of law, or provide your own recommendation (as long as, in both cases, preference is given to, or you clearly identify, organisations that hold a Quality Mark).

- *Note* that it is good practice to provide direct assistance wherever possible.

Referral

- For referrals – your procedure **must** include, as a minimum, the practical steps to be taken to identify appropriate service providers, including giving first consideration to those with a Quality Mark, and the circumstances in which use of a service without the Quality Mark might be appropriate.

- The process you adopt for referrals (usually documented in your procedure) **must** ensure that in *all* instances:

- The client is told what role your organisation will take and what service(s) they should expect from the new service provider.

- Any feedback that is later given (by the client) on the service provided by the new service provider is recorded and reviewed.

- Information about advice or assistance already given (and any relevant documentation) is forwarded to the new service provider.

- Any cost implications identified are discussed with the client (i.e. as a minimum this means explaining the relevant charging information shown in the CLS Legal Adviser Directory) and noted on file.

B1 Signposting and Referral

Requirements:

B1. 3	Maintaining and reviewing referral records and data
B1. 3	Records of referrals are maintained (including records of all instances where no suitable service provider could be found), and reviewed at least annually.
B1.	Ensuring that supplier information is up to date
B1. 4	Access to the CLS Legal Adviser Directory is available, and there is a process to ensure that details about alternative service providers are kept up to date.

Definitions:
(These qualify the requirements and are mandatory where the word "must" appears)

B1.3	**Maintaining and reviewing referral records and data**
	• You **must** have a process (usually documented in your procedure) to ensure that:
	o Records for all referrals identify, as a minimum, the client or case, who made the referral, to whom the client was referred (justifying the selection of any service without a Quality Mark), and the reason for referral (e.g. related to the scope of the matter type, case capacity or to the limits of the mediator's competence).
	o Records are kept every time a suitable provider could not be found when the need for a referral had been identified, and these records include the subject matter and what (if anything) was done to progress the client's case further.
B1.4	**Ensuring that supplier information is up to date**
	• Access to the CLS Legal Adviser Directory **must** be available and **must** contain correct information about your organisation (or steps **must** have been taken to correct errors).
	• Note: The CLS Legal Adviser is accessible either via the Community Legal Advice website (**www.communitylegaladvice.org.uk**) or via the Community Legal Advice national helpline (**0845 345 4 345**)
	• You **must** demonstrate that you have access to current details (i.e. telephone number(s), type(s) of service offered, opening times, charging information, languages offered and disabled access availability) for any alternative service providers used.

17

689

Quality Mark Standard for Mediation

This page has been left blank intentionally.

Issue 1: 12/'02

690

C RUNNING THE ORGANISATION
Members of the Community Legal Service (CLS) must have structures and procedures that ensure effective management of the organisation and its resources.

Requirement C1	Organisational Structure
Purpose:	It is important that all members of staff know to whom they report and who reports to them, and can identify those with relevant key departmental and organisational responsibilities. In addition, it is fundamental that organisations are independent of any undue pressure, and that they abide by agreed practices for dealing with serious misdemeanours.
Requirement C2	Resource Provision
Purpose:	It is important that organisations produce key information about their resources, and that they monitor the information to ensure that their service strategy can be fulfilled.
Requirement C3	Financial Control
Purpose:	It is important that organisations produce key financial information and monitor this information regularly, in order to ensure that financial resources are properly and effectively managed.
Requirement C4	Suitable Premises / Off-Site Facilities
Purpose:	It is important that organisations have arrangements in place to ensure that their facilities are suitable for dealing with two or more parties before, during and after the mediation process. The facilities must ensure privacy for clients.

19

Quality Mark Standard for Mediation

C1 Organisational Structure

Requirements:

C1.1	Your staff structure
C1.1	A document is available to all members of staff that identifies them, their current jobs and lines of responsibility.

C1.2	Key roles and decision-making structure
C1.2	A document is available to all members of staff that identifies those with key roles and decision-making responsibilities.

Definitions:

(These qualify the requirements and are mandatory where the word "must" appears)

C1.1   Your staff structure

- As a minimum, your document **must** show details for all individuals who work within the part of your service for which you are seeking, or want to maintain, the Quality Mark, including all support staff.

- Details **must** include each person's name and job title, and the document **must** demonstrate to whom they report (if anyone) and who (if anyone) reports to them.

- As a minimum, the structure **must** include the name and job title for every member of staff (including volunteers) working in the relevant Quality Mark area(s), and **must** be accessible to all those individuals.

C1.2   Key roles and decision-making structure

- The person's name, job title and main responsibilities **must** be given for: all individuals responsible for the management of the organisation as a whole (including any working outside the part of the service for which you are seeking, or want to maintain, the Quality Mark); individuals responsible for the management of a department; and for the individuals with overall responsibility for finance and quality.

- The person with ultimate responsibility for meeting the Quality Mark **must** be identified (see requirement G3.1).

- Those with authority to deal with complaints, those with mediation review responsibilities, and supervisors (including professional practice consultants) **must** be identified. Where any of these responsibilities falls with external personnel, these individuals **must** be shown.

- The document **must** be updated to reflect changes of staff or to job titles or responsibilities within three months of that change.

20   Issue 1: 12/'02

692

C1 Organisational Structure

Requirements:

C1.3   Management committees

C1.3	Where a management committee runs an organisation, the committee demonstrates independence.

C1.4   Membership of recognised representative bodies

C1.4	The Ultimate focus of the Quality Mark is on the client. Mediators who **undertake publicly funded family mediation** should be members of and regulated by a member organisation of the Family Mediation Council.

Definitions:

(These qualify the requirements and are mandatory where the word "must" appears)

C1.3	Management committees
	• Funding bodies **must** remain a minority within the committee membership (no more than 50% of members on the committee should be funders), the governing document **must** be detailed, and the relationship between the committee and those running the organisation **must** be clear.
	• Where a management committee is involved in running the organisation, the decision-making process **must** be identified from its written constitution, together with the definition of its role, quorum and terms of reference (including any sub-committees).
	• Up-to-date lists of members **must** be kept, together with an identification of roles and responsibilities. You **must** have a written description of the management structure and designate the responsibilities of individuals within it. The relationship between the responsibilities of the management committee and those of any paid or volunteer staff of the organisation **must** also be clear. This information could be provided as a family tree.
C1.4	**Membership of recognised representative bodies**
	• Mediators who undertake publicly funded family mediation should be members of and **regulated by a member organisation of the Family Mediation Council.** Charities should comply with regulation by the Charity Commission, while local authority organisations should comply with the requirements of their local authority.
	•

21

693

C2 Resource Provision

Requirements:

C2.1	Annual service performance review
C2.1	A process for reviewing levels of service performance against the service delivery aims on an annual basis.

C2.2	Analysing resource/service capacity
C2.2	An analysis of the resources required in order to meet the service delivery aims outlined in the business plan.

Definitions:

(These qualify the requirements and are mandatory where the word "must" appears)

C2.1   Annual service performance review

- You **must** have a written procedure that is in effective operation so that those responsible for running the organisation can keep service performance under review. Your procedure **must** detail how and what you intend to monitor in terms of actual performance, and the key targets against which you will compare. The items to be monitored might include:

  ○ Number of new clients seen.

  ○ Hours of mediation carried out.

  ○ Number of mediation cases completed.

  ○ Percentage of clients from target area(s).

- Findings from reviews **must** be noted and fed into the annual business plan review process (at A1). Even where a review identifies no danger to the plan's objectives and no major opportunities for expansion, a note to this effect **must** be made. Where a review does identify something that may impact on your ability to deliver, you **must** demonstrate that action has been taken.

C2.2   Analysing resource/service capacity

- You **must** consider your service's capacity in the light of available resources, so that you plan to deliver a service that is based on individuals' caseloads and responsibilities.

- The background information for this review will be detailed on personal files and in the job specification for any position being recruited (see Section D). However, for this purpose, information about mediators' estimated capacity (in terms of numbers of cases and responsibilities) and availability **must** be compiled for the department(s) or organisation, so that decisions can be made about the overall capacity of the service.

- Performance information **must** be collected on an ongoing basis, and this **must** be cross-checked with your service delivery aims to ensure that your business plan remains on track. In addition, you **must** feed into the process any other information relevant to service delivery which has been collected (e.g. from monitoring questionnaires, from complaints or from referral feedback). The main resources reviewed will be human; however, other resources, such as buildings and equipment, may feature.

23

Appendix 8 Ethical Standards and Accreditation

C3 Financial Control

Requirements:

C3.1	Financial processes
C3.1	Financial management must be exercised in line with agreed statements of financial policies, procedures and authorities.

C3.2	Independent financial review
C3.2	Financial review by an independent source.

C3.3	Financial reviews and service provision
C3.3	An analysis of financial information that has been used to assist in reviewing the provision of services.

Definitions:

(These qualify the requirements and are mandatory where the word "must" appears)

C3.1   Financial processes

- You **must** be able to provide the auditor with evidence that you produce the required minimum financial information (and any additional financial information that you say you produce).

- You **must** be able to provide the auditor with evidence as to how often financial information is produced, and how it is used to assist in the financial management of the organisation (i.e. who reviews the figures, how often, and for what purpose). This may be documented in your procedure where you choose not to disclose the content of financial documents to the auditor.

- Auditors will not need to consider the content of financial information produced in terms of the detail contained in the information, but will require sight of the relevant documents. You can maintain financial information in any recognised format.

C3.2   Independent financial review

- You **must** provide written confirmation from an independent accountant that the organisation's accounts have been either certified or audited to their satisfaction.

- An accounting period **must** last no longer than 18 months, and each one **must** begin immediately the previous one ends, and confirmation that accounts have been certified/audited to the accountant's satisfaction **must** cover the last accounting period.

C3.3   Financial reviews and service provision

- Financial information, like service performance (in C2) **must** be reviewed at least every six months to ensure confidence in the continuing financial position of the organisation. Findings **must** then feed into the business-planning process, so that decisions can be taken about what changes (if any) need to be made to the service being delivered.

- You **must** be able to provide the auditor with evidence to confirm that the review of overall finances has been carried out every six months (alongside the review of the business plan as required in A1.2), usually evidenced by providing the documents reviewed or the minutes of a review meeting (see guidance).

C3.5   Public liability insurance

C3.5   Display of public liability insurance certificate in each office.

C3.5   Public liability insurance

- Public liability insurance certificates **must** be on display in every office where mediation takes place.

25

697

Quality Mark Standard for Mediation

C4 Suitable Premises / Off-Site Facilities

Requirements:

C4.1	Facilities to ensure that clients wait separately
C4.1	Facilities to ensure that, where appropriate, clients can wait separately prior to the mediation.

C4.2	A minimum of two suitable rooms
C4.2	A minimum of two suitable rooms to ensure that clients can be seen separately or separated if necessary.

C4.3	Identification of the mediation service
C4.3	In mixed services, the mediation service is clearly identified when answering the telephone.

C4.4	Facilities for children
C4.4	Suitable child facilities, are available where appropriate.

C4.5	Privacy for clients
C4.5	Privacy must be ensured for both clients, both in the room where mediation takes place, and prior to the commencement of the session.

Issue 1: 12/'02

Definitions:

(These qualify the requirements and are mandatory where the word "must" appears)

C4.1   **Facilities to ensure that clients wait separately**
• Facilities **must** be available to enable clients to wait separately prior to the mediation, where appropriate.
C4.2   **A minimum of two suitable rooms**
• In some instances, clients will need to be seen separately, or a form of shuttle mediation will take place. In such situations, there **must** be two separate rooms, thereby ensuring client privacy. Additionally, in some other circumstances, clients may need to be separated, and for this reason it is important to have two rooms.
C4.3   **Identification of the mediation service**
• It is essential that, in mixed services, the mediation service is clearly identified as being separate from any other service (i.e. advice service) run from the same premises.
C4.4   **Facilities for children**
• Where a service consults children as part of the mediation process, it **must** ensure that suitable child facilities, such as play materials, are available.
C4.5   **Privacy for clients**
• The service **must** have access to facilities to ensure client privacy as appropriate.

27

This page has been left blank intentionally.

D PEOPLE MANAGEMENT
Members of the Community Legal Service (CLS) must ensure that members of staff and volunteers are treated fairly, and that they possess or develop the skills and knowledge required to meet clients' needs.

Requirement D1	Roles, Responsibilities, Recruitment and Equal Opportunities for Staff and Volunteers
Purpose:	To ensure that everyone is clear about what their job entails, so that their contribution to the service is recognised and their potential is realised, without discrimination.
Requirement D2	Induction, Appraisal and Training
Purpose:	Attention must be given to staff and volunteer development if your service is to meet its potential, with clients given a quality service.
Requirement D3	Supervisors – Including Professional Practice Consultants (PPC) - Family Mediation Services and Community Mediation Services
Purpose:	To ensure that supervisors are in place with the requisite skills and experience to underpin the delivery of quality mediation sessions for the client. *Also see D4 for operation of the supervisory role.*
Requirement D4	Operation of the Supervisory Role – Family Mediation Services and Community Mediation Services
Purpose:	To ensure that members of staff and volunteers are supported so that they deliver a quality service, and so that their professional knowledge and skills are being developed continuously.
Requirement D5	Individual Competence – Family and Community Mediators
Purpose:	To ensure that all mediation and intake/suitability sessions undertaken are conducted by competent staff.

29

D1 Equal Opportunities Policy/Fair Treatment of Staff

Requirements:

D1.1 & D1.2	**Job descriptions, person specifications, key responsibilities and objectives**
D1.1	A current job description is available for every member of staff, and a job description and person specification is available for every post to be recruited.
D1.2	All staff know their current key responsibilities and objectives, and these are documented.

Definitions:

(These qualify the requirements and are mandatory where the word "must" appears)

D1.1 & D1.2	Job descriptions, person specifications, key responsibilities and objectives

- Documents **must** be available for all staff who are directly or indirectly involved in that part of your service for which you are seeking, or wish to maintain, the Quality Mark

- Documents **must** be sufficiently detailed and accurate to ensure that:

  o   Staff are clear about what is expected of them in their roles.

  o   Documents can be used for appraisal purposes (see D2.2).

  o   Documents can be used as a basis for reviewing training and development needs (see D2.3).

  o   Documents identify the skills, knowledge, experience and attributes required for the post, and outline the job purpose and lines of accountability.

D1: Roles, Responsibilities, Recruitment and Equal Opportunities for Staff

Requirements:

D1.3   Non-discrimination in the provision of services - Equality and Diversity Standard

D1.3   You **must** have a written Equality and Diversity Policy that is in effective operation. This policy **must** be available to all staff and **must** as a minimum meet the requirements of the Equalities and Diversity standards as shown. The standard is tailored to the size of the organisation.

There **must** be a named person with responsibility for implementing E & D in the policy and in any document showing lines of responsibilities and key decision makers.

It must also outline the action to be taken if any breaches occur.

31

703

| D1. | **Non-discrimination in the provision of services - Equality and Diversity Standard** |

LEVEL 1 (Fewer than 5 employees)
Organisations with fewer than 5 employees, are required provide a written document that demonstrates the organisations commitment to Equality and Diversity legislation. In addition, you will be required to provide written assurance that the appropriate level of the Equality and Diversity Standard will be achieved following any recruitment that will increase the organisation to 5 or more employees.

LEVEL 2 (5 to 49 Employees)
All organisations with between 5 and 49 employees must have a standard that achieves criteria 1-4 listed below

1. All organisations must provide an equal opportunities policy in respect of race, gender, disability, sexual orientation, age, religion/belief that covers at least:

   a. Recruitment, selection, training, promotion, discipline and dismissal

   b. Discrimination, harassment and victimisation making it clear that these are disciplinary offences within the organisation

   c. Identification of senior position with responsibility for the policy and its effective implementation

   d. How this policy is communicated to your staff

2. Effective implementation of the policy in the organisation's recruitment practices, to include open recruitment methods such as the use of job centres, careers services and press advertisements

3. Regular reviews of the policy (at least every three years)

4. Regular monitoring of the number of job applicants from different gender, disability and ethnic groups (at least annually)

LEVEL 3 (50 or more Employees)
All organisations with 50 or more employees must have a policy that achieves criteria 1- 4 in Level 2 and the additional criteria 5 –9 listed below

5. Provide written instructions to managers and supervisors on equality in recruitment selections, training promotion, discipline and dismissal of staff.

6. All managers, and any staff responsible for recruitment and selection have undergone equality training. This should be in effect by April 2011.

Continued over

7. In addition to criteria 4 (level 2) carry out monitoring, annually, on the number of employees from different gender, disability, age and ethnic groups by grade when:
    a. In post
    b. Applying for posts
    c. Taking up training and development opportunities
    d. Promoted
    e. Transferred
    f. Disciplined and dismissed
    g. Leaving employment

8. There is a process in place to review monitoring data which includes details on how to deal with circumstances where under representation of the groups listed above is identified (e.g. taking positive action, identifying specific training etc)

9. Regular reporting and consultation on equality issues with the workforce.

LEVEL 4 (250 or more Employees)
All organisations with 250 or more employees must have a standard that achieves criteria 1-9 and

10. Check that criteria 1- 9 are being used effectively

11. Where the review of monitoring data (set out in criteria 8 above) identifies under representation, you should:

   - Seek professional advice on the employment issues identified. This could be from EHRC or an in-house equality representative the equality unit in their employment advisory services

   - Take appropriate action. This may include identifying specific training needs or taking positive action to increase employee diversity where under representation is identified.

Notes
Employees in relation to the E&D standard refers to staff employed in the services of the organisation covered by the Specialist Quality Mark

Guidance on an equality and diversity policy and categories for Ethnic monitoring forms will be available on the LSC website.

A definition of positive action is available on the EHRC website:
http://www.equalityhumanrights.com/your-rights/rights-in-different-settings/shops-and-services/when-discrimination-is-lawful/positive-action/

33

Quality Mark Standard for Mediation

This page has been left blank intentionally

Issue 1: 12/'02

706

D1.4	Operating an open recruitment process
D1.4	An open recruitment process.

D1.5	Safety
D1.5	A documented procedure to ensure staff, volunteer and client safety throughout the mediation process.

D1.4   Operating an open recruitment process

- For your recruitment process to be considered "open", you **must** be able to demonstrate that, for each available permanent vacancy, the job is offered to the most suitable individual, on the basis of an objective and consistent assessment against requirements that you set relating to the role's key tasks and responsibilities, as well as any relevant personal attributes that you seek.

  o Notes show that the process assessed the skills, experience and attributes advertised as being required, and that it was applied consistently.

  o All short-listed candidates (as a minimum) **must** be able to obtain feedback from assessment (if they request it), with assessment records being kept for all applicants and candidates, whether short-listed or not, for at least 12 months.

D1.5   Safety

- As a minimum, your written procedure **must**:

  o Ensure that a sole member of staff/volunteer is never left alone with client(s) on the premises.

  o Detail the procedures to be followed in the event of any violence toward staff, volunteers or clients.

35

707

D2 Induction, Appraisal and Training

Requirements:

D2.1	Induction
D2.1	An induction process for people who join the organisation.
D2.2	**Performance review and feedback**
D2.2	Performance appraisal of all members of staff is undertaken at least annually.

                                                                                                        Issue 1: 12/'02

Definitions:

(These qualify the requirements and are mandatory where the word "must" appears)

D2.1   Induction
 	
• Induction **must** begin within two months of joining (unless justifiable reasons have been recorded), and your process **must** cover *all* of the areas listed below:
 	
    ○   The organisation's aims.
 	
    ○   The management/staff structure and where the new post fits into it.
 	
    ○   The recruit's role and the work of their department or team.
 	
    ○   The organisation's policies on non-discrimination, quality, customer care and complaints.
 	
    ○   The office procedures manual and/or other work instructions/processes relevant to the post.
 	
    ○   Terms and conditions of employment, and welfare and safety matters.
 	
• Records confirming induction (content and date(s)) for each individual **must** be kept.

D2.2   Performance review and feedback • Annual appraisals **must** be conducted for all members of staff other than with the auditor's agreement. • Appraisal records **must** detail existing and future objectives, and be signed by the individual being appraised and the person performing the appraisal. • *Note* that these records may be kept on individuals' personal files (i.e. not necessarily in a central file).

D2 Induction, Appraisal and Training

Requirements:

D2.3	Individual training and development plans
D2.3	Individual training and development plans are produced, which are reviewed at least annually, and with the review recorded.

D2.4	Training records
D2.4	All training is recorded.

Definitions:

(These qualify the requirements and are mandatory where the word "must" appears)

D2.3   Individual training and development plans

- Plans **must** include any training needs and/or development opportunities identified:
    - During appraisals, mediation reviews and supervisory sessions.
    - From business or service reviews (see A1.2).
    - As a result of recognising that a required skill is not available in the organisation.
- The plans **must** outline what is to be achieved (i.e. the aim), how it is to be achieved (i.e. the method), and over what timescale.
- Assessment of training needs and development opportunities **must** cover organisational, managerial and/or mediation competence as necessary.
- Training records **must** include the dates of external and in-house training courses attended (or given), the course titles, and the names of course providers.

D2.4   Training records

- Training records **must** include the dates of external and in-house training attended, the course titles and the names of the course providers.
- These records may be kept on individual's personal files as opposed to central records.

    Issue 1: 12/'02

D3a Supervisors

Requirements:

D3.1   Named category supervisor

D3.1   A named supervisor or professional practice consultant (PPC) to supervise mediators for each category of work (Property and Finance, Children only *or* AIM (All Issues Mediation: Property and Finance, and Children matters)), who is accessible to mediators.

Definitions:

(These qualify the requirements and are mandatory where the word "must" appears)

D3.1   Named category supervisor

- The Auditor **must** be sent details (in writing and within four weeks) whenever a supervisor leaves or is changed, including the name and date of leaving of the outgoing supervisor and the name of the new person, their date of appointment and how they qualify as a supervisor, or outlining satisfactory arrangements to recruit, and steps taken to control, quality of work in the interim.

External Supervisors (from other organisations):

- External supervisors may be authorised at the auditor's discretion. In order to be considered, they **must** meet D3.2, D3.3 and D4.2 in full, their role **must** be formalised by a contract, and supervisory arrangements **must** be documented in detail. External supervisors **must** be included in the staff plan and key roles structure (see C1.1 and C1.2), and their performance appraisals **must** be appraised. Finally, an external supervisor **must** be able to demonstrate that such an arrangement will not be detrimental to supervisory duties they carry out for any other Quality Mark organisation (see guidance for further details).

Accessibility:

- The organisation **must** show how the supervisor maintains accessibility, and **must** be able to demonstrate control over the quality of work (e.g. by the supervisor being accessible by telephone or email), especially if the supervisor is not office based (e.g. by being accessible by telephone or e-mail).

Deputy Supervisors:

- A deputy supervisor (who may not meet all the requirements at D3.2 and D3.3) can be named and can carry out functions usually performed by the supervisor, under their supervision (i.e. the supervisor **must** demonstrate that they maintain overall responsibility). Deputy supervisors **must** be denoted as such on the key roles structure (at C1.2) and they **must** have a training and development plan (D2.3) that is specifically designed to provide the skills and experience necessary for them to be able to meet all of the supervisory requirements in the future. A deputy may also act as a temporary supervisor in the supervisor's absence, and in such instances you need not justify the nomination nor carry out an appraisal after ten days.

Temporary Supervisors:

- A temporary supervisor (who may not meet all the requirements) can be nominated to cover periods of absence or sickness, but you **must** be able to explain the

---

39

grounds on which that person was nominated, and one performance appraisal **must** be carried out (within 28 days) should the period of cover extend beyond ten consecutive working days. *Note* that delegation to a deputy **must** not extend beyond four weeks continuously, or eight weeks in any calendar year, without the authority of the auditor.

D3 Supervisors

Requirements:

D3.2 Supervisory skills

D3.2 Supervisors must be registered as a supervisor by a member organisation of the Family Mediation Council and have successfully completed a mediation supervision training course organised by a Member Organisation of the Family Mediation Council.

Definitions:

(These qualify the requirements and are mandatory where the word "must" appears)

D3.2   Supervisory skills • The supervisor **must** demonstrate that they are registered as a supervisor by a Member Organisation of the Family Mediation Council • The MQM standard may in future recognise other organisations to register supervisors who have similar registration systems as the named body above.

Quality Mark Standard for Mediation

D4 Operation of the Supervisory Role

Requirements:

D4.1	Case allocation
D4.1	Processes to ensure that staff are allocated cases according to the role they are required to fulfil and on the basis of their competence and capacity.

D4.2	Systems of supervision
D4.2	Effective systems of supervision exist that are tailored to the competence of individual members of staff.

D4.3	Limits of individual competence and referral
D4.3	All members of staff know the limits of their own capacity and are aware of the need to inform their supervisor if a case is beyond their capacity.

Issue 1: 12/'02

Definitions:

(These qualify the requirements and are mandatory where the word "must" appears)

These requirements apply to all mediators and to all supervisors.

D4.1   Case allocation

- Supervisors **must** be able to demonstrate that staff only undertake work that is appropriate for their role (see individual job profiles at D1.1), and that it falls within their limits in terms of competence and capacity. It is not a requirement that supervisors allocate work on a day-to-day basis, but, where they do not, services **must** be able to demonstrate how work is allocated so that it incorporates the supervisor's assessments.

D4.2   Systems of supervision

- Arrangements for supervision **must** be tailored to each member of staff and each volunteer according to their knowledge, skills and experience, and **must** be not less than one hour per quarter one-to-one supervision.

- Supervisors **must** be able to demonstrate control over the quality of work produced by the staff and volunteers they supervise (including work that has been the subject of a transaction criteria audit), and **must** demonstrate how they ensure that the skills and knowledge of staff and volunteers skills and knowledge are being developed continuously through supervision.

- Supervision sessions **must** be recorded, including date, type of session, cases and issues discussed, areas of action /change and relevant timescales.   Supervision sessions do not have to be one-to-one sessions with individual mediators, and can be performed with a group of mediators at the same time.

- If services make use of group supervision, they **must** also ensure that at least two of the supervision sessions per year for each individual mediator are one to one.   If there are issues of bad practice, these **must** be dealt with by way of one-to-one supervision.

- The supervisor **must** make the decision as to whether group supervision or one-to-one supervision is the most appropriate, and this decision **must** be justifiable to the auditor.

D4.3   Limits of individual competence and referral

- Staff and volunteers **must** be able to demonstrate referral of cases internally (or externally where appropriate), or explain the point at which they would refer a case that had reached the limit of their competence.

- Exceptions may be made on a case-by-case basis, only where the referral is not possible due to the specific circumstances of the client (e.g. their mental state), the urgency of the case, or the lack of availability of an appropriate person to refer to.

43

D4 Operation of the Supervisory Role

Requirements

D4.4	Access to reference materials
D4.4	Ready access to current relevant and up-to-date reference material, as documented by the service provider.
D4.5	Updating information on best practice and procedure to staff
D4.5	A process exists for giving timely information to staff about changes in law, practice and procedure that are pertinent to the service they deliver.

Definitions:

(These qualify the requirements and are mandatory where the word "must" appears)

These requirements apply to all mediators and to all supervisors.

D4.4	**Access to reference materials**
	• Current reference materials **must** be available.
	• You **must** be able to demonstrate how materials are kept up to date and made available to staff.
D4.5	**Updating information on best practice and procedure to staff**
	• Supervisors **must** demonstrate how they become aware of relevant changes in legislation, practice and procedure, and then how they make sure that the knowledge of the staff they supervise is also kept up to date.

D5a Individual Competence – Family Mediators

Requirements:

D5.1	**Individual competence**
D5.1	Mediators must be assessed as competent by one of the following routes:
	• Successful completion of the competence assessment process managed by member organisations of the Family Mediation Council.
	• Practitioner membership of the Law Society Family Mediation Panel.

Definitions:

(These qualify the requirements and are mandatory where the word "must" appears)

D5.1	**Individual Competence**
	• Member Organisations of the Family Mediation Council provide competence assessment.
	• Where organisations choose The Law Society Panel Membership route, the following membership is required:
	o At preliminary audit, general membership **must** be obtained;
	o At pre Quality Mark audit, practitioner membership **must** be obtained.

45

Quality Mark Standard for Mediation

This page has been left blank intentionally.

Issue 1: 12/'02

E RUNNING THE SERVICE	
Members of the Community Legal Service (CLS) must have processes and procedures that ensure an effective and efficient service to their clients.	
Requirement E1	**File Management**
Purpose:	To ensure that cases are properly managed and controlled, both overall (from an organisational perspective) and individually (so that they are acted upon appropriately and punctually).
Requirement E2	**File Review**
Purpose:	An independent review of work enables organisations to monitor the quality of mediation and service being provided, as well as allowing early intervention where concerns are raised, and for training and development needs to be quickly identified and acted upon.

E1: File Management

Requirements:

E1.1   Access to files

E1.1   Quality Mark auditors must have access to appropriate files/client records.

▪   **Definitions:**
The definitions below qualify the requirement and are mandatory where the word "must" appears.
Where the sentence or paragraph begins with the word "Note", it contains information to help you (see also the separate Guidance document) and is not mandatory.

E1.   Access to files
<ul><li>Auditors will require access to client files for audit purposes. Arrangements must be in place to ensure that client confidentiality must not be breached (see Section F6.2). Clients need to be made aware that it is possible that their file may be audited, and permission should be obtained from the client.</li><li>Where an organisation holds an LSC contract for the mediation work, additional requirements are in place for producing lists of client files from the date of the Quality Mark application; see contract for further information.</li></ul>

47

Quality Mark Standard for Mediation

E1.2	File management procedure(s)

E1.2 Documented procedures are effective in:

(a) Identifying potential conflicts of interest.

(b) Locating files and tracing documents, correspondence and other items relating to any case that has been closed for less than six years.

(c) Maintaining a back-up record of key dates.

(d) Monitoring files for inactivity at pre-determined intervals.

- **Definitions:**

The definitions below qualify the requirement and are mandatory where the word "must" appears.

Where the sentence or paragraph begins with the word "Note", it contains information to help you (see also the separate Guidance document) and is not mandatory.

E1.2 **File management procedure(s)**

Conflict of interest

- The procedure **must** identify when a potential conflict of interest could arise, the process that is followed, and who is responsible for the process, and as a minimum, how to deal with circumstances where:

  o The case may involve disputes with the organisation, a member of its staff or management committee, or a funder.

  o A dispute that the mediator or service knows to be based on false information.

  o A case where the mediator has acquired any relevant information in any private or professional capacity.

  o Where mediation services are offered as part of a practice/consortia offering other professional services, a mediator from that practice/consortia may not act as a family mediator for any client who has received other professional services from that practice/consortia unless the mediator is able to demonstrate that the information given to other professionals at the practice/consortia has no bearing on the issues to be addressed in the mediation, and that the client has given personal consent to that person acting as a mediator, having been informed of the potential conflict of interest.

Locating files and tracing contents

- The procedure **must** allow you to access files (at least those containing correspondence) from your on-site filing system or from archive, for files closed up to six years ago.

Back-up recording of key dates

- Definitions of "key dates" **must** be documented, which, as a minimum, **must** include court return dates, where they apply. The procedure(s) **must** outline the back-up system mediators use to ensure that they are alerted (other than by their own diaries), as well as identifying who is responsible for recording and monitoring key dates records and how often this is done.

Monitoring files for inactivity

- The procedure(s) **must** outline the process and identify how frequently reviews will take place. There **must** be justification for any interval longer than three months.

E1 File Management

Requirements:

E1.3	Mediation files are logical and orderly
E1.3	Mediation files presented in an orderly and logical manner, with key information readily apparent to someone other than the person who normally has conduct of the case.

E1.4	Confidentiality in mixed practices
E1.4	In mixed practices, mediation files are must be stored confidentially.

E1.5	Recording information in client files
E1.5	A documented procedure must be in place to detail the information that is to be recorded on the file during each mediation session.

49

Definitions:

(These qualify the requirements and are mandatory where the word "must" appears)

E1.4   Confidentiality in mixed practices
• A mixed practice is one that offers both mediation and other services (e.g. solicitor/mediator practice). Files relating to the mediation service **must** be kept confidentially, separate from any files relating to another service.

E1.3   Mediation files are logical and orderly

As a minimum, key dates and any funding limitations must be shown together in a prominent place on the file (i.e. on the outside or on the flysheet/inside cover of a paper file, or in a summary section of a computerised file), and the case status or latest action must be evident from the file. Documents must be stored securely and correspondence must be filed in chronological order.

E1.5   Recording information in client files
• The written procedure **must** detail the information that should be recorded on client files during or after each mediation session, and as a minimum **must** include:
○ Who attended each session (and, if others attended, their relationship to the clients).
○ The agreement of both parties to mediation (unless a formal written agreement exists), and any appropriate ground rules.
○ Information relevant to the mediation.
○ Relevant issues and proposals of either party.
○ Relevant options identified during the session.
○ Any action to be taken (by either party or the mediator).
○ The outcome of the session and issues for the next session where appropriate.

E2 Mediation Review

Requirements:

E2.1   Mediation review procedure(s)

E2.1   Documented procedure(s) ensure that:

(a) For each mediator member of staff, both the number of mediations to be reviewed, and the frequency and method of reviews, have been determined according to that person's experience, expertise and quality of work (subject to minimum requirements).

(b) The sample of work reviewed for each member of mediation staff can be demonstrated to be representative of their overall caseload.

(c) Review findings are communicated in accordance with a (written) procedure to relevant member(s) of staff.

(d) Corrective action is completed within a reasonable timescale and to the satisfaction of the reviewer in accordance with a (written) procedure.

51

Definitions:

(These qualify the requirements and are mandatory where the word "must" appears)

E2.1   Mediation review procedure(s)

- The independent review of mediation delivered by individuals can be performed in two ways. Either:

    o   Review of files containing a record of the mediation session(s) and evidence that internal procedures have been followed, *or*

    o   Review of the mediation session as it happens (i.e. by a co-mediator or an additional mediator observer) together with a review of the file to ensure that internal procedures have been followed.

Numbers, frequency and method

- You **must** document the number of files to be reviewed, the frequency, and (where other than file content only, e.g. one to one) the method(s) of review, for each mediator (to whom cases have been allocated) and you **must** be able to justify these to the auditor on the basis of experience, expertise, caseload and on any findings that have implications for the quality of their work (e.g. previous mediation reviews). *Note* that while review frequency **must** be justified (as above), it will not ordinarily be possible to justify mediation reviews that are less frequent than every three months. If mediators are not currently working or there are a small number of cases available to review, it may not be appropriate to review files if this would mean reviewing the same files over and over again. However when mediator begin work again, it may be appropriate to increase the number of files reviewed to ensure that the period spent not working has not resulted in a reduction in quality.

Representative samples

- You **must** be able to demonstrate that the files selected for review reflect the range of work conducted by each individual over the period of a year. You are likely to have a process to ensure that this happens and may want to document the categories of work covered alongside the numbers of files to be reviewed and the method to be used (see E2.1(a)), although it is not a requirement to do so.

Communicating review findings

- Your procedure **must** outline how the individual is to become aware that a file has been reviewed, how the review findings (including any corrective action identified) will be communicated, and within what timescales. You may want to have different processes and/or timescales for reviews in which corrective action is identified, as opposed to those where it is not.

Corrective action

- Your procedure **must** set out the process you use to ensure that corrective action has been completed to the satisfaction of the reviewer, and within the timescale agreed (and that the timescale for completion and for review of corrective action can be justified to the auditor in terms of the significance of error, the risk posed to you, the client or a funder, and the urgency required).

Issue 1: 04/02

E2 Mediation Review

Requirements:

E2.2   Process management

E2.2   The review process is managed by the mediation supervisor.

E2.3   Mediation reviews

E2.3   All reviews are independent and carried out by a suitably qualified individual (see definitions).

E2.4   Review (and any corrective action) is evident on file

E2.4   Conduct of a mediation review (and details of any corrective action to be taken) is evident from the case file.

Definitions:

(These qualify the requirements and are mandatory where the word "must" appears)

E2.2   Process management

- The supervisor **must** be able to demonstrate that mediation review processes and procedures are followed, and that they are aware of the status of reviews and all findings, including any reviews not carried out by them personally, and of findings from periodic monitoring.

E2.3   Mediation reviews

- Reviews **must** be carried out by a mediator who has not had conduct of the mediation, and who has successfully undergone the competence assessment process in the appropriate area of work (see section D), ideally by the supervisor, although the following also applies:

- All reviews (other than for supervisors, of their own work; see guidance) **must** be carried out by the supervisor, other than where one of the following applies:

  o   Reviews by a temporary supervisor may occur for short holiday periods and in exceptional circumstances (where the conditions for temporary supervisors will apply).

  o   Reviews have been delegated to deputy supervisors with the prior authority of the auditor, unless the individual also meets D3.2 in full (i.e. the competence requirements for supervisors), in which case prior authority is not required.

  o   Procedural checks (only) have been delegated to other members of staff.

  o   Prior authority has been granted (by the auditor) to allow someone else to conduct routine or specific reviews (to a maximum of 50% of files to be reviewed) (see guidance).

E2.4   Review (and any corrective action) is evident on file

- Files that have been reviewed **must** contain a note that, as a minimum, confirms the date of review and the identification of the reviewer. Where corrective action was

53

725

identified, it **must** also include details of the action to be taken and the timescale within which it **must** be completed. *Note* that it may also be appropriate to identify the person whose work is being reviewed, where more than one person has conducted work on the file.

- A separate note is not required where you retain a copy of the review record (see E2.5 below) on file, and where this details any corrective action to be taken, and relevant timescales (as required above).

E2 Mediation Review

Requirements:

E2.5   A detailed record is kept of all mediation reviews

E2.5   A comprehensive record of findings is produced for each mediation review.

E2.6   Monitoring mediation review records

E2.6   Records of mediation reviews are monitored at least annually, with action taken to improve performance where negative trends are identified.

Definitions:
(These qualify the requirements and are mandatory where the word "must" appears)

E2.5   A detailed record is kept of all mediation reviews

- Records **must** be kept together (centrally and/or on the individual's personal files), but **must** be presented in a way that is easy to manage (e.g. to monitor samples and corrective action, to identify trends and to conduct performance appraisals).
- Each record **must** provide:
  - Key mediation review information, including:
    - File reference.
    - Date of review.
    - Mediator and reviewer identification.
    - Method (where it may be other than file content only, e.g. one to one).
  - A note which confirms that each of the following has been checked and found satisfactory, or details of any adverse findings in respect of:
    - Quality of mediation.
    - Action proposed or taken.
    - Adherence to organisational procedures.
  - Evidence about corrective action (i.e. whether corrective action was required or a training need identified, and, in either case, a summary of the problem or scope for improvement, the action proposed and subsequent confirmation of completion).
- The record may be in the form of a single document completed at the end of each review, or may be a collection of copies of the review forms if a standard form is used.

E2.6   Monitoring mediation review records

- *From October 2003*, as a minimum, you **must** show that all records are reviewed at least once a year to identify recurring or emerging trends in performance (for individuals and/or departments and/or the organisation as a whole), and that action is taken wherever negative trends are identified.

55

This page has been left blank intentionally.

Appendix 8 Ethical Standards and Accreditation

676,185,927,201Mediation Quality Mark Standard

F MEETING CLIENTS' NEEDS

Members of the Community Legal Service (CLS) must have processes and procedures that ensure that clients receive information and mediation services to meet their needs.

Requirement F1	Before Mediation
Purpose:	To ensure that the relevant systems are in place to inform the client about the mediation service prior to the commencement of mediation.
Requirement F2	During Mediation
Purpose:	To ensure that the relevant systems are in place to inform the client throughout the mediation process.
Requirement F3	After Mediation
Purpose:	To ensure that the relevant systems are in place to inform the client of the outcome of the mediation process.
Requirement F4	Children
Purpose:	To ensure that the relevant systems are in place to protect any children who might be at risk, and to consider the views of any children directly involved in the mediation process.
Requirement F5	Costing Structures
Purpose:	To ensure that clients are aware of any costs that they may incur during the mediation process.
Requirement F6	Confidentiality, Privacy and Fair Treatment
Purpose:	To ensure that clients receive a confidential and private service, and are treated fairly throughout the mediation process.
Requirement F7	Use of Approved Suppliers
Purpose:	To ensure that quality is maintained where part of the service is delivered by another supplier, i.e. translators, etc.

57

729

Quality Mark Standard for Mediation

This page has been left blank intentionally.

Appendix 8 *Ethical Standards and Accreditation*

Quality Mark Standard for Mediation

This page has been left blank intentionally.

731

F1 Before Mediation

Requirements:

F1.1   Suitability of mediation
F1.1   A system to identify the suitability of mediation for a case, based on consideration of the clients, dispute and all the circumstances of the case.

F1.2   Information regarding the mediation process
F1.2   Information provided to the client regarding the mediation process, before the process begins.

F1.3   Right to seek independent legal advice
F1.3   A system to ensure that mediators check at the beginning and throughout the mediation process that parties have considered the need for, and/or received, independent legal advice.

Definitions:

(These qualify the requirements and are mandatory where the word "must" appears)

F1.1   Suitability of mediation

- A screening system **must** be in place to identify whether a case is suitable for mediation. The system **must** consider:
  - o   The clients.
  - o   The dispute.
  - o   The circumstances (including previous instances of domestic violence or abuse and other power imbalances).
- Where it is concluded that mediation is not suitable, potential clients **must** be informed of this in writing (note, the letter does not need to state the reasons for unsuitability of mediation). A note should be kept on file.
- Evidence of the operation of the system will be required on audit, either by reviewing of case files or by reviewing a central system.

F1.2   Information regarding the mediation process

- Organisations **must** ensure that information is given to the client (either verbally or in writing) about the mediation process. This information **must** be given before a mediation session begins and **must** include information on:
  - o   An overview of the mediation process.
  - o   Note-taking.
  - o   Confidentiality, including where confidentiality may be waived due to safety issues arising in respect of the other parties and associated people (including children).
  - o   The independence and impartiality of mediators.

    ○   The voluntary nature of participation.

    ○   Other complementary services where relevant, e.g. Relate.

    ○   Information from all organisations regarding their complaints processes.

- Where this information is given to the clients verbally, a note **must** be made on the file to reflect this.

F1.3   Right to seek independent legal advice

- Organisations **must** ensure that clients are made aware of their right to seek independent legal advice at the start of, and throughout, the mediation process, including the availability of publicly funded legal help where appropriate. This information may be given in writing or verbally to the client, and, where it is given verbally, a note of this **must** be recorded on the file.

F1 Before Mediation

Requirements:

F1.4   Client/Mediator safety

F1.4   A written procedure/statement detailing how client and mediator safety is maintained.

Definitions:

(These qualify the requirements and are mandatory where the word "must" appears)

F1.4   Client/Mediator safety

- There **must** be a written procedure/statement in place which details how client safety on arrival and departure is ensured, and, further, how client and mediator safety is maintained throughout the mediation.

F2 During Mediation

Requirements:

F2.1   Specifics relating to the mediation process

F2.1   A process in place to ensure that specific information relating to the commencement of the mediation process is confirmed in writing to the parties as soon as possible.

F2.2   Information to clients during the process

F2.2   A process in place to ensure that clients are kept informed during the mediation process.

F2.3   Specific complementary services

F2.3   A process to ensure that mediators consider specific complementary services throughout the process.

59

Definitions:

(These qualify the requirements and are mandatory where the word "must" appears)

F2.1   Specifics relating to the mediation process
 	
• There **must** be a process in place to ensure that the following information will be confirmed in writing to the parties as soon as possible after the decision has been made that the case is suitable for mediation:
 	
   o   Date and venue of the mediation session.
   o   Name of the mediator(s) involved, and to whom complaints should be addressed.
   o   Any relevant key dates the client(s) has/have told the mediator about.
   o   Any action to be taken (by either party or mediator).
   o   Any limits on the mediator's ability or willingness to mediate.
   o   The availability of independent legal advice.

F2.2   Information to clients during the process
 	
• There **must** be a process in place to ensure that, during the mediation, you write to clients, at a minimum, in the following circumstances:
 	
   o   When there is any change in planned action.
   o   If it becomes clear that mediation is no longer appropriate.
   o   If there is a change in mediator responsible.

F2.3   Specific complementary services
 	
• Family mediation services **must** have a process in place to ensure that mediators consider whether either party has a need for information on the following:
 	
   o   A welfare benefits supplier who has obtained the Specialist Quality Mark.
   o   A marital counselling agency.
   o   A financial adviser.
   o   A child counselling service.
   o   An organisation with a Legal Services Commission (LSC) civil contract in family law.

F3 After Mediation

Requirements:

F3.1   Outcome of the mediation process

F3.1   A process to ensure that the outcome of the mediation process and follow-up actions are communicated in writing to all parties.

F3.2   Independent legal advice

F3.2   Clients are reminded in writing of their right to independent legal advice.

F3.3   Additional information

F3.3   A process in place to ensure that:

- Clients are reminded that reconciliation remains an option, if appropriate.

- Where financial disclosure has been made, all parties sign to state whether financial disclosure has been full or partial.

Definitions:

(These qualify the requirements and are mandatory where the word "must" appears)

F3.1   Outcome of the mediation process

- There **must** be a process in place to ensure that:
  - o   **For family mediation involving property or financial matters**, a written memorandum of understanding is produced, together with a letter confirming its meaning and effect if the document itself does not already make this clear.
  - o   **For non-financial and non-property family mediation issues and for community mediation issues**, a written outcome statement is produced listing key actions that parties are willing to take. (*Note* for community mediation services this **must** be signed by all parties.)
  - o   **If no agreement is reached**, the mediator writes to all parties explaining the outcome of the mediation and any further action that is to be taken by either party or the mediator.
  - o   In all cases, original documents are returned to the client, if appropriate.
  - o   In all cases, clients are told in writing of any storage arrangements for their files.
  - o   If appropriate, clients are offered, in writing, a review in the future.
  - o   Copies of the memorandum of understanding, outcome statement or result of the mediation, where an agreement has not been reached, **must** be provided or sent to all parties within ten working days of the last mediation session.

F3.2   Independent legal advice

- Clients **must** be informed in writing of their right to independent legal advice, regardless of the outcome of the mediation. A standard blanket statement at the bottom of the memorandum of understanding, outcome statement or written letter, where no agreement has been reached, would satisfy the auditor that this requirement has been met.

F3.3   Additional information

- The files **must** show that clients are reminded that reconciliation is an option where appropriate, and the files **must** contain, where financial disclosure has been made, a statement regarding whether financial disclosure is full or partial, which has been signed by the parties.

F4 Children and Child Protection

Requirements:

F4.1   Documented child protection procedure

F4.1   A documented child protection policy that outlines the principles on which decisions about child protection are taken, and a documented child protection procedure that outlines the specific steps to be taken where a concern about child safety is raised.

F4.2   Procedures for addressing the role of children in mediation

F4.2   A documented procedure to ensure that, in considering whether or not children are to be directly consulted by the mediator, the mediator addresses and records on the file:

- Whether, and to what extent, each child should be given the opportunity to express their wishes and feelings in the mediation.
- The purpose of the consultation.
- Parental and child consent.
- The wishes and feelings of each child.

63

737

Appendix 8   Ethical Standards and Accreditation

Definitions:

(These qualify the requirements and are mandatory where the word "must" appears)

F4.1	**Documented child protection procedure**
	• If your organisation works to a recognised body's child protection policy rather than your own, you **must** clearly document this and have ready and immediate access to such a policy. The child protection procedure **must** be specific to the local mediation service.
F4.2	**Procedures for addressing the role of children in mediation**
	• Mediators **must** show from the file that the key areas shown in the requirements have been considered, and the outcome of this consideration **must** be recorded on the file. It is essential that child confidentiality is preserved, the only exception being where child protection issues arise.

F5 Costing Structures

Requirements:

F5.1   Charge to the client
F5.1   Clients are informed in writing at the start of the process if there is a charge for any aspect of the mediation service.

F5.2   Cost updates
F5.2   Where charges are made, clients are updated in writing every six months about the current cost.

F5.3   Litigation costs
F5.3   Clients are informed in writing of the potential cost implications of matters proceeding to court

Definitions:

(These qualify the requirements and are mandatory where the word "must" appears)

F5.1   Charge to the client
• If your organisation charges for some, or all, of its mediation service, you **must** give an indication at the outset of the mediation of the total likely cost to be incurred by the client. This estimate **must** include a breakdown to show the pricing structure.

F5.2   Cost updates

• Where clients are charged for services, the organisation **must** send a written cost update where there have been significant changes in the planned activities, and in any case at least every six months, to detail:
 	
   o   Costs to date.
 	
   o   A revision or confirmation of the original estimate.

F5.3   Litigation costs
• Clients **must** be informed in writing of the potential cost implications of matters proceeding to courtrather than mediation (i.e. statutory charge or contributions), to enable clients to assess the cost benefit of the mediation process. The cost implications estimates **must** be based on the best available information.

65

739

F6 Confidentiality, Privacy and Fair Treatment

Requirements:

F6.1   A written confidentiality policy

F6.1   A written confidentiality policy that covers all information given to the organisation about the client and their case.

F6.2   Privacy

F6.2   Arrangements are in place to ensure privacy in meetings with clients.

▪ **Definitions:**

The definitions below qualify the requirement and are mandatory where the word "must" appears.

Where the sentence or paragraph begins with the word "Note", it contains information to help you (see also the separate Guidance document) and is not mandatory.

F6.1   A written confidentiality policy

- If your organisation works to a recognised body's confidentiality policy rather than your own, you **must** clearly document this and have ready and immediate access to such a policy.

- Your organisation **must** have a specific local confidentiality procedure, which **must** detail:

  o Circumstances where the organisation may need to breach confidentiality (e.g. if required to do so by court, or where child protection is an issue (see Section F4.1)).

  o Procedures outlining how confidentiality of information is maintained, to ensure that information is not passed from one party to the other without the party's consent.

  o Is understood by all staff in the organisation who have access to case information (i.e. not only casework staff).

  o Where confidentiality might be a particular issue (including, for example, where more than one organisation shares the same premises, your procedure **must** include guidance specifically on how confidentiality will be maintained in those circumstances.

  o *Note* also that legislation requires the protection of clients' data by you and also by anyone with whom you share it.

  o If your organisation is not an LSC contract holder this it **must** include a process for obtaining the clients consent for their file to be disclosed for audit.

F6.   Privacy

- You **must** be able demonstrate to the auditor that that you have facilities (or that you make efforts) to discuss matters with the client in a private location.

F7 Use of Approved Suppliers

Requirements:

F7.1   Non-discrimination when using other suppliers

F7.1	A written non-discrimination policy, in place, and available to all staff, when instructing or using other suppliers, and precluding discrimination on the grounds of race, colour, ethnic or national origins, sex, marital status or sexual orientation, disability, age or religion or belief.

F7.   Selection of suppliers

F7.2	Suppliers are selected on the basis of objective assessment, other than in exceptional cases.

- **Definitions:**

The definitions below qualify the requirement and are mandatory where the word "must" appears.

Where the sentence or paragraph begins with the word "Note", it contains information to help you (see also the separate Guidance document) and is not mandatory.

Members of the CDS (with a Specialist Quality Mark in Crime) should note that any caseworker/fee-earner who has been designated by them (including police station agents and unassigned counsel) is not defined as a supplier for this purpose, and F5 does not apply.

F7.   Non-discrimination when instructing suppliers

- Your policy **must** outline the action to be taken if any breaches occur.

- You must take reasonable steps to ensure that the supplier complies with the Race Relations Act 1976 and also as far as possible, the Commission for Racial Equality's Employment code of practice.

- (http://www.homeoffice.gov.uk/docs/racerel1.html)
  (http://www.cre.gov.uk/gdpract/employ_cop.html).

- *Note* that this policy is only part of the equal opportunities framework required by the Quality Mark; a single document may cover all areas (see also A3.1 (provision of services) and D1.3 (selection, treatment and behaviour of staff)).

- *Note* that you may adopt an existing model policy, but may need to include additional grounds in order to meet the Quality Mark minimum requirements (see Guidance).

F7.2   Process for selection, use and evaluation of other service providers

- Other than in exceptional circumstances, the process in place **must** ensure that the supplier has been selected on one of the following grounds:

  o The supplier's details appear in a central register, and there is evidence of the criteria (including at least quality of service, value for money, speed of response and expertise) against which they were assessed before inclusion. *Or:*

67

741

        o   The supplier holds the Quality Mark.

- "Exceptional circumstances" are those where you need to use a new supplier on a one-off occasion because of the nature and type of service you require. Where this happens, you **must** make a note of the circumstances on the client's file.

- The process **must** also ensure that:

        o   Clients are consulted during the selection process.

        o   The service provider is evaluated.

        o   Negative evaluations are reflected on the central register (with due regard given to the law relating to defamation, discrimination and data protection).

F7.3	**Clients are informed in writing**
F7.3	Clients are informed in writing if there is a charge to them for the use of other suppliers.

F7.3	**Clients are informed in writing**
	• Clients **must** be informed in writing if there is a charge that they will incur for the use of the approved supplier.

This page has been left blank intentionally.

69

743

G   COMMITMENT TO QUALITY
All members of the Community Legal Service (CLS) are committed to improving quality of their service.

Requirement G1	Complaints
Purpose:	Complaints are important as they tell you how well a service is meeting client expectations, and provide information that could inform improvements to the service.
Requirement G2	Client Feedback
Purpose:	To encourage clients to feedback about how well their needs are being met by the service provided. This feedback will enable the organisation to monitor its service and make informed service improvements.
Requirement G3	Quality Review
Purpose:	To ensure that the organisation has a named representative who is responsible for ensuring that all quality procedures used within the organisation are up to date and reviewed at least annually.

70

744

G1 Complaints

Requirements:

G1.1   Informing clients about how and to whom they should complain

G1.1   Work practices show that clients have information about what to do if they have a problem with the service provided.

G1.2   Complaints procedure

G1.2   There is a procedure for identifying and dealing with complaints.

▪   Definitions:

The definitions below qualify the requirement and are mandatory where the word "must" appears.

Where the sentence or paragraph begins with the word "Note", it contains information to help you (see also the separate document) and is not mandatory.

G1.1   Informing clients about how and to whom they should complain

-
- Wherever a file has been opened (see F1.2 for the definition), you **must** provide details of how and to whom they should complain, in writing, at the outset of the case.
- Where a file is not opened (e.g. where the client is given one-off mediation), other than where the advice is given by telephone, you **must** advise the client about whom to approach if they are dissatisfied with the service provided.

71

G1.2   Complaints procedure

- Your procedure **must** contain details of, at least, *all* of the following:

- The definition of a complaint.

- Who has responsibility for complaints handling (generally and ultimately in the organisation, including who is responsible for complaints made about the person who would ordinarily have ultimate responsibility).

- How complaints are identified.

- How complaints are recorded.

- How to identify the cause of a complaint and respond to it (including acknowledging complaints and telling the client when they will receive a substantive response, explaining to whom they should take matters if they remain dissatisfied at any stage, providing options for redress and for correcting any underlying problem or unsatisfactory procedure or process).

- The process for reviewing complaints (i.e. what is reviewed, by whom and when); see also G1.3 below.

- Your procedure **must** be compliant with the Family Mediation Councils Code of Conduct.

G1 Complaints

G1.3   Central record and annual review

G1.3	A central record of every complaint made, which is reviewed annually to identify trends.

- **Definitions:**

The definitions below qualify the requirement and are mandatory where the word "must" appears.

Where the sentence or paragraph begins with the word "Note", it contains information to help you (see also the separate document) and is not mandatory.

G1.3   Central record and annual review

- Details of complaints received (e.g. face to face, over the telephone or in writing) **must** be held in a central record, and copies of any documentation (usually correspondence) showing how the complaint was resolved **must** be available (i.e. either on the central record, or held in the case file with a cross reference in the central record).

- The central record **must** be reviewed at least annually to identify trends and to determine whether action can be taken, as a result, to improve the service being delivered.

- The results (i.e. trends identified and any action proposed as a result) of the annual review (or at least one review if you carry out more than one a year) **must** be documented.

G2 Client Satisfaction Feedback

Requirements:

G2.1   Client feedback procedure

G2.1   A client satisfaction feedback procedure in place that includes *all* of the following:

- A comprehensive feedback mechanism.

- Details on how and when the client gives feedback.

- The frequency and methodology of analysis of submitted feedback.

73

747

- Definitions:

The definitions below qualify the requirement and are mandatory where the word "must" appears.

Where the sentence or paragraph begins with the word "Note", it contains information to help you (see also the separate document) and is not mandatory.

G2.1   Client feedback procedure

- You **must** have a written procedure that encourages clients to provide feedback about the quality of service they received.

Client feedback mechanism

- As a minimum, your feedback mechanism **must** cover the following areas:

  o Whether the service was approachable and friendly?

  o Whether the client was kept informed?

  o Whether the information explained sufficiently to the client?

  o Were matters managed in a competent and timely manner?

How and when the client gives feedback

- Data collection **must** take place at least once a year, and the sample you use **must** be sufficient to encourage meaningful response data.

- *Note* that you can make your own decisions about how and when the client gives feedback. Ordinarily, the method will be by questionnaire, although this need not necessarily be the case. You might choose to seek feedback in all cases (e.g. by sending a questionnaire with the closing letter or by asking clients to complete one at the final meeting), or you might want to seek the information on a sample basis (e.g. from all clients in the first week of every month, or all clients in three months out of 12).

Frequency and methodology

- *Note* that, as above, it is for you to decide how often and by what method you will review completed client feedback. Generally it is good practice to review all feedback as it is received, as this provides the best opportunity to identify any feedback that should be handled as a complaint, and to respond to it accordingly. Analysis of the feedback will, however, be less frequent; here you will want to strike a balance between having sufficient feedback to identify trends and having too much to process at once.

G2.2   Annual review and outcome

G2.2   Client feedback is reviewed at least annually, with the review findings and outcome documented.

74

748

▪   Definitions:

The definitions below qualify the requirement and are mandatory where the word "must" appears.

Where the sentence or paragraph begins with the word "Note", it contains information to help you (see also the separate document) and is not mandatory.

G2.2   Annual review and outcome
• Review documentation **must** include feedback findings (trends identified) and outcomes from the review (of action proposed to resolve concerns or to improve the service) and **must** be kept for at least three years. • Original feedback material and materials reviewed (e.g. completed feedback questionnaires and an analysis of findings) **must** be retained for at least twelve months and made available to the auditor on request.

G3 Quality Review

Requirements:

G3.1   Appointing a quality representative
G3.1   A named individual responsible for overseeing all quality procedures used by the organisation.

G3.2   Up-to-date quality procedures
G3.2   All quality procedures are up to date and reviewed at least annually.

G3.   Process control
G3. 3   The Quality Representative is aware of instances where processes have been identified as failing to meet the Quality Mark standard, and can show what response has been made.

- **Definitions:**

The definitions below qualify the requirement and are mandatory where the word "must" appears.

Where the sentence or paragraph begins with the word "Note", it contains information to help you (see also the separate document) and is not mandatory.

G3.1   Appointing a Quality Representative

- An individual **must** be appointed to have responsibility for ensuring that quality procedures are up to date and are accurate (see G3.2 below) across all offices. .

- The individual(s) appointed **must** be entitled to update the quality procedures (or authorise updates to the quality procedures) as and when required.

- The individual(s) appointed **must** be available (to the auditor) throughout all audits.

- You **must** notify your auditor, in writing, as soon as possible and certainly within 28 calendar days of a change of Quality Representative.

G3.2   Up - to - date quality procedures

- All quality procedures **must** show the date they became effective and/or the issue number, and there **must** be a process in place for recording dates of amendments to procedures (this includes procedures maintained on computer systems).

- All quality procedures **must** be reviewed at least annually to check that they are up to date and accurate on paper and in practice.

G3.3   Process control

- As a minimum, all instances in which processes (for which requirements have been given in the Quality Mark standard) have been identified as having failed, which may lead to a Critical Quality Concern or General Quality Concern being raised at audit, **must** be brought to the attention of the Quality Representative.

- The Quality Representative **must** be able to demonstrate what response was made, which, where appropriate, **must** include action to avoid further repetitions (e.g. by requiring reviewers to target file reviews to consider certain issues, by checking that specific training is planned for certain staff, or by introducing a quality procedure to cover the relevant process.

---

2. Appendix 1: Quality Concerns and Observations

2.1 Observations

- Examples of **observations** include: (1) Mediation review is in effective operation, but on audit it is identified that a small proportion of corrective action has not been closed out; (2) Only 90% of mediation reviews are undertaken correctly, but there is evidence that the procedure is working under normal circumstances; (3) A procedure or plan, required to be updated every six months, was updated only after eight months.

2.2 Classification of Quality Concerns by Requirement

- Where an auditor has not been able to identify sufficient evidence to satisfy the requirements, this will lead to a quality concern being recorded. In summary there are 89 requirements within the standard of which 51 have been classified as "**critical**" i.e. relating to quality of advice, competence or client care and where a quality concern is identified would normally be classified as "**critical**".

- The following table is based on the assumption that documented plans/procedures were submitted with the Quality Mark application. Where any required documented plans/procedures are not submitted with the application, and are therefore not available during the desktop audit, the recommendation will be to refuse the application.

MQM Requirement	Preliminary Audit	Pre and Post QM Audit	Written Procedures
A1.1	General	General	Business plan
A1.2	General	General	
A2.1	General	General	
A2.2	General	General	
A3.1	**Critical**	**Critical**	Non-discrimination policy
A3.2	General	General	
B1.1	**Critical**	**Critical**	
B1.2	**Critical**	**Critical**	Signposting and referral procedure
B1.3	General	General	
B1.4	General	General	
B2.1	General	General	
C1.1	General	General	
C1.2	General	General	
C1.3	General	General	
C1.4	General	General	Authority to obtain status enquiry
C2.1	General	General	
C2.2	General	General	
C3.1	General	General	
C3.2	General	General	
C3.3	General	General	
C3.4	**Critical**	**Critical**	
C3.5	General	General	
C4.1	General	General	
C4.2	General	General	
C4.3	General	General	
C4.4	General	General	
C4.5	General	General	
D1.1	General	General	

77

Quality Mark Standard for Mediation

MQM Requirement	Preliminary Audit	Pre and Post QM Audit	Written Procedures
D1.2	General	General	
D1.3	Critical	Critical	Non-discrimination policy
D1.4	General	General	
D1.5	Critical	Critical	Safety procedure
D2.1	General	General	
D2.2	General	General	
D2.3	Critical	Critical	
D2.4	General	General	
D3a.1	Critical	Critical	
D3a.2	Critical	Critical	
D3a.3	Critical	Critical	
D4.1	Critical	Critical	
D4.2	Critical	Critical	
D4.3	Critical	Critical	
D4.4	Critical	Critical	
D4.5	Critical	Critical	
D5a.1	Critical	Critical	
D5b.1	Critical	Critical	
D5b.2	Critical	Critical	
E1.1	Critical	Critical	
E1.2	Critical	Critical	File management procedures
E1.3	General	General	
E1.4	Critical	Critical	
E1.5	General	General	
E2.1	Critical	Critical	File review procedures
E2.2	Critical	Critical	
E2.3	Critical	Critical	
E2.4	Critical	Critical	
E2.5	Critical	Critical	
E2.6	Critical	Critical	
F1.1	Critical	Critical	
F1.2	Critical	Critical	
F1.3	Critical	Critical	
F1.4	Critical	Critical	Client/mediator safety procedure
F2.1	Critical	Critical	
F2.2	Critical	Critical	
F2.3	Critical	Critical	
F3.1	Critical	Critical	
F3.2	Critical	Critical	
F3.3	Critical	Critical	
F4.1	Critical	Critical	Child protection procedure
F4.2	Critical	Critical	
F5.1	Critical	Critical	
F5.2	Critical	Critical	
F5.3	Critical	Critical	
F6.1	General	General	
F6.2	Critical	Critical	
F7.1	Critical	Critical	Non-discrimination policy
F7.2	Critical	Critical	
F7.3	General	General	
G1.1	Critical	Critical	
G1.2	Critical	Critical	Complaints procedure

78

752

MQM Requirement	Preliminary Audit	Pre and Post QM Audit	Written Procedures
G1.3	**Critical**	**Critical**	
G2.1	General	General	Client feedback procedure
G2.2	General	General	
G3.1	General	General	
G3.2	General	General	
G3.3	General	General	

79

753

3. Appendix 2 - Logo Guidance

- If you are an applicant, unless we grant you prior written permission, you **must** not in any way imply that you are, or will be, Quality Marked (either in full or provisionally). If we do grant you prior written permission, you **must** comply with any conditions that we specify.

- You may publicise and promote your status as Quality Marked (in full or provisionally) in any reasonable manner consistent with the spirit and intention of the Quality Mark agreement.

- You **must** not say or do anything that is, or is likely to be, misleading to clients or potential clients regarding your status as Quality Marked (full or provisional), or to advertise or associate with any other services that could in any way imply that they are endorsed, associated or otherwise part of the Community Legal Service.

- If we consider that you are publicising or promoting in a manner that is not consistent with the spirit and intention of the Quality Mark agreement, or may be misleading to clients (or potential clients), we may direct you to cease such publicity or promotion. If we do direct you to cease such publicity or promotion, you **must** comply with the direction without delay.

- You acknowledge that we own all rights in any promotional items.

- You **must** not alter or amend any promotional items without our prior written permission.

- You acknowledge that any promotional items that are owned by us, and designated as such, at all times remain in our ownership.

- You **must** use promotional items in accordance with any guidelines that we issue about them.

- Further guidelines on the use of the CLS logo (permitted colour, size, etc.) are provided as part of this guidance. Guidelines are issued by the LSC (in the form of a "logo pack") upon grant of the Quality Mark.

Definitions

"Promotional Items" means any logos, certificates, display materials, information, literature and other items supplied, or approved in writing, by us for use in connection with the Quality Mark.

4. Appendix 3 – Quality Mark Agreement

Set out below is an example of the agreement used for the MQM standard. Please note that this agreement will only be used where the Quality Marked supplier does **not** hold a contract with the LSC (e.g. mediation contract). Where an organisation holds such a contract with the LSC, that contract applies instead.

- If we agree that you meet the requirements for the Quality Mark for Mediation, we will grant your application and send you a Quality Mark for Mediation certificate. If any of the information in, or to be included in, your certificate changes, we will issue a replacement.

- If we refuse your application you may, within 21 days of the date of the refusal notice, submit an appeal in accordance with our published appeal procedure.

- Provided you continue to hold a current certificate, this agreement will stay in force. You may end it by giving us one month's notice. You may not assign it or otherwise dispose of it or any rights under it. When this agreement ends, all rights and obligations under it end, unless otherwise stated. This agreement does not create any right enforceable by any person not a party to it.

- Your certificate may include additional agreement terms. While you hold a current certificate, you:

  o **must** continue to meet the requirements for the Quality Mark for Mediation and **must** demonstrate this when required to by us.

  o **must** allow us, on no less than 14 days' notice, to attend your premises to verify, by audit or otherwise, your compliance with this agreement.

  o **must** not say or do anything misleading about your status under this agreement.

  o **must** provide us with information for entry in the CLS Directory.

  o **must** tell us if any information recorded in your certificate changes, and of any material changes to the information you gave us in your application.

  o **must** tell us of any change in your legal identity, of any sale or transfer of your business, of any change in your ownership or control, if any insolvency proceedings are commenced against you, and if any criminal proceedings are commenced against you or any of your personnel in connection with your operations.

  o may use, in accordance with guidance, the CLS Quality Mark and items bearing it, issued by us in connection with the CLS.

- We will give you six months' notice of any changes to the terms of this agreement or to the requirements for the Quality Mark for Mediation. We will not make any major changes without first consulting The Law Society, the UK College of Family Mediations, Mediation UK, Advice Services Alliance, the Lord Chancellor's Department and any bodies whose names we have published as consultees.

- You **must** provide us with any information you hold that we are required by law to obtain from you. We will keep all confidential information concerning your or your clients' affairs strictly confidential unless we are required by law to disclose it or are

81

755

required to disclose it to parliament. This obligation continues after this agreement has ended.

- You acknowledge that you are not an agent or partner of ours and **must** not act as if you were.

- You **must** indemnify us without delay in respect of all liabilities we incur as a result of: (a) injury to our personnel or their property while they are on your premises for the purpose of this agreement, and which is either caused by your negligence or in respect of which you are entitled to indemnity under a policy of insurance; and (b) any claim by a third party in respect of any act or default committed by, or for, you unless the act or default was ours.

- You **must** not try to bribe any of our personnel or any person who may perform services for, or who is associated with, us or the Community Legal Service.

- Any of our functions under this agreement may be performed by a body authorised by us.

- If you breach this agreement, if you gave us false information in your application, if insolvency proceedings are commenced against you or if any criminal proceedings or professional disciplinary proceedings are commenced against you or any of your personnel in connection with your operations, we may suspend or cancel your certificate on one month's notice.

- If we give you notice suspending or cancelling your certificate you may, within 21 days of the date of the notice, submit an appeal in accordance with our published appeals procedure.

- After all relevant appeal procedures have been exhausted, any remaining disputes between you and us that arise after the grant of your application shall be decided under the Arbitration Act 1996. The arbitration shall be in accordance with the Legal Services Commission arbitration scheme run by the Chartered Institute of Arbitrators and shall be final and binding.

- Provided, if applicable, we have reasonably operated the appeals procedure, where we have acted in good faith but are in breach of this agreement, we shall not be under any liability to you under this agreement or otherwise for any loss or damage. "Loss or damage" includes any loss of anticipated profits, as well as any consequential or economic loss or damage, arising from the breach.

82

5. GLOSSARY OF TERMS

Term	Definition
Community Legal Advice	Community Legal Advice consists of a national helpline **0845 345 4 345**, a website, www.communitylegaladvice.org.uk and a series of free printed legal information leaflets. The national helpline offers free and confidential legal advice in debt, education, employment, housing and welfare benefits and tax credits. The helpline also enables members of the public to find details of their local advice providers and order CLA Leaflets. The website contains a CL Legal Adviser Directory search facility, electronic versions of the CL Leaflets and an Advice Search facility, which provides details of other websites offering legal advice and information.
CLS Legal Adviser Directory	This contains details of members of the CL and CDS. Retaining access to the Directory and ensuring that your details are up to date are requirements of the SQM (see A1.2, B1.2 and B1.4). The Directory details can be accessed via the Community Legal Service Direct website (www.communitylegaladvice.org.uk) and their national helpline 0845 345 4 345.
Legal Aid	This is also now known as CLS funding (for civil cases) and CDS funding (for criminal cases).
Legal Services Commission (LSC)	The Legal Services Commission (LSC) runs the legal aid scheme in England and Wales.
Observation	Observations can be raised during the audit against any requirement within the MQM. These will form part of the audit report but will not result in recorded quality concerns. They will be noted on the audit report as areas where the quality requirements are not fully complied with but where there is evidence that the organisation has a clear commitment to fully meeting the standard. For some observations the organisation may be required to submit details of the (proposed) corrective action.
Organisation	Those parts of the service where you are seeking or want to maintain a Quality Mark. You may know this as the "firm", the "office" or the "agency".
Policy	A statement of intent, e.g. your non-discrimination policy.
Procedure	A written description of a process. You must be able to demonstrate that all staff members are aware of what the correct procedures and processes are, and must ensure that they are following them.
Term	Definition
Process	The procedure operating in practice (i.e. without reference to a written set of instructions). The auditor will need to see evidence that the process is in effective operation and meets the requirements outlined in this document. In some instances processes are known as work practices.

83

Quality concern	Where an auditor has not been able to identify sufficient evidence to satisfy the requirements this will lead to a quality concern being recorded. Quality concerns are defined as either "general" or "critical", depending on which requirement the quality concern is raised against (see Section 5 and Annex A).
Recognised representative bodies	A representative body that is recognised by the LSC as an umbrella body e.g. The Family Mediation Council.
Referral and signposting	Methods of ensuring that individuals receive advice from an appropriate alternative service provider whenever your organisation cannot help them;, either where you cannot help them initially before any service has been provided (i.e. signposting), or where you cannot help then further in a current matter where a client relationship has already been established (i.e. referral).
Signposting	The process whereby the service provides the CLS Directory and/or the information to the client who is then responsible for making contact with the other provider.
Staff	Individuals who work in the part of the service for which you are seeking or want to maintain a Quality Mark. Staff includes all mediators, all support staff, all partners and/or managers, and includes both paid and voluntary staff.
Supervisor	A person who is able to recognise best practice and who can provide appropriate guidance and assistance to staff in the delivery of a quality service. This includes professional practice consultants.

Appendix 9

Concerns and Complaints

A   Civil Mediation Council

CIVIL MEDIATION COUNCIL
MEMBERS' COMPLAINTS RESOLUTION SERVICE
complaintsresolution@civilmediation.org

1. One of the objectives of the Civil Mediation Council is to promote standards and good practice in mediation. Integral to the concept of good practice is a means of resolving disputes or complaints that may occasionally arise about the conduct of the mediator, mediation organisation or mediation trainer ('members').

2. Ordinarily these will be resolved by the system that has been put in place by the member as part of good practice. But there may be instances (and experience suggests that these will be rare) where the system does not resolve complaints and disputes about the member.

3. The CMC does not believe that it should take on a regulatory role and determine or decide such matters. It does, however, believe that it is appropriate to the CMC's wider promotion of mediation for it to offer CMC members who find that they face an unresolved complaint a further option.

4. The CMC has announced that from 1st January 2008 members of the CMC will have access to a complaints resolution service whereby either a member, or a client of a member, who has exhausted the member's own complaints process, can refer the matter to the CMC for resolution. Resolution, of course, will be through mediation.

5. The process is simple. The CMC has a panel of 20 mediators who have each conducted at least 20 mediations who are prepared to work on a fixed fee basis to resolve complaints. The list is maintained by the CMC's administrator admin@civilmediation.org and is both regionally and mediation organisation diverse to avoid the risk of conflict – and to minimise travel costs.

6. The procedure for using the scheme is that either the member, or the client of the member, should contact the administrator who will establish (1) that the complaint is about a member; and (2) that the complaint has been through and exhausted the member's own complaints process.

7. The Registrar will then contact the other disputant to confirm that they are willing to use the CMC's Complaints Resolution Service. If so the administrator

will send the disputants a standard agreement to mediate and once it has been completed will conduct a basic conflict check before choosing three candidate names from the panel.

8. These candidates will be asked by the administrator whether they have any objection to being offered as mediators under the scheme to the matter involving the member. If they do not then they will be put forward to the disputants for a choice to be made.

9. In default of agreement by the disputants, then provided the disputants wish to continue to use the scheme, the administrator will forward three further and similarly checked names to the President of the CMC for an appointment to be made.

10. Once the mediator has been appointed, the administrator will agree a date, time, and a venue and the matter will proceed in the normal way. The disputants will bear the cost of the venue (if any) and any travel, each paying half.

11. The mediation will be time limited to two hours plus any reading. The mediator will act for a fixed fee of £250+VAT which the CMC will bear.

12. To use this service, please contact by email the administrator at complaintsresolution@civilmediation.org.

B   CEDR

Complaints procedure[1]

We set high standards across the full range of services we offer. We aim to achieve those standards all of the time. Although seldom used, we have a procedure for dealing with complaints that ensures they are given proper attention.

CEDR aims to provide a responsive and timely service to all our clients, we will:

- treat all complaints seriously and deal with them properly;
- resolve complaints promptly; and
- learn from complaints and take action to improve our service.

Please address all complaints to the appropriate department, or to:

Danny McFadden, CEDR Director
Centre for Effective Dispute Resolution
International Dispute Resolution Centre
70 Fleet Street
LONDON
EC4Y 1EU

Tel: +44 (0) 20 7536 6022, E-mail: dmcfadden@cedr.com

---

1   Reproduced with the kind permission of CEDR. Please visit www.cedr.com to check for latest version of this document as these documents are updated and existing versions can become out of date.

Your complaint will then be handled in accordance with our complaints procedure.

What we will need to know

- Your name, and details of how to contact you

- Details of your complaint

- What you would like to happen

What you can expect from us

We will:

- Acknowledge the receipt of your complaint within five working days with an indication of how long it will take to send you a detailed response. (If you do not receive an acknowledgement within this timeframe please contact us in the event that it has not been received.)

- Investigate your complaint carefully and thoroughly.

- Write back to you with a full reply within 14 working days (occasionally we may need longer than this but this will be indicated in the acknowledgment letter).

- Should you not be satisfied with the response, the matter will be referred to CEDR's Chief Executive to be considered further and may include a meeting with all concerned parties in an effort to reach a satisfactory conclusion.

You will not be treated any less favourably as a result of complaining about our services.

We would also encourage you to provide us with compliments and feedback if we have exceeded expectations so that we can pass this on the person/team involved and learn from things we are doing right as well as from our mistakes.

C   CORE Solutions Group[2]

Concerns or Complaints

We seek excellence in all that we do and that includes the way in which we handle any concerns or complaints that are raised. Although rarely used, we have a procedure for dealing with concerns and complaints that ensures that these are given proper attention and that they help us to make improvements in our service, as well as providing redress if appropriate.

If you have any concerns about the service provided by Core Mediation or by any of its mediators, please contact either John Sturrock or Pamela Lyall as soon as convenient. We undertake to address your concerns as soon as we reasonably can and to discuss with you any issues which you wish to raise. If it is not possible to resolve matters by discussion, we undertake to engage an independent mediator to help to address matters in a constructive way and to explore the most appropriate way to achieve a solution.

---

2   This document is reproduced with permission from the Guide to Mediation Services published by Core Solutions Group. Core Solutions Group is Scotland's pre-eminent provider of mediation services to business, organisations and the professions in Scotland. www.core-solutions.com.

We will seek to:

- treat all complaints and concerns (both verbal and written) seriously and confidentially
- record all complaints and concerns
- resolve complaints and concerns promptly
- learn from complaints and concerns and improve our service delivery as a result

Please address all concerns and complaints to:

John Sturrock
Chief Executive john.sturrock@core-solutions.com

Pamela Lyall
Director of Mediation Services pamela.lyall@core-solutions.com

Core Solutions Group Limited
Rutland House
19 Rutland Square
Edinburgh
EH 2 1BB
Tel: 0131 221 2520

Please provide us with:

- Your name and address and how you can be contacted
- Details of your concern or complaint
- An explanation of what you would like to happen

What Core will do:

- Acknowledge receipt of your concern or complaint within 7 working days with an indication of how long it will take to provide a detailed response. (If you do not receive an acknowledgement within this timescale, please contact us.)
- Investigate your concern or complaint thoroughly and carefully
- Write back to you with a full and detailed response, usually within 14 working days
- Should you not be satisfied with the response, refer the matter to the Civil Mediation Council's Complaints Resolution Service for a free independent mediation.

For more information, or to arrange a without commitment discussion contact us at tel no 0131 221 2520
email: laura.rutherford@core-solutions.com

D   NMI (Netherlands Mediation Institute)[3]

NMI Complaints scheme

NMI has a complaints scheme, the purpose of which is to promote the quality of services relating to mediation in general, and to provide a procedure for the adequate handling of complaints in the shortest possible time in particular. The provisions of the complaints scheme are as follows.

Article 1 – Definitions

In this complaints scheme the following terms have the following meaning:

The NMI:	the Foundation 'Stichting Nederlands Mediation Instituut', having its registered office in Rotterdam.
Director:	the managing director of the NMI.
Adjudicator:	the person designated by the Director in consultation with the Executive Board of the NMI to handle a complaint.
Code of Conduct:	the code of conduct for Mediators laid down by the NMI.
Complaint:	any expression of dissatisfaction regarding the performance of a Mediator addressed verbally or in writing to the NMI by or on behalf of the Complainant.
Complainant:	the party or its representative involved in a mediation who has lodged a complaint.
Mediator:	the mediator(s) registered with the NMI against whom the complaint is directed.
Complaints Scheme:	this complaints scheme.

Article 2 – Procedure

2.1   If the Complainant submits a Complaint to the NMI or the Mediator and such Complaint cannot be immediately solved, it shall be passed on to the Adjudicator. In such case the Complainant must present the Complaint – insofar as it has not yet been presented – to the NMI in writing, clearly describing the complaint and the reasons therefor (written notification).

2.2   When lodging his Complaint the Complainant must in any case state:

- his name, address, telephone number and fax number (if any) and e-mail address (if any);
- the name of the Mediator;

---

3   Reproduced with the kind permission of the Nederlands Mediation Instituut – NMI. For further information please visit www.nmi-mediation.nl.

- a concise description of the mediation to which the Complaint relates;

- a concise description of the Complaint.

2.3   The NMI shall record the date of receipt of the Complaint lodged by the Complainant. If the Complaint is not solved immediately after the Complainant has lodged it with the NMI, the NMI shall inform the Adjudicator within two weeks after receipt of the written notification of the Complaint and of the information referred to in Article 2.2. The NMI shall make any (other) documents which the Complainant has enclosed with his Complaint available to the Adjudicator.

2.4   The Adjudicator shall ensure that the Complaint, in accordance with the principles of a fair hearing of all parties if the Complainant and/or the Mediator desire(s) such, is adequately handled and that the Complaint is handled within a period of six weeks after the date on which the Adjudicator has received the notification of the Complaint and the information and documents from the NMI as referred to in Article 2.3. This period may be extended once by a maximum of four weeks. The Adjudicator must give the Complainant and the Mediator advance notice of an intended extension.

If the Complainant and the Mediator agree to this, the complaint may be handled by telephone.

2.5   The Adjudicator is not authorized to give a binding decision or impose sanctions.

2.6   The Adjudicator shall make a proper record of the date on which he has received the information and the documents from the NMI as referred to in Article 2.3, and the procedure he has followed, including any agreements he has made with the Complainant and/or the Mediator.

2.7   The Adjudicator shall inform the Complainant in writing that if the Complaint has not led to a satisfactory result, the Complainant may bring it before the Foundation 'Stichting Tuchtrechtspraak Mediators', in accordance with the Rules of the Foundation 'Stichting Tuchtrechtspraak Mediators' in force in respect of mediators.

2.8   Except with regard to the Executive Board and the Director of the NMI, the Adjudicator is under the obligation to maintain confidentiality concerning all information of which he has become possessed during the handling of the Complaint.

Article 3 – Records and internal information

3.1   The NMI shall keep records of all Complaints received by the NMI.

3.2   The Adjudicator shall inform the Director in writing concerning the handling of every Complaint he has dealt with, as soon as he has dealt with the Complaint. He shall furnish the Director with all documentation relating to the Complaint and the handling thereof, including the record referred to in Article 2.6.

3.3   The NMI shall file the documents relating to the Complaint after it has been handled.

3.4   The Director shall periodically inform the Executive Board of the NMI concerning the handling of the Complaints received by the NMI.

3.5   Based on the information received, the Director in consultation with the Executive Board of the NMI shall take such measures as they may deem necessary.

Article 4 – Final provisions

4.1   This Complaints Scheme and the procedure for the handling of Complaints as described herein shall be exclusively governed by Dutch law.

4.2   Any disputes relating to this Complaints Scheme and/or the procedure for the handling of Complaints as described herein, between the Complainant and/or the Mediator and/or the NMI shall in the first instance be resolved by mediation in conformity with the NMI Mediation Rules, as worded on the day of commencement of the mediation. Any disputes that have not been resolved by mediation – insofar as no other method of resolving the dispute has been agreed in writing between the parties – shall be exclusively decided upon by the Dutch courts.

4.3   This Complaints Scheme has been drawn up and may be amended by the NMI. In all cases not provided for by this Complaints Scheme, the Executive Board of the NMI shall decide.

E   IMI[4]

DISCIPLINARY COMMISSION PROCESS

The IMI Disciplinary Commission operates a fast, local, cost-effective process for considering and resolving complaints against IMI Certified Mediators and, in appropriate circumstances, applying sanctions. The process involves up to three steps – the Informal Complaints Process, the Disciplinary Commission Process and the Disciplinary Appeals Board.

The IMI Disciplinary Commission process is not intended to replace any complaint or disciplinary process of an IMI Certified Mediator's professional body, or any applicable national process that may be invoked, but offers Complainants an alternative process

1. IMI Informal Complaints Process

All complaints regarding an IMI Certified Mediator's non-compliance with the IMI Code of Ethical Conduct must first be made through the IMI Complaints Process. If this fails to resolve the matter, the Complainant may file a formal request with the IMI's Disciplinary Commission.

1A   A party in a mediation who believes that an IMI Certified Mediator has failed to comply with the IMI Code, and who wishes to submit a complaint, is invited first to raise the matter with the Mediator in person within one month of the occurrence of the alleged breach. If the matter cannot be resolved promptly through discussion

---

4   Reproduced with the kind permission of the International Mediation Institute (IMI). For further information and to download IMI documents free of charge please visit www.IMImediation.org.

with the Mediator (potentially with the assistance of an independent mediator), the Complainant is asked to file a written complaint under the IMI Informal Complaints Process within a period of two months from the occurrence of the alleged breach.

1B   To activate the IMI Informal Complaints Process, the Complainant is requested to complete the Complaint Initiation Form [link] and send it electronically to IMI. Within one week, IMI will acknowledge receipt and send a copy to the IMI Certified Mediator whose conduct is the subject of the complaint.

1C   Within two weeks of receipt of the Complaint Initiation Form, IMI will appoint a Neutral to handle the complaint. The Neutral, who shall be independent of the Complainant and of the IMI Certified Mediator, shall strive to ensure that the Complaint is handled within a period of six weeks after the date on which the Complaint Initiation Form is filed with IMI. In exceptional circumstances, this period may be extended once by a maximum of four weeks but the Neutral must give the Complainant and the Mediator advance notice of any intended extension. The Neutral will determine how the complaint will be handled in the interests of a fair hearing for both the Complainant and the Mediator.

1D   After hearing the parties and determining the facts, the Neutral will issue to the Complainant and the Mediator a non-binding opinion and, if appropriate, a non-binding recommendation. This will be summarized and filed with IMI, where it will be received in confidence. The Neutral shall not be authorized to give a binding decision or to impose sanctions, and will inform the Complainant that if the Neutral's opinion or recommendation does not resolve the matter, the Complainant may activate the IMI Disciplinary Commission Process in accordance with these Rules.

1E   The Neutral will be obliged to maintain the confidentiality of all information relating to the Complaint, with the sole exception of the written summary referred to in paragraph 1D above which will be filed in confidence with IMI.

2. Purpose and Sanctions of the IMI Disciplinary Commission Process

2A   The IMI Disciplinary Process may be activated by a party in a mediation to seek redress for an alleged breach of the IMI Code of Conduct if the IMI Informal Complaints Scheme has not resolved the issue to the satisfaction of the Complainant. The Disciplinary Process involves the IMI Disciplinary Commission and, if necessary, the IMI Appeals Board.

2B   At the conclusion of the Disciplinary Process, the Disciplinary Commission and the Appeals Board will issue a decision with one of the following outcomes:

■ Uphold the complaint but without any sanction

■ Issue a written warning

■ Issue a written reprimand

■ Suspend the Mediator's IMI Certification(s) for up to one year

■ Permanently withdraw the Mediator's IMI Certification(s)

■ Recommendation as to costs of the Disciplinary Process.

2C   As an additional sanction, the Disciplinary Committee and the Appeals Board may instruct publication of the decision and sanction that has been imposed, in a manner determined by the Committee or the Board, as well as notification to the Mediator's professional indemnity insurers. 'The Mediator's professional indemnity insurers will also be informed' is a suggested wording.

2D   When imposing the sanction of suspension or permanent withdrawal of the Mediator's IMI Certification(s), the Disciplinary Commission and the Appeals Board may determine that this sanction (where it applies to a suspension, in whole or in part) will not be implemented, unless the Disciplinary Commission determines on a subsequent occasion that the Mediator is guilty of some other breach of the Code of Conduct within a period not exceeding two years

3. Composition of Disciplinary Commission and Appeals Board

3A   Members of the Disciplinary Commission shall be appointed from time to time by the Board of Directors of IMI. The Chair of the Disciplinary Commission will be appointed by the Board of Directors of IMI, will be independent of IMI and will not be an IMI Certified Mediator.

3B   The Appeals Board shall comprise the Chair of the Board of Directors of IMI and the Co-Chairs of the IMI Standards Commission, both of whom shall be independent of IMI.

3C   Members of the Disciplinary Commission will not be members of the Appeals Board and members of the Appeals Board will not be members of the Disciplinary Commission.

3D   The members of the Disciplinary Commission and the Appeals Board shall each be appointed for a term of four years and shall be eligible for reappointment.

3E   The Chair of the Disciplinary Commission will appoint three members of the Commission to form the

Disciplinary Panel to preside over a complaint, supported by a Secretary drawn from the staff of IMI or from any other source determined by the Chair.

4. Disciplinary Panel and Appeal Board Appointments

4A   A member of the Disciplinary Commission and of the Appeals Board may decline an appointment to a Disciplinary Panel, or may be challenged by the Complainant or by the Mediator, in the event of actual or potential conflict of interest or for any other reason which could compromise impartiality.

4B   Any challenge by the Complainant or Mediator must be presented to the IMI Secretary no later than 7 days after notification of the identity of the Disciplinary Panel, and be fully supported by reasons. The Chair of the Disciplinary Commission will make a final and binding decision over the challenge, and if the challenge is upheld, will appoint a replacement member of the Disciplinary Panel. If the challenge should relate to a member of the Appeals Board, and is upheld, the Board of Directors of IMI will appoint a substitute, against which no further challenge shall be accepted.

4C   The parties shall be informed in writing of all decisions relating to appointments to the Disciplinary Panel and Appeal Board.

5. Disciplinary Panel Procedure

5A   Any party to a mediation process at which an IMI Certified Mediator acted as mediator pursuant to the IMI Code of Ethical Conduct who believes that any provision of the Code may have been breached by the Mediator, and whose complaint is not resolved to their satisfaction by the IMI Informal Complaints Process, may file a formal written complaint with the IMI Disciplinary Commission using the <u>Disciplinary Panel Complaint Form</u> [link]. The Disciplinary Commission shall inform the Mediator against whom the complaint is directed of the filing of the Form by sending the Mediator a copy.

5B   The Chair of the Disciplinary Commission shall declare a complaint to be inadmissible if the complainant has also taken action under any code of conduct or ethics of any mediation or professional organization, or filed any legal proceedings against the Mediator in any country, and shall dismiss any apparently frivolous or vexatious complaint, or any complaint which has not in good faith passed through the IMI Informal Complaints Process. The Chair will accompany the inadmissibility or dismissal notice with a statement of reasons and will inform the complainant and the Mediator of the fact.

5C   The Chair will as soon as possible after having received notice of an admissible and properly-filed complaint, appoint a Disciplinary Panel of three members of the Disciplinary Commission to hear the complaint and the Mediator's case and decide upon the outcome.

5D   The Disciplinary Panel shall determine the appropriate process in each case, which may involve one or more Hearings in person, be conducted by written, electronic or telephonic communications, or any suitable combination. The Disciplinary Panel will in all cases strive to understand all relevant facts, and allow each of the parties the full opportunity to present their respective cases and to rebut. The parties shall have the right to be assisted by counsel during the complaint, and the Disciplinary Panel may call and hear witnesses and experts. The sessions of the Disciplinary Panel shall be private.

5E   The Disciplinary Panel will strive to reach a decision within eight weeks after the filing of the complaint. The decision of the Disciplinary Panel shall be accompanied by reasons. A decision of the Disciplinary Commission will become effective as from the day on which such decision has become final and conclusive.

5F   The Disciplinary Panel shall immediately send a copy of their decision to the:

- Complainant
- Mediator against whom the complaint is directed
- Secretary of the Disciplinary Commission.

6. Appeal from a Decision of the Disciplinary Commission

6A   Within a period of four weeks after receipt of the decision of the Disciplinary Panel, the Complainant or the Mediator may lodge an appeal with the IMI Appeals

Board. The appeal procedure shall be commenced by filing the <u>Notice of Appeal Form</u> [link] with IMI. The appeal shall be handled at a session of the Appeals Board which shall be held as soon as possible after receipt of the appeal, and in any event within four weeks of that date.

6B   The appeal shall suspend the enforcement of the decision of the Disciplinary Panel.

6C   The provisions of Clause 5B-F in relation to the Disciplinary Panel Procedure shall also apply, with any necessary adaptations, to the handling of the appeal by the Appeals Board.

6D   Decisions of the Appeals Board will be final and binding in all respects.

7. Confidentiality

The members of the Disciplinary Commission and the Appeals Board and IMI are under an obligation to maintain confidentiality of all information to which they become exposed during the Disciplinary Commission Process except to the extent that publication of a final and binding decision may be ordered.

8. Publication

IMI will have the power to publish the decisions of the Disciplinary Commission or of the Appeals Board in such manner(s) as it may deem appropriate. IMI will not disclose the identity of the parties unless ordered to do so by the final and binding decision.

9. Dispute Resolution

9.1   This Complaints Process and the procedure for the handling of Complaints as described herein shall be exclusively governed by Dutch law.

9.2   Any disputes relating to this Complaints Process and/or the procedure for the handling of Complaints as described herein, between the Complainant and/or the Mediator and/or the IMI shall in the first instance be resolved by mediation in conformity with the Mediation Rules of the Netherlands Mediation Institute, as worded on the day of commencement of the mediation. Any disputes that have not been resolved by mediation – insofar as no other method of resolving the dispute has been agreed in writing between the parties – shall be exclusively decided upon by the courts of The Netherlands.

F   College of Mediators[5]

Complaints procedure

1. Statement of purpose

The College of Mediators [the College] sets, promotes, improves and maintains the highest standards of professional conduct for those practising and working in the field of mediation. This procedure aims to help maintain and encourage those high standards. This procedure sets out when and how complaints   relating to a mediator's practice should be dealt with by the College.

2. Scope and application

2.1 The College expects that all mediation services will have complaints procedures of their own and expects that these will be used before the College becomes involved. Every effort should be made for a complaint to be dealt with promptly and directly first by the mediator[s] concerned and, if applicable, by their mediation service.

2.2 A professional practice consultant [PPC] is deemed to be a mediator for the purposes of this procedure and 'mediation practice' shall include a PPC's practice as both a mediator and a PPC.

2.3 A complaint can be made by a client, or a mediator [including a PPC], who has cause to believe that a mediator's practice has been in breach of the Code of Practice of the College. The mediators must be members of the College.

2.4 The College will consider a fresh complaint only when all other complaints procedures have been exhausted. It is not, therefore, an appeal procedure in relation to any prior complaints procedures.

2.5 There is no charge for using the Complaints Procedure.

2.6 A complaint can be made by a mediation client who has cause to believe that a mediator's practice has been in breach of the Code of Practice of the College. The mediator must be a member of the College.

2.7 A complaint must be made within 6 months of the practice from which the complaint arises. If a complaint is made after this time limit an explanation for the delay must be given and the College will have discretion to take this into account.

2.8 A complaint will be dealt with by the Complaints Panel of the College

2.9 Once a complaint is raised with the College every effort will be made to resolve it in an informal way through direct contact with all concerned. (see point 4.5 below) The resort to informal attempts to resolve the complaint will not jeopardise the right of the complainant to proceed with the Complaints Procedure as set out below.

.   **Registered Office: Alexander House Telephone Avenue Bristol BS1 4BS
Tel:0117 904 7223; www.collegeofmediators.com; Company Number 03145073**

---

5   This document is reproduced with the kind permission of the College of Mediators. The College website is a regularly updated source of information and resources so for the most up to date material please visit www.collegeofmediators.co.uk.

2.10 In order for a complaint to be properly considered, those involved may not claim confidentiality. By virtue of their membership of the College, a mediator cannot claim confidentiality in respect of the subject matter of a complaint. Neither may a client as the College is entitled to monitor the practice of its members through professional channels for the purposes of quality control, professional development and the maintenance of high standards of practice.

3.How a complaint should be made.

3.1 A complaint must be made in writing to the College. If other means are needed the College will be pleased to give assistance upon receiving a request to do so.

3.2 The College will require full information concerning those involved, including the name[s] of the mediator[s] concerned, and demonstrating that all the prior complaints procedures have been fully exhausted. Supporting documents must be presented in full. The College will contact directly all those involved including the Professional Practice Consultant concerned.

4. Management of complaints.

4.1 Upon receipt of a complaint in writing, the College will acknowledge receipt in writing within 7 days and enclose a copy of this document and of the Code of Practice of the College.

4.2 The Chair of the Complaints Panel will determine whether or not the complaint falls within the scope of the procedure.

4.3 The mediator[s] and their Professional Practice Consultant[s] will be informed that a complaint has been made and a copy of the complaint will be sent to them for comment.

4.4 A response to the complaint from the mediator[s], in consultation with their Professional Practice Consultant[s], will be expected in writing normally within 28 days of the date of the letter from the College. . If the response to a complaint is made after 28 days an explanation for the delay will be given.

4.5 A member of the Complaints Panel will make direct contact with all those concerned and will make an informal attempt to resolve the complaint [including an offer of mediation], where this is appropriate.

4.6 Should the matter remain unresolved, this member of the Complaints Panel will subsequently send all the relevant written information received and a record of any discussions/ actions taken to the Chair of the Complaints Panel. The Complaints Panel will consider the complaint on the basis of written submissions only unless otherwise agreed with the College [as in 3.1 above]. The member undertaking the preliminary enquiries as set out above will not participate as a member of the Complaints Panel in the formal consideration of the complaint.

4.7 All complaints received by the College will be dealt with as promptly as possible. The aim is to do so within 3 months of receipt of the complaint. Any delays will be notified to all concerned.

. **Registered Office: Alexander House Telephone Avenue Bristol BS1 4BS Tel:0117 904 7223; www.collegeofmediators.com; Company Number 03145073**

4.8 The College will consider as final the decision of its Complaints Panel.

5. The Composition and Function of the College Complaints Panel.

5.1 The Complaints Panel will be appointed by the Governors of the College and will agree its own Chair and will be composed of a maximum of four members.

5.2 An alternative member or members must be used if there is any question of any conflicts of interest.

5.3 If the complaint is upheld, the Complaints Panel may recommend that the mediator[s] make[s] such amends as are considered appropriate [including, where appropriate, restitution of fees] and may also recommend that disciplinary proceedings against the mediator[s] be initiated.

5.4 The deliberations of the Complaints Panel will be confidential.

6. Notification of proceedings

The College will disseminate [anonymously] to its members general professional practice issues learned from matters raised under the Complaints Procedure.

app Bd Govs 10/08

. **Registered Office: Alexander House Telephone Avenue Bristol BS1 4BS
Tel:0117 904 7223; www.collegeofmediators.com; Company Number 03145073**

Appendix 10

Further Reading and Resources

A Further bibliography of books and articles

Abramson, H., Chew, P. and Nolan-Haley, J. *International Conflict Resolution: Consensual ADR Processes*. West, 2005.

Abramson, H. I. *Mediation Representation: Advocating in a Problem-Solving Process*. National Institute for Trial Advocacy, 2004.

Ackerman, R. M. 'Disputing Together: Conflict Resolution and the Search for Community'. *Ohio State Journal on Dispute Resolution*, 2002, 18, pp 27–92.

Alexander, N. *Global Trends in Mediation*. Kluwer Law International, 2006.

American Arbitration Association. *ADR and the Law – 21st Edition*. JurisNet LLC, 2007.

Arrow, K., Mnookin, R. H., Ross, L., Tversky, A. and Wilson, R. (eds). *Barriers to Conflict Resolution*. W. W. Norton, New York, 1995.

Avruch, K. *Culture and Conflict Resolution*. United States Institute of Peace Press, Washington DC, 1998.

Axelrod, R. *The Evolution of Cooperation*. Basic Books, New York, 2006.

Baruch Bush, R. and Folger, J. *The Promise of Mediation*. Jossey-Bass, San Francisco, 1994.

Batchelder, H. 'Mandatory ADR in Common Interest Developments: Oxymoronic or Just Moronic'. *Thomas Jefferson Law Review*, 2000, 23, p 227.

Benjamin, R. *The Effective Negotiation and Mediation of Conflict: Applied Theory and Practice Handbook*, 2007.

Benjamin, R. *The Guerrilla Negotiator: Effective Strategies for Reaching Agreement and the Mediation of Conflict*, 2004.

Bercovitch, J., Kremenyuk, V. and Zartman, W. (eds). *The SAGE Handbook of Conflict Resolution*. Sage Publications Ltd, 2008.

Blumberg, M. 'Why Good Engineers Make Bad Decisions: Some Implications for ADR Professionals'. *Penn State Law Review*, 2003, 108, p 137.

Bordone, R. and Moffitt, M. *The Handbook of Dispute Resolution*. Jossey-Bass, 2005.

Boulle, J and Nesic, M., *Mediation: Principles, Process, Practice*, Tottel Publishing, 2001.

Bowling, D. and Hoffman, D. *Bringing Peace into the Room: How the Personal Qualities of the Mediator Impact the Process of Conflict Resolution*. Jossey-Bass, 2003.

Brand, M. 'Consensus Building and Smart Growth (Recent Research in Environmental Disputes)'. *Conflict Resolution Quarterly*, 2003, 21, pp 189–209.

Brazil, W. D. 'Court ADR 25 Years After Pound: Have we Found a Better Way'. *Ohio State Journal on Dispute Resolution*, 2002, 18, pp 93–150.

Brogan, M. and Spencer, D. *Mediation Law and Practice*. Cambridge University Press, 2007.

Brooker, P. 'Survey of Construction Lawyers' Attitudes and Practice in the use of ADR in Contractors' Disputes'. *Construction Management and Economics*, 1999, 17, pp 757–765.

Friedman, G. and Himmelstein, J. *Challenging Conflict: Mediation through Understanding*, American Bar Association, 2008.

Fuller, L. 'Mediation: its Form and its Functions', *Southern California Law Review*, 1971, p 44.

Galanter, M. 'The Vanishing Trial: An Examination of Trials and Related Matters', *Federal Journal of Empirical Legal Studies*, 2004, 1, pp 459–570.

Genn, H. *Court-based ADR Initiatives for Non-Family Civil Disputes: the Commercial Court and the Court of Appeal*, Lord Chancellor's Department Research Secretariat, London, 2002.

Golann, D. *Mediating Legal Disputes*, Little, Brown, 1996.

Goleman, D. *Working with Emotional Intelligence*, Bantam, 1998.

Hasson, R. and Slaikeu, K. *Controlling the Costs of Conflict: How to Design a System for your Organization*, Jossey-Bass, 1998.

Hetherington, L. and Frascogna, X. M. *The Lawyer's Guide to Negotiation: A Strategic Approach to Better Contracts and Settlements*, American Bar Association, 2001.

Hofstede, G. and Hofstede, G. J. *Cultures and Organizations: Software of the Mind*, McGraw-Hill, 2004.

Hofstede, G. *Culture's Consequences: International Differences in Work-Related Values*. Volume 5, Cross-cultural Research and Methodology Series, SAGE Publishers, 1982.

Honeyman, C., Schneider, A. K. et al (ed). *The Negotiator's Fieldbook: The Desk Reference for the Experienced Negotiator*, American Bar Association, 2007.

Imgrogno, A. R. 'Using ADR to Address Issues of Public Concern: Can ADR Become an Instrument for Social Oppression', *Ohio State Journal on Dispute Resolution*, 1998, 14, p 855.

Intrater, K. A. and Gann, T. G. 'The Lawyer's Role in Institutionalizing ADR', *Hofstra Labour and Employment Law Journal*, 2000, 18, p 469.

Jeong, H. *Understanding Conflict and Conflict Analysis*, Sage Publications Ltd, 2008.

Jones, T. S. 'Conflict Resolution Education: The Field, the Findings and the Future', *Conflict Resolution Quarterly*, 2004, 22, pp 233–268.

Justice, T. and Jamieson, D. *The Facilitator's Fieldbook: Step-by-Step Procedures, Checklists and Guidelines*, AMACOM, 2006.

Katsh, E. and Rifkin, J. *Online Dispute Resolution: Resolving Conflicts in Cyberspace*, Jossey-Bass, 2001.

Kent, J. C. 'Getting the Best of Both Worlds: Making Partnerships Between Court and Community ADR Programs Exemplary', *Conflict Resolution Quarterly*, 2005, 23, pp 71–85.

Kolb, D. M. and Associates. *When Talk Works: Profiles on Mediators*, Jossey-Bass, San Francisco, 1994.

Kovach, K. *Mediation: Principles and Practice*, West, 2004.

Krivis, J. and Lucks, N. *How to Make Money as a Mediator: 30 Top Mediators Share Secrets to Building a Successful Practice*, Jossey-Bass, 2006.

La Rue, H. C. 'The Changing Workplace Environment in the New Millennium: ADR is a Dominant Trend in the Workplace', *Columbia Business Law Review*, 2000, p 453.

Larson, D. A. 'Online Dispute Resolution: Technology takes a Place at the Table', *Negotiation Journal*, 2004, 20.

Lauchli, U. M. *Cross-Cultural Negotiations, with a Special Focus on ADR with the Chinese*, 2000, 26, p 1045.

Lederach, J. P. *Preparing for Peace: Conflict Transformation Across Cultures*, Syracuse University Press, New York, 1995.

Lenski, T. *Making Mediation Your Day Job: How to Market Your ADR Business Using Mediation Principles You Already Know*, iUniverse Inc., 2008.

Levy, D. 'The Role of Apology in Mediation', *New York University Law Review*, 1997, 72(5), p 1165.

Lise, E. C. 'ADR and Cyberspace: the Role of ADR in on-line Commerce, Intellectual Property and Defamation', *Ohio State Journal on Dispute Resolution*, 1996, 12, p 193.

Love, L., Menkel-Meadow, C., Schneider, A. and Sternlight, J. *Dispute Resolution: Beyond the Adversarial Model*, Aspen Publishers, 2004.

MacNaughton, A. L. and Martin, J. G. *Environmental Dispute Resolution: An Anthology of Practical Solutions*, American Bar Association, 2002.

Masters, J. and Rudnick, A. *Improving Board Effectiveness: Bringing the Best of ADR into the Boardroom – A Practical Guide for Directors*, American Bar Association, 2005.

Mayer, B. *Beyond Neutrality – Confronting the Crisis in Conflict Resolution*, Jossey-Bass, San Francisco, 2004.

Mayer, B. *Conflict and Resolution*, Jossey-Bass, San Francisco, 2000.

Mayer, B. *Staying with Conflict: A Strategic Approach to Ongoing Disputes*, Jossey-Bass, 2009.

McCabe, J. 'Uniformity in ADR: Thoughts on the Uniform Arbitration Act and Uniform Mediation Act', *Pepperdine Dispute Resolution Law Journal*, 2002, 3, p 317.

McGrath, A. 'The Corporate Ombuds Office: An ADR Tool No Company Should be Without', *Hamline Journal of Public Law and Policy*, 1996, 18, p 452.

Menkel-Meadow, C. and Wheeler, M. *What's Fair: Ethics for Negotiators*, Jossey-Bass, San Francisco, 2004.

Menkel-Meadow, C. 'Toward Another View on Legal Negotiation: the Structure of Problem Solving', *UCLA Law Review*, 1984, Vol 31, p 754.

Menkel-Meadow, C. 'The Lawyer as Consensus Builder: Ethics for a New Practice',*Tennessee Law Review*, 2002, 70, pp 63–119.

Menkel-Meadow, C., Love, L. P. and Schneider, A. K. *Mediation: Practice, Policy and Ethics*, Aspen Publishers, 2006.

Merrills, J.G. *International Dispute Settlement*, Cambridge University Press, Cambridge, 2005.

Mnookin, R., Peppet, S. and Tulumello, A. *Beyond Winning: Negotiating to Create Value in Deals and Disputes*, Belknap Harvard, Cambridge, Massachusetts, 2004.

Mnookin, R. H. and Others. *Barriers to Conflict Resolution*, W. W. Norton and Company, 1995.

Moore, C. *The Mediation Process* (2nd ed), Jossey-Bass, San Francisco, 1996.

Moore, C. W. *The Mediation Process: Practical Strategies for Resolving Conflict*, Jossey-Bass, 2003.

Mosten, F. S. *Mediation Career Guide: A Strategic Approach to Building a Successful Practice*, Jossey-Bass, 2001.

Nelson, R. *Nelson on ADR*. Thomas Carswell, 2003.

O'Keefe, E. *Tools for Conflict Resolution: A Practical Program Based on Peter Senge's 5th Discipline*. Scarecrow Education, 2004.

O'Leary, R. and Bingham, L. B. *The Collaborative Public Manager: New Ideas for the Twenty-first Century*, Georgetown University Press, 2009.

Orrego Vicuna, F. *International Dispute Settlement in an Evolving Global Society: Constitutionalization, Accessibility, Privatization*, Cambridge University Press, Cambridge/New York, 2004.

Palmer, M. and Roberts, S. *Dispute Processes: ADR and the Primary Forms of Decision-Making*. Cambridge University Press, 2005.

Patrick, J. Equal Opportunities and Anti-Discriminatory Practice, in Liebmann, M. (ed). *Community and Neighbourhood Mediation*, Cavendish Publishing, London, 1998.

Picker, B. *Mediation Practice Guide: A Handbook for Resolving Business Disputes*, American Bar Association, 2004.

Pirie, A. *Alternative Dispute Resolution: Skill, Science and the Law,* Irwin Law, Toronto, 2000.

Ponte, L. M. 'Broadening Traditional ADR Notions of Disclosure: Special Considerations for Posting Conflict Resolution Policies and Programs on E-Business Web Sites', *Ohio State Journal on Dispute Resolution,* 2002, 17, pp 321–340.

Princen, T. *Intermediaries in International Conflict,* Princeton University Press, 2006.

Pruitt, D. G. and Another, in Afzalur M. F. (ed), *The Process of Mediation: Caucusing, Control and Problem Solving.* Praiger Publishers, New York, 1989.

Pryor, W. and O'Boyle, R. M. *Public Policy ADR: Confidentiality in Conflict* 1992, 46, p 2207.

Reuben, R. *Corporate Governance: A Practical Guide for Dispute Resolution Professionals,* American Bar Association, 2005.

Riskin, L. 'The Contemplative Lawyer: On the Potential Contributions of Mindfulness Meditation to Law Students and Lawyers and their Clients', *Harvard Negotiation Law Review,* June 2002, Vol 7, p 1.

Riskin, L. 'Understanding Mediators' Orientations, Strategies and Techniques: a Grid for the Perplexed', *Harvard Negotiation Law Review,* 1996, Vol 1, p 38.

Roberts, M. *Developing the Craft of Mediation: Reflections on Theory and Practice,* Jessica Kingsley Publishers, 2007.

Rothschild, J. H. 'Dispute Transformation, the Influence of a Communication Paradigm of Disputing, and the San Francisco Community Boards Program', in Engle Merry, S. and Milner, N. (eds) *The Possibility of Popular Justice: A Case Study of Community Mediation in the United States,* University of Michigan Press, Ann Arbor, 1995.

Rule, C. *Online Dispute Resolution for Business,* Jossey-Bass, 2002.

Sanders, P. *The Work of UNCITRAL on Arbitration and Conciliation,* Kluwer Law International, London/The Hague, 2004.

Shell, G. R. *Bargaining for Advantage: Negotiation Strategies for Reasonable People* (2nd ed), Penguin, 2006.

Sherman, E. F. 'Confidentiality in ADR Proceedings: Policy Issues Arising from the Texas Experience', *South Texas Law Review,* 1997, 177, p 541.

Smyth, G. 'Considering Democracy and ADR: Diversity Based Practice in Public Collaborative Processes', *Windsor Review of Legal and Social Issues,* 2005, 19, p 13.

Steger, D. P. *Peace Through Trade: Building the World Trade Organization,* Cameron May Ltd, London, 2004.

Tihanyi, K. Z. and Du Toit, S. F. 'Reconciliation through Integration? An Examination of South Africa's Reconciliation Process in Racially Integrating High Schools', *Conflict Resolution Quarterly,* 2005, 23, pp 25–41.

Ury, W. *The Power of a Positive No: How to Say No and Still Get to Yes.* Bantam, 2007.

Ury, W. *The Third Side: Why We Fight and How We Can Stop,* Penguin, 2000.

Victorio, R. M. 'Internet Dispute Resolution (iDR): Bringing ADR into the 21st Century'. *Pepperdine Dispute Resolution Law Journal,* 2000, 1, p 279.

Vraneski, A. and Richter, R. 'What's News? Reflections of intractable environmental conflicts in the news: Some promises, many premises (Colloquy: Recent Research in Environmental Disputes)'. *Conflict Resolution Quarterly,* 2003, 21, pp 239–262.

Wallensteen, P. *Understanding Conflict Resolution: War, Peace and the Global System,* Sage Publications Ltd, 2007.

Winslade, J. and Another. *Narrative Mediation: A New Approach to Conflict Resolution.* Jossey-Bass, San Francisco, 2000.

Wissler, R. L. 'The Effectiveness of Court-Connected Dispute Resolution in Civil Cases',*Conflict Resolution Quarterly,* 2004, 22, pp 55–88.

Zartman, W. and Faure, G. O. *Escalation and Negotiation in International Conflicts,* Cambridge University Press, 2006.

B   Mediation videos and DVDs

Aaron and Golann, *Mediators at Work: A Case of Discrimination?* 2004

Alexander, *Cooking up a Compromise: Resolving Disputes Through Mediation*, Asian Productions, 2009.

Bond Dispute Resolution Centre QLD Australia, *Mediating a Partnership Dispute*, 2004

CEDR, *Mediation of a Personal Injury case*, 2005

CEDR, *Mediation of a Business case*, 2009

CPR Institute New York, *Mediation in Action*, 1994

CPR Institute New York, *Resolution Through Mediation*, 2003

Golann and Aaron, *Mediators at Work: Breach of Warranty?* 1999

Golann D., *Representing Clients in Mediation – How Advocates can Share a Mediator's Powers*, 2000

Global Mediation Services Ltd/Colin Wall (Hong Kong), Dooley (the Contractor) v National Industrial Process Enterprises Corporation (NIPEC) (the Employer), 2008

Himmelstein J. and Friedman G., *Saving the Last Dance: Mediation through Understanding*, 2001

JAMS Foundation, *Mediating a Sexual Harrassment Case: What would you do?* 2003

LEADR, Sous Chef or Sue Chef

Phillips J., *Mediation Madness*, 2003

PLI, *Mediation Advocacy*, Due for release in 2010

C   Other resources

CPR Institute New York, *ADR Podcast Program,* www.cpradr.org

www.familymediationhelpline.co.uk

www.nationalmediationhelpline.com

Appendix 11

Mediation Organisations

A   Selection of mediation organisations

(i) UK

Academy of Experts
www.academy-experts.org.uk

ADR Chambers (UK) Limited
www.adrchambers.co.uk

ADR Group
www.adrgroup.co.uk

Association of Northern Mediators
www.northernmediators.co.uk

Centre for Effective Dispute Resolution
www.cedr.co.uk

The Chartered Institute of Arbitrators (CIArb)
www.arbitrators.org.uk

Civil Mediation Council
www.civilmediation.org

CMP Resolutions
www.conflictmanagementplus.com

Core Mediation
www.core-mediation.com

Family Mediation Association (FMA)
www.thefma.co.uk

Globis
www.globis.co.uk

In Place of Strife
www.mediate.co.uk

Law Society
Legal Services Commission
www.legalservices.gov.uk

Littleton Dispute Resolution Services Ltd
www.littletonchambers.com

National Family Mediation (NFM)
www.nfm.org.uk

Relationships Scotland
www.relationships-Scotland.org.uk

Resolution (formerly SFLA)
www.resolution.org.uk

Royal Institution of Chartered Surveyors
www.rics.org

Scottish Mediation Network
www.scottishmediation.org.uk

TCM (Total Conflict Management)
www.tcmsolutions.co.uk

UK College of Family Mediators (UKCFM)
www.ukcfm.co.uk
www.collegeofmediators.co.uk

(ii) Europe

Austria	ARGE Wirtschaft Mediation www.arge-wirtschaftmediation.at	
	Osterreichischer Bundesverband der MediatorInnen (OBM) www.oebm.at	
Belgium	Brussels Centre for Mediation and Arbitration www.cepani.be	
	Brussels Mediation Centre www.bbmc-mediation.be	
	Mediation Familiale www.mediationfamiliale.be	
Denmark	Mediation Center www.medationcenter.dk	
	Mediationsinstituttet www.mediationsinstituttet.com	
France	CMAP www.cmap.fr	

Germany	German Association for Business Mediation www.dgmw.de
Greece	Hellenic Mediation Association www.hellenic-mediation.gr
Italy	ADR Center www.adrcenter.com
	The Chamber of National and International Arbitration of Milan www.camera-arbitrale.com
Luxembourg	Le Centre de Mediation du Barreau de Luxembourg (CMBL) www.centre-mediation.lu
Netherlands	Netherlands Mediation Institute (NMI) www.nmi-mediation.nl
	Het Amsterdams ADR Instituut www.adrinstituut.nl
Poland	House of Mediation www.houseofmediation.eu
	Ministertwo Sprawiedliwisci (Ministry of Justice) www.ms.gov.pl
Russia	Chamber of Commerce and Industry of the Russian Federation www.tpprf-arb.ru
Slovenia	Concordia Mediation Institute www.mediacija.net
	Family Mediation Institute www.mirabi.org
	Slovenian Mediators Association www.slo-med.si
Spain	The Bar Association www.imac.es
Sweden	The SCC Mediation Institute www.sccinstitute.com
Switzerland	Swiss Chamber of Commercial Mediation www.mediationchamber.ch
	Federation of Swiss Mediation Associations www.infomediation.ch

(iii) International

CPR Institute
www.cpradr.org

ICC
www.iccwbo.org

IMI
www.imimediation.org

LCIA
www.lcia-arbitration.com

Appendix 12

ODR (on-line dispute resolution) Providers

A Selection of providers

ClickNsettle.com	www.clicknsettle.com
Cybersettle	www.cybersettle.com
Ussettle.com	www.ussettle.com
AllSettlecom	www.allsettle.com
Settle Online	www.settleonline.net
Settle Smart	www.settlesmart.com
Eresolution	www.eresolution.ca
WEBdispute.com	www.webdispute.com
Icourthouse	www.i-courthouse.com
Internet Neutral	www.internetneutral.com
Online Mediators	www.onlinemediators.com
Square Trade	www.squaretrade.com
Enterprise Mediation	www.enterprise-mediation.com
Dispute Manager	www.disputemanager.com
Intersettle	www.intersettle.co.uk
MARS	www.resolvemydispute.com
The Claim Room	www.themediationroom.com
WeCanSettle	www.wecansettle.com
AAA University	www.aaauniversity.org

Appendix 13

Mediation Laws

A EU Mediation Directive

DIRECTIVE 2008/52/EC OF THE EUROPEAN PARLIAMENT AND OF THE COUNCIL of 21 May 2008 on certain aspects of mediation in civil and commercial matters

THE EUROPEAN PARLIAMENT AND THE COUNCIL OF THE EUROPEAN UNION,

Having regard to the Treaty establishing the European Community, and in particular Article 61(c) and the second indent of Article 67(5) thereof,

Having regard to the proposal from the Commission,

Having regard to the Opinion of the European Economic and Social Committee (1),

Acting in accordance with the procedure laid down in Article 251 of the Treaty (2),

Whereas:

(1) The Community has set itself the objective of maintaining and developing an area of freedom, security and justice, in which the free movement of persons is ensured. To that end, the Community has to adopt, inter alia, measures in the field of judicial cooperation in civil matters that are necessary for the proper functioning of the internal market.

(2) The principle of access to justice is fundamental and, with a view to facilitating better access to justice, the European Council at its meeting in Tampere on 15 and 16 October 1999 called for alternative, extra-judicial procedures to be created by the Member States.

(3) In May 2000 the Council adopted Conclusions on alternative methods of settling disputes under civil and commercial law, stating that the establishment of basic principles in this area is an essential step towards enabling the appropriate development and operation of extrajudicial procedures for the settlement of disputes in civil and commercial matters so as to simplify and improve access to justice.

(4) In April 2002 the Commission presented a Green Paper on alternative dispute resolution in civil and commercial law, taking stock of the existing situation as

785

concerns alternative dispute resolution methods in the European Union and initiating widespread consultations with Member States and interested parties on possible measures to promote the use of mediation.

(5) The objective of securing better access to justice, as part of the policy of the European Union to establish an area of freedom, security and justice, should encompass access to judicial as well as extrajudicial dispute resolution methods. This Directive should contribute to the proper functioning of the internal market, in particular as concerns the availability of mediation services.

(6) Mediation can provide a cost-effective and quick extrajudicial resolution of disputes in civil and commercial matters through processes tailored to the needs of the parties. Agreements resulting from mediation are more likely to be complied with voluntarily and are more likely to preserve an amicable and sustainable relationship between the parties. These benefits become even more pronounced in situations displaying cross-border elements.

(7) In order to promote further the use of mediation and ensure that parties having recourse to mediation can rely on a predictable legal framework, it is necessary to introduce framework legislation addressing, in particular, key aspects of civil procedure.

(8) The provisions of this Directive should apply only to mediation in cross-border disputes, but nothing should prevent Member States from applying such provisions also to internal mediation processes.

(9) This Directive should not in any way prevent the use of modern communication technologies in the mediation process.

(10) This Directive should apply to processes whereby two or more parties to a cross-border dispute attempt by themselves, on a voluntary basis, to reach an amicable agreement on the settlement of their dispute with the assistance of a mediator. It should apply in civil and commercial matters. However, it should not apply to rights and obligations on which the parties are not free to decide themselves under the relevant applicable law. Such rights and obligations are particularly frequent in family law and employment law.

(11) This Directive should not apply to pre-contractual negotiations or to processes of an adjudicatory nature such as certain judicial conciliation schemes, consumer complaint schemes, arbitration and expert determination or to processes administered by persons or bodies issuing a formal recommendation, whether or not it be legally binding as to the resolution of the dispute.

(12) This Directive should apply to cases where a court refers parties to mediation or in which national law prescribes mediation. Furthermore, in so far as a judge may act as a mediator under national law, this Directive should also apply to mediation conducted by a judge who is not responsible for any judicial proceedings relating to the matter or matters in dispute. This Directive should not, however, extend to attempts made by the court or judge seised to settle a dispute in the context of judicial proceedings concerning the dispute in question or to cases in which the court or judge seised requests assistance or advice from a competent person.

(13) The mediation provided for in this Directive should be a voluntary process in the sense that the parties are themselves in charge of the process and may organise it as they wish and terminate it at any time. However, it should be possible under national law for the courts to set time-limits for a mediation process. Moreover, the courts should be able to draw the parties' attention to the possibility of mediation whenever this is appropriate.

(14) Nothing in this Directive should prejudice national legislation making the use of mediation compulsory or subject to incentives or sanctions provided that such legislation does not prevent parties from exercising their right of access to the judicial system. Nor should anything in this Directive prejudice existing self-regulating mediation systems in so far as these deal with aspects which are not covered by this Directive.

(15) In order to provide legal certainty, this Directive should indicate which date should be relevant for determining whether or not a dispute which the parties attempt to settle through mediation is a cross-border dispute. In the absence of a written agreement, the parties should be deemed to agree to use mediation at the point in time when they take specific action to start the mediation process.

(16) To ensure the necessary mutual trust with respect to confidentiality, effect on limitation and prescription periods, and recognition and enforcement of agreements resulting from mediation, Member States should encourage, by any means they consider appropriate, the training of mediators and the introduction of effective quality control mechanisms concerning the provision of mediation services.

(17) Member States should define such mechanisms, which may include having recourse to market-based solutions, and should not be required to provide any funding in that respect. The mechanisms should aim at preserving the flexibility of the mediation process and the autonomy of the parties, and at ensuring that mediation is conducted in an effective, impartial and competent way. Mediators should be made aware of the existence of the European Code of Conduct for Mediators which should also be made available to the general public on the Internet.

(18) In the field of consumer protection, the Commission has adopted a Recommendation (1) establishing minimum quality criteria which out-of-court bodies involved in the consensual resolution of consumer disputes should offer to their users. Any mediators or organizations coming within the scope of that Recommendation should be encouraged to respect its principles. In order to facilitate the dissemination of information concerning such bodies, the Commission should set up a database of out-of-court schemes which Member States consider as respecting the principles of that Recommendation.

(19) Mediation should not be regarded as a poorer alternative to judicial proceedings in the sense that compliance with agreements resulting from mediation would depend on the good will of the parties. Member States should therefore ensure that the parties to a written agreement resulting from mediation can have the content of their agreement made enforceable. It should only be possible for a Member State to refuse to make an agreement enforceable if the content is contrary to its law, including its private international law, or if its law does not provide for the enforceability of the content of the specific agreement. This could be the case if the obligation specified in the agreement was by its nature unenforceable.

(20) The content of an agreement resulting from mediation which has been made enforceable in a Member State should be recognised and declared enforceable in the other Member States in accordance with applicable Community or national law. This could, for example, be on the basis of Council Regulation (EC) No 44/2001 of 22 December 2000 on jurisdiction and the recognition and enforcement of judgments in civil and commercial matters (1) or Council Regulation (EC) No 2201/2003 of 27 November 2003 concerning jurisdiction and the recognition and enforcement of judgments in matrimonial matters and the matters of parental responsibility (2).

(21) Regulation (EC) No 2201/2003 specifically provides that, in order to be enforceable in another Member State, agreements between the parties have to be enforceable in the Member State in which they were concluded. Consequently, if the content of an agreement resulting from mediation in a family law matter is not enforceable in the Member State where the agreement was concluded and where the request for enforceability is made, this Directive should not encourage the parties to circumvent the law of that Member State by having their agreement made enforceable in another Member State.

(22) This Directive should not affect the rules in the Member States concerning enforcement of agreements resulting from mediation.

(23) Confidentiality in the mediation process is important and this Directive should therefore provide for a minimum degree of compatibility of civil procedural rules with regard to how to protect the confidentiality of mediation in any subsequent civil and commercial judicial proceedings or arbitration.

(24) In order to encourage the parties to use mediation, Member States should ensure that their rules on limitation and prescription periods do not prevent the parties from going to court or to arbitration if their mediation attempt fails. Member States should make sure that this result is achieved even though this Directive does not harmonise national rules on limitation and prescription periods. Provisions on limitation and prescription periods in international agreements as implemented in the Member States, for instance in the area of transport law, should not be affected by this Directive.

(25) Member States should encourage the provision of information to the general public on how to contact mediators and organisations providing mediation services. They should also encourage legal practitioners to inform their clients of the possibility of mediation.

(26) In accordance with point 34 of the Interinstitutional agreement on better law-making (3), Member States are encouraged to draw up, for themselves and in the interests of the Community, their own tables illustrating, as far as possible, the correlation between this Directive and the transposition measures, and to make them public.

(27) This Directive seeks to promote the fundamental rights, and takes into account the principles, recognised in particular by the Charter of Fundamental Rights of the European Union.

(28) Since the objective of this Directive cannot be sufficiently achieved by the Member States and can therefore, by reason of the scale or effects of the action,

be better achieved at Community level, the Community may adopt measures in accordance with the principle of subsidiarity as set out in Article 5 of the Treaty. In accordance with the principle of proportionality, as set out in that Article, this Directive does not go beyond what is necessary in order to achieve that objective.

(29) In accordance with Article 3 of the Protocol on the position of the United Kingdom and Ireland, annexed to the Treaty on European Union and to the Treaty establishing the European Community, the United Kingdom and Ireland have given notice of their wish to take part in the adoption and application of this Directive.

(30) In accordance with Articles 1 and 2 of the Protocol on the position of Denmark, annexed to the Treaty on European Union and to the Treaty establishing the European Community, Denmark does not take part in the adoption of this Directive and is not bound by it or subject to its application,

HAVE ADOPTED THIS DIRECTIVE:

Article 1

Objective and scope

1. The objective of this Directive is to facilitate access to alternative dispute resolution and to promote the amicable settlement of disputes by encouraging the use of mediation and by ensuring a balanced relationship between mediation and judicial proceedings.

2. This Directive shall apply, in cross-border disputes, to civil and commercial matters except as regards rights and obligations which are not at the parties' disposal under the relevant applicable law. It shall not extend, in particular, to revenue, customs or administrative matters or to the liability of the State for acts and omissions in the exercise of State authority (*acta iure imperii*).

3. In this Directive, the term 'Member State' shall mean Member States with the exception of Denmark.

Article 2

Cross-border disputes

1. For the purposes of this Directive a cross-border dispute shall be one in which at least one of the parties is domiciled or habitually resident in a Member State other than that of any other party on the date on which:

(a)   the parties agree to use mediation after the dispute has arisen;

(b)   mediation is ordered by a court;

(c)   an obligation to use mediation arises under national law; or

(d)   for the purposes of Article 5 an invitation is made to the parties.

2. Notwithstanding paragraph 1, for the purposes of Articles 7 and 8 a cross-border dispute shall also be one in which judicial proceedings or arbitration

following mediation between the parties are initiated in a Member State other than that in which the parties were domiciled or habitually resident on the date referred to in paragraph 1(a), (b) or (c).

3. For the purposes of paragraphs 1 and 2, domicile shall be determined in accordance with Articles 59 and 60 of Regulation (EC) No 44/2001.

Article 3

Definitions

For the purposes of this Directive the following definitions shall apply:

(a) 'Mediation' means a structured process, however named or referred to, whereby two or more parties to a dispute attempt by themselves, on a voluntary basis, to reach an agreement on the settlement of their dispute with the assistance of a mediator. This process may be initiated by the parties or suggested or ordered by a court or prescribed by the law of a Member State. It includes mediation conducted by a judge who is not responsible for any judicial proceedings concerning the dispute in question. It excludes attempts made by the court or the judge seised to settle a dispute in the course of judicial proceedings concerning the dispute in question.

(b) 'Mediator' means any third person who is asked to conduct a mediation in an effective, impartial and competent way, regardless of the denomination or profession of that third person in the Member State concerned and of the way in which the third person has been appointed or requested to conduct the mediation.

Article 4

Ensuring the quality of mediation

1. Member States shall encourage, by any means which they consider appropriate, the development of, and adherence to, voluntary codes of conduct by mediators and organizations providing mediation services, as well as other effective quality control mechanisms concerning the provision of mediation services.

2. Member States shall encourage the initial and further training of mediators in order to ensure that the mediation is conducted in an effective, impartial and competent way in relation to the parties.

Article 5

Recourse to mediation

1. A court before which an action is brought may, when appropriate and having regard to all the circumstances of the case, invite the parties to use mediation in order to settle the dispute. The court may also invite the parties to attend an information session on the use of mediation if such sessions are held and are easily available.

2. This Directive is without prejudice to national legislation making the use of mediation compulsory or subject to incentives or sanctions, whether before or after judicial proceedings have started, provided that such legislation does not prevent the parties from exercising their right of access to the judicial system.

Article 6

Enforceability of agreements resulting from mediation

1. Member States shall ensure that it is possible for the parties, or for one of them with the explicit consent of the others, to request that the content of a written agreement resulting from mediation be made enforceable. The content of such an agreement shall be made enforceable unless, in the case in question, either the content of that agreement is contrary to the law of the Member State where the request is made or the law of that Member State does not provide for its enforceability.

2. The content of the agreement may be made enforceable by a court or other competent authority in a judgment or decision or in an authentic instrument in accordance with the law of the Member State where the request is made.

3. Member States shall inform the Commission of the courts or other authorities competent to receive requests in accordance with paragraphs 1 and 2.

4. Nothing in this Article shall affect the rules applicable to the recognition and enforcement in another Member State of an agreement made enforceable in accordance with paragraph 1.

Article 7

Confidentiality of mediation

1. Given that mediation is intended to take place in a manner which respects confidentiality, Member States shall ensure that, unless the parties agree otherwise, neither mediators nor those involved in the administration of the mediation process shall be compelled to give evidence in civil and commercial judicial proceedings or arbitration regarding information arising out of or in connection with a mediation process, except:

(a) where this is necessary for overriding considerations of public policy of the Member State concerned, in particular when required to ensure the protection of the best interests of children or to prevent harm to the physical or psychological integrity of a person; or

(b) where disclosure of the content of the agreement resulting from mediation is necessary in order to implement or enforce that agreement.

2. Nothing in paragraph 1 shall preclude Member States from enacting stricter measures to protect the confidentiality of mediation.

Article 8

Effect of mediation on limitation and prescription periods

1. Member States shall ensure that parties who choose mediation in an attempt to settle a dispute are not subsequently prevented from initiating judicial proceedings or arbitration in relation to that dispute by the expiry of limitation or prescription periods during the mediation process.

2. Paragraph 1 shall be without prejudice to provisions on limitation or prescription periods in international agreements to which Member States are party.

Article 9

Information for the general public

Member States shall encourage, by any means which they consider appropriate, the availability to the general public, in particular on the Internet, of information on how to contact mediators and organisations providing mediation services.

Article 10

Information on competent courts and authorities

The Commission shall make publicly available, by any appropriate means, information on the competent courts or authorities communicated by the Member States pursuant to Article 6(3).

Article 11

Review

Not later than 21 May 2016, the Commission shall submit to the European Parliament, the Council and the European Economic and Social Committee a report on the application of this Directive. The report shall consider the development of mediation throughout the European Union and the impact of this Directive in the Member States. If necessary, the report shall be accompanied by proposals to adapt this Directive.

Article 12

Transposition

1. Member States shall bring into force the laws, regulations, and administrative provisions necessary to comply with this Directive before 21 May 2011, with the exception of Article 10, for which the date of compliance shall be 21 November 2010 at the latest. They shall forthwith inform the Commission thereof. When they are adopted by Member States, these measures shall contain a reference to

this Directive or shall be accompanied by such reference on the occasion of their official publication. The methods of making such reference shall be laid down by Member States.

2. Member States shall communicate to the Commission the text of the main provisions of national law which they adopt in the field covered by this Directive.

Article 13

Entry into force

This Directive shall enter into force on the 20th day following its publication in the *Official Journal of the European Union.*

Article 14

Addressees

This Directive is addressed to the Member States. Done at Strasbourg, 21 May 2008.

For the European Parliament
The President
H.-G. PÖTTERING
For the Council
The President
J. LENARČIČ

B   UNCITRAL Model Law on International Commercial Conciliation[1]

Article 1. Scope of application and definitions

1. This Law applies to international1 commercial2 conciliation.

2. For the purposes of this Law, 'conciliator' means a sole conciliator or two or more conciliators, as the case may be.

3. For the purposes of this Law, 'conciliation' means a process, whether referred to by the expression conciliation, mediation or an expression of similar import, whereby parties request a third person or persons ('the conciliator') to assist them in their attempt to reach an amicable settlement of their dispute arising out of or relating to a contractual or other legal relationship. The conciliator does not have the authority to impose upon the parties a solution to the dispute.

---

1   Reproduced with the kind permission of UNCITRAL. For further information please visit www.uncitral. org.

4. A conciliation is international if:

(a) The parties to an agreement to conciliate have, at the time of the conclusion of that agreement, their places of business in different States; or

(b) The State in which the parties have their places of business is different from either:

    (i)   The State in which a substantial part of the obligations of the commercial relationship is to be performed; or

    (ii)   The State with which the subject matter of the dispute is most closely connected.

5. For the purposes of this article:

(a) If a party has more than one place of business, the place of business is that which has the closest relationship to the agreement to conciliate;

(b) If a party does not have a place of business, reference is to be made to the party's habitual residence.

6. This Law also applies to a commercial conciliation when the parties agree that the conciliation is international or agree to the applicability of this Law.

7. The parties are free to agree to exclude the applicability of this Law.

8. Subject to the provisions of paragraph 9 of this article, this Law applies irrespective of the basis upon which the conciliation is carried out, including agreement between the parties whether reached before or after a dispute has arisen, an obligation established by law, or a direction or suggestion of a court, arbitral tribunal or competent governmental entity.

9. This Law does not apply to:

(a) Cases where a judge or an arbitrator, in the course of judicial or arbitral proceedings, attempts to facilitate a settlement; and

(b) [. . .]

Article 2. Interpretation

1. In the interpretation of this Law, regard is to be had to its international origin and to the need to promote uniformity in its application and the observance of good faith.

2. Questions concerning matters governed by this Law which are not expressly settled in it are to be settled in conformity with the general principles on which this Law is based.

Article 3. Variation by agreement

Except for the provisions of article 2 and article 6, paragraph 3, the parties may agree to exclude or vary any of the provisions of this Law.

Article 4. Commencement of conciliation proceedings

1. Conciliation proceedings in respect of a dispute that has arisen commence on the day on which the parties to that dispute agree to engage in conciliation proceedings.

2. If a party that invited another party to conciliate does not receive an acceptance of the invitation within thirty days from the day on which the invitation was sent, or within such other period of time as specified in the invitation, the party may elect to treat this as a rejection of the invitation to conciliate.

Article 5. Number and appointment of conciliators

1. There shall be one conciliator, unless the parties agree that there shall be two or more conciliators.

2. The parties shall endeavour to reach agreement on a conciliator or conciliators, unless a different procedure for their appointment has been agreed upon.

3. Parties may seek the assistance of an institution or person in connection with the appointment of conciliators. In particular:

(a) A party may request such an institution or person to recommend suitable persons to act as conciliator; or

(b) The parties may agree that the appointment of one or more conciliators be made directly by such an institution or person.

4. In recommending or appointing individuals to act as conciliator, the institution or person shall have regard to such considerations as are likely to secure the appointment of an independent and impartial conciliator and, where appropriate, shall take into account the advisability of appointing a conciliator of a nationality other than the nationalities of the parties.

5. When a person is approached in connection with his or her possible appointment as conciliator, he or she shall disclose any circumstances likely to give rise to justifiable doubts as to his or her impartiality or independence. A conciliator, from the time of his or her appointment and throughout the conciliation proceedings, shall without delay disclose any such circumstances to the parties unless they have already been informed of them by him or her.

Article 6. Conduct of conciliation

1. The parties are free to agree, by reference to a set of rules or otherwise, on the manner in which the conciliation is to be conducted.

2. Failing agreement on the manner in which the conciliation is to be conducted, the conciliator may conduct the conciliation proceedings in such a manner as the conciliator considers appropriate, taking into account the circumstances of the case, any wishes that the parties may express and the need for a speedy settlement of the dispute.

3. In any case, in conducting the proceedings, the conciliator shall seek to maintain fair treatment of the parties and, in so doing, shall take into account the circumstances of the case.

4. The conciliator may, at any stage of the conciliation proceedings, make proposals for a settlement of the dispute.

Article 7. Communication between conciliator and parties

The conciliator may meet or communicate with the parties together or with each of them separately.

Article 8. Disclosure of information

When the conciliator receives information concerning the dispute from a party, the conciliator may disclose the substance of that information to any other party to the conciliation. However, when a party gives any information to the conciliator, subject to a specific condition that it be kept confidential, that information shall not be disclosed to any other party to the conciliation.

Article 9. Confidentiality

Unless otherwise agreed by the parties, all information relating to the conciliation proceedings shall be kept confidential, except where disclosure is required under the law or for the purposes of implementation or enforcement of a settlement agreement.

Article 10. Admissibility of evidence in other proceedings

1. A party to the conciliation proceedings, the conciliator and any third person, including those involved in the administration of the conciliation proceedings, shall not in arbitral, judicial or similar proceedings rely on, introduce as evidence or give testimony or evidence regarding any of the following:

(a) An invitation by a party to engage in conciliation proceedings or the fact that a party was willing to participate in conciliation proceedings;

(b) Views expressed or suggestions made by a party in the conciliation in respect of a possible settlement of the dispute;

(c) Statements or admissions made by a party in the course of the conciliation proceedings;

(d) Proposals made by the conciliator;

(e) The fact that a party had indicated its willingness to accept a proposal for settlement made by the conciliator;

(f) A document prepared solely for purposes of the conciliation proceedings.

2. Paragraph 1 of this article applies irrespective of the form of the information or evidence referred to therein.

3. The disclosure of the information referred to in paragraph 1 of this article shall not be ordered by an arbitral tribunal, court or other competent governmental authority and, if such information is offered as evidence in contravention of paragraph 1 of this article, that evidence shall be treated as inadmissible. Nevertheless, such information may be disclosed or admitted in evidence to the extent required under the law or for the purposes of implementation or enforcement of a settlement agreement.

4. The provisions of paragraphs 1, 2 and 3 of this article apply whether or not the arbitral, judicial or similar proceedings relate to the dispute that is or was the subject matter of the conciliation proceedings.

5. Subject to the limitations of paragraph 1 of this article, evidence that is otherwise admissible in arbitral or judicial or similar proceedings does not become inadmissible as a consequence of having been used in a conciliation.

Article 11. Termination of conciliation proceedings

The conciliation proceedings are terminated:

(a) By the conclusion of a settlement agreement by the parties, on the date of the agreement;

(b) By a declaration of the conciliator, after consultation with the parties, to the effect that further efforts at conciliation are no longer justified, on the date of the declaration;

(c) By a declaration of the parties addressed to the conciliator to the effect that the conciliation proceedings are terminated, on the date of the declaration; or

(d) By a declaration of a party to the other party or parties and the conciliator, if appointed, to the effect that the conciliation proceedings are terminated, on the date of the declaration.

Article 12. Conciliator acting as arbitrator

Unless otherwise agreed by the parties, the conciliator shall not act as an arbitrator in respect of a dispute that was or is the subject of the conciliation proceedings or in respect of another dispute that has arisen from the same contract or legal relationship or any related contract or legal relationship.

Article 13. Resort to arbitral or judicial proceedings

Where the parties have agreed to conciliate and have expressly undertaken not to initiate during a specified period of time or until a specified event has occurred arbitral or judicial proceedings with respect to an existing or future dispute, such an undertaking shall be given effect by the arbitral tribunal or the court until the terms of the undertaking have been complied with, except to the extent necessary for a party, in its opinion, to preserve its rights. Initiation of such proceedings is not of itself to be regarded as a waiver of the agreement to conciliate or as a termination of the conciliation proceedings.

Article 14. Enforceability of settlement agreement4

If the parties conclude an agreement settling a dispute, that settlement agreement is binding and enforceable . . . [*the enacting State may insert a description of the method of enforcing settlement agreements or refer to provisions governing such enforcement*].

C   Council of Europe Recommendation No.R(98)1 of the Committee of Ministers to Member States on Family Mediation2

COUNCIL OF EUROPE COMMITTEE OF MINISTERS

RECOMMENDATION No. R (98) 1 OF THE COMMITTEE OF MINISTERS TO MEMBER STATES ON FAMILY MEDIATION

(Adopted by the Committee of Ministers on 21 January 1998 at the 616th meeting of the Ministers' Deputies)

1. The Committee of Ministers, under the terms of Article 15.b of the Statute of the Council of Europe,

2. Recognising the growing number of family disputes, particularly those resulting from separation or divorce, and noting the detrimental consequences of conflict for families and the high social and economic cost to states;

3. Considering the need to ensure the protection of the best interests and welfare of the child as enshrined in international instruments, especially taking into account problems concerning custody and access arising as a result of a separation or divorce;

4. Having regard to the development of ways of resolving disputes in a consensual manner and the recognition of the necessity to reduce conflict in the interest of all the members of the family;

5. Acknowledging the special characteristics of family disputes, namely:

–   the fact that family disputes involve persons who, by definition, will have interdependent and continued relationships;

–   the fact that family disputes arise in a context of distressing emotions and increase them;

–   the fact that separation and divorce impact on all the members of the family, especially children;

6. Referring to the European Convention on the Exercise of Children's Rights, and in particular to Article 13 of this convention, which deals with the provision of mediation or other processes to resolve disputes affecting children;

---

2   Reproduced by kind permission of Council of Europe. For further information please visit www.coe. int.

7. Taking into account the results of research into the use of mediation and experiences in this area in several countries, which show that the use of family mediation has the potential to:

–   improve communication between members of the family;

–   reduce conflict between parties in dispute;

–   produce amicable settlements;

–   provide continuity of personal contacts between parents and children;

–   lower the social and economic costs of separation and divorce for the parties themselves and states;

–   reduce the length of time otherwise required to settle conflict;

8. Emphasising the increasing internationalisation of family relationships and the very particular problems associated with this phenomenon;

9. Realising that a number of states are considering the introduction of family mediation;

10. Convinced of the need to make greater use of family mediation, a process in which a third party, the mediator, impartial and neutral, assists the parties themselves to negotiate over the issues in dispute and reach their own joint agreements,

11. Recommends the governments of member states:

i.   to introduce or promote family mediation or, where necessary, strengthen existing family mediation;

ii.   to take or reinforce all measures they consider necessary with a view to the implementation of the following principles for the promotion and use of family mediation as an appropriate means of resolving family disputes.

Principles of family mediation

I. Scope of mediation

a.   Family mediation may be applied to all disputes between members of the same family, whether related by blood or marriage, and to those who are living or have lived in family relationships as defined by national law.

b.   However, states are free to determine the specific issues or cases covered by family mediation.

II. Organisation of mediation

a.   Mediation should not, in principle, be compulsory.

b.   States are free to organise and deliver mediation as they see fit, whether through the public or private sector.

c.   Irrespective of how mediation is organised and delivered, states should see to it that there are appropriate mechanisms to ensure the existence of:

–   procedures for the selection, training and qualification of mediators;

–   standards to be achieved and maintained by mediators.

III. Process of mediation

States should ensure that there are appropriate mechanisms to enable the process of mediation to be conducted according to the following principles:

i.   the mediator is impartial between the parties;

ii.   the mediator is neutral as to the outcome of the mediation process;

iii.   the mediator respects the point of view of the parties and preserves the equality of their bargaining positions;

iv.   the mediator has no power to impose a solution on the parties;

v.   the conditions in which family mediation takes place should guarantee privacy;

vi.   discussions in mediation are confidential and may not be used subsequently, except with the agreement of the parties or in those cases allowed by national law;

vii.   the mediator should, in appropriate cases, inform the parties of the possibility for them to use marriage counselling or other forms of counselling as a means of resolving their marital or family problems;

viii.   the mediator should have a special concern for the welfare and best interests of the children, should encourage parents to focus on the needs of children and should remind parents of their prime responsibility relating to the welfare of their children and the need for them to inform and consult their children;

ix.   the mediator should pay particular regard to whether violence has occurred in the past or may occur in the future between the parties and the effect this may have on the parties' bargaining positions, and should consider whether in these circumstances the mediation process is appropriate;

x.   the mediator may give legal information but should not give legal advice. He or she should, in appropriate cases, inform the parties of the possibility for them to consult a lawyer or any other relevant professional person.

IV. The status of mediated agreements

States should facilitate the approval of mediated agreements by a judicial authority or other competent authority where parties request it, and provide mechanisms for enforcement of such approved agreements, according to national law.

V. Relationship between mediation and proceedings before the judicial or other competent authority

a.   States should recognise the autonomy of mediation and the possibility that mediation may take place before, during or after legal proceedings.

b.   States should set up mechanisms which would:

  i.   enable legal proceedings to be interrupted for mediation to take place;

  ii.   ensure that in such a case the judicial or other competent authority retains the power to make urgent decisions in order to protect the parties or their children, or their property;

iii.   inform the judicial or other competent authority whether or not the parties are continuing with mediation and whether the parties have reached an agreement.

VI. Promotion of and access to mediation

a.   States should promote the development of family mediation, in particular through information programmes given to the public to enable better understanding about this way of resolving disputes in a consensual manner.

b.   States are free to establish methods in individual cases to provide relevant information on mediation as an alternative process to resolve family disputes (for example, by making it compulsory for parties to meet with a mediator), and by this enable the parties to consider whether it is possible and appropriate to mediate the matters in dispute.

c.   States should also endeavour to take the necessary measures to allow access to family mediation, including international mediation, in order to contribute to the development of this way of resolving family disputes in a consensual manner.

VII. Other means of resolving disputes

States may examine the desirability of applying, in an appropriate manner, the principles for mediation contained in this recommendation, to other means of resolving disputes.

VIII. International matters

a.   States should consider setting up mechanisms for the use of mediation in cases with an international element when appropriate, especially in all matters relating to children, and particularly those concerning custody and access when the parents are living or expect to live in different states.

b.   International mediation should be considered as an appropriate process in order to enable parents to organise or reorganise custody and access, or to resolve disputes arising following decisions having been made in relation to those matters. However, in the event of an improper removal or retention of the child, international mediation should not be used if it would delay the prompt return of the child.

c.   All the principles outlined above are applicable to international mediation.

d.   States should, as far as possible, promote co-operation between existing services dealing with family mediation with a view to facilitating the use of international mediation.

e.   Taking into account the particular nature of international mediation, international mediators should be required to undergo specific training.

Index

[all references are to paragraph number and Appendix]

810